creating competitive advantage

@e-biz

manager's notebook

Flag Football

Thurs.
9th @ 9:00 pm

Sat. 18th @ 12:00 pm

Thurs. 30th @ 9:00 pm

Thurs. Oct 14th @ 7:00 pm

-Tues-
Oct 26 @ 9:00 pm

Apt# 374-3402 Mike

Small Business Management

ENTREPRENEURSHIP AND BEYOND

SECOND EDITION

Small Business Management

ENTREPRENEURSHIP AND BEYOND

Timothy S. Hatten
Mesa State College

Houghton Mifflin Company
Boston   New York

Executive Editor: George T. Hoffman
Associate Sponsoring Editor: Joanne Dauksewicz
Marketing Manager: Steven W. Mikels
Senior Project Editor: Fred Burns
Production/Design Coordinator: Jodi O'Rourke
Senior Manufacturing Coordinator: Marie Barnes

Cover Illustration: William James © Stock Illustration Source

Photo Credits
Chapter 1: page 3, Boston Beer Company; page 20, Carol Klucas. **Chapter 2:** page 33, Jeff Greenberg, Photo Edit; page 42, Jim Mone/AP/Wide World. **Chapter 3:** page 71, BRIAN SMALES PHOTOGRAPHER; page 84, Rudi Von Briel/Photo Edit. **Chapter 4:** page 105, Adam Tanner/The Image Works; page 108, Sunny Drewel. **Chapter 5:** page 137, © Auntie Anne's, Inc.; page 139, Jeff Greenberg/Photo Edit. **Chapter 6:** page 190, Corbis. **Chapter 7:** page 201, Andy Freeberg; page 214, Marc Romanelli/The Image Bank/Getty Images. **Chapter 8:** page 233, Paul Kennedy; page 257, SRC Corporation. **Chapter 9:** page 269, Steve Skoll; page 273, St. Petersburg Times. **Chapter 10:** page 297, Jeff Greenberg/Photo Edit; page 306, Jeff Greenberg/Photo Edit. **Chapter 11:** page 331, AP/World Wide Photos; page 337, Judy Gelles/Stock Boston. **Chapter 12:** page 363, Mike Steinberg/Black Star; page 369, Wrebbit Inc. **Chapter 13:** page 391, Pac Van, Indianapolis, IN; page 403, John Elk/Stock Boston. **Chapter 14:** page 427, Photo Edit; page 453, Mark Richard/Photo Edit. **Chapter 15:** page 467, Lonely Planet Publications; page 488, David McIntyre/Black Star. **Chapter 16:** page 499, Roger Mastrianni. **Chapter 17:** page 531, Masterfile; page 548, Karen Preuss/The Image Works. **Chapter 18:** page 569, Jim Bounds/AP/Wide World; page 585, The Loranger Manufacturing Company.

Printed in the U.S.A.

Library of Congress Control Number: 2001133282

ISBN: 0-618-12848-4

2 3 4 5 6 7 8 9—DOW—06 05 04 03 02

To Jill, Paige, Brittany, and Taylor

Brief Contents

Contents

9 Small Business Finance 268

10 The Legal Environment 296

Small Business Marketing: Place   390

 Small Business Marketing: Price and Promotion   426

Preface

Are you thinking about starting your own business some day? For many students, preparation for small business ownership begins with a course in small business management. As a teacher, my goal has been to help students fulfill their dreams of becoming entrepreneurs and achieving the independence that comes with small business success. The purpose of this text is the same.

The theme of this book revolves around creating and maintaining a *sustainable competitive advantage* in starting and managing your small business. Running a small business is difficult in today's rapidly evolving environment and at no other time has the importance of holding a competitive advantage been greater. Every chapter in this book can be used to create your competitive advantage—whether your idea, your product, your location, or your marketing is the key to your business. Running a small business is like being in a race with no finish line. You must strive for continual improvement to satisfy the changing wants and needs of your customers. This book can help you run your best race.

The writing style is personal and conversational. I have tried to avoid the excessive use of jargon by explaining topics in simple, understandable language. The book is written in first person, present tense because I, the author, am speaking directly to you, the student. I believe that a good example can help make the most complex concept more understandable and interesting to read. Examples were carefully selected from the business press and from small business owners I have known to strengthen the flow of material and to reinforce important points.

New to This Edition

In preparing for this second edition, I have incorporated suggestions from teachers and students who have used the previous edition. In addition, an advisory board of educators from around the country was consulted to help me determine the best ways to meet the needs of students in this course. Here are some of the changes that have been made in this edition:

- Revised chapters have been thoroughly updated and include more emphasis on important topics such as e-commerce, technology, and managing change in a global environment.
- The financial and legal aspects of small business management have been moved forward to lay the groundwork for later study and to help you understand and appreciate the importance of financial and legal matters early on.
- Learning objectives, chapter topics, and summary points have been closely correlated to allow you to easily focus in on the most important concepts.

- "What Would You Do?" exercises have been added to each chapter, giving you the opportunity to visualize yourselves as small business managers, solving problems and making decisions as you would in actual situations.
- Chapter closing cases have been added to describe real-world business situations and to provide the opportunity for you to further apply what you have learned.

Important Boxed Features

To help highlight important issues in small business management, a variety of boxed features have been included. "Creating Competitive Advantage" boxes focus on the text's main theme of business success through competitive advantage. "Manager's Notebook" inserts provide specific "how to" tips and practical advice. "Reality Check" boxes illustrate text concepts through current, real-world examples. A box called "@e-biz" focuses on the importance of e-commerce to today's small businesses. Examples of topics included in each insert follow:

Creating Competitive Advantage

- Preserving the spirit of entrepreneurship
- Advantages of inner-city businesses
- Green marketing
- How to beat the competition
- Frustration solvers
- Motivating more with less
- Hiring right
- Benchmarking your way to competitive advantage

Manager's Notebook

- Good, bad, and ugly business plans
- Computerized accounting packages
- Financial status checklist
- Turn up the tap on your cash flow
- What to do before you talk to your banker
- Which advertising medium should you use?
- Can you motivate?
- Productive disciplinary steps

Reality Check

- Entrepreneurial mistakes
- Can you serve two bottom lines?
- Startup myths and realities
- Plastic finance—tempting, but risky
- Getting it there just in time
- Don't give away the farm with special offers
- How good is good enough?

@e-biz

- Cool B-plan tools
- Surf your way to a new franchise
- Shopping for a business online
- Finding financing online
- Online marketing
- Big-time products for small niches
- Online global power
- Online training

Effective Pedagogical Aids

The pedagogical features of this book are designed to complement, supplement, and reinforce material from the body of the text. To enhance critical thinking and show practical applications of running a small business you will find the following features:

- **Part Introductions** provide a concise description of the materials that follow, helping you to better understand how chapters within each section are correlated and how each section of the text fits within the whole.
- **Chapter Opening Vignettes,** along with **Reality Checks** and extensive use of examples throughout the book, show you what *real* small businesses are doing.
- Each chapter begins with **Learning Objectives,** which directly correlate to the chapter topic headings and coverage. These same objectives are then revisited and identified in each **Chapter Summary.**
- A **Running Glossary** in the margins brings attention to important terms as they appear in the text.
- **Questions for Review & Discussion** allow you to assess your retention and comprehension of the chapter concepts.
- **Questions for Critical Thinking** will prompt you to apply what you have learned to realistic situations.
- **What Would You Do?** exercises are included to stimulate effective problem solving and classroom discussion.
- **Experience This . . .** provides exercises for student experiential practice.
- **Chapter Closing Cases** present actual business scenarios, allowing you to think critically about the management challenges presented and further apply chapter concepts.
- **Two Complete Business Plans,** one for a retail business and one for a service business, provide you with excellent examples to follow in creating your own business plan.

Complete Package of Support Materials

This edition of *Small Business Management: Entrepreneurship and Beyond* provides a support package that will encourage student success and increase instructor effectiveness.

Student Support Materials

GoVenture CD. This fun and exciting business simulation program allows you to virtually experience the challenges and satisfactions of small business management. As you take on the role of entrepreneur/manager, you are faced with the myriad decisions that must be made—from what type of business you will launch, to what your measures of success will be, to how to keep control of inventory. So much real-life detail is built into this program that you will feel that you are indeed going through a "dry run" of the day-to-day realities of small business management.

Student Web Site. This valuable resource will include "Searching the Internet" exercises and links to help you find out more about small business management. Online self-tests for each chapter will give you immediate feedback on your progress in remembering and understanding the material. You will also find additional sample business plans that you can use as reference materials, as well as longer case studies that you can easily download to complete assignments.

Instructor Support Materials

Instructor's Web Site. This password-protected site includes valuable tools to help instructors design and prepare for the course. Downloadable PowerPoint Slides, lecture outlines, and a sample syllabus will help teachers plan effective classroom sessions. Comments on "Searching the Internet" exercises will also be provided.

PowerPoint Slide Presentations. New author-created PowerPoint slides have been specially developed for this edition. The package contains over 350 slides, providing a complete lecture for each chapter and including key figures from the text. Instructors with Microsoft PowerPoint can use the presentations as is, or edit, delete, and add to them to suit their specific classroom needs.

Instructor's Manual and Test Bank. The comprehensive Instructor's Resource Manual has been written by the text author and presents learning objectives for each chapter, a brief chapter outline, comprehensive lecture outlines, answers to review and discussion questions, as well as teaching notes for the Questions for Critical Thinking, What Would You Do? incidents, and end-of-chapter cases.

The test bank is also author-created and contains over 1,800 items. Each chapter contains a variety of true/false, multiple-choice, and short-answer essay questions. To ensure quality, the test bank has been thoroughly checked and reviewed by small business management instructors.

Computerized Test Bank. This electronic version of the printed Test Bank allows instructors to generate and change tests easily on the computer. The program will print an answer key appropriate to each version for the test you have devised, and it allows you to customize the printed appearance of the test. The program also includes an online testing system, which makes it possible for instructors to administer tests via a network system, modem, or personal computer. A Gradebook feature grades the tests and allows instructors to set up a new class, record grades, analyze grades, and produce class and individual statistics.

Videos. A diverse collection of professionally produced videos can help instructors bring lectures to life by providing thought-provoking insights into real-world companies, products, and issues. A Video Guide accompanies the program and is designed to help instructors integrate text content with the video series.

Acknowledgments

There are so many people to thank, some who made this book possible and some who made it better. Projects of this magnitude do not happen in a vacuum and, even though my name is on the cover, many talented people have contributed skills. Lynn Guza and Ellen Derrick have played key roles in its history. The entire group of Houghton Mifflin sales reps has a major impact on the success of this book. I appreciate their efforts.

George Hoffman is the executive editor who saw potential in my work. I am lucky that he is my editor and even more fortunate that he is my friend. Joanne Dauksewicz—wow! She is my fantastic associate sponsoring editor who accomplishes a difficult job with a kindness and sincerity that are unusual in this business. Fred Burns deserves a medal for coordinating the production process even though I was in Iceland at the time. There are many other people whose names I unfortunately do not know who have worked their magic making the beautiful book you hold in your hands; I sincerely thank them. Thanks to Tom Liesz, Morgan Bridge, Joan Winn, Leo Paul Dana, and other faculty contributors.

I would like to thank the many colleagues who have reviewed this text and provided feedback concerning their and their students' needs.

Allen C. Amason, University of Georgia
Walter H. Beck, Sr., Reinhardt College
Rudy Butler, Trenton State College
Michael Cicero, Highline Community College
Richard Cuba, University of Baltimore
Gary M. Donnelly, Casper College
Arlen Gastinau, Valencia Community College West
Doug Hamilton, Berkeley College of Business
Philip G. Kearney, Niagara County Community College
Mary Beth Klinger, College of Southern Maryland
Paul Lamberson, University of Southern Mississippi—Hattiesburg
MaryLou Lockerby, College of Dupage—Glen Ellyn
Norman D. McElvany, Johnson State College
Milton Miller, Carteret Community College—Morehead City
Bill Motz, Lansing Community College
Grantley E. Nurse, Raritan Valley Community College
Cliff Olson, Southern Adventist University
Roger A. Pae, Cuyahoga Community College
Nancy Payne, College of Dupage—Glen Ellyn
Julia Truitt Poynter, Transylvania University
George B. Roorbach, Lyndon State College
Marty St. John, Westmoreland County College
Joe Salamone, SUNY Buffalo
Bernard Skown, Stevens Institute of Technology
William Soukoup, University of San Diego
Jim Steele, Chattanooga State Technical Community College
Raymond Sumners, Westwood College of Technology

Charles Tofloy, George Washington University
Warren Weber, California Polytechnical
Alan Zieber, Portland State University

Finally, to my family. . . . Saying thanks and giving acknowledgment is not enough for the patience, sacrifice, and inspiration you have provided. My wife, Jill, our children, Paige, Brittany, and Taylor—you are the best. The perseverance and work ethic needed for a job of this magnitude were instilled in me by my father, Drexel, and mother, Marjorie—I don't know how you did it, but I appreciate it.

About the Author

Timothy S. Hatten is associate professor of marketing at Mesa State College in Grand Junction, Colorado, where he has served as chair of business administration and director of the MBA program. He received his Ph.D. from the University of Missouri—Columbia. He earned his M.A. at Central Missouri State University and his B.A. from Western State College in Gunnison, Colorado.

Dr. Hatten has been passionate about small and family businesses his whole life. He grew up with the family-owned International Harvester farm equipment dealership in Bethany, Missouri, which his father started. Later, he owned and managed a Chevrolet, Buick, and Cadillac dealership with his father, Drexel, and brother, Gary.

Timothy Hatten is a Fulbright Scholar who taught small business management and entrepreneurship at Reykjavik University in Iceland. He has also taught business planning at the Russian–American Business Center in Magadan, Russia.

Since entering academia, he has been active bringing students and small businesses together through the Small Business Institute program. He counsels and leads small-business seminars through the Western Colorado Business Development Corporation. Dr. Hatten approached writing this textbook as if it were a small business. His intent was to produce a product (in this case, a book) that would benefit his customers (students and faculty).

Dr. Hatten's adopted home on the western slope of Colorado has provided him the opportunity to share his love of the mountains with his family—wife, Jill, and children, Paige, Brittany, and Taylor.

Please send questions, comments, or suggestions to: thatten@mesastate.edu

The Challenge

When most people think of American business, corporate giants like General Motors, IBM, and Wal-Mart generally come to mind first. There is no question that the companies that make up the *Fortune 500* control vast resources, produce products and services that set world standards, and employ many people. But as you will discover in these first two chapters, small businesses and the entrepreneurs who start them play a vital role in the American economy. **Chapter 1** illustrates the economic and social impact of small businesses. **Chapter 2** discusses the process and factors related to entrepreneurship.

1

Small Business:
An Overview

ON PATRIOT'S DAY 1985, Jim Koch (pronounced "cook") started Boston Beer Company. Koch brewed his beer, Samuel Adams, according to a family recipe from the 1870s. Although he had never been in the beer business before, he became at age 37 a sixth-generation brewer. Intending to compete directly with the best imports, Koch advertised beer with patriotic slogans like "Declare your independence from foreign beer." The namesake of the beer was a revolutionary war hero who helped organize the Boston Tea Party.

Like many entrepreneurs, Koch started his business on a shoestring: $100,000 from personal savings and $250,000 borrowed from family and friends—a small amount for a brewery. To reduce overhead expenses, he arranged to use the excess capacity of a brewery in Pittsburgh. For the first several years, Koch was the company's only salesperson, traveling from bar to bar enticing bartenders to taste samples of Samuel Adams that he carried in his briefcase. Sometimes up to 15 calls were needed before getting the sale. Even after the company had grown to revenues of $7 million with 28 employees, Koch still spent two-thirds of his time making sales.

Samuel Adams was not made for the mass market. At first it was brewed in batches of only 6,500 cases each. Koch marketed the beer to people tired of drinking "ordinary" beer and willing to pay for premium quality. Koch enjoyed saying that major breweries spill more beer in a minute than he made in a year. Quality was his focus, not quantity.

Samuel Adams has been voted Best Beer in America at the Great American Beer Festival four times in its ten-year existence. It was the first American beer in the twentieth century to satisfy the stringent German purity laws enabling it to be sold in the German market. Premium ingredients costing up to ten times more than those used by competitors are needed to maintain this level of quality. Appropriately, Boston Beer Company ads stress product and process—not image—by not featuring muscle-bound men or bikini-clad women. Because Samuel Adams was the first beer to have a freshness date stamped on its label, Koch wrote a radio ad touting that "Maybe other beer commercials want you to think that if you drink their beer, you'll get lucky. But I can guarantee with Samuel Adams, you'll always get a date." Anheuser-Busch later mimicked the practice.

Koch has a passion for quality and always strives to fill a niche market. He wanted to produce the best (and strongest, at 20 percent alcohol, and most expensive, at $200 per bottle) beer possible to celebrate the year 2000. Boston Beer produced only 3,000 bottles of Samuel Adams Millennium, and Koch personally signed and numbered every one. He likened the mixture to a fine bourbon or port with flavors of malt, oak, vanilla, butterscotch, pear, and just a hint of cinnamon. First-rate packaging must accompany first-rate beer. Each cobalt-blue bottle has platinum lettering topped with a natural cork and sealing wax fitted into a cherrywood box. Not exactly an everyday brew, but a good illustration of the extent Koch is willing to go in breaking new ground in the niche beer market.

In a short time, from austere beginnings, Boston Beer Company has become a $50 million business. Samuel Adams is no longer brewed in small batches, but the quality remains high. The company is the first to enter the chasm between *micro*brewery and *major* brewery. Its incredible growth and success have come from its fanatical attention to quality, its use of marketing tools that no other microbrewery had used—advertising, merchandising, and hard selling—and the perseverance of its founder, Jim Koch, an entrepreneur with a vision.

Sources: Adapted from Jennry McCune, "Brewing Up Profits," *Management Review,* April 1994, 16–20; James Koch, "Portrait of the CEO as Salesman," *Inc.,* March 1988, 44–46; Gerry Khermouch, "Marketers of the Year—Jim Koch," *Brandweek,* 8 November 1993, 42; Stanley Angrist, "Brewing America," *Forbes,* 6 April 1987, 172; John Persinos, "Heady Brews: Amber Waves of Grain," *Venture,* January 1988, 58–61; Laura Loro, "The Marketing 100—Jim Koch," *Advertising Age,* 5 July 1993, s–22; Peter Corbett, "Microbrew Boom Starting to Lose Fizz," *The Arizona Republic,* 30 April 1999; "Samuel Adams Millennium World's Most Astonishing Beer to Become World's Most Expensive," *PR Newswire,* 10 November 1999.

▬ What Is Small Business?

As the driver of the free enterprise system, small business generates a great deal of energy, innovation, and profit for millions of Americans. According to the Internal Revenue Service, almost 25 million tax returns were filed in 1998 that included income from a small business.[1] This figure excludes farmers, who constitute another 2 million people whose primary occupation is operating a small business. What a great time to be in (and be studying) small business! Check out the following facts. Did you realize that small businesses

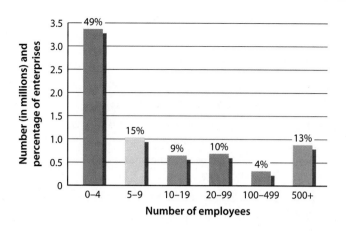

FIGURE 1.1
Almost All Businesses Are Small Businesses

Source: U.S. Small Business Administration, "Small Business Answer Card 2000," sba.gov/advo/stats

- Represent over 99 percent of *all* businesses (payroll of fewer than 500 people)?
- Employ 52 percent of all nongovernment employees?
- Employ 38 percent of private employees in the high-tech sector?
- Create virtually all net new jobs?
- Represent 96 percent of all exporters of goods?
- Receive 35 percent of federal contract dollars?[2]

Small businesses include everything from the stay-at-home parent who provides day care for other children, to the factory worker who makes after-hours deliveries, to the owner of a chain of fast-food restaurants (see Figure 1.1). Over 9 million Americans operate "sideline" businesses, part-time enterprises that supplement the owner's income. Another 12 million people make owning and operating a small business their primary occupation. Seven million of these employ only themselves—as carpenters, independent sales representatives, freelance writers, and other types of single-person businesses. Nearly 5 million businesses have fewer than 100 employees. About 80,000 businesses have 100 employees or more, whereas only 15,000 businesses have 500 or more workers on their payroll.

Size Definitions

The definition of **small business** depends on the criteria for determining what is "small" and what qualifies as a "business." The most common criterion used to distinguish between large and small businesses is the number of employees. Other criteria include sales revenue, the total value of assets, and the value of owners' equity. The Small Business Administration (SBA), a federally funded agency that provides loans and assistance to small businesses, has established definitions of business size that vary by industry. These definitions are based on annual sales revenues or number of employees and are assigned by Standardized Industrial Code (SIC) to each of seven main industries: construction, manufacturing, mining, transportation, wholesale trade, retail trade, and service.[3] In general, manufacturers with fewer than 500 employees are classified as small, as are wholesalers with fewer than 100 employees, and retailers or services with less than $5 million annual revenue. Some selected exceptions to those standard size limitations can be seen in Table 1.1.

small business A business is generally considered small if it is independently owned, operated, and financed; has fewer than 100 employees; and has relatively little impact on its industry.

TABLE 1.1
How Big Can a Small Business Be?

SIC Code	Description by Industry	Annual Sales (Millions) or Number of Employees
1521	General building contractor	$17.0
2211	Broadwoven fabric mills, cotton	1,000 employees
2511	Wood furniture manufacturer	500 employees
3411	Metal can fabrication	1,000 employees
3571	Electronic computer manufacturer	1,000 employees
4724	Travel agency	$ 1.0
4212	Garbage and refuse collection w/o disposal	$ 6.0
5311	Department store	$20.0
5511	Motor vehicle dealer (new and used)	$21.0
5651	Family clothing store	$ 6.5
5961	Catalog and mail order	$18.5
6531	Real estate agents and managers	$ 1.5
7378	Computer maintenance and repair	$18.0
7819	Motion picture and video production	$21.5

Source: Small Business Administration, www.sba.gov

Why is it important to classify businesses as big or small? Aside from academic discussion of the contributions of each, these classifications are important in that they determine whether a business may qualify for SBA assistance and for government set-aside programs, which require a percentage of each government agency's purchases to be made from small businesses.

Types of Industries

Some industries lend themselves to small business operation more than others do. In construction, for instance, 86.8 percent of companies in the industry are classified as small by the SBA. Manufacturing industries have long been associated with mass employment, as well as mass production, yet SBA data show that 28.9 percent of manufacturers are classified as small.

Over 60 percent of all retail businesses are small, employing a total of 10.6 million people in selling goods to ultimate consumers. More than three out of every four wholesale businesses are small, as 4.5 million people are employed by these intermediaries.

The industry that employs the greatest number of people in small business, however, is services. Over 13 million people (51.5 percent of the total) are employed by small businesses that provide a broad range of services from restaurants to lawn care to telecommunications.

As indicated by industry percentages and by sheer numbers of employees, small businesses are important to every industry sector (see Figure 1.2).

For purposes of discussion in this book, we will consider a business to be small if it

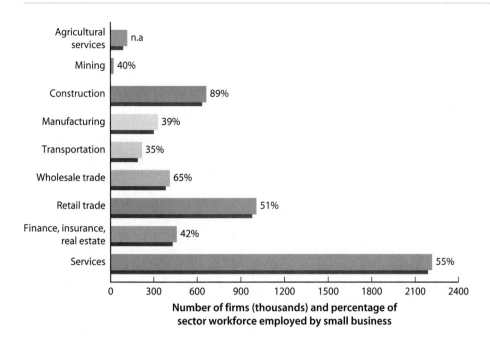

Agricultural services — n.a
Mining — 40%
Construction — 89%
Manufacturing — 39%
Transportation — 35%
Wholesale trade — 65%
Retail trade — 51%
Finance, insurance, real estate — 42%
Services — 55%

0   300   600   900   1200   1500   1800   2100   2400

Number of firms (thousands) and percentage of sector workforce employed by small business

- *Is independently owned, operated, and financed.* One or very few people run the business.

- *Has less than 100 employees.* Although SBA standards allow up to 500 or more for some types of businesses, the most common limit is 100.

- *Has relatively little impact on its industry.* Boston Beer Company, described in the chapter opener, has sales of $50 million. Although this is an impressive figure, Boston Beer is still classified as a small business because it has little influence on the Anheuser-Busch or Miller breweries with 1994 sales of $11.5 billion and $2.92 billion, respectively.[4]

Small Business in the American Economy

Until the early 1800s, all businesses were small in the way just described. Most goods were produced one at a time by workers in their cottages or in small artisan studios. Much of the U.S. economy was based on agriculture. But with the Industrial Revolution, mass production became possible. Machinery like Samuel Slater's textile machinery, Eli Whitney's cotton gin, and techniques like Samuel Colt's use of interchangeable parts in producing firearms changed the way business was conducted. Factories brought people, raw material, and machinery together to produce large quantities of goods.

Although early manufacturers were small, by the late 1800s businesses grew rapidly in industries that relied on economies of scale for their profitability. *Economy of scale* is the lowering of costs through production of larger quantities: The more units you make, the less each costs. For example, Andrew Carnegie founded U.S. Steel, Henry Ford introduced the assembly line for manufacturing automobiles, and Cornelius Vanderbilt speculated in steamships and railroads. Although these individuals had begun as entrepreneurs, their companies eventually came to dominate their industry. The costs of competing with them became prohibitively high as the masses of capital they had accumulated formed a barrier to entry for newcomers to the industry. The subsequent industrialization of America decreased the impact of new entrepreneurs over the first half of the twentieth century.[5] Small businesses still existed during this period, of course, but the economic momentum that large businesses gathered kept small businesses in minor roles.

The decades following World War II also favored big business over small business. Industrial giants like General Motors and IBM, and retailers like Sears, Roebuck, flourished during this period by tapping into the expanding consumer economy.

In the late 1950s and early 1960s, another economic change began. Businesses began paying more attention to consumer wants and needs, rather than focusing solely on production. This paradigm shift was called the **marketing concept;** finding out what people want and then producing that good or service, rather than making products and then trying to convince people to buy them. With this shift came an increased importance of the service economy. The increased emphasis on customer service by businesses adopting the marketing concept started to provide more opportunities for small business. The **service sector** of our economy is made up of jobs that produce services for customers rather than tangible products. The growth of this sector is important to small businesses because they can compete well in it.

The importance of service businesses is illustrated by changes in traditional measuring tools. The prestigious Fortune 500 list of the largest businesses in the United States radically changed by including service businesses for the first time in 1995.[6]

The service industry is growing by leaps and bounds. As we enter the twenty-first century, service businesses dominate the economies of the United States, Canada, Australia, and Western Europe. What factors have led to this phenomenal growth? Part of the growth in services can be traced to the fact that the post–World War II economic boom years provided consumers with more money but less time to perform many of the services that they had previously performed for themselves. They had money to pay to have these services done for them. In addition, consumers' increased income meant that they could acquire more possessions, which led to increased demands for maintaining and preserving those possessions. Finally, rapid advances in telecommunications and computer technology have inaugurated entire new industries devoted to organizing, storing, and transmitting information for both personal and commercial uses. Small service businesses create competitive advantage by offering customers more time for other things. Because service organizations comprise such a large proportion of U.S. economic activity, in each chapter of this book we'll look at specific ways in which small businesses are innovating and prospering in this field.

marketing concept The business philosophy of discovering what consumers want and then providing the good or service that will satisfy their needs.

service sector Businesses that provide services, rather than tangible goods.

Recent Growth Trends

By the early 1970s, corporate profits had begun to decline, while costs increased. Entrepreneurs like Steve Jobs of Apple Computer and Bill Gates of Microsoft started small businesses and created entirely new industries that had never before existed. Managers began realizing that bigger is not necessarily better, that economy

Maximum Efficiency

What's your image of the U.S. steel industry? If you think of cavernous buildings, housing giant blast furnaces capable of transforming iron ore, coal, and limestone into millions of tons of molten metal every single year, you're seeing only part of the picture. During the early 1980s, the major U.S. steel producers were battered by foreign competitors who capitalized on their weaknesses: oversized, outdated production facilities; high costs; and inflexible and overly bureaucratic management structures. However, in the last decade, the steel industry has been magically transformed by an aggressive group of small firms, called *minimills,* which produce between 200,000 and 1 million tons of steel per year.

A minimill is a relatively small, electric-powered steel mill that melts down scrap steel to manufacture various steel products. This radically different production process saves money on costly labor, raw materials, and the expensive machinery needed to produce steel from iron ore. (However, a major concern of minimill manufacturers is maintaining product quality, because their raw materials consist of scrap steel containing a variety of impurities and alloys.) These small firms concentrate on producing only a few products and are usually much more efficient than most of their larger rivals. Because of their efficiency, they have been growing and adding capacity while larger U.S. steel companies have been restructuring, downsizing, and otherwise struggling to survive in a changed global environment.

What's the story behind the success of these steel minimills? To better understand the role of these small businesses in the turnaround of the steel industry, let's take a closer look at one—Nucor Corporation of North Carolina. Nucor operates several minimills that produce basic steel products such as joists, decking, and steel bars. Nucor is extremely efficient at making steel—its sales revenues have grown at an annual compounded rate of more than 20 percent during the last decade. The company began with the reorganization of a nearly bankrupt company called Nuclear Corporation of America. To help control both quality and costs, Ken Iverson, who was chosen as the company's chief executive officer (CEO), designed a decentralized company structure with only four management levels. At the top level is Iverson and the company's president. The second level includes vice presidents, each of whom serves as a general manager of one of the company's minimills, joist plants, and other divisions. At the third level are the department heads—sales managers, division controllers, and managers of melting and casting. And the fourth level includes the first-line supervisors.

Iverson delegated all decisions dealing with manufacturing operations to the individual plants. He believed that managers closest to the action had the knowledge to best deal with changes and to take appropriate steps. Iverson also tied worker compensation directly to production, awarding bonuses for each extra ton of production. These bonuses can sometimes almost double a production worker's paycheck. Managers' financial rewards are similarly dependent on continued productivity. Finally, Nucor's workers have excelled in suggesting innovative ideas for improving productivity and quality. So, although Nucor has reached over $4 billion in annual sales, it continues to prosper by "acting small."

Sources: "Business: Growing Pains," *Economist,* 16 October 1999, 68; Donald F. Barnett and Robert W. Crandall, *Up from the Ashes: The Rise of the Steel Minimill in the United States* (Washington, DC: Brookings Institution, 1986); John Ortman, "Nucor's Ken Iverson on Productivity and Pay," *Personnel Administrator,* October 1986, 46–108; *Wall Street Journal,* 10 May 1991, A1, A4; F. C. Barnes, "A Nucor Commitment," in *Strategic Management: Text and Cases,* 5th ed., ed. James M. Higgins and Julian W. Vincze (Fort Worth, TX: Dryden Press, 1993); and John A. Byrne, "How Entrepreneurs Are Reshaping the Economy—And What Big Companies Can Learn," *Business Week, Enterprise Edition,* October 1993, 12–18.

of scale does not guarantee lower costs. Other startups, such as Wal-Mart and The Limited, dealt serious blows to retail giants like Sears because their organizational structures were flatter, they were faster in responding to customers' changing desires, and they were more flexible in changing their products and services.

In the 1980s, then again in the 1990s, U.S. business saw a period of "merger mania," when businesses acquired other businesses purely for the sake of growth, not because a natural fit would be created. This period was short-lived because most of the mergers and acquisitions were financed heavily, often with *junk bonds*—funds borrowed at very high interest rates. This debt left the newly expanded businesses at a disadvantage and was often followed by a string of bankruptcies and layoffs. A relatively new term entered the business vocabulary—**downsizing.** Downsizing involved the reduction of a business's work force in order to shore up dwindling profits. Any segment of a business in which its owner did not have special skills was put up for sale, eliminated, or sent out for someone else to do, or *outsourced.* The impact of downsizing on small business was twofold. Many people who lost their jobs with large businesses started small businesses of their own. These new businesses often do the work that large businesses no longer perform themselves—temporary employment, cleaning services, and independent contracting, for example.

The trend of people's working in their homes either via telecommuting or as the owner of their own home-based business may put the study of the history of business into perspective. Have we now come full circle to where we were in the early 1800s, with all business conducted in private cottages? We probably will not continue that far, but the question does illustrate the importance of studying history—it can repeat itself.

Large businesses will always be needed, but in an environment in which competition, technology, and the desires of the marketplace change quickly, as it does in the economy of the twenty-first century, entry barriers fall. Small businesses are better able to take advantage of changing conditions. As Ted Stolberg, a venture capitalist who invests in small businesses, says, "The capital advantage big businesses sometimes have is being eliminated. The technology is helping smaller companies beat up the big guys."[7]

INCREASED BUSINESS STARTUPS.   Indeed, the rate of small business growth has more than doubled in the last 30 years. In 1970, 264,000 new businesses were started.[8] In 1980, that figure had grown to 532,000, reaching 647,000 by 1990 and 799,000 in 1997! Although a lot of attention tends to be paid to the failure rate of small businesses, many more people are going into business for themselves. Nine new businesses are formed for every one that fails.[9]

INCREASING INTEREST AT COLLEGES AND UNIVERSITIES.   The growing economic importance of small business has not escaped college and university campuses. In 1971, only 16 schools in the United States offered courses in entrepreneurship. By 1993, that number had grown to 370.[10] Today there are over 400.

What can explain this phenomenal growth of interest in small business? For one thing, it parallels the explosion in small business formation. For another, mistakes made in running a small business are expensive in terms of both time and money. More students today are present or prospective business owners who want to make as many of those mistakes as possible on paper and not in reality.

downsizing The practice of reducing the size of a business. Downsizing affects small businesses in two ways: people who have lost their jobs often start their own businesses, and small businesses often provide services that downsized businesses no longer perform themselves.

Small Business as Employer

Small businesses generate employment when they are started and when they expand. The SBA Office of Advocacy is compiling a comprehensive file of longitudinal data called Business Information Tracking System (BITS). Data are becoming available although with a three- to four-year time lag. BITS data show that the smallest microbusinesses (1 to 4 employees) produced an increasingly large proportion of new jobs from 1994 to 1995: 500,000 net new jobs (jobs created minus jobs lost) from startups and another 500,000 through expansions. Small businesses with 19 to 99 employees created another 576,000 net new jobs over the same time period. Of the net new jobs generated from 1970 to 1999, small businesses created virtually all of them.[11] This contribution is even more impressive when you consider that the total number of U.S. jobs increased by 50 percent during this period. According to research conducted by Cognetics, Inc., of Cambridge, Massachusetts, 11.1 million net new jobs were added to the U.S. economy from 1994 to 1998. Firms with 1 to 4 employees created all 60.2 percent of those net new jobs. During the same five-year period, firms with 5 to 19 employees created another 18.3 percent, whereas those with 500 or more employees had a net loss of jobs.[12]

Seven of the ten industries adding the most new jobs in 1998 were dominated by small business. Among small businesses, the most jobs created were in the following industries:

Business services	563,000 net new jobs
Engineering and management services	231,000
Special trade contractors (electricians, plumbers, and so on)	168,000
Wholesale trade, durable goods	134,000
Amusement and recreation sector	115,000
Social services	114,000
Restaurants	110,000
Personnel supply services (such as temporary employment agencies)	50,000

No big surprise that the fastest-growing small businesses as we begin the twenty-first century are technology related. Programmers, management consulting services, and training businesses have fared the best recently. The Bureau of Labor Statistics projects that small businesses will continue to create a large majority of the new jobs in the U.S. economy at least through 2005. Typically, many new jobs are created by the food service sector. Restaurants are expected to produce over 1 million new jobs from 1994 to 2005.

Work Force Diversity ▬

The U.S. work force is becoming more diverse. The perceived homogeneity of the business world, as depicted in television shows of the 1950s, sharply contrasts with the reality of the twenty-first century (see Table 1.2). Trends of an aging population,

TABLE 1.2 **The U.S. Work Force Is Changing**	Percentage of the Work Force			
	1965	**1980**	**1990**	**1996**
Women	35.0	42.0	45.0	46.1
African Americans	6.5	9.4	10.1	11.1
Hispanics	—	5.6	7.5	10.7
Asians	—	1.0	2.6	4.6

Source: U.S. Small Business Administration, Office of Advocacy, 1999.

increasing birthrate of minority groups, more attention to the needs and abilities of people with handicaps, and more women entering the work force are changing the way our nation and our businesses operate. The intent of most civil rights laws (covered in Chapter 10) is to ensure that all groups are represented and that discrimination is not to be tolerated. Wheels of change tend to move slowly, and inequities exist for all groups of people, but progress is being made.

Business Responds to Diversity

The response by businesses to the diversification of the work force has been mixed. Research has shown that many companies are aware of and concerned about the effects of demographic shifts on their work force and markets. Yet their response so far has concentrated more on the recruitment of minorities than on initiatives to improve their long-term retention, such as training, education, and support.[13] A study of 1,400 companies by the Hay Group reported that nearly two-thirds responded that adapting to work force diversity over the next two years was either "important but not a priority" or "not very important."[14] Still, some businesses have proven how variety in the work force can pay off.

Certain large companies like Levi Strauss and Hoechst Celanese have turned diversity to their own advantage. Levi's has established a strict set of corporate goals, or "aspirations," for its work environment. Levi's states that it will "value a diverse work force (age, sex, ethnic group, and so on) at all levels of the organization. . . . Differing points of view will be sought; diversity will be valued and honestly rewarded, not suppressed."[15] Levi's believes that a varied work force will lead to unique and creative perspectives among its workers. Levi's chairman and CEO, Robert Haas, great-great-grandnephew of the company's founder Levi Strauss, believes in multiformity not because it is "politically correct," but because of the interconnection between the personal success of the people involved and the success of the company. So far, the connection between diversity and profit has not been proven, but Levi's adheres to its vision.

Ernest Drew, CEO of chemical producer Hoechst Celanese, learned the value of diversity during a company conference. A group of 125 top company officials, primarily white men, were separated into groups with 50 women and minority employees. Some of the groups comprised a variety of races and genders; some were composed of white men only. The groups were asked to solve a problem concerning corporate culture and how to change it. According to Drew, the multiformed teams produced the broadest solutions. "They had ideas I hadn't even thought of," he recalled. "For the first time, we realized that diversity is a strength as it relates to problem solving."[16] Drew now believes that a varied work force is needed at every level of an organization. Drew's realization, of course, applies to businesses of any size. Talent and teamwork are among the most valued qualities to look for in an employee.

Small Business's Opportunity for All

How does diversity affect small business ownership? Businesses owned by women and minorities are growing at a faster rate than all businesses combined. According to the Small Business Administration, women own and operate one-third (over 7.1 million) of all proprietorships in the United States.[17] From 1987 to 1997, the rate of women entering business increased 89 percent to 8.5 million; African American–owned businesses grew by 108 percent to 1.4 million: Hispanic-owned businesses grew by 232 percent to 1.4 million; Asian-owned companies rose 180 percent to 1.1 million.[18] The growth rate for all firms during the period was 111 percent. These data show that when faced with the choice of working for someone else or working for themselves, people from widely varied backgrounds are finding opportunities in small businesses.

Considering the number of problems that most small business owners face, perhaps more small business owners will find the same answer that Ernest Drew found—that diversity in the workplace can provide creative problem-solving ideas.

The Expanding Marketplace: Small Business Opportunities ▬

It may come as a surprise, but big businesses need small businesses. Actually, a symbiotic relationship exists between large and small businesses. For instance, John Deere Company relies on hundreds of vendors, many of which are small, to produce component parts for its farm equipment. Deere's extensive network of 3,400 independent dealers comprising small businesses provides sales and service for its equipment. These relationships enable Deere, the world's largest manufacturer of farm equipment, to focus on what it does best, while at the same time creating economic opportunity for hundreds of individual entrepreneurs.

Small businesses perform more efficiently than larger ones in several areas. For example, although large manufacturers tend to enjoy a higher profit margin due to their economies of scale, small businesses are often better at distribution. Most wholesale and retail businesses are small to link large manufacturers more efficiently with the millions of consumers spread all over the world.

Downsizing, Outsourcing, and Strategic Alliances

outsourcing Occurs when a company hires another business to provide goods or services rather than producing them itself.

As large businesses continue to trim the size of their organizations, many turn to outsourcing as a way to do more with fewer employees. **Outsourcing** means that a company hires another, usually smaller, business to produce components and perform needed activities. None of the major U.S. automobile manufacturers makes more than half of the parts used to build cars and trucks. Chrysler outsources two-thirds of its components.[19] Nike makes none of its own shoes. If you choose the right outsourcer, the people in your business are free to concentrate on what they know best. Through outsourcing, small and large businesses form what is called a *strategic alliance*—a contract or commitment to work together to produce goods and services.

Honda Motor Corporation provides a clear illustration of how outsourcing and strategic alliances can lead to more efficient modes of production. Honda chose Donnelly Corporation of Holland, Michigan, to produce external mirrors for its U.S.-made cars. Although Donnelly did not make external mirrors at the time (only internal ones), Honda liked how Donnelly treated its workers—encouraging them to make use of their intelligence and imagination, as well as their manual labor skills. This type of working philosophy, Honda's managers believed, amounts to a partnership with suppliers as opposed to an adversarial relationship. The payoff to Donnelly was big—$5 million in sales the first year.[20] Since Donnelly signed with Honda, it has taken off—literally. It penned agreements to supply Ford, Nissan, Toyota, and finally Lear jets. Sales in 1997 jumped to $700 million![21]

Just as many small businesses today perform specific tasks for large businesses, small business owners are increasingly turning to other companies for needed goods and services. A survey of 400 CEOs of fast-growing businesses showed that 68 percent outsourced their payroll responsibilities, 48 percent hired another business to handle their tax compliance, and 46 percent farmed out their employee benefits and claims administration.[22]

The former chairman of General Electric, John G. Welch, Jr., has said that "Size is no longer the trump card it once was in today's brutally competitive world—a marketplace that is unimpressed with logos and sales numbers but demands, instead, value and performance."[23] Because they are flexible and efficient, today's small businesses can provide the "value and performance" that the market demands.

Niche Marketing

niche marketing Marketing that focuses on service of small groups, or segments, of a market.

The flexibility of small businesses to respond to the needs of their customers, whether they be large businesses, consumers, or firms located in another country, is their ability to market to niches. **Niche marketing** is defined as serving a small segment or group of customers. Small businesses enjoy the advantage of being able to profitably serve smaller niches than can their larger counterparts. For example, Olmec Corporation, maker of ethnic toys, has chosen a niche in the gigantic toy market. Olmec was one of the first to produce ethnic toys and still has the niche largely to itself. Currently, the large toy manufacturers are not making toys for this market because they believe there is not enough demand to justify large production

Flying Solo

Jody Severson got tired of managing employees, shuffling paperwork, and "sweating payroll every Sunday night." Bill Collier lost his job of 33 years at IBM. Ellen Leanse could not imagine raising her children while working 80-hour weeks as an executive at Apple Computer. Paul Farrow found himself at a crossroads the day that his job as vice president of finance and manufacturing for an environmental service company no longer existed. Paul Taylor designs clothing for tree trimmers.

What do these five people have in common? More than you might think. They are all new business soloists.

Severson, Collier, Leanse, Taylor, and Farrow all started businesses that allowed them to do what they do very well. They work for themselves—by themselves. Severson became a political consultant in South Dakota thriving on the independence and advantages a solo business provides: low overhead, no worries about anyone else's salary, and picking the work he wants to do. Severson, like many soloists, depends on technology to communicate with customers and distribute his service. His laptop computer, fax machine, and cordless phone counter any geographical disadvantage he might face from being located in South Dakota.

Collier provides an example of the situation that 600,000 salaried personnel or managers faced in the mid-1990s. Forced from his previous position due to corporate downsizing, he turned to self-employment for survival. Collier formed Multiprocessor Diagnostics, where he produces and markets software that test-programs computer multiprocessors.

Leanse has maintained many of her business contacts from Apple, which have developed into an ever-increasing web of referrals and new business. She now provides marketing consultation to high-tech companies.

While Farrow was on a family vacation in Maine, he chanced upon the opportunity for a new career and a new identity for himself. He wanted more than to own his own company. He wanted to be the company, all by himself. So Farrow created a *virtual corporation* making kayaks for the masses.

Farrow used his knowledge of manufacturing, his passion for the environment, and his observation of a large unsatisfied market to produce an inexpensive kayak made of recycled plastic for people who had never before considered kayaking. Virtual corporations like Farrow's Walden Paddlers require many strategic partnerships by using the skills of many other people and organizations to complement the skills of the entrepreneur. This allows one person, like Paul Farrow, to design, produce, and market a technically sophisticated kayak by himself.

Being a tree climber by trade, Paul Taylor knew the difficulties of finding work clothing tough enough to last and still be comfortable. He had a friend from his high school days whose sister worked in the children's clothing industry introduce him to clothing and textile manufacturers. Taylor used the approach common in small business of relying on informal connections to get Arborwear going. Arborwear produces work pants, shirts, and belts, and Taylor tests them close to home while he still operates his other business, Taylor Tree Service.

Soloists are a new hybrid of business owner and their numbers are growing. It is estimated that 20 million Americans' primary occupation is now owner of a solo business. Soloists are not empire builders. They are not getting rich, but by offering specialized professional services, they are changing the way business is done. And they are inventing new varieties of self-employment.

Sources: Adapted from Tom Ford, "A Hard Climb to Try Solo," *Crain's Cleveland Business,* 10 May 1999, 13; Anne Murphy, "Do-It-Yourself Job Creation," *Inc.,* January 1994, 36–48; and Edward O. Wells, "Virtual Realities," *Inc.,* August 1993, 50–58.

runs or national marketing campaigns. Therefore, Olmec could put itself in danger if it succeeds in creating a much larger market for minority-oriented toys, because larger competitors might be attracted to enter the field.

Small Business in a Global Marketplace

By striving for flexibility, creativity, and closeness to the customer, small businesses deliver satisfaction along with quality products and services

The same competitive advantages (unique skills, talents, and products) that have made a small business successful in local markets may also create advantage in foreign markets. Because small businesses are especially suited to satisfying niche markets quickly, they are and will continue to be important players in international trade. As the world becomes more of a global marketplace, many opportunities are emerging for small businesses, especially those that can take advantage of technological advances.

Small businesses are serious players in international business. Of the 112,854 manufacturers involved in exporting products, about 96 percent had fewer than 100 employees; 63 percent had fewer than 20 employees. (In terms of quantities of goods exported, however, large companies still predominate.) The top 100 exporters account for over half of the goods sent abroad.[24] But manufacturing isn't the only area in which small businesses are advancing globally. In Chapter 15, we will discuss how small businesses are involved in exporting, international licensing, international joint ventures, establishing operations in other countries, and importing.

▬ Secrets of Small Business Success

When large and small businesses compete directly against each other, it may seem that large businesses have a better chance of winning. However, small businesses have certain inherent factors that work in their favor. You will improve your chances of success in running a small business if you identify your competitive advantage, remain flexible and innovative, cultivate a close relationship with your customers, and strive for quality.

Competitive Advantage

competitive advantage The facet of a business that is done better than everyone else. A competitive advantage can be built from many different factors.

To be successful in business, you have to offer your customers more value than your competitors do. That value gives the business its **competitive advantage.** For example, say that you are a printer whose competitors offer only black-and-white printing. An investment in color printing equipment would give your business a competitive advantage, at least until your competitors purchased similar equipment. The stronger and more sustainable your competitive advantage, the better your chances of winning and keeping customers. You must have a product or service that your business provides better than the competition, or the pressures of the marketplace may make your business obsolete (see Chapter 11).

Changing Their Stripes

Consider the example set by Edward Kaplan and Gary Cless, two electromechanical engineers. Working at Teletype, a subsidiary of AT&T's Western Electric, the two men were designing teleprinters, a precursor to fax machines. Because they didn't like working for a large corporation, they decided to go into business together. One of their products was a paper-tape punch machine that punched out designs to program machine tools. They rapidly became the market leaders in that industry, but Kaplan and Cless were closely monitoring how computers and technology were changing the way businesses worked. They believed that the newly emerging business of bar coding was what they should focus on in the future.

Kaplan and Cless started their next company, Zebra Technologies, in 1982, to make industrial bar code label printers. And the demand for their products positively exploded. Today, bar codes produced by Zebra software and printed on Zebra printers can be found everywhere, from hospitals to zoos to steel plants. And inevitably, the company attracted global competitors because of its success. However, Zebra continues to prosper by selling high-end printers while its competitors sell mostly cheaper models.

Kaplan and Cless nonetheless recognize that they must cultivate more midsize companies to broaden their customer base. To this end, they've introduced a more moderately priced line of bar code printers that smaller companies can afford. Obviously, the two founders of Zebra Technologies are people who know how to "change their stripes"—that is, how to survive in a rapidly evolving marketplace.

Sources: Vanessa Richardson, "Companies to Watch," *Money*, April 1999, 56; and Toddi Gutner Block, "Riding the Waves," *Forbes*, 11 September 1995, 182–183.

FLEXIBILITY. In order to take advantage of economies of scale, large businesses are usually concerned with devoting resources to produce large quantities of products over long periods of time. This commitment of resources limits their ability to react to new and quickly changing markets as small businesses do. Imagine the difference between making a sharp turn in a loaded 18-wheel tractor trailer and a small pickup. Now apply the analogy to large and small businesses turning in new directions. The big truck has a lot more capacity, but the pickup has more maneuverability in reaching customers.

INNOVATION. Real innovation has come most often from independent inventors and small businesses. The reason? The research and development departments of most large businesses tend to concentrate on the improvement of the products the company already makes. This practice makes sense for companies trying to profit from their large investments in plant and equipment. At the same time, it tends to discourage the development of totally new ideas and products. For example, telecommunications giant AT&T has an incentive to improve its existing line of telephones and services to better serve its customers. But the idea of inventing a product that would make telephones obsolete would threaten its investment.

Small businesses have contributed many inventions that we use daily. The long list would include zippers, air conditioners, helicopters, computers, instant cameras, audiotape recorders, double-knit fabric, fiber-optic examining equipment, heart valves, optical scanners, soft contact lenses, airplanes, and automobiles, most of which were later produced by large manufacturers. In fact, many say that the greatest value of entrepreneurial companies is the way they force larger competitors to respond to innovation. Small businesses innovate new technology, markets, products, and ideas.

creative destruction The replacement of existing products, processes, ideas, and businesses with new and better ones.

Economist Joseph Schumpeter called the replacement of existing products, processes, ideas, and businesses with new and better ones **creative destruction.** It is not an easy process. Although change can be threatening, it is vitally necessary in a capitalist system.[25] Small businesses are the driving force of change in the development of new technology.

Recently the SBA researched types of innovation and the role played by small businesses. The four types of innovation are

- *Product innovation.* Developing a new or improved product.

- *Service innovation.* Offering a new or altered service for sale.

- *Process innovation.* Inventing a new way to organize physical inputs to produce a product or service.

- *Management innovation.* Creating a new way to organize business's resources.

The most common types of innovation relate to service and product. Thirty-eight percent of all innovations are service related, and 32 percent are product related. Interestingly, the majority of innovations were found to have originated from the smallest businesses, those with 1 to 19 employees. Over three-fourths of service innovations are generated by very small businesses, which also generate 65 percent of both product and process innovations.[26]

The process of creative destruction is not limited to high technology or to the largest companies. A small business owner who does not keep up with the market risks being left behind. Creative destruction occurs in mundane as well as exotic industries, such as chains of beauty salons replacing barber shops.[27] Knowledge is the key to innovation and advancement. For this reason, it is important for you to keep current with business literature by reading periodicals, such as *Inc., Fast Company,* or *Fortune Small Business,* which cover small business topics, and any specialized trade journals that exist for your type of business. Many business schools also have executive education programs, which range from two days to a year or longer, specifically designed for small business owners.[28]

CLOSE RELATIONSHIP TO CUSTOMERS.   Small business owners get to know their customers and neighborhood on a personal level. This closeness allows small businesses to provide individualized service and gives them firsthand knowledge of customer wants and needs. By contrast, large businesses get to "know" their customers only through limited samples of marketing research (which may be misleading). Knowing customers personally can allow small businesses to build a competitive advantage based on specialty products, personalized service, and quality, which enable the small business to compete with the bigger business's lower prices gained through mass production. For this reason, you should always remember that the rapport you build with your customers is what makes them come back again and again.

PRODUCT QUALITY.   One of the management buzzwords of the 1980s was *total quality management (TQM).* Companies have adopted TQM principles as a way to demonstrate their commitment to quality on every level of the business. The philosophy of total quality management is based on the work of W. Edwards Deming, who developed a list of 14 points for managers to follow in achieving world-class quality (described in Chapter 16). Basically, **quality** refers to all the features and characteristics of a product or service that affect its ability to satisfy a customer's wants and needs.

Val Verutti is quality support manager for Granite Rock Company, a construction materials manufacturer. For Verutti, the key to producing quality is being able to measure the results. "If you set goals and lofty ideals, without means of measuring," he states, "you're just kidding yourself."[29] Verutti should know something about quality—Granite Rock won the Malcolm Baldrige National Quality Award for the small business category.

Some companies subscribing to the TQM philosophy have found that it can be expensive, time consuming, and complex. It can result in more attention being paid to administering the TQM program than to customers or to products. Many managers, especially small business owners who are strapped for resources, now look for **return on quality (ROQ),** which means paying the closest attention to parts of your product or business that are most important to your customers and your bottom line. Quality for its own sake, in areas that don't matter to customers or that don't produce a payoff in improved sales, profits, or increased market share, waste the company's effort and resources[30] (see Chapter 16).

quality The features and characteristics of a product that allow it to exceed customer expectations.

return on quality (ROQ) The act of concentrating attention to produce quality in areas most important to customers.

Getting Started on the Right Foot

Before starting your business, you will want to make sure you have the tools to succeed. Look for a market large enough to generate a profit, sufficient capital, skilled employees, and accurate information.

MARKET SIZE AND DEFINITION. Who will be buying your product or service? Marketing techniques help you find out what consumers want and in what quantity. With this information, you can make an informed decision about the profitability of offering a particular good or service. Once you conclude that a market is large enough to support your business, you will want to learn what your customers have in common and about their likes and dislikes, in order to serve them better and remain competitive.

GATHERING SUFFICIENT CAPITAL. Too often, entrepreneurs try to start a business without sufficient startup capital. The lifeblood of any young business is cash; starting on a financial shoestring hurts your chances of success. Profit is the ultimate goal, but inadequate cash flow cuts off the blood supply (see Chapter 8).

You may need to be creative in finding startup capital. A second mortgage, loans from friends or relatives, a line of credit from a bank or credit union, or a combination of sources may be sufficient. Thorough planning will give you the best estimate of how much money you will need. Once you have made your best estimate, double it—or at least get access to more capital. You'll probably need it.

FINDING AND KEEPING EFFECTIVE EMPLOYEES. Maintaining a capable work force is a never-ending task for small businesses. Frequently, small business owners get caught up in urgency to "fill positions with warm bodies" before spending enough time on the selection process. You should hire, train, and motivate your employees before opening for business (see Chapter 17).

Once established, you must understand that your most valuable assets walk out the door at closing time. Your employees are valuable assets because it is their skill, knowledge, and information that make your business successful. These intangible assets are called **intellectual capital.**

intellectual capital The valuable skills and knowledge that employees of a business possess.

GETTING ACCURATE INFORMATION. Managers at any organization will tell you how difficult it is to make a decision before acquiring all the relevant information. This difficulty is compounded for the aspiring small business owner, who does not yet possess the expertise or experience needed to oversee every functional area of the business, from accounting to sales. Consult a variety of sources of information, from self-help books in your local library to experts in your nearest Small Business Development Center. A more accurate picture can be drawn if you consider several vantage points.

Understanding the Risks of Small Business Ownership

The decision to start your own business should be made with a full understanding of the risks involved. If you go in with both eyes open, you will be able to anticipate problems, reduce the possibility of loss, and increase your chances of success. The prospect of failure should serve as a warning to you. Many new businesses do not get past their second or third years. Running a small business involves much more than simply getting an idea, hanging out a sign, and opening for business the next

Kent and Darcie Krueger started sitstay.com for pet owners who love dogs as much as Kent and Darcie do.

SitStay.com Stays Focused

Make a profit by selling pet supplies on the web? It must be impossible because Pets.com had so much money it ran multiple ads on the Super Bowl (to the tune of $2 million plus per 30-second ad) with a cute sock puppet dog as spokes-pooch before it became one of the biggest dot.com fizzles. Pets.com created great brand awareness, but it had a problem with its business model of emphasizing deep discounts on all pet products. In its last quarter of business, Pets.com lost $277,000 on sales of $9.3 million. It regularly sold products for less than it paid for them. Here's a good point to make in the first chapter of a textbook about running your own business—You can't sell stuff for less than you pay for it and stay in business—it's that simple.

Kent and Darcie Krueger know that their business SitStay.com needs to make money. They started the high-end dog supply web site as a hobby for Belgium-shepherd dog owners. As people started depending on the Kruegers for advice, Kent and Darcie realized they had the beginnings of a customer base. They didn't try to raise tens of millions of dollars to buy up-to-the-second technology, hire the most tech-savvy employees, or bombard the world with prime-time advertising. They generated word-of-mouth goodwill, upgraded phones, computers, software, and warehouse space only when they had the cash in hand.

They had a customer base but needed stuff to sell, so they approached M.I. Industries about selling their all natural pet treats. M.I. agreed but was wary to the point of requiring cash for the first order—a single box of Macho Stix (appropriately named because they are made from the male genitalia of beef cattle). The company doesn't try to be all things to all pet owners. SitStay.com concentrates its relatively small product selection (about 1,500 items) targeting dog owners who want quality products for their pets. After four years of operation, SitStay.com has 19,000 customers and $900,000 of annual revenue, with 4 human and 4 canine employees.

SitStay.com is a great illustration, because it exhibits the traits of a well-run business—not a stereotypical Internet business.

Source: Jill Hecht Maxwell, "Sit! Stay! Make Money! Good Company," from *Inc.: The Magazine for Growing Companies*. Copyright © 2001 by Goldhirsh Group/Inc Pubg. Reproduced by permission of Goldhirsh Group/Inc Pubg in the format textbook via Copyright Clearance Center.

day. You need a vision, resources, and a plan in order to take advantage of the opportunity that exists.

What Is Business Failure?

Even though business owners start their ventures with the best of intentions and work long, hard hours, some businesses do fail. Dun & Bradstreet, a financial research firm, defines a *business failure* as a business that closes

- Due to actions such as bankruptcy, foreclosure, or voluntary withdrawal from the business *with a financial loss to a creditor.*

- Because it is involved in court action such as receivership (taken over involuntarily) or reorganization (receiving protection from creditors).

According to this definition, 76 out of 10,000 businesses failed in 1998.[31] More detailed information on failure rate by industry for 1998 is shown in Figure 1.3. You

FIGURE 1.3
Business Failure Rate per 10,000 Firms

Source: Statistical Abstract of the United States (Washington, DC: U.S. Government Printing Office, 1999), 561.

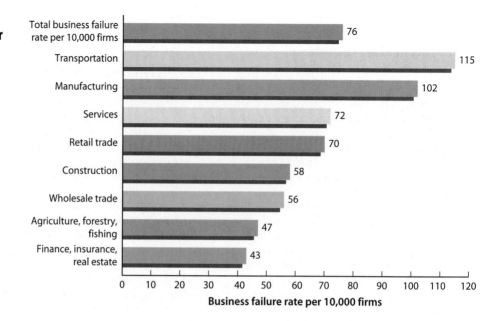

Business failure rate per 10,000 firms

Total business failure rate per 10,000 firms	76
Transportation	115
Manufacturing	102
Services	72
Retail trade	70
Construction	58
Wholesale trade	56
Agriculture, forestry, fishing	47
Finance, insurance, real estate	43

can see that businesses within the agriculture, forestry, and fishing industries enjoy the lowest industry failure rate, whereas businesses within the transportation industry suffer the highest rate. Still, a considerable variance of failure rates exists within industries. The table in the Reality Check box illustrates the five riskiest and the five safest businesses. If you are considering starting an amusement or recreation service business, the failure rate of 578 businesses per 10,000 carries much more meaning to you on the risk you face than the figure of 76 per 10,000 for all businesses.

Causes of Business Failure

The rates of business failure vary greatly by industry and are affected by factors such as type of ownership, size of the business, and expertise of the owner. The most common causes of business failure, however, are inadequate management and financing (see Figure 1.4).

Although financial problems are listed as the most common cause of business failure, consider management's role in controlling them. Could business failure due to industry weakness be linked to poor management? Yes, if the owner tried to enter an industry or market with no room for another competitor or was slow to respond to industry changes. High operating expenses and an insufficient profit margin also reflect ineffective management. Finally, business failure due to insufficient capital also suggests inexperienced management.

INADEQUATE MANAGEMENT. Business management is the efficient and effective use of resources. For small business owners, management skills are especially desirable—and often especially difficult to obtain. Lack of experience is one of their most pressing problems. Small business owners must be generalists; they do not have the luxury of specialized management. On the one hand, they may not be able

Source: DILBERT reprinted by permission of United Features Syndicate, Inc.

to afford to hire the full-time experts who could help avert costly mistakes. On the other hand, their limited resources will not permit them to make many mistakes and stay in business. As a small business manager, you will probably have to make decisions in areas in which you have little expertise.

The manager of a small business must be a leader, a planner, and a worker. You may be a "top gun" in sales, but that skill could work against you. You might be tempted to concentrate on sales while ignoring other equally important areas of the business, such as record keeping, inventory, and customer service.

INADEQUATE FINANCING. Business failure due to inadequate financing can be caused by improper managerial control as well as shortage of capital. On the one hand, if you don't have adequate funds to begin with, you will not be able to afford the facilities or personnel you need to start up the business correctly. On the other hand, if you do possess adequate capital but do not manage your resources wisely, you may be unable to maintain adequate inventory or keep the balance needed to run the business.

There are a lot of ways to fail in business. You can extend too much credit. You can fail to plan for the future or not have strategic direction. You can overinvest in

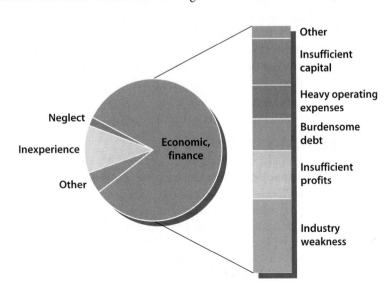

FIGURE 1.4

The Causes of Business Failures Are Many and Complex.

Source: Business Failure Record, The Dun & Bradstreet Corporation, NFIB Foundation/VISA Business Card Primer, as shown in William J. Dennis, Jr., *A Small Business Primer* (Washington, DC: National Foundation of Independent Business, 1993), 23. Reprinted by permission of National Federation of Independent Business.

Risky Business

Riskiest Types of Business	Business Failure Rate per 10,000
Amusement and recreation services	578
Oil and gas extraction	166
Lumber and wood manufacturing	106
General building contractors	101
Furniture and home furnishing stores	99
Safest Types of Business	**Business Failure Rate per 10,000**
Personal services	39
Insurance agents and brokers	28
Legal services	25
Health services	21
Private educational services	13

Source: Bruce Phillips, Small Business Administration Office of Economic Research, cited in *Inc., The State of Small Business,* 16 May 1995, 20.

fixed assets or hire the wrong people. Identifying mistakes that can be made is only part of the problem. Figuring out how to avoid them is the hard part.[32]

Business Termination

business termination When a business ceases operation for any reason.
business failure When a business closes with a financial loss to a creditor.

There is a difference between a **business termination** and a **business failure.** A *termination* occurs when a business no longer exists for any reason. There are many reasons for a business to be terminated. The owner may have an opportunity to sell his or her business to someone else for a healthy profit. The owner may be ready to move on to a new business or to retire, or may have simply lost interest in the business. The market for the business's product may have changed or become saturated. Perhaps the owner decided it was more attractive to work for someone else. In other cases, businesses may change form. A partnership may be restructured as a corporation, or a business may simply move to a new location. Businesses that undergo such changes are considered terminated even though they continue in another form.

Failure-Rate Controversy

Almost everyone has heard the story about the supposedly high rate of failure for small businesses. "Did you know that 90 percent of all new businesses fail within one year?" the story usually begins, as if to confirm one's worst fears about business ownership. For educators and businesspeople, this piece of modern folklore is known as "the myth that would not die." Actually, only about 18 percent of all new businesses are forced to close their doors with a loss to creditors.[33] The rest either closed voluntarily or are still in business.

Entrepreneurial Mistakes

No one likes to think about failing. Yet many small business owners invite failure by ignoring basic rules for success. One of the most common mistakes is failing to look toward the future, in the belief that planning is too hard or time consuming. Planning what you want to do with your business, where you want it to go, and how you're going to get it there are prerequisites for a sound business. But that doesn't mean you can't change your plans as circumstances dictate. Rather, your plan should provide a roadmap for your business, showing you both the expressways and the scenic route—and, of course, the detours.

Another common mistake is failing to understand the commitment and hard work that are required for making a business a success. Having to work long hours and do things you don't enjoy because there's no one else to do them are part and parcel of owning a small business. But often, when you have the freedom of being your own boss, the hard work and long hours don't seem so demanding!

Another mistake that small business owners make, particularly in rapidly growing businesses, is not hiring additional employees soon enough or not using existing employees effectively. There comes a point in the growth of a business when it's no longer possible for the manager to do it all, and it's often difficult for the manager to give up control. Yet it's important to recognize that delegating tasks to others isn't giving up control—it's giving up the execution of details.

The last type of mistake that we want to look at involves the financials. Inaccurate estimates of cash flow and capital requirements can swamp a business quickly. Figuring the correct amount of money needed for starting a business is a tough balancing act. Asking for too little may hinder growth and may actually jeopardize survival. But asking for too much might cause lenders or investors to hesitate. An important rule to remember in terms of arranging financing or calculating cash flow projections is to figure the unexpected into your financial plans. In this way, you can have more of a cushion to fall back on when things don't go exactly according to plan. After all, without the right amount of capital, it's impossible to succeed.

Sources: Richard Monk, "Why Small Businesses Fail," *CMA Management,* July/August 2000, 12–13; Udayan Gupta, "How Much?" *Wall Street Journal,* 22 May 1995, R7; and Stephanie N. Mehta, "Small Talk: An Interview with Wendell E. Dunn," *Wall Street Journal,* 22 May 1995, R16ff.

Sometimes researchers include business terminations in their failure-rate calculations, resulting in an artificially high number of failures. Economic consultant David Birch describes the misinterpretation of economic data as "like being at the end of a whisper chain. It's a myth everyone agrees to."[34] Fortunately for small business owners, the myth is not a fact.

Starting a business does involve risk, but the assumption of risk is part of life. The divorce rate in 1995 was 44 per 10,000.[35] Of every 10,000 students who start college, how many fail to graduate? Would you decide not to get married because the divorce rate is too high? Were you afraid to go to college because of the dropout rate? The point to remember is that if you have a clear vision, know your product and your market, and devote the time and effort needed, small businesses can and do succeed.

Over the past several decades, the number of new businesses that have opened has exceeded the number that have closed. Table 1.3 shows a net business formation for a recent 25-year period. Data from the SBA show that the average new firm formation rate averaged 13 percent for the years 1982 through 1993.[36]

TABLE 1.3 **U.S. Startups** **Versus Failures**	Number of New Incorporations	Number of Failures
1970	264,000	10,748
1975	326,000	11,432
1980	532,000	11,742
1985	663,000	57,078
1990	647,000	60,747
1997	798,917	84,342

Source: Statistical Abstract of the United States (Washington, DC: U.S. Government Printing Office, 1999), 560.

What's Ahead?

Because small businesses vary so greatly, it is difficult to generalize about them. Examples and illustrations used to describe how to operate a small business may be appropriate for most but still not fit the exact business you have in mind. The following chapters will attempt to lead you through the process of starting and operating your own successful small business.

SUMMARY

The characteristics of small business.

Small businesses include a wide variety of business types that are independently owned, operated, and financed. Although specific size definitions exist for each type of business, manufacturers with fewer than 500 employees, wholesalers with fewer than 100 employees, and retailers or services with annual revenue of under $3.5 million are considered small. By itself, each individual small business has relatively little impact in its industry.

The role of small business in the U.S. and global economies.

Small businesses provided the economic foundation on which the U.S. economy was built. Small businesses are creating new jobs while large businesses are eliminating jobs. Small businesses are more flexible in the products and services they offer. Most real product innovations come from small businesses. Small businesses are rapidly becoming important players in international trade.

The importance of diversity in the marketplace and the workplace.

Small businesses are responding as the population becomes more diverse. Businesses owned by women and minorities are growing at a faster rate than the overall rate of business growth. Diversity is important in small business, not because of affirmative action compliance, but because a wide range of viewpoints and personal backgrounds can improve problem solving.

Ways to court success in a small business venture.

To prevent your small business from becoming another casualty in business failure statistics, you must begin with a clearly defined competitive advantage. You must offer a product or service that people want and are willing to buy. You must do *something* substantially better than your competition. You must remain flexible and innovative, stay close to your customers, and strive for quality.

The causes of small business failure.

Ineffective and inefficient management, which shows up in many ways, is the number one cause of business failure. Inadequate financing, industry weakness, inexperience, and neglect are other major causes.

QUESTIONS FOR REVIEW & DISCUSSION

1. How would you define *small business?*

2. Name a company that seems large but might be classified as small because it has relatively little impact on its industry.

3. Large businesses depend on small businesses. Why?

4. Define *outsourcing,* and describe its impact on small business.

5. Why are small businesses more likely than large businesses to be innovative?

6. Explain the term *creative destruction.*

7. How can being close to your customers give you a competitive advantage?

8. How would you show that small business is becoming a more important part of the economy?

9. The text compares the failure rate of small business with the divorce rate in marriage and student failure rate in college. Are these fair comparisons?

10. Describe four causes of small business failure. How does the quality of management relate to each of these causes?

11. Describe the techniques that a business with which you are familiar has used to prevent business failure.

12. How would the computer industry be different today if there were no businesses under 500 employees? Would personal computers exist?

13. Predict the future of small business. In what industries will it be involved? What trends do you foresee? Will the failure rate go up or down? Will the importance of small business increase or decrease by the year 2020?

1. The chapter discussed the evolution of small business in the American economy. With the rapid popularity of Internet businesses in the late 1990s and the bust in 2000, what is the next stage of small business evolution? Is the Internet just another business tool, or is it going to re-create the way business is done again?

2. Is creative destruction just another economic theory for the foundation of capitalism? Build a case supporting your answer.

Experience this...

This chapter discussed the failure rate of small business. Call your local Small Business Development Center, and ask if the local business failure rate matches the SBA rate questioned in the chapter.

WHAT WOULD **YOU** DO?   No. 1

Clark Childers is all of 17 years old and already president of his own successful small business, QuikSkins Boat Covers of Corpus Christi, Texas. Even at such a young age, Childers pulled together several key ingredients to launch his business: a comprehensive business plan, product prototypes, available funding, and an untapped market.

Childers loves to sail. But one thing he hates about the hobby is taking his small Sunfish sailboat apart after sailing and packing up all the boat's parts. This chore could easily consume 15 to 20 minutes each time. Then Childers realized that he could make his pastime much more enjoyable if he found a way to cover his Sunfish in just a few minutes. So he designed a fabric cover to fit around the mast, cover the boat, and protect the boat's removable parts (rudder, centerboard, and tiller). The cover even included a pocket for the sail.

Childers's first product prototype worked well, but his initial attempts at mail order and marketing to local boat shops weren't as successful. Demand was so small that only a family friend was needed to hand-sew the boat covers as they were ordered. However, Childers knew he had a good product that other Sunfish enthusiasts would be excited about. So he wrote to the president of the boat's manufacturer, Sunfish/Laser, Inc., describing his product. And his strategy paid off with an order for 300 boat covers!

To begin production, Childers first had to find financing. He obtained a bank loan, cosigned by his mother. Then he had to find an affordable production facility that could turn out the product quickly and reliably. Childers wanted to ensure that paying production expenses didn't eat up all his profits. And he had only six weeks from the time he signed the contract with Sunfish/Laser to deliver the 300 covers. He considered manufacturers in Corpus Christi, which he realized would allow him only to break even on his expenses. After someone suggested that he look to Mexico for a possible partner, he found a firm in Piedras Negras called Tight Stitches, which not only met the production deadline, but charged $30 less per cover than the lowest bid he had received in Corpus Christi. That 300-cover order propelled QuikSkins Boat Covers to 1994 sales of $45,000, with profits topping $20,000.

What advice does Clark Childers have for other small business owners? He says the main lesson he learned was to be open to nontraditional ways of operating. Childers continued working with Tight Stitches, but also partnered with a Corpus Christi workshop for people with disabilities to manufacture some of his other products. Using a foreign factory or a manufacturing shop made up of workers with disabilities may *sound* risky to some small business owners, but for Childers, it has proven profitable.

Source: Clark Childers and Susan Biddle Jaffe, "Setting Sail on a New Venture," *Nation's Business*, October 1995, 6.

QUESTIONS

1. Pretend that you're Clark Childers and (like every business in existence) if you don't get some customers for your product, your business is facing shutdown. Write a letter to the president of Sunfish/Laser, Inc., that would persuade the president to place an order. Of course, the president of Sunfish/Laser doesn't care if your little business succeeds or fails, so your persuasion must concentrate on the advantages and benefits that Sunfish/Laser will receive from buying your covers.

2. Break into teams and discuss what Childers did correctly in getting his business started. What problems could he possibly run into, and how could he address them?

WHAT WOULD **YOU** DO? | No. 2

Tara Phillips is a young entrepreneur trying to redefine underwear—or at least the way it's designed and bought. While working in media relations for Intel, Phillips found enhanced web sites inspiring. She visualized a process in which customers would click on options to design underwear using 3-D virtual characters as models. Thus she started an online company selling customizable undergarments. Phillips' final ensemble of virtual female characters had quirky personalities and story lines—hooks that Phillips hoped will keep her target market of 18-to-34-year-old females coming back.

Source: Victoria Neal, "Online Undies," *Business Start-ups*, March 2000, 17.

QUESTIONS

1. Evaluate the business idea of Tara's business. Why would customers want to design and buy their underwear online? What is their competitive advantage?

2. Look at Figure 1-4, "Causes of Business Failure." If the business goes under (as it eventually did), what do you think will be the most likely reason?

Small Business Lessons from the Movies

Want to inspire your organization? Earn the undying loyalty of employees? Turn crises into triumphs? Start by renting these 10 videos.

Every year around Christmas, Susan Schreter takes a refresher course in leadership. Her teacher is always the same: George Bailey, the sweetly earnest hero of *It's a Wonderful Life,* who risks his livelihood to prove that compassionate banking need not be an oxymoron. "Every time I see that movie, I want to be more like George," says Schreter, CEO of Coupons4Everything.com, a Seattle-based start-up that offers coupons and rebates for consumer goods over the web. "He reminds me that the important thing is to be respected, not as a rich entrepreneur but as a socially minded, successful member of a community."

Schreter's paean to the saint of Bedford Falls came in response to a recent *Inc.* survey that asked small-company CEOs and senior executives to name the movies that inspired business leaders best. The question isn't a frivolous one: movies—like Shakespeare—are becoming a staple of business school curricula, as professors screen *Wall Street* to teach ethics and leaven Tom Peters with Tom (Jerry Maguire) Cruise. "Films are a catalyst. They present dramatic problems, crises, and turnarounds," explains John K. Clemens, who incorporates works like *Hoosiers* and *Citizen Kane* into his graduate management and executive education courses at Hartwick College, in Oneonta, N.Y., and is the coauthor of *Movies to Manage By: Lessons in Leadership from Great Films* (NTC/Contemporary Publishing Group, 1999). "Films beg to be interpreted and discussed, and from those discussions businesspeople come up with principles for their own jobs."

Academic validation notwithstanding, *Inc.* magazine writers expected the cold shoulder when they recently asked approximately 100 readers to don Roger Ebert hats. Company builders, after all, are generally too busy to haunt the local cineplex, let alone mull the business implications of what they might see there. Or so they thought. To their surprise, almost two-thirds of those surveyed responded, many almost immediately. Some wrote or called several times to tweak their lists, while others left impassioned voice mail messages extolling their favorites. "If you haven't seen it, rent it today," these messages almost invariably concluded.

A few respondents described movies that had influenced their professional lives. One CEO said that *Baby Boom,* in which Diane Keaton trades the corporate piranha pool for motherhood and a gourmet baby food start-up, inspired her to go into business for herself. Another used insights gleaned from the Bill Murray comedy *What About Bob?*—about a psychiatric patient tormenting his shrink—to help him cope with a problem employee.

More often, however, readers praised films that grapple with ethical and personal quandaries played out by realistically nuanced characters. "The best leadership films deal with the fundamentals, such as the presence or absence of integrity and trust," says Clemens. "In *Citizen Kane,* for example, you see the classic trajectory of early integrity followed by its loss as the character climbs the power grid. In *Dead Poets Society,* Keating, an English teacher at a prep school, is fired, and there's a suicide. But he has enormous integrity. And at the end you have to ask yourself, 'Did he succeed or fail?'—which is a wonderful question for anyone interested in leadership."

Readers, no doubt, will disagree with the inclusion of some of the films listed here and become apoplectic over the exclusion of others. But that's to be expected. As the Academy Awards remind us each year: Filmmaking is both an art and a science. Film ranking is neither.

Following is a list of movies that ranked highly in the *Inc.* survey. Yes, some of them were made before most students were born, but they *are* available as rentals. To see a description and analysis of these titles go to this book's web page under cases at http://business.college .hmco.com/students.

Apollo 13 (1995)
The Bridge on the River Kwai (1957)
Dead Poets Society (1989)
Elizabeth (1998)
Glengarry Glen Ross (1992)
It's a Wonderful Life (1946)
Norma Rae (1979)
One Flew over the Cuckoo's Nest (1975)
Twelve Angry Men (1957)
Twelve O' Clock High (1949)

Source: Adapted from "Everything I Know About Leadership, I Learned from the Movies," by Buchanan and Hofman, from *Inc.: The Magazine for Growing Companies.* Copyright © 2000 by Goldhirsh Group/Inc Pubg. Reproduced with permission of Goldhirsh Group/Inc Pubg in the format textbook via Copyright Clearance Center.

QUESTIONS

1. What are your personal screen inspirations? What lessons do these or other movies provide in running a small business?

2. In addition to the movies cited in this case, think of other titles for business lessons like *Risky Business, Wall Street,* and *Tucker.* What lessons do they provide?

3. What movies portray leaders who think creatively, who keep their heads, who manage communication, and as for failure, well, that's just not an option (a line from *Apollo 13*)?

4. Since the intent of movies is artistic, rather than educational, what movie lessons illustrate the *opposite* of what a manager should do or say?

2

Small Business Management, Entrepreneurship, and Ownership

After reading this chapter, you should be able to:

- Articulate the differences between the small business manager and the entrepreneur.

- Discuss the steps in preparing for small business ownership.

- Enumerate the advantages and disadvantages of self-employment.

- Characterize the three main forms of ownership—sole proprietorship, partnership, and corporation—and their unique features.

DO YOU HAVE what it takes to be an entrepreneur? Do you personally know an entrepreneur? Do you act and think like him or her? Becoming an entrepreneur is one of the most exciting careers going. The big question now is to see how much you have in common with other entrepreneurs. Take the quiz and see.

Directions: Indicate True or False.

Entrepreneurs:

True	**False**	1.	Dislike working for others.
True	**False**	2.	Possess an above-normal energy quotient.
True	**False**	3.	Can balance work and family life.
True	**False**	4.	Involve spouses and children in the enterprise.
True	**False**	5.	Often copy the successful ideas of others.
True	**False**	6.	Frequently sell one business and start another.
True	**False**	7.	Usually obtain an M.B.A. before starting a business.
True	**False**	8.	Like to establish a right way to do something and stick to it.
True	**False**	9.	Value teamwork above everything.
True	**False**	10.	Use other people's money to begin a business.
True	**False**	11.	Often go into business with a friend.
True	**False**	12.	Cut corners on quality to raise margins.
True	**False**	13.	Underprice the competition to get a leg up.
True	**False**	14.	Must lower ethical norms to compete.
True	**False**	15.	Are perfectionists and hate making mistakes.

Now that you have answered this entrepreneurship quiz, compare your responses with those of successful entrepreneurs, found at the end of this chapter on pages 66–67. Good luck!

Source: Dick Irish, "Do You *Really* Want to Be an Entrepreneur?" First published in *The Costco Connection*, November 1997, 32–33. Reprinted by permission of the author.

■■ The Entrepreneur-Manager Relationship

entrepreneurship The process of identifying opportunities for which marketable needs exist and assuming the risk of creating an organization to satisfy them.

small business management The ongoing process of owning and operating an established business.

What is the difference between a small business manager and entrepreneur? Aren't all small business owners also entrepreneurs? Don't all entrepreneurs start as small business owners? The terms are often used interchangeably, and although there is overlap between them, there are enough differences for them to be studied separately. Entrepreneurship and small business management are both *processes,* not isolated incidents.

Entrepreneurship is the process of identifying opportunities for which marketable needs exist and assuming the risk of creating an organization to satisfy them. An entrepreneur needs the vision to spot opportunities and the ability to capitalize on them. **Small business management,** by contrast, is the ongoing process of owning and operating an established business. A small business manager must be able to deal with all the challenges of moving the business forward—hiring and retaining good employees, reacting to changing customer wants and needs, making sales, and keeping cash flow positive, for example.

The processes of entrepreneurship and small business management each present challenges and rewards as the business progresses through different stages.

What Is an Entrepreneur?

An entrepreneur is a person who takes advantage of a business opportunity by assuming the financial, material, and psychological risks of starting or running a company.

An entrepreneur is a person who sees an opportunity and assumes the risk of starting a business to take advantage of the opportunity or idea. The risks that go with creating an organization can be financial, material, and psychological. The term *entrepreneur,* a French word that dates from the seventeenth century, translates literally as "between-taker" or "go-between."[1] It originally referred to men who organized and managed exploration expeditions and military maneuvers. The term has evolved over the years into a multitude of definitions, but most include the following behaviors:

■ *Creation.* A new business is started.

■ *Innovation.* The business involves a new product, process, market, material, or organization.

■ *Risk assumption.* The owner of the business bears the risk of potential loss or failure of the business.

- *General management.* The owner of the business guides the business and allocates the business's resources.

- *Performance intention.* High levels of growth and/or profit are expected.[2]

All new businesses require a certain amount of entrepreneurial skill. The degree of entrepreneurship involved depends on the amount of each of these behaviors that is needed.

Entrepreneurship and the Small Business Manager

Entrepreneurship involves the startup process. Small business management focuses on running a business over a long period of time. Although you cannot study one without the other, they are different. In managing a small business, most of the "entrepreneuring" was done a long time ago. Of course, a good manager is always looking for new ways to please customers, but the original innovation and the triggering event that launched the business make way for more stability in the maturity stage of the business.

The manager of a small business needs perseverance, patience, and critical thinking skills to deal with the day-to-day challenges that arise in running a business over a long period of time.

Staying Fresh

What happens to that opportunity-seeking, entrepreneurial spirit as a small business grows? Does achieving stability mean the end of entrepreneurship? What can you, as a small business manager, do to maintain the creative, daring, innovative approaches that made your business successful in the first place, while building a "business that lasts"?

Often, as a small business achieves marketplace and financial successes and grows in size, it loses those bold, ingenious risk-seeking attitudes, actions, and approaches that helped make it successful. For instance, employees may, for whatever reasons, become resistant to taking risks and making changes. But it doesn't have to be that way! A successful and growing small business can be well structured, organized, under control, and yet still maintain an organizational environment where entrepreneurial attitudes can flourish. How? Let's look at some suggestions that can help small businesses preserve that spirit of entrepreneurship.

Develop an Appropriate Control System. It's important to get feedback about decisions that have been made by employees. Yet your control system should imply trust, so that employees can make decisions without feeling as if someone is always looking over their shoulder.

At Indus Group, a management software developer in San Francisco, founder Bob Felton wanted employees to use their judgment, not bureaucratic rules, to guide their actions. He uses e-mail to keep up with them. Every Friday, all employees type up a one-page summary of what they worked on that week, what their plans are for the coming week, and what obstacles they ran into.

Emphasize Responsibility, Not Just Authority. In a young firm, employees tend to feel personally responsible for what happens to the company. In older firms, where authority is centralized in levels of management, people often feel less inclined to pursue opportunities and change on their own initiative. How can you instill a sense of employee commitment in your established firm?

At BAI International, a Tarrytown, New York–based market research firm, employees are encouraged to "make things work" by improving both the work environment and the work product. President and owner Kathy Knight asks employees to get involved by speaking up about work-related decisions. Because they are involved in these decisions, employees feel a sense of responsibility to the company.

Determine the Kinds of Failure Your Company Can Tolerate. Failure and mistakes are an inevitable part of business life. One of the hallmarks of an entrepreneurial company is that failures are seen as valuable learning experiences. Of course, lapses in ethical decision making can have serious consequences and should not be tolerated. Yet when individuals fail because they lack the skills or application of needed effort, or because of uncontrollable external influences, managers should look for ways to address the causes and remedies of those mistakes so that they can be avoided in the future.

Create and Nurture Teams and Teamwork. A growing company inevitably becomes more complex. The number of its products and the size of its markets have probably increased, and it may pursue new technologies or aggressive growth strategies. Organizing employee teams offers a way to empower employees to stay on top of all the changes for you. Teams facilitate empowerment in varying ways, some by cross-training employees to increase the general skill level, others by asking employees to specialize in a certain area. However they are structured, teams assist problem solving by giving employees a sense of direction.

At Published Image, a small Boston firm that publishes documents for shareholders of 11 mutual fund companies, president and founder Eric Gershman reorganized employees into four self-managed teams. Gershman says that creating the teams helped to halt chronically high employee turnover and to keep customers coming back while increasing profits. Gershman feels that it was the teams' close focus on clients' needs that helped his company manage its rapid growth.

Encourage Functional Excellence in All Positions. Although every manager wants quality people in all functional areas, hiring specialists is typically cost prohibitive for the small business. So you may have to try other options. At Playground Environments, Inc., a small maker of playground equipment in Speonk, New York, all core employees are trained to do several jobs. From product innovation, to developing marketing plans, to taking turns cooking lunch for everyone in the office, employees are expected to contribute in different functions as needed. By working in these different jobs, the company's employees get to see how all the pieces fit together and why it is important for each job to be done in an excellent manner.

Promote Continuous Adaptive Organizational Change. To build a company atmosphere that supports opportunity-seeking behavior and change, the small business manager should reward individuals who come up with bold, innovative ideas. Nothing can kill the risk-taking spirit faster than criticizing employees who want to try something new. Restless invention, not staid complacency, should be the credo of a growing business that wants to maintain that entrepreneurial spirit.

Sources: Howard Stevenson and José Carlos Jarrillo-Mossi, "Preserving Entrepreneurship as Companies Grow," *Journal of Business Strategy,* Summer 1986, 10–23; Leslie Brokaw, "Thinking Flat," *Inc.,* October 1993, 88; Roberta Maynard, "Are Your Employees Helping Your Company Grow?" *Nation's Business,* April 1994, 10; Michael Selz, "Testing Self-Managed Teams, Entrepreneur Hopes to Lose Job," *Wall Street Journal,* 11 January 1994, B1ff; and Gail Buchalter, "Making a Difference," *Forbes,* 9 May 1994, 164–165.

A Model of the Startup Process ▰

The processes of entrepreneurship and small business management can be thought of as a spectrum with six distinct stages that can be identified for each (see Figure 2.1).[3] The stages of the entrepreneurship process are innovation, a triggering event, and implementation. The stages of the small business management process are growth, maturity, and harvest.

The **entrepreneurship process** begins with an *innovative idea* for a new product, process, or service, which is refined as you think it through. You may tell your idea to family members or close friends to get their feedback as you develop and cultivate it. You may visit a consultant at a local Small Business Development Center for more outside suggestions for your innovative business idea. Perhaps you even wake up late at night thinking of a new facet of your idea. That is your brain working through the creative process subconsciously. The time span for the innovation stage may be months or even years before the potential entrepreneur moves on to the next stage. Usually a specific event or occurrence sparks the entrepreneur to proceed from thinking to doing—a **triggering event.**

When a triggering event occurs in the entrepreneur's life, he or she begins bringing the organization to life. This event could be the loss of a job, the successful gathering of resources to support the organization, or some other factor that sets the wheels in motion.

Implementation is the part of the entrepreneurial process when the organization is formed. This can also be called the "entrepreneurial event."[4] Risk increases at this stage of the entrepreneurial process because a business is now formed. The innovation goes from being an idea in your head to committing resources to bring it to reality. The commitment needed to bring an idea to life is a key element in entrepreneurial behavior. Implementation involves one of the following: (1) introducing new products, (2) introducing new methods of production, (3) opening new markets, (4) opening new supply sources, or (5) industrial reorganization.[5]

Entrepreneurship is the creation of new organizations.[6] By defining entrepreneurship in terms of the organization rather than the person involved, en-

entrepreneurship process The stage of a business's life that involves innovation, a triggering event, and implementation of the business.

triggering event A specific event or occurrence that sparks the entrepreneur to proceed from thinking to doing.

implementation The part of the entrepreneurial process when the organization is formed.

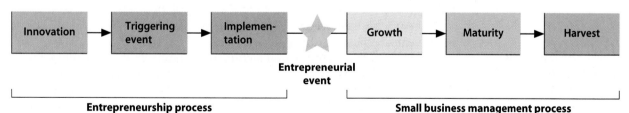

FIGURE 2.1

The Startup Process

The stages of entrepreneurship and small business management.

Source: Based on, with additions to, Carol Moore, "Understanding Entrepreneurial Behavior: A Definition and Model," in *Academy of Management Best Paper Proceedings,* ed. J. A. Pearce II and R. B. Robinson, Jr., 46th Annual Meeting of the Academy of Management, Chicago, 1989, 66–70. See also William Bygrave, "The Entrepreneurial Paradigm (I): A Philosophical Look at Its Research Methodologies," *Entrepreneurship: Theory and Practice,* Fall 1989, 7–25.

small business management process The stage of a business's life that involves growth, maturity, and harvest.
growth Achievement of a critical mass in the business, a point at which an adequate living is provided for the owner and family, with enough growth remaining to keep the business going.
maturity The stage of the organization when the business is considered well established.

harvest The stage when the owner removes himself or herself from the business. Harvesting a business can be thought of as picking the fruit of years of labor.

environmental factors Forces that occur outside the business which have an impact on the business and its owner.

trepreneurship ends when the creation stage of the organization ends. This is the point where the **small business management process** begins. The rest of this text will concentrate on the process of managing a small business from growth through harvest.

The small business manager guides and nurtures the business through the desired level of **growth.** The growth stage does not mean that every small business manager is attempting to get his or her business to Fortune 500 size. A common goal for growth of small businesses is to reach a critical mass, a point at which an adequate living is provided for the owner and family, with enough growth remaining to keep the business going.

The **maturity** stage of the organization is reached when the business is considered well established. The survival of the business seems fairly sure, although the small business manager will still face many other problems and challenges. Many pure entrepreneurs do not stay with the business until this stage. They have usually gone on to other new opportunities before this point. Small business managers are more committed to the long haul. This stage could be as short as a few months (in the case of a fad product) or as long as decades. Maturity in organizations can be similar to maturity in people and in nature. It is characterized by more stability when compared to the growth and implementation stages. Of course, organizations should not become too complacent or stop looking for new ways to evolve and grow, just as people should continue learning and growing throughout their lives.

In the **harvest** stage, the owner removes himself or herself from the business. Harvesting a business can be thought of as picking the fruit of years of labor. In his book *The Seven Habits of Highly Effective People,* Steven Covey says that one of the keys of being effective in life is "beginning with the end in mind."[7] This advice applies to effectively harvesting a business also. Therefore, it is a time that should be planned for carefully.

Harvest can take one of many forms. The business can be sold to another individual who will step into the position of manager. Ownership of the business could be transferred to its employees via an employee stock ownership plan (ESOP). It can be sold to the public through an initial public offering (IPO). The business could merge with another existing business to form an entirely new business. Finally, the harvest could be due to failure, in which case the doors are closed, the creditors paid, and the assets liquidated. Although made in a different context, George Bernard Shaw's statement "Any darned fool can start a love affair, but it takes a real genius to end one successfully" can also apply to harvesting a business.

Not every business reaches all stages. Maturity cannot occur unless the idea is implemented. A business cannot be harvested unless it has grown.

Figure 2.2 adds **environmental factors** to our model to show what is going on outside the business at each stage of development. Management guru Peter Drucker points out that innovation occurs as a response to opportunities within several environments.[8] For example, other entrepreneurs serve as role models when we are in the innovation and triggering event stages. Businesses in the implementation and growth stages must respond to competitive forces, consumer desires, capabilities of suppliers, legal regulations, and other forces. The environmental factors within which a business must operate change from one stage to the next.

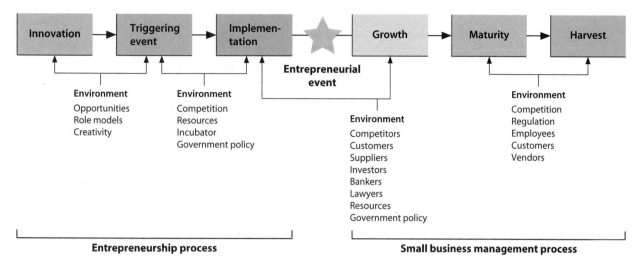

FIGURE 2.2

Environmental Factors Affecting the Startup Process

At each stage in the startup process, the small business owner must confront a new set of concerns. Here the arrows show what those concerns are and how they overlap.

Source: Based on, with additions to, Carol Moore, "Understanding Entrepreneurial Behavior: A Definition and Model," in *Academy of Management Best Paper Proceedings,* ed. J. A. Pearce II and R. B. Robinson, Jr., 46th Annual Meeting of the Academy of Management, Chicago, 1989, 66–70. See also William Bygrave, "The Entrepreneurial Paradigm (I): A Philosophical Look at Its Research Methodologies," *Entrepreneurship: Theory and Practice,* Fall 1989, 7–25.

The personal characteristics of the entrepreneur or the small business manager that are most significant in running a business will vary from one stage to the next. As you will see in the following section, personal characteristics or traits are not useful in predicting who will be a successful entrepreneur or small business manager, but they do affect our motivations, actions, and effectiveness in running a small business (see Figure 2.3). For example, in the innovation and triggering event stages, a high tolerance for ambiguity, a strong need to achieve, and a willingness to accept risk are important for entrepreneurs. In the growth and maturity stages, the personal characteristics needed to be a successful small business manager are different from those needed to be a successful entrepreneur. For example, the small business manager needs to be persevering, committed to the long run of the business, a motivator of others, and a leader.

The business changes as it matures also. In the growth stage, attention is placed on team building, setting strategies, and creating the structure and culture of the business. In the maturity stage, more attention can be directed to specific functions of the business. The people within the business gravitate toward, specialize in, and concentrate on what they do best, be it marketing, finance, or managing human resources.

The purpose of the entrepreneurship and small business management model is to illustrate the stages of both processes and factors that are significant in each. The purpose of this book is to assist you as you proceed from the innovation stage through the management of your successful business to a satisfying harvest.

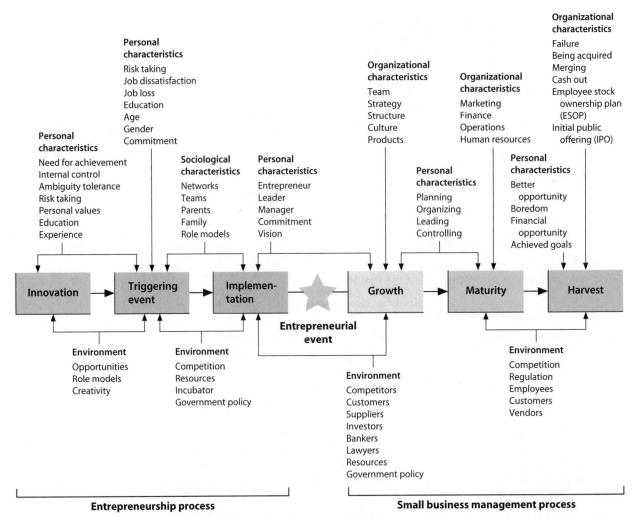

Personal characteristics
Need for achievement
Internal control
Ambiguity tolerance
Risk taking
Personal values
Education
Experience

Personal characteristics
Risk taking
Job dissatisfaction
Job loss
Education
Age
Gender
Commitment

Sociological characteristics
Networks
Teams
Parents
Family
Role models

Personal characteristics
Entrepreneur
Leader
Manager
Commitment
Vision

Organizational characteristics
Team
Strategy
Structure
Culture
Products

Personal characteristics
Planning
Organizing
Leading
Controlling

Organizational characteristics
Marketing
Finance
Operations
Human resources

Organizational characteristics
Failure
Being acquired
Merging
Cash out
Employee stock
  ownership plan
  (ESOP)
Initial public
  offering (IPO)

Personal characteristics
Better
  opportunity
Boredom
Financial
  opportunity
Achieved goals

Innovation → **Triggering event** → **Implementation** → ⭐ **Entrepreneurial event** → **Growth** → **Maturity** → **Harvest**

Environment
Opportunities
Role models
Creativity

Environment
Competition
Resources
Incubator
Government policy

Environment
Competitors
Customers
Suppliers
Investors
Bankers
Lawyers
Resources
Government policy

Environment
Competition
Regulation
Employees
Customers
Vendors

Entrepreneurship process

Small business management process

FIGURE 2.3

A Model of the Entrepreneurship/Small Business Management Process

In each stage of the startup process, different personal characteristics will be more important to the owner as the business takes on new attributes. This model shows how entrepreneurial skills are required early in the process, giving way to management skills once the business is established.

Source: Based on, with additions to, Carol Moore, "Understanding Entrepreneurial Behavior: A Definition and Model," in *Academy of Management Best Paper Proceedings,* ed. J. A. Pearce II and R. B. Robinson, Jr., 46th Annual Meeting of the Academy of Management, Chicago, 1989, 66–70. See also William Bygrave, "The Entrepreneurial Paradigm (I): A Philosophical Look at Its Research Methodologies," *Entrepreneurship: Theory and Practice,* Fall 1989, 7–25.

▬ Your Decision for Self-Employment

Because you have chosen to study small business management, you may be considering the prospect of starting your own business now or at some time in the future. What are some of the positive and negative aspects of self-employment? Why have other people chosen this career path? What do they have in common? What resources did they have available? How can you prepare yourself for owning a small business? The answers to these questions may help you decide if owning a small business is right for you.

Pros and Cons of Self-Employment

Owning your own business can be an excellent way to satisfy personal as well as professional objectives. Before starting your own business, you should be aware of the payoffs and drawbacks involved.

Most people starting their own businesses seek the opportunities of independence, an outlet for their creativity, a chance to build something important, and rewards of money and recognition (see Figure 2.4).

OPPORTUNITY FOR INDEPENDENCE.   To many people, starting their own business means having control over their own lives. That is why owning their own business is attractive to so many people. They don't feel that working for someone else will enable them to reach their full potential. They feel restrained by the organization or by their boss. For such people, business ownership can offer a way to realize their talents, ambitions, or vision. The search for independence has led many people to leave jobs with large corporations to strike out on their own.

OPPORTUNITY FOR A BETTER LIFESTYLE.   The desire to use one's own skills fully is the most common motivation for self-employment. It may enable you to provide a good or service that other people need while enjoying what you do. The lifestyle provided by owning your own business can make going to work fun. Starting a business could be a creative outlet that would give you the opportunity to use a combination of your previously untapped talents.

The challenge presented by running a business is attractive to most entrepreneurs who may be bored working for someone else. The only limitations you

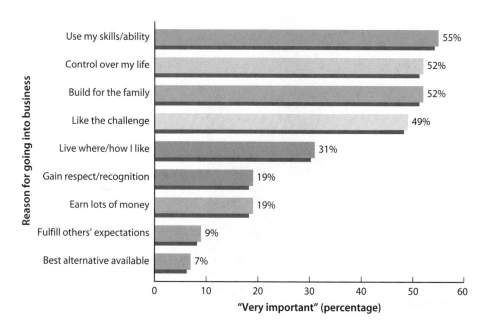

FIGURE 2.4

Independence Is the Primary Reason Most People Go into Business for Themselves

Reasons for going into business by relative importance.

Source: Arnold C. Cooper et al., New Business in America, NFIB Foundation/VISA Business Card Primer, as shown in William J. Dennis, Jr., *A Small Business Primer* (Washington, DC: National Federation of Independent Business, 1993), 31.

We All Sing for Ginseng

Paul Hsu initially came to the United States from Taiwan in 1969 to pursue a career in social work. Five years later, Hsu decided that his knowledge of Asian culture and traditions were his competitive advantage and started his own business, Hsu's Ginseng Enterprises. He began exporting North American ginseng to Asia, where the plant is used as a treatment for a variety of ailments. Within a year, Hsu's small part-time business had become a full-time job. The company has since expanded into farming its own ginseng, even opening a division in Malaysia. By starting this business, Hsu found a way to profit from his skills and knowledge *and* to do something he enjoyed!

Source: Excerpt from Paul Hsu, "Profiting from a Global Mindset." Reprinted by permission, *Nation's Business*, June 1994. Copyright 1994, U.S. Chamber of Commerce.

face arise from a challenge to your own perseverance and creativity, not from barriers placed before you by other people or the constraints of an organization.

About half of small business owners are motivated by familial concerns (see Figure 2.4). They may feel that self-employment is the best way to provide for their children, or they may wish to have a legacy to pass on. Children, in turn, may enter the family business out of self-interest or to help ease their parents' burden.

OPPORTUNITY FOR PROFIT. Less than 20 percent of small business owners expressed a desire to earn lots of money. Most people do not start businesses to get rich, but to earn an honest living. Nonetheless, the direct correlation between effort and compensation is a powerful motivation to work hard. The fact that you can keep all the money you earn is a powerful motivator for many entrepreneurs.

Entrepreneurs see needs then create products to satisfy them. Here Patricia Greene shows how one of her ergonomically designed garden tools increases power and reduces work.

From Accidental Startup to Sure Thing

reality check

Small business owners go into business for incredibly varied reasons and means. Here are two examples to illustrate how differently two businesses can start up—one by design and planning, one by chance and luck.

Dan Hoard and Tom Bunnell were on a quest for fun and adventure while backpacking in Australia. The sun was hot, so Hoard did what any self-respecting, uninhibited free spirit would do (or anyone who thought of it)—he cut off his pant leg and stuck it on his head. He was just having fun; he didn't intend to create a $3 million clothing business. "We would sit in front of the mirror and cry laughing," remembers Bunnell.

Thus was born the Mambosok ("It sounded festive," Hoard explains). Research and development consisted of driving around the Pacific Northwest in a beat-up van. Their business plan didn't exist. They were flying by the seat, er, leg of their pants.

Bunnell was a bartender and expected to sell a few of their first 1,000 Mambosoks to his bar patrons. They were gone in two weeks! This success led Bunnell to formulate two hypotheses:

1. The market for this product does exist.

2. Drinking impairs your judgment. (This could be a combination.)

Hoard and Bunnell sold $200,000 worth in six months. They sold $1 million worth in the second year and $3 million in 1993. They even picked up some business savvy along the way. Hoard and Bunnell realized that the product life cycle for Mambosoks would probably be rather short and that competition would certainly enter with knock-off products. This led the Seattle funsters to extend their product line to more than 60 items of Mambosok wear. Amazing what doing something fun and funky can turn into! Seattle-based Gerry Sportwear purchased Mambosok in 1997 in order to capture the youth and snowboard markets, and changed the name to Mambino for a catchier, cuter image. Perhaps you have the next big, fun, accidental business just waiting to happen to you.

By sharp contrast, if any startup company ever looked like a sure thing, it would be Cardinal Technologies. Harold Krall, now CEO of Cardinal, and six other managers from RCA left the company together to form their new business to manufacture computer-related equipment like modems, monitors, and desktop systems. Without even realizing it at the time, they followed a path that is prototypical of how the most successful U.S. companies begin.

First, they knew their industry inside and out, and they knew how to run a business. They started with a full slate of management—a CEO and specialists in marketing, finance, manufacturing, engineering, sales, and systems. Most had grown up in family businesses before taking management positions with RCA. Second, they had contacts within the industry: suppliers, marketing allies, and contacts who would become customers. They began the business as a team and have forged even stronger bonds.

Third, even though they were beginning a capital-intensive business, they had a healthy financial start. The 7 partners and the 13 other former RCA employees pooled $800,000 of their own money to get things rolling. They were also wise enough to trade away some equity for cash. A healthy respect for debt has kept the company virtually debt free.

A real key to Cardinal's success is that it didn't ever look like a startup. The experience of the team kept them from ever being mistaken for novices. Even though the business was new, the players were not. Although the founders surely went through most of the same traumas that any founders experience, the outside world didn't see them.

Sources: Adapted from Nancy J. Kim, "Gerry Rebranded," *Puget Sound Business Journal,* 23 October 1998, 3A, reprinted by permission of bizjournals.com; Kristina Grish "Gerry Sportwear Moves Labels into Four-Season Business," *Sporting Goods Business,* r. 32, n. 10 21 June 1999, 21, reprinted by permission of Sporting Goods Business Magazine; Anne Murphy, "Founded on Frolic," in "Where Great Ideas for New Businesses Come From," by Tom Ehrenfeld *Inc.: The Magazine for Growing Companies,* September 1993, 54–57, copyright © 1993 by Goldhirsch Group/Inc. Pubg, reproduced with permission of Goldhirsh Group/Inc Pubg in the format textbook via Copyright Clearance Center; and Leslie Brokaw, "Guaranteed Success," *Inc.: The Magazine for Growing Companies,* March 1993, 66–68, copyright © 1993 by Goldhirsch Group/Inc Pubg, reproduced with permission of Goldhirsh Group/Inc Pubg in the format textbook via Copyright Clearance Center.

RISKS OF SELF-EMPLOYMENT. Small business ownership offers ample opportunities to satisfy your material and psychological needs, but it also poses certain risks of which you should be aware. Personal liability, uncertain income, long working hours, and frequently limited compensation while the business grows are some of the disadvantages of self-employment. Not having anyone looking over your shoulder may leave you with fewer places to turn for advice when the going gets tough. And even though you are your own boss, you are still answerable to many masters. You must still respond to customer demands and complaints, keep your employees happy, obey government regulations, and grapple with competitive pressures.

The uncertainty of your income is one of the most challenging aspects of starting a business. There is no guaranteed paycheck at the end of the pay period, as exists when you are working for someone else. Your young business will require you to pump any revenue generated back into it. As the owner, you will be the last person

Not All Happy Endings

Mary and Phil Baechler started their company, Racing Strollers, in 1984 with a rented garage and a phone listing in *Runner's World* magazine. A devoted runner, Phil had designed a stroller, the Baby Jogger, with three bicycle wheels that enabled him to take their six-month-old child with him when he went running. The product was very successful, and the business grew quickly. Within ten years, Racing Strollers had become a $5 million company. Unfortunately, the Baechlers differed in their levels of interest in the business. This compounded the strain of living and working together. Mary became hooked on the challenges of running a growing business, whereas Phil wanted to cultivate a life away from work. Phil couldn't understand why Mary always chose work over family. Mary couldn't understand why Phil wouldn't always put in the extra effort for the business. Can two people with different obsessions live in peace?

Mary thinks the secret might be in accepting the other person the way he or she is, but they couldn't do that for each other. Mary wanted to change Phil into a manager, embroiled in every detail of the business. Phil longed for the sweet girl he had met 15 years earlier. At some point, Mary chose the business over her marriage. The pressure she felt to build the business is common to entrepreneurs. She used typical rationalizations, like "as soon as this current problem is over, I'll spend more time with the family" and "I just gotta get through this month," to justify her actions to herself.

Small problems in the marriage accumulated, building a wall one brick at a time—critical comments made in passing, patterns of neglect here and there. Soon the success of the business brought in offers from prospective buyers and very different reactions from the Baechlers. Phil saw the business as a winning lottery ticket to be cashed in. Mary couldn't let go of it.

The Baechlers' marriage ended because they had different answers to the fundamental question: Why are we here? Phil is an artist and designer who wanted financial security from the business which would allow him to play golf and paint in Hawaii. Mary loved being needed by the business. She needed the thrills and magic that the problems and victories of running a business provided. They still loved each other, but they couldn't love each other *and* run a business together.

Can you separate family and business? How can you maintain a balance between them? When is enough sacrifice enough?

Sources: Mary Baechler, "Death of a Marriage," *Inc.,* April 1994, 74–78; and Matthew Goldstein, "Breaking Up Is Hard to Do," *Crain's New York Business,* 28 September 1998, 27.

to be paid, and you will probably have to live on your savings for a while. Going through the first year of business without collecting a salary is common for entrepreneurs.[9]

The reliable, if dull, nine-to-five work schedule is another luxury small business owners must do without. To get your business off the ground during the critical startup phase, you may find yourself being the company president during the day and its janitor at night. Owning and running a business require a tremendous commitment of time and effort. You must be willing to make sure that everything that must be done gets done.

When you own a business, it becomes an extension of your personality. Unfortunately, it can also take over your life, especially at the beginning. Families, friends, and other commitments must sometimes take a back seat to the business. This problem is complicated by the fact that people often start businesses in their child-rearing years. Married couples going into business together face a volatile mix of business and marital pressures that do not always lead to happy endings.

Traits of Successful Entrepreneurs

Since the early 1960s, researchers have tried to identify the personal characteristics that will predict those people who will be successful entrepreneurs. The conclusions of 30 years of research indicate that there are no personality characteristics that predict who will be a successful entrepreneur before entering business. Successful small business owners and entrepreneurs come in every shape, size, and color, and from all backgrounds. Still, in this section we will briefly examine some characteristics seen among individuals who tend to rise to the top of any profession. The point to remember when you are considering owning a business is that no combination of characteristics guarantees success. People possessing all these traits have experienced business failure.

What are some prerequisites for becoming a successful entrepreneur? You need a *passion* for what you are doing. Caring very deeply about what you are trying to accomplish through your business is imperative. If you go into business with a take-it-or-leave-it, it-will-go-or-it-won't attitude, you are probably wasting your time and money. *Determination* is also critical. You must realize that you have choices and are not a victim of fate. You need to believe that you can succeed if you work long enough and hard enough. Finally, you need a deep *knowledge* of the area in which you are working. Your customers see you as a reliable source in solving their wants and needs. These are three characteristics that virtually every successful entrepreneur possesses.[10] Having perseverance, the technical skills to run a business, and belief in yourself are more important than any specific psychological trait you could exhibit.

A pioneer in entrepreneurial research, David McClelland, identified entrepreneurs as people with a higher **need to achieve** than nonentrepreneurs.[11] People with high need to achieve are attracted to jobs that challenge their skills and problem-solving abilities. They avoid goals that they think would be almost impossible to achieve or ones that would guarantee success. They prefer tasks in which the outcome depends on their individual efforts.

Locus of control is a term used to explain how people view their ability to determine their own fate. Entrepreneurs tend to have a stronger internal locus of control than people in the general population.[12] People with high internal locus of control believe that the outcome of an event is determined by their own actions. Luck,

need to achieve The personal quality linked to entrepreneurship in which people are motivated to excel and choose situations in which success is likely.

locus of control A person's belief concerning the degree to which internal or external forces control his or her future.

creating
competitive
advantage

Hispanic Fingers Go Walking

Martha Rubi and Monica Vega-Christie are two Hispanic immigrants who display a trait that hundreds of thousands of other immigrants have shown over the past century—a flair for entrepreneurship. Rubi has talent in marketing and advertising, whereas Vega-Christie's skills lean toward graphic design and publication. They spent two years soul-searching and trying to identify an unsatisfied niche they could fill. They finally decided on "Paginas Amerillas de Colorado" or the Spanish version of "The Colorado Yellow Pages."

The first edition of Paginas Amerillas saw 50,000 copies distributed free throughout metropolitan Denver supermarkets, churches, the Denver Hispanic Chamber of Commerce, and the Mexican Consulate. For the second edition in 1999, they plan to expand distribution toward becoming statewide by including the cities of Fort Collins, Colorado Springs, and Grand Junction.

The specialized Yellow Pages is smaller than its English-language counterparts, but it does have advantages. For example, advertising businesses do not have to compete against similar or identical businesses, and many of the target market prefer to patronize Hispanic-owned businesses whenever possible.

Rubi and Vega-Christie understand the patrons of their guide who come here without education or money and with little knowledge of English. Rubi was born in Cuernavaca, Mexico, and made her way to Colorado via the Denver-Cuernavaca Sister Cities exchange program. While in Denver, she earned a scholarship to attend Metropolitan State College. Vega-Christie brought experience as a graphic designer and art director from her home of Lima, Peru, to design and lay out Spanish-language newspapers in Washington, D.C., and Virginia.

The need for the Paginas Amarillas guide is founded in the obstacles Hispanic immigrants face as Spanish-only speakers. The guide is more than advertising. It includes metric conversions and important local community information on everything from purchasing a car to finding a physician. Rubi says, "We are able to focus 100 percent of our efforts on this business because we have a true experience of being immigrants and moving to a new and foreign place."

Source: Adapted from Lorenzo Chavez, "Guide Serves Niche," *Denver Business Journal,* 12 June 1998, 19A. Reprinted by permission of bigjournals.com.

---

chance, fate, or the control of other people (external factors) are less important than one's own efforts.[13] When faced with a problem or a difficult situation, internals look within themselves for solutions. Internal locus of control is the force that compels many people to start their own businesses to gain independence, autonomy, and freedom.

Successful entrepreneurs and small business owners are innovative and creative. *Innovation* results from the ability to see, conceive, and create new and unique products, processes, or services. Entrepreneurs see opportunities in the marketplace and visualize creative new ways to take advantage of them.

How do entrepreneurs tend to view *risk taking?* A myth about entrepreneurs is that they are wild-eyed, risk-seeking, financial daredevils. While acceptance of financial risk is necessary to start a business, the prototypical entrepreneur tends to accept moderate risk only after careful examination of what he or she is about to get into.

Scott Schmidt does not see himself as reckless. Schmidt is the entrepreneurial athlete who started what has become known as "extreme skiing." Basically, he jumps from 60-foot cliffs on skis for a living. Ski equipment companies sponsor him for endorsements and video production. If you saw him from the ski lift, you would

A small business manager needs perseverance, patience, and intelligence to meet the ongoing challenges of keeping a company vibrant.

say, "That guy is a maniac for taking that risk." The same is often said of other entrepreneurs by people looking in from outside the situation. Actually, Schmidt very carefully charts his takeoff and landing points. An analogy can be drawn between Schmidt's adventurous style of skiing and the risks of starting a new business.

Entrepreneurs carefully plan their next moves in their business plans. Once they are in the air, entrepreneurs must trust their remarkable talent to help them react to what comes their way as they fall. Entrepreneurs don't risk life and limb, because they look for ways to minimize their risks by careful observation and planning, just as Schmidt precisely plans his moves. They commonly do not see unknown situations as risky because they know their strengths and talents, are confident of success, and know the playing field. In similar fashion, Scott Schmidt doesn't consider himself reckless. He considers himself very good at what he does.[14] That is a typical entrepreneurial attitude.

Other traits that are useful in owning your own business are: high level of energy, confidence, orientation toward the future, optimism, desire for feedback, high tolerance for ambiguity, flexibility/adaptability, and commitment. If one characteristic of the entrepreneurial personality stands out above all others across all types of businesses, it would have to be *incredible tenacity.*

Preparing Yourself for Business Ownership

How do you prepare for an undertaking like owning your own business? Do you need experience? Do you need education? The answer to both questions is always "yes." What kind and how much? These are tougher to answer because it depends on the type of business you plan to enter. The experience you would need to open a franchised bookstore would be different from that needed for an upscale restaurant.

Entrepreneurs and small business owners have higher education levels than the general public. About 60 percent of new business owners have had at least some college (see Figure 2.5).[15] Exceptions exist—people have dropped out of school and gone on to start successful businesses—so it is difficult to generalize. But in a majority of cases, we can conclude that more education increases the chances of success. Note should be taken that, for the most successful small businesses, the CEOs of Inc. 500 companies have significantly higher education levels (see Figure 2.5).

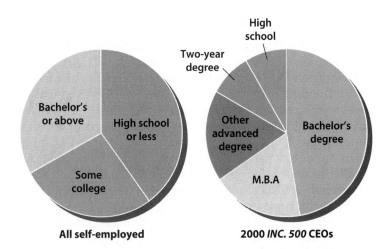

All self-employed   **2000 *INC. 500* CEOs**

FIGURE 2.5

Education Level of New Business Owners

Although individual exceptions exist, small business owners as a group have more formal education than the general population, and Inc. 500 CEOs have even higher education levels.

Sources: U.S. Small Business Administration, Office of Advocacy, "Characteristics of Small Business Employees and Owners," www.sba.gov/stats; and "Data Mine—The CEOs," *The 2000 Inc. 500 Almanac,* 58.

A Domain of Your Own

Your starting point for e-business is establishing your domain name. A domain name is important because of the Internet's addressing procedures. Every computer on the Internet has an Internet protocol (IP) address, which is a unique string of four numbers separated by periods, such as 111.111.1.1. How many of these could you remember? Not many, so a domain name system has been created to assign a unique name to each numeric IP address.

Beyond the technical aspects, a domain name that will stick in customers' minds brings customers in to your e-business. Some benefits of establishing a business domain name include:

■ *Adding credibility to your business.* You look more professional through a web presence. Your credibility is enhanced if your domain name is registered and unique, as opposed to obtaining one free through your Internet service provider (ISP), which would look like www.yourisp.com/~yourbusiness. Not too inspiring for people sending you money!

■ *Adding mobility to your Internet presence.* If you don't own your own URL (domain name), you will lose it every time you change web hosts or service providers.

■ *Building your brand.* If your domain name matches your business name, it is that much more recognizable and easier for customers to remember and return to.

So how do you get a domain name? You may be surprised to find out how simple it is to check name availability. But don't be frustrated if all the clever names you dream up are already protected. Since 1993, Network Solutions Incorporated has had an exclusive contract with the U.S. government to register top-level domain names that end in .com, .net, or .org—about 50 to 75 percent of all Internet domains. In 1998, the U.S. government formed the nonprofit Internet Corporation for Assigned Names and Numbers (ICANN) to transfer administration of domain names to the private sector and open it up to competition.

Currently, it costs $70 to register a domain name for the first two years, with a $35 annual renewal fee. With new competition, the price is expected to drop. To get a domain name, go to the Network Solutions home page and enter your name in question. If it is available, Network Solutions will guide you through the simple registration process. Check it out.

Source: "@e-biz: A Domain of Your Own", from www.allbusiness.com. Reprinted by permission.

Entrepreneurship and small business management are the fastest-growing subjects in business schools across the country.[16] In 1971, Karl Vesper of the University of Washington found that 16 U.S. schools offered a course in entrepreneurship. In his 1993 update, that number had grown to 370.[17] Even that number appears to have grown since the last count. Some of the nation's top business schools, such as Babson College, the Wharton School of the University of Pennsylvania, Harvard Business School, the University of Southern California, the University of California at Los Angeles, as well as many other four-year colleges and community colleges, are offering degrees in entrepreneurship and small business management. Up until very recently, leaders of most business schools argued that entrepreneurship could not be taught. However, the increased academic attention is constructing a body of knowledge on the processes of starting and running small businesses, which proves that entrepreneurial processes can and are being learned.[18]

The SBA and other nonacademic agencies offer start-your-own-business seminars to prospective entrepreneurs. Executive education programs offered through college extension departments are providing curricula specifically designed for entrepreneurs and small business owners.[19] These one-day to one-year programs provide valuable skills without a degree.

Obtaining practical experience in your type of business is an important part of your education. You can learn valuable skills from all types of jobs which will prepare you for owning your own business. For example, working in a restaurant, in retail sales, or in a customer service department can hone your customer relations skills, which are crucial in running your own business but difficult to learn in a classroom.

The analytical and relational skills that you learn in formal educational settings are important, but remember that your future development depends on lifelong learning. (Commencement, after all, means "beginning"—the beginning of your business career!) Finally, don't overlook hobbies and other interests in preparing for self-employment. Participating in team sports and student organizations, for instance, can cultivate your team spirit and facility in working with others. Your marketing skills can be improved through a knowledge of languages or fine art. Sometimes an avocation can turn into a vocation. For example, more than one weekend gardener has become a successful greenhouse owner. Many small business owners get their ideas for what types of businesses they want to run from their favorite pastimes.

No amount of experience or education can completely prepare you for owning your own business. Because every person, situation, and business is different, you are certainly going to encounter situations for which you could not have prepared. Get as much experience and education as you can, but at some point you must "take off and hang on." You have to find a way to make your business go.

Forms of Business Organization ▬

One of the first decisions you will need to make in starting a business is choosing a form of ownership. This section will lead you through your options and present the advantages and disadvantages of each.

Several issues should be considered when making this decision. To what extent do you want to be personally liable for financial and legal risk? Who will have controlling interest of the business? How will the business be financed? The three basic legal structures you can choose for your firm are sole proprietorship, partnership, or corporation, with specialized options of partnerships and corporations available.

About 73 percent of all businesses that exist in the United States are sole proprietorships, making them the most common form of ownership (see Figures 2.6, 2.7, and 2.8). Although a majority of businesses are proprietorships, they account for only about 5 percent of the total revenue generated and about 22 percent of the net profits earned. Corporations bring in 89 percent of business-generated revenue and 72 percent of the net income earned, although they make up only about 20 percent of the total. Partnerships are a minority, with 7 percent of the total number, 5 percent of the revenue, and less than 11 percent of the net income earned.

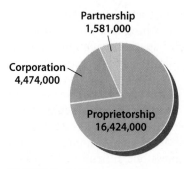

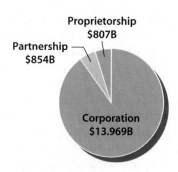

FIGURE 2.6
Ownership Forms of U.S. Businesses

Although the sole proprietorship is the most common business form in the United States, corporations produce the majority of revenue and net income.

Source: Statistical Abstract of the United States (Washington, DC: U.S. Government Printing Office, 1999), 540.

FIGURE 2.7
Sales Revenue by Ownership Type

Source: Statistical Abstract of the United States (Washington, DC: U.S. Government Printing Office, 1999), 540.

FIGURE 2.8
Net Income by Ownership Type

Source: Statistical Abstract of the United States (Washington, DC: U.S. Government Printing Office, 1999), 540.

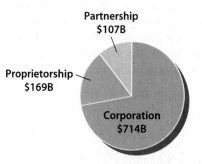

FIGURE 2.9
Growth in the Business Population

Business tax returns filed by form of business and year.

Source: Statistical Abstract of the United States (Washington, DC: U.S. Government Printing Office, 1999), 545.

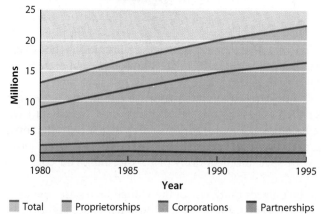

Figure 2.9 shows that proprietorships increased in number and as a percentage of the total of the 22 million small businesses that existed in the United States from 1980 to 1995. This illustrates the rise of very small businesses. The number of corporations grew gradually, whereas the number of partnerships remained relatively

constant. Changes in tax laws have an effect on the number of businesses of each type that are formed.

There is no single best form of organization. The choice depends on your short- and long-term needs, your tax situation, and your personal preferences, abilities, and resources. Don't confuse legal form of ownership with the size of the business. When you walk into a small neighborhood business, can you assume that it is a sole proprietorship? Not necessarily. A one-person flower shop may be a corporation, or a multimillion-dollar factory could be a sole proprietorship.

The Sole Proprietorship

A **sole proprietorship** is a business that is owned and operated by one person. There are no legal requirements to establish a sole proprietorship. In most states, if you are operating under a name other than your full first and last legal names, you must register the business as a trade name with the state department of revenue (see Table 2.1).

sole proprietorship A business owned and operated by one person.

ADVANTAGES. As the owner of a sole proprietorship, you have complete control of the business. The sole proprietorship is well suited to the aspiring entrepreneur's desire for independence. You don't have to consult with any partners, stockholders, or boards of directors. As a result of this independence, you are free to respond quickly to new market needs. Because you make all the decisions and bear all the responsibility, you do not have to share profits with anyone. You may have a smaller pie, but it's all *your* pie. As Mel Brooks in the movie *History of the World, Part I,* said, "It's good to be the king." No one else in the business tells you what to do, criticizes your mistakes, or second-guesses your decisions.

A sole proprietorship is easy to set up. There are fewer legal requirements and restrictions than with a partnership or a corporation. Legal and license costs are at a minimum. An inexpensive business license from the city or county clerk is all that is usually required, unless your type of business requires special permits. For example, businesses selling food must be inspected by health departments. Otherwise, you need only hang your sign on the door and let the world know you are in business. The fast, simple way in which a proprietorship can be formed reduces startup costs and stress.

The Internal Revenue Service (IRS) regards business and owner in a sole proprietorship as a single entity. If your business shows a loss the first year or two (which is common), those losses can be deducted from any other income for the year. This tax advantage is short-lived, however. The tax code states that your business must make money three out of five years. According to the IRS, only money-making ven-

TABLE 2.1 **Balancing the Advantages and Disadvantages of Sole Proprietorships**	Advantages	Disadvantages
	Independence	Unlimited liability
	Easy to set up	Limited resources
	Easy to close	Limited skills
	Tax benefits	Lack of continuity

"You can't call in sick, Harold, you're self-employed"

Source: H. Bosch/Cartoon Features Syndicate.

tures are considered businesses. Anything else is a hobby. Still, this deduction can give you a boost if you are starting your business on a part-time basis and have other income.

Just as proprietorships are easy to open, they are easy to close. If you choose, you can liquidate your assets, pay your bills, turn off the lights, take your sign off the door, and you are out of business. This is not the case with partnerships and corporations.

unlimited liability The potential to lose more than an owner has invested in a business.

DISADVANTAGES. The biggest disadvantage of sole proprietorships is **unlimited liability.** This means that as a sole proprietor, you are personally liable for all debts incurred by the business. If the business should fail, you could lose more than you invested in it. Personal assets, such as your home and car, might have to be liquidated to cover the business debt. Thus, although there are few caps on the potential for return with a sole proprietorship, there are similarly few caps on the amount you could lose.

The sole proprietorship is the most difficult form of business for which to raise capital from outside sources. As one individual, you have access to fewer financial resources than a group of people could gather. Lenders believe that their chances of seeing a return on their investment are reduced in a sole proprietorship and, therefore, they are not as likely to loan money.

The total responsibility of running a sole proprietorship may mean independence, but it can also be a disadvantage. As you are limited to the amount of capital you can raise, you are also limited to and by your own skills and capabilities. You may be an expert in some areas of running a business but be deficient in others.

Total responsibility can also mean a lack of continuity in the business. If you should become unable to work through illness, disability, or death, the business will cease to exist. Long vacations can become virtually impossible to take.

The Partnership

If two or more people are going into business together, they have two choices: form a partnership or a corporation. A **partnership** is defined as an association of two or more persons to carry on as co-owners of a business for profit. Legally you can have a partnership without a written agreement (although it is not recommended), so the paperwork requirements for starting a partnership are about the same as for a proprietorship.

When you form a partnership with friends, family, or associates, you may not think it is necessary to have a written agreement, because you are so familiar with each other. You do. Problems are inevitable for every partnership. An agreement that is well thought out when the partnership is formed can save the business—and a friendship—later. Without a written agreement, a partnership operates according to the rules of the state under the Uniform Partnership Act (UPA). The intent of the UPA is to settle problems between partners. For example, without a written agreement that states otherwise, each partner shares equally in the profit and management of the business.

Partners should bring complementary skills and resources to the alliance to give it a better chance of success. For instance, if one partner has creative abilities, the other partner should have a good business sense. Partners may also complement one another by providing different business contacts or amounts of capital. Think of the relationship this way: If both partners possess the same qualities, one of them probably isn't needed.

There are two types of partnerships: general and limited. Most of this discussion will focus on the **general partnership,** which is more common. In a general partnership, each partner faces the same personal liability as a sole proprietor. In a limited partnership, at least one of the partners has limited liability. This section will concentrate on general partnerships, with limited partnerships discussed at the end of the section.

ADVANTAGES. The biggest advantage of partnerships should be the pooling of managerial talent and capital to create a product or service that is better than any of the partners could have created individually (see Table 2.2).

Access to additional capital is an advantage of partnerships. Partners can pool their money, and credit is easier to obtain than for a proprietor. The reason for this is that the creditor can collect the debt from any one or all of the partners. Partnerships can benefit from more management expertise in decision making.

The tax advantages of a partnership, as for a proprietorship, are usually there because partners pay taxes as individuals. The partnership must file an informational return that reports how much money the partnership earned or lost during the tax year and what share of the income or loss belongs to each partner. Therefore, profits are taxed only once on each partner's share of the income.

partnership An association of two or more persons to carry on as co-owners of a business for profit.

general partnership A business structure in which the business owners share the management and risk of the business.

TABLE 2.2 **Balancing the Advantages and Disadvantages of Partnerships**	Advantages	Disadvantages
	Pooled talent	Unlimited liability
	Pooled resources	Potential for management conflict
	Easy to form	Less independence than proprietorships
	Tax benefits	Continuity or transfer of ownership

Partnerships are easy to create. Like a proprietorship, all you need are the appropriate business licenses and a tax number, and you're in business—for better or for worse.

DISADVANTAGES. As with sole proprietorships, a disadvantage of partnerships is that the general partners carry the burden of unlimited liability. Each general partner's liability is not limited to the amount of his or her investment but extends to his or her personal property as well. Even if the partnership agreement specifies a defined split in profits, each partner is 100 percent responsible for all liabilities.

In a partnership, you may be held liable for the negligence of your partners. A great deal of trust, a comprehensive agreement, and a good lawyer are needed. Similarly, each partner may act as an agent of the partnership. This means that any partner can enter into a contract for the partnership, incurring debt or other responsibilities, or selling assets, unless limited by the articles of partnership. The choice of a business partner is much like choosing a partner for marriage. You need to know and be able to live with the other person's character, work habits, and values to make sure you are compatible.

The potential for managerial conflict within the partnership is one of the most serious problems that can threaten its viability. If partners disagree on matters that involve core issues, such as future direction of the business, the partnership could literally split at the seams.

The four Sasson brothers were looking ahead when they started Scopus Technology, a high-tech firm, in 1991. Recognizing that each had a strong ego, they minimized managerial overlap by each taking on a different function of the business—one in marketing, one in operations, another in technology, and the fourth controlling the financial management of the business. After three years, Scopus Technology had 70 employees and annual revenues of $8 million. They consider the secret of their success to be the fact that they had so clearly divided responsibilities among themselves and had hired a salaried president to act as referee.[20] The move paid off. Scopus was purchased by Siebel Systems in 1998 for $460 million.[21]

If a common reason to go into small business is independence, going into a partnership limits that independence. For example, what happens if you want to reinvest profits in the business, but your partner wants to start having your business meetings in Hawaii and have the company buy each of you new cars? Some resolution must be found, or the entire business could be in jeopardy. Being a partner requires compromise and cooperation.

Although the ability to raise capital is higher with a partnership than with a proprietorship, a partnership still cannot usually gather as many resources as a corporation.

Another financial problem could occur when the partnership decides to retain some of its income and reinvest it in the business. All partners must still pay income tax on their share of the partnership's income, even if they do not receive those funds. This could be financially difficult for some partners.

Continuity can be a problem for partnerships. Difficulties arise if a partner wants to withdraw from the partnership, dies, or becomes unable to continue in the business. Even if the partnership agreement identifies the value of each owner's share, the remaining partners may not have the financial resources to buy out the one who wants to leave. If a partner leaves, the partnership is dissolved. The remaining partners must either find a new partner to bring in, contribute additional capital themselves, or terminate the business. This problem can be avoided in advance by including a buy-sell agreement in the articles of partnership. This agreement spells out what will happen if one of the partners wants to leave voluntarily, becomes disabled, or dies. A sensible solution is a "right of first refusal" clause, which requires the selling partner to give the remaining partners first chance at buying the share. This proactive solution is highly recommended for all partnerships and corporations.

THE LIMITED PARTNERSHIP. The **limited partnership** was created to avoid some of the problems of a general partnership while retaining its basic benefits. A limited partnership must have at least one general partner who retains unlimited liability and all other responsibilities discussed in the general partnership section. Any number of limited partners with limited liability is allowed. Limited partners are usually passive investors. All they can lose is the amount they invest in the business. With very few exceptions, limited partners cannot participate in management of the business without losing their protection. Limited partnerships are a good way for the general partners to acquire capital—from the limited partners—without giving up control, taking on debt, or going through the process of forming a corporation.

> **limited partnership** A business structure in which one or more of the owners may be granted limited liability as long as one partner is designated as a general partner with unlimited liability.

The cost and complication of organizing a limited partnership can be as high as for forming a corporation. A document called a "limited partnership agreement" is required in most states. This agreement identifies each partner's potential liability and the amount of capital each partner supplies. Most limited partnerships are formed for real estate investment because of the tax advantages to the limited partners, who can write off depreciation and other deductions from their personal taxes.[22]

THE UNIFORM PARTNERSHIP ACT (UPA). Signed in 1914, the UPA covers most legal issues concerning partnerships and has been adopted by every state in the Union except Louisiana. The intent of the UPA is to settle problems that arise between partners. The best way for partners to protect their individual interests and the interests of the business is to draft their own articles of partnership. But because partnerships can be formed by two people verbally agreeing to hang up a sign and start a business, not all of them write such articles. Even if the partners do not draw up a written agreement, the UPA provides an amount of protection and regulation for them, including

- All partners must agree to any assignment of partnership property.

- Each partner has one vote, no matter what percentage of the partnership he or she owns, unless a written agreement states otherwise.

- Accurate bookkeeping records are required, and all partners have the right to examine them.

- Each partner owes loyalty to the partnership by not doing anything that would intentionally harm the partnership or the other partners.

- Partners may draw on their share of the profits. This provides partners access to their own capital.

- Salaries must be part of a written agreement. If a loss is incurred, partners must pay their share.[23]

ARTICLES OF PARTNERSHIP. The formal contract between the principals, or people forming a partnership, is called the **articles of partnership.** The purpose of the contract is to outline partners' obligations and responsibilities. As a legal docu-

> **articles of partnership** The contract between partners of a business that defines obligations and responsibilities of the business owners.

ment, it helps to prevent problems from arising between partners and provides a mechanism for solving problems that do arise. A partnership agreement can save your business and your friendship. Articles of partnership usually specify

- The name, location, and purpose of the partnership.

- The contribution of each partner in cash, services, or property.

- The authority of each partner and the need for consensual decision making. For example, large purchases (over $5,000) or contracts could require the approval of a majority of the partners.

- The management responsibilities of each partner; for example, that all partners shall be actively involved and participate equally in the management of the operation of the business.

- The duration of the partnership. Many partnerships are created to last indefinitely. Partnerships that exist for a specific period of time or for a specific project, such as building a new shopping center, are called **joint ventures.**

- The division of profits and losses. Distribution of profits or losses does not have to be exactly equal. Distribution could be allocated according to the same percentages that the partners contributed to the partnership. If not exactly equal, the division must be clearly stated.

- The salaries and draws of partners. How will partners be compensated? After the decision is made on how to divide profits and losses at the end of the accounting period, you need to specify how each will be paid. A *draw* is the removal of expected profits by a partner.

- The procedure for dispute settlement or arbitration. Even with a partnership agreement, disputes can still arise. Providing an agreement for mediation or arbitration to solve serious disagreements can save a costly trip to court.

- The procedure for sale of partnership interest. This section should provide veto power to partners should a partner try to sell his or her interest in the business.

- The procedure for addition of a new partner. You should specify whether the vote for adding a new partner will have to be a simple majority or unanimous.

- The procedure for absence or disability of a partner. No one likes to consider an accident, illness, or death of a partner, but provisions should be defined.

- The procedure and conditions for dissolving the partnership.

joint venture A partnership that is created to complete a specified purpose and is limited in duration.

The Corporation

corporation A business structure that creates an entity separate from its owners and managers.

closely held corporation A corporation owned by a limited group of people. Stock is not traded publicly.

The **corporation** is the most complicated business structure to form. In the eyes of the law, a corporation is an autonomous entity which has the legal rights of a person, including the ability to sue and be sued, to own property, and to engage in business transactions. A corporation must act in accordance with its charter and the laws of the state in which it exists. These laws vary by state.

This section is concerned with the type of corporation most common among small businesses—a **closely held corporation.** This means that relatively few people (usually fewer than ten) own stock. Most owners participate in management, and those who don't are usually family or friends. By contrast, corporations that sell shares of stock to the public and are listed on a stock exchange are called **public corporations.** Public corporations must comply with more detailed and rigorous federal, state, and Securities Exchange Commission (SEC) regulations, such as disclosing financial information in the company's annual report. These are different animals from the closely held corporations of small businesses.

This discussion will begin with the regular or C corporation. Later we will look at variations called the "S corporation" and the "limited-liability company (LLC)." The **C corporation** is a separate legal entity which reports its income and expenses on a corporate income tax return and is taxed on its profits at corporate income tax rates.

ADVANTAGES. By far the biggest advantage of forming a corporation is the limited liability it offers its owners. In a corporation, the most you stand to lose is the amount you have invested in it. If the business fails or if it is sued, your personal property is protected from creditors (see Table 2.3).

An example of how limited liability can be an advantage to a small business can be shown in the case of Kathy, owner of a local pub. Kathy is worried that one of her employees might inadvertently or intentionally serve alcohol to a minor or to an intoxicated person. If the intoxicated person were to get into an automobile accident, Kathy could be sued. In addition to buying liability insurance, Kathy has also incorporated her business so that her personal assets will be protected in the event of a lawsuit.

Corporations generally have easier access to financing, because bankers, venture capitalists, and other lending institutions tend to regard them as being more stable than proprietorships or partnerships. Corporations have proved to be the best way to accumulate large pools of capital.

Corporations can take advantage of the skills of several people and draw on their increased human and managerial resources. Boards of directors can bring valuable expertise and advice to small corporations.

Finally, because a corporation has a life of its own, it continues to operate even if its stockholders change. Transfer of ownership can be completed through the sale of the stock.

DISADVANTAGES. Complying with requirements of the state corporate code poses disadvantages not faced by proprietorships or partnerships. Even the smallest corporation must file articles of incorporation with the secretary of state, adopt bylaws, and keep records from annual stockholder and director meetings. Directors must meet to show that they are setting policy and are actively involved

public corporation A corporation that sells shares of stock to the public and is listed on a stock exchange.

C corporation A separate legal entity that reports its income and expenses on a corporate income tax return and is taxed on its profits at corporate income tax rates.

TABLE 2.3 **Balancing the Advantages and Disadvantages of Corporations**	Advantages	Disadvantages
	Limited liability	Expensive to start
	Increased access to resources	Complex to maintain
	Transfer of ownership	Double taxation

in running the corporation. All these requirements are needed to prevent the IRS, creditors, or lawsuits from removing the limited liability protection. If a corporation does not operate as a corporation, the limited-liability protection of the directors and stockholders could be denied, holding them personally responsible for corporate liabilities. This process is referred to as "piercing the corporate veil."[24]

The legal and administrative costs incurred in starting a corporation can be a sizable disadvantage. Self-incorporation kits exist, but be careful about going through the incorporation process without the aid of an attorney. The cost of incorporating can easily reach $1,000 before the business is even open.

Corporate profits face double taxation in that the profits are taxed at the corporate level first and can be taxed again once the profits are distributed to stockholders. If a stockholder also works in the corporation, he or she is considered to be an employee and must be paid a "reasonable wage," which is subject to state and federal payroll taxes.

Even the limited liability a corporation affords does not completely protect your personal property. If you use debt financing or borrow money, lenders will probably expect you to secure the loan with your personal property. Therefore, if the business must be liquidated, your personal property can be attached.

If you sell stock in your corporation, you are giving up some control of your business. The more capital you need to raise, the more control you must relinquish. If large blocks of stock are sold, you may end up as a minority stockholder of what used to be your own business. Raising capital in this way may be necessary for growth, but you will have to relinquish some control.

articles of incorporation A document to describe the business which is filed with the state in which a business is formed.

FORMING A CORPORATION. The process of incorporating your business includes the following steps. You must prepare **articles of incorporation** and file them with the secretary of state in the state in which you are incorporating. You must choose a board of directors, adopt bylaws, elect officers, and issue stock. At the time you incorporate, you must also decide whether to form a C corporation, an S corporation, or a limited-liability company.

You are not required to use an attorney to file articles of incorporation, but attempting the process and making a mistake could end up costing you more than an attorney would have charged for the job. Although states vary in their requirements, articles of incorporation usually include

- *The name of your company.* The name you choose must be registered with the state in which it will operate. This registration prevents companies from operating under the same name, which could create confusion for the consumer. Your corporation's name must not be deceptive about its type of business.

- *The purpose of your corporation.* You must state the intended nature of your business. Being specific about your purpose will give financial institutions a better idea of what you do. Incorporating in a state that permits very general information in this section allows you to change the nature of your business without reincorporating.

- *The names and addresses of the incorporators.* Some states require at least one incorporator to reside in that state.

- *The names and addresses of the corporation's initial officers and directors.*

■ *The address of the corporation's home office.* You must establish headquarters in the state from which you receive your charter or register as an out-of-state corporation in your own state.

■ *The amount of capital required at time of incorporation.* You may need to deposit a specified percentage of the par value (the value that you place on your stock) of the capital stock in a bank before incorporation.

■ *Capital stock to be authorized.* In this section, you specify the types of stock and the number of shares that the corporation will issue.

■ *Bylaws of the corporation.* A corporation's bylaws are the rules and regulations by which it agrees to operate. Bylaws must stipulate the rights and powers of shareholders, directors, and officers; the time and place for the annual shareholder meeting and the number needed for a quorum (the number needed to transact business); how the board of directors is to be elected and compensated; the dates of the corporation's fiscal year; and who within the corporation is authorized to sign contracts.

■ *Length of time the corporation will operate.* Most corporations are established with the intention that they will operate in perpetuity. However, you may specify a duration for the corporation's existence.

Some small business owners minimize the legal costs of forming a corporation by doing much of the background work themselves. Software companies have jumped on this do-it-yourself bandwagon. For instance, the PC Law Library, published by Cosmi Corporation of Rancho Dominguez, California, contains over 200 legal documents for both business and personal situations. Nolo Press of Berkeley, California, a publisher of legal reference books, has developed Nolo's Partnership Maker®. This software provides 84 standard and alternative clauses that can be included in a partnership agreement. It also provides step-by-step help for understanding each clause in a partnership agreement.

If you decide to go this route, it is highly advisable to have an attorney familiar with your state's incorporation or partnership laws review your papers just to make sure that all the required information has been covered.

Specialized Forms of Corporations

You have two other options to consider in addition to the C corporation. S corporations and limited-liability companies are corporations that are granted special tax status by the Internal Revenue Service. A competent tax advisor can assist you to determine whether one of these options could provide a tax advantage for your business.

S CORPORATION. An **S corporation** provides you with the limited liability protection of a corporation while enjoying the tax advantages of a partnership. Forming an S corporation will allow you to avoid the double-taxation disadvantage of regular corporations and to offset losses of the business against your personal income tax. The S corporation files an informational tax return to report its income and expenses, but it is not taxed separately. Income and expenses of the S corpora-

S corporation A special type of corporation in which the owners are taxed as partners.

tion "flow through" to the shareholders in proportion to the number of shares they own. Profits are taxed to shareholders at their individual income tax rate. To qualify as an S corporation, you must meet the following requirements:

■ Shareholders must be individuals, estates, or trusts—not other corporations.

■ Nonresident aliens may not be shareholders.

■ Only one class of outstanding common stock can be issued.

■ All shareholders must consent to the election of the S corporation.

■ State regulations specify the portion of revenue that must be derived from business activity, not from passive investments.

■ There may not be more than 35 shareholders.[25]

limited-liability company (LLC) A relatively new type of corporation which taxes the owners as partners yet provides a more flexible structure than an S corporation.

LIMITED-LIABILITY COMPANY (LLC). A relatively new form of ownership, the **limited liability company (LLC),** is quickly becoming the "hot" business form on its way to becoming the entity of choice for the future. Recognized by the IRS in 1988, LLCs offer the protection of limited liability of a corporation and the tax advantages of a partnership without the restrictions of an S corporation. As with many new developments, the LLC is still evolving. For example, although the LLC is provided pass-through treatment for federal taxation, individual states may tax it differently. Most states tax the LLC as a partnership, whereas others, such as Florida, tax the LLC as a corporation.[26] Check with your tax accountant to see how LLCs are taxed in your state.

The owners of an LLC are called "members." Unlike the situation for C and S corporations, shares of stock do not represent the ownership by the members. Rather, the rights and responsibilities of members are specified by the operating agreement of the LLC, which is like a combination of bylaws and a shareholder agreement in other corporations. LLCs offer small business owners greater flexibility than either C or S corporations. This flexibility is provided to the members by their writing of the operating agreement. The operating agreement can contain any provision for the LLC's internal structure and operations. LLCs are not constrained by the regulations imposed on C and S corporations, such as who can and cannot participate, what the LLC can or cannot own, or how profits and losses are allocated to members. For example, the owners of an LLC can allocate 50 percent of the profit to a person who owns 30 percent of the business. This is not allowable in C or S corporations.

You should seriously consider forming an LLC if you need flexibility in the legal structure of your business, desire limited liability, and prefer to be taxed as a partnership rather than as a corporation.

nonprofit corporation A tax-exempt corporation that exists for a purpose other than making a profit.

THE NONPROFIT CORPORATION. The **nonprofit corporation** is a tax-exempt organization formed for religious, charitable, literary, artistic, scientific, or educational purposes. Nonprofit corporations depend largely on grants from private foundations and public donations to meet their expenses. People or organizations that contribute to a nonprofit can deduct that contribution from their own taxes. Assets dedicated to nonprofit purposes cannot be reclassified. If its directors decide to terminate the corporation, its assets must go to another nonprofit organization.[27] The details of forming and running a nonprofit corporation are beyond the interest of most readers of this book. To learn more about this business form, consult the sources listed in the endnotes.

SUMMARY

■■■ **The differences between the small business manager and the entrepreneur.**

An entrepreneur is a person who recognizes an opportunity and assumes the risk involved in creating a business for the purpose of making a profit. A small business manager is involved in the day-to-day operation of an established business. Each faces significant challenges, but they are at different stages of development in the entrepreneurship/small business management model.

■■■ **The steps in preparing for small business ownership.**

The entrepreneurship process involves an *innovative* idea for a new product, process, or service. A *triggering event* is something that happens to the entrepreneur that causes him or her to begin bringing the idea to reality. *Implementation* is the stage at which the entrepreneur forms a business based on the idea. The first stage of the small business management process is *growth,* which usually means the business is becoming large enough to generate enough profit to support itself and its owner. The *maturity* stage is reached when the business is stable and well established. The *harvest* stage is when the small business manager leaves the business through either its sale, merger, or failure.

■■■ **The advantages and disadvantages of self-employment.**

The advantages of self-employment include the opportunity for independence, the chance for a better lifestyle, and the potential for significant profit. The disadvantages include the personal liability you face should the business fail, the uncertainty of an income, and the long working hours.

■■■ **The characteristics of the forms of small business ownership.**

There are several choices for the form of ownership of your small business. The most common is the sole proprietorship. If you choose a partnership, you could form a general partnership, in which all partners are fully liable for the business, or a limited partnership, in which at least one partner retains unlimited liability. A corporation offers its owners limited liability. In forming a corporation, you are creating a legal entity that has the same rights as a person. Variations of corporations include S corporations, limited-liability companies, and nonprofit corporations.

QUESTIONS FOR REVIEW & DISCUSSION

1. What do entrepreneurs do that distinguishes them from any other person involved in business?

2. How could a person be both a small business manager and an entrepreneur?

3. Why may personality characteristics be good predictors of who will be a successful entrepreneur?

4. If a friend told you that entrepreneurs are high risk takers, how would you set the story straight?

5. Describe the significance of triggering events in entrepreneurship. Give examples.

6. How is small business management different from entrepreneurship?

7. Why would an entrepreneur be concerned about harvesting a business that has not yet been started?

8. Explain why people who own a small business may not enjoy pure independence.

9. In light of your answer to question 8, why is the desire for independence such a strong motivator for people to become self-employed?

10. If personal characteristics or personality traits do not predict who will be a successful entrepreneur, why are they significant to the study of entrepreneurship or small business management? Which characteristics do you think are most important?

11. Is a college degree in entrepreneurship an oxymoron?

12. Sole proprietorships make up 76 percent of all U.S. businesses and generate 6 percent of all business revenue. Only 18 percent of all sole proprietorships are incorporated, but they generate 90 percent of all revenue. What do these statistics tell you about the two forms of ownership?

13. Under what conditions would you consider joining a partnership? Why would you avoid becoming a partner?

14. What is the difference between limited and general partners?

15. When would forming a limited-liability company be more advantageous than a C corporation or a partnership?

QUESTIONS FOR **CRITICAL THINKING**

1. Think of an activity that you love to do; it could be a personal interest or a hobby. How could you turn your passion for this activity into a business? What questions would you have to answer for yourself before you took this step? What triggering events in your personal life would it take for you to start this business?

2. Imagine that the principal from the high school you attended (and graduated from) called to invite you to make a presentation to a newly founded entrepreneurship club at the school. What would you tell this group of high school students about owning their own business as a career option?

Experience
this...

Do you really know what it's like to start a business? Interview a person you consider an entrepreneur to get some insight. Because time is valuable, have a set of questions prepared before the interview. The following set may be a place for you to start:

1. How did you develop a vision for your business?

2. How long did you envision this business before you took action to start it?

3. What triggering event prompted you to take action to start this business?

4. What are the most important entrepreneurial characteristics that have helped you succeed?

5. What were your biggest challenges?

6. What would you do differently the next time you start a business?

WHAT WOULD **YOU** DO?	No. 1

"Gardeners love this crap." That's the slogan for Pierce Ledbetter's Memphis, Tennessee–based company, Zoo Doo. In 1990, while still a student at Cornell University, Ledbetter returned home to Memphis and talked the managers at the local zoo into selling him composted animal manure from the enormous amounts produced by the zoo's animals daily. Why would any sane individual want animal manure? Well, it's extremely rich in soil nutrients. Wanting to cash in on the gardening craze just beginning to sweep across the United States, Ledbetter saw a marketing opportunity. He began selling his "Zoo Doo" in attractively designed pails. He even had the unique idea of having the manure compressed into various animal-shaped sculptures that gardeners could place in their gardens to decompose naturally and organically. His designs caught the eye of garden centers and mass merchandisers across the United States. Ledbetter's Zoo Doo now claims sales of about $1.5 million.

But having a great product and a great slogan isn't enough to make any small business a success. It's important to choose a form of business ownership that best meets your individual needs, goals, and constraints. Factors such as availability of adequate funding, amount of management expertise, product liability possibilities, and willingness to share decision making can influence which form of ownership is most appropriate.

Source: Cyndee Miller, "Entrepreneur Steps Firmly into the Field of Manure," *Marketing News,* 22 June 1992, 15, 18.

QUESTIONS

1. Put yourself in Pierce Ledbetter's shoes (and watch where you step!) Discuss the advantages and disadvantages of organizing Zoo Doo as a sole proprietorship, a partnership, or a corporation. Think of all the possible factors that might influence your choice.

2. Now that you've looked at the various ways to organize Zoo Doo, it's time to convince your management professor at Cornell University of your decision. Write a letter describing the approach you've decided to take in organizing your Zoo Doo business and why.

WHAT WOULD YOU DO?   No. 2

Entrepreneurs have to look for a niche. Hoby Buppert knew that he couldn't go head to head with the likes of Coke and Pepsi as he was writing a business plan in his last semester at Cornell University. The soft drink industry is huge, and Hoby looked at several different approaches to enter the market—the homespun/old-fashioned approach, the nutraceutical/herb-enhanced approach, and the new/exotic flavor approach. The 27-year-old had seen the popularity of highly caffeinated beverages in European dance clubs, so he created his own soft drink made from the naturally caffeinated Amazonian Guarana berry.

Buppert launched BAWLS (Brazilian American Wildlife Society) in Miami with the help of a $200,000 bank loan. What sets BAWLS apart from other soft drinks (in addition to the Guarana berry) is the distinctive packaging: a bumpy, cobalt-blue, 10-ounce glass bottle. He used his own van to deliver BAWLS to local clubs and cafés until Arizona Distribution picked his product up and expanded coverage to 16 states.

QUESTIONS

1. What approach would you use to capture a niche of the soft drink market? No preservatives? Include floating multicolored gel gumballs? Come up with an offensive name?

2. What are the biggest challenges Hoby Buppert faced (and you would) in creating a new soft drink? (*Hint:* Achieving distribution and shelf space is number one.)

ANSWERS TO CHAPTER OPENER QUIZ

---

1. **True.** Many entrepreneurs are fired or quit for a variety of reasons. Bumping their heads on glass ceilings often frustrates women. Entrepreneurs seldom get ahead by getting along. The only people entrepreneurs are glad to work for are customers.

2. **True.** Entrepreneurs often need less than five hours of sleep per night—*and like it!*

3. **False.** Many entrepreneurs have difficulty maintaining a balance between work and family. Perhaps some are successful because they have little personal life.

4. **True.** Related to question 3 above, those entrepreneurs who do maintain a work-family balance involve the whole family in the business. We often see this in first-generation immigrants who come to America and begin businesses. Involving the whole family is a great way to keep overhead expenses down. Business involvement also keeps down resentment from family members who would otherwise be isolated.

5. **True.** Entrepreneurs often take ideas from many sources and look for ways to combine and improve them.

6. **True.** Entrepreneurs' strength lies in getting started, and they often grow bored running businesses once they are well established. Even if they don't become bored, many entrepreneurs lack the management skills to keep their operations going and must bring in professional managers.

7. **False.** M.B.A.'s are trained to be managers, but the degree doesn't mean they have what it takes to be an entrepreneur. Academic pedigree does not mean that a person has (a) the needed personality traits, (b) a money-making opportunity identified, or (c) the persistence needed to find resources.

8. **False.** Entrepreneurs love to experiment with *new* rules and procedures, not necessarily accepted ones. This is why they don't often fit well in large organizations.

9. **False.** The maverick tendencies of entrepreneurs do not suit them to be real team players. If on a team, entrepreneurs are usually the captain.

10. **False.** Money must often come from many sources, but *no one*—not friends, family, or bankers—will help with startup funds unless you put your house and life savings on the line.

11. **False.** Partnerships can be described as "marriage without the sex." Friendships are more often than not destroyed when combined with commerce. Going out on your own means just that—not venturing out with John, Betty, or Sue.

12. **False.** Quality is what counts when you're building the name of your business. The entrepreneurs who leave jobs working for someone else do so because they are tired of working with colleagues and bosses who don't care enough. When it comes to starting a business, "good enough" isn't.

13. **False.** Marketing research tells the entrepreneur what to charge. Underpricing literally "gives the farm away"; overpricing denies the business any chance of success.

14. **False.** Ethical standards of successful entrepreneurs typically rise. A solid business is built on a foundation of trust. Your word, especially as an entrepreneur, is your bond.

15. **False.** Entrepreneurs must make so many decisions, so quickly, on such a wide variety of topics, that they may be right about one out of every three times. Anyone who can't stand to make mistakes should work for someone who can. Many entrepreneurs have had three or four ventures fail before one goes. Entrepreneurs must have the ability to cope with repeated failure.

Start Temps CZ Starts Up

Karin Genton-L'Epée was between management jobs when she learned of a new and exciting business opportunity in Prague, the capital of the Czech Republic. She had moved there from Paris, attracted by a job in a recruitment ad placed by Agency Start, the Prague franchise of Start Holland, an executive search agency. A native of France, Karin was fluent in English, proficient in German, and had a basic knowledge of Czech. She was 40 years old, single, with a background in wholesaling, retail sales, and general management. Before coming to Prague, she had worked as a consultant in international distribution and marketing in Paris and New York.

In Prague, Karin first worked for an Italian caterer and then became general manager for Macadam, a clothing retailer, where she had no trouble working with and managing Czech employees. Karin's administrative assistant, Barbara, acted as interpreter and office manager. Although Karin helped open three new stores, she disagreed with the retailer's strategic direction and resigned. Shortly afterward she met Frans Hoekman, Agency Start's owner.

New Business Idea   Frans had an idea for opening a temporary-employment agency for blue-collar workers. He had clients who were interested in temporary factory workers, but had been unable to find them through Agency Start. Frans believed that the best way was to establish a separate agency that specialized in temporary work contracts. However, he was not in a position to invest either the time or money necessary to open another business.

Frans envisioned a service that would "help both those companies in financial trouble who want to lay off workers and those who wish to hire them" by shifting workers between companies as demand warranted. "Production highs and lows in different firms do not coincide," he observed. Frans saw a market for a service that could match excess workers at one company with production demand in another.

Although she knew nothing about temporary employment, Karin was intrigued by Frans's idea. She began to collect information about the Czech labor market, then she and Frans approached Start Holland. The corporation supplied a grant to develop a business plan. Two months after Karin submitted the plan, Start approved the proposal to open offices in each of the Republic's seven regions, aiming for 15 to 19 within three years. Karin set a deadline for opening the first office in Kladno, an industrial city near Prague.

Laying the Foundation   Karin hired Barbara, 20, her assistant at Macadam, and Angela, 22, to set up the central Prague office. Both part-timers were fluent in English and Czech. Meanwhile, Frans hired Martin S., 26, as financial director. Martin was Czech, but had grown up in Canada, had worked for a year in cost analysis for Philip Morris, and then served for three months as assistant financial controller for Trane Air Conditioning. Karin expected Martin to set up the financial and accounting procedures, take the lead in preparing the employment contracts, and supervise Barbara and Angela in the day-to-day office administration.

Karin hired Richard K., 25, to manage the Start Temps office in Kladno. Richard had tried to start a recruitment agency in Prague with three friends, but had sold his share over disagreements involving software design and office management. Richard understood employment issues in the Czech Republic and wanted to design his own operation, but had no experience with legal contracts. He thought Karin and Martin would handle the legal issues.

While the Czech Labor Code did not recognize temporary employment as such, the Czech Parliament had recently expanded the definition of "employer" for income tax withholding purposes. By doing so, the government acknowledged the right to hire employees to work for a third party, a common practice among construction contractors. Nevertheless, Czech workers, used to guaranteed positions with well-defined job descriptions, found temporary employment a foreign concept. For their part, Czech managers were used to following well-established norms and working within familiar bureaucratic systems.

Karin knew that contracts for client companies and employees would have to be carefully worded to operate within the evolving legal system, a challenge complicated by legally mandated health benefits and retirement accounting. "Anyone can set up an individual placement office and match a few people with a few companies and make money," said Karin. "Small guys can make it, but we want to expand. Kladno will be our blueprint. We can't do each contract from scratch. We need a system."

The Deadline Nears   As her self-imposed deadline for opening the Kladno office approached, Karin saw several issues. She was the only one who seemed to feel the need for clear and precise documents. Barbara and Angela did what they were told, but did not understand what else needed to be done. Martin was trying to understand the accounting system, but was not delegating adequately. There seemed to be some question whether the Kladno office would open or not.

Source: Adapted from "Start Temp CZ" case by Joan Winn. From *Entrepreneurship Theory and Practice* 24(3), Spring 2000. Reprinted by permission of the author. To read the entire case, visit the *Small Business Management: Entrepreneurship and Beyond* web site at http://business.college.hmco.com/students.

QUESTIONS

1. Would you describe Karen as an entrepreneur? If so, what entrepreneurial traits can you identify in her?

2. What unique challenges did she face in the Czech Republic?

3. Referring to Figure 2.3, Model of Entrepreneurship/Small Business Management, identify Karin's position at different points in the case.

4. How could Karin have been more prepared for entrepreneurship?

Planning in Small Business

Getting a small business started and keeping it successful does not happen by accident. Planning is required in order to gather the resources needed and to allocate them wisely. While some successful businesses have been formed without a formal plan, none was created without planning. The most important thing about business planning is not the written plan that is produced; it is the strategic thinking that goes into the writing. These two chapters will take you through several facets of business planning. **Chapter 3** discusses social responsibility and strategic planning. **Chapter 4** concentrates on the operational side of business planning.

Social Responsibility, Ethics, and Strategic Planning

After reading this chapter, you should be able to:

Recognize the relationship between social responsibility, ethics, and strategic planning.

Identify the levels of social responsibility.

Discuss how to establish codes of ethics for your business.

List the steps in the strategic planning process.

Suggest ways to influence the organizational culture of your new business.

GREAT HARVEST BREAD is not your run-of-the-mill flour mill—it grows businesses and business owners. Pete and Laura Wakeman started baking delicious homemade wheat bread in their Durham, Connecticut, garage in 1972. To work their way through college, they would load the bread up and sell it by the roadside on a card table. After they graduated, Pete and Laura took a trip west. While trekking across Montana from Yellowstone to Glacier, they fell in love with the town of Great Falls. Pete worked on local wheat farms while Laura worked as a nutritionist for Great Falls schools. They combined the skills they developed in Connecticut with Montana wheat and opened their first bakery in 1976. They often sold a day's inventory in an hour.

Friends and acquaintances wanted to learn to make bread and run a bakery like the Wakemans. The first Great Harvest Bakery opened in Kalispell, Montana, in 1978. Two years later, they began franchising nationwide. By 1998, Great Harvest had 130 bakeries in 35 states and annual revenues of $60 million.

How did they grow so fast? By selling franchises that are different from normal. They don't insist on standardized procedures or impose top-down regulations. Rather, they promote localized innovation and encourage fast learning. Although they have an operating manual of best practices, owners run their bakeries as they see fit—on one condition: they learn along the way with other owners in the Great Harvest system.

After a week of training at company headquarters in Dillion, Montana, owners visit two existing franchises in other parts of the country. Chief Operating Officer Tom McMakin says this is when the education really begins. "New owners learn more from their peers than they do from bureaucrats." Great Harvest has developed a concept called "the Learning Community," a cross-pollenization of ideas facilitated through e-mail, corporate extranet, a newsletter, bakery travel, and an annual convention. Great Harvest communication between franchises is so impressive that Microsoft chose it from 200 companies to feature in its latest technology advertising campaign. Microsoft's message is simple—the software giant's products help Great Harvest and its franchise owners communicate with one another and build their businesses.

A guiding principle of Great Harvest is to value freedom over security. The company is a network of free and independent owners, who have the freedom to succeed or fail. The company defined their product not as the bread, but as the simple freedom to be your own boss. Where else do businesses offer free slices of hot, fresh bread to the sheer delight of each customer? It may seem strange to others to give away a lot of bread over the breadboard, but as Great Harvest bakery owner Jack Corkey (Herndon, Virginia) says, "It's why we got into this business. It's more important than money."

Great Harvest Bakery is a good example of a company that understands the value of profit but also understands that the value of people is higher. (Look for its mission statement later in this chapter.)

Sources: Great Harvest franchise disclosure statement; Heath Row, "Great Harvest Reaps Benefits of Team-work," *Financial Post*, 15 December 1998; Diana Setterberg, "Technology-Aided Bread Franchise to Open in Butte, MT," *Montana Standard*, 29 June 1999; and Heath Row, "Great Harvest's Recipe for Growth," *Fast Company*, December 1998, 44–45. The Great Harvest Mission Statement is reprinted by permission of Great Harvest.

The Relationship Between Social Responsibility, Ethics, and Strategic Planning

What do concepts like social responsibility and ethics have to do with strategic planning in business? They are rarely covered together in textbooks, but the connection between them is especially strong in small businesses because of the inseparability of the owner and the business. The direction in which the business is heading is the same direction the owner is going. What is important to the business is important to the owner. In many cases, a small business is an extension of the owner's life and personality.

Strategic planning is the guiding process used to identify the direction for your business. Strategic planning spells out a long-term game plan for operating your business. Social responsibilities are the obligations of a business to maximize the positive impact it has on society and minimize the negative impact. Ethics are the rules of moral values that guide decision making—your understanding of the difference between right and wrong.

Let's look at the relationship between social responsibility, ethics, and strategic planning in the following way. When you assess your company's external environment for opportunities and threats, you identify what you might do. When you look at your internal strengths and weaknesses, you see what you can do and cannot do. Your personal values are ingrained in the business; these are what you want to do. Your ethical standards will determine what is right for you to do. Finally, in responding to everyone who could be affected by your business, social responsibility guides what you should do.

So, are social responsibility, ethics, and strategic planning connected? When we are talking about small business, absolutely. In fact, at a very fundamental level, they are more difficult to separate than to connect.

Social Responsibilities of Small Business

Social responsibility means different things to different people. In this chapter, we will define it as the managerial obligation to take action to protect and improve society as a whole, while achieving the goals of the business.[1] The manager of a socially responsible business should attempt to make a profit, obey the law, act ethically, and be a good corporate citizen.

Your level of commitment to these responsibilities and the strategic planning process you conduct form the heart of your business, the foundation and philosophy on which the business rests. Knowing what is important to yourself, your business, and everyone affected by its actions (social responsibility), is significant in deciding where you want to go and how to get there (strategic planning). The business you start or operate takes on a culture or a set of shared beliefs of its own. When you create a business, *your* values have a strong influence on the culture of the business you create. The values and culture of your business are demonstrated by your socially responsible (or irresponsible) actions.

Social responsibilities are the obligations of a business to maximize the positive impact it has on society and minimize the negative impact. There are four levels of social responsibility: economic, legal, ethical, and philanthropic (see Figure 3.1).[2] Although the primary responsibility of a business is economic, our legal system also enforces what we, as a collective group or society, consider proper behavior. Each firm and person decides what is ethical, or what is right beyond legal requirements.

social responsibility The obligations of a business to have a positive impact on society on four levels—economic, legal, ethical, and philanthropic.

Philanthropic Goodwill

Be a good corporate citizen.
Contribute resources to the community; improve quality of life.

Ethical Responsibility

Be ethical.
Obligation to do what is right, just, and fair. Avoid harm.

Legal Obligations

Obey the law.
Law is society's codification of right and wrong. Play by the rules of the game.

Economic Responsibility

Be profitable.
The foundation on which all other levels rest.

FIGURE 3.1

The Pyramid of Social Responsibility

The four interconnected areas in which businesses are expected to act in a responsible manner.

Source: "The Pyramid of Corporate Social Responsibility: Toward the Moral Management of Organizational Stakeholders." Reprinted with permission from BUSINESS HORIZONS (July/August 1991). Copyright ©1991 by the Board of Trustees at Indiana University, Kelley School of Business.

Finally, a business can be expected to act like a good citizen and help improve the quality of life for everyone. Although all four of these obligations have always existed, ethical and philanthropic issues have received considerable attention recently.

Economic Responsibility

As a businessperson in a free enterprise system, you have not only the fundamental right but also the responsibility to make a profit. You are in business because you are providing a good or a service that is needed. If you do not make a profit, how can you stay in business? If you don't stay in business, how can you provide that good or service to people who need it?

Historically, the primary role for business has been economic. Entrepreneurs assume the risk of getting into business because profit is their incentive. If you don't attend to the economics of your business, you can't take care of anything else. Therefore, the economic responsibilities of your business would include a commitment to being as profitable as possible; to making sure employees, creditors, and suppliers are paid; to maintaining a strong competitive position; and to maintaining efficient operation of your business.

Economist Milton Friedman emphasizes the economic side of social responsibility. Friedman contends that business owners should not be expected to know what social problems should receive priority or how many resources should be dedicated to solving them. He states, "There is one and only one social responsibility of business: to use its resources and energy in activities designed to increase its profits so long as it stays within the rules of the game . . . [and] engages in open and free competition, without deception and fraud."[3] His point of view is that business revenues that are diverted to outside causes raise prices to consumers, decrease employee pay, and may support issues with which some of the business's stakeholders do not agree. Basically, Friedman's argument is that businesses should produce goods and services and let concerned individuals and government agencies solve social problems.

Legal Obligations

Above making a profit, each of us is expected to comply with the federal, state, and local laws that lay the ground rules in which we must operate. Laws can be seen as society's codes of right and wrong, which exist to ensure that individuals and businesses do what is considered right. These codes change all the time as laws are added, repealed, or amended in an attempt to match public sentiment. Regulation of business activity generally falls into four groups of laws that protect (1) consumers, (2) the competition, (3) the environment, and (4) equality and safety.

The category of consumer protection became popular when Ralph Nader started the consumer movement in the early 1960s. Beginning with his safety campaign in the automotive industry, Nader and the consumer activist group he formed, Nader's Raiders, have fought to protect the safety and rights of consumers. Consumer activism has taken the form of letter-writing campaigns, lobbying of government agencies, and boycotting of companies that are perceived to be irresponsible. Of course, consumer protection did not start in the 1960s. Laws protecting consumers from unsafe business practices go back to 1906, when the Pure Food and Drug Act was passed largely in response to Upton Sinclair's 1905 book about the meat-packing industry, *The Jungle*. Today, government agencies such as the Consumer Product Safety Commission and the Food and Drug Administration (FDA) set safety standards and regulations for consumer products, food, and drugs.

Laws that protect competition go back to the Sherman Antitrust Act of 1890, which prohibits monopolies. These laws see competition and unrestrained trade as checks and balances on businesses providing quality products and services at reasonable prices. The Federal Trade Commission (FTC) enforces many of these laws.

Laws protecting the environment were passed beginning in the 1960s also to set minimum standards for business practices concerning air, water, and noise. The Environmental Protection Agency (EPA) was created to enforce many of these laws.

The 1960s saw the passage of legislation regarding equality in the workplace. The Civil Rights Act of 1964 prohibits discrimination in employment on the basis of race, color, sex, religion, or national origin. The Equal Employment Opportunity Commission (EEOC) enforces these laws. Although the Americans with Disabilities Act (ADA) of 1990, equal employment opportunity (EEO), and affirmative action regulate diversity in the workplace (see Chapter 10 for more details on these issues), a small business owner must keep the big picture in mind. The key to managing diversity is to see people as individuals with strengths and weaknesses, and to create a climate where everyone can contribute to the best of his or her ability.[4]

Sexual harassment is a problem in small businesses, although it generally doesn't receive as much public attention as multimillion-dollar corporate settlements. Sexual harassment can damage a person's dignity, productivity, and eagerness to come to work, which is costly to that person and to the business.[5] EEOC guidelines define sexual harassment as unwelcome sexual advances, requests for sexual favors, and other verbal or physical conduct of a sexual nature when (1) sexual activity is required to get or keep a job or (2) a hostile environment is created in which work is unreasonably difficult.[6] The legal costs associated with a sexual harassment lawsuit average $200,000 per complaint for those investigated and found to be valid before the suit ever gets to court. Sexual harassment cost U.S. businesses over $1 billion in legal fees and actual damages from 1994 to 1999.[7] To help keep your small business free of harassment, the American Management Association recommends that you

- Have a clear written policy prohibiting sexual harassment.

- Hold mandatory supervisory training programs on policies and prevention of harassment.

- Ensure that the workplace is free of offensive materials.

- Implement a program for steps to take when a complaint of harassment is received.

- Keep informed of all complaints and steps taken.

- Make sure the commitment against harassment exists at every level.[8]

Ethical Responsibility

Although economic and legal responsibilities are shown in Figure 3.1 as separate levels of obligation, they actually coexist because they represent the minimum threshold of socially expected business behavior. Ethics are the rules of moral values that guide decision making by groups and individuals. They are a person's fundamental orientation toward life—what he or she sees as right and wrong. Ethical responsibilities of a business are how its decisions and actions show concern for what its stakeholders (employees, customers, stockholders, and the community) consider fair and just.

Changes in ethical standards and values usually precede changes in laws. As shown in the previous section on legal obligations, society's expectations changed dramatically in the 1960s, which led to new laws. Changing values cause constant interaction between the legal and ethical levels of social responsibility.

Even businesses that set high ethical standards and try to operate well above legal standards have difficulty keeping up with expectations that perpetually rise. As a case in point, late in 1994, The Body Shop encountered direct and specific criticism of some of its business practices. Critics began to question whether or not The Body Shop was being honest in its advertising and its public image. One of the most vocal critics was journalist Jon Entine. A year-long investigation by Entine led him to make certain allegations against The Body Shop in the September/October 1994 issue of *Business Ethics.* Selected allegations follow:

- Despite its reputation as an innovative natural cosmetics company, cosmetics experts say the company uses many outdated, off-the-shelf product formulations filled with nonrenewable petrochemicals.

- The company has a documented history of quality control problems, including selling "contaminated" products and products that contain formaldehyde. Former Body Shop quality control managers and one of its own consulting scientists made these assertions.

- The Body Shop's charitable contributions and its progressive environmental standards don't match up to what the company claims it does.

About three weeks after the publication of these allegations, T. Gordon Roddick (founder Anita Roddick's husband and chairman of The Body Shop) responded with a letter to subscribers of *Business Ethics,* disputing the information in the article. He stated that "Of the 22 sources named in the article, 10 were disgruntled former employees or franchisees, current competitors, or disappointed bidders for our business, all of whom obviously have personal reasons for wanting to make The Body Shop look bad."

But that wasn't the end of this intriguing story. In the middle of November 1994, subscribers to *Business Ethics* received a letter from the publisher stating that The Body Shop had obtained the mailing list of the magazine through deceptive means and used it without permission to send Roddick's letter to subscribers, and that Entine and the publisher stood by the facts stated in the article.

It's hard to know whether or not the criticisms against The Body Shop were fully justified or whether this is a situation in which a company that has loudly and visibly pronounced itself as socially responsible and ethical was just an easy target for critics. But the fact remains that a business that makes such claims about itself had better be able to stand up to scrutiny. It's a lesson that The Body Shop learned the hard way.[9]

In addition to Roddick, other owners and their businesses that began small and have led the way in social responsibility include Paul Hawkin of Smith & Hawkin, Ben Cohen and Jerry Greenfield of Ben and Jerry's Ice Cream, and Yvon Chouinard of Patagonia.[10]

Philanthropic Goodwill

Philanthropy is the highest level illustrated on the social responsibility pyramid of Figure 3.1. This includes businesses participating in programs that improve the quality of life, raise the standard of living, and promote goodwill. The difference between ethical responsibility and **philanthropic goodwill** is that the latter is seen not so much as obligations but as contributions to society to make it a better place. Businesses that do not participate in these activities are not seen as unethical, but those that do tend to be seen in a more positive light.

Philanthropic activity is not limited to the wealthy or to large corporations writing seven-digit donation checks. Average citizens and small businesses can be and are philanthropic. A small business can sponsor a local Special Olympics meet, contribute to a Habitat for Humanity project, lead a community United Way campaign, or sponsor a Little League baseball team. Albert Vasquez allows a church group to convert his Tucson, Arizona, El Saguarito Mexican food restaurant into a worship center on Sunday mornings. Kerry Stratford, co-owner of Boelts Bros. Associates, and his partners have donated over 500 hours in their studios in 1999 creating designs and advertising for nonprofit groups.[11]

One small business owner can make a difference. Pierre Omidyar started a small business that didn't stay small for long. Omidyar founded the online auction site eBay. In 1998, he and his wife Pamela met for brunch at the home of Jerry Yang, co-founder of Yahoo! to discuss money with a total of 40 couples. They didn't talk

philanthropic goodwill The level of social responsibility in which a business does good without the expectation of anything in return.

Making Good

Do you have to be the owner of a big corporation, flush with cash, to be able to make a contribution to your city or neighborhood? Not necessarily. Small businesses all over the country are recruiting their modest resources—including their products, skills, customers, and suppliers—to help make their communities better places. Not every small business can mount a national campaign against social problems, as Ben & Jerry's or The Body Shop has done. But your commitment and creativity can make a contribution more important than money to your community.

Giving your product away may be a starting point. Laury Hammel is general manager and principal owner of Longfellow Clubs, a health and recreation company in Wayland, Massachusetts. Hammel has founded five nonprofit foundations, is involved in ten such organizations, and participates in many local charities and community events. But his favorite charitable act is donating the use of Longfellow Club facilities to kids with special needs. In his Handi-Racket Tennis Program, handicapped kids learn to play tennis. Hammel has similar programs for swimming and basketball. The three programs bring in about 50 disabled children from the Wayland area each week. Although Hammel estimates that he gives up about $3,000 per year in court and club fees, he says his program takes more initiative than money. Hammel is committed to working with these children, even if the programs sometimes get in the way of club members' desires.

No matter how large or small, a social purpose injects humanity into your business. The perception of business as being soulless has existed for so long that many owners love a chance to show an amount of social concern through their company.

Source: Adapted from "Making Good," by Ellyn Spragins, from *Inc.: The Magazine for Growing Companies.* Copyright ©1993 by Goldhirsh Group/Inc Pubg. Reproduced with permission of Goldhirsh Group/Inc Pubg in the format textbook via Copyright Clearance Center.

about how to make it, but how to give it away. The group had a total worth of over $30 billion, and they were all under 35 years old. The group hopes to stimulate a new type of philanthropy in the same way they have created a new economy. The Omidyars and others of the new superrich want to take an active role in seeing that their money is used for worthwhile purposes that make a real difference, not for self-perpetuating entities that are wasteful and inefficient. The Omidyar foundation has created a new approach that it calls "venture philanthropy." It gives money to charities that follow solid business plans and meet established benchmarks.[12]

Ethics and Business Strategy

ethics The rules of moral values that guide decision making—your understanding of the difference between right and wrong.

Business **ethics** means more than simply passing moral judgment about what should and should not be done in a particular situation. It is part of the conscious decisions you make about the directions you want your business to take. It is a link between morality, responsibility, and decision making within the organization.[13]

The American public has serious concerns about the ethical standards of people they deal with and the decisions they make. Figure 3.2 shows the perception of the American public that the ethical standards of small business owners are considerably higher than those of members of Congress, lawyers, and large business executives.

A poll by RISEbusiness published in *Business Week* magazine asked people who run small and large businesses whether they found certain business practices to be acceptable or unacceptable. Compare their responses to your own (see Figure 3.3).

code of ethics The tool with which the owner of a business communicates ethical expectations to everyone associated with the business.

Codes of Ethics

A **code of ethics** is a formal statement of what your business expects in the way of ethical behavior. It can serve as a guide for employee conduct to help employees de-

FIGURE 3.2

Groups Perceived to Have Unethical Standards

Source: "Groups Perceived to Have Unethical Standards" graph, from "USA Snapshots", *USA Today*, 3 September 1992. Copyright 1992, USA TODAY. Reprinted with permission.

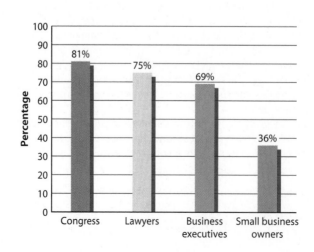

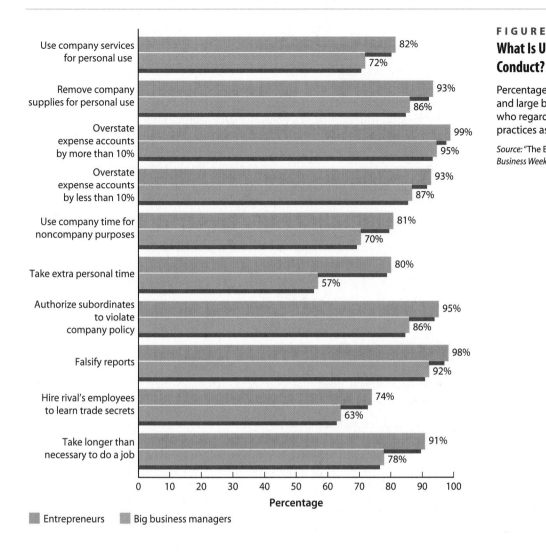

FIGURE 3.3

What Is Unacceptable Conduct?

Percentage of entrepreneurs and large business managers who regard questionable practices as unacceptable.

Source: "The Entrepreneurial Ethic," *Business Week,* 5 October 1998.

termine what behaviors are acceptable. Because the purpose of a code of ethics is to let everyone know what is expected and what is considered right, it should be included in an employee handbook (see Chapter 17 on human resource management).

Your code of ethics should contain a reflection of *your* ethical ideals, be concise in order to be remembered, be written clearly, and apply equally to all employees, regardless of level of authority.[14] Your expectations and the consequences of breaking the code should be communicated to all employees. Small businesses, especially in fast-paced, high-tech industries, often ignore formal codes of conduct because of their push for rapid growth. This mistake can cause expensive legal problems later.

An explicit code of ethics and the expectation that employees must adhere to it can reap many benefits for your small business, including

1. Obtaining high standards of performance at all levels of your work force.
2. Reducing anxiety and confusion over what is acceptable employee conduct.
3. Allowing employees to operate as freely as possible within a defined range of behavior.

4. Avoiding double standards that undermine employee morale and productivity.
5. Developing a public presence and image that are consistent with your organization's ideals.[15]

If you want to maintain and encourage ethical behavior in your business, it must be part of your company's goals. By establishing ethical policies, rules, and standards in your code of ethics, you can treat them like any other company goal, such as increasing profit or market share. Establishing ethical goals allows you to take corrective action by punishing employees who do not comply with company standards and by rewarding those who do. If your code of ethics is supported and strictly enforced by you and your management team, it will become part of your company's culture and will improve ethical behavior. If your managers and employees see your code of ethics as a window-dressing façade, it will accomplish nothing.

Include a frequently asked questions (FAQs) section in the code of ethics section of your employee handbook. Have these FAQs relate specifically to your industry because your new employees will probably have the same questions.[16]

Ethics Under Pressure

Businesses face ethical dilemmas every day. How can they maintain high ethical standards when the effects will hit their bottom line?

> You run a construction company and receive a bid from a subcontractor. You know a mistake was made and the bid is accidentally 20 percent too low. If you accept the bid, it could put the subcontractor out of business. But accepting it will improve your chance of winning the contract for a big housing project. *What do you do?*[17]

Robert George, CEO of Medallion Construction Company of Merrimack, New Hampshire, was the manager who faced this dilemma. Medallion was bidding to become the general contractor of a $2.5 million public housing contract. An electrical contractor from the area submitted a bid that was $30,000, or 20 percent, lower than the quotes from four other subcontractors. Subcontractor bids come in only a few hours before the general contractors must deliver their bids, so that subcontractors can't be played off against each other. Robert George was tempted to take the bid that he knew was a mistake because it would have almost guaranteed that Medallion would win the contract. Then he reconsidered for several reasons. Accepting the bid could have caused problems if the subcontractor went belly up once the project was under way. Then he would have to find a replacement, which would cause time delays and cost overruns.

Aside from pragmatic problems, the ethical ramifications troubled George. He asked himself, "Is it fair to allow someone to screw up when they don't know it and you do?" He decided that the money wasn't worth the damage to his reputation or putting a fellow small businessperson under. George called the subcontractor and said, "Look, I'm not going to tell you what your competitors bid, but your number is very low—in my opinion, too low." The subcontractor withdrew his bid. Medallion still won the contract.

A year later, the same subcontractor submitted another low bid on a different project. This time the low bid was intentional. The subcontractor offered a 2 percent discount because he remembered how honestly George had treated him earlier.

Sometimes high ethics can have material rewards. Having a reputation for high ethical standards can give you an "ethical edge," a competitive advantage for your business. Being known for doing what is right can help you attract talented people, win loyal customers, forge relationships with suppliers, and earn the public's trust.

> You spend months trying to negotiate a deal to sell your equipment in Japan. You deliver your product, as agreed, but the Japanese distributor tells you it is not what the customer expected. The distributor wants you to reengineer the equipment even though it clearly meets the written specifications. *What do you do?*

David Lincoln is president of Lincoln Laser Company, a manufacturer located in Phoenix. Lincoln thought he had a done deal with a distributor from Japan who had spent months scrutinizing Lincoln's $300,000 machine that scans printed circuit board wiring for very small cracks or breaks. The distributor finally ordered eight machines. Unfortunately, the Japanese client wasn't happy after delivery. Lincoln said, "They thought it should inspect *every type* of printed circuit board, even though we explained repeatedly that it was suitable only for a certain class of boards." To change the machine so that it could inspect every type of circuit would require Lincoln to have the software rewritten, pull engineers from another project, and borrow funds to pay for the additional work.

Ethical dilemmas can be magnified by differences in language, culture, and business practices.

Lincoln's first instinct was to say, "This is what you agreed to, we supplied what we said we would. You bought it, pay up." He could have said "no" and been acting ethically according to common business practices in the United States, but he decided to go beyond his basic obligation and do what he felt was the right thing. Lincoln reflected on the differences between American and Japanese customers. Lincoln had expected Japanese customers to act like American clients without realizing the differences in adaptation levels between the two groups. The company hadn't taken time to become sensitive to cultural differences. Fortunately, Lincoln was able to secure financing to accommodate its customers—keeping its ethical principles, its credibility, and the Japanese market intact.

Here are some more ethical situations to consider:

- You own a high-tech business in a very competitive industry. You find out that a competitor has developed a scientific discovery that will give it a significant competitive advantage. Your profits will be severely cut, but not eliminated, for at least a year. If you had some hope of hiring one of your competitor's employees who knows the details of their secret, would you hire him or her?

- A high-ranking government official from a country where payments regularly lubricate decision-making processes asks you for a $200,000 consulting fee. For this fee, he promises to help you obtain a $100 million contract that will produce at least $5 million of profit for your company. What do you do?

- You recently hired a manager who is having a problem with sexual harassment from another manager. She informs you, as the business owner, what is happening and is considering legal action. Unfortunately, you have been so busy dealing with incredible growth that you haven't had a chance to write formal policies. What do you do?

- An advertising agency has created and released a marketing and advertising campaign for your consumer product. The campaign has proven to be offensive to some minority groups (who do not buy your product) and have expressed their objections. However sales for your product have increased by 45 percent since the campaign started. What do you do?[18]

Can You Serve Two Bottom Lines?

When Tom and Gun Denhart moved from Connecticut to Portland, Oregon, to start their own business, they had modest goals. Tom wanted to get out of the high-pressure rat race of advertising he faced with Ogilvy & Mather in New York. Tom and Gun wanted to make a living selling high-quality Swedish products for children. They created what quickly became the ideal workplace. Unfortunately, they found that putting the needs of their employees, the community, and society first can be hazardous to the health of a business.

The business they created is called Hanna Andersson (named after Gun's grandmother). They sold upscale children's clothing made from Swedish cotton via mail order. Tom used his advertising skills to create award-winning, understated masterpieces of direct mail. The market of successful baby boomers was ripe in the early 1980s. They were ready to spend money on their young children. Competition didn't exist, so Hanna Andersson flourished. Their startup could have come from a storybook. Operating out of their garage and a spare room until their second year, Hanna soon reached $40 million annual sales while retaining the atmosphere of a family-run shop. Sales and number of employees doubled annually for the first five years. They were not only creating a company, they were creating their own counterculture. From the start the company was not about baby clothes or money; it was about serious social responsibility, creating opportunities for people to be fulfilled at work and "to do the right thing."

By conscious design, the workplace created was one of perks, benefits, and contributions. Local charities received 5 percent of pretax profits. When profits were in the millions, this yielded six-figure gifts. Their crown jewel initiative was the Hannadown program. Customers would receive a 20 percent discount on their next purchase for returning used Hanna clothing. The returned goods were distributed to needy children across the country. Employee benefits were incredible. Half of all child care costs were paid by the company. Part-time and seasonal employees working 30 hours per week received full benefits. They had flextime, family-leave time, sick time, and even lunchtime was subsidized with a light gourmet employee cafeteria. They were paid cash bonuses, had profit-sharing and tuition reimbursement programs, and received deep product discounts. Employee parking cost the company $80,000 per year.

Success was calculated by what the Denharts and other socially responsible entrepreneurs called the "double bottom line": one for profit, one for good works. Profits, revenue, and good works flowed freely, and Gun thought that the money would always flow to them as long as they did the right thing—but it didn't. The tide started to turn, not because of a single problem, but because of a combination of problems. Two years of recession made customers less willing to shell out $38 for overalls for a two-year-old. There had been management mistakes in trying to fix things that weren't broken, such as radical changes to a great catalogue. When the company started in 1984, it was alone in the market. By 1991, it realized that worthy competitors like Lands' End, L. L. Bean, Oshkosh, Gymboree, and Gap Kids were out there. Most companies could have made adjustments to compensate for the competition, but most companies were not saddled with cost structures that paid for sky-high benefits and contributions. Mary Roberts, now company president, said, "We thought we were immune to worldly cares. Suddenly, we had to face the fact that we were part of the real world."

Costs had to be reduced, and inefficiencies had to be improved. Benefit cuts and even some layoffs sent tremendous shock waves through the culture that was used to protection and pampering. Gail Johnson, vice president of operations, stated that "Topping the to-do list was reeducating employees and weaning them of the sense of entitlement that years of prosperity had bred." The many cost-cutting adjustments are helping the company get back on its feet. Sales are climbing slowly, and attention is being paid to the bottom line. Values are not being abandoned, just modified. Gun realizes that having high values is easy, but maintaining them is difficult when the going gets tough. Doing the right thing by employees isn't the same as doing the smart thing for the business.

What do you do when the current well-being of employees clashes with the future well-being of the company? How do you tell what the "right" thing to do is at any given time? Would a strategic plan have helped management to be socially responsible and to monitor changing competitive and customer environments so adaptations could have been made *before* serious problems existed?

Source: Adapted from "Can You Serve Two Bottom Lines?" by Anne Murphy, from *Inc.: The Magazine for Growing Companies.* Copyright © 1994 by Goldhirsh Group/Inc Pubg. Reproduced with permission of Goldhirsh Group/Inc Pubg in the format textbook via Copyright Clearance Center.

Inner-City Action

When *Inc.* magazine and the Initiative for a Competitive Inner City (ICIC) compiled the Inner City 100 to look into a window of the new U.S. economy, they were surprised at what they saw. The 100 companies had an average annual compound growth rate of 44 percent, and collectively they created 4,695 jobs between 1993 and 1997.

Although many people assume that little economic activity occurs in inner-city neighborhoods well known for problems, the opposite is actually true. Inner cities are a hotbed of entrepreneurship. What competitive advantages could draw businesses to these areas? Michael Porter and Anne Habiby identified four principal competitive advantages:

creating competitive advantage

- *A strategic location at the core of major urban areas, highways, and communication nodes with potent logistical advantages.* Inner-city businesses that are logistics-savvy understand the proximity to customers and to transportation infrastructure as their key advantages.

- *An underutilized work force with high retention amid a tight overall national labor market.* For the past few decades, the most pressing human resource issue facing the U.S. economy has been the creation of jobs. Finding workers will be the critical issue for the next decade. Fueling the new economy with labor will arise largely from the available and growing inner-city work force. More than 54 percent of the work force will come from minority communities, many of which are concentrated in cities and inner cities. The challenge will be to attract, train, and retain this mix of workers.

- *An underserved local market with substantial purchasing power which can support many more retail and service businesses than it now has.* As standards of living improve in inner-city neighborhoods, the quantity of goods and services demanded in those areas will increase. The real opportunity to create self-sustaining income and wealth for inner-city residents is ultimately through the private sector—not more expensive and failed government programs. If just 100 inner-city businesses created 4,695 jobs between 1995 and 1997, what could a concerted effort to foster entrepreneurship produce?

- *Opportunities for companies to link up with and provide outsourcing for competitive clusters (for example, health care and tourism) in the regional economy.*

Source: Adapted from "A Window on the New Economy" by Michael Porter and Anne Habiby, from *Inc.: The Magazine for Growing Companies.* Copyright © 1999 by Goldhirsh Group/Inc Pubg. Reproduced with permission of Goldhirsh Group/Inc Pubg in the format textbook via Copyright Clearance Center.

creating competitive advantage

Green Marketing

Efforts of businesses to act in a socially responsible manner toward the environment are usually called *green marketing*. Small businesses can show concern for the environment (and cut costs at the same time) by recycling paper products and office supplies, by using environmentally benign products, and by using environmentally safe product packaging. Each business must decide how it can have the greatest positive environmental impact. Not every business can affect the air pollution from vehicles or ozone depletion, but every business must recognize the power of the green movement and the rise in environmental consciousness. Incorporating a green marketing program can be aided by the following guidelines:

- Environmentalism is not a passing fad. It is strongly supported.

- The number of people concerned about environmental issues is growing. They buy environmentally friendly products.

- Green marketing can be a sustainable competitive advantage leading to long-term profit.

- Green marketing involves the actual production of your product, raw material procurement, and disposal.

- A successful green marketing strategy depends on effective communication and continuous monitoring.

- Green marketing needs to be integrated into the strategic planning process.

Sources: Jacquelyn Ottman, "Green Marketing: The Systems That Surround You," *Business*, July/August 2000, 29; Ted Rakstis, "Business Rethinks, Refines, Recycles, and Recoups," *Kiwanis Magazine*, August 1993, 43–49; and Stephen McDaniel and David Rylander, "Strategic Green Marketing," *Journal of Consumer Marketing* 10, no. 3 (1993): 4–10.

Small businesses that understand and serve their customers can thrive.

Hire a Hacker???

Hacking. You know, the electronic snooping practice of breaking into someone else's computer system without permission. Sometimes hackers are just curiously looking around to see what they can see. Sometimes their intent is much, much worse. Hacking obviously crosses ethical lines. The question is: How can you prevent it? Or, better, how can you catch a hacker? John Klein believes the old saying that it takes one to know one. Hackers, that is.

Klein started and runs Rent-a-Hacker (www.rent-a-hacker.com), a computer security consulting firm, by contracting a network of 300 freelance computer security experts (hackers) throughout the world. Whenever a client calls Klein, he handpicks a specialist to match the situation. Klein's hackers use their computer powers for good, not evil.

To catch offenders, Klein says, "The trick was not just blocking them out, but finding out who they were. But it's delicate. It's like a chess game. First mistake loses."

One of Klein's top guns is Kelvin Wong. As an Australian juvenile, Wong had hacked such high-profile sites as nasa.gov, army.mil, and usda.gov. But before he got busted, Wong turned from the dark side. "I was turning 18, I didn't want to go to jail," he said. Klein was impressed with Wong's innate network knowledge and hired him to be chief operating officer. Good move.

The Computer Security Institute's (www.gocsi.com) most recent annual survey indicated that 90 percent of the businesses and organizations had suffered computer security breaches within 12 months, and 70 percent had been serious. The total loss from theft, fraud, and sabotage was over $265 million. Makes Rent-a-Hacker's hourly rate of $175 and up seem cheap.

Klein directs his business toward small businesses and individuals by taking more of a real-world perspective than his larger competitors. He realizes that there are 14-year-old kids out there who can hack in ways that many with degrees in computer science would never dream of. Rent-a-Hacker knows those hacking tools and the unconventional thinking used to create them. That's why using the 300-plus contractors, each with a specialty, works. No one person, firm, or software can cover all the bases necessary. Klein points out that prepackaged security scanners like Network Associates CyberCop focus on common security holes and can't deal with creative attacks that hackers dream up. "Most of the time, what trips up system administrators is that they think like system administrators and not like hackers."

Some hackers want data, but more thrive on the creativity challenge required to exploit a system. Wong says that some of the biggest hacks have been through some of the simplest holes. He adds that *zero-day* (brand new) tactics come up all the time. Hackers also *backdoor*, or create secret entryways by modifying server software.

Do you know what you're up against in protecting your small business's computer system against hackers? If not, then go where the bad boys go—but be careful.

www.antionline.com   Ins and outs of hacker activity.
www.gosci.com   Current security research and tips.
www.hackers.com   Archives of underground text files and hacker shareware.
www.securityfocus.com   Invaluable security portal with news, downloads, and advance attack notice.

Source: Christopher Null, "How to Hire a Hacker," *Smart Business for the New Economy,* July 2000, 112–118. Reprinted by permission of Ziff-Davis, Inc.

@e-biz

Strategic Planning

strategic plan A long-term planning tool used for viewing a business and the environments in which it operates in broadest terms.

Recall from Chapter 1 that poor management is the major cause of business failure. The first function of good management, therefore, is good planning. A **strategic plan** is a long-range management tool that helps small businesses be proactive in the way they respond to environmental changes. The process of strategic planning provides an overview of your business and all the factors that may affect it in the next three to five years. This will help you formulate goals for your business to take advantage of opportunities and avoid threats. From your goals you can determine the most appropriate steps you need to take to accomplish them—an action plan.

At the beginning of this chapter, the question was posed about the connection between social responsibility, ethics, and strategic planning. If the intent of the strategic planning process is to produce a working document for your business to follow, the relationship can be seen in the following way. When you assess your company's external environment for opportunities and threats, you identify what you *might do.* When you look at the internal strengths and weaknesses, you see what you *can do* and *cannot do.* Your personal values are ingrained into the business; these are what you *want to do.* Your ethical standards will determine what is *right for you to do.* Finally, in responding to everyone that could be affected by your business, social responsibility guides what you *should do.* When viewed in this manner, not only are social responsibility, ethics, and strategic planning connected, it isn't possible to separate them.

The Strategic Planning Process

Writing a strategic plan generally involves a six-step sequential process. Figure 3.4 shows that the strategic planning process begins with (1) formulating your mission statement, (2) completing an environmental analysis, (3) performing a competitive analysis, (4) analyzing your strategic alternatives, (5) setting your goals and strategies, and (6) setting up a control system.

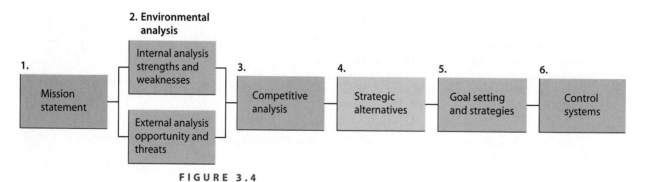

FIGURE 3.4

The Strategic Planning Process

The six sequential steps to drafting a strategic plan.

MISSION STATEMENT. A **mission statement** provides direction for the company by answering the question: What business are we really in? The mission statement should be specific enough to tell the reader something about the business and how it operates. It should *not* be a long, elaborate document that details all of your business philosophies. By carefully identifying the purpose, scope, and direction of your business, the mission statement communicates what you want your business to do and to be. It is the foundation on which all other goals and strategies are based.

mission statement The description of the reason an organization exists.

Another value of a mission statement is the commitment you make by printing and publicizing your strategy and philosophy. You have more incentive to stick to your ideas and expect others to follow them if they are written and shared than if you keep them to yourself.

Management consultant and author Tom Peters writes that a company's mission statement should be 25 words or less in length.[19] This brevity will allow everyone in the organization to understand and articulate it.

The company from the chapter opener, Great Harvest, is dedicated to finding the best people in the world who share their values, their love of life, and their passion to run a good business. Those values can be summed up by their brief, but heartfelt, mission statement:

■ Be loose and have fun.

■ Bake phenomenal bread.

■ Run fast to help customers.

■ Create strong, exciting bakeries.

■ Give generously to others.

Good mission statements, like Great Harvest's, maintain a balance between ideas and reality. From Great Harvest's statement, you can tell what it wants to achieve and how. It says what the business is and is not. Does Great Harvest intend to diversify into wedding cakes and frozen pies to become a major force in the baking industry? No, the company intends to focus on making and selling the best bread possible.

Because the mission statement is the heart of the strategic planning process, you can see in Great Harvest's statement and principles the connection between strategic planning and social responsibility. You can even see evidence of the pyramid of social responsibility in its stated principles. The importance of making a profit identifies economic responsibility. The principle of treating each other with respect and dignity incorporates ethics into its strategic plan. The company's principle of contributing positively to the community and the environment shows ethics and philanthropy.

ENVIRONMENTAL ANALYSIS. Large and small businesses must operate in constantly changing environments. The ability to adapt to change is a major determinant of success or failure for any business in a free enterprise system. Essentially, environmental analysis is the process in which a manager examines what is going on within any sector that could affect the business, either within the business or outside of it.

SWOT analysis The step of strategic planning in which the managers identify the internal strengths and weaknesses of a business and the opportunities and threats that exist outside the business.

Environmental analysis is also called **SWOT analysis** because you examine **S**trengths, **W**eaknesses, **O**pportunities, and **T**hreats. An analysis of the *internal*

Strategic Cabinetry

The importance of having a strategic plan cannot be overemphasized. Businesses of any size can develop competitive advantage through the strategic thinking needed to write a strategic plan. One company that recognized the importance of strategic planning early is Woodpro Cabinetry, Inc., of Cabool, Missouri, a small bathroom cabinet manufacturer located in the rolling hills of the Missouri Ozarks. Owner and president LeRoy Walls knew that competition was heating up and that the marketplace was changing. He realized that, to help ensure future prosperity, his company needed a document to guide its decisions. So, in the early 1990s, LeRoy and several Woodpro employees began developing in earnest a strategic plan for the company. The results of their hard work can be found in a document of over 200 pages entitled "Woodpro Strategic Plan." The document, contained in a three-ring binder, covers a wide variety of important information, such as

- *The Mission Statement.* One of the first elements that you see in Woodpro's strategic plan is its mission statement, which establishes that Woodpro seeks to be the *best* on-time producer and distributor of affordable-quality bath cabinetry. But having a mission statement is just the first step in a strategic plan.

- *The Environmental and Competitive Analysis.* Formulating appropriate strategies also requires an environmental and competitive analysis. Woodpro's strategic plan describes what the company's managers see as its strengths (positive internal characteristics and resources) and weaknesses (negative internal characteristics and lack of resources); opportunities (positive external environmental trends), and threats (negative external environmental trends). Woodpro's strategic plan, internal strengths and weaknesses, and external opportunities and threats are analyzed for each of the company's functional areas (marketing, manufacturing, human resources, and communication). For instance, its "Marketing Threats" section warns that "Competitors are broadening their product offerings" and that "More manufacturers are targeting home center stores." The company's 15 top competitors are then analyzed by products, services, customers, and operations, with the information presented in eight separate tables. The "Operations Weaknesses" section notes that the company's "raw material usage volumes are too low to capture industry competitor cost advantages" and that a "preventive maintenance program is not yet in place." Woodpro's managers can use this vital information to strengthen the company's productivity and assure the stability and growth of its market share. Woodpro's managers admit that gathering competitor data hasn't been a high priority of theirs for very long, but they recognize the importance of knowing what the competition is doing. The competitor analysis in the strategic plan provides a good start to knowing the competition.

- *Strategic Alternatives, Goals, and Chosen Strategies.* Each of the functional sections in Woodpro's strategic plan ends with a description of specific strategies and desired outcomes. Thus the goal stated under the topic "Marketing Promotion," in the "Marketing" section is "To increase awareness of Woodpro's attributes, philosophies, product offerings, and how we help sell our cabinetry, we will establish better communication and rapport with customers, potential customers, and neighbors." To accomplish this goal, the plan states that its strategy is to become better known in the American Midwest through advertising and trade shows, and to use public relations tactics to gain recognition among cabinet retailers and cabinet manufacturers. In the "Human Resource" section, one stated goal is "To provide a computerized system for entry and reporting of innovations, personal reminders, things to do, and strategies and plans." The strategies for achieving this goal are to improve reporting and control of project teams and process teams. Another strategy is to turn the strategic planning group into a team with ongoing responsibilities.

■ *Putting Strategies into Action.* A written plan by itself isn't enough to ensure success. It needs to be put into action. Woodpro's strategic plan describes specific details for implementing each strategy. For instance, the "Marketing" section asserts that, to become better known in mid-America through advertising and trade shows, managers must develop direct-mail advertising programs, attend national trade shows, and use national magazine advertising.

■ *Setting Up Controls.* This is one area where Woodpro's strategic plan isn't as thorough as it could be. Although the plan does identify specific actions that will be monitored, specific control techniques aren't described. In the "Marketing" section, for example, Woodpro is to monitor the accomplishment of its strategies by determining if a direct-mail advertising program was developed, if national trade shows were attended, and if national magazine advertising was used. However, the means for evaluating the degree of success are not stated.

Once Woodpro's strategic plan was completed, it wasn't thrown on a shelf to gather dust. Instead, it was openly shared with all company employees, directors, and financial partners. It is constantly used. Whenever decisions need to be made or problems crop up, the strategic plan reminds employees and managers alike what Woodpro is striving to achieve.

Source: Woodpro Business Plan, Woodpro Cabinetry, Inc., Cabool, Missouri.

environment identifies strengths and weaknesses that exist within your own business. An analysis of the *external* environment identifies opportunities and threats—factors outside your control—that may affect your business.

Because of their speed, flexibility, and sensitivity to customer preferences, small businesses are in a position to take advantage of changes in the environment rapidly. Environmental analysis is important to small businesses because they have fewer resources to risk. No business can afford many mistakes, but the larger the operation, the more breadth it generally has to absorb the cost of errors. A small business may be significantly affected by environmental changes that a larger business could more easily weather.

EXTERNAL ANALYSIS. Opportunities are positive alternatives that you may choose to help attain your company's mission. Although you should always be scanning for opportunities, you cannot pursue every one. Your strategic plan will help you identify those that are right for your business.

Threats are obstacles to achieving your mission or goals. They are generally events or factors over which you have no personal control. A change in interest rates, new government regulations, or a competitor's new product might threaten your business. You might not be able to control these threats, but you can prepare for them or take positive action to cope with them. Threats and opportunities can be found by scanning developments in the following environments:

■ *Economic.* A lot of economic data readily available on the international and national levels are very valuable to small businesses operating in smaller, more isolated markets. As a small business owner, you need to be aware of economic conditions that affect your target markets, such as unemployment rates, interest rates, total sales, and tax rates within your community.

- *Legal/regulatory.* Some factors can affect small businesses in more than one environment. For example, the passage of the North American Free Trade Agreement (NAFTA) changes regulations and the competitive environment. With regulations altered to encourage trade between the United States, Canada, and Mexico, many small businesses find a wealth of new opportunity in new markets. Other businesses see the changes as a threat with new competition. The voice of small business was also heard in Washington, as delegations of small business representatives from all 50 states brought nearly 300 policy recommendations when they met for the White House Conference on Small Business in the summer of 1995.

- *Sociocultural.* What members of society value and desire as they pass from one life stage to another has an effect on what they purchase. For example, increased popularity of tattoos for teens and twenty-somethings means opportunity for skin artists who are able to provide this service in a small business. Will the next opportunity for an entrepreneur be an innovative new process for removing those tattoos?

- *Technological.* Technology is the application of scientific knowledge for practical purposes. Few environmental forces have caused as much excitement in the business community as the creation of the Internet. Entrepreneurs are scrambling to find ways to take advantage of the opportunities of e-business.

- *Competitive.* Actions of your competitors are considered forces within your competitive environment. You face a difficult task in not only tracking what your competitors are currently doing, but also in predicting their reactions to your moves. If you drop the price of your product to gain more market share, will competing business managers react by holding their prices constant or by cutting their prices below yours? This could escalate into an expensive price war.

Are opportunities and threats easy to identify? No, and they never have been. Writer Mark Twain once said, "I was seldom able to see an opportunity until it had ceased to be one."

INTERNAL ANALYSIS. An internal analysis assesses the strengths and weaknesses of your company. It identifies what it is that your company does well and what it could do better. Internal analysis is important for two reasons. First, your personal opinion of your own business will be biased, at best, and could provide an unrealistic view of the capacity and potential of your business. We tend to look at ourselves through proverbial rose-colored glasses.

Second, internal analysis is important in matching the strengths of your business with opportunities that exist. The idea is to put together a realistic profile of your business to determine if you are able to take advantage of opportunities and react to the threats identified in the environmental analysis. This isn't as easy as it sounds, because you have to view your environments not as if they are snapshots, but as several videos playing at once. The key is to match opportunities that are still unfolding with resources that are still being acquired.[20]

Although most of us have no problem identifying our strengths, some of us may need help realizing our weaknesses. The following diagnostic tests can help you evaluate your business realistically:

- Visit your newest, lowest-level employee. Can he or she tell you why the business exists? name major competitors? say what you do well? list major customers? If not, your vision isn't coming across.

- Can that same employee describe what he or she is doing to contribute to your competitive advantage?

- Ask a long-term employee how things went yesterday. If you get answers like "Okay" or "Fine . . . just fine," you may have a potential problem. If you hear specifics, consider it a good sign.

- Observe what the business looks like after hours. Are things neat and orderly, or does it look like a tornado struck? Although neatness doesn't guarantee success, you should be able to find the checkbook, phone book, and most of the furniture.

- Observe your business during work hours. Invent a reason to be where you can watch and hear what goes on. What impression do you get of the business?

- Select a few customers at random to call or visit. Ask them how they were *honestly* treated the last time they were in your business.

- Call your business during the busiest part of the day. How quickly is the phone answered? Is the response efficient, friendly, surly, or overly chatty?

- Ask a friend to visit your business as a mystery shopper. Would he or she come back again?[21]

COMPETITIVE ANALYSIS/COMPETITIVE ADVANTAGE. Without analysis, competition can also be viewed with bias. Competitors are rarely as slow, backward, and inferior in all areas as we would like to believe they are. Competition should be viewed as formidable and serious. In the competitive analysis, you are trying to identify *competitive weaknesses*. In what areas is the competition truly weak and therefore vulnerable? Some bias may be removed if you are as specific as possible in writing your competitive analysis. For example, instead of saying that your competitors offer poor service, qualify your remarks with references to return policies, delivery, schedules, or fees.

The heart of your company's strategy and reason for being in business is your *competitive advantage*. You must do *something* better than everyone else; otherwise your business isn't needed (see Chapter 11). Your competitive advantage must be sustainable over time to remain a benefit to you. If it can be easily copied by competitors, you have to find a new way to stay ahead.

Sometimes people mistake a gimmick for competitive advantage. For example, suppose a microbrewery accidentally adds blue food coloring to a vat of beer, which becomes a surprise hit with its regular customers. Could this brewery sustain this advantage? No, it's really a gimmick, because competitors could just as easily add blue food coloring to their beer with little lapse of time, negating the microbrewery's advantage. By contrast, the microbrewery might find greater competitive advantage by using unique combinations of ingredients when brewing its beer or refining its process of production to be truly distinctive.

Competitive advantage can be enhanced through *positioning*. Positioning is creating an image for your business or its products and is achieved by differentiating your good or service from your competition's offering. Positioning and images are created in people's minds through comparing your products or services with those of competing companies. The more unique people view your product to be when compared with others, the stronger your position will be in the market. You accomplish positioning through your marketing efforts (see Chapter 11).

How can you analyze the competition? The process of gathering competitive intelligence doesn't have to be prohibitively expensive. A little effort and creativity

Competitive Analysis: How to Beat the Competition

Rank your business and the four competitors you have identified for each of the following areas. Rank the business from "1" to "5," with "5" being the lowest and "1" being the highest. Assign only one "1" per area, one "2," and so on through "5." No ties are allowed, so you end up with a ranked list of the five companies. This exercise will help you improve your competitive position and possibly point out new areas for competitive advantage to you.

Areas of Comparison (For example only; add or delete areas that most apply to your business.)

1. *Image.* How do consumers perceive the reputation and the physical appearance of the business?

2. *Location.* Is the business convenient to customers for distance, parking, traffic, and visibility?

3. *Layout.* Are customers well served with the physical layout of the business?

4. *Atmosphere.* When customers enter the business, do they get a feeling that it is appropriate for your type of business?

5. *Products.* Can customers find the products they expect for your type of business?

6. *Services.* Do customers receive the quantity and quality of services they expect?

7. *Pricing.* Do customers perceive the prices charged to be appropriate for the quality of the products sold? Do they receive the value they expect?

8. *Advertising.* Does the advertising of the business reach its target market?

9. *Sales methods.* Are customers comfortable with the methods the business uses to sell products?

Areas of Comparison	Your Business	Competitor A	Competitor B	Competitor C	Competitor D
1. Image					
2. Location					
3. Layout					
4. Atmosphere					
5. Products					
6. Services					
7. Pricing					
8. Advertising					
9. Sales methods					
TOTALS					

combined with keeping your eyes open can yield a lot of information. Here are common ways that can help small business owners gather information for compiling their competitive analyses:

■ Read articles in trade publications. A proliferation of specialized publications in every industry makes your gathering easier; for example, *Progressive Grocer* if you are selling food products, or *Lodging Hospitality* if you are interested in travel accommodations.

- Listen to what your customers and salespeople say about competitors. These groups make the most frequent comparisons of you and the competition.

- Keep a file on key competitors. Information is useless unless you can access it easily. Include published information, notes of conversations, or competitors' sales, product, or service brochures. These readily available sources of information can help you determine how competitors position themselves.

- Establish a regular time, perhaps a monthly meeting, to meet with key employees to evaluate the information in these competitive information files.

- Attend industry trade shows, exhibits, and conferences. A lot can be learned from competitors' booths and through the networking (or socializing) that goes on at such events.

- Buy competitors' products and take them apart to determine their quality and other advantages. Consider incorporating the best elements of competing products into your products. This process is called *reverse engineering* and is part of a process of establishing comparison standards called *benchmarking.*

- Consult published credit reports on your competitors. Companies like Dun & Bradstreet (D&B) make standard credit reports available. See what D&B says about the competition.[22]

STRATEGIC ALTERNATIVES. The process of defining strategic alternatives begins by identifying problems based on information gained in earlier steps. The process continues with drafting a list of alternatives; thus, it is a two-step process—identify what is wrong and what you can do about it.

Problem identification is the most difficult part of strategic planning. It takes thorough SWOT and competitive analyses and a lot of analytical thinking to pinpoint problems like a current strategy that no longer suits your environment or a mismatch between your strengths and an opportunity that you have identified. Bracing one of your weaknesses and preparing for an upcoming threat are problems that demand your attention. If completion of your SWOT and competitive analyses identifies no major problems or new strategies needed, don't fix anything. Always look to be proactive, but don't ignore the status quo either.

DILBERT reprinted by permission of United Features Syndicate, Inc.

creating competitive advantage

Do Your Homework

Erick Laine Chaitman, president and CEO of Aleas Corp., New York knife producer, has some advice for other small business owners trying to choose markets strategically. First, when scouting for a country to enter, Aleas looks for a place where its basic sales and marketing approach successful in the U.S. will work. It has found that, when it departs from techniques that work here, sales get tougher. For example, it varied its approach when it entered Korea—with limited success and much higher expenses until it figured out what worked.

Chaitman recommends easing up the learning curve if possible. The firm entered Costa Rica because it's a small country, but easy to enter; it's stable; it has a high literacy rate; and it has a high average income for the region. It was also a good place to learn. Aleas had a chance to develop Spanish-speaking managers and plans to use what it has learned in Costa Rica as a steppingstone to the rest of Latin America.

Strategically, the approach will work no matter what country you are located in. Find markets similar to your own in which you can use tried-and-true techniques as you expand internationally.

Source: "Do Your Homework," *Chief Executive, Little Big Corp. Supplement,* 1998, 8–9. Reprinted by permission of RMSREPRINTS.COM.

Few problems can be solved with a single solution or with the first one that comes to mind. Therefore, after you have identified a problem, your next step is to generate a list of alternative solutions. Try to come up with as many alternatives as possible. Once you've exhausted the possibilities, evaluate whether they would solve your particular problem or work in your company. However, don't evaluate possibilities as you generate ideas, as this stifles creativity. Once your list of alternative strategies is compiled, you need to anticipate the result of each and consider the impact on your company's resources, environment, and people.

Although there is a strong temptation to list alternatives and strategies informally in one's mind, research has shown that getting ideas down on paper creates a wider range of strategies and alternatives.[23] Most strategic theorists stress that creativity and insightful thinking are the bases for strategic change.[24]

GOAL SETTING AND STRATEGIES. Your mission statement sets the broadest direction for your business. SWOT and competitive analyses help you refine or change direction. The goals that you set must stem from your mission statement. Goals are needed before you can build a set of strategies. As the cliché goes, "If you don't put up a target, you won't hit anything." Goals need to be

- *Written in terms of outcomes rather than actions.* A good goal states where you want to be, not how you want to get there. For example, a goal should focus on increasing sales rather than on your intention to send one of your brochures to every address in town.

- *Measurable.* You must be able to tell if you accomplish a goal or not. To do this, you must be able to measure the outcome you want to accomplish.

- *Challenging yet attainable.* Goals that are too easy to accomplish are not motivating. Goals that are not likely to be accomplished are self-defeating and decrease motivation.

- *Communicated to everyone in the company.* You will find that a team effort is difficult to produce if some of your players don't know the goals.

- *Written with a time frame for achievement.* Performance and motivation increase when people have goals with a time frame as compared with open-ended goals.

Writing usable goals isn't easy at first. If you state that your goal is to be successful, is that a good goal? It sounds positive, it sounds nice. But is it measurable? No. How can you tell whether or not you achieve your goal? You can't, because there is no defined outcome. There is also no time frame. Do you intend to be successful this year? by the time you are 90? Goals need the characteristics listed previously to be useful.

Although you will have only one mission statement, you will have several business-level goals that apply to your entire organization. Each functional area of your business (for example, marketing, finance, human resources, and production) will have its own set of specific goals that will relate directly to achieving your business-level goals (see Figure 3.5). Even if you are the only person performing marketing, finance, human resource management, and production duties, these areas of your small business must still be addressed individually.

- Your *mission statement* describes who you are, what your business is, and why it exists.

- A *business-level goal* describes what you want your overall business to accomplish in order to achieve your company mission.

- A *function-level goal* describes the performance desired of specific departments (or functional areas, such as marketing, production, and so on) in order to achieve your business-level goals.

- A *strategy* is a plan of action that details how you will attain your function-level goals.

In the final stage of goal setting, specific strategies are developed to accomplish your goals. For example, a *marketing strategy* would be to hire Jerry Seinfeld to be

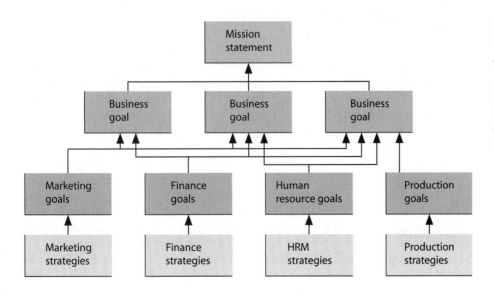

FIGURE 3.5

Levels of Goals

The goals you set for each functional area of your small business should help you achieve the overall goals of your business, which in turn focus on your mission statement.

spokesperson for your new standup comedy computer program. This strategy should help you attain your *function-level marketing goal* of capturing 20 percent market share of the total comedy software market. Your marketing goal should help you attain your *business-level goal* of increasing third-quarter profits by 8 percent, which in turn ensures that you accomplish your company *mission* of satisfying the entertainment needs of lonely computer operators and thereby earning a profit.

Function-level goals and strategies must coordinate with one another and with business-level goals for the business to run smoothly. For example, the marketing department may develop a strategy of advertising on the Internet that will bring in orders from all over the globe. This is great as long as the production department can increase capacity, the human resource department can hire and train enough new employees, and all other areas of the business are prepared. Each functional area must see itself as an integral part of the entire business and act accordingly.

CONTROL SYSTEMS. Planning for the future is an inexact science. Very rarely do the actual outcomes of your plans match exactly what you anticipated. When things don't turn out as you planned, you must ask, "Why was there a deviation?" Having a control process built into the planning process will help answer this question.

Your strategic plan, including all of its separate parts, sets a standard of comparison for your business's actual performance. The purpose of control systems is to provide you with information to start the planning process all over again. After checking your controls, you either readjust the standards of your plan or create new goals for your plan, and off you go for another planning period. This is why goals must be written in terms of outcomes rather than actions; measurable, challenging, yet attainable; communicated; and written with a time frame for achievement. You need to collect accurate data about what you have done so you can compare this information with your planned standards. Control systems don't need to be expensive and elaborate. They should be simple enough to become a natural part of your management process.

Strategic Planning in Action

Strategic plans are different from business plans (see Chapter 4). Business plans and strategic plans support each other and overlap to a degree, but seek to accomplish different purposes. Business plans are written primarily to test the feasibility of a business idea, acquire financing, and coordinate the startup phase. Strategic plans are needed both before the business is started and continuously while it is in operation, to match the direction of the business with changes that occur within its environments.

Strategic planning addresses strategic growth—where you are going. Business planning addresses operational growth—how you will get there. Strategic planning looks outward from the business at the long-term prospects for your products, your markets, your competition, and so on. Business planning or organizational growth focuses on the internal concerns of your business, such as capital, personnel, and marketing. Eventually, the two plans converge as your long-term strategic goals will be strongly influenced by operational decisions made when the business was

Strategic planning requires you to broaden your thinking and forces you to look at the general issues over the next three to five years—countering the realities of the competitive world with concrete plans instead of wishful thinking.

started.[25] Strategic planning requires you to broaden your thinking and forces you to look at general issues over the next three to five years—countering the realities of the competitive world with concrete plans instead of wishful thinking. Most sections will not be extremely detailed but will provide outlines for direction. Business planning, on the other hand, needs to be as detailed as possible.

Planning is difficult and many small business owners would like to ignore it. The reason the planning process is difficult is because it forces you to identify realities that exist in a competitive world rather than rely on emotions, guesses, and assumptions.

What is the best kind of strategic or business plan to write? The one that you will *use!* A balance must be struck between floundering with no direction and drowning in a detached, strangling planning process based on hard data that really are not hard. You need to remember that the *planning process* is actually more important and valuable than the plan that is created because of the *strategic thinking* required to write it.

When you begin writing the first draft of your plan, don't worry about the fine points of its structure—simply get your ideas on paper. Once written, you should revise your plan to reorder your ideas into a logical and clear format. An informal plan written in a format that you are comfortable with and will use is 100 percent better than a formal plan that fits someone else's definition of "correct" form but sits on a shelf.

Get advice and suggestions from as many sources as practical when you are formulating your plans. Talk to colleagues, bankers, accountants, other executives, and lawyers for their input. If your business is already in operation, including employees in decisions is a great way to show them their opinions count. They can all provide valuable insight to your plans.

Establishing a Business Culture ▬

Organizational culture can be defined as a set of values, beliefs, goals, norms, and rituals that members of the organization share. You could say that culture is "the way we do things around here." Culture is created by a manager's belief about how to manage himself or herself and the employees, and how to conduct business.[26]

organizational culture A set of values, beliefs, goals, norms, and rituals that members of the organization share.

If you expect ethical behavior, you must act ethically yourself and reward ethical behavior. If you do not express and model desired behavior and goals, a culture will evolve on its own. If ethical behaviors are not valued by your business, you may be rewarding unethical behavior.

Gaps between your ethical beliefs and those of your employees can develop. For example, you may believe that the culture of your business encourages respect for each other, but your reward system may communicate to your employees that you want them to compete against one another. Because of this belief, they may intentionally or unintentionally sabotage each other's work to win the reward.[27] Rewards and punishments need to be consistent with your business's true culture. A basic premise of management is "the things that get rewarded are the things that get done."

creating
competitive
advantage

Strategic Planting

Lorraine Miller owns and operates a plant store in Salt Lake City called Cactus and Tropicals. Her company sells unusual and unique plants, at both the wholesale and the retail levels. In addition, some of her 35 employees tend about 2 million plants under commercial maintenance contracts. Not wanting to rest on her laurels, so to speak, Miller devised a goal to reenergize herself and her company. She decided that she wanted Cactus and Tropicals to go from $1 million in sales per year to $5 million. And she also wanted to create a business culture in which employees would continue to be motivated and committed to the customer. To accomplish these goals, Miller started off by drafting a six-point mission statement that reflected ambitions for the company *and* for her employees. Miller says, "I wanted to create a space where my employees can grow, too." So, even small business owners who have received visible and very public tributes to their success must still deal with putting their plans into action.

Source: Excerpt from "Profits in Bloom," by Michael Barrier. Reprinted by permission, *Nation's Business,* October 1995. Copyright 1995, U.S. Chamber of Commerce.

SUMMARY

■■■■ The relationship between social responsibility, ethics, and strategic planning.

The social responsibility and ethics of your business are the commitments you make to doing what is right. Strategic planning is the process of deciding where you want your business to go and how it will get there. All three concepts work together to form the foundation on which your entire business rests.

■■■■ Levels of social responsibility.

You have an economic responsibility to make your business profitable. Without profit, your business could not contribute anything else. Your legal obligation to obey the law shows the minimum behavior expected to be part of society. Your ethical responsibility covers your obligation to do what is right, without intentionally harming others. Philanthropic goodwill is contributing to others without expecting anything in return.

■■■■ Importance of a code of ethics.

Business ethics means more than deciding what should and should not be done in a particular situation. It supplies the fundamental basis for the course you want your business to take. A code of ethics is a way for you to communicate your ethical expectations to everyone involved in your business. The code should represent your ethical ideals, be concise enough to be remembered, be written clearly, and apply to everyone in the organization.

▨▨▨   **Steps in the strategic planning process.**

The strategic planning process includes defining your mission statement, conducting an environmental analysis (internal and external, or SWOT, analysis), analyzing the competition, identifying strategic alternatives, setting goals, and establishing systems to measure effectiveness.

▨▨▨   **The importance of establishing an organizational culture.**

Organizational culture is the set of values, beliefs, goals, norms, and rituals shared by members of the organization. Culture is created by a manager's belief about how to manage himself or herself, the employees, and the business. If the manager expects ethical behavior, he or she must act ethically and consistently reward this behavior. Employees will be mostly likely to do what is expected and rewarded by the business's culture.

QUESTIONS FOR REVIEW & DISCUSSION

1. Write a brief summary of the connection between social responsibility, ethics, and strategic planning in a small business setting.

2. Discuss the four groups of laws that generally regulate business activity in this country, and give some historical background on the major laws that affect all entrepreneurs today.

3. Define the purpose of a code of ethics, and write a brief code that would be suitable for a small business.

4. Although a certain practice may be widely accepted in the business community and be perfectly legal, does that necessarily mean it is *always* moral? Qualify your answer with examples.

5. Write a mission statement for a small business that not only functions as a strategic planning guide but also incorporates the company's philosophy of social responsibility and ethical standards.

6. Explain how cultural differences between countries can have either a positive or a negative effect on an entrepreneur who is pursuing a contract either outside the United States or with persons of different ethnic backgrounds in the United States.

7. Why is environmental analysis more crucial to the small business owner than to larger corporations?

8. You are an entrepreneur and wish to perform a self-evaluation of your business environment. How would you go about this task? Be specific about what you hope to discover through the evaluation of your employees, product, management, and so on.

9. What is the value of competitive analysis to the small business owner? What sorts of things should you know about your competition, and what analytical methods can you use to find out this information?

10. Goal setting is a major part of the entrepreneur's business plan. Outline specific methods for setting goals that are realistic, fit into the overall mission of the company, and can be related to the strategic planning process that is in place at the organization.

11. Discuss the concept of organizational culture as it relates to the small business environment. What is the role of the manager/owner in the organizational culture?

QUESTIONS FOR **CRITICAL THINKING**

1. How can a small business show that it is socially responsible? Think of evidence of social responsibility (like sponsoring a Little League team) that a small business can demonstrate.

2. What does strategic planning mean to the small business owner? How does the size of the organization affect the strategic planning process, and how much input should be sought from outside sources while outlining the strategic plan?

Experience this...

You have small businesses in the area where you live making impacts on your local society, for both good and ill. Identify two local companies—one that is a good citizen and one that is not. Find newspaper and magazine articles to support your classifications (so that you are dealing with as many data and as little opinion as possible). Write a two- to three-page paper explaining the possible strategic business implications of their actions. Will either small business need to change in the near future as a consequence of past behavior?

WHAT WOULD **YOU DO?**   No. 1

Some small businesses, by the very nature of what they produce or market, find it difficult to clarify how they're going to fulfill the four levels of social responsibility (economic, legal, ethical, and philanthropic). However, by using strategic planning, even companies in somewhat controversial and questionable industries can define how they're going to be socially responsible. Take, for instance, Grand Casinos of Minneapolis. As more and more states have legalized gambling in selected locations, Lyle Berman, CEO of Grand Casinos, has been there to develop and manage the casinos. His company has been so successful that it ranked first on *Fortune's* list of America's 100 fastest-growing companies. Yet Grand Casino's business—gambling—still tends to arouse definite controversy. Obviously, Berman could use strategic planning to help identify areas in which his company could fulfill its social responsibilities.

QUESTION

1. You're in charge of strategic planning for Grand Casinos. The company has plans to open and manage a casino in rural Iowa. Community residents have asked you and your strategic planning team to attend a town meeting to discuss the casino. You'll need to prepare a description of how your company is fulfilling its social responsibility. (Use Figure 3.1 as a guide.) Other members of the class will act as community residents. Prepare your questions and concerns for confronting the Grand Casinos team.

WHAT WOULD **YOU** DO?	No. 2

Take a look at another small business in an industry that often is publicly criticized for its products. Boisset USA is a producer and marketer of high-quality, affordable wines. Yet Jean Charles Boisset, president of Boisset USA, has committed his company to supporting charitable causes—one in particular that the company supports is Oklahoma-based Feed the Children. Ten percent of gross profit on every bottle of two of the company's products, Christophe Vineyards and the French-imported J. C. Boisset, goes to Feed the Children. Currently, that amounted to funding for 3 million meals for needy children. The goal is to fund 5 million meals each year, and the company appears to be on track to meet that particular goal, but planning is needed to reach the goal.

QUESTIONS

1. You've been hired by Boisset USA to prepare a strategic plan. Draft an outline of a strategic plan for the company which takes into consideration all the components of strategic plans, including the social responsibility and ethics aspects.

2. Here we have two companies, both in industries that often arouse public criticism and controversy. How can they connect social responsibility, ethics, and strategic planning?

Sources: Richard S. Teitelbaum, "America's 100 Fastest-Growing Companies," *Fortune*, 17 April 1995, 75–84; and Lynn Keillor, "Fighting Hunger with Wine," *Business Ethics*, July/August 1995, 25.

CHAPTER CLOSING CASE	No. 3

Testing the Limits

Testing the limits is an apt description of Yvon Chouinard in both his personal and professional life, which tend to overlap to the point of being indistinguishable. Chouinard, a life-long avid outdoors adventurer, is the founder and owner of Patagonia, Inc., the Ventura, California–based maker and retailer of outdoor clothing and equipment. His unique approach to managing his business is an interesting story of how a business owner can succeed—and succeed, not just in the usual sense of being profitable, but in a variety of ways that some businesspeople might consider atypical—by following his dream.

This story begins in 1957 when the 19-year-old Chouinard began selling handmade mountain-climbing equipment out of his car. Frustrated with the standard climbing pitons (pegs pounded into rock or ice as a climbing support) that were used and then left behind, Chouinard had designed a removable hard-steel piton that could be used repeatedly and with less waste. His other innovative designs revolutionized mountain climbing equipment.

By 1964 Chouinard had moved to the coastal city of Ventura, California, in search of good surf, where he eventually set up shop in a tin shed behind a meatpacking plant. His legendary reputation among extreme adventurers attracted other self-described "dirt bags" and "fun hogs" seeking work. Chouinard hired workers not on the basis of any particular business skills but because they had climbed, surfed, or fished with him and wanted to work with him because it seemed like a fun thing to do. Chouinard's management style included making decisions from the "gut." For instance, when he realized that his climbing pitons were severely pitting and scarring rock faces, Chouinard denounced them in an essay in the company catalog about "clean climbing." At that time, such products constituted 70 percent of his company's sales. He then introduced an environmentally responsible aluminum alternative.

By the early 1970s Chouinard had added a line of outdoor clothing that became so immensely popular that he created a new name for it: Patagonia. (The name comes from the southern region of Argentina.) The 1980s were a bonanza for the company as it continued to post increasing sales revenues. Customers bought not only Patagonia's products—rain gear, foul-weather sailing wear, ski clothes, and casual pants, shirts, and shorts—but the lifestyle they represented. By the late 1980s Patagonia offered 375 different styles and the company's annual growth rate was nearly 30 percent.

Patagonia was regularly heralded in the business press for its atypical business atmosphere. With an on-site sand volleyball court for aggressive lunchtime matches, surfboards propped in office corners for employees to catch the best afternoon waves, and a company cafeteria serving gourmet pizzas and fresh-cut organic vegetables, the company's image was "one of cool Patagonia people selling cool products to cool people."

However, that image was tarnished in 1991 when Patagonia, whose sales had become flat, found itself with a warehouse full of stuff that wasn't selling. Expenses had spiraled out of control and the company faced a cash crunch, so it took on millions of dollars in additional debt just to stay afloat. An uncertain economic environment and a mild winter contributed to the problems.

Chouinard also found himself at a crossroads in deciding what he wanted for his business. Chouinard and his wife Malinda (who is co-owner) sought counsel from Michael Kami, president of the Center for Strategic Management in Miami. In Kami's blunt assessment, entrepreneurial businesses like Patagonia that were at the outer limits of their capacity generally had two options: sell the company or adopt a more "normal" or businesslike management style. The Chouinards and key company colleagues went on a retreat to Argentina to discuss the "next 100 years." They concluded that the only way to reconcile the company's values with its environmental impact was to "use the company as a tool for social change." But what exactly did this assertion mean? Sidestepping Kami's advice, it established a policy of "slow growth" to return the company to its original mission of producing the highest-quality products and donating a portion of its profits to environmental groups.

To achieve this new goal, Chouinard downsized the company by 20 percent, cut the clothing line by 30 percent, reduced catalog production from four to two times a year, and replaced the direct-mail tactic of prospecting with rented mailing lists. Chouinard described the change to customers in an essay called "Reality Check" in the fall 1991 catalog. "Everything pollutes," he wrote. "Well, last fall you had a choice of five ski pants; now you may choose between two. This is, of course, un-American, but two styles of ski pants are all that anyone needs."

The company's accountant said that Patagonia became a much better company from a traditional financial management perspective because of the slow, controlled growth. At the same time, the company's commitment to social accountability has made a difference. To some entrepreneurs, Chouinard's decision to live within self-prescribed limits may seem to contradict the American ethic of pursuing growth at any cost. Yet Chouinard has learned from his life-long pursuit of risk sports that one should never exceed one's resources. "The ultimate is to be right on the edge, but you never go over it because then you'd be dead," he said. "Living on that edge and breaking a lot of the rules in business to do things our own way is what unifies the company."

Chouinard's visionary management style arises from his strong philosophical principles about the relationship between business and the environment. It's best reflected in the simple description of the company's mission: "Building really good products for your friends and being able to do some good." His idea of "doing good" means donating 1 percent of the company's annual sales to environmental groups. And Patagonia's commitment to priorities beyond the bottom line is a critical success factor: In 1994, Chouinard was named one of the retailing industry's "Entrepreneurs of the Year." Today the company manufactures and retails outdoor clothing and equipment worldwide. By the end of its fiscal year in April 1995, Patagonia's sales had reached $150 million and checks written to environmental groups totaled $1.5 million. Chouinard and Patagonia's current managers know that they need to keep focused on the company's values. They've recently reaffirmed those core principles: commitment to the environment, dedication to employees and community, and pursuit of highest quality. A glowing testament to the company's ability to do this comes from one of its competitors, Jack Gilbert, president of Mountain Hardware of Berkeley, California. "It would appear to be difficult to stay on the cutting edge over such an extended period, and to be true to such lofty environmental goals, but Patagonia manages to do both well," Gilbert said. "Plus, they're honorable businesspeople, a company which is true to its word." Chouinard's approach to business and sports has marked him as an innovator. And he has proven that you can "test the limits" and succeed.

Sources: "Retailing's Entrepreneurs of the Year," *Chain Store Age Executive,* December 1994, 46–50; Polly LaBarre, "Patagonia Comes of Age," *Industry Week,* 3 April 1995, 42–48; and Mary Scott, "Interview with Yvon Chouinard," *Business Ethics,* May/June 1995, 31–34.

QUESTIONS:

1. How and why did Chouinard start his business? Is this typical for small business owners? Explain.

2. Can company growth become a problem? What are some ways that small business owners or managers can solve this problem?

3. Do you think that many small business owners or managers make decisions from the "gut"? What are the advantages of doing so? What might the drawbacks be?

4. What role have Chouinard's personal values played in the company's growth and operations?

5. Why does a nontraditional approach to doing business appear to work for Patagonia? Could it work for other companies? Why or why not?

4

The Business Plan

After reading this chapter, you should be able to:

- Explain the purpose and importance of the business plan.

- Describe the components of a business plan.

- Recognize the importance of reviewing your business plan.

IN OCTOBER AND November of 1998, your author had the opportunity to teach the process of writing business plans to budding entrepreneurs in the Russian far east city of Magadan. Magadan is a city of 130,000 located on the Sea of Okhotsk, not far below the Arctic Circle. The University of Alaska–Anchorage has set up Russian-American Business Training Centers throughout the Russian far east as a means of developing entrepreneurship—a much-needed commodity in this economically troubled country.

There is no question that entrepreneurship—with the creation of new businesses with new products and ideas—is the engine that runs a free market economy like the one Russia is trying to establish. But a very real question remains: How do you start that engine of new business in times of economic crisis? At a time when many Russians had not been paid for 6, 9, even 12 months or more, the fuel (currency) to run the engine is scarce. Still, over 40 aspiring entrepreneurs enrolled in my classes to learn the process of writing a business plan.

When resources are scarce, the need for creativity and innovation increases. This was evident in Magadan. Although the banks had no money to make loans, students identified "alternative sources" of finance in their business plans, such as extensive use of barter of goods and services, and multiple friends and family from whom to borrow small amounts of money. They demonstrated the essence of "bootstrapping"—the perseverance and desire to make business happen despite formidable obstacles. Remember the term *bootstrapping*, or picking yourself up by your own bootstraps, as you consider self-employment.

What types of businesses were planned? As wide a variety as you find in the class you are probably in now. A range of cafés, an importer of used cars and trucks, a crematorium, and a 900-million-ruble expansion and upgrade of the Magadan airport. I found a preponderance of talent in artistic areas. A man named Dmitri, who was trained as a geologist, had built and collected machinery for cutting, shaping, and polishing stone. During the summer, he would scour the hills in the Magadan area collecting agate, geodes, and other stone and minerals. He then spent the long Russian winters in his workshop where he would transform them into beautiful chess sets, mosaics, and other creations. He and a partner wrote a business plan to export his treasures.

If entrepreneurship involves identifying a need and creating a business to satisfy that need (and it does), then my entrepreneurial prize went to a man named Anatoli. Anatoli has been trained as an electrical engineer, and like many of us, he likes to see what he can find in salvage piles. One day Anatoli found a compact heating element, and he immediately thought of a new use for this relic. Magadan, like most Russian cities, has a central, coal-fired heating plant where water is heated then sent via underground pipes to all business and government buildings and apartments, finally reaching cast-iron radiators to heat the rooms. Since underground means permafrost, this is not the most efficient system ever designed. When the system is operating at peak performance, you can still see your breath indoors. At worst, when the city coal supply runs short, the entire heating system is shut down for hours. Anatoli adapted the heating element he found to electrically heat the water as it comes into an individual apartment's radiator. Anatoli wrote a business plan to import similar heating elements that could be retrofitted to existing heating units and keep Russian apartments more comfortable. Now that's an entrepreneur with a plan!

■ Every Business Needs a Plan

Successful small business owners know where they want to go and find a way to get there. To see their dreams of owning a business become a reality, they know they must plan each step along the way. Starting a business is like going on vacation—you don't reach your destination by accident. Whether you want to hike through Denali National Park in Alaska or sell frozen yogurt to tourists in Miami, you need a map and adequate provisions.

business plan A document describing a business that is used to test the feasibility of a business idea, to raise capital, and to serve as a road map for future operations.

The Plan

A **business plan** is a written document that demonstrates persuasively that enough products or services can be sold at a profit for your firm to become a viable business. Planning is an essential ingredient for any successful business. Although we all create mental plans, those thoughts need to be committed to writing before starting a business.[1] Planning can help find omissions and flaws in our ideas by allowing other people to critically review and analyze our plans.

A business plan gives the reader the *what, when, where, why,* and *how* your business will accomplish its objectives and tells *who* will be involved in running it. When planning, you need to define the goals of your business, determine the actions that need to be taken to accomplish them, gather and commit the resources needed, and aim for well-defined targets. A business plan can be the difference between running a business proactively and reactively. When NASA launched Apollo 7, the first manned spacecraft to land on the moon, it didn't aim at the moon. It pointed the rocket to the point in space where the moon would be, considering the time needed to get there.[2]

The Purpose

The three primary reasons for writing business plans are to aid you in determining the feasibility of your business idea, to attract capital for starting up, and to provide direction for your business after it is in operation.

PROVING FEASIBILITY. Writing a business plan is one of the best ways to prevent costly oversights. Committing your ideas to paper forces you to look critically at your means, goals, and expectations. Many people thinking of starting a small business get caught up in the excitement and emotions of the process. It is a truly exciting time! Unfortunately, business decisions based purely on emotion are often not the best long-term choice.

Wanting to have a business does not mean that a market exists to support your desire. You may love boats and want to build a business around them, but if you live 100 miles from the nearest body of water and are unwilling to move, it is unlikely that you can create a viable boat business. Norm Brodsky is a successful entrepreneur and writes a column in *Inc.* magazine titled "Street Smarts." Brodsky states, "The initial goal of every business is to survive long enough to see whether or

Linen & Lace

Sunny Drewel of St. Louis, Missouri, used her well-researched and well-written business plan to help line up financing for her new business, Linen & Lace. Linen & Lace is a mail-order catalogue business in which Drewel sells unique imported and domestic linen and lace products. Twice a year, a full-color catalogue containing 30 pages (or even more!) of pictures of the company's elegant products is sent to a mailing list that now numbers around 375,000 names. Currently, Linen & Lace's annual sales are approaching $1.5 million. But Drewel's business is thriving because she thoroughly researched her market, customers, and product, and formulated a well-written business plan.

Source: Claire Buhl, "Captivated by Lace," *Nation's Business,* October 1995, 16.

Linen & Lace uses its catalogue and web site to support each other.

not the business is viable—no matter what type of business, or how much capital you have. You never know for sure if a business is viable until you do it in the real world."[3] Writing your plan can help remove strong personal emotions from the decision-making process. You need to be passionate about the business you are in, but emotion must be balanced and tempered with logic and rationality.

ATTRACTING CAPITAL. Almost all startups must secure capital from bankers or investors. One of the first questions a banker or investor will ask when approached about participating in a business is "Where is your plan?" You need to appreciate bankers' position. They have to be accountable to depositors for the money entrusted to their care. Bankers in general are financially conservative, so before they risk their capital, they want assurance that you are knowledgeable and realistic in your projections. Therefore, a complete business plan is needed before you can raise any significant capital. Your business plan will show that you know what you are doing and have thought through the problems and opportunities.[4]

PROVIDING DIRECTION. Business plans should provide a road map for future operation. You have heard the clichés "Can't see the forest for the trees" and "It's difficult to remember that your initial objective was to drain the swamp when you're up to your hips in alligators." These illustrations apply to starting a small business in that so much of your time can be filled with immediate problems (management by spot fire, or paying attention to the latest dilemma to flare up) that you have trouble concentrating on the overall needs of the business. By having a road map to refer to, you are more likely to stay on course.

The Practice: Guidelines for Writing a Business Plan

No rigid formula for writing business plans exists that would fit every new business. Plans are unique to each business situation. Still, general guidelines should be followed.

CONSIDER YOUR AUDIENCE. You need to show the benefit of your business to your reader. Investors want their money to go into market-driven businesses, which satisfy wants and needs of customers, rather than technology-driven ones, which focus more on the product or service being made than on what people want.[5]

KEEP IT BRIEF. Your business plan should be long enough to cover all major issues facing the business, yet not look like a copy of *War and Peace*. Your final plan should be complete yet concise. Including financial projections and appendices, your plan should be less than 40 pages long. Your first draft will probably be longer, but you can sharpen your ideas by editing to 40 pages or less.

POINT OF VIEW. Try to write your business plan in the third person (do not use "I" or "we"). This helps maintain objectivity by removing your personal emotions from the writing process.

Cool B-Plan Tools

Need to write a business plan and want to look for some online help? There is no shortage. Many web pages provide a plethora of information, ranging from free to a long way from free. Check out some of these and other business planning web pages:

CCH Business Owner's Toolkit (www.toolkit.cch.com/tools/tools.tools.stm) You'll find free sample business plans written for service, retail, and manufacturing businesses—in downloadable files. These could come in handy for the "Experience this . . ." at the end of this chapter.

BizPlanit.com (www.bizplanit.com) This site is set up by consultants who, for fees a long way from zero, will review and critique your plan section by section for $750 or draft your plan from scratch for $8,500. Yikes! Good incentive to write your own plan. There are a lot of freebies on this site also: advice, links, and a newsletter.

Ohio State University Fact Sheet: Organizing a Business Plan (www.ag.ohio-state.edu/~ohioline/cd-fact/1101.html) A long URL, but a lot of straight-shooting information.

North of the Border Business Plan (www.sb.gov.bc.ca:80/smallbus/workshop/sample.html) The British Columbia Business Service Centre created this model plan helpful for most small businesses.

The Queen Mother of Business Plan Sites (www.sba.gov/starting/businessplan.html) In addition to all the other information regarding your small business at the Small Business Administration web site, you will find some outstanding business plan advice.

CREATE A PROFESSIONAL IMAGE. The overall appearance should be professional and attractive but not extravagant. Having your document laser-printed on white paper, with colored-stock cover, dividers, and spiral binding, is fine. Think of the message your business plan will send to bankers and investors: having it bound in leather with gold leaf–trimmed pages is not a good sign. Does it appear that you really need the money or will spend it wisely? Conversely, what might they think of

Fast Track to Venture Capital

Daniel Lubin is a financier with D. H. Blair & Co., a New York investment banking firm that provides funding for new businesses. Each year D. H. Blair & Co. receives 3,000 business plans, and Lubin reads most of them. What is the first thing he looks for in a plan? A lie or bad information—a reason to throw it out. The sheer number of plans requires Lubin to spend about as much time with each plan as you hope your next visit to the dentist lasts.

When asked for an example of a plan that sent him scrambling for the company checkbook, Lubin holds up Pierce Lowrey, Jr.'s, plan for Imtech, a startup that provides mailroom, word processing, printing, and other information-output services for large corporations. Lowrey's plan eventually won him $4.5 million in an initial public offering backed by Blair. The high points of his plan are summarized:

- *Executive summary.* In very few words, Lowrey hit three points that made the venture capitalists (VCs) sit up and take notice immediately. First, Lowrey showed that the company had a critical proprietary edge that no other company held. Second, his financial goals were attractive—break even in the first 18 months with a 20 percent return on investment. Finally, Lowrey displayed his proven track record. Management experience is the most important factor to most VCs. Lowrey had started ten other successful businesses within 15 years, the last of which was sold to NCR Corporation.

- *Analysis of the competition.* Even though the industry was young, Lowrey identified and discussed three competitors. His thorough, realistic investigation of the market impressed Blair that Lowrey, not his competitors, had the edge.

- *Information about management.* The longest section of Lowrey's plan—five pages. Lowrey showed that his skills as CEO would complement those of the rest of the management team. Even though not all of Imtech's key slots were filled, Lowrey included a detailed job description for each position.

- *Financial projections.* Venture capitalists are suspicious of projections that appear "juiced up" or not grounded in reality. A red flag is an income statement that shows steady, even growth on every line—an indicator that a software program, not an in-depth analysis, was driving the numbers. Lowrey's financials contained appropriate footnotes and the assumptions on which the numbers rested.

Writing plans for one year into the future is difficult—planning five years out is almost impossible. Although venture capitalists want plans to be as realistic as possible, few hold entrepreneurs accountable to their initial plan. Lowrey's plan, however, has shown uncanny accuracy. His projected third-year sales were $27 million—actual sales came in at $25 million. A good plan.

a business plan scratched out on a Big Chief tablet with a crayon? Would it look as if you were really serious about your business?

As you write the first draft of your plan, have several people who are not involved in your business read your work to get their initial reactions. Do they quickly grasp the essence of your proposal? Are they excited about your idea? Do they exclaim, "Wow!"? Getting feedback while you are still writing the plan can help you refine your work and get the reader to say "Wow!"

WHERE TO GET HELP. Who should write the business plan for your proposed venture? You should! The person who is best qualified and who receives the most benefit from the planning process is the person who is going to implement the plan. It is *your* business, and it needs to be *your* plan. With that stated, can you get aid in writing the plan? Of course, you can and should get help if you need it. You can get assistance in writing your business plan from:

> *Free or inexpensive business planning assistance is available to entrepreneurs from such sources as Small Business Development Centers.*

- One of the many paperback guides written on business plans available at any bookstore.

- The Small Business Administration home page at www.sba.gov

- Your local Small Business Development Center.

- A local SCORE (Service Corp of Retired Executives) chapter.

- Your local Chamber of Commerce.

- A college or university near you.

Computer software is available to perform many functions of our daily lives. We can balance our checkbook or design our dream house. Although software packages can make our lives easier, you need to be careful in not using them to generate a "cookie-cutter" business plan. Filling in a few blanks on a master document does not produce a workable business plan any more than a paint-by-numbers kit pro-

Good, Bad, and Ugly Business Plans

In their jobs, loan officers at a bank and small business consultants are constantly examining business plans. A discussion with them about good and poor business plans reveals that they've seen the gamut from excellent to just plain awful. Let's look at selected pages from two specific examples of business plans—one well written and one that needs a lot of revision. (Needless to say, the poorly written business plan has been altered to protect the identity of the writer.)

Company A Selected pages from that plan follow in Figure 4.1(a).

Company B Jay's Quarterback Club was the idea for a sports bar and restaurant in Norcross, Georgia. When Jay M. went looking for financing of his idea, however, he found that potential investors and lenders were reluctant to loan him the startup capital. A close look at his business plan reveals mistakes that might explain their reluctance. Selected pages from that plan follow in Figure 4.1(b).

FIGURE 4.1(a)
A professional-looking report, with sound financial projections, is essential to prospective business owners. Of the hundreds of loan proposals that an investor or banker must sort through each year, only a fraction will be funded.

Excalibur Traditional Men's Clothier, Ltd. (Excalibur)

Executive Summary

This is what quality is all about: the customer's perception of excellence.
And quality is our response to that perception.
-Tom Peters

Excalibur Traditional Men's Clothier, Ltd. (Excalibur), by and through its owners, has created this comprehensive business plan in order to invite First of America Bancorp to assist Excalibur in raising the needed capital of $80,000 to begin the operations of a men's clothing store in Monroe, Michigan.

The Program
The development of Excalibur can be attributed to the two principal investors, B. Mark Springsteel and Karl E. Hall. A men's clothing store, yes, but that is where the similarity ends. By reintroducing an old concept "customer service and satisfaction," Excalibur intends to aggressively promote its *value-added* pricing policy to attract the professional businessman. It is the intention of Excalibur to assist the executive in image building through successful marketing of the proper apparel for his position in the company. Inasmuch as the only available service is off-the-rack-type purchasing, Excalibur intends to tailor-make to the needs of the customer. Excalibur will also provide the service of going to the office of the executive for proper measurements and selection of fabric, color, and styling. Excalibur is confident that the professional male is more than willing to pay for this type of value-added service. A survey of the Monroe area indicated there was no store that catered to the executive.

   The principals of Excalibur are confident there is a strong demand for this type of merchandise that is not available in the Monroe area. Monroe is a bedroom community for both the Detroit Metro and Toledo areas; however, the principals discovered that executives preferred to shop in their home community as opposed to either metropolitan area, provided that the merchandise they sought was available to them.

The Plan
Financial projections for Excalibur indicate an investment of approximately $80,000, in addition to the principals' investment of $100,000, is required for a startup cost in order to initiate operations. These funds will be committed to beginning inventory and store equipment and supplies, and will provide working capital for the first year of operations.

The Players
Excalibur has three distinct and complementary players. B. Mark Springsteel, president, brings to Excalibur his expertise in the area of finance and marketing along with retail sales and management experience. Karl Hall, treasurer, with his varied background in accounting and finance, has the hands-on experience and know-how of the internal workings of a small business. Craig Hall, who will manage the store, in the past developed his own clientele base while employed with a men's retail store in the Monroe area. His ease with people and his ability to merchandise add to the diversity of this group.

The Game Summary
Collectively, the players have spent the past five months developing the concept and image of Excalibur. With confidence in their abilities, knowledge, and professionalism, the players anticipate a net profit in the first year of operations.

---

duces art. Because your business will be different from others, you need to emphasize *your* competitive advantage and show *your* objectives.

   This is not to imply that you should not use word processing, spreadsheets, or graphics packages to produce your plan. You should, because they can be extremely helpful. This caveat is against "canned" business plans. If you do wish to investigate business planning software, check out Jian's BizPlanBuilder Interactive and Palo Alto Software's Business Plan Pro, but remember that writing a business plan is as much an art as it is a science.[6]

JAY'S QUARTERBACK ~~CULB~~ CLUB

Proposed Business

My idea is to open a bar/restaurant that have a sports theme. Sports are big business right now and the timing is perfect. I think that people are really interested in sports and will be willing to pay good money for this type of dining experience. People eat out a lot and my business will give them another place to spend their money.

Marketing Research and Marketing Plan

I've done some research in the community and haven't seen any restaurant or bar like Jay's Quarterback Club. Since there's nobody else doing this type of business, I won't have no direct competition. So marketing expenses will be minimal. Perhaps I'll run some newspaper advertisements and put out coupons iif I need to when sales aren't enough to help me pay the expenses.

Operations Plan

As soon as I get word on my financing, I'll start looking for an appropriate location for my business. If I can't find something that fits my needs, I'll just build one. I've been checking into suppliers for food and other materials I'll need. I feel confident that I can dedvelop good contacts and have reliable sources.

As far as employees goes, with the level of business that I know we can accomplish in the first few months of operations, I will be hiring 4 additional employees: cook, bartender, and 2 waitpersons. This will leave me free to do the scheduling, ordering, and managing.

Sales Projections

I've worked in restaurants in the past and have a lot of experience there so I believe that my bar/restaurant can make lots of money. I believe that my first year's sales will be $500,000 and expenses will be $410,000. That means I'll make $90,000. I intend to have several cost controls but, still it's really hard to tell exactly what my expenses will be, though. In the second year, because we'll be familiar to the customer, I know we can increase sales by 20% for total revenue of $510,000. I think I can hold my expenses constant at $90,000.

Conclusion

Since I've had a lot of experience working in restaurants, I am positive that I can make this venture work. The theme will be unique and there's not anyone else doing this, so there shouldn't be any problem attracting paying customers. If you'd like more information, I'd be happy to share my idea for Jay's Quaterback Club with you in person. Just call me at my home number. Thanks for your consideration.

FIGURE 4.1(b)
A sloppy appearance can hurt the chances of your plan being taken seriously by lenders and investors.

Business Plan Contents

A business plan should be tailored to fit your particular business. Write the plan yourself, even if you seek assistance from lawyers, accountants, or consultants. In 40 pages or less, the plan should present your strengths clearly and in a logical order.

Although a plan's contents vary from business to business, its structure is fairly standardized. Your plan should contain as many of the following sections as appropriate for your type of venture.[7] Not every business will require every one of these sections. For example, if your business is a startup, it won't have a history section, but you can describe *your* management experience.

Cover Page

The cover page should include the name of the business, its address and phone number, and the date the plan was issued. If this information is overlooked, you have a problem if a potential investor tries to reach you to ask additional questions (or send a check).

Table of Contents

You want the business plan to be as easy to read as possible. An orderly table of contents will allow the reader to turn directly to the sections desired.

Executive Summary

executive summary A condensed abstract of a business plan used to spark the reader's interest in the business and to highlight crucial information.

The **executive summary** gives a one- to two-page overview of your entire plan. This is the most important section of the plan because readers do not want to wade through 35 to 40 pages to get the essential facts. If you do not capture the reader's attention here, he or she is certainly not likely to read the rest of the plan.

The executive summary should include

- *Company information.* What product or service you provide, your competitive advantage, when the company was formed, your company objectives, and the background of you and your management team.

- *Market opportunity.* The expected size and growth rate of your market, your expected market share, and any relevant industry trends.

- *Financial data.* Include financial forecasts for the first three years of operations, equity investment desired, and long-term loans that will be needed.

This is a lot to condense into two pages, but remember the concise executive summary that Pierce Lowrey, Jr., used in his plan for Imtech (see Reality Check, "Fast Track to Venture Capital," p. 110). If you truly understand something, you can explain it simply.

Although the executive summary is the first section of the plan, it should be written last. You are condensing what you have already written into the summary, not expanding the summary to fill the plan. A hint for writing the executive summary is: As you compose all the other sections of the plan, highlight a few key sentences that are important enough to include in your executive summary. To see examples of executive summaries, refer to the two complete plans included in Appendix A.

Company and Industry

In this section you should describe the background of your company, your choice of legal business form, and the reasons for the company's establishment. How did your company get to the point where it is today? Give company history by going into some detail describing what your business does and how it satisfies customers' needs. How did you choose and develop your products or services to be sold? Don't be afraid to describe any setbacks or missteps you have taken along the way to forming your business. They represent reality, and leaving them out could make your plan and projections look "too good to be true" to lenders or investors.

You should also describe the industry you operate within. One helpful way to draw the line between what and whom to include in your industry is to consider possible substitutes that your customers have for your product. If you own a business that sells ice cream, do your customers view frozen yogurt or custard as a possible substitute for your ice cream? If so, you should consider businesses that sell these substitutes as part of your industry. What competitive reactions and industry-wide trends can you identify? Who are the major players in your industry? Have any businesses recently entered or exited? Why did they leave?

Lenders want to see that you have a clear understanding of how your industry operates. Specifically, which of Porter's Five Forces (threat of new entrants, bargaining power of customers, threat of substitutes, bargaining power of suppliers, and rivalry among existing competitors; see Chapter 11) are rated as high or low for the industry you intend to enter?[8]

Products or Services

Once you have given the background of your company, you can go into detail describing your product or service. How is your product or service different from those currently on the market? Are there any other uses for your product that could increase current sales? Include drawings or photos if appropriate. Describe any patents or trademarks that you hold, as these give you a proprietary position that can be defended. Describe your competitive advantage. What sets your product or service apart as better than the competition's?

What is your product's potential for growth? How do you intend to manage your product or service through the product life cycle? Can you expand the product line or develop related products? This gives you a chance to discuss potential product lines as well as current ones.

Marketing Research and Evaluation

Evidence that a market exists for your business is much more convincing than an unsubstantiated claim or guesswork. Present the facts you have gathered on the size and nature of your markets. An investor will want to know if a large enough market exists and if you can be competitive in that market. State market size in dollars and units. Give your sales forecast by estimating from your marketing research how many units and dollars worth of your product you expect to sell in a given time period. That sales forecast becomes the basis for projecting many of your financial statements. Indicate your primary and secondary sources of data, and the methods you used to estimate total market size and your market share.

MARKETS. You must identify your target markets and then concentrate your marketing efforts on these key areas. These markets must have some commonly identifiable need that you can satisfy. What do the people who buy your product have in common with one another? There could be a demographic characteristic (for example, 18- to 25-year-old females), a psychographic variable (similar lifestyles, usage rate of product, or degree of loyalty), a geographic variable (anyone who lives within a five-mile radius of your business), or other variable used to segment your markets. Describe actual customers who have expressed a desire to buy your product. What trends do you expect to affect your markets?

MARKET TRENDS. Markets and consumer tastes change, so you will need to explain how you will assess your customers' needs over time. A danger of segmentation and target marketing is the belief that those segments and markets will stay the same. Identify how you will continue to evaluate consumer needs so that you can improve your market lines and aid new product development.

COMPETITION. Among three or four primary competitors, identify the price leader, the quality leader, and the service leader. Realistically discuss the strengths and weaknesses of each. Compare your products or services with those of competitors on the basis of price, product performance, and other attributes.

This section offers a good opportunity to include the SWOT analysis you completed in the strategic planning chapter (Chapter 3). Identify the strengths and weaknesses of your business and the opportunities and threats that exist outside your business.

MARKET SHARE. Because you have identified the size of your market and your competitors, you can estimate the market share you intend to gain. Market share refers to your sales in relation to the total industry sales expressed as a percentage. It can effectively be shown and explained using a pie chart.

Your job in writing the marketing research section of your business plan is to convince the reader that a large enough market exists for your product for you to achieve your projected sales forecasts.

MARKETING PLAN Your marketing plan shows how you intend to reach your sales forecast. You should start by explaining your overall marketing strategy by identifying your potential markets and deciding the best ways to reach them. Include your marketing objectives (what you want to achieve) and the strategies you will use to accomplish these objectives.

PRICING. Your pricing policy is one of the most important decisions you will have to make. The price must be "right" to penetrate the market, to maintain your market position, and especially to make profits. Compare your pricing policies with those of the competitors you identified earlier. Explain how your gross margin will allow you to make a profit after covering all expenses. Many people go into business with the intent of charging lower prices than the competition. If this is your goal, explain how you can do this and still make a profit: through greater efficiency in manufacturing or distributing the product, through lower labor costs, lower overhead, or whatever else allows you to undercut the competition's price.

You should discuss the relationship between your price, your market share, and your profits. For example, by charging a higher price than the competition, you may reduce your sales volume but hold a higher gross margin and increase the bottom line.

PROMOTION. How will you attract the attention of and communicate with your potential customers? For industrial products, you might use trade shows and advertise in trade magazines, via direct mail, or through promotional brochures. For con-

I'm Starting a Dot-Com, Do I Still Need a Business Plan?

So, you plan to start an Internet-based business and have read many stories of dot-com startups with no more than an idea getting money thrown their way. They didn't seem to need a business plan, so why should you? Good question. Until the dot-com stock shakeup in the spring of 2000, many people seemed to think that the traditional rules of business no longer applied. A technology plan was more important than a marketing plan or five-year income projections. But, of course, no matter what format your business utilizes, a good plan will help you broadly figure out where you are going and how to get there, in addition to the specific needs of your business.

So what's different for an Internet startup? Courtney Wood, a senior manager for Ernst & Young's business incubator, states that "in the E age, speed to market is everything." You may not have the time luxury of exploring many different strategic models for your e-biz. Wood suggests that it is better to choose a sizable chunk of your long-term business plan to concentrate on its viability, rather than get bogged down in proving your comprehensive model (a process she calls the "60 percent solution"). Get that crucial 60 percent ironed out and to the market the quickest, in order to win a customer base and validate your business.

Fortunately, the speed at which change occurs in Internet industries also speeds the information available on the research front. When writing financial projections and a business description for your e-biz, you may find it useful to read SEC registration statements for other Internet companies.

Some specific ways business plans are changing from traditional models follow:

- It must allow for, but not be driven by, specific protocols that guide short-term implementation.

- It must promote ultraswift action.

- It demands an organizational culture that will tolerate one or more—often completely different—organizational structures and still allow principals to function as a team.

- It must allow for on-the-spot exploration of opportunity and confrontation of threats. This requires constant, open communication and knowledge sharing.

Need another motivation to prevent your Internet business from burning out like a meteor shower? Check out a site devoted to those recently flamed at www.dotcomfailures.com, with a tag line of "Kick 'em while they're down." Nice.

Sources: Jill Andresky Fraser, "Do I Need to Plan Differently for a Dot-com Business?" *Inc.,* July 2000, 142–143; Paul Willax, "Today's Small Business Plan Requires Fluidity," *Long Island Business News,* 18 February 2000, 37A; and Claire Tristram, "The Shame of Dot-coms," *Computerworld,* 7 August 2000, 52–53.

sumer products, describe your advertising and promotional campaigns. You should also give the advertising schedule and costs involved. Examples of advertising or brochures may be included in the appendix of the business plan.

PLACE. Describe how you intend to sell and distribute your products. Will you use your own sales force or independent sales representatives or distributors? If you will hire your own sales force, describe how it will be structured, the sales expected per salesperson per year, and the pay structure. Your own sales force will concentrate more on your products by selling them exclusively. If you will use sales representatives, describe how they will be selected, the territories they will cover, and the rates they will charge. Independent sales representatives will also be handling products and lines other than yours, but they are much less expensive for you because they are not your employees. Your place strategy describes the level of coverage (local, regional, or national) you will use initially and as your business grows. It includes the channels of distribution you will use to get and to sell products.

SERVICE POLICIES. If you sell a product that may require service, such as cameras, copy machines, or bicycles, describe your service and warranty policies. These policies can be important in the customer's decision-making process. How will you handle customer service problems? Describe the terms and types of warranties offered. Explain whether you will provide service via your own service department, subcontract out the service work, or return products to the factory. Also state whether service is intended to be a profit center or a breakeven operation.

Manufacturing and Operations Plan

The manufacturing and operations plan will stress elements related to your business's production. It will outline your needs in terms of facilities, location, space requirements, capital equipment, labor force, inventory control, and purchasing. Stress the areas most relevant to your type of business. For instance, if you are starting a manufacturing business, outline the production processes and your control systems for inventory, purchasing, and production. The business plan for a service business should focus on your location, overhead, and labor force productivity.

GEOGRAPHIC LOCATION. Describe your planned location and its advantages and disadvantages in terms of wage rates, unionization, labor pool, proximity to customers and suppliers, types of transportation available, tax rates, utility costs, and zoning. Again, you should stress the features most relevant to your business. Proximity to customers is especially important to a service business, whereas access to transportation will be of greater concern to a manufacturing business.

FACILITIES. What kind of facilities does your business need? Discuss your requirements for floor space (including offices, sales room, manufacturing plant space, and storage areas), parking, loading areas, and special equipment. Will you rent, lease, or purchase these facilities? How long will they remain adequate: One year? Three years? Is expansion possible?

MAKE-OR-BUY POLICY. In a manufacturing business, you must decide what you will produce and what you will purchase as components to be assembled into the finished product. This is called the "make-or-buy decision." Many factors go into this decision (see Chapter 12). In your business plan, you should justify the advantages of your policy. Describe potential subcontractors and suppliers.

CONTROL SYSTEMS. What is your approach to controlling quality, inventory, and production? How will you measure your progress toward the goals you have set for your business?

LABOR FORCE. At the location you have selected, is there a sufficient quantity of adequately skilled people in the local labor force to meet your needs? What kinds of training will you need to provide? Can you afford to offer this training and still remain competitive? Training can be one of those hidden costs that can turn a profit into a loss.

Management Team

A good management team is the key to transforming your vision into a successful business. Show how your team is balanced in technical skills (possessing the knowledge specific to your type of business), business skills (the ability to successfully run a business), and experience. As in building any team, the skills and talents of your management team need to complement one another. Include a job description for each management position, and specify the key people who will fill these slots. Can you show how their skills complement one another? Have these individuals worked together before? An organization chart can be included in the appendix of your plan to graphically show how these positions fit together. Résumés for each key manager should also be included in the appendix.

A successful management team unites people with complementary business knowledge, technical skills, and life experience.

State how your key managers will be compensated. Your chances of obtaining financing are very slim unless the managers are willing to accept substantially less than their market value for salary while the business is getting started. Managers must be committed to putting as many proceeds as possible back into the business.

Discuss the management training your key people have had and may still need. Be as specific as possible on the cost, type, and availability of this management or technical training.

Like your managers, you may need professional assistance at times. Identify other people with whom you will work, including a lawyer, a certified public accountant, an insurance agent, and a banker. Identify contacts you have supporting you in these areas.

Timeline

Outline the interrelationship and timing of the major events planned for your venture. In addition to helping you calculate your business needs and minimize risk, the timeline is also an indicator to investors that you have thoroughly researched potential problems and are aware of deadlines. Keep in mind that people tend to underestimate the time needed to complete projects. Your time schedule should be realistic and attainable.

Critical Risks and Assumptions

All business plans contain implicit assumptions, such as how your business will operate, what economic conditions will be, and how you will react in different situations. Identification and discussion of any potentially major trends, problems, or risks that you think you may encounter will show the reader that you are in touch with reality. These risks and assumptions could relate to your industry, markets, company, or personnel.

This section gives you a place to establish alternate plans in case the unexpected happens. If potential investors discover unstated negative factors after the fact, they can quickly question the credibility of you and the business. Too many businesses are started with only a plan A and no thought to what will happen if X, Y, or Z occurs.[9] Possible contingencies that you should anticipate are

- *Unreliable sales forecasts.* What will you do if your market does not develop as quickly as you predicted or, conversely, if your market develops too quickly? Each situation creates problems. Sales that are too low cause serious financial problems. Sales that are too high can cause bottlenecks in production, difficulties in purchasing enough products from vendors or suppliers, trouble hiring and scheduling employees, or dissatisfied customers who must wait longer than they expected for your product or service.

- *Competitors' ability to underprice or to make your product obsolete.*

- *Unfavorable industrywide trends.* Not long ago, businesses that produced asbestos made up a thriving industry supplying products for automotive and building construction firms. Then reports linking asbestos with cancer drastically affected the demand for that product and virtually eliminated the industry.

- *Appropriately trained workers not as available as predicted.*

- *Erratic supply of products or raw materials.*

- *Any one of the 10,000 other things you didn't expect.*

Benefits to the Community

Your new business will have an impact on many other people besides yourself. Describe the potential benefits to the community that the formation of your business could provide.

- *Economic development.* Number of jobs created (total and skilled), purchase of supplies from local businesses, the multiplier effect (which shows the number of hands that new dollars brought into the community pass through before exiting).

- *Community development.* Providing needed goods or services, improving physical assets or the appearance of the community, contributing to a community's standard of living.

- *Human development.* Providing new technical skills or other training, creating opportunities for career advancement, developing management or leadership skills, offering attractive wages, and providing other types of individual growth.

Exit Strategy

Every business will benefit by devoting some attention to a succession plan. Before you begin your business is a good time to consider how you intend to get yourself (and your money) out of it. Do you intend to sell it in 20 years? Will your children take it over? How will you prepare them for ownership? Do you intend to grow the business to the point of an initial public offering (IPO)? How will investors get their money back?

Financial Plan

Your financial plan is where you demonstrate that all the information from previous sections, such as marketing, operations, sales, and strategies, can all come together to form a viable, profitable business. Potential investors will closely scrutinize the financial section of your plan to ensure it is feasible before they become involved. Projections should be your best estimates of future operations. Your financial plan should include the following statements (existing businesses will need historical statements and pro forma projections, whereas startups will only have projections):

- Sources and uses of capital (initial and projected)
- Cash flow projections for three years
- Balance sheets for three years
- Profit-and-loss statements for three years
- Breakeven analysis

We will discuss how to prepare these documents in later chapters. (See Chapter 8 for cash flow projections, balance sheets, and profit-and-loss statements, and

Calvin and Hobbes
by Bill Watterson

Chapter 9 for sources and uses of capital.) With the financial statements, you need to show conclusions and important points, such as how much equity and how much debt are included, the highest amount of cash needed, and how long the payback period for loans is expected to be.

SOURCES AND USES OF FUNDS. This simple form shows where your money is coming from and how you are spending it (see Figure 4.2).

CASH FLOW. The most important financial statement for a small business is the **cash flow statement,** because if you run out of cash, you're out of business. A cash flow statement shows you that, from your opening cash balance, you add all the money that comes into your business for a given time period (week, month, quarter); then you subtract all the money you spend for the same time period. The result is your closing cash balance, which becomes your opening balance for the next time period (see Figure 4.3).

You should project a cash flow statement by month for the first year of operation and by quarter for the second and third years. Cash flow shows you what the highest amount of working capital will be. This can be especially critical if your sales are seasonal in nature or cyclical.

BALANCE SHEET. The **balance sheet** shows all the assets *owned* by your business and the liabilities, or what is *owed* against those assets. The difference between the two is what the company has *earned,* or the net worth of the business, which is also called "capital." From the balance sheet, bankers and investors will calculate some key ratios, such as debt to equity and current ratio (see Chapter 8) to help determine the financial health of your business. You need to prepare balance sheets ending each of the first three years of operation (see Figure 4.4).

sources and uses of funds A financial document used by startup businesses which shows where capital comes from and what it will be used for.

cash flow statement A financial document that shows the amount of money a business has on hand at the beginning of a time period, receipts coming into the business, and money going out of the business during the same period.

balance sheet A financial document that shows the assets, liabilities, and owner's equity for a business.

FIGURE 4.2

The Sources and Uses of Funds Worksheet

A sources and uses of funds sheet shows where money comes from and what it is used for.

Sources of Funds:

Debt:
Term loans $ _____
Refinancing of old debt   _____
Lines of credit   _____
Line 1   _____
Line 2   _____
Mortgage   _____

Equity:
Investments   _____
Total Sources: $ _____

Uses of Funds:
Property $ _____
Inventory   _____
Equipment (itemize)

                                    _____
                                    _____
                                    _____
                                    _____

Working capital   _____
Cash reserve   _____

Total Uses: $ _____

Opening cash balance

Add: Cash receipts
           Collection of accounts receivable
           New loans or investment
           Other sources of cash
               Total receipts

Less: Utilities
           Salaries
           Office supplies
           Accounts payable
           Leased equipment
           Sales expenses
           Loan payments
           General expenses
               Total disbursements

Cash increase (or decrease)
Closing cash balance

FIGURE 4.3

Sample Components of a Cash Flow Statement

A cash flow statement shows you how money enters and exits your business.

FIGURE 4.4

Balance Sheet

A balance sheet shows what you own and whom you owe.

For year ended [month] [day], [year]	YEAR 1	YEAR 2	YEAR 3
Current Assets			
Cash	$ _____	$ _____	$ _____
Accounts Receivable	_____	_____	_____
Inventory	_____	_____	_____
Supplies	_____	_____	_____
Prepaid Expenses	_____	_____	_____
Fixed Assets			
Real Estate	_____	_____	_____
Equipment	_____	_____	_____
Fixtures and Leasehold Improvements	_____	_____	_____
Vehicles	_____	_____	_____
Other Assets			
License	_____	_____	_____
Goodwill	_____	_____	_____
TOTAL ASSETS	$ _____	$ _____	$ _____
Current Liabilities			
Accounts Payable	_____	_____	_____
Notes Payable (due within 1 year)	_____	_____	_____
Accrued Expenses	_____	_____	_____
Taxes Owed	_____	_____	_____
Long-Term Liabilities			
Notes Payable (due after 1 year)	_____	_____	_____
Bank Loans	_____	_____	_____
TOTAL LIABILITIES	$ _____	$ _____	$ _____
NET WORTH (assets minus liabilities)	$ _____	$ _____	$ _____

profit-and-loss statement
A financial document that shows sales revenues, expenses, and net profit or loss.

PROFIT-AND-LOSS STATEMENT. Don't expect the pro forma **profit-and-loss statement** for your business plan to be a finely honed, 100 percent accurate projection of the future. Your objective is to come up with as close an approximation as possible of what your sales revenues and expenses will be. In making your projections, it is helpful to break sales down by product line (or services) and to determine a best-case scenario, a worst-case scenario, and a most likely scenario somewhere between the two extremes.[10]

Start with the left-hand column to show what your sales and expenses would be under the worst of conditions (see Figure 4.5). Assume that you have difficulty getting products, that the weather is terrible, that your salespeople are out spending all

F I G U R E   4 . 5
Profit-and-Loss Projection

Projecting the best and the worst that could happen helps you calculate what your profits or losses are likely to be.

	Low	Most Likely	High
SALES:			
Product/service line 1	$ _____	$ _____	$ _____
Product/service line 2	_____	_____	_____
Product/service line 3	_____	_____	_____
Product/service line 4	_____	_____	_____
TOTAL SALES REVENUE			
Cost of Goods Sold:			
Product/service line 1	_____	_____	_____
Product/service line 2	_____	_____	_____
Product/service line 3	_____	_____	_____
Product/service line 4	_____	_____	_____
TOTAL COST OF GOODS SOLD	$ _____	$ _____	$ _____
GROSS PROFIT	$ _____	$ _____	$ _____
EXPENSES:			
Variable:			
Payroll	$ _____	$ _____	$ _____
Sales commission	_____	_____	_____
Freight and delivery	_____	_____	_____
Travel and entertainment	_____	_____	_____
Semivariable:			
Advertising/promotion	_____	_____	_____
FICA/payroll tax	_____	_____	_____
Supplies	_____	_____	_____
Telephone	_____	_____	_____
Fixed:			
Rent	_____	_____	_____
Utilities	_____	_____	_____
Property taxes	_____	_____	_____
Dues and subscriptions	_____	_____	_____
TOTAL EXPENSES	_____	_____	_____
Profit before depreciation	_____	_____	_____
Depreciation	_____	_____	_____
NET PROFIT	$ _____	$ _____	$ _____

Note: Expense items for your business will vary from these three categories. For illustration purposes only.

their time playing golf instead of selling, that the state highway department closes the road that runs in front of your only location for repairs. Imagine that anything bad that can happen will. Now, in the right-hand column, make projections as if everything goes exactly your way. What would your sales and expenses be if customers with cash in their hands are waiting in line outside your door every morning at opening time, if suppliers rearrange their schedules so you never run out of stock, and if competitors all close their doors for a month of vacation just as you are beginning operations. This is a lot more fun, but not any more likely to happen than the first scenario, although either could happen. Your most realistic estimate will fall between the two in the center column.

Question and test your projections. Is there enough demand for you to reach your sales goal? Do you have enough space, equipment, and employees to reach your sales goal? Break your sales down into number of units, then the number of units bought per customer, and then the number of units sold per day.[11] When viewed this way, you may find that every person in town would have to buy 8 bagels per day, 365 days per year, for you to achieve your sales projections for your proposed bagel shop. Obviously, you would need to revise your goal, expand your menu, do more to control your expenses, or convince people to eat more bagels than is humanly possible for your business to succeed.

BREAKEVEN ANALYSIS. How many units (or dollars' worth) of your products or service will have to be sold to cover your costs? A breakeven analysis will give you a sales projection of how many units or dollars need to be sold to reach your **breakeven point;** that is, the point at which you are neither making nor losing money (see Figure 4.6; see also Chapter 14).

breakeven point The point at which sales and costs are equal and a business is neither making nor losing money.

To reinforce your financial projections, you may want to compare them to industry averages for your chosen industry. *Robert Morris Associates Annual Statement* publishes an annual index showing industry averages of key manufacturing, wholesale, and retail business groups. Compare your projected financial ratios with industry averages to give the reader an established benchmark (see Chapter 8).

Appendix

Supplemental information and documents not crucial to the plan, but of potential interest to the reader, are gathered in the appendix. Résumés of owners and principal managers, advertising samples, brochures, and any related information can be included. Different types of information, such as résumés, advertising samples, or-

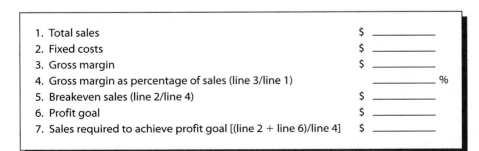

FIGURE 4.6

Breakeven Analysis

At what point will you make money?

1. Total sales	$ _____
2. Fixed costs	$ _____
3. Gross margin	$ _____
4. Gross margin as percentage of sales (line 3/line 1)	_____ %
5. Breakeven sales (line 2/line 4)	$ _____
6. Profit goal	$ _____
7. Sales required to achieve profit goal [(line 2 + line 6)/line 4]	$ _____

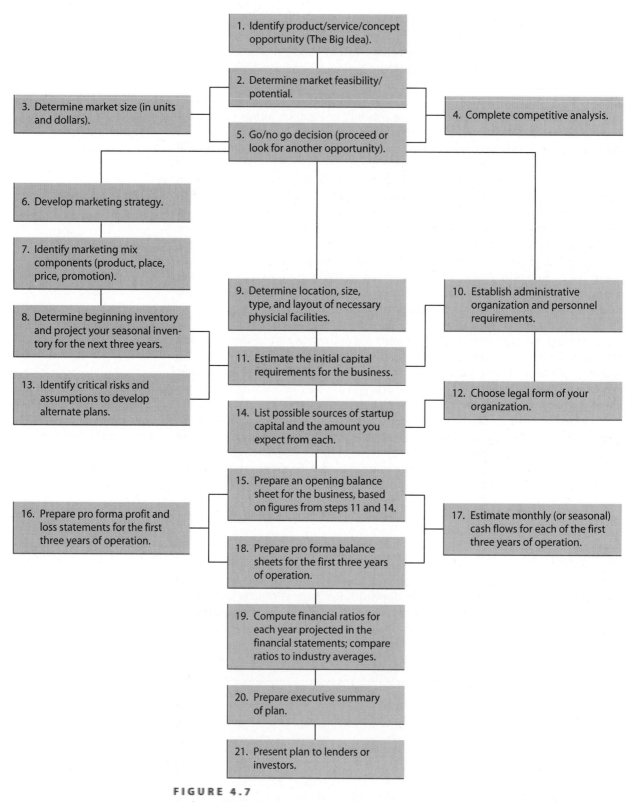

FIGURE 4.7
Business Plan

The progressive steps in writing a business plan.

ganization chart, and floor plan, should each be given a separate appendix labeled with successive letters of the alphabet (Appendix A, Appendix B, and so on). Be sure to identify each appendix in your table of contents (for example, "Appendix A: Advertising Samples").

Review Process

Writing a business plan is a project that involves a long series of interrelated steps. Beginning with your idea for a business, you want to determine its feasibility through the creation of your business plan. The technique illustrated in Figure 4.7 will allow you to identify the steps you need to take in writing your plan. Steps connected by lines show that lower-numbered steps need to be completed before moving on to higher-numbered ones. Steps that are parallel show that these take place simultaneously. For example, steps 6 through 10 can be completed at the same time, and all must be accomplished before you can estimate how much capital you need in step 11.

Like any project involving a number of complex steps and calculations, your business plan should be carefully reviewed and revised before you present it to potential investors. After you have written your plan, rate it yourself as lenders and investors will evaluate it (see Manager's Notebook, "How Does Your Plan Rate?").

Business Plan Mistakes

Often, we can learn from the mistakes of others. Writing business plans is no exception. Bankers and investors who view hundreds of business plans a year look for reasons to reject proposed plans. This practice helps them to weed out potentially unworthy investments and to identify the likely winners—the most organized, focused, and realistic proposals.

Your business plan says a lot about your level of financial and professional knowledge. How can you keep investors focused on your ideas while keeping your plan out of the "reject" pile? It helps to avoid the most common errors.

- *Submitting a "rough copy."* Your plan should be a cleanly typed copy without coffee stains and scratched-out words. If you haven't worked your idea out completely enough to present a plan you're proud of, why should the investor take you seriously?

- *Depending on outdated financial information or industry comparisons.* It is important to be as current as possible to convince the investor that you are a realistic planner.

- *Trying to impress financiers with technojargon.* If you can't express yourself in common language in your business plan, how will you be able to market?

- *Making unsubstantiated assumptions.* Explain how and why you reach your conclusions at any point in the plan. Don't assume that the competition will roll over without a fight or that phenomenal growth will begin the moment you get the money.

- *Being overly optimistic.* Too much "blue sky and rainbows" will lead the investor to wonder if your plan is realistic. Describe potential pitfalls also, and how you would cope with them.

■ *Misunderstanding financial information.* Even if you get help from an accountant in preparing your financials, be sure you understand and can interpret what they say.

■ *Ignoring the macroenvironment.* How will competitors react to your business? What other economic factors are likely to change? Considering the business climate and environment will help demonstrate the breadth of your understanding.

■ *Avoiding or disguising potential negative aspects.* You will give the impression that you are either naive or devious, and lenders find neither trait especially charming.

■ *Having no personal equity in the company.* If you aren't willing to risk your own money in the venture, why should the investor? A vested interest in the business will help to convince potential lenders that you will work as hard as possible to make the business succeed. Or, if you have only invested $1,000, is it reasonable to seek $20 million in capital?

Sources: Guy Kawasaki, "Needbucks.com," *Forbes*, 10 January 2000, 188; Scott Clark, "Great Business Plan Is Key to Raising Venture Capital," *Portland Business Journal,* 31 March 2000, 36; and J. T. Broome, Jr., "How to Write a Business Plan," *Nation's Business,* February 1993, 29–30.

How Does Your Plan Rate?

On the following checklist, take the perspective of a potential lender or investor in rating your own plan. Rate each section with an A-through-F grading scale, with A being the highest, best grade. Would you want to invest *your* money in a business that doesn't earn an A in as many categories as possible? Use your rating to identify areas that can be improved.

	Grade	Model (A+) Plan
Buiness Description		
Company	_____	Simply explained and feasible
Industry	_____	Growing in market niches that are presently unsatisfied
Products	_____	Proprietary position (quality exceeds customer's expectations)
Services	_____	Described clearly; service level exceeds customer expectations
Previous success	_____	Business has past record of success
Competitive advantage	_____	Identified and sustainable
Risks turned into opportunities	_____	Risks identified and shown how minimized
Orientation of business	_____	Market oriented, not product oriented
Marketing		
Target market(s)	_____	Clearly identified
Size of target market(s)	_____	Large enough to support viable business
User benefits identified	_____	Benefit to customers clearly shown
Management Team		
Experience of team	_____	Successful previous experience in similar business
Key managers identified	_____	Managers with complementary skills on team

Financial Plan

Projections	_____	Realistic and supported
Rate of return	_____	Exceptionally high; loans can be paid back in less than one year
Participation by owner	_____	Owner has significant personal investment
Participation by others	_____	Other investors already involved

Plan Packaging

Appearance	_____	Professional, laser-printed, bound, no spelling or grammatical errors
Executive summary	_____	Concise description of business that prompts reader to say, "Wow!"
Body of plan	_____	Sections of plan appropriate and complete
Appendices	_____	Appropriate supporting documentation
Plan standardized or custom	_____	Plan custom-written for specific business, not "canned"

SUMMARY

▬▬ *The importance of the business plan.*

Business plans are important (1) to raise capital, (2) to provide a road map for future operations, and (3) to prevent oversights.

▬▬ *The components of a business plan.*

The major components of a business plan include cover page, table of contents, executive summary, company and industry, products or services, marketing research and evaluation, marketing plan, manufacturing and operation plan, management team, timeline, critical risks and assumptions, benefits to the community, financial plan, and appendix.

▬▬ *The review process.*

Like any project involving a number of complex steps and calculations, your business plan should be carefully reviewed and revised before you present it to potential investors. After you have written your plan, evaluate it as you think lenders and investors will.

QUESTIONS FOR REVIEW & DISCUSSION

1. Why wouldn't a 100-page business plan be four times better than a 25-page business plan?

2. Should you write a business plan even if you do not need outside financing? Why or why not?

3. Who should write the business plan?

4. If successful companies like Pizza Hut have been started without a business plan, why does the author claim they are so important?

5. Why do entrepreneurs have trouble remaining objective when writing their business plans?

6. Why do some prospective business owners refuse to plan?

7. Why is the executive summary the most important section of the business plan?

8. Talk to the owner of a small business. Did he or she write a business plan? a strategic plan? If he or she received any assistance, where did it come from?

QUESTIONS FOR **CRITICAL THINKING**

1. When you reach the point of your career when you are ready to start your own business (or your next one), will you write a business plan before beginning? Why or why not? If you would choose to start a business without a business plan, what would be a better alternative for testing feasibility?

2. You are an investor in small businesses, and you have three business plans on your desk. Which of the following do you think would be the best bet for an investment (if you could pick only one)?

   a. A recent college grad, full of energy and ideas, but short on experience

   b. A middle-management corporate refugee desiring a business of her own after frustration with bureaucratic red tape

   c. A serial entrepreneur who has previously started seven businesses (three of which were huge successes, whereas four failed, losing entire investments)

Experience this...

Do a keyword Internet search for "business plans." When you find a sample business plan that interests you, complete a thorough analysis of it. How do the section headings compare with the headings described in this chapter? Have any sections been added or deleted? Does the executive summary make you say, "Wow, this is a great idea!"? Complete a review process of the business plan you found using Figure 4.7 and Creating Competitive Advantage, "How Does Your Plan Rate?" Does the plan appear to be a feasible idea for a business? Do you find any "holes" in the plan? If this were a plan for your business, would you proceed? Why or why not? If you were an investor approached for financing this plan, would you put your money into this business without being able to run it? Why or why not?

Select one of the three startup companies described below to complete the questions at the end of the exercise.

Company A. Salad in a bag, sold in the produce section of supermarkets. Now that's an idea whose time has come! Busy, time-starved consumers will like the convenience of washed and premade salads. And they'll particularly appreciate the fact that they're not only getting something fast, they're getting something healthy. Fresh Express International of Salinas, California, sees fresh bagged salads as a prime business opportunity.

Company B. Taking aerial photographs for a living isn't for the timid of heart—or stomach. Fickle weather conditions (particularly in Milwaukee, Wisconsin), strict insurance requirements, and soaring fuel costs are just a few of the variables that Skypix has to deal with. Yet the demand—both commercial and individual—for custom aerial photographs is strong and growing.

Company C. Sassy Scents isn't only the name but also an apt description of this San Antonio–based business. Sassy Scents manufactures and markets home fragrance products including potpourri, wax chips, candles, and incense. The company intends to break into the intensely competitive gift market by taking on some of the industry's biggest and best-known competitors, such as Claire Burke and Aromatics. You wouldn't really expect a business that calls itself "sassy" to be timid, now would you?

QUESTIONS

1. Write an executive summary for the company you choose. (You should refer to the section on Business Plan Contents to refresh your memory of executive summary contents.)

2. Break into small groups (three or four per group) comprising students who selected the same company. Each student will write a brief business plan outline in addition to the executive summary and will take turns presenting them to the rest of the group as if they were potential financial lenders. Present your plan in the most positive light so that the "lenders" will react favorably toward your business. Meanwhile, the financial lenders will look for holes in your business plan, so be sure to cover all the areas.

Early one morning your telephone rings. It is your small business/entrepreneurship professor who tells you he just received notification of winning the first Nobel Prize in Entrepreneurship. His plane leaves soon for Stockholm to pick up the award, so he won't be in class today. Because you are one of the star students in this class, he asks you to conduct class today covering Chapter 4, "The Business Plan." Write an outline of how you would teach this class and what you would cover to effectively teach this material. Would you lecture? How would you keep discussion going? Would you show business plan samples? Where would you find them? Would you show web pages? Which ones? You can do anything (except cancel class!!!) that your professor would do, but *what would you do?*

Oyster Communications: Is the World Its Oyster?

Entrepreneur Margot Langstaff has followed a winding road in the development of Oyster Communications. The firm had its beginnings in *The Colorado Guide to Financial Sources for the Entrepreneur and Small Business Owner* that Margot, a Harvard MBA, successfully published out of her Denver home. The guide came about through Margot's involvement with a Chamber of Commerce task force that studied small business financing. She recognized the need for such a publication, obtained an SBA loan to produce it, and contacted business organizations, banks, and accounting firms to learn what information was available. At any given time, she had 5 to 18 contract employees working on the book.

Building on the Guide   Langstaff's guide attracted the attention of USWest Communications and American Express, both asking about similar information for other states. USWest was setting up a web site for its business customers and was interested in using the book as content. C.J. Juleff, a vice president at the Colorado Banking Association, was interested in distributing the book to her organization's members. C.J. also introduced Margot to Kenton Kuhn, CEO of Intellinet, the Denver firm that had designed the banking group's web site.

C.J.'s idea was to provide online financial information to trade associations and municipalities. Kenton knew that Intellinet had the capabilities to provide graphics and solicit online advertising for such an effort. But Kenton also saw the larger possibilities in linking small businesses directly to the financial institutions listed in Margot's guide. C.J. and Kenton proposed setting up a partnership with Margot to provide online financial information and referrals. Intellinet had the programming skills, C.J. had the association contacts, and Margot understood the content and knew how to sell any products they might design.

Oyster Begins to Develop   "The world is our oyster," said C.J., and so Oyster Communications was born as a marketing and distribution company, with Intellinet providing technical support. The guide would be a subsidiary or division, and Oyster would license and brand it for different corporate clients, as, for example, *The American Express Guide to Financial Sources*. C.J. quit her job, and she and Margot began to contact lending institutions and associations.

Margot and C.J. envisioned an automated system that matched a small business with the appropriate funding source, using an online screening process. Oyster would earn a commission on these loan referrals. However, the task was daunting because funding could come from thousands of sources in twelve financing categories (commercial banks, investment banks, SBA lenders, business and finance brokers, commercial finance companies, venture capitalists, angel capital networks, micro-loan companies, factors, and leasing, state, and federal programs).

C.J. noted that online loan approvals allow a small business manager to avoid the humiliation of begging for money or being turned down because of poor credit or an inadequate business plan. Kenton said that Oyster would offer anonymity, "and we're doing the bank's screening for them."

Oyster began to evolve into an information network. Using its system, a business owner would submit financial information that Oyster would collate with credit bureau information and score for creditworthiness. Oyster would then direct the applicant to appropriate financing sources based on acceptable norms for different loan programs and lending institutions. If no financing options were available, the system would send the applicant to an educational site containing business plan templates and information on improving credit ratings.

A Strategic Alliance Saves Money   Oyster considered contracting for an existing credit scoring program to assess loan risk at an annual cost of $18,000. Then the Oyster partners learned of Affinity Technologies, which specialized in automating mortgage loans and credit card applications and was looking for strategic alliances. Affinity had the expertise to create the software Oyster needed and wanted to improve its name recognition among bankers.

As negotiations with Affinity began, the National Black Chamber of Commerce announced it would hold its annual conference in Denver. The Chamber had 163 chapters and 60,000 members. Margot sent the chairman the remaining inventory of her guide to distribute to attendees, pointing out that online lending leveled the playing field for loan approval. Margot was sure that if she could get a contract with the Black Chamber, the big banks would sign on as lenders.

Margot said, "Right now we have no idea what all this will look like in six to eight months. The technology is moving fast, and, to be perfectly frank, we don't have a business plan. But Kenton and I have built companies before, so we know what is entailed and the type of infrastructure that's needed. We don't have it down on paper, but we know the type of staffing and wrap-up that we will need very, very fast—as soon as that first contract is written."

Source: Adapted from "Oyster Communications," by Joan Winn. *From Entrepreneurship Theory & Practice,* 23(2), Winter 1998. Reprinted by permission of the author. To read the entire case, visit the *Small Business Management: Entrepreneurship and Beyond* web site at http://business.college.hmco.com/students.

QUESTIONS

1. How would a business plan have helped Oyster Communications?

2. What would you emphasize in writing a business plan for Oyster?

3. Oyster is obviously a very dynamic, changeable business. Why write a plan for this type of business?

Early Decisions

A small business owner has three primary options for getting into business: A franchise can be purchased, an existing business can be bought, or a new venture can be created. While each has advantages and disadvantages, which one is right for your business? Circumstances may mean that only one or two of these options are available to you, but the correct path depends on several factors that will be explored as Early Decisions. **Chapter 5** introduces us to franchising; **Chapter 6** covers the purchase of an existing business; and **Chapter 7** focuses on the excitement and risks of starting from scratch.

5

Franchising

After reading this chapter, you should be able to:

- **Establish what a franchise is and how it operates.**

- **Articulate the difference between product (or trade-name) franchises and business-format franchises.**

- **Compare the advantages and disadvantages of franchising.**

- **Explain how to evaluate a potential franchise.**

- **Explore franchising in the international marketplace.**

THE BUSTLING NEON COMMERCIALISM of any large American shopping mall seems an unlikely outlet for a product created amid the rural charm of Pennsylvania's Amish farmland. Yet that product, a soft pretzel, made by a company called Auntie Anne's, is taking the nation's malls by storm. Headquartered in Lancaster County, Pennsylvania, Auntie Anne's is a fast-growing treats franchise that sells freshly made, delicious soft pretzels. Anne Beiler, who was raised in this Amish area, founded the company in 1988 when she began making soft pretzels to replace a pizza business she had managed at an Amish farmer's market. Business was so brisk that Beiler expanded first from one to two booths and then began refining her pretzel recipe. Like many successful businesses, chance played an important role in the company's history. When a supplier inadvertently delivered the wrong ingredients, Beiler added them to her original pretzel recipe, and the mix-up ended up making the pretzels taste better!

The first thing you notice about an Auntie Anne's franchise location is its delightful smell, which Sean Kelly, director of marketing for the parent company, laughingly refers to as the "sweet smell of success." Because the bulk of the stores' sales are to impulse shoppers, the aroma of freshly baked pretzels is an important sales tool. Franchisees also use free product sample distribution throughout the malls, frequent-user programs, and brochures (extolling everything from the way the pretzels are made, to their health benefits, to suggested dip recipes) to market the products effectively. The company has since branched into selling related merchandise, primarily coffee mugs designed with traditional Amish quilt patterns and tumblers decorated with artwork about Lancaster County.

Auntie Anne's now has over 580 franchise stores. The majority of these stores are located in shopping center food courts, but the company is experimenting with alternative locations, such as Wal-Marts, train stations, and airports. It is also expanding into Indonesia, Malaysia, the Philippines, Singapore, Thailand, and Israel. Franchise expansion grows steadily at 60 to 70 units per year, and the company receives more than 400 inquiries per month for new franchises. In this chapter you will learn about the process of franchising, including the different types of franchising systems, the advantages and disadvantages of franchises, and how to go about selecting a franchise. Maybe you, too, will one day savor the sweet smell of success in a franchise business.

Sources: Hoover's Company Capsule Database, no. 58148, 7 September 1999; Jaqueline Kochak, "A New Twist," *Restaurant Business*, 15 September 1998, 80–81; and Milford Prewitt, "Auntie Anne's Promo Showcases Sweet Smell of Success," *Nation's Restaurant News*, 27 February 1995, 12ff.

▬ About Franchising

franchise A contractual license to operate an individually owned business as part of a larger chain.

franchisor The parent company that develops a product or business process and sells the rights to franchisees.

franchisee The small business person who purchases the franchise in order to sell the product or service of the franchisor.

Over the past 50 years or so, franchising has become a very attractive means of starting and operating a small business. Some of the most familiar franchises are McDonald's, H&R Block, AAMCO Transmissions, GNC (General Nutrition Centers), and Dairy Queen. A **franchise** is an agreement that binds a **franchisor** (a parent company of the product, service, or method) with a **franchisee** (a small business that pays fees and royalties for exclusive rights to local distribution of the product or service). Through the franchise agreement, the franchisee gains the benefit of the parent company's expertise, experience, management systems, marketing, and financial help. Franchisors benefit by expanding their operations by building a base of franchisees rather than using their own capital and resources.

Background

Franchising dominates the fast-food, automobile, and lodging segments of the U.S. economy.

Franchises have experienced growth since the 1950s. However, contrary to popular belief, they did not originate with McDonald's. They have existed since the early 1800s.

In the 1830s, Cyrus McCormick was making reapers, and Isaac Singer began manufacturing sewing machines. As America's economic system was beginning to shift from one based on agriculture and small business to one based on industry and big business, business methods needed to change also. Early manufacturers also had to provide distribution and were faced with the choice of setting up a company-owned system or developing contracts with independent firms to represent them. The choice was not easy. Direct ownership guaranteed complete control and ensured quality levels of service. On the other hand, direct ownership was expensive and difficult to manage. McCormick and Singer were two of the first to use agents in building sales networks quickly, at little cost to themselves.[1] This use of exclusive agents laid the groundwork for today's franchising. The exclusive contractual agreement between franchisor and franchisee has evolved past agency, but it has become a viable business alternative.

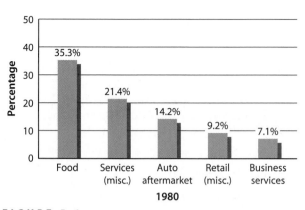

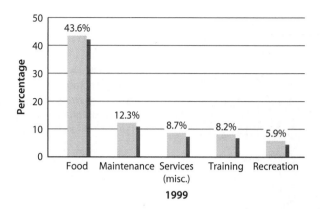

FIGURE 5.1
Franchise 500

The composition of the Franchise 500 has changed from 1980 to 2000.

Source: Franchise Fact Sheet, International Franchise Association, 5 June 1995.

Franchising Today

Today, franchising is represented in almost every industry. More than 600,000 U.S. businesses are franchised. Interest in international franchising is growing quickly. In 1999, franchised businesses had annual sales of $1 trillion![2]

Although the number of franchises has been increasing since the 1950s, the 1980s were a real boom period. Franchise sales in 1980 were $336 billion. Sales jumped to $714 billion in 1990—a 112 percent increase. See Figure 5.1 to compare how the *Entrepreneur* Franchise 500 has changed over the years.

Franchises are an important part of the American economic landscape.

Fast Facts

The International Franchise Association underwrote a research study conducted by FRAN-DATA Corporation and the University of Missouri–Columbia to create a statistical basis for accurate answers to key questions about franchising. Data from the study's 1,156 companies representing 18 main industry segments were drawn from state-registered Uniform Franchise Offering Circulars (UFOCs). Some interesting findings emerged.

- 95 percent of study's population charged an initial franchise fee of less than $40,000
- 2 percent with an initial franchise fee of more than $50,000
- 80 percent of all companies with an initial investment average of $240,000 or less
- 17 percent of franchisors that do not require a contribution to an advertising fund
- 33 percent of franchisors in operation longer than 12 years
- 15 percent of franchisors in operation 1 year or less
- 61 percent of the companies with a total system population (number of franchises) of 11 to 500 units
- 21 percent of the companies with a system size of 10 units or less
- 73 percent of companies that offer an exclusive territory to franchisees

Source: "New Franchising Study Most Comprehensive View of Unique Concept to Date," *PR Newswire,* 9 November 1998, Lexis-Nexis Academic Universe search.

Franchising Systems

The two types of franchises are *product* (or *trade-name*) *franchises* and *business-format franchises.* These two forms are used by producers, wholesalers, and retailers to distribute goods and services to consumers and other businesses.

Product (Trade-Name) Franchising

product (trade-name) franchising A type of franchising in which the franchisee agrees to purchase the products of the franchisor or to use the franchisor's name.

Product (trade-name) franchising allows the franchisee (or dealer) to buy products from the franchisor (or supplier) or to license the use of its trade name. This approach typically connects a single manufacturer with many dealers. The idea is to make products available to consumers in a specific geographic region through exclusive dealers. Soft-drink bottlers and gasoline stations use this type of franchising. Auto manufacturers also use this system to make their cars, service, and parts available. Your local Chevrolet dealer, for instance, has full use of the Chevrolet trade name, brand names (like Corvette), and logos (like the bow tie symbol) to promote the dealership in your area. Product franchisors regulate their franchisees' locations to avoid excessive competition between them. Chevrolet would not allow a new dealership that sells its products across the street from your established local dealer.

Business-Format Franchising

Business-format franchising is more of a *turnkey* approach to franchising. This means that the franchisee purchases not only the franchisor's product to sell, but also the entire way of doing business, including operation procedures, marketing packages, physical building and equipment, and full business services. Business-format franchising is commonly used in fast-food restaurants and lodging establishments, such as hotel and motel chains. McDonald's and Burger King use business-format franchising.

business-format franchising A type of franchising in which the franchisee adopts the franchisor's entire method of operation.

Why Open a Franchise? ▬

If you are considering the purchase of a franchise, you should compare its advantages and disadvantages to those of starting a new business or buying an existing nonfranchised business (see Chapters 6 and 7). You should also determine whether the unique characteristics of franchising fit your personal needs and desires. Some small business owners would rather assume the risk and expense of starting an independent business than have to follow someone else's policies and procedures. Others prefer the advantages that a franchise's proven system can provide. Sometimes it makes sense not to reinvent the wheel (see Table 5.1).

Franchisee's Perspective	Franchisor's Perspective	
Advantages	*Advantages*	**TABLE 5.1** **The Advantages and Disadvantages of Franchising**
1. Proven product or service	1. Expansion with limited capital	
2. Marketing expertise	2. Multiple sources of capital	
3. Financial assistance	3. Controlled expansion	
4. Technical and managerial assistance	4. Motivated franchisees	
5. Opportunity to learn business	5. Bulk purchasing discounts	
6. Quality control standards		
7. Efficiency		
8. Opportunity for growth		
Disadvantages	*Disadvantages*	
1. Fees and profit sharing	1. Loss of control	
2. Restrictions of freedom	2. Sharing profit with franchisees	
3. Overdependence or unsatisfied expectations	3. Potential for disputes with franchisees	
4. Risk of fraud or misunderstanding		
5. Termination of the agreement		
6. Performance of other franchisees		

Advantages to the Franchisee

For the franchisee, there are eight major advantages of franchising: proven product or service, marketing expertise, financial assistance, technical and managerial assistance, an opportunity to learn the business, quality control standards, efficiency, and opportunity for growth.[3]

PROVEN PRODUCT. The advantage of selling a proven product or service is the greatest benefit to a franchisee. Customers are aware of the product; they know the name and what to expect. For example, travelers may not know anything about the Ramada Inn in Colorado Springs, but they know of Ramada's reputation and are more likely to stay there than at some independent, unknown motel.

MARKETING EXPERTISE. Franchisors spend millions of dollars on national or regional advertising to help build an image that independent businesses could not afford. Franchisors also develop print, broadcast, and point-of-purchase advertising. Local franchisees do share in these advertising costs, usually based on their gross revenues.

FINANCIAL ASSISTANCE. Some franchisors provide financial assistance to new franchisees. This assistance typically comes in the form of trade credit on inventory or overhead reduction by the franchisor's choosing, purchasing, and owning buildings and real estate.

PROFESSIONAL GUIDANCE. A franchise can provide a source of managerial and technical assistance not available to an independent business. You can benefit from the accumulated years of experience and knowledge of the franchisor. Most franchisors provide training, both as preparation for running the business and as instruction after the business is going. This training can allow a person without prior experience to be successful in owning a franchise. A good franchisor is available to provide day-to-day assistance and to give you someone to turn to if a crisis arises. In addition, franchisees can receive a great deal of technical assistance, such as store layout and design, location, purchasing, and equipment.

OPPORTUNITY TO LEARN. Although it is not usually advisable to go into a business in an unfamiliar field, franchising can provide an opportunity to be successful doing exactly that. This can be helpful for a midcareer change of direction. In fact, some franchisors prefer their franchisees not to have experience in that particular field. These franchisors would prefer to train from scratch so there are no bad habits to break.

RECOGNIZED STANDARDS. Franchisors impose quality standards for franchisees to follow, a feature that might not seem advantageous at first. If independence is your motive for self-employment, why would you want to meet standards set by someone else? The benefit, though, is that the practice ensures consistency to customers. Consumers can walk into a McDonald's anywhere in the world and know what to expect. A franchisor's quality control regulations help franchisees to maintain high standards of cleanliness, service, and productivity. As a franchisee, you will benefit from standardized quality control, because if another franchisee in your organization provides inferior service, it will affect attitudes toward *your* business.

EFFICIENCY. Because of increased efficiency, a franchise can sometimes be started and operated with less capital than it takes to start an independent business. Franchisors have already been through the learning curve and worked most of the bugs out of the process. Inventory needs, such as what to stock and what will sell quickly, are known before you open the doors, so you won't be wasting money on equipment, inventory, or supplies that you don't need. Many franchisors often provide financial resources for startup and working capital for inventory.

POTENTIAL FOR BUSINESS GROWTH. If you are successful with a franchise, you will often have the opportunity to multiply that success by expanding to other franchises in other locations. Most franchisors have provisions to open other territories.

Franchising can increase your chances of success in business and provide many things you might not otherwise have access to. These seven advantages have one theme in common—the opportunity to benefit from someone else's experience. You have the chance to learn from someone else's mistakes.

Disadvantages to the Franchisee

There are drawbacks to franchising also. You must give up some control, some decision-making power, and some freedom. The disadvantages to the franchisee include fees and profit sharing, restrictions of freedom, overdependence, fraud or misunderstanding, termination of the agreement, and performance of other franchisees.

COST OF FRANCHISE. The services, assistance, and assurance in buying a franchise come at a price. Every franchisor will charge a fee and/or a specified percentage of sales revenue (see Table 5.2). The disadvantage to the franchisees is that they are usually required to raise most of the capital before they begin operations. The total investment can range from $500 for a windshield repair franchise to $45 million for Hilton Inn.

These fees and percentages may begin to seem excessive after you have been in business for a while and see their impact on your bottom line. It is not uncommon for franchisees to be grateful for the assistance a franchisor provides in starting the business, only to become frustrated by the royalties paid a few years later.

RESTRICTIONS ON FREEDOM OR CREATIVITY. Restrictions on freedom may be a problem for some franchisees. This is especially true because most people open their own business because of a desire for independence. Franchises have policies and procedures that must be followed to maintain the agreement. The size of your market will be limited by territorial restrictions. You may feel that some products, promotions, or policies may not be appropriate for your area, but you have little recourse after the franchise agreement has been signed.

OVERDEPENDENCE OR UNSATISFIED EXPECTATIONS. Even though a franchisee is bound by contractual agreement, overdependence on the franchisor can still be a problem. Franchisors do not always know what is best for local conditions. The franchisee must be willing and able to apply his or her own managerial decisions in running the business in the best way for the local market. The flip side

TABLE 5.2	Franchise	Franchise Startup Fee	Costs	Royalty (Percentage)
Getting In	Maaco Auto Painting & Bodyworks	$30K	$224.5K	8%
	Meineke Discount Mufflers	$25K	$152K–276K	to 7%
	Jazzercise, Inc.	$650	$1.8K–20.6K	to 20%
	Snip N' Clip	$10K	$51.8K	5%
	Signs First	$7.5–17.5K	$28K–100K	6%
	Big Apple Bagels	$25K	$205K–342K	5%
	Rocky Mountain Chocolate Factory	$19.5K	$113K–213K	5%
	KFC	$25K	$1.1M–1.7M	4%
	Burger King	$40K	$235K–2.3M	3.5–6%
	Baskin-Robbins	$30K	$180K–429K	5.9%
	Taco John's	$15K–22.5K	$495K–658K	4%
	Subway	$10K	$63.5K–175K	8%
	Super 8 Motels	$24K+	$254K–2.3M	5%
	Merry Maids	$16K–24K	$32K–50K	5%–7%
	Together Dating Service	$50K–80K	$98K–185K	5%
	McDonald's	$45K	$478K–1.4M	12.5+%
	CD Warehouse	$15K–20K	$128K–169K	5%
	Closet Factory	$28K–40K	$100K–198K	5.75%
	Frank & Stein	$20K	$170K–300K	6%
	Keller Williams Realty	$18K	$114K–245K	6%
	Sylvan Learning Centers	$38K–46K	$121K–219K	8–9%
	Pro Golf Discount	$50K	$252K–1.1M	2.5%

Source: "22nd Annual Franchise 500," *Entrepreneur,* January 2001, 174–269.

of overdependence is a franchisor that does not provide all the assistance that the franchisee expected.

RISK OF FRAUD OR MISUNDERSTANDING. Less-than-scrupulous franchisors have been known to mislead potential franchisees with promises that are not delivered. To avoid being taken by fraudulent franchises, be sure to consult an attorney and talk with as many current franchisees as possible. Do not think that because the agreement looks standard, you should not understand every section, especially the fine print.

PROBLEMS OF TERMINATION OR TRANSFER. Difficulty in terminating the franchise agreement or having it terminated against your will can be a disadvantage to the franchisee. Before entering into the franchise, you should understand the section of the agreement that describes how you can get out of the agreement. For instance, what if you want to transfer your rights to a family member, or sell the franchise to someone else, or otherwise terminate your agreement? What provisions does the contract make for you to renew the agreement? Most franchise agreements are made for a specific period of time—typically, between 5 and 20 years. Some may be renewed for perpetuity if both parties agree. Otherwise, both sides must consider franchise renewal when the term of the agreement expires. Check the agreement to see if the franchisee has a right of first refusal, which means that the franchisee must decline to continue the agreement before the franchisor can offer the franchise to someone else. Check to see if the franchisor must provide "just cause" for termination or must give a definite reason why the agreement is not continued. Remember that a franchise is a contract. Any questions regarding it should be directed to your legal council.

POOR PERFORMANCE OF OTHER FRANCHISEES. Poor performance on the part of other franchisees can lead to problems for you. If the franchisor tolerates substandard performance, a few franchisees can seriously affect the sales of many others. Customers view franchises as an entire unit, because the implicit message from franchises is that "we are all alike"—for good or bad. If customers are treated unsatisfactorily in one location, they are likely to believe the same treatment will occur elsewhere.

Advantages to the Franchisor

Now let's look at franchising from the franchisor's perspective. Franchisors also face advantages and disadvantages. The positive aspects include decreased capital investment when compared with forming so many outlets independently, multiple sources of capital coming into their business, expansion of the business happening much faster than if they were in business alone, the synergy created by a group of motivated franchisees, and the volume discounts of bulk purchasing.

EXPANSION WITH SMALLER CAPITAL INVESTMENT. From the perspective of the franchisor, the biggest advantage of offering franchises is the expansion of its distribution sources with limited equity investments. The franchise fees from franchisees provide capital to the franchisor. The franchisor therefore does not have to borrow from lenders or attract outside investors. For a business with limited capital, franchising may be the only viable way to expand by providing franchisees an opportunity to share the financial burden for all to succeed.

MULTIPLE SOURCES OF REVENUE. Franchisors often have several sources of revenue built into franchise agreements. These sources include the franchise fee, which is paid when the agreement is signed, a percentage of the franchise's monthly gross operating revenues, and revenue from selling the necessary products and supplies to the franchisees. For example, a fast-food restaurant can have a franchise fee of up to $200,000; pay 3 to 8 percent of monthly gross sales as a royalty fee; and be required to purchase all food items (from hamburger to condiments), office supplies, and restaurant supplies (napkins, coffee filters, paper cups) from the franchisor.

CONTROLLED EXPANSION. When compared with the expansion of a corporate chain, expanding via franchising can be accomplished with a simpler management structure. Very rapid growth of a corporation can be more of a problem than an opportunity if the growth outpaces central management's capacity to control and monitor it. When this happens, problems with inconsistency, communications, and especially cash flow generally appear. Although franchisors still face these problems to some degree, the franchise network reduces them.

Once Burned . . .

After fighting fires with the New Orleans Fire Department for 25 years and making it to district chief, the last way Delo Breckenridge expected to get burned was by an unscrupulous franchisor. In fact, he was taken to the cleaners—literally—to the tune of $40,000.

The franchise operation Breckenridge signed on with, Automated Micro Dry Cleaning Centers, sold a system whereby customers were to drop off clothes to be dry-cleaned in a sorting machine located in an office building storefront. There the clothes were to be retrieved by a worker, cleaned, and then returned to the original location. When he picked up his or her clothes, the customer would pay with a credit card swiped through a machine. "It was supposed to work kind of like a jukebox," Breckenridge says. Yet when he went to California for a demonstration, the model didn't work. Breckenridge knows that he should have backed out at that point, but a franchise salesman kept calling him a "wussy," and the insult worked: Breckenridge sank his money into the system.

Breckenridge has received absolutely nothing in return for his investment except letters from the franchisor stating, in effect, that there were problems with the machines and that the company was out of money, and asking him to send more. And Breckenridge wasn't alone in this nightmare. Nineteen other franchisees were also suckered in. He laments, "It's kind of like getting a new car and wrecking it the first day without having any insurance. I'll be paying $600 a month on my bank loan for the next five years."

It might seem that Breckenridge must have been some sort of ignorant fool to have gotten duped like this—but his background indicates otherwise. Not only is he an expert in his profession, he graduated from Louisiana State University with a degree in economics. His father was a lawyer, and his mother was a respected journalist for the New Orleans *Times-Picayune* newspaper. His lesson: He now wishes he had contacted other franchisees and talked to them before signing on.

Thoroughly researching a potential franchise, particularly one that is newly established or unfamiliar to you, and doggedly asking questions until you get the information you need to make an intelligent decision is just smart business. And, as Breckenridge now admits, you must never let someone use insults to push you into making a bad decision.

Source: Andrew Serwer, "Trouble in Franchise Nation," *Fortune*, 6 March 1995, 115–129.

MOTIVATED FRANCHISEES. Because franchisees own their own business, they are almost always more highly motivated to make it succeed than an employee working for someone else. Franchisees have a direct personal interest in the entire operation, so they are inspired to perform and create positive synergy within the franchise.

BULK PURCHASING. Centralized purchasing of products and supplies allows franchisors to take advantage of volume discounts, because they are buying for all the franchise locations. This can increase profit margins and hold down costs for franchisees.

Disadvantages to the Franchisor

Problems exist in every method of business, and franchising is no exception. Maintaining control is the biggest disadvantage to franchisors. Others are profit sharing and potential disputes with franchisees.

LOSS OF CONTROL. Franchisees who do not maintain their businesses not only reflect poorly on the other franchisees, but on the franchisor also. Although the franchisor does control the organization to the limit of the franchise agreement, franchisees are still independent businesspeople. After the franchise agreement has been signed, the franchisor must get permission from franchisees before any products or services are changed, added, or eliminated. Permission is often negotiated individually. This makes adapting products to meet changing customer needs very difficult for the franchisor, especially if a wide variety of consumer tastes are being served over a large geographic area.

One way franchisors have dealt with this problem is by establishing some company-owned units. Because these are not independently owned businesses, the franchisor can test-market new products, services, and procedures in them. This can give the franchisor a way to track and respond to changing customer needs, as well as examples to use when negotiating with franchisees.

PROFIT SHARING. If franchisees expect (and are able) to recover their initial investment within two or three years, they could be yielding 30 to 50 percent return on investment. This can provide motivation for the franchisees, but it is also profit the franchisor is not making with a company-owned unit.

FRANCHISEE DISPUTES. Friction between franchisees and franchisors may arise over such issues as payment of fees, expansion, and hours of operation. These potential conflicts point to the importance of communication between both sides and having a clearly written franchise agreement.

Selecting a Franchise ▬■

Choosing the right franchise is a serious decision. Investing in a franchise represents a big commitment of time and money. Determine what you need in a business and evaluate what several different franchises can offer you and your customers.

Evaluate Your Needs

The choice of which franchise to buy is not an easy one. You need to find a franchise opportunity that matches your interests, skills, and needs. Ask yourself the following questions to help determine whether or not franchising is the route to small business ownership for you:

- How much equity capital will you need to purchase the franchise and operate it until your income equals your expenses? Where are you going to get it?

- Are you prepared to give up some independence of action to secure the advantages offered by the franchise?

- Do you really believe you have the innate ability, training, and experience to work smoothly and profitably with the franchisor, your employees, and your customers?

- Are you ready to make a long-term commitment to working with this franchisor, offering its product or service to your public?[4]

Do Your Research

Inc., Fortune Small Business, the *Wall Street Journal, Success,* and *Entrepreneur* are general business periodicals that contain advertising and articles related to franchising. Trade journals and magazines that specialize in franchising are *Franchise, Franchising Opportunities World,* and *Quarterly Franchising World.*

Trade associations can be valuable sources of information when you are investigating franchise opportunities. The major trade association of franchising is the International Franchise Association (IFA), publisher of *The Franchise Handbook,* which gives you an idea of requirements, expectations, and assistance for each franchise. Table 5.3 shows examples of franchise descriptions from this handbook. The IFA is a leading source of information for franchisors and franchisees, offering publications on industrywide data as well as company-specific information. You can contact the IFA for information, at 1350 New York Avenue NW, Suite 900, Washington, DC 20005-4709, (202) 628-8000, www.franchise1.com

© The 5th Wave, www.the5thwave.com

TABLE 5.3
Franchise Information

Marble Slab Creamery
3100 S. Gessner, # 305
Houston, TX 77063
www.marbleslab.com
Contact: marbleslab@marbleslab.com

Company Description: Marble Slab Creamery offers homemade, superpremium ice cream that is prepared to order on a marble slab. Customers can create their own ice cream concoctions by combining any flavor of ice cream with "mixins" such as fresh fruit, candy, cookies or nuts. The ice cream & mixins are then folded together on a frozen marble slab & served on a freshly baked waffle cone. Other products include smoothies, shakes, sundaes, banana splits, ice cream pies/cakes, specialty coffees & bakery items.

# of Franchised Units:	190
Company-Owned Units:	1
In Business Since:	1983
Franchising Since:	1984
Franchising Fee:	$23,000
Royalties:	6%
Capital Requirements:	$250,000 net worth, $50,000 liquid
Financing Options:	None

Training and Support: Assistance is available on site selection, lease negotiation, architectural layout and construction supervision. A ten-day training program in Houston, Texas is required.

Seeking Franchisees: In the U.S., Canada, Central America, Eastern Europe, Middle East, Mexico, South America, Western Europe.

Play It Again Sports
Grow Biz International, Inc.
4200 Dalhberg Dr.
Minneapolis, MN 55422-4837
www.playitagainsports
Contact: mpeterson@growbiz.com

Company Description: Play It Again Sports buys and sells new and used sporting goods. Stores carry items like golf clubs and bags, baseball bats and gloves, in-line skates, and fitness equipment. Play It Again Sports is owned by Grow Biz International, which also franchises Music Go Round, Once Upon a Child, Plato's Closet, and Re-Tool.

# of Franchised Units:	556
Company-Owned Units:	2
In Business Since:	1983
Franchising Since:	1988
Franchise Fee:	$20,000
Capital Requirements:	$153,000–$265,000 total investment. $50,000–$75,000 startup cash
Financing Options:	Assistance in preparation of a comprehensive business plan.

Training and Support: Training includes such topics as site selection, lease negotiations, store build-out, POS inventory management, business operating system, evaluating product, local store marketing.

TABLE 5.3
**Franchise Information
(continued)**

Subway
325 Bic Dr.
Milford, CT 06460
www.subway.com
Contact: franchise@subway.com

Company Description: Today, it is the world's largest and fastest growing franchise. In 1965, it was 17-year-old Fred DeLuca and family friend Peter Buck's tiny sandwich shop started as a way to get through college. Subway ranked number one in *2001 Entrepreneur* magazine's Franchise 500 by offering a healthy alternative to fast-food restaurants. Over 50% of franchises purchased are sold to existing owners who choose to reinvest.

# of Franchised Units:	12,682 in the U.S., 1,491 in Canada, 1,074 in other countries
Company-Owned Units:	1
In Business Since:	1965
Franchising Since:	1974
Franchise Fee:	$10,000
Royalty Fee:	8%
Capital Requirements:	$63,400–$175,000

Financing Options: Franchise fee financing available. Startup financing available. Equipment leasing available.

Training and Support: 2 weeks training at 3 locations: Connecticut, USA; Costa Rica and Australia. Follow up support given by field staff and headquarters' staff.

General Nutrition Centers
GNC Franchising
300 Sixth Ave.
Pittsburgh, PA 15222
www.gncfranchising.com

Company Description: In 1935 David Shakarian started a health-food store in Pittsburgh called Lackzoom. It specialized in yogurt (which his father introduced to the U.S.) but also carried health-food products such as honey and grains. Today, as the leading national specialty retailer of vitamins, minerals, herbs & sports nutrition supplements, GNC capitalizes on the accelerating trend toward self-care. GNC was ranked America's #1 franchise by *Entrepreneur* magazine in 1998/99.

# of Franchised Units:	1,368 in the U.S., 2 in Canada, 311 in other countries
Company-Owned Units:	2817
In Business Since:	1935
Franchising Since:	1988
Franchise Fee:	$35,000/$27,500
Royalty Fee:	6%
Capital Requirements:	$100K net worth—$60K cash liquidity requirement

Financing Options: GNC offers direct company financing for startup fees, equipment, inventory and accounts receivable to qualified individuals.

Training and Support: New franchisees receive three weeks of initial training, including an intensive one-week training class at corporate headquarters.

Choice Hotels International
10750 Columbia Pike
Silver Spring, MD 20901
www.choicehotels.com
Contact: franchise_info@choicehotels.com

Company Description: Started in 1939 by a group of Southern motel owners as a discussion of the motel industry. FBI director J. Edgar Hoover had warned that motels were used as bases of operations by gangsters. Choice Hotels is a chain that includes Sleep, Comfort, Quality, Clarion, Rodeway, and Econo Lodge. Choice combines consistency, high quality & price-value advantage to create a pleasant guest experience & opportunity for hotel developers.

# of Franchised Units:	3,250 in the U.S., 236 in Canada, 947 in other countries
Company-Owned Units:	0
In Business Since:	1939
Franchising Since:	1962
Franchise Fee:	$25K–50K, $4M–$6M total investment
Capital Requirements:	$750K net worth requirement, $200K cash liquidity requirement

Financing Options: Assistance with preparing mortgage applications for major renovations or conversions

Training and Support:	Yes

Dunkin' Donuts
14 Pacella Park Dr.
Randolph, MA 02368
www.dunkin-baskin-togos.com

Company Description: In 1946, William Rosenberg founded Industrial Luncheon Services, a company that delivered meals and snacks to workers in the Boston area. That success led him to start the Open Kettle, a doughnut shop in Quincy, MA. Two years later he changed the name to Dunkin' Donuts. Today, they sell donuts, muffins, bagels, coffee, and fruit drinks.

# of Franchised Units:	3,732 in the U.S., 205 in Canada, and 1,368 in other countries
Company-Owned Units:	2
In Business Since:	1950
Franchising Since:	1955
Franchise Fee:	$40,000
Capital Requirements:	$200,000 cash liquidity requirement, net worth minimum $400,000
Financing Options:	Yes
Training and Support:	Yes

TABLE 5.3

Franchise Information (continued)

TABLE 5.3 **Franchise Information (continued)**	Gingiss Formalwear 2101 Executive Dr. Addison, Il 60101 www.gingiss.com Contact: gingiss@gingiss.com
	Company Description: In 1936, after having a difficult time renting tuxedos for his sister's wedding, Benjamin Gingiss borrowed $500 and opened the first Gingiss Formalwear in Chicago. Now, the world's largest tuxedo specialist has 255 stores renting and selling men's/boy's formalwear for proms, weddings and other special occasions.
	# of Franchised Units: 170 in the U.S.
	Company-Owned Units: 85
	In Business Since: 1936
	Franchising Since: 1968
	Franchise Fee: $15,000
	Royalty Fee: 7–8%
	Capital Requirements: Total investment of $94,700–$242,700.
	Financial Requirements: $200K net worth requirement, $50K cash liquidity requirement.

Source: Entrepreneur Franchise 500 issue (January 2001), www.entrepreneur.com

OTHER INFORMATION SOURCES. The American Franchise Association (AFA), based in Chicago, and the American Association of Franchisees and Dealers (AAFD), headquartered in San Diego, are trade associations that provide information and services, represent the interests of members, and were formed to help negotiate better terms and conditions from franchisors. The AAFD has developed a Franchisee Bill of Rights as a code of ethical business conduct for franchised businesses.[5] Women in Franchising, Inc. (WIF), also located in Chicago, (312) 431-1467, www.infonews.com specializes in training women and minorities for advancement in franchising.[6]

On Yahoo!, under the Business and Economy category, Small Business Information, you will also find a link to additional franchise information, called FranNet. FranNet (http://www.frannet.com) can provide you with information to help you select the right franchise. The Franchise Handbook Online is a comprehensive franchise directory devoted to providing useful information about franchising opportunities and franchising companies. The Franchise Handbook Online address is http://www.franchise1.com. Additional information on franchises can be found on any of the popular search engines by doing a keyword search using "franchise." Better yet, go to a full-text online database like ABI-INFORM or Lexis-Nexis to search for general and company-specific information on franchises.

You might also want to check out the Better Business Bureau's web site (found at http://www.bbb.org/bbb). At this site, you'll find a publications directory, membership list, and contact information for Better Business Bureaus nationwide. You can also access the bureau's newsletter, check the scam alerts, and even file a complaint online. Another source of franchise information is the Institute of Management and Administration's page, which provides links to hundreds of other business sites, including many industry-specific resources (http://ioma.com/ioma).[7]

From the Horse's Mouth

A good place to get information about a particular franchise is from the people currently running one. Try asking the following questions to get the straight scoop:

- What does the business cost to operate on a monthly basis?

- How long did it take to break even?

- How profitable is the franchise?

- How much does the company charge for advertising fees? (Be careful if this number is more than 1 percent to 3 percent of gross sales.)

- Does the money go toward ads in the local market or mainly toward building the parent company's national image? (You should expect about 50 percent to benefit the franchisee.)

- How many units have failed?

- How rapid is unit turnover?

- How many stores does the parent company own? (About 25 percent is acceptable. Too many could weaken franchisee bargaining power; too few could indicate a weak system.)

- Would you buy the franchise again? (The bottom line.)

Remember when you are talking with these current franchise owners that many of them are struggling to internally validate the decision they have made regarding this business. They will often tell you that things are going great, sales are up, and they would definitely do it all over again. They may be trying to convince themselves. To get a realistic picture of what you are facing, push for getting them to tell you *exactly* how much profit they have made in each year of operation. Will you be able to go for two years without making a profit? That may be the case.

Sources: Todd D. Maddocks, "Write the Wrongs," *Entrepreneur,* January 2001, 152–155; and Laurel Allison Touby, "Should You Buy a Franchise?" *Working Woman,* October 1991, 68–69.

QUESTIONS TO ASK. When you have a general idea of the franchise you are interested in, contact the company for a copy of its disclosure statement. Before you sign the required contracts with a chosen franchisor, talk to current and former franchisees. They can provide priceless information that you could not learn anywhere else.

Once you have found a franchise you would consider (or possibly a few to choose from), consider your opportunity by asking yourself the following questions about the franchise:

- Did your lawyer approve the franchise contract you are considering after he or she studied it paragraph by paragraph?

- Does the franchise call on you to take any steps which are, according to your lawyer, unwise or illegal in your state, county, or city?

- Does the franchise give you an exclusive territory for the length of the franchise, or can the franchisor sell a second or third franchise in your territory?

- Is the franchisor connected in any way with any other franchise company handling similar merchandise or services? If so, what is your protection against this second franchisor organization?

- Under what circumstances can you terminate the franchise contract and at what cost to you, if you decide for any reason at all that you wish to cancel it?

- If you sell your franchise, will you be compensated for your goodwill, or will the goodwill you have built into the business be lost by you?

Evaluate what the franchisor will offer you and your customers by asking the following questions about the franchisor:

- How many years has the firm offering you a franchise been in operation?

- Has it a reputation for honesty and fair dealing among the local firms holding its franchise?

- Has the franchisor shown you any certified figures indicating exact net profits of one or more going firms which you personally checked with the franchisee(s)?

- Will the firm assist you with
    - A management training program?
    - Capital?
    - An employee training program?
    - Credit?
    - A public relations program?
    - Merchandise ideas?

- Will the firm help you find a good location for your new business?

- Is the franchising firm adequately financed so that it can carry out its stated plan of financial assistance and expansion?

- Is the franchisor a one-person company or a corporation with an experienced management trained in depth (so that there would always be an experienced person at its head)?

- Exactly what can the franchisor do for you that you cannot do for yourself?

- Has the franchisor investigated you carefully enough to assure itself that you can successfully operate one of its franchises at a profit to both of you?

- Does your state have a law regulating the sale of franchises, and has the franchisor complied with the law?

Analyze the Market

What do you know about your market, the people buying your product or service? In answering the following questions, determine whether a franchise is the best way to match what the franchisor has to offer with your skills and your customers' needs:

1. Have you made any study to determine whether the product or service that you propose to sell under franchise has a market in your territory at the prices you will have to charge?

Sell Ice Cream in Alaska? Yeah, Right!

Some good ideas may not always appear so good at first glance, a point that Julia and Eric Henderson will tell you. The success of their Baskin-Robbins ice cream store in Wasilla, Alaska, seems to defy logic. The Hendersons don't know why their Alaskan neighbors like ice cream so much, even when the mercury in the thermometer takes a nose dive—but apparently they do. Julia thinks all the snow reminds people of ice cream. Because there isn't much to do in the winter if you don't ski, the shop gives the people in the town of 4,000 a place to socialize.

Eric is the principal in the local middle school. Julia ran a restaurant with her sister before deciding she wanted to open a BR. "Initially, Baskin-Robbins was skeptical about selling ice cream to Alaskans," Eric says. But demographic research showed serious growth potential. Wasilla has twice as many kindergartners and first-graders as high school seniors. That statistic showed the Hendersons that there was a real potential for growth. It was also a good indicator of their target market—kids everywhere love ice cream, no matter what the temperature. Revenue for the first six months of operation was projected to be $250,000, 72 percent above initial expectations.

Source: Adapted from Meg Whittemore, "Winds of Change in Franchising," *Nation's Business,* January 1994, 49–55.

2. Will the population in your proposed territory increase, remain static, or decrease over the next five years?
3. Will the product or service you are considering be in greater demand, about the same, or in less demand five years from now?
4. What competition already exists in your territory for the product or service you contemplate selling?
   a. Nonfranchise firms?
   b. Franchise firms?

Disclosure Statements

Franchisors are required by the Federal Trade Commission (FTC) to provide **disclosure statements** to prospective or actual franchisees. Comparing disclosure statements from each franchise you are considering will help you identify risks, fees, benefits, and restrictions involved. Figure 5.2 provides a sample table of contents for a disclosure statement. The entire document can be several hundred pages long. As a prospective franchisee, you would want to read the document carefully and consult a lawyer to review the franchise agreement. Disclosure statements identify and provide information on 20 items, each of which is defined below.

1. *The franchisor.* Information identifying the franchisor and its affiliates and describing their business experience.
2. *Business experience of the franchisor.* Information identifying and describing the business experience of each of the franchisor's officers, directors, and management personnel responsible for franchise services, training, and other aspects of the franchises in the franchise program.

disclosure statement Information that franchisors are required to provide to potential franchisees.

> *Don't assume that the disclosure statement tells you everything you need to know about the franchise.*

FIGURE 5.2
Franchise Disclosure Statement

Table of Contents

Section

1. Franchisor and Any Predecessors
2. Identity and Business Experience of Persons Affiliated with the Franchisor
3. Litigation
4. Bankruptcy
5. Developer's/Franchisee's Initial Franchise Fee or Other Initial Payment
6. Other Fees
7. Franchisee's Initial Investment
8. Obligation of Franchisee to Purchase or Lease from Designated Sources
9. Obligations of Franchisee to Purchase or Lease in Accordance with Specifications or from Approved Suppliers
10. Financing Arrangements
11. Obligations of the Franchisor: Other Supervision, Assistance, or Services
12. Exclusive Area or Territory
13. Trademarks, Trade Names, and Service Marks
14. Patent and Copyrights
15. Obligation of Franchisee to Participate in the Actual Operations of the Franchise
16. Restrictions on Goods and Services Offered by Developer/Franchise
17. Renewal, Termination, Repurchase, Modification, and Assignment of the Franchise Agreement and Related Information
18. Arrangements with Public Figures
19. Statement of per-Franchise Average Gross Sales and Ranges of Gross Sales for the Year Ended Month, Day, Year
20. Other Franchises of the Franchisor
21. Financial Statements
22. Contracts

EXHIBIT A Franchise Agreement
EXHIBIT B Area Development Agreement
EXHIBIT C Preliminary Agreement
EXHIBIT D Royalty Incentive Rider
EXHIBIT E Disclosure Acknowledgment Statement
EXHIBIT F List of Franchisees as of Month, Day, Year
EXHIBIT G List of Franchisees Who Have Ceased Doing Business in the One (1)-Year Period Immediately Preceding Month, Day, Year
EXHIBIT H Financial Statements of Franchisor

3. *Litigation.* A description of the lawsuits in which the franchisor and its officers, directors, and management personnel have been involved.
4. *Bankruptcy.* Information about any previous bankruptcies in which the franchisor and its officers, director, and management personnel have been involved in the past 15 years.
5. *Initial fee.* Information about the initial franchise fee and other initial payments that are required to obtain the franchise. The franchisor must also tell how your fee will be used and whether you must pay in one lump sum or if you can pay in installments. If every franchisee does not pay the same amount, the franchisor must describe the formula for calculating the initial fee.
6. *Other fees.* A description of the continuing payments franchisees are required to make after the franchise opens, and the conditions for receiving refunds.
7. *Estimate of total initial investment.* The franchisor must provide a high-range and a low-range estimate of your startup costs. Included expenses would cover real estate, equipment and other fixed assets, inventory, deposits, and working capital.

8. *Purchase obligations.* Information about any restrictions on the quality of goods and services used in the franchise and where they may be purchased, including restrictions requiring purchases from the franchisor or its affiliates.

9. *Financial assistance available.* Terms and conditions of any assistance available from the franchisor or its affiliates in financing the purchase of the franchise.

10. *Product or service restrictions.* A description of restrictions on the goods or services that franchisees are permitted to sell. This could include whether you are required to carry the franchisor's full line of products or if you can supplement them with other products.

11. *Exclusive territory.* A description of any territorial protection or restrictions on the customers with whom the franchisee may deal. Recently franchisees of Subway sandwich shops have alleged that the franchisor has placed franchises too close together and overlapped territories.[8] This practice cuts into the sales volume and market size of individual stores.

12. *Renewal, termination, or assignment of franchise agreement.* A description of the conditions under which the franchise may be repurchased or refused renewal by the franchisor, transferred to a third party by the franchisee, and terminated or modified by either party.

13. *Training provided.* A description of the training program provided to franchisees, including location, length and content of training, cost of program, who pays for travel and lodging, and any additional or refresher courses available.

14. *Public figure arrangements.* A disclosure of any involvement by celebrities or public figures in promoting the franchise. If celebrities are involved, you need to be told if they are involved in actual management and how they are being compensated.

15. *Site selection.* A description of any assistance in selecting a site for the franchise that will be provided by the franchisor. Some franchises, like McDonald's, complete all site analysis and make all location decisions without input from franchisees. Others give franchisees complete discretion in site selection.

16. *Information about franchisees.* You will receive information about the present number of franchises; the number of new franchises projected; and how many have been terminated, chose not to renew, or were repurchased. Franchisors must give you the names, addresses, and phone numbers of all franchisees located in your state; contact several of them.

17. *Franchisor financial statements.* The audited financial statements of the franchisors are included to show you the financial condition of the company.

18. *Personal participation of franchisees.* A description of the extent to which franchisees must personally participate in the operation of the franchise. Some permit franchisees to own the franchise yet hire a manager to run the business. Others require franchisees to be personally involved.

19. *Earning capacity.* A complete statement of the basis for any earnings claims made to the franchisee, including the percentage of existing franchises that have actually achieved the results that are claimed. Franchisors do not have to make any projections of what a franchisee may earn, but if they do, they must also describe the basis and assumptions used to make claims.

20. *Use of intellectual property.* The franchisor must describe your use of its trademarks, trade names, logos, or other symbols. You should receive full use of them because they comprise a great deal of the value of a franchise.[9]

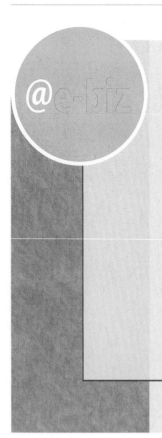

Surf Your Way to a New Franchise

As you have read in this chapter, the Federal Trade Commission (FTC) requires franchisors to provide prospective franchisees with extensive disclosure information about the franchisor and its business. This is a good thing for franchisees, because signing a franchise contract represents a major long-term commitment of both money and time. You want as much information as you can get, right? The FTC tries to correct the imbalance of power between franchisors and potential franchisees with required information. But paper copies of all this documentation has been a great expense to franchisors. The solution? Once again—the Internet.

A proposed FTC amendment to the Franchise Rule adds an entire section that allows a franchisor to provide its disclosure statement via the Internet. This change cuts costs for franchisors and speeds access of information to franchisees. Franchisor costs can be as low as $5 to $10 per document after development and implementation costs of $2,500 to $10,000 per year, according to FRANDATA. This compares favorably to a FRANDATA estimate of $40 per paper disclosure statement for printing and mailing costs and about $60 per document for administrative costs.

You potential franchise entrepreneurs can immediately access and compare multiple disclosure statements side by side during the shopping stage. Several concerns from both sides have been raised, but overall the proposal has been largely supported. At this writing, the FTC is involved with some minor rewording, but you will soon be able to log on to www.franchisedisclosure.com and surf your way to a new franchise.

Source: Perry Siatis, "Assessing the FTC's Proposed Franchise Rule Provisions Involving Electronic Disclosure," *Brigham Young University Law Review*, no. 2 (2000): 713–748.

The FTC revised the Uniform Franchise Offering Circular (UFOC) in the spring of 1994. The changes were made to replace much of the "legalese" wording of disclosure statements with plain English and to provide more standardized information for comparing franchises.[10]

When you receive a disclosure statement, you will be asked to sign and date a statement that you received it. The franchisor may not accept any money from you for ten working days from the time you sign the disclosure. This allows you the time to study, evaluate, and prepare your financing.

The Franchise Agreement

franchise agreement The legal contract that binds both parties involved in the franchise.

The **franchise agreement** is a document that spells out the rights and obligations of both parties in a franchise. It is a contract defining the precise, detailed conditions of the legal relationship between the franchisee and the franchisor. Its length, terms, and complexity will vary from one franchise and industry to another, in order to maintain the delicate balance of power between franchisees and franchisors.[11] It may or may not be possible for you to negotiate the contents of the contract, depending on how long the franchisor has been established and the current market conditions.

You should remember that the franchisor wrote the contract and that most of the conditions contained in it are weighted in the franchisor's favor. Read it carefully yourself, but never sign a franchise agreement without getting your lawyer's opinion. Make sure your attorney and accountant have experience with franchising. Some of the most important topics that you should understand in franchise agreements are fees to be paid, how the agreement can be terminated or renewed, and your rights to exclusive territory.

FRANCHISE, ROYALTY, AND ADVERTISING FEES. The **franchise fee** is the amount of money you have to pay to become a franchisee. Some agreements require you to have a percentage of the total franchise fee from a nonborrowed source, meaning that you can't borrow it. Agreements may or may not allow you to form a corporation to avoid personal liability.

franchise fee The one-time payment made to become a franchisee.

Royalty fees are usually a percentage of gross sales that you pay to the franchisor. Remember that royalties are calculated from gross sales, not from profits. If your business generates $350,000 of sales and the royalty fee is 8 percent, you have to pay $28,000 to the franchisor whether you make a profit or not. And you still have all your other operating expenses to cover.

royalty fee The ongoing payments that franchisees pay to franchisors—usually a percentage of gross sales.

When comparing two franchises, look at the combination of franchise fees and royalties. For example, franchise X charges $25,000 for the franchise fee and 10 percent royalty (not including advertising fees), and franchise Y charges a $37,500 franchise fee with 5 percent royalty (no advertising fees either). Assume that gross sales for each franchise would be $250,000 per year. The total fee you would pay for either would be $50,000 for the first year. But for each year after the first, you would pay $25,000 ($250,000 × 10%) with franchise X and only half that with franchise Y ($250,000 × 5%).

If the franchise agreement requires you to pay advertising fees, you want to be sure that a portion of the fee goes to local advertising in your area. If you operate a

Training

Providing excellent training in all areas of operating a franchise isn't only one of the benefits of franchising, it's an absolute necessity for both franchisor and franchisee to succeed. For a service franchise, training in outstanding customer service is one of the most important topics to be covered. American Leak Detection is a company that looks for leaks of any type in businesses and homes, and corrects them. When the company, based in Palm Springs, California, began franchising in the mid-1980s, founder and president Dick Rennick recognized how important it was to provide franchisees with a strong program of customer service training. "We're a lot more high tech than baking a cookie. We have to make sure the customer is treated properly." The company's training program for franchisees is intense. It's six weeks long, 50 hours a week. And during five of those weeks, new franchisees are out in the field actually going to job sites around the country. A 90-day home-study program follows this hands-on training. The benefit of this type of extensive customer service training is the payoff in satisfied customers, whose demand for the services provided by American Leak Detection continues to grow.

creating competitive advantage

Source: Echo Montgomery Garrett, "Why Franchising Works: Training and Support," *Inc.*, September 1995, 88–95.

franchise on the outer geographic fringe of the franchise's operations, the franchisor could spend all of your advertising dollars where there is a greater concentration of other franchises, but none of *your* customers.

When it comes to total fees in franchising, you generally get what you pay for, and if a deal looks too good to be true (unlimited potential earnings with no risk), it probably is.[12]

TERMINATION OF THE FRANCHISE AGREEMENT. The agreement should state how you as the franchisee may lose your franchise rights. Also described should be the franchisee's obligations if you choose to terminate the agreement. Make sure the franchisor must have to show "good cause" to terminate the agreement. Because some states require this clause, it means there must be a good reason to discontinue the deal.

TERMS AND RENEWAL OF AGREEMENT. This section identifies how long the agreement is in effect and the renewal process. Most franchises run from 5 to 15 years. Will you have to pay a renewal fee, or possibly worse, negotiate a whole new franchise agreement? Because fees and royalties are generally higher for well-established franchises, your royalties and fees would probably go up if you have to sign a new agreement 10 years from now.

EXCLUSIVE TERRITORY. You need to know the geographical size of the territory and the exclusive rights the franchisee would have. Franchisors may identify how many franchises a territory can support without oversaturation and then issue that many, regardless of specific locations. Rights of first refusal, advertising restrictions, and performance quotas for the territory are addressed in this section.[13]

This issue of exclusive territory is the subject of much controversy in the franchising world. Patrick Leddy, Jr., had run a Baskin-Robbins franchise for 13 years when he learned that the franchisor was planning to open a new store less than two miles away from his. He protested, but Baskin-Robbins opened the store anyway. Leddy's sales plunged. He tried to sell his store but could not find a buyer because of his declining sales. Many franchisees are using examples like Leddy's to call for a federal law to prevent what they call widespread unfair treatment by franchisors.[14]

In reviewing the franchise opportunity, a potential franchisee should gather and verify the accuracy of the information included in the franchise agreement and all other information provided by the franchisor. This process is called **due diligence.** It means doing your homework and investigating the franchise on your own, rather than accepting everything the franchisor says at face value. This is a big commitment, so investigate. Some information you can find yourself; some you will need professional assistance to gather and interpret.

due diligence The process of thoroughly investigating the accuracy of information before signing a franchise (or any other) agreement.

Get Professional Advice

Consult a lawyer and a CPA *before* you sign any franchise agreement. Ask your accountant to read the financial data in the company's disclosure statements to determine whether the franchisor would be able to meet its obligation to you if you buy

Communication Is the Key

The franchisor-franchisee relationship is unique in the world of business. Jan Kirkham and Timothy McGowan of Management 2000, a franchise consulting firm, have examined hundreds of franchises at every stage of development and have concluded that most problems between franchisors and franchisees result from misunderstandings about their relationship. Often, neither fully understands what is expected of the other. They recommend that franchisors communicate the following points to franchisees:

- Unit-to-unit consistency is imperative to the success of franchising. Each franchise must look, act, and feel like all the others to the customers. Lack of consistency dilutes the investment made by all franchisees in the system, because uniformity is a large part of what they are buying.

- Franchisees are not competitors, even if they are located in the same market. All parties involved in the agreement need to work as a team to develop the franchise name. An advantage that franchises have over independent businesses is the *synergy* that is created in a strong franchise system. Synergy exists when the total output is greater than the sum of the individual inputs; that is, $2 + 2 = 5$.

- The franchisor and franchisee have an interdependent relationship. Each side must accept responsibility and accountability for the success of the system. The franchisor is not responsible for making the franchisee successful. Effort and trust must flow in both directions.

- The franchisee must understand the purpose of the initial franchise fee and the ongoing royalty fees. The initial franchise fee protects the franchisee by covering the expenses of selecting quality franchisees; training and support of franchisees prior to opening; covering costs of developing and organizing the franchise and related systems; paying for trademark and trade name registration and protection; and ensuring compliance with various laws. The royalty fees are paid from generated revenue, because the use of the franchisor's brand name attracts customers and the operating system gets customers to come back, whereas the support services provided by the franchisor help the franchisee acquire and develop the ability to use the brand name and operating system to get and keep customers.

Source: Adapted from Jan Kirkham and Timothy McGowan, "Strengthening and Supporting the Franchise System," in *The Franchising Handbook* (New York: AMACOM American Management Association, 1993), 297.

creating competitive advantage

a franchise. Then ask a lawyer who is familiar with franchise law to inform you of all your rights and obligations contained in the franchise agreement—it *is* negotiable, but you have to push. Query your lawyer about any state or local laws that would affect your franchise. The cost of consulting professionals is small compared to the amount of time and money you will invest in a franchise. Do not assume that the disclosure statement tells you everything you need to know about the franchise. That is not the intent of the document.

■ International Franchising

Overseas franchising has become a major activity for U.S. companies faced with constantly increasing levels of domestic competition. Companies like KFC, Pizza Hut, and Taco Bell are signing almost no new franchises domestically, but are still rapidly adding foreign operations.[15]

Ray Kroc, who built McDonald's into a franchise giant, once said, "Saturation is for sponges." What Kroc was saying is that by expanding less crowded or underserved markets, you can increase sales and profits.

Canada is a growing market for U.S. franchises because it is close and its markets are similar. With the passage of the North American Free Trade Agreement (NAFTA), franchise opportunities in Mexico are expected to increase. For example, TCBY Enterprises is quickly opening stores in Mexico after the agreement ended the 20 percent import duty on yogurt going into Mexico.[16] Both Eastern and Western European and Pacific Rim countries (especially Taiwan, Thailand, Indonesia, and Singapore) are also attractive for franchise expansion. When expanding abroad, franchisors must be sensitive to the demographic, economic, cultural, and legal climates of the host country.[17]

The success of U.S. franchises is spreading all over the globe. In response, many governments are enacting legislation to regulate franchise operations. Following are some highlights of franchise legislation from a variety of countries:

■ *United States*. You have read throughout this chapter the federal legislation regarding disclosure statements, registration requirements, and restrictions on the sale and offering of franchises.

■ *Canada*. Unlike the United States, Canada has no federal legislation uniquely directed toward franchising. Only the province of Alberta has a specific franchise law, which relates to timely disclosure of information.

■ *France*. Although French law does not specify the word *franchising*, disclosure documents are required to be received by franchisees 20 days prior to execution of the franchise agreement.

■ *Mexico*. The Industrial Property Law calls for disclosure; however, the franchisor may, if desired, exclude any confidential information that would benefit a competing franchise system.

■ *Brazil*. Federal law does not seek to regulate the relationship between franchisor and franchisee, but again, the franchisee must receive full information at least 10 days before execution of franchise agreement.

■ *Spain*. In January 1996, the Spanish government enacted a Retail Trade Act that requires franchisors to register company name with federal government and disclose full information in writing to potential franchisees.

■ *Australia*. The Australian government enacted the Franchising Code of Conduct in 1998 to help franchisees make an informed decision.

■ *Indonesia*. The government of Indonesia passed a Government Regulation on Franchising in 1997 to provide order in the business of franchising and protection to consumers.

- *Russia.* The Civil Code of Russia regulates the contractual agreement between franchisors and franchisees.

- *Republic of China.* According to legislation passed in 1997, prospective franchisees must receive specific information at least ten days before signing an agreement.[18]

SUMMARY

▬▬ **What franchising is and how it operates.**

Franchising is a legal agreement that allows a franchisee to use a product, service, or method of the franchisor in exchange for fees and royalties. A franchisee is an independent businessperson who agrees to operate under the policies and procedures set up by the franchisor.

▬▬ **The difference between product (or trade-name) franchises and business-format franchises.**

Product or trade-name franchises allow the franchisee to purchase the right to use the trade name of the manufacturer and to buy or sell the manufacturer's products. Business-format franchises allow the franchisee to duplicate the franchisor's way of doing business.

▬▬ **The advantages and disadvantages of franchising.**

Eight major advantages of franchising exist for the franchisee: proven product or service, marketing expertise, financial assistance, technical and managerial assistance, opportunity to learn, quality control standards, efficiency, and opportunity for growth. The primary disadvantages to the franchisee include fees and profit sharing, restrictions of freedom, overdependence, unsatisfied expectations, termination of the agreement, and performance of other franchisees.

▬▬ **Evaluating the franchise opportunity.**

When evaluating a franchise opportunity, send for a copy of the company's disclosure statement (the company is required to send it to you), research the company through business periodicals, talk to current and former franchisees, and check with the International Franchise Association.

▬▬ **Franchising in the international marketplace.**

Franchises are rapidly exploring international expansion when faced with saturated domestic markets. Foreign markets are often less crowded and more underserved.

QUESTIONS FOR **REVIEW & DISCUSSION**

1. What is the difference between a franchise, a franchisee, and a franchisor?

2. How would you explain the difference between franchises and other forms of business ownership?

3. Why would you prefer to buy a franchise rather than start a new business or buy an existing business?

4. Why is franchising important in today's economy?

5. What is the difference between product or trade-name franchises and business-format franchises? Give an example for each that has not been cited in the text.

6. What are the biggest advantage and the biggest disadvantage of franchising? Justify your answer.

7. What do you expect to get in return for paying a franchise fee?

8. What is a royalty fee?

9. Is the disclosure statement the *only* source of information you need to check out a potential franchise? Why or why not?

10. In reading topics included in a franchise agreement, who do you think controls most of the power in a franchise: the franchisee or the franchisor? Explain.

11. What are the potential sources of conflict between franchisees and franchisors?

12. You are worried that someone else will buy a specific franchise in your area before you do. Would it be all right to sign the franchise agreement before talking to your lawyer or accountant if you intend to meet with them later? Explain.

13. If you are the franchisee of a bookstore and are offered twice the business's book value, should you or the franchisor collect the additional money? Take a position and justify it.

14. What do you think will be the growth areas (in products, services, and geographical areas) for franchises in the near future?

QUESTIONS FOR **CRITICAL THINKING**

1. Explain how a franchise could be considered a partnership. What makes a franchise agreement simpler than a partnership that you would start with another individual?

2. After having read about entrepreneurship in Chapter 2, would you consider someone who buys a franchise an entrepreneur? Does franchising stifle entrepreneurship?

Contact a local franchise owner and set up an appointment to visit. Ask if you can see a copy of the franchise agreement, or at least discuss the terms and conditions of the agreement with the franchisor.

Experience this...

WHAT WOULD **YOU** DO? No. 1

Say you're convinced that purchasing a franchise is your method of choice for becoming a small business owner. Before you jump in, though, you'd better do your homework. For this exercise, we'll first present some basic information about two possible franchise operations, then it's your turn.

Snip 'N Clip (SNC Franchise Corporation). This franchisor began business in 1958 and started franchising in 1985. Its business is providing all kinds of hair care procedures. There are 84 locations throughout the United States, 43 of which are owned by franchisees. The initial franchise fee is $10,000, and total investment ranges from $50,950 to $58,450. The company doesn't offer financing.

Yogen Fruz Worldwide. This frozen yogurt dessert finished number one in *Entrepreneur* magazine's 1999 Franchise 500. Yogen Fruz began franchising in 1987, selling frozen yogurt and ice cream. There are 4,879 independent franchises and 17 company-owned ones in 2000. There is a $25,000 franchise fee and royalties of 6 percent Startup costs range from $25,000 to $250,000. The company offers financing for franchise fee, startup costs, equipment, and inventory.

QUESTIONS

1. Of the two franchises presented, draft a business plan outline for the one that you would be interested in.

2. Divide the class into teams to discuss the merits and potential drawbacks of each of these franchises.

WHAT WOULD **YOU** DO? No. 2

Tricon Global Restaurants is the franchisor for KFC, Taco Bell, and Pizza Hut. Having 29,000 franchises in 83 countries makes communication difficult. Most franchisors assemble bulky three-ring binders mailed to franchisees and maintain a phone line for franchisees to call with questions and problems. Tricon recently developed a Brand Toolkit CD-ROM software which includes extensive volumes of marketing data, digitized images, and forms. The software contains historical and current trademark materials; point-of-purchase materials, including instructions on building menu boards; primary and secondary market research data, including questionnaires for franchisees to use; and a help section.

QUESTIONS

1. What benefits does the Brand Toolkit provide to franchisees? to the franchisor?

2. The Brand Toolkit is a major improvement over three-ring binders and phone calls, but what other tools or techniques could improve communications between franchisees and franchisors?

CHAPTER CLOSING CASE   No. 5

Flapjack Chain Runs Out of Dough

One thing Sytje's Pannekoeken Huis Family Restaurants never lacked was name recognition. The chain of casual-dining establishments was well-known for its puffy pancakes, windmill-kitsch décor, and waitresses decked out in Dutch-style skirts and bodices. But as financial troubles mounted in the 1990s the 15-restaurant chain's low revenues matched its low-country motif. Starting in 1991, the company lost money every year on flat revenues of approximately $10.5 million. Last year, Pannekoeken finally removed its finger from the dike and was washed away by Chapter 7 liquidation.

Company CEO Todd Novaczyk, a former Wendy's franchise owner, had bought the Pannekoeken restaurants, based in Edina, Minnesota, with the help of a partner in 1983, expanding them from four company restaurants to ten. The company also had five franchisees. But while Pannekoeken did a brisk breakfast trade, it faced the challenge, common to many family restaurants, of increasingly lackluster dinner sales.

Former Pannekoeken employees describe Novaczyk, who did not return *Inc.'s* calls, as a likable, caring boss, who prior to the 1990s had paid scrupulous attention to the business. "We had no problem dealing with Todd back then," says Tasos Psomas, who still operates a Pannekoeken restaurant in Rochester, Minnesota, as an independent business, "The restaurants were busy; advertising was nice; menu changes and development were coming down all the time."

But in the early 1990s, restaurant managers and franchise owners witnessed a drop in corporate quality checks, less attention to detail, and a dearth of effective advertising. That happened about the same time that the corporation was pursuing acquisitions and new dining concepts that it hoped would boost revenues.

In late 1993 Novaczyk announced his intent to purchase a small bar-and-grill chain in Seattle called Yankee Diner. The deal to convert some Pannekoeken restaurants to Yankee Diners fell through in 1994, but the plan revealed the company president's new attitude.

"Novaczyk was really intent on an acquisition strategy, but he didn't have his base covered," says Dick Lee, a marketing consultant who worked with Pannekoeken in 1993 and 1994. "Pannekoeken was his only base, and it needed a lot of attention."

Another acquisition plan fell through in 1994, the same year that Pannekoeken lost $2 million. Soon franchisees began to mutiny, refusing to pay franchise fees. Then in March 1996, the Minnesota Department of Revenue delivered a deathblow when it raided Pannekoeken's corporate-owned restaurants, seizing money and, in some cases, furniture and equipment to satisfy a $300,000 sales-tax debt.

The company filed for Chapter 11 the day after the highly publicized raid. Business dropped 50 to 60 percent and Chapter 7 liquidation followed six months later.

Today four former Pannekoeken franchisees are still doing business independently while corporate assets are in the hands of a bankruptcy trustee, who is sorting through a long list of creditors.

One creditor is waitress Kathleen Contons, who claims she's owed $2,000 in wages. She also never recovered her good winter coat, which was locked inside the restaurant where she had worked for nine years. But, Contons says, "more than anything else I was hurt because I didn't get to say good-bye to my customers."

Source: "Obit: Flapjack Chain Runs Out of Dough", by Tom Fudge, from *Inc.: The Magazine for Growing Companies,* Oct. 1, 1997, 25. Copyright (c) 1997 by Goldhirsh Group Inc Pubg. Reproduced with permission of Goldhirsh Group Inc Pubg in the format textbook via Copyright Clearance Center

QUESTIONS

1. How does this case illustrate problems associated with franchises from both the franchisee and franchisor perspectives?

2. What was the primary cause of death of this business? Secondary cause? What could have been done to prevent bankruptcy?

6

Taking Over an Existing Business

After reading this chapter, you should be able to:

- Compare the advantages and disadvantages of buying an existing business.

- Propose ways of locating a suitable business for sale.

- Identify ways to measure the condition of a business and determine why a business would be sold.

- Differentiate tangible and intangible assets, and assess the value of each.

- Calculate the price to pay for a business.

- Describe what makes a family business different from other types of business.

IN THE MID–1940s, Paul Bardeen came up with a way to make jack-o'-lanterns better than the boring old traditional triangle-shaped eyes and nose. Bardeen wanted to make Halloween special for his children, so he used his creativity and innovation to make pumpkin carvings intricate and exotic by using drills and small saws. The Bardeen family shared their methods of creating vegetable masterpieces with friends and family. Local newspapers featured their creations, and the tradition continued.

When Paul died in 1983, his son, John, a Denver business owner, decided that he and his sisters, Dione, Janice, Pat, and Kathie, would begin selling pumpkin-carving kits as a tribute to their father. The kits included instructions, patterns, and plastic saws, drills, and scrapers. In 1986, a test market of 6,000 kits did well enough to warrant hiring a Chicago marketing company and a national public relations firm that forecast 1987 sales of 600,000 kits. Armed with such hopeful numbers, Pumpkin Masters borrowed $425,000 to produce 235,000 kits. Sales were a disaster. The marketing firm sold only 50,000 kits. The PR firm generated little PR. Kits were piled up in a warehouse, 10 percent of them with no saw blades.

Some fast talking and family action convinced bankers to extend the terms of their loan. They quickly fired the marketing and PR firms, hired their own sales representatives, and began inspecting the contents of each kit. The company took off the very next year when a customer stepped up with volunteer public relations work. By not taking "no" for an answer, this customer convinced the ABC television network to show pumpkins carved with portraits of *Monday Night Football* announcers when the Denver Broncos played the Indiana Colts on Halloween night. Sales took off due to this publicity. The Bardeen family did not forget the origin of Pumpkin Masters' success. Each year they carve 300 promotional pumpkins of celebrities like Jay Leno, Katie Couric, Rosie O'Donnell, and Elvis, and works of art from *American Gothic* to the Mona Lisa, which are seen on TV, newspapers, magazines, and at events across the country every October.

Because they are a privately held company, they don't have to release financial figures, but 1998 sales were up to 2 million kits. They were honored in 1998 with a nomination for the Blue Chip Enterprise Initiative award for small businesses that have overcome challenges. No doubt their father would be proud of the accomplishments and cooperation of these siblings. Does it really get any better than that?

Sources: Thomas Love, "Creating Demand for a New Product," *Nation's Business,* August 1998, 11; and Pumpkin Masters company information.

▬ The Business Buyout Alternative

> *Existing businesses must be scrutinized carefully to determine whether they are a worthy investment of your time and money.*

Say you are a prospective small business owner. You possess the necessary personal qualities, managerial ability, and capital to run a business, but you haven't decided on the approach you should take to get into business. If you aren't inheriting a family business, then you have three choices for getting started: You may buy out an existing establishment, acquire a franchised business, or start a new firm yourself. This chapter will discuss the many factors to be considered in buying an existing business and taking over a family business.

Advantages of Buying a Business

The opportunity to buy a firm already in operation appears attractive for a number of reasons. Like franchising, it offers a way to avoid some beginners' hazards.[1] The existing firm is already functioning—maybe even a proven success. Many of the typical serious problems should have been either avoided or corrected by now. It appears to be like a ship after its "shakedown cruise," a new automobile after the usual small adjustments have been made, or a computer program that has been "debugged."

Buying an existing business is becoming a more popular way for people to own a small business. In a recent year, over 250,000 businesses valued at less than $5 million each changed hands.[2]

There are several advantages to buying an existing business as compared with the other methods of getting into business. Because customers are used to doing business with the company at its present address, they are likely to continue doing so once you take over. If the business has been making money, you will break even

	TABLE 6.1
Advantages	**The Advantages and Disadvantages of Buying a Business**
1. Established customer base at present location	
2. Customers familiar with location	
3. Planning can be based on known historical data.	
4. Supplier relationship already in place	
5. Inventory and equipment in place	
6. Experienced employees	
7. Possible owner financing	
Disadvantages	
1. Image difficult to change	
2. Employees may be ones whom you would not choose.	
3. Business may not have operated the way you like and could be difficult to change.	
4. Possibly obsolete inventory and equipment	
5. Financing costs could drain your cash flow and threaten the business's survival.	
6. The business's location may be undesirable, or a good location may be about to become not so good.	
7. Potential liability for past business contracts	

sooner than if you start your own business from the ground up. Your planning for an ongoing business can be based on actual historical figures, rather than relying on projections, as with a startup. Your inventory, equipment, and suppliers are already in place, managed by employees who already know how to keep the business going. Financing may be available from the owner. If the timing of the deal occurs when you are ready to buy a business and the owner needs to sell for a legitimate reason, you may get a bargain (see Table 6.1).

Disadvantages of Buying a Business

Or is this business that you're considering, in fact, more like a used car that is a "lemon"? Most people don't sell their cars until they feel they need considerable mechanical attention. Is the same true of selling businesses?

There are disadvantages to buying an existing business as a way to become your own boss. The image of the business already exists and is difficult to change. The employees who come with the business may not be the ones whom you would choose to hire. The previous owners have established precedents that may be difficult to change. The way the business operates may be outmoded. The inventory or equipment may be outdated. The purchase price may create a burden on future cash flow and profitability. You may pay too much for the business due to misrepresentation or inaccurate appraisal. The business's facilities or location may not be the best. You may be held liable for contracts left over from previous owners.

Do . . . Due Diligence

A new facet of entrepreneurship is evolving as entrepreneurs look to buy rather than start businesses. As a buyout entrepreneur, preparation is the key to a successful business purchase. You need to analyze your own skills, find good advisors, write a business plan, and, most importantly, do "due diligence."

Due diligence begins with the overall financial health of the company. What trends have occurred with revenues, expenses, and profit margins? Have they grown, stagnated, or declined? Are the products going to be made obsolete in the foreseeable future? If the small business does not have audited financial statements signed by an accountant (and many don't) then insist on seeing the owner's tax returns (because it's harder to lie about those). Beyond financials, check the local county courthouse to look for any existing or pending litigation or liens filed against the business or owners. The Better Business Bureau can tell you about past or current complaints.

Vern Crosby almost cut corners in due diligence and came close to paying quite a price. Crosby was in charge of marketing for a Maryland-based company that provided facilities, janitorial, and grounds maintenance for military bases across the United States. The company's annual revenue was $1 million when Crosby started, and because of his marketing skills, sales shot to $8.5 million, then $15 million within five years. The partner owners began fighting and announced they wished to part ways. They offered Crosby right of first refusal to purchase the business.

Given his track record with the company, Crosby thought he knew everything he needed. He conducted his own appraisal. He received input from an accountant and a mentor, but no one else, not even a lawyer. Bad move. Crosby's offer of $2 million was accepted for assets valued at $600,000 plus $1.2 million of debt.

If you understand anything about purchasing a business, catch this—if you purchase the stock of a business, you're getting not just the assets but all the liabilities, debt, litigation, and history of the company. Vern Crosby just about got caught on this point.

Crosby found out that the company he planned to buy hadn't been paying its vendors, so he began digging deeper. He had a hard time tracking cash flow through the business, because the owners had been commingling money among several businesses they owned. He says, "They were robbing Peter to pay Paul. It was a nightmare once you got into it." Amazingly, he was still anxious to buy. Finally, the banks that were providing financing found that the tax debt was actually over $1 million, rather than the $250,000 stated. That killed the deal.

Ironically, the feuding owners' sons co-owned two businesses, and they, too, were fighting—to the point where they wanted out. Crosby learned his lessons about due diligence the first time and conducted proper investigation with the help of an accountant and an acquisitions attorney to handle the valuation. He ended up purchasing both businesses and continues to run them separately.

Source: Joyce Jones, "Shopping for an Enterprise," *Black Enterprise,* September 1998, 75–83.

How Do You Find a Business for Sale?

If you have decided that you're interested in purchasing an existing business and have narrowed your choices down to a few types of businesses to consider, how do you locate one to buy? Perhaps you are currently employed by a small business. Is there a chance that it may be available sometime soon? Because you know the inner workings of the business, it might be a good place to start. Newspaper advertising is a traditional place for someone who is actively trying to sell a business to start. Don't stop your quest with the newspaper, however, because many good opportunities don't get advertised. Word of mouth through friends and family may turn up businesses that don't appear to be available through formal channels.

People who counsel small businesses on a regular basis, such as bankers, lawyers, accountants, and Small Business Administration representatives, can be good sources for finding firms for sale. Real estate brokers often have listings for business opportunities, which include real estate and buildings.

Don't overlook a direct approach to finding a business. If you have been a regular customer of an establishment and have an attraction to it, why not politely ask the owner if he or she has ever thought of selling it? The timing may be perfect if the owner is considering a move to another part of the country or is exploring another new business. Perhaps this is an unlikely way to find a business, but what do you have to lose by asking?

Nearly every city has one or more **business brokers.** Most inspect and appraise a business establishment offered for sale before listing and advertising it. Some also assist a buyer in financing the purchase, but not all of them will provide you with the same level of service. A few will work very hard for you in trying to find a business that matches your talents and needs. Most will tell you what is available at the moment, but not much more than that. Some will do you more harm than good. Remember, business brokers normally receive their commission from the seller, so their loyalty is to the seller—not to you.

Unfortunately for prospective buyers, however, something approaching a "business opportunities racket" has developed in many cities: the practice of selling unprofitable businesses to unwary buyers who are usually inexperienced in running a business. The ruse is most common in the retail field, where a single business unit can wreck a dozen or more owners through successive sales and resales to a steady stream of newcomers, each confident that he or she can succeed where others have failed. Naturally, the brokers who promote these sales make more commission the more frequently the business changes hands. Check for recommendations from bankers, accountants, and other businesspeople who have used the broker in the past. You need to be on guard to keep from being included among that group immortalized by the late P. T. Barnum, who allegedly said, "There's a sucker born every minute."

Brokers take classes and pass examinations to become certified business intermediaries (CBIs). To find a reliable business broker, contact the International Business Brokers Association at 118 Silver Hill Road, Concord, MA 01742, (508) 369-5254, or check www.ibba.org

To examine the ins and outs of buying an existing business, there are a couple of unique information sources on the Internet that you might find useful. One of these is the World M&A Network (found at http://raptor.cqi.com/MandA/). This site contains hundreds of listings of companies for sale, possible merger candidates, and corporate buyers. (The only possible drawback is that this network focuses on midsized companies.) Another source is the National SBDC (Small Business Development Center) Research Network (found at http://www.smallbiz.sunycentral.edu/). This site provides information to Small Business Development Centers about small business and entrepreneurial opportunities. And don't forget to link to the Better Business Bureau (http://www.bbb.org/bbb) to check the business scams that are currently described.

> *Don't overlook the direct approach to finding a business for sale. If you are attracted to a business where you have been a customer, why not politely ask the owner if he or she has thought of selling?*

business broker A business that brings sellers of their businesses together with potential buyers.

Shopping for a Business Online

Bored with shopping for a business to buy the old-fashioned ways, like with classified ads and business brokers? Then, of course, go online. While browsing through www.allbusiness.com (another great information source for small business), I clicked on "Buying a Business" and found my way to www.bizbuysell.com. It proved to be a very comprehensive site for buying or selling a business.

Bizbuysell.com turns out to be a database of over 10,000 established businesses for sale. You begin by choosing where you want your business to be. All 50 states, plus Africa, Asia, Australia/New Zealand, Canada, the Caribbean, Central America, Europe, and South America, are represented. Next, you choose the type of business you are looking for. You can choose all SIC codes or pick from 17 retail, 20 service, 20 manufacturing, 2 wholesale, 3 construction, 8 transportation, 7 finance, and several other miscellaneous categories.

The information concerning the 10,000 businesses on bizbuysell.com is well organized and thorough. No teasers or blind leads. You are told current business location and what the business does. Asking price, annual gross revenue, and cash flow are posted at the top of each page. You get a summary description of the business, year established, number of employees, market outlook, competition, terms of sale, reason for selling the business, and contact information.

This is a fun and informative site, whether you are just shopping around or seriously in the market for a business. If you are ready to take the big step but want more information, you can purchase a *Buyer's Workbook* from bizbuysell.com. This workbook includes worksheets for cash requirements and pricing, plus checklists for site visits, due diligence, disclosure, and closing.

Sources: www.allbusiness.com and www.bizbuysell.com

▬ What Do You Look For in a Business?

To successfully analyze the value of any business, you should have enough experience to recognize specific details that are most relevant in this type of business. You need enough knowledge to take information provided by sales, personnel, or financial records and both evaluate the past performance of the business and predict probable future developments. You need objectivity in order to avoid excess enthusiasm that might blind you to the facts. Don't let emotions cloud your decisions.

At a minimum, you should ask the following questions to gather information about the business you consider buying:

- How long has the business existed?
  - Who founded it?
  - How many owners has it had?
  - Why have others sold out?
- What is the profit record?
  - Is profit increasing or decreasing?
  - What are the true reasons for the increase or the decrease?

- What is the condition of the inventory?
  - Are the goods new or obsolete?

- Is the equipment in good condition?
  - Who owns it?
  - Are there liens against any of it?
  - How does it compare with competitors' equipment?

- How long does the lease run?
  - Is it a satisfactory lease?
  - What are its conditions?
  - Can it be renewed?

- Are there dependable sources of supply?
  - Are any franchises or other special arrangements expiring soon?

- What about present and future competition?
  - Are new competitors or substitute materials or methods visible on the horizon?

- What is the condition of the area around the business?
  - Are traffic routes or parking regulations likely to change?

- Does the present owner have family, religious, social, or political connections that have been important to the success of the business?

- Why does the present owner want to sell?
  - Where will he or she go?
  - What is he or she going to do?
  - What do people (customers, suppliers, local citizens) think of the present owner and of the business?

- Are personnel satisfactory?
  - Are key people willing to remain?

- How does this business, in its present condition, compare with one that you could start and develop yourself in a reasonable amount of time?[3]

General Considerations

If you aspire to entrepreneurship by buying out an existing business, don't be rushed into a deal. Talk with the firm's banker and verify account balances with its major customers and creditors. Be sure you get any verbal understanding in writing from the seller.

Put the earnest money in escrow with a reputable third party. Before an agreement to purchase is signed, have all papers checked by your accountant and attorney.

If the business you are buying involves inventory, you need to be familiar with the bulk sales provisions of the Uniform Commercial Code. The law varies from state to state, but it generally requires a seller to provide a list of all business creditors and amounts due to each buyer. Then you as the buyer must notify each creditor that the business is changing hands. This protects you from claims against the merchandise previously purchased.

manager's
notebook

Look Before You Leap

Businesses constantly change hands and have for hundreds of years. But the process of buying a business is no less confusing now than it ever has been. The following steps are a compilation of answers from experts in the business-selling world to questions like: How do I find the right company? How much should I pay for it? What should I watch for? The common thread that runs through the comments is that business buyers rarely think hard enough about the real personal and professional questions they should be asking. The outcome of their search ends up focusing on timing and opportunity (read "luck") instead of on a clear understanding of the role the business will play in their life.

1. Make sure you shouldn't be starting a company instead of buying an existing business.

2. Determine the kind of business you want and whether you're capable of running it.

3. Consider the lifestyle involved in running your own business.

4. Consider the location. Where in the world, country, state, and town do you want to be for a long time?

5. After you've determined the kind of business you're after, find the right company.

6. Have lenders lined up in advance.

7. Choose the right seller. (If it's so great, why does the owner want out?)

8. Do research before setting the initial price.

9. Make sure your letter of intent is specific.

10. Don't skimp on due diligence.

11. Be skeptical.

12. Don't forget to assess the employees.

13. Make sure the final price reflects the real value.

Source: Jay Finegan, "The Insider's Guide," *Inc.*, October 1991, 27–36.

Why Is the Business Being Sold?

When the owner of a business decides to sell it, the reasons the owner tells prospective buyers may be somewhat different from those known to the business community, and both of these may be somewhat different from the actual facts. There are at least as many factors that could contribute to the sale of a business as there are reasons for business liquidations. Be careful. Business owners who are aware of future problems (such as a lost contract for a strong line of merchandise or a new law that will affect the business unfavorably) may not tell you all that they know. For a prospective buyer, a discussion with the firm's customers and suppliers is recommended. Check with city planners about proposed changes in streets or routing of transportation lines that might have a serious effect on the business in the near future.

Although anyone can be misled or defrauded, a savvy business buyer with good business sense will rely on his or her ability to analyze the market, judge the competitive situation, and estimate the profits that could be made from the business, rather than rely on the present owner's reasons for selling. These "reasons" are often too hard to verify.

Financial Condition

A study of the financial statements of the business will reveal how consistently the business has rewarded its previous owner's efforts. As a perspective purchaser, you must answer several questions. Will this income be satisfactory to you and your family? If it is not, could that income be increased? You will want to compare the firm's operating ratios with industry averages in order to detect where costs could be reduced or more money is needed.

The seller's books alone should not be taken as proof of stated sales or profits. You should also inspect bank deposits for at least five years or for as long as the present owner has operated the business.

When analyzing the financial statements of the business, don't rely strictly on the most recent year of operation. Profits can be artificially pumped up and expenses cut temporarily for almost every business. Check to see if the business employs the same number of people as in previous years; most businesses can operate short-handed for a while to cut labor expenses. Maintenance on equipment, vehicles, or the building can be cut to increase short-term profit figures. Profits that show on the books may also be overstated by insufficient write-off of bad debts, inventory shortages and obsolescence, and underdepreciation of the firm's fixed assets.

Ask to see the owner's tax returns. This shouldn't be a problem if everything is legitimate. Compare bills and receipts with sales tax receipts. Reconcile past purchases with the sales and markup claimed. Make certain that all back taxes have been paid. Make sure that interest payments and other current obligations are not in arrears.

Realize that the financial information that you need to analyze the business is sensitive information to the seller, especially if you two don't know each other. You can decrease the seller's suspicions about your using this information to aid a competing business or some other improper use by writing a letter of confidentiality.

INDEPENDENT AUDIT. Before any serious discussion of purchasing a business, an independent audit should be conducted. This will identify the condition of the financial statements. You will want to know whether the business's accounting practices are legitimate and its valuation of inventory, equipment, and real estate is realistic.

Even audited statements need some subjective interpretation. For example, owners may underreport their income for tax reasons. A family member may be on the payroll and paid a salary although unneeded by the business. Business owners who use a company car or a credit card for nonbusiness purposes also misrepresent their business expenses.

THE PROFIT TREND. Financial records of the business can tell you whether sales volume is increasing or decreasing. If it is going up, which departments or product

Letter of Confidentiality

Johnnie Bronco, CEO
Bronco Products, Inc.

Dear Mr. Bronco:

It was a pleasure to talk with you last week concerning the possible purchase of your produce business. Our conversation has brought my interest in your business to the point where I would like to examine your financial records for the past five years. With the company records I also wish to see tax returns filed for that period of time.

I realize that this information is confidential in nature and that you are concerned about improper use of these records. I assure you that I request this information strictly for the purpose of making a purchase decision regarding your business and the terms of the deal. The only persons to whom I will disclose this confidential information are my spouse, my attorney, and my accountant. I will obtain signed confidentiality statements from them before showing them your records.

I will return all of your records, including any copies made, within two weeks of their delivery to me. Thank you for your trust. I will not violate it, and I look forward to continuing our business transaction.

Sincerely,

James Rocky

---

lines account for the increased volume? Did the increased volume lead to increased profitability? Many businesses have failed by concentrating on selling volume goods at such low margins that making net profits was impossible.

If the sales volume is decreasing, is it due to the business's failure to keep up with competition or its inability to adjust to changing times? Or is the decline simply due to a lack of effective marketing?[4]

Interpret net profit of the business you are considering in terms of the amount of capital investment you will have to make in the business as well as sales volume. In other words, a $5,000 annual net profit from a business that requires a $10,000 investment and sales of $20,000 is much more attractive than a business that generates the same profit but requires a $100,000 investment and sales of $200,000.

THE EXPENSE RATIOS. Industry averages comparing expenses to sales exist for every size and type of business. Industrywide expense ratios are calculated by most trade associations, many commercial banks, accounting firms, university bureaus of business research, and firms like Dun & Bradstreet and Robert Morris Associates.

For example, Robert Morris Associates (RMA) publishes industry averages for 392 specific types of businesses (by SIC number) in manufacturing, wholesale, retail, and service sectors in *RMA Annual Statement Studies*.[5] Comparisons are made by percentages of assets, liabilities, and income data. RMA also provides industry averages of 16 common financial ratios, such as current ratio, quick ratio, sales/working capital, and sales/receivables. (These and other financial ratios are explained further in Chapter 8.)

Imagine you are interested in buying a health club. The location is good, the advertising has caught your attention for several months, and the equipment is state of the art. You are very excited about the possibilities and are now looking over the financial statements. You divide the total current assets by the total current liabilities to calculate the club's current ratio. You get a current ratio of 0.5, knowing that this figure shows the ability of a business to meet its current obligations. You want to get an idea of management performance, so you divide the profit before taxes by total assets and multiply by 100 (to convert to a percentage). This computation gives you 4.8 percent. You ask yourself, "Are a current ratio of 0.5 and an operating ratio of 4.8 percent good or bad for a health club?" They could be either. You need something to compare them with to tell you whether they are in line. You go to the library at a nearby university to compare your figures with RMA industry averages. You look in the RMA reports under "Service—Physical Fitness Facilities (SIC #7991)" and find the median current ratio listed at 0.9 and the median percentage profit before taxes divided by total assets at 7.5 percent. Your figures are well below industry average, so you decide you need to dig deeper to find out why such large deviations exist between the business you are interested in buying and the average for other similar-sized businesses in the health club industry.

Operating ratios are standards or guides for comparison. Their effective use depends on your ability to identify problems that exist and to change conditions that have caused any ratios to be appreciably below the standard.

OTHER MEASURES OF FINANCIAL HEALTH. Profit ratios are excellent indicators of a business's worth, but you should also examine other aspects of its financial health. A complete financial health examination consists of the calculation and interpretation of a variety of other financial ratios in addition to those relating to profit. Of particular interest to you and your accountant will be

1. The working capital and the cash flow of the business: Is there enough to adequately keep the business going?
2. The relationship between the firm's fixed assets and the owner's tangible net worth.
3. The firm's debt load or leverage.

What Are You Buying?

When buying an existing business, the value of that business comes from what the business owns (its assets and what it earns), its cash flow, and the factors that make the business unique, such as the risk involved (see Figure 6.1).

Tangible Assets

The **tangible assets** of a business, such as inventory, equipment, and buildings, are generally easier to place a fair market value on than intangible assets, such as trade names, customer lists, and goodwill.

tangible assets Assets that a business owns which can be seen and examined.

FIGURE 6.1

What Should You Pay?

The price you offer for a business should begin with adding the value of tangible and intangible assets to the profit potential of the business.

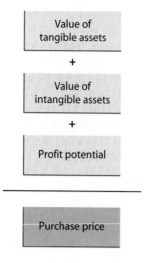

If the firm is selling its accounts receivable, you should determine how many of these are collectible and discount them accordingly. Receivables that are 120 days or older are not worth as much as those less than 30 days old, because the odds are greater that you will not collect them. This is called "aging accounts receivable." Of the other tangible assets of a business up for sale, inventories and equipment should be examined the most closely, because they are most likely to be outdated and therefore worth less than the seller is asking.

THE INVENTORY.   Inventory needs to be timely, fresh, and well balanced. An indication that the business has been well managed is an inventory of goods that people want, provided in the proper sizes, designs, and colors, and priced to fit the local buying power and purchasing habits.

Your biggest concern about inventory is that you aren't buying "dead" stock (merchandise that has no, or very little, value) that the seller has listed as being worth its original value. The loss in value of dead stock should be to the original buyer, and you must be sure that the loss is not passed on to you as part of the sale.

THE EQUIPMENT.   It is important that a business be equipped with current, usable machines and equipment. Book value for electronic office equipment, especially computers, becomes outdated quickly.[6] A cash register designed for the bookkeeping requirements of a generation ago will not record the information now required for tax reporting or scan UPC codes for efficient inventory control.

Often, the usefulness of the firm's equipment was outlived long ago and its value depreciated. The owner has delayed so long in replacing equipment that it has no trade-in value, and without this discount the owner finds the prices of new equipment to be exorbitant. This reason alone could lead to the decision to sell the business. Anything the owner makes on the fixtures and equipment is new, clear profit, an extra bonus on his period of operation.

The Declining Value of Aging Accounts Receivable

Accounts receivable represent cash that's owed to you. However, all accounts receivable are not equal. Those that have been owed to you the longest are worth the least because they are the least likely to be collected. In other words, the longer it takes someone to pay his or her account, the more likely it is that he or she is never going to pay it. Therefore, in valuing a business for sale, the cash value of long overdue accounts needs to be reduced to reflect the odds that they're not going to be paid. This process is called "aging accounts receivable." Let's look at a simple example.

Determining how much to reduce the value of old accounts should be based on the debtor company's past payment trends. In the hypothetical example of a company we'll call Fabio's Floral Wholesalers, let's say that accounts receivable 30 days and under have a 100 percent likelihood of being paid. Those accounts 31 days to 60 days old have had a 70 percent probability of being paid; those 61 days to 90 days old have had a 50 percent probability; and those over 90 days have had a 25 percent probability of being paid. Keep in mind that these percentages were determined by looking at the company's accounts receivable history—a fair and logical request to make of the business owner. Now let's see how the valuation process works.

Accounts Receivable	Probability Percentage	Book Value	Aged Value
30 days and under	100	$ 75,000	$ 75,000
31 to 60 days	70	50,000	35,000
61 to 90 days	50	30,000	15,000
Over 90 days	25	30,000	7,500
Total Value		$185,000	$132,500

You can see from this simple example that there's a significant difference in the aged value and the book value of the accounts receivable: $52,500! So when you're buying an existing business, play it smart and be sure to value accounts receivable accurately.

Sources: R. Lawrence Nicholson, "Aging Criteria Help Reduce Accounts Receivable," *Healthcare Financial Management,* June 1984, 56–58; and Calvin D. Byl, "Reporting Accounts Receivable to Management," *Business Credit,* October 1994, 43–44.

Intangible Assets

Businesses are also made up of **intangible assets** that may have real value to the purchaser. Among these are goodwill; favorable leases and other advantageous contracts; and patents, copyrights, and trademarks.

GOODWILL. **Goodwill** is an intangible asset that enables a business to earn a higher return than a comparable business with the same tangible assets might generate. Few businesses that are for sale have much goodwill value.

We all know businesses in existence for years that have not established enough goodwill for the average customer to see the business as being "special." If strong competition existed, such companies would have been driven out of business long

intangible assets Assets that have value to a business but are not visible.

goodwill The intangible asset that allows businesses to earn a higher return than a comparable business with the same tangible assets might generate.

DILBERT reprinted by permission of United Features Syndicate, Inc.

ago. From a consumer preference standpoint, they are at the bottom of the scale. This public attitude cannot be changed quickly. A good name can be ruined in far less time than it takes to improve a bad one.

A successful business has goodwill as an asset. Taking over a popular business brings with it public acceptance that has been built up over a period of many years, which is naturally valuable to the new owner.

LEASES AND OTHER CONTRACTS. A lease on a favorable location is a valuable business asset. If the selling firm possesses a lease on its building, or if it has any unfulfilled sales contracts, you should determine whether the lease and other contracts are transferable to you or whether they must be renegotiated.

PATENTS, COPYRIGHTS, AND TRADEMARKS. Intellectual property can also be a valuable intangible asset. Protection of your machine, process, or a combination of the two against unauthorized use or infringement lasts for only a limited period of time, after which they are open to use by others. Thus it is important for the prospective buyer of an existing business to determine precisely when the firm's patent rights expire and to value these rights based on the time remaining.

Copyrights offer the best protection for books, periodicals, materials prepared for oral presentation, advertising copy, pictorial illustrations, commercial prints or labels, and similar intellectual property. Unlike patent rights, copyrights are renewable.

Registered trademarks provide offensive rights against unauthorized use or infringement of a symbol, such as the Mercedes-Benz star or McDonald's arches, used in marketing goods. The function of trademarks is to identify specific products and to create and maintain a demand for those products. Because trademark protection lasts as long as the trademark is in continuous use, you should consider its value when purchasing a business that owns a trademark.

Personnel

When purchasing a business, the people working there must be considered just as important as profits and production. Retention of certain key people will keep a successful business going. New employees rarely come in as properly trained and steady workers. To help you estimate expenses related to finding, hiring, and training new employees, you will want to know if there are enough qualified people presently employed. Will any of these people depart with the previous owner? Are there any key individuals who may be unwilling or unable to continue working for you? The loss of a key person or two in a small business can have a serious impact on future earnings.

The Seller's Personal Plans

As a prospective purchaser of an existing business, you should not feel that all sellers of businesses have questionable ethical and moral principles. Just remember that "Let the buyer beware" has been a reliable maxim for years. There are laws against fraud and misrepresentation, but intent to defraud is usually very difficult to prove in court.

Reduce risk by writing protective clauses into contracts of sale, such as a **noncompete clause,** in which the seller promises not to enter the same kind of business as a competitor within a specified geographical area for a reasonable number of years. If the seller resists agreeing to such a clause, it may be a signal that he or she intends to enter into a similar business in the future.

noncompete clause A provision often included in a contract to purchase a business which restricts the seller from entering the same type of business within a specified area for a certain amount of time.

How Much Should You Pay? ▬

Even if you don't plan to buy an existing business, the methods of evaluating one are useful in appraising the success of any firm.

When you make a substantial financial investment in a business, you should expect to receive personal satisfaction as well as an adequate living. A business bought at the wrong price, at the wrong time, or in the wrong place can cost you and your family more than the dollars invested and lost. After you have thoroughly investigated the business, weighed the information collected, and decided that the business will satisfy your expectations, a price must be agreed on.

Determining the purchase price for a business involves several important factors: (1) valuation of the firm's tangible net assets; (2) valuation of the firm's intangible assets, especially any goodwill that has been built; (3) expected future earnings; (4) the market demand for the particular type of business; and (5) the general condition of the business (including completeness and accuracy of the records, employee esprit de corps, and physical condition of facilities).[7]

Approaches to valuing a business that focus on the value of the business's assets are called **balance sheet methods of valuation.** These are most appropriate for businesses that generate earnings primarily from their assets, rather than from the contributions of their employees. Approaches that focus more on the profits or cash flow a business generates are called **income statement methods of valuation.**

balance sheet method of valuation A method of determining the value of a business based on the worth of its assets.

income statement method of valuation A method of determining the value of a business based on its profit potential.

Tire Kicking for Beginners

In 1987, Lauren Karpinski, then the director of international trade and customs for accounting firm Arthur Andersen, faced a tough choice: to accept a transfer from her Orlando office or stay close to her family. Family ties won. "But I told my husband," she recalls, "that if I were going to leave a perfect job, I wanted to buy a business." Her second requirement was to buy it fast—within six weeks, while still on her employer's payroll.

So began the nightmare for the Karpinskis, who spent $750,000 to buy a Port Canaveral marina that was probably worth no more than $550,000. Their biggest error: They relied on financial numbers that were incomplete, vague, and in some cases downright inaccurate. Although Dolphin's Leap Marina is profitable today, with about $800,000 in annual revenues, the Karpinskis' experience provides a casebook lesson in how not to evaluate a possible purchase.

Karpinski admits that, despite her accounting firm background, she was naive, largely because she was so eager to do a deal. "We were given a compilation on an accountant's letterhead," she explains. (A compilation is simply a list of sales and other business results, without any elaborate information such as footnotes or accountants' opinions about the reliability of the numbers. A more thorough analysis—a limited financial review—applies generally accepted accounting standards. A full audit includes tests of the accuracy of line items such as inventory.)

The couple was easily satisfied, though, because the compilation "showed the correct trends," Karpinski recalls. But she concedes that "we didn't realize that the categories on the list were much too general and that all kinds of numbers were combined to hide losses." Case in point: Beer, bait, and tackle were listed on a single line, even though the margins and buying patterns for each were wildly different.

Also, the list of the marina's assets was inaccurate, and what's more, the Karpinskis didn't receive the list until the close. That left them with no time to physically verify the accuracy of asset valuations, which the couple never considered doing in any case. "There were items that didn't even belong to the marina. They belonged to vendors," Karpinski says. Other items were overvalued. One painful example: A compressor valued at more than $1,000 was a hollow shell. Worse, the Karpinskis relied on a single appraisal, which had valued the marina on its sales potential, not on realities such as current sales.

Karpinski's advice to others? "Insist on at least a limited financial review, and sit down with the company's accountant to make sure you understand every single line. If you can't talk to the accountant, don't do the deal."

She also urges that you "request a full list of assets prior to the closing and verify all important items. Make sure assets exist, that they don't belong to anyone else, that they work, and that they're worth what you're told they're worth." And she recommends obtaining at least two appraisals, reflecting more than one appraisal method.

What Are the Tangible Assets Worth?

As stated earlier, the worth of tangible assets is what the balance sheet method of valuation seeks to establish. Their value is determined according to

- *Book value.* What the asset originally cost or what it is worth from an accounting viewpoint; the amount shown on the books as representing the asset's value as a part of the firm's worth.

■ *Replacement value.* What it would cost to buy the same materials, merchandise, or machinery today; relative availability and desirability of new items must be considered.

■ *Liquidation value.* How much the seller could get for this business, or any part of it, if it were placed on the open market.

There are significant differences in these three approaches to determining value. Book value may not hold up in the marketplace. Buildings and equipment may not be correctly depreciated, whereas land may have appreciated. Replacement value may not be a reliable figure because of opportunities to buy used equipment. Replacement value is significant as a measure of value only in comparison to what it would cost to start your own business.

Liquidation value is the most realistic approach in determining the value of tangible assets to the buyer of a business. This value may represent the lowest figure that the seller would be willing to accept.

You have to determine the value of the following physical assets before serious bargaining can begin:

1. Cost of the inventory adjusted for slow-moving or dead stock
2. Cost of the equipment less depreciation
3. Supplies
4. Accounts receivable less bad debts
5. Market value of the building

Don't make an offer for a business based on the seller's asking price. You may feel as if you got a real bargain if you talk the seller down to half of what the seller is asking—but half might still be twice as much as the business is worth.[8]

What Are the Intangible Assets Worth?

An established business may be worth more than the sum of its physical assets, and its owner may be likely to be unwilling to sell for liquidation value alone. The value of a business's intangible assets is difficult to determine. Intangible assets are the product of a firm's past earnings, and they are the basis on which its earnings are projected.

Goodwill is the term used to describe the difference between the purchase price of a company and the net value of the tangible assets. Goodwill is the most difficult asset to set a value on that the seller will think is fair. It includes intangible, but very real, assets with real value to the prospective purchaser. Goodwill can be regarded as (1) compensation to the owner for his or her losses on beginner's mistakes you might have made if you started from scratch, and (2) payment for the privilege of carrying on an established and profitable business.[9] It should be small enough to be made up from profits within a reasonably short period.

What is goodwill worth? To determine a company's goodwill, you can start by using the income statement method of valuation. To do this you should capitalize your projected future earnings at an assumed rate of interest that would be in excess of the "normal" return (earnings adjusted to remove any unusual occurrences like a lawsuit settlement or a one-time gain from the sale of real estate) in that type and size of business. The capitalization rate is a figure assigned to show the risk and expected growth rate associated with future earnings.

For example, suppose that the liquidation value of the firm's tangible net assets is $224,000 and that the normal before-tax rate of return on the owner's investment in this business is 15 percent, or $33,600 per year. We will assume that the actual profit during the past few years has averaged $83,600, exclusive of the present owner's salary (which may have been overstated or understated).

From the profit, we will deduct a reasonable salary for the owner or manager—what he or she might earn by managing this type of business for someone else. If we assume a going-rate annual salary of $40,000, then the excess profit to be capitalized (that is, the amount of profit based on goodwill) is $10,000 ($83,600 minus $40,000 salary minus a normal profit of $33,600).

The rate of capitalization is negotiated by the buyer and the seller of the business. The capitalization rate should be appropriate to the risk taken. The more certain you are of the estimated profits, the more you will pay for goodwill. The less certain you are (the higher you perceive your risk to be) the less you will pay.

If you assume a 25 percent rate of return on estimated earnings coming from goodwill, then the value of the intangible assets is $10,000/0.25, or $40,000. Usually this relationship is expressed as a ratio or multiplier of "four times (excess) earnings." You would expect to recover the amount invested in goodwill in no more than four years. When you put these two figures together, you come up with an offering price of $264,000 for the business—net tangible assets of $224,000 at liquidation value plus goodwill valued at $40,000. The calculations for this price are shown in Table 6.2.

If the average annual net earnings of the business before subtracting the owner's salary (line 4) were $73,600 or less, then there would be no goodwill value. Even though the business may have existed for a long time, the earnings would be less than you could earn through outside investment. In that case, your price would be determined by capitalizing the average annual profit (net earnings minus all expenses and owner's salary) by the normal or expected rate of return on investment in this business. For example,

$$\$73,600 - \$40,000 = \$33,600 = \text{Profit}$$
$$\$33,600/0.15 = \$224,000 = \text{Offering Price}$$

Valuing goodwill is a highly subjective process. The value of intangible assets comes down to what you think they are worth and what you are willing to pay. You will need to negotiate with the seller to reach a consensus.

TABLE 6.2 **Calculating the Purchase Price of an Existing Business**		
1. Adjusted value of tangible net worth		$224,000
2. Earning power at 15%		$ 33,600
3. Reasonable salary for owner or manager		40,000
		$ 73,600
4. Average annual net earnings before subtracting owner's salary		$ 83,600
5. Extra earning power of business (line 4 − total of lines 2 and 3)		$ 10,000
6. Value of intangibles using four-year profit figure for moderately well established firm in (4 × line 5)		40,000
7. Offering price (line 1 + line 6)		$264,000

Buying Your Business ▬

To complete the purchase of your business, you need to negotiate the terms of the deal and prepare for the closing.

The Terms of Sale

After agreeing on a price for the business, the terms of sale need to be negotiated. Few buyers are able to raise the funds required to pay cash for a business. A lump-sum payment may be in neither the buyer's nor the seller's best interests for tax reasons, unless the seller intends to reinvest in another business. Paying in installments is often the most practical solution.

By building installment payments into your cash flow projection, you should be assured that the business can be paid for out of earnings. Installments assure the seller that his investment in the business will be returned on a tax-deferred basis, as opposed to paying all taxes at one time with a lump-sum payment. With an installment sale, the seller has some motivation to help with the buyer's success.

A seller may need to take steps to make the business more affordable. One way to do this is known as "thinning the assets." The seller can adjust the assets to be more manageable for the new owner in one or more of the following ways:

- Separate real estate ownership from business ownership. The new owner leases rather than purchases the building. The buyer has less to borrow, and the seller receives a steady rental income.

- Lease equipment and/or fixtures in the same manner as real estate.

- Sell off excess inventory.

- Factor accounts receivable or carry the old accounts.

Closing the Deal

When you and the seller have reached an agreement on the sale of the business, several conditions must be met to ensure a smooth, legal transaction. Closing can be handled by using either a settlement attorney or an escrow settlement.

A settlement attorney acts as a neutral party to draw up the necessary documents and represents both the buyer and the seller. Both parties meet with the settlement attorney at the agreed-upon closing date to sign the papers after all the conditions of the sale have been met, such as financing being secured by the buyer and a search completed to determine whether any liens against the business's assets exist.

In an escrow settlement, the buyer deposits the money, and the seller provides the bill of sale and other documents to an escrow agent. You can find an escrow agent at most financial institutions, such as banks and trusts that have escrow departments, or through an escrow company. The escrow agent holds the funds and documents until proof is shown that all conditions of the sale have been completed. When the conditions are met, the escrow agent releases the funds and documents to the rightful owners.

Taking Over a Family Business

> *Family businesses account for more than 50 percent of U.S. GDP.*

A fourth route into small business (besides starting from scratch, buying an existing business, or franchising) is taking over a family business. This alternative offers unique opportunities and risks.

What Is Different About Family Businesses?

Family businesses are characterized by two or more members of the same family who control, are directly involved in, and own a majority of the business. Family businesses make up 80 percent of all businesses in the United States and comprise nearly 50 percent of the nation's gross domestic product (GDP).[10] Family businesses are obviously an important part of our economy, but what makes them different from nonfamily businesses? Two factors are (1) the complex interrelationships of family members interacting with each other and interacting with the business, and (2) the intricate succession planning needed.

creating competitive advantage

Keeping the Family Fires Burning

It's one thing to create a competitive advantage in a business, and it's another to keep it into the third generation of ownership. But that's exactly what Barcelona, Spain–based Puig has done. Puig sells fashion goods, haute couture, and perfume, among other product lines. In 1998, it won the Distinguished Family Business World Award from the International Institute for Management Development of Lausanne, Switzerland. Puig is most noted for the governing system and unique protocols developed to run its 4,000-employee worldwide enterprise.

The founders of Puig developed a family council which now is composed of one representative from each branch of the second generation and one representative from the third generation (all of whom are over the age of 30). The council meets twice per year, creates standing family orders, and wrote a family handbook which is in essence a family business code of conduct for behavior and protocol. Included in the protocol is a rule that any family member who serves in an executive capacity must have a university degree and a minimum of five years' experience outside the company. There is a prohibition against in-laws serving on the board of directors. Other practices that set this family business apart are

- Each generation develops its own entrepreneurial way for the business.

- The third generation is further professionalizing top levels of management by adding a nonfamily senior manager.

- This round of the succession planning process (second to third generations) has lasted six years.

- Even before internationalization was common for Spanish businesses, Puig began a global strategy 35 years ago.

Source: Vivian Pospisil, "All in the Family," *Industry Week*, October 1998, 14. Reproduced by arrangement with Reprint Management Service.

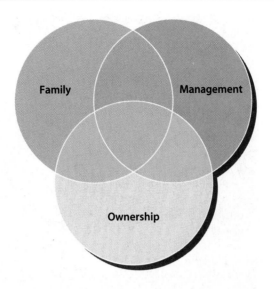

FIGURE 6.2
Family Business Perspectives

The family business owner views the business and what goes on within it from three different overlapping perspectives.

Complex Interrelationships

When you run a family business, you have three overlapping perspectives on its operation (see Figure 6.2).[11] For example, suppose a family member needs a job. From the family perspective, you would see this as an opportunity to help one of your own. From the ownership perspective, you might be concerned about the effect of a new hire on profits. From a management perspective, you would be concerned about how this hire would affect nonfamily employees.

Everyone involved in a family business will have a different perspective, depending on each one's position within the business. The successful leader of this business must maintain all three perspectives simultaneously.

Planning Succession

Many entrepreneurs dream of the time when they will be able to "pass the torch" of their successful business on to their children. Unfortunately, many factors, such as jealousy, lack of interest, or ineptitude, can cause the flame to go out. Less than one-third of family businesses survive through the second generation, and fewer than one in ten makes it through the third generation.[12] The major cause of family business failure is lack of a business succession plan. There appear to be four reasons for family inability to create such a document.

1. It is difficult for senior family members to address their own mortality.
2. Many senior family members are concerned that the way younger family members run the business will maintain its success. Only 20 percent are confident of the next generation's commitment to the business.[13]
3. Transfer of control is put off until too late because of seniors' concern for their personal long-term financial security.
4. Seniors (like most small business owners) are too personally tied to the business and lacking in outside interests to be attracted to retirement.[14]

Family businesses can unite personal and professional connections.

If the potential successor wants to take over the family business, he or she must gain acceptance and trust within the organization (see Figure 6.3). When a family member enters the business, he or she is not usually immediately accepted by non-family employees. This skepticism increases when that person moves up to a leadership position within the business. The successor must earn credibility by showing

FIGURE 6.3

Succession Model of Family Business

Passing on the ownership of a family business is a difficult process. The successor must earn the trust of employees before becoming a successful leader.

that he or she is capable of running the business. Only after being accepted and earning credibility will the new manager have legitimate power and become successful as the new leader.[15]

General Family Business Policies

Because family businesses have unique situations and problems, they need a set of policies to deal with such situations, which are not needed in other types of businesses. David Bork, a family business consultant, makes the following suggestions as part of a family employment policy. A set of policies like these can help prevent problems such as animosity from nonfamily employees, which can decrease their motivation and productivity.

- When hiring family members, they must meet the same criteria as nonfamily employees.

- In performance reviews, family members must meet the same standards as nonfamily employees.

- Family members should be supervised by nonfamily employees when possible.

- If family members are under age 30, they are only eligible for "temporary" employment (less than one year).

- No family member may stay in an entry-level position permanently.

- All positions will be compensated at fair market value.

- For family members to seek permanent employment, they must have at least five years' experience outside the company. Family members must prove their worth to another employer to be useful here.[16]

Want more information about family businesses? Check out www.fambiz.com (over 300 articles on family business issues and additional links) and http://www.familybusinessmagazine.com/index.html (*Family Business* magazine online).

SUMMARY

■■■■ **The advantages and disadvantages of buying an existing business.**

The advantages of buying an existing business include the fact that it is an already functioning operation; customers are used to doing business with it; and you will break even sooner than if you started from the ground up. The disadvantages include the difficulty of changing the business's image or the way it does business; outdated inventory and equipment; too high a purchase price; poor location; and liabilities for previous contracts.

How to find a business for sale.

Newspaper advertising is one source, and word of mouth through friends and family may be another. Bankers, lawyers, accountants, real estate brokers, business brokers, and Small Business Administration representatives can be other good sources.

The means of measuring a business's condition and why a business would be sold.

Profitability, profit trends, comparison of operating ratios to industry standards, and total asset worth are all measures of the financial health of a business. There are as many reasons for selling a business as there are businesses to sell. As a prospective buyer, you must learn to cut through what is said to determine the realities of a situation. You must develop an ability to analyze a market and estimate potential profits and worth.

The difference between tangible and intangible assets.

Tangible assets are those that "cast a shadow." Real estate, inventory, and equipment are important tangible assets. Intangible assets, though unseen, are no less valuable. Goodwill, merchandise franchises, leases and contracts, and patents, copyrights, and trademarks are examples.

The price to pay for a business.

The offering price to pay for a business is calculated by adding the adjusted value of tangible assets to the value of intangible assets (including goodwill, if appropriate).

What makes family businesses different from other types of businesses?

The two primary differences between family businesses and other businesses are the complex interrelationships among family members and their interaction in the business, and the intricate succession planning needed.

QUESTIONS FOR REVIEW & DISCUSSION

1. What are some arguments for buying an established business rather than starting one yourself?

2. In buying an established business, what questions should you ask about it? From whom might you seek information about the business?

3. Identify and discuss some of the more important factors to consider in appraising a business.

4. Which is more important in appraising a business: profitability or return on investment? Discuss.

5. Should one ever consider purchasing a presently unsuccessful business (that is, a business with relatively low or no profits)? Explain.

6. What factors warrant special attention in appraising a firm's (a) inventory? (b) equipment? (c) accounts receivable?

7. What should a prospective buyer know about the seller's inventory sources and other resource contacts? How is this information obtained?

8. Does competition help or hurt a business? Explain.

9. Discuss the ways in which the tangible assets of a business may be valued. What is the most realistic approach to true value? Why?

10. What is goodwill, and how may its value be determined?

11. How can a buyer determine the rate of return to use in evaluating the worth of a business?

12. What is an installment sale? What are its advantages to the buyer of a business? to the seller of a business?

13. What is meant by "thinning the assets"? Cite examples.

14. Discuss the advantages of dealing through a business broker. What precautions should one take when dealing with a business broker?

QUESTIONS FOR **CRITICAL THINKING**

1. Say that you are analyzing the financial records of the business you have been thinking about buying. You discover that, although the firm has excellent current and quick asset ratios by industry standards (current assets are higher than current liabilities), its cash is low and it hasn't paid its bills on time. What might have caused this? Would this influence your decision to buy the business?

2. A mother believes that all the family's children should have equal ownership of the family business regardless of their participation in the business. The father sees the situation completely differently. He believes that the children who are actively involved should receive more ownership. How can this dispute be resolved?

Look in your local Yellow Pages for the name of a business broker in your community. Call the broker and ask about the process of buying an existing business. What terms and conditions are common? What businesses does the broker currently represent?

Experience
this...

Master of Music (MM) is a retail music store located in South Bend, Indiana. At its two locations, one downtown and the other in the Heritage Mall, MM sells musical instruments, sheet music, and musical accessories. It also provides music lessons—piano and guitar—for school-age students and adults. Michelle Smith has owned the business for 20 years and wants to sell out so that she can retire to "someplace warm." This type of business is exactly what you've been looking for, but you want to make sure you pay a fair market price for it. Smith has provided you with the financial information you requested.

Income Statements for Masters of Music

	1997	1998	1999	2000	2001
Revenues:					
Retail Sales	1,500,000	1,200,000	1,500,000	1,550,000	1,720,000
Music Lessons	78,000	80,000	80,000	83,000	82,000
Total Revenue	1,578,000	1,280,000	1,580,000	1,633,000	1,802,000
Expenses:					
Cost of Goods Sold	780,000	830,000	860,000	875,000	927,000
Salaries and Wages	120,000	125,000	138,000	140,000	157,000
Other Operating Expenses	145,000	157,000	160,000	172,000	175,000
Marketing Expenses	57,000	65,000	72,000	83,000	90,000
Other Expenses (including insurance, interest, etc.)	55,000	50,000	63,000	70,000	78,000
Income Before Taxes	421,000	53,000	287,000	293,000	375,000
Income Taxes (33%)	138,930	17,490	94,710	96,690	123,750
Net Income	282,070	35,510	192,290	196,310	251,250

Balance Sheets for Masters of Music

Assets:					
Cash	105,000	65,000	93,000	98,000	117,000
Accounts Receivable	39,800	49,000	43,700	45,000	50,200
Inventory	947,000	986,00	993,000	1,200,000	1,205,000
Building	542,000	542,000	542,000	542,000	542,000
Furniture Fixtures	213,000	213,000	233, 000	249, 000	252,000
Less Accumulated Depreciation	87,000	79,200	73,000	68,000	67,100
Total Assets	1,759,800	1,775,800	1,831,700	2,066,000	2,099,100
Liabilities:					
Accounts Payable	32,000	43,000	30,000	35,000	28,000
Line of Credit	500,000	500,000	530,000	550,000	550,000

Roosevelt Federal	151,000	149,000	176,000	180,000	185,000
Sales Tax Payable	45,000	36,000	45,000	46,500	51,600
Other Payables	17,000	28,000	28,000	30,000	31,500
Total Current Liabilities	745,000	756,000	809.000	841,500	846,100
Long-Term Notes/Leases	375,000	375,000	343,000	343,000	343,000
Total Liabilities	1,120,000	1,131,000	1,152,000	1,184,500	1,189,100
Stockholder's Equity:					
30,000 shares at $15/share	450,000	450,000	450,000	450,000	450,000
Retained Earnings	189,800	194, 800	229,700	431,500	460,000
Total Liabilities and Stockholders' Equity	1,759,800	1,775,800	1,831,700	2,066,000	2,099,100

QUESTIONS

1. Calculate a range of values for Masters of Music. Use both the balance sheet method of valuation and the income statement method. Be sure to note your assumptions on your valuations.

2. Students are to break into groups of four, with each group divided into pairs. One pair will act as sellers, and the other pair will act as buyers, for which each pair will set their own value for Masters of Music. Negotiate a sale for the company. Be prepared to justify your estimation of value.

WHAT WOULD **YOU** DO?	No. 2

A family in the Pacific Northwest owns a retail clothing store. Two brothers worked the business. Their mother is president of the company. Sibling rivalry had been a problem while the boys were growing up, and now that they are in the family business together, it is reappearing. In addition to her role as president, mom often found herself in the role of referee and "chief emotional officer" when the young men fought. Neither the continued rivalry between the brothers nor the mother's need to intervene between them contributed to a normally functional business. The family realizes that their business system is entangled with their family system, but they are not sure what to do about it.

QUESTIONS

1. What should the mother do for her family (and her business) to operate more normally?

2. Would bringing in a nonfamily manager with direct line control over each brother help or cause more problems? How can they ever decide who will eventually take over control of the business?

Preston's Cleaners

Family businesses are often described as constituting the "bedrock" of America—especially by politicians on the campaign trail. However, those same politicians are creating a tangle of laws and regulations that are threatening to strangle the family business as families attempt to pass the business from one generation to the next. Preston's Cleaners is a classic example.

Preston's Cleaners was incorporated in 1969 by Mark and Sylvia Preston of Lincoln, Illinois, and eventually taken over by the Prestons' son Glen. Having received a degree in business, Glen worked in Tennessee for ten years as a manager for a large publicly owned company. Then his parents began looking for someone besides themselves to manage the family dry cleaning business. After a year of wavering back and forth, Glen decided in 1991 to return home and buy into the family firm. But, Glen admits, the actual transfer of the business from parents to son has been like walking a financial tightrope.

The company run by Mark and Sylvia had a single location—a "package plant" as it's called in the industry, where both the customer service facility and the dry cleaning equipment were housed. However, Glen realized that in order to support both his family—a wife and two young daughters—and his parents, he would need a larger volume of business. So he decided to double the size of the first store and to add a second location. Although the site he chose for Preston's #2 was not in a "demographically desirable" area, Glen said, he received a good deal from the landlord, who was also the landlord for Preston's #1. At Preston's #2, Glen installed a shirt laundry making it the first cleaners to wash shirts "in-house" rather than sending them to a commercial laundry operation. The dry cleaning equipment was still located at Preston's #1. Although it was an expensive proposition, Glen felt that he gained control over the quality of the cleaning process. However, his competitors soon added their own shirt laundries.

One of Preston's competitive advantages is that it provides pickup and delivery service to homes and businesses. However, this service has had its drawbacks too. For instance, Glen recalled that one of his delivery employees was caught stealing goods from customers' homes, which he had hidden in the attic of another customer's home. Because the employee had access to customers' homes, it was easy for him to both steal and stash the goods. And, it was pretty safe, really. After all, how often do people actually go into their attics? He was finally caught when the customer whose attic was the storage site had to stay home unexpectedly one day with a sprained ankle and heard someone enter her house and go up into the attic. After calling the police, she retrieved a pistol and was able to get off a shot, hitting the employee in the ankle as he was coming down the stairs. That's when she discovered that her attic had become the storage site for goods stolen from other customers' houses. Needless to say, Glen fired the employee immediately and revised the way that pickups and deliveries were made.

In Glen's first three years, sales volume continued to increase, so he considered opening a third location. Because the northeast side of the city was growing rapidly, he decided that Preston's #3 should be located there and found a new strip shopping center in the area that offered a very attractive demographic location. However, Glen's biggest competitors also decided to build stores in the area. Still Glen went ahead with his plans and opened Preston's #3 in 1994. The store provided drop-off and pickup service, but did not have any cleaning equipment, thus reducing his capital expenses.

Unfortunately, 1995 was a bad year for the entire dry cleaning industry. Although Glen did not detect any significant decrease in sales revenues, five new competitors opened their doors, which could affect future sales. And Glen, who had always been pretty confident in his ability to project sales, found that none of his past guidelines fit.

One factor affecting the overall climate, he felt, was the economy, because of the concerns it caused his customers about their job security. The stagnant retail sales of clothing that resulted also had an impact on the dry cleaning business. Fewer clothes purchased meant fewer clothes to be dry cleaned or laundered. Not only were customers taking fewer clothes in to be cleaned, they were leaving them for longer periods of time. For instance, Preston's inventory used to be 8 days; it has become closer to 24 days.

Changes in people's lifestyles and expectations further threaten the demand for dry cleaning services. For instance, Glen sensed that the trend toward more casual dressing could ultimately affect his sales revenues. His target market had always been professionals— doctors, attorneys, managers, accountants, and so forth. As firms institute practices such as "casual Fridays," the number of suits, ties, and other professional clothing that need to be cleaned is likely to decline.

Glen cited globalization and other market pressures as having an impact on his business. It used to be that the big-name clothing manufacturers would stand behind their products. Now, as manufacturers chase price and negotiate contracts all over the world, often at the expense of quality, the local dry cleaner has to deal with the shoddily made clothes that customers bring in for cleaning. When these clothes fall apart easily, the angry customer sometimes blames the closest suspect—the dry cleaner—for the problem.

Finally, Glen noted the labor shortage that he faced in 1995. Finding good employees and keeping them has always been a problem for small service businesses. But Glen found it particularly trying in 1995. He tells this story: "I hired a young man (I'll call him Joe) who appeared to be a hard worker. One of the requirements for this particular job is that you have to be at work at 4 A.M. During his first couple of weeks on the job, Joe was catching a ride with a friend, but that individual didn't have to be at work until 5 A.M. and got tired of getting up earlier than he really needed to. I decided that Joe had potential and I wanted to keep him. So I went out to a local used-car auction and bought a 1982 blue Cadillac for $760 and loaned it to Joe. He appreciated the gesture and for the next couple of weeks was at work right on time. Then, one Friday afternoon, Joe turned the keys over, saying he'd found a better-paying job. He quit and I haven't seen him since. Now my wife is hollering at me to get that darned car out of the driveway. I don't know what else I can do to get or keep good employees."

All of these factors led Glen to shut down Preston's #2. "You're in business to make a profit," he said. "It didn't make a profit." Then he added, "You can have the best product, the best-quality product, but if people don't have money to pay for it, you won't be in business." He said he continues to struggle with the plans for transferring the business from his parents to himself without incurring a significant, and potentially costly, tax bite. He recommends getting as much advice on the process as you can.

Despite all the pressures and risks, Glen doesn't regret making the decision to come back in the family business. For one thing, he said, his parents are there for him and they back him completely. Also he enjoys the freedom to make his own decisions. He still strongly believes in the power of family businesses, although he is worried about the climate that they face.

Source: Personal interview with the owner, March 1996. The story of Preston's Cleaners describes a real situation, although the names and locations have been disguised at the owner's request.

QUESTIONS

1. Research family businesses at the library. How prevalent are they? What types of issues and challenges do family businesses face? In what ways is Preston's Cleaners a "typical" family business?

2. Preston's Cleaners is obviously a service-type business. Would Glen Preston have faced similar problems if the family business were in manufacturing? Why or why not?

3. Look at the location decision behind Preston's #2. Do you think this is a typical way for small business owners to make this decision? What are the problems with doing so? How would you have made this decision?

4. What are Preston's Cleaners' competitive advantages? Are they sustainable? Might the company develop other competitive advantages? Describe.

5. Glen Preston described some of the challenges that his industry faces. Do you think a small business owner needs this information? Why or why not?

6. Although there are no financials included, Glen states that he shut down Preston's #2 because it didn't make a profit. Do you think you would have made the same decision? Are there some instances when a small business might keep a location open even though it's not making a profit? Explain.

7. Discuss the implications of Glen's statement, "You can have the best product, the best-quality product, but if people don't have money to pay for it, you won't be in business."

8. What do you think the advantages of starting or running a family business are? What are the drawbacks?

7 Starting a New Business

After reading this chapter, you should be able to:

- Discuss the advantages and disadvantages of starting a business from scratch.

- Describe types of new businesses and discuss the common characteristics of fast-growth companies.

- Evaluate potential startups and suggest sources of business ideas.

- Explain the most important points to consider when starting a new business.

IN 1977, BRIAN MAXWELL was ranked third in the world in marathon running, with a personal best of 2:14:43. Despite his efforts and training, a sensitive stomach prevented him from improving on his 2:14. If he ate anything before a race, he would get digestive problems and cramps during the race. Yet if he didn't eat anything, he had no energy left for the final miles.

Out of frustration with his condition, Maxwell, aided by biochemist and runner Bill Vaughan, sought to create a high-energy, easily digestible food bar for athletes. The pair first began experimenting with different grains, proteins, textures, and flavors. They were making progress when, after two years of tests, Jennifer Biddulph, a runner and student majoring in food science, joined them. For three more years the group would make up batches at home and product-test them at races every weekend.

In February 1986, Maxwell and Biddulph took a big jump toward turning a hobby into a business. With their combined life savings (the couple married in 1988), they contracted a single production run of 40,000 PowerBars. Word-of-mouth promotion spread quickly through the close-knit running and cycling community. Mail-order sales in 1987 were $400,000. PowerBar's marketing philosophy was, and still is, "We have a good product that works. All we have to do is get athletes to try it." Maxwell and Biddulph spent half of their promotion budget on direct marketing—sponsoring events and giving away bars at road races "at 7:00 A.M. in the rain," as Maxwell put it. The other half of the budget went for simple print and broadcast advertisements produced by Maxwell and Biddulph. It worked. Between 1987 and 1991, sales grew 6,915 percent, from $400,000 to $6.7 million. PowerFoods, the company's name, ranked 22nd on the 1992 *Inc.* list of the 500 fastest-growing companies in America. By 1993, revenue grew to nearly $14 million. By 1998, sales exploded to $50 million. Jennifer Maxwell was honored as winner of *Working Woman* magazine's 1999 Entrepreneurial Excellence Award.

Although few young companies have such extraordinary success, PowerFoods' founders are not unlike many other entrepreneurs. A need in their lives motivated them to find a solution. That solution also satisfied a need in other people's lives. The initial focus was not on creating a business. That was more of a by-product—a means to an end. Their focus was to simply solve a problem. PowerBar was purchased by Switzerland-based Nestlé in February 2000 for $375 million.

Can you identify some problem or need that exists? Can you come up with a solution to that problem or need? Do you have the perseverance to stay focused and follow through? If you answer "yes" to these three questions, you are well on your way to starting a successful business.

Sources: Adapted from Bob Wischnia, "PowerPlay," *Runner's World,* June 1994, 90–95; Aiden McNulty, "Raising the Bar," *Success,* August 1998, 29; and Betsy Wiesendanger, "1999 Entrepreneurial Excellence Award Winner: Jennifer Maxwell," *Working Woman,* May 1999, 48.

▬ About Startups

Starting a business from the ground up is more difficult than buying an existing business or a franchise, because nothing is in place. There is also more risk involved. However, to many people the process of taking an idea through all the steps, time, money, and energy needed to become a viable business is the essence of entrepreneurship. The period in which you create a brand new business is an *exciting* time.

Do you want to be totally independent at work? If so, you may be ready to start your own business.

Do you think you would like to be totally independent? Can you set up an accounting system readable to you and acceptable to your bank and the Internal Revenue Service? Can you come up with a promotional campaign that will get you noticed? Are you willing to devote the time and resources needed to succeed? Can you find sources of products, components, or distribution? Can you find employees with the skills your business will need? If so, you may be ready to start your own business.

Advantages of Starting from Scratch

When you begin a business from scratch, you have freedom to mold your new creation into whatever you feel is appropriate. Other advantages of starting from scratch include the ability to create your own distinctive competitive advantage. Many entrepreneurs thrive on the challenge of beginning a new enterprise. You can feel pride when creating something that didn't exist before and in realizing your own goals. The fact that the business is all new can be an advantage in itself—there is no carryover baggage of someone else's mistakes, location, employees, or products. You establish your own image.

© 1992 by Patrick Hardin

Disadvantages of Starting from Scratch

The risk of failure is higher with startups than with purchasing existing businesses or franchises. You may have trouble identifying market needs in your area that you are able to satisfy. You have to inform people that your business exists—it can be tough to get noticed. You have to deal with thousands of details that you didn't foresee, from how to choose the right vendors, to where to put the coffeepot, to where to find motivated employees.

Types of New Businesses

No matter what type of business you are starting, your most important resource is your time. Nothing happens until you make it happen. You have to create and build on the enthusiasm that will attract others to your idea and your business. In the beginning, the only thing you have is your vision, and only you will be responsible for its success.

Frustration Solvers

The labor-intensive nature of service businesses is evident in the company that brothers James and Peter Kovolsky started in Charlotte, North Carolina. James had worked his way through college putting together unassembled manufactured products for people. He could—and did—construct just about anything—bicycles, toys, bookshelves, office furniture, you name it. When James and Peter were both laid off from their sales jobs in 1991, they decided to start their own business, Frustration Solvers, which would take advantage of their skills and allay people's fears of those three simple words "Some Assembly Required." They've since developed close relationships with stores that sell toys, office furniture, lawn and garden supplies, sporting goods, and home improvement goods. The stores do not pay the brothers directly but allow their salespeople to give Frustration Solvers' phone number to customers. Obviously, the brothers have identified a true market niche, because company revenues have tripled every year since 1992, reaching over $1 million in 1995. The Kovolsky brothers are considering franchising or seeking investors to help fund the company's growth. Says James, "The business is out there. We've got retailers calling us from other states." By identifying a critical customer need, the Kovolskys started a profitable service business.

Source: From "Putting It All Together" by Dorothy Elizabeth Brooks, *Nation's Business* (September 1995). Copyright 1995, U.S. Chamber of Commerce. Reprinted by permission of *Nation's Business.*

As the service industry plays an ever-greater role in the U.S. economy, startup businesses become more popular. The reason? Service businesses tend to be more **labor intensive,** or dependent on the services of people, as opposed to manufacturing businesses, which are more **capital intensive,** or dependent on equipment and capital.

labor-intensive business A business that is more dependent on the services of people than on money and equipment.

capital-intensive business A business that depends greatly upon equipment and capital for its operations.

Start by finding out all you can about your industry and trade area from books, newsletters, trade publications, magazines, organizations, and people already in business. After all your questions and investigation, if you are ready for the challenge, you will find several possible routes in starting your business.

Let's look at a few of those routes that people take, aside from the typical goal of a low-growth, stable startup, which provides the small business owner a comfortable, modest living.

E-Businesses

e-business A business that shares information, maintains customer relationships, and conducts transactions by means of telecommunications networks.

Nothing has changed the small business landscape like the Internet. It is the ultimate in one-to-one connections—which is where small businesses have always thrived. You can begin an **e-business** with relatively low overhead and potentially reach markets all over the world. But keep in mind that the Internet, though a powerful tool, doesn't make all other business metrics obsolete. You still have to make a profit, keep employees happy and motivated, provide customer service, and offer a product that customers are willing to turn over their hard-earned money to get. Unlike popular opinion at one time, electronic business is not all about "click here to buy." More likely is the model of "click here to get more information," "click here to start the just-in-time inventory flow," or "click here to let a new employee go through the orientation process."[1]

There is considerable difficulty describing electronic business in a few paragraphs, because one simple model does not exist. Your e-biz may be something as simple as taking a current avocation (like tying flies for fishing or making custom pillows) and selling your concoctions on eBay, business to consumer. You may not ever personally touch a product, but provide value by connecting other businesses, business to business. In these few paragraphs we won't get into the technical details of mips, megs, and browsers. You, as a webpreneur, will need understanding at the leading edge of technology. Unfortunately (or fortunately), that edge moves so quickly that we can't do justice to it here. What we can cover here are basic characteristics a successful web business must possess.

- *Have a sound business strategy, beginning with having a good reason to be online.* But how do you commit to long-term strategic planning in an economy that moves at the speed of the Internet? John Noble, vice president of corporate Internet strategy at Putnam Investments, suggests that you need to figure out which strategic moves you want to make first. Then figure out how to use technology to accomplish your strategy. If you make decisions based strictly on what is technically possible today, you will be out of position in 6 to 12 months. Internet strategy has become a two-pronged field: you need ideas and the capacity to execute them. Internet strategy has become more of a team effort among people who provide an overarching vision and the information technology (IT) people who turn those visions into reality.[2]

- *Have a clear market analysis and create traffic coverage.* Believe it or not, not everyone is on the web! Are your customers? If they aren't, why are you? The "if you build it, they will come" model seldom works.[3] As with brick-and-mortar businesses, you need to generate traffic into your site. You begin this by registering your site with search engines. For registration, you need to think of "meta tags," or keywords that are associated with your business.[4] While thinking of your Internet "location," you need to register your business name with InterNIC. You can register directly with one of several providers, such as Register.com and NetworkSolutions.com

- *Design an attractive, functional web site.* Your web page needs to be attractive, clear, and efficient. *Inc.* magazine created web awards for the best small business sites. Their panel of judges found six common problem themes for all the sites they evaluated.
  - *Mistake 1: Putting form before function.* Bells and whistles can get in the way of your actual intent. Just because you can put flashing, dancing animals on your web page doesn't mean that you should.
  - *Mistake 2: Putting simply your company brochure online.* All communication media have their own inherent advantages. Use them. The Internet allows you to create, so don't just scan in what has already been done.
  - *Mistake 3: Having features that don't work properly.* Few things turn Internet users off faster than error messages. People who might have bought from you will quickly move on if things don't work as expected.
  - *Mistake 4: Making life difficult for users.* Extras like background music slow downloading. Remember that not all users have up-to-the-nanosecond screaming machines, blazing connections, or big-screen monitors. Slow downloads are death.
  - *Mistake 5: Making it hard for people to buy.* If people want to impulse-purchase, make the process for them to order overwhelmingly clear. One site showed customers a product, but required them to order over the phone.

■ *Mistake 6: Inadequately measuring the bottom-line impact.* Is your web site contributing to your business return on investment (ROI) when you consider all the fixed and recurring costs of your web presence?[5]

secure method for payments Internet communications protocol to encrypt data transmitted between computers.

■ *You need a **secure method for payments.*** To be a real e-biz player, you will need payment software, a merchant account, payment-processing services, and a gateway to connect all of these elements securely. In order to accept or send electronic payments, open an account with your merchant bank. This bank will set up accommodations to secure payment transfers from credit card companies. Finding a merchant bank for processing credit cards may not be easy. Check out Signio (www.signio.com), CyberCash (www.cybercash.com), and Authorize.net (www.authorize.net). Setup fees run $500 to $1000, plus $40 to $80 per month, plus 20 to 60 cents per transaction.[6]

Home-Based Businesses

The fastest-growing segment of business startups comprises those operated out of people's homes. According to the American Association of Home-Based Businesses (AAHBB), the number of people running businesses from home is over 24 million.[7]

home-based business A popular type of business that operates from the owner's home, rather than from a separate location.

About 30 percent of **home-based businesses** deal with financial or computer-related services. Two reasons stand out as advantages for this type of business: schedule flexibility and low overhead.

Technology has had a lot to do with making this trend possible. Notebook computers, DSL and cable Internet connections, wireless modems, faxes and PDAs (Personal Digital Assistants, such as a Palm Pilot), cellular phones, and laser printers contribute to flexibility, with quality results from working at home. The idea is becoming more widely accepted.

Meg Gottemoller left her position as a vice president of Chase Manhattan Bank in New York to start her own communications and training consultancy. Martha Gay runs her own corporate research business from her home in Fort Washington, Pennsylvania. Both of these businesses are successful because they take advantage of *corporate outsourcing.* As larger companies reduce the size of their work force, they must contract out work that was once done by their own workers. This outsourcing provides many opportunities for small businesses.

Running a business out of your home can provide flexibility in your personal life, but it takes serious organization and self-discipline. Let's look at some of the advantages and disadvantages

ADVANTAGES OF A HOME-BASED BUSINESS

■ Control over work hours

■ Convenience

■ Ability to care for domestic responsibilities (like children, parents, household)

■ Low overhead expenses

■ Lack of workplace distractions (coworkers popping in, chatting around the coffee machine)

■ Decreased commute time

■ Tax advantages

DISADVANTAGES OF A HOME-BASED BUSINESS

- Difficulty setting aside long blocks of time
- Domestic interruptions
- Informal, cramped, insufficient workspace at home
- Demands on family members to cooperate
- Lack of respect (Will people think you are unemployed or doing this as a hobby?)
- Lack of workplace camaraderie (Houses can get quiet and lonely.)
- Zoning issues[8]

So, what kind of businesses can you run from your home? According to *Entrepreneur's Startup* magazine, some possibilities include specialty travel tours, computer consultant, personal chef, concierge service, web site consultant, event planner, cart or kiosk business, translation service, feng shui consultant, online auctioneer, and technology writer. Check out these and other articles to brainstorm ideas.[9]

Starting a Business on the Side

Many people start businesses while keeping their regular job. Although it is often not recommended as a way to enter business, the Bureau of Labor Statistics estimates that just over 1.2 million people did so in 1997.[10] Working a full-time job while getting a business going may require superhuman organizational skills and discipline, yet there can be advantages. A transitional period can allow you to test the waters without complete immersion in the marketplace. You can also prepare yourself psychologically, experientially, and financially, so that when—or if—you leave your job, you will have a running start. Before taking this route, however, you should be absolutely clear on your company's moonlighting policy and avoid doing anything that might resemble a conflict of interest. Moonlighting policies could include not starting an identical business or soliciting current customers.

Fast-Growth Startups

Not every new business can be or desires to be a hypergrowth company like Power-Foods, with its nearly 7,000 percent growth rate, as we saw in the chapter opener. The average percentage sales growth from 1995 to 1999 for Inc. 500 companies was 1,632%. But *Inc.* magazine compiled its own database of Inc. 500 businesses (see Figure 7.1). From these data *Inc.* identified characteristics and patterns of similarity that these fast-growth companies shared.

1. *They rely on team effort.* In contrast with low-growth firms, most fast-growth companies are started by partnerships. In an increasingly complex and competitive environment, teams can deal with a much wider range of problems than can an individual operating alone. One-half of the fast-growth CEOs owned less than 50 percent of their business's equity.

FIGURE 7.1

2000 Inc. 500 by the Numbers

Information about companies that made the Inc. 500.

Source: "Data Mine," *Inc. 500,* 17 October 2000, 57–65.

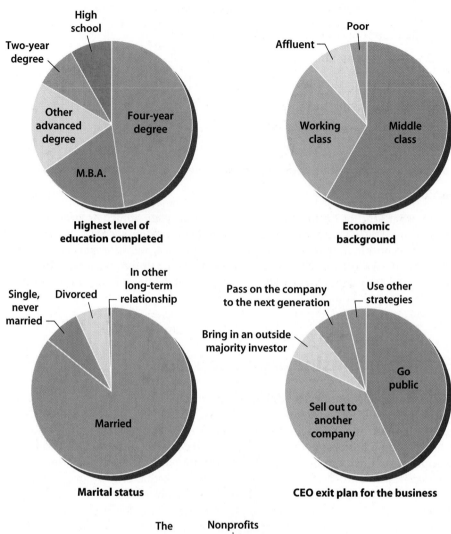

Highest level of education completed

Economic background

Marital status

CEO exit plan for the business

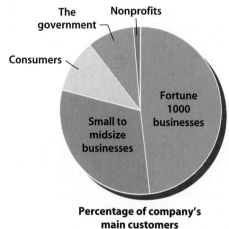

Percentage of company's main customers

2. *They're headed by people who know their line of work.* A majority of high-growth CEOs had at least ten years of experience in the industry. This contrasts with just a few years of prior experience for owners of low-growth companies.

3. *They're headed by people who have started other businesses.* Research shows that 63 percent of the founders of high-growth companies had started other companies, and 23 percent had started three or more. This compares to only 20 percent of all business owners who had been self-employed previously. Some 61 percent started in the founder's home.

4. *They're headed by men.* The number of firms owned by women increased twice as fast as all businesses did in the 1990s. But 93 percent of fast-growth companies have male CEOs. This does not by any means suggest inferior female management. Possible explanations could be that women as a group have not yet gained the business experience needed to form fast-growth firms or that rapid growth has not been a primary goal of female CEOs.

5. *They're high tech.* Of the fast-start companies, 47 percent label themselves "high tech." Services make up a full 56 percent, which is another indicator of the importance of the service sector in our economy. Computer software and services was the largest sector, represented at 38 percent.

6. *They're better financed—but not by much.* This factor is harder to measure because of the subjectivity in determining what is "well financed." Sixteen percent of Inc. 500 companies started with less than $1,000 and 26 percent began with between $1,000 and $10,000. Only 21 percent had initial startup capital of over $100,000. Ninety-two percent of CEOs used personal assets at startup. After the startup phase, 83 percent raised money with a bank line of credit. One and a half million dollars was the median amount of additional finance after startup.[11]

7. *Their markets aren't just local.* Successful companies are expanding their horizons. A majority of Inc. 500 companies gets more than half of its revenue outside the home region, and 38 percent are international players. They are looking for **strategic alliances** also. One third have agreements with large companies, which expand their markets.[12]

> **strategic alliance** A partnership between two businesses that join forces to produce a product or serve a market that neither could do alone. Often used as a means to enter a foreign market.

Evaluating Potential Startups

The first thing you need to start your own business is an idea. But not every idea is a viable business opportunity. You must be able to turn this idea into a profitable business. How do you tell an idea from an opportunity? Where do people come up with viable business ideas that are opportunities?

Business Ideas

Although there is no shortage of ideas for new and improved products and services, there is a difference between ideas and opportunities. But are they all business opportunities? Harvard business professor Jeffry Timmons states that a business opportunity has the qualities of being attractive, durable, and timely, and is anchored in a product or service that creates or adds value for its buyer or end user.[13] Many ideas for new products and businesses do not add value for customers or users. Maybe the time for the idea has yet to come, or maybe it has already passed.

Consider the idea for a new device for removing the crown caps that were common on bottles of soft drinks for many years. You could concoct an exotic and ingenious tool that would be technically feasible to produce, but is there an opportunity to build a business from it? Not since soft drink and beer companies switched to resealable bottles and screw-off tops to solve the same consumer problem that your invention does.[14] Good idea—no opportunity.

An idea that is too far ahead of the market can be just as bad as one too far behind consumer desires. In 1987, Jerry Kaplan left his job as a software writer for Lotus Development to start Go Computers because he thought the world was ready for portable, pen-based computers. He had some big-time backing from IBM and AT&T, who pitched in $75 million to help with startup. He had a vision of salespeople, lawyers, insurance adjusters, and millions of other people writing away on Go computers as if they were paper. Unfortunately, consumers at the time didn't find computers that could recognize their handwriting and that could convert it into print so that it was usable. Fourteen years later, many consumers regularly use a PDAlike palm-sized computer which can do just that. Even with a great idea, a talented leader, and strong financial backing, Go Computers sold only 20,000 units and lasted only three years—it was ahead of its market. When Go closed, Kaplan believed that "A new class of computing devices will come into being . . . it's just a question of when."[15] He was right. A startup, even one with substantial resources, can't wait for technology or markets to catch up with an idea.

You've probably heard of the term **window of opportunity.** These windows constantly open and close (sometimes rapidly) as the market for that product ("product" meaning either goods or services) or business changes. Products go through stages of introduction, growth, maturity, and decline in the **product life cycle.** During the introduction stage, the window of opportunity is wide open because there is little or no competition. As products progress through this cycle, competition increases, consumer expectations are higher, and profit margins are lower so the window of opportunity is not open as wide (see Figure 7.2).

window of opportunity A period of time in which an opportunity is available.

product life cycle Stages that products in a marketplace pass through over time.

FIGURE 7.2
Windows of Opportunity at Stages of the Product Life Cycle

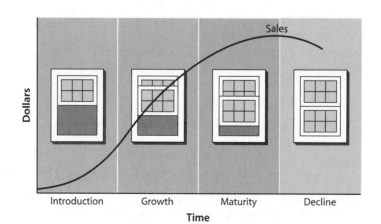

Startup Myths and Realities

The human mind has a remarkable ability to rationalize just about anything. If we want to do something, we can often tell ourselves something that sounds right—whether it is reality or not. You can build competitive advantage only by basing actions on reality—not myth. The following myths may add some perspective to starting a business:

Myth 1: I'm Smart—I Can Just Wing It *Reality:* Face it—you need a plan. One of the few things that a group of small business lenders, advisors, and consultants would agree on is the need for a business plan. New York business consultant Jim Gabe reminds us that "an entrepreneur's perception isn't always in step with reality."

Myth 2: I Can Do It on a Shoestring *Reality:* While no one ever has *enough* money, having too *little* can be doom. Thomas Dandrige of State University of New York at Albany states, "People forget that most businesses require a great deal of spending before they can begin to develop cash flow." Having money is not as important to a business as having a product that people want, but you have to have enough money for you and the company to survive until it can support itself.

Myth 3: No Sweat, I Have a Great Idea *Reality:* According to William E. Dunn of University of Pennsylvania's Wharton School, "About 5 percent of the success equation is having a good idea." Great ideas are an important start for businesses, but ideas alone won't get you far. You also need the resources, skills, and products to make a business.

Myth 4: I've Got Nothing Better to Do *Reality:* You cannot start a successful small business halfheartedly. Starting a business because you have been laid off your job and just need something to do is not a good idea. The level of commitment associated with making a quick buck is a long way from the reality needed for success in starting a new business.

Myth 5: Maybe Starting a Business Will Help Our Marriage *Reality:* A risky bet. The stress involved in starting a business can amplify marital weaknesses. Marriage counselors advise people not to start businesses until they are emotionally stable. The distraction of personal problems takes away from your ability to concentrate on your new business.

Myth 6: A Bad Economy Will Mean Fewer Competitors *Reality:* Maybe, but it can also make the survivors fiercer competitors. Bank loans and customers with money may be more difficult to find.

Myth 7: I'm Mad as Hell and I'm Not Going to Take It Anymore *Reality:* The frustration that you have built up with your current job can be a good rationale for starting your own business, if your anger is focused on positive outcomes. Anger in general won't get you ahead. W. L. Gore was a frustrated chemist with Du Pont Co. because he didn't think Teflon was being used to its potential. He quit to start his own business, W. L. Gore & Associates. The company grew to $1 billion annual revenue from Gore-Tex, the Teflon-based waterproof fabric.

Myth 8: If I Can't Think of Anything Else, I'll Open a Bar *Reality:* Despite common opinion, restaurants and bars are not easy businesses to start or run. The rationale that everyone likes to eat and drink does not hold up. Having dined out regularly or bellied up to a bar does not qualify as experience in this business. Dunn advises, "You have to know customers and know how to solve their problems. You have to be better and cheaper to get their business."

reality
check

Optimally, you want to get through while the window is still opening—if the opportunity is the right one for you. To tell whether you should pursue an opportunity, ask yourself the following questions about your business idea:

- Does your idea solve a consumer want or need? This can give you insight into current and future demand.

- If there is a demand, are there enough people who will buy your product to support a business? How much competition for that demand exists?

- Can this idea be turned into a *profitable* business?

- Do you have the skills needed to take advantage of this opportunity?

- Why hasn't anyone else done it? If others have, what happened to them?

In the idea stage of your thinking (before you actually pursue an opportunity), discuss your idea with a wide variety of people to get feedback. Although praise may make you feel good at this stage, what you really need are people who can look for objectivity and possible flaws, and point out the shortcomings of your idea.

The final answer to whether your idea is an opportunity that you should follow will come from a combination of research and intuition. Both are valuable management tools, but don't rely exclusively on either. Although research has kept some good ideas from becoming products or businesses, it has kept many more bad ones from turning into losing propositions. Do your homework; thoroughly investigate your possibilities. But don't get "analysis paralysis," which prevents you from acting because you think you need more testing or questioning—while the window of opportunity closes. Managerial decision making is as much an art as it is a science. There are times when you have to make decisions without having every last shred of evidence possible. Get all the information that is practical, but also listen to your gut instincts.

Where Business Ideas Come From

The National Federation of Independent Business reports that prior work experience generates a majority of ideas for new businesses for both men and women, although it is a more common source for men. Women look slightly more to hobbies and personal interests for ideas for their businesses (see Figure 7.3).

FIGURE 7.3

Sources of New Business Ideas Among Men and Women

Prior work experience is the most common source of ideas for new businesses for both men and women.

Source: Arnold C. Cooper et al., "New Business in America," 1990, NFIB Foundation/VISA Business Card Primer, in William W. Dennis, Jr., *A Small Business Primer* (Washington, DC: National Federation of Independent Business, 1993), 17. Reprinted by permission of National Federation of Independent Business.

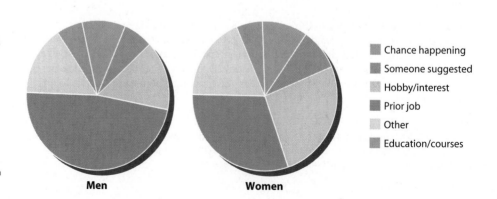

Men **Women**

Chance happening
Someone suggested
Hobby/interest
Prior job
Other
Education/courses

Ideas Aplenty, Ideas Galore

reality check

You get great ideas for new businesses or products all the time, right? Of course you do (because you are reading this book)! Following you will find examples of people who have taken ideas from mind to matter:

Company: Misty Mate, Tempe, Arizona
Time from idea to startup: 2 years
Initial investment: $80,000

Steve Utter was not surprised by what employees of his Phoenix-based construction company kept telling him—they were hot working in the Arizona sun in the summertime. He tried operating from before sunrise until about noon—better for employees but a real productivity killer. Then he saw the fog nozzle they used to spray insecticide into a fine mist. Utter thought about the possibilities of connecting such a nozzle to a portable water tank his workers could use to spray themselves and keep down their body temperature. These workers served as willing guinea pigs as Utter refined the idea. The original combination tank, hose, and nozzle was a hit, and Utter applied for a patent. Other construction companies bought the devices for their overheated employees. The price has dropped from $175 for the original down to $25 for the current fanny-pack model, but revenue has climbed to $7 million in 1997.

Company: Steeplechase Software, Ann Arbor, Michigan
Time from idea to startup: 6 months
Initial investment: $30,000

Mike Klein knows how the cartoon character Dilbert feels—an enthused employee takes an innovative product idea to management, which states that it would never work. Klein knew the idea would work, so he raised $30,000 and went into business. Klein's idea came from listening to customers of his former employer, Allen-Bradley, a unit of Rockwell International. Customers would complain that the mainframe computer system used to run the factory lines was complicated. Klein's idea involved simplifying the expensive mainframe system with less expensive PCs. When he pitched his idea to management in early 1992, he was frustrated to hear responses like "That's not how we operate here" and "It'll be a decade before PCs run the factory floor." To Klein, a decade translated to a five-year open window of opportunity—so he jumped through while the window was open. Sales have grown by 400 percent per year from 1993 to 1998. At the time Steeplechase Software was started, big companies didn't understand the value of entrepreneurial thinking that went beyond the current revenue stream.

Ideas are not hard to find, but their potential can be hard to see. Entrepreneurs bring ideas to life. Ideas often come from businesses they are already in and markets they already serve, from customer comments or employees' suggestions. Innovative ideas are often just the assembly of two known things, put together in a different way. Look around—make new connections.

Source: Samuel Fromartz, "How to Get Your First Great Idea," *Inc.*, April 1998, 91–94.

PRIOR WORK EXPERIENCE. Experience can be a wonderful teacher. Working for someone else in your area of interest can help you to avoid many errors and begin to build competitive advantages. It gives you the chance to ask yourself, "What would I do differently, if I ran this business?"

Starting a new business can mean doing work you love.

corridor principle Opportunities that become available to an entrepreneur only after the entrepreneur has started a business.

One startup may even lead to another. Seeing opportunities for new ventures after starting the first is known as the **corridor principle.**[16] Entrepreneurs start second, third, and succeeding businesses as they move down new venture corridors that did not open to them until they got into business. As we saw with fast-growth startups, 63 percent of fast-growth CEOs had started other companies in the past, suggesting that one idea really does lead to another.

Research by Karl Vesper of the University of Washington shows that big ideas occur to small business owners almost twice as often after the business is already running as before it begins.[17] This illustrates that experience pays off whether you are working for someone else or for yourself.

HOBBIES AND AVOCATIONS. Turning what you do for pleasure into a part-time or full-time business is a possibility that you should consider. It helps ensure that your business will be one that you enjoy and understand. If you enjoy fishing, could there be an opportunity for you to use your skills to become a guide? If you love pets, could you channel your affections into a dog-grooming or pet-sitting business?

Bill Sargent of Murtaugh, Idaho, has been a woodworker for years, but after he retired from farming in 1999, he started making projects that have become a second career. Sargent makes ballpoint pens out of sagebrush. He found that the light tan, twisted, aromatic wood can be crafted into a unique gift. He even won $200 in a statewide competition for Idaho-made products. He says that his pens "catch people's attention because they have seen sagebrush grow but they never knew you could make anything out of it." Finding the right working stock is no small feat—a trunk that appears to be four or five inches in diameter is usually three or four pieces twisted like a rope. After cutting and trimming, a piece of sage may produce enough wood for a dozen pens—or none at all. To glean, cure, trim, and shape a single pen on his lathe, Sargent spends about 45 minutes that retail for $15. So he won't get rich, but Sargent enjoys crafting his unique creations.[18]

CHANCE HAPPENING OR SERENDIPITY. *Serendipity* means finding something valuable that you were not looking for. Sometimes business opportunities come to you unexpectedly. The ability to recognize them takes an open mind, flexibility, a sense of adventure, and good business sense.

Dorothy Noe, who ran an antique shop, was initially disappointed that her customers were less interested in her merchandise than in the frilly curtains that decorated the store windows. After numerous customers had told her, "I'll pay whatever for them," she gave in and started a curtain business called Dorothy's Ruffled Originals. A production problem existed because Dorothy hated to sew. She solved that by forming a cottage industry of local seamstresses to begin sewing her elaborate curtains. Dorothy got her curtains hung in doctors' offices, restaurants, and businesses all over Wilmington, North Carolina. Dorothy's Ruffled Originals has grown to a business selling $10 million worth of home decor products.[19]

Brother and sister Ethan and Abby Margalith had to borrow a truck in the summer of 1973 to move a few things to a local swap meet. Both were just out of high school and out of work. While driving the truck to the swap meet, they realized that moving could be their summer job. Their first truck was a 1944 weapons carrier that they got for free by rescuing it from a mudslide. Starving Student Moving Company became the low-priced alternative to other movers with full uniforms and high prices. The Margaliths used their sense of humor in their advertising—one ad stated that they offered "24-hour service for lease breakers." Even without knowing what they were doing, they had more business than they could handle. Ethan has stated that it wasn't until he got to law school that he realized he and his sister were really running a business. He finished law school but decided that the moving business is fun, exciting, and profitable, so he stayed in business with his sister. By 1999, Starving Students had 35 locations from California to Virginia. They have proudly moved families, companies, government agencies like the U.S. Secret Service and the FBI, and even celebrities like Cher, Jerry Seinfeld, and Tom Hanks—and it all started with digging a truck out of the mud![20]

Hung Van Thai has struggled to make his entrepreneurial ideas work in a very tough environment—communist Vietnam. Thai started his first two private businesses successfully, only to have the government take them away. The first was a soap manufacturing operation that had sales of $5,000 a day, half of which was net profit. But government authorities shut down his operations because he was undercutting the state-owned soap producers. After that, Thai started his second business making plastic slippers. Again, because of his success, he attracted government attention. But this time, Thai offered to turn his business into a state-owned facility if the government would leave him alone, and his offer was accepted. In the late 1980s, as the Vietnamese government began easing up on economic controls, Thai saw his chance to once again start his own private company. His third startup, Hunsan Co., a manufacturer and retailer of sports shoes, has since thrived. Hunsan sales have topped $12 million. Thai hopes to become a viable player in the intensely competitive global shoe industry. He's living proof that the corridor principle—whereby one business naturally leads to another—is alive and well in the global marketplace.[21]

Antique dealer Dorothy Noe recognized that her customers were more eager to buy her decor—frilly curtains—than her merchandise. Undaunted, Noe started a new business selling curtains. Annual sales have reached $10 million.

Keep Creativity Alive

Once you have your business up and going (because of your creativity), how do you keep yourself and others in your business creative? Creativity is a matter of providing the proper business environment—your key to sustaining a competitive advantage. Almost every business has a creative pool with potential that is greater than its performance. Six elements of creativity are

- Alignment
- Self-initiated activity
- Unofficial activity
- Serendipity
- Diverse stimuli
- Intracompany communication

Let's look at these elements one at a time. Alignment refers to interests and actions of employees directed toward company goals. An airline flight attendant noticed that company policy required ten cardboard coffeepot lids on each flight, although only half were regularly used. She suggested that only five be stocked. Because each lid cost only 1.5 cents, the suggestion hardly seemed worthwhile. Soon managers realized that five fewer lids would save 7.5 cents per flight, and 2,300 flights per day would lead to $62,000 savings per year.

Self-initiated activity encourages employees to pick a problem they are interested in and feel able to solve. Stick with ideas; great ideas often look the worst at first (or second) glance. Silly Putty started as a wartime substitute for rubber!

Unofficial activity breaks people out of their regular boxes. Japan Railways (JR) East was building a new bullet-train line through the mountains of Japan. Water caused problems in digging a tunnel, and engineers drew up plans to drain it away. Line workers found another use: they drank it. One maintenance worker thought it tasted so good that the company should sell it as a premium bottled water. Although JR East was not in the bottled water business, their Oshimizu water now generates $60 million in annual sales.

Serendipitous discovery is a fortunate accident in the presence of sagacity (keenness of insight) by making connections between things that may seem unconnected. Mike Stephenson's epiphany occurred during a lunch meeting with his accountant, a German investor, and miscellaneous lawyers in a noisy Manhattan restaurant. Stephenson is president of Great Lakes Hybrids, a supplier of agricultural seeds. He got caught up reading the label on a bottle of wine. It was a very personalized message that described growing conditions and things the grapes had gone through, along with a family message from the vineyard owner—with his signature. Stephenson thought "Hey, we should do this with our products." Signing their names to bags of corn seed and personal statements about quality were a good idea. They had been looking for a way to break their products out of commodity status and get away from selling on price. His people back at Great Lakes Hybrids got the idea but had many questions that pushed and shaped the idea. The new product line called Signature Seed more than doubled company sales to $18 million.

Diverse stimuli provide fresh insight into a project already started or into entire new vistas. What you can't tell is how a person will react to a particular stimulus. What grabs one person's attention will be completely ignored by another person.

Intracompany communication means people within the same company exchanging information. Small companies often don't have as much difficulty in this area as larger ones, but for purposes of creativity, formal communication channels are not worth much. Don't have all your company communication via e-mail and meetings (both are creativity killers). Get people from as many different areas of the business together as much as possible—that's when creativity can flourish.

Sources: Susan Greco, "Where Great Ideas Come From," *Inc.,* April 1998, 76–86; and Sam Stern, "How Companies Can Be More Creative," *HR Magazine,* April 1998, 59.

Getting Started ▬

Most of the topics involved in starting your own business are covered in detail in other sections or entire chapters of this book. Let's look at what else is needed to get a business off the ground.

What Do You Do First?

You must first decide that you want to work for yourself rather than for someone else. You need to generate a number of ideas for a new product or service that people will buy, until you come up with the right opportunity that matches your skills and interests.

Whether you are starting a business because you have a product or service that is new to the world or because your product or service is not available locally, you have to get past the questions: Is there a need for this business? Is this business needed here? Is it needed now? These questions address the most critical concern in getting a business off the ground—the feasibility of your idea. Owning a business is a dream of many Americans, but there is usually a gap between that dream and bringing it to reality. Careful planning is needed to bridge that gap.

The Importance of Planning to a Startup

Before you begin your business, you should start by writing a comprehensive business plan (see Chapter 4). A business plan not only helps you determine the direction of your business and keeps you on track after it opens, it will be required if you need to borrow money to start your business. It shows your banker that you have seriously evaluated the business opportunity and how you will be able to pay back the loan.

Business Startup from the Left Side of the Brain

Larry Broderick is one analytical-thinking kind of guy. So much so that, when *Inc.* magazine ran an issue devoted to Startups, it spotlighted eight different styles—Broderick was labeled "The Rationalist." He is now CEO of Denver-based SteelWorks, which makes metal shapes sold to the do-it-yourself crowd via home improvement centers, lumberyards, and hardware stores. He earned the *Inc.* moniker through the process of analyzing businesses to start or buy.

Broderick is a refreshing change from the typical entrepreneurs we often read about—"a budding entrepreneur falls in love with an idea and naively embraces misguided assumptions about the cost, the time, and the customers needed to turn said idea into a viable enterprise." He created a 37-point checklist to help him evaluate during his 18-month business hunt. In fact, Broderick stated that "I think it's a huge mistake to love a business. When a business gets to be like one of your children, you can't be objective and you make a lot of bad decisions." Now no one is saying that you can run a business you don't care about (not for too long or too successfully, at least). The checklist is a tool for detaching emotion from the business process.

Although it may sound cold, Broderick-type analysis makes a lot of sense. With the correction in the stock market in 2000, a lot of funding for startups dried up, and investors started requiring a higher degree of "adult supervision" in businesses. So it is smart to apply rigorous criteria *before* the business begins. Broderick's checklist allows the entrepreneur to rate whether each of the criteria is positive or negative and to what extent this is true (circling two positive or negative signs indicates the intensity of the rating).

Broderick's Checklist

1. Specific Business
   + + – – Market
   + + – – Sources of Supply
   + + – – Customers
   + + – – Nature of Products
   + + – – Price Stability of Products
   + + – – Capital-intensive/Labor-intensive
   + + – – Union Versus Nonunion
   + + – – Environmental Concerns
   + + – – Regulatory Environment
   + + – – Existing Relationships with Customers/Vendors
   + + – – Quality of Personnel at Target
   + + – – Available Personnel to Bring to Target
   + + – – High, Medium, or Low Tech
   + + – – Point of Target in Business Cycle
   + + – – Overall Industry

2. Competition
   + + – – Profile of Competition
   + + – – Mom-and-Pop Competition
   + + – – Will Vendors Go Directly to Consumers?

3. Financial
   + + – – Profit Margins
   + + – – Float (how fast to pay vendors compared to speed customers pay)
   + + – – Seasonality
   + + – – Industry Stability
   + + – – Cost of Target
   + + – – Size of Target
   + + – – Control Considerations
   + + – – Minimum Rate of Return on Investment
   + + – – Cash Flow
   + + – – Exitability

4. Potential
   + + – – Growth Potential
   + + – – Efficiency of Target
   + + – – Computerization of Target

5. General
   + + – – Advisor Opinions
   + + – – Personal Experience/Expertise
   + + – – Gut Feel

Source: Joshua Hyatt, "The Death of Gut Instinct," *Inc.,* January 2001, 38–44.

In addition to writing your business plan, you will need to decide and record other important steps in starting your business, primarily

- *Market analysis.* For your small business to be successful, you have to get to know your market by gathering and analyzing facts about your customers in order to determine the demand for your product. Market analysis takes time and effort, but it does not have to be statistically complex or expensive. Who will buy your product? What do your customers have in common with each other? Where do they live? How much will they spend?

- *Competitive analysis.* Your business needs a competitive advantage that separates it from competitors. Before you can develop your own uniqueness, you need to know what other businesses do and how they are perceived.

  An exercise to help you remove some of the subjectivity of the competitive analysis process begins with you identifying four of your direct competitors. Then set up a grid on which you will rank your business with your competitors.

- *Startup costs.* How much money will you need to start your business? Before you can seek funding, you need to itemize what your expenses will be (see Figure 7.4). Although some of these expenses will be ongoing, others will be incurred only when you start business. There will be many expenses that you do not expect; therefore, add 10 percent to your subtotal to help offset them.

Capital equipment assets (computers, office equipment, fixtures, and furniture) have a life of more than one year. List the equipment you need with the rest of your startup costs. Beware of the temptation to buy the newest, most expensive, or fastest

FIGURE 7.4

How Much Money Will You Need?

Expense	Estimated Cost
Capital equipment	_____
_____	_____
_____	_____
_____	_____
Beginning inventory	_____
Legal fees	_____
Accounting fees	_____
Licenses and permits	_____
Remodeling and decorating	_____
Deposits (utilities, telephone)	_____
Advertising (preopening)	_____
Insurance	_____
Startup supplies	_____
Cash reserve (petty cash, credit accounts)	_____
Other expenses:	_____
_____	_____
_____	_____
_____	_____
Subtotal startup expenses:	$ _____
Add 10% safety factor:	_____
TOTAL STARTUP EXPENSES	$ _____

equipment available before you open your doors. You don't have any revenue yet, and more small businesses have failed due to lack of sales than from lack of expensive "goodies." Is good used equipment available? Should you lease rather than buy it? If sales do materialize, you can replace used equipment with new from actual profits.

- *The legal form of your business.* As discussed in Chapter 2, when starting a business you need to consider the appropriate legal form of business. Your decision will be based on tax considerations, personal liability, and cost and ease of organizing.

- *The location of your business.* Consider how important the location of your business is to your customers (see Chapter 13). If customers come to your business, your location decision is critical. If your business comes to them, or if you don't meet with them face to face, location is a less critical decision.

- *Your marketing plan.* The marketing decisions you need to make before you open your business include who your customers are, how you will reach your potential customers, what you will sell them, where it will be available, and how much it will cost (see Chapter 11).

Some aspects of starting your business are not included in the business plan. Now let's look at what your business will focus on, how you will approach customer service, the licenses you will need to acquire, and the taxes you must withhold to begin business.

manager's
notebook

Information Technology: Your Silent Partner

Information technology (IT) is rapidly changing the way organizations large and small are doing business. As costs have continued to decrease and capabilities have increased, small business owners and managers are wholeheartedly embracing the benefits offered by information technology. In fact, results from a recent survey of small business owners showed that the overwhelming majority of them felt that information technology was a critical or important factor in helping them work faster and smarter.

Information technology gives you a competitive advantage in starting a small business. In fact, a high-tech office is becoming more of a necessity than a luxury for the small business owner. IT can increase your productivity when resources are stretched tightly.

A growing amount of computer hardware and software is being designed for small businesses. You can find software to help you with all facets of planning for your business, provide you with legal advice, or furnish your business with order forms, invoices, business letters, and other forms to run your business on computer disk. Hardware that combines printer, copier, fax, and scanner functions into one machine affordable to small businesses can hold down your equipment costs. Internet service providers (ISPs) can open access to new customers, investors, and information to small businesses.

As you're organizing your startup, you might find IT useful in different areas of your business. Let's take a closer look at what IT can do for you and how you can use it to create competitive advantage.

- *Simplify your organizational structure.* Computers linked in networks allow information to be shared simultaneously and instantly among employees. The result is that employees anywhere can easily access information about marketing, sales, finances, operations, or whatever else they might need to do their jobs properly. For instance, you might decide to use an e-mail system in your small business to communicate both internally and externally. This type of communication creates a much more open organizational structure because you, your employees, customers, and others can freely communicate.

■ *Make operations more efficient and effective.* IT can help your startup run more efficiently and effectively whether you have a manufacturing or a service business. For instance, computer inventory systems can help a small manufacturer keep close tabs on the amount and type of inventory in the warehouse. Or, if you're a retail firm, you might use a point-of-sale system to calculate daily sales, control inventory, and read product bar codes as customers check out. For instance, Katie Patterson of Irving, Texas, uses a complete point-of-sale system at her bakery store to help her track sales and estimate demand for holidays such as Valentine's Day and Christmas. A personal information management system can help you manage time—your most valuable asset.

■ *Limit the number of employees.* IT enables many small businesses to operate with fewer full-time employees and to utilize freelancers or part-timers as needed for certain projects or tasks. At Rickard Associates of Hopewell, New Jersey, for instance, owner Wendy Rickard publishes magazines and marketing materials with the help of one full-time assistant and a part-time employee. However, she also utilizes freelance artists and editors across the United States, and she is able to communicate with them via the Internet and America Online. Her small business operates just as effectively as if these people were physically in the office.

■ *Enhance new product development.* Many small businesses live and die by their adeptness at developing new products. IT can play a role through capabilities such as computer-aided design (CAD) software programs, in which product designs are developed and manipulated on the computer screen before a physical model is built. Computer information systems that funnel customer comments about current and future products to product designers can also be useful.

■ *Enhance customer service.* This is another area in which IT can have a major impact. For instance, build marketing consistency and customer service by including your e-mail address and web page URL on all communications with customers. Desktop publishing packages can provide your small business with a way to cost-effectively design attractive marketing pieces, customer newsletters, or catalogues. Another IT application that can enhance customer service is a customer database with which you can keep track of customer names, addresses, phone numbers, recent order history, special orders, and so forth. For example, Gary L. Mead of Lompoc, California, owns a pizza parlor called Mi Amore Pizza & Pasta. He's able to compete with the likes of Pizza Hut, Domino's, and Little Caesar's because he uses database and direct-marketing technologies to personalize his marketing efforts. Of course, telephones are critical for your business operation, but e-mail can free you from the phone, because communications can be stored if you are not available to talk on the phone. A wireless modem in your laptop computer allows you to transmit or receive e-mail while you are on the go.

One challenge of IT is keeping up with all the information coming your way. The average office worker receives a staggering 201 pieces daily.

Sources: Thomas A. Stewart, "Managing in a Wired Company," *Fortune*, 11 July 1994, 44–56; Ira Sager, "The Great Equalizer," *Business Week, Special Bonus Issue*, 1994, 100–107; Gary McWilliams, "Mom and Pop Go High Tech," *Business Week*, 21 November 1994, 82–90; Bronwyn Fryer, "How to Succeed with Software," *Working Woman*, November 1995, 55–60; Gary McWilliams, "Small Fry Go Online," *Business Week*, 20 November 1995, 158–164; and Timothy O'Brien, "The Electronic Edge," *Wall Street Journal Report—Small Business*, 15 October 1993, R12.

How Will You Compete?

Before you begin your small business, consider what you want to be known for. Because no business can be all things to all people, you need to realize what your customers value and strive to exceed their expectations. For instance, if your customers value low price, you must set up your business to cut costs wherever possible, so that you can keep your prices low. If your customers value convenience, you need to set up your business with a focus on providing speed and ease for them. In providing value to your customers, we can identify three disciplines on which companies compete: operational excellence, product leadership, and customer intimacy.[22] In choosing to focus on one of these disciplines, you are not abandoning the other two. Instead, you are defining your position in consumers' minds. Visualize your choice of discipline by picturing each as a mountain on which you choose to compete by raising the expectation level of customers in that area (see Figure 7.5). By becoming a leader in that discipline, you are better able to defend against competing companies below you.

Companies that pursue **operational excellence** know that their customers value low price and concentrate on the efficiency of their operations to hold down costs. They don't have the very best products or cutting-edge innovations. They strive to offer good products at the lowest price possible. Dell Computer is an example of a company that competes on operational excellence.

Companies that are **product leaders** constantly innovate to make the best products available even better. This kind of commitment to quality is not inexpensive, but product leaders know that price is not the most important factor to their customers. New Balance athletic shoes are known for their technical excellence, not for their inexpensive price or their customer service.

Companies that focus on developing **customer intimacy** are not looking for a one-time sale. They seek to build a long-term, close working relationship with their customers. Their customers want to be treated as if they are the company's only customer. The Lands' End operator you speak with on the telephone sees records of clothing sizes, styles, and colors from your previous orders as soon as you call. Customer-intimate companies offer specific rather than general solutions to their customers' problems.

operational excellence Creates a competitive advantage by holding down costs to provide customers with the lowest-priced products.

product leadership Creates a competitive advantage based on providing the highest-quality products possible.

customer intimacy Creates a competitive advantage by maintaining a long-term relationship with customers through superior service.

Customer Service

Your business relationship with your customers does not end with the sale of your product or service. Increasing your level of customer service and adopting professional standards are critical, especially in an industry where all competitors appear to be the same. Satisfying the customer is not a means to achieve a goal; *it is the goal.* Customer service can be your competitive advantage.

FIGURE 7.5

On Which Mountain Will You Compete?

When setting up your small business, you must decide how you will satisfy your customers. Do you need to offer them the best product, the best price, or the best service?

The importance of a startup business's providing an emphasis on the highest-quality customer service cannot be overstated. When her father suddenly became ill, Deborah Silverberg took over the family's commercial floor contracting business, AnchorMann Enterprises of St. Louis, MO. Despite a recession, she increased the size of the business tenfold—basically starting the business all over again. She expanded service to other cities and bought out a competitor. For Silverberg, making customers happy is an essential part of her strategy for success. As one of the only companies in the flooring industry with its own maintenance department, AnchorMann Enterprises is able to offer longer warranties on its products than can its competitors. Silverberg admits that this advantage is "not mind-boggling. But it's unique enough to get people to do business with us rather than the competition."[23]

Licenses, Permits, and Regulations

If your business has no employees, you have fewer legal requirements to meet. First, let's look at the common requirements for all businesses. You need to file your business name with the secretary of state of the state in which you are forming your business. This is to make sure that the name you have chosen for your business is not registered by another company. If it is, you will have to find another name for your business.

You must obtain the appropriate local licenses from the city hall and county clerk's office before you start your business. Find out if you can operate your business in the location you have picked by checking local zoning ordinances. You may need a special permit for certain types of businesses. For example, if your business handles processed food, it must pass a local health department inspection.

Most states collect sales tax on tangible property sold. If your state does, you must apply for a state sales tax identification number to use when paying the sales taxes you collect. Contact the department of revenue in your state for information regarding your requirements. Many types of businesspeople, such as accountants, electricians, motor vehicle dealers, cosmetologists, and securities dealers, require specific licenses. These licenses are obtained from the state agency that oversees that type of business.

Very few small businesses are likely to need any type of federal permit or license to operate. If you will produce alcohol, firearms, tobacco products, meat products, or give investment advice, contact an attorney regarding regulations.

Taxes

When your business begins operation, you must make advance payments of your estimated federal (and possibly state) income taxes. Individual tax payments are due in four quarterly installments—on the 15th day of April, June, September, and January. It is important for you to remember to set money aside from your revenues so that it will be available when your quarterly taxes are due. The Internal Revenue Service is not known for its sense of humor if funds are not available.

If your business is a sole proprietorship, you report your self-employment income on Schedule SE of IRS Form 1040, and any income or loss on Schedule C of IRS Form 1040. A partnership reports partnership income on IRS Form 1065 and each partner reports his or her individual share on Schedule SE and Schedule E. Corporations file tax returns on IRS Form 1120. Any payment you make over $600 for items like rent, interest, or services from independent contractors must be shown on Form 1096, and copies of Form 1099 must be sent to the people you paid.

When you begin employing other people, you become an agent of the U.S. government and must begin collecting income and social security taxes. You must get a federal Employer Identification Number, which identifies your business for all tax purposes. Your local IRS office will supply you with a business tax kit with all the necessary forms. You withhold 7.51 percent of an employee's wages for social security tax, and you must pay a matching 7.51 percent employer's social security tax. Pay both halves of the tax quarterly with your payroll tax return.

independent contractor
Person who is not employed by a business and, unlike employees, is not eligible for a benefit package.

If a person provides services to your business but is not an employee, he or she is considered to be an **independent contractor.** Because independent contractors are considered to be self-employed, you do not have to withhold social security tax, federal or state income taxes, or unemployment taxes from their earnings—an obvious advantage to you. Because of the advantage of classifying a person as an independent contractor rather than an employee, the IRS imposes stiff penalties on businesses that improperly treat employees as independent contractors.

You must deposit a percentage of each employee's earnings for federal and state unemployment tax with a federal tax deposit coupon. The federal unemployment tax rate is 6.2 percent of the first $7,000 per employee, but a credit of up to 5.4 percent is allowed for state unemployment tax. In reality, only 0.8 percent goes to federal tax. The state rate you pay depends on the amount of claims filed by former employees. The more claims, the higher your unemployment tax, within certain limits.

SUMMARY

The advantages and disadvantages of starting a business from scratch.

When starting a business from scratch, the small business owner is free to establish a distinct competitive advantage. There are no negative images or prior mistakes to overcome, as may occur when purchasing an existing business. The creation of a new business builds pride of ownership. However, the risk of failure is higher for a startup because there are more questions regarding the size and existence of a market for the business.

The common types of new businesses and characteristics of fast-growth companies.

E-businesses have completely changed the small business landscape. Other types of new businesses are home-based businesses and part-time businesses. Some small businesses start with the intention of becoming hypergrowth companies. These companies are generally led by teams of people with experience starting that type of business (usually high-tech manufacturing). They are well financed and constantly look to expand into new markets.

Evaluating potential startups and ideas.

When a new product idea is introduced to the market, the window of opportunity is open the widest (assuming it is a product that people want and will buy), because little competition exists. As a product progresses through the product life cycle, the window of opportunity closes, as more competition enters the market and demand declines.

Most people get ideas for new businesses from prior employment. Turning a hobby or outside interest into a business is also common. Ideas may come from other people's suggestions or spring from information gained while taking a class. Sometimes business ideas occur by chance.

Getting started.

The entrepreneur needs to begin with questioning the feasibility of his or her idea. Then, to bridge the gap between dream and reality, careful planning is needed. Entrepreneurs need to carefully consider the costs of starting a new business, and they must analyze the market and competitive landscape to ensure their competitive advantage.

Providing customers with outstanding service during and after the sale of a product is of utmost importance in business startups. Customer service is the basis for establishing a long-term relationship with customers.

Startups also have legal requirements. Entrepreneurs must file the business name with the state of origin and obtain local business licenses and any industry-specific permits. They must also apply for a tax identification number in order to collect and process sales taxes.

QUESTIONS FOR **REVIEW & DISCUSSION**

1. Compare and contrast the advantages and disadvantages of starting a business from the ground up. Be sure to include the different types of businesses in your analysis.

2. Define "hypergrowth" companies, and evaluate the reasons for their phenomenal rate of growth. What are the most valid explanations for the rate of success found in these companies?

3. Explain the concept "window of opportunity" as it relates to new startups, from idea conception through the final decision about whether or not to turn the idea into a reality.

4. Entrepreneurs get their ideas for business startups from various sources. Elaborate on these sources, and analyze which ones are the most reliable indicators for the new business owner with regard to future success.

5. Once a decision has been made to start up a new business, give some examples of things the new entrepreneur should immediately investigate in order to ensure to the maximum extent possible that the business will "get off the ground."

6. Is a business plan really necessary even for a very small startup business? How much market analysis and competitive analysis should the new entrepreneur conduct prior to startup?

7. What are some of the tangible resources that the new entrepreneur might need in order to go into business? What are some options for obtaining capital for a business that is brand new and therefore has no financial history?

8. After startup, what is the *single* most important tool the small business owner has at his or her disposal to ensure the success of the business? Why is it so crucial?

9. What are some examples of consumer preferences and values? What are some examples of things the new business owner can do to ensure capturing some of the market for the good or service being produced?

10. Discuss the legal ramifications of starting your own business. Where should the new entrepreneur go to get information and advice regarding laws that govern the type of business that is being promoted?

QUESTIONS FOR **CRITICAL THINKING**

1. What criteria do you see as most critical when differentiating an idea from an opportunity?

2. Many entrepreneurs test the waters of a market by starting a sideline business. What are the advantages and disadvantages of selling items on Internet auctions like eBay? Is a person who regularly has 20 or 25 items for sale at any given time an entrepreneur? What types of products would be most appropriately sold in this manner?

Experience this...

A good idea is nothing more than a tool in the hands of an entrepreneur. Take a class session to conduct a brainstorming exercise to stimulate creativity. Brainstorming begins by defining a purpose. In this case we want to generate ideas for a business that undergraduate business students can start before they graduate. Choose a student to serve as the facilitator, who will record *every* idea on the board—with no criticism or negatives. Encourage brainstorming to occur spontaneously and abundantly (although you may wish to set a parameter that the idea be legal in nature). Students should strive to fill a known or perceived void. Don't spend time getting committed to one idea.

Once a sizable list has been generated (about 50 ideas, or when the exercise runs out of gas), identify the most promising ideas. Refine and prioritize the ideas. Have the group choose about 10 percent (5 or 6 ideas) and discuss their opportunity potential. Could they stand on their own as viable opportunities—or, better yet, could 2, 3, or all 6 be combined in a feasible venture?

WHAT WOULD **YOU** DO? | No. 1

Todd Holmes and Louis Amoroso enjoy going out to a bar and having a beer. In the early nineties, they noticed a trend—beer drinkers like trying out different high-quality, regional beers. Research into industry statistics disclosed the same trend. Since 1988, overall beer consumption had been flat, but the combined volume of 460 U.S. microbrewers had grown an average of 46 percent a year. So the 24-year-old pals put their heads together to find a way they could tap into this trend, and came up with two prospects. But they weren't sure of the approach they wanted to take. The first prospect was that they could start their own microbrewery—a small, regional brewery producing fewer than 15,000 barrels a year. As a manufacturer, they'd make their own regional beer and market it. Or they might try a different approach by acting as a distributor. Here their idea was to set up a beer-of-the-month club that would send subscribers a different regional beer every month. What do *you* think about these two startups that Holmes and Amoroso could pursue to take advantage of this market trend?

Sources: James M. Clash, "Beer Bash," *Forbes*, 5 December 1994, 66–69; and "Beer Across America," *Success*, September 1995, 34.

QUESTIONS

1. Draft a proposal for the startup business in this example that you feel has the greatest potential. Be sure to consider all the aspects of being a manufacturer versus being a distributor.

2. Working together in teams of two or three individuals, discuss the relative merits of each of Holmes's and Amoroso's possibilities. Develop a bulleted list of pros and cons for each approach.

WHAT WOULD **YOU** DO? | No. 2

Carrie Ann thinks she is onto an opportunity. She has watched the trend of tattoos and body art increasing for several years. She now believes the trend is leveling off and that in the near future many people who had gotten tattoos will want them removed. In anticipation, she has developed a nonsurgical approach to tattoo removal that consists of a cream applied to the tattoo. The area is then covered with gauze, and the cream must be reapplied every day for two weeks. At the end of two weeks, the tattoo is gone. A tube of Carrie Ann's cream will retail at about $50.

QUESTIONS

1. Carrie Ann is concerned about the timing of releasing her product. She is not sure the window of opportunity is open wide enough at this time for her business to succeed, but she worries that, if she waits for the opportunity to develop, another product will beat her as first to market. How would you advise her in her opportunity analysis?

2. Carrie Ann's business could become a fast-growth player as described in this chapter. What would she need to do to become a fast-growth company?

Turning James Prosek into "James Prosek" the Brand

James Prosek, 23, is not going into business for himself; he's going into business as himself. At least that's how his big sister Jennifer, 30, sees the plan. Jennifer is part owner of Jacobs & Prosek, a $1.5 million public relations firm based in Stamford, Conn. As an MBA candidate at Columbia University's School of Business, Jennifer and her classmates developed a 67-page business plan to turn "James Prosek" into a profit-making concern.

Capitalizing on Fame   When James was a 20-year-old Yale undergraduate, he parlayed his passion for fishing into an encyclopedic coffee-table book, *Trout: An Illustrated History*, which has sold more than 60,000 copies. His watercolors of the angling world fetch as much as $6,000. He has published two more books. His fans include *Rolling Stone* magazine founder Jann Wenner and broadcaster Tom Brokaw, who fished with Prosek in front of NBC news cameras.

Jennifer wants to help James garner the multimillion-dollar opportunities available through his fame in the literary, art, and fishing worlds. She spends much of her free time dreaming up ways her brother can generate ever-greater revenues ($220,000 in one recent year). Yet James says his foremost objective "is to be recognized as a relatively serious author and painter."

Setting Profit Goals   The business plan's goal is to post revenues of close to $3 million with $1.5 million in profits within three years. The plan identifies James as company president, creative director, and product manager for books and fine art. The company's purpose is to help James establish a diversified product line and a brand image—to put James's stamp of approval on everything from smoked-trout gift baskets to fish-theme wrapping paper, calendars, and even throw rugs, already available for $40 apiece. James, however, has reservations: "I don't want the licensing stuff to take over from books. I don't want to become known for throw rugs."

The "James Prosek" business plan is a bid for James to become the personification of a brand like Martha Stewart. While the comparison makes James frown, Jennifer has found it helpful in talking up the plan to potential investors. James may resist the comparison, but "James Prosek's" goal is to transform the individual from a fish aficionado to standard-bearer for an entire way of life. Despite representing simplicity and naturalness, the "James Prosek" lifestyle will be highly accessorized. The company's overriding mission, says the plan, is "to awaken the minds of all individuals to the beauty of the natural world, trout, and the experience of fishing through the words, paintings, products, and services of James Prosek." As Jennifer says, "I was always frustrated that he had more notoriety than he did dollars. One of my dreams has been, 'Can we leverage all this great exposure James has been getting?'"

Own One Word   Such personal-brand models as the one Jennifer would like to establish already exist, say experts such as Al Ries, coauthor of *Positioning: The Battle for Your Mind*. This branding is what practically every CEO wants these days. "I say to them, 'Think of a word you can own in the mind,'" says Ries. "Regardless of whether you're good at everything, you should emphasize one aspect of your personality and de-emphasize everything else. Become known for one thing."

Right now, James is simply a professional-services provider. He gets paid only if he produces something. The business plan concedes that he can create only so many paintings or write so many books. And none of that is guaranteed. The plan warns that "personal injury could seriously affect Prosek's ability to write and paint." Unlike accountants or consultants, James can't recruit junior partners, taking a percentage of their billings.

James is not slavishly following the business plan. For example, he decided not to host the TV show the plan described. The show would have featured James fishing with top-drawer CEOs and "could have been a huge opportunity," says Jennifer. James says, "I couldn't see the shape of it. I sometimes entertain things just so my sister won't be discouraged."

James expressed reservations about a travel-tour package that Jennifer developed. Jennifer found a partner to finance and market the tour, but the advertising made James uneasy. "They ran a full-page ad in *Yale Alumni Magazine* that said 'created and hosted by James Prosek,'" he says. "I was not going to be there for more than two or three days. I think the tour idea is a great one, but the idea of using me as a poster boy is the unsettling part." As it turned out, only four people signed up for the $10,900 tour and it was canceled.

"The biggest problem is James's personal struggle with wanting to be commercial," Jennifer says. "Nine out of 10 things I offer James, which can be profitable, he'll decline. If I were James Prosek, I'd grow the empire."

Source: Adapted from "Brand in the Making" by Mike Hofman, from *Inc.: The Magazine for Growing Companies*, Oct. 1999, 52–62. Copyright © 1999 by Goldhirsh Group/Inc Pubg. Reproduced with permission of Goldhirsh Group/Inc Pubg in the format textbook via Copyright Clearance Center.

QUESTIONS

1. Describe the niche that 23-year-old James Prosek is filling with his diversified product line. What "business" is he really in as himself?

2. Analyze the opportunities and challenges that James and Jennifer face in creating this business.

3. What would your advice be to them? Do you agree with Al Ries's suggestion to "become known for one thing"?

4. Is James committed enough to start and run this business, or is he being manipulated?

Financial and Legal Management

As a small business owner you will need to depend on the advice of several professionals—most significantly, accountants, lenders, and lawyers. But in order to make the best decisions for your business from their advice, you need a basic understanding of accounting systems, financial management, and the law. You have to understand your own accounting system and financial statement analysis; ways to finance your business; and the laws and regulations that apply to your business. **Chapter 8** covers accounting systems and financial statements and their use; **Chapter 9** discusses small business financial needs; and **Chapter 10** examines the legal environment of small business.

8

Accounting Records and Financial Statements

After reading this chapter, you should be able to:

- Discuss the importance and uses of financial records to a small business.

- Itemize the accounting records needed for a small business.

- Explain the 11 ratios used to analyze financial statements.

- Illustrate the importance of and procedures for managing cash flow.

KEN AND MARJORIE FOUST took a typical approach to operating their small business when they started it two years ago. Ken is general manager of ElectriCraft, an electrical contracting company in Denver. Marjorie owned the business and handled the bookkeeping, payroll, and accounts receivable and payable, which took about 30 hours per week to complete. Marjorie was also studying electrical engineering full time. So, in order for Marjorie to have a life, something had to go. The Fousts ran a classified ad for a part-time bookkeeper. Lance and Deanna Gildea, owners of The Accounting Department (TAD), responded to the Fousts' ad. TAD is an online accounting service based in San Diego which is now saving the owners of ElectriCraft a lot of time and money.

TAD handles all of ElectriCraft's accounting and bookkeeping needs, like payroll, accounts receivable and payable, financial statement preparation, and taxes, at about one-third the cost of hiring an in-house bookkeeper. Plus Marjorie got her life back, because now she spends only ten minutes a day scanning source documents which are transmitted to TAD for processing, rather than the 30 hours a week she spent doing the work herself.

Deanna Gildea, owner and president of TAD, calls her company a "one-stop shop" outsourcing bookkeeping, accounting, and tax preparation services—services that many small businesses have trouble affording by hiring their own qualified staff. TAD has 10 employees (all of whom telecommute) who serve their 45 clients. Services provided range from basic to full-service outsourcing, real-time or near-real-time accounting, access to high-end accounting software applications, and 24–7 client access to their accounts. Clients tend to come from small construction, high-tech, and nonprofit companies.

TAD's online accounting service begins with clients' scanning source documents, such as invoices, contracts, and bank statements. TAD provides a Visioneer Strobe Pro

Scanner free, as part of the service contract for accounts of more than $1,500 per month, or for $250 for smaller accounts. The scanned documents are sent to TAD, where they are updated into the client's account. Customers can go to TAD's home page (www .tadepartment.com), sign into their secure client page, and view, print, or download reports, checks, and other information. Not only does each client have its own electronic filing cabinet, it also has access to its own assigned bookkeeper, CPA, and tech support person.

The cost of such online service can mean as much as 50 percent savings. For example, a business with up to five employees, 26 to 50 invoices a month, and 61 to 100 billings per month could pay between $1,418 and $1,900 a month for bookkeeping. Not bad.

Source: Antoinnette Alexander, "Pioneers on the Virtual Frontier," *Accounting Technology*, January/February 2000, 18–24.

> *The accounting process helps you to translate numbers—the language of business—into plain English.*

Are you intimidated by the thought of accounting systems, with row after row and column after column of numbers? If you are, you aren't alone. But you shouldn't be frightened by or dread the numbers of your business, because accounting isn't about making rows and columns of numbers. It is about organizing and communicating what's going on in your business. Think of numbers as the language of business.

Computers help us take piles of raw data and turn them into usable information with which to make managerial decisions. For example, consider a marketing research project you have conducted. You have received thousands of completed questionnaires, each with 20 responses. You would have a very hard time interpreting these thousands of pages because they contain raw, unprocessed *data*. If you were to enter all your data into a statistical program on a computer, you could organize these data into means, trends, and a few meaningful numbers, or *information*, which would allow you to make marketing decisions.

DILBERT reprinted by permission of United Features Syndicate, Inc.

Accounting systems accomplish a similar purpose. Think of all the piles of checks, receipts, invoices, and other papers your business generates in a month as data. Everything you need to know about the financial health of your business is in those piles, but it is not in a usable form. Accounting systems funnel piles of data into usable information by recording every transaction that occurs in your business in journals, then transferring (or posting) them into ledgers. The process is basically the same whether you use pencil and paper or an accounting program on a PC. From the ledger you make financial statements like a balance sheet, income statement, and statement of cash flow. These statements communicate what is going on in your business much better than the piles of papers you started with.

The last step in the accounting process is to take certain numbers from your financial statements to compute key ratios which can be compared to industry averages or historical figures from your own business to help you make financial decisions. The intent of this chapter is not to turn you into an accountant, but rather to help you understand the communication process—or language—better (see Figure 8.1).

So how is a new entrepreneur supposed to get the accounting process started? How can you create an orderly system from nothing without expertise in accounting? Many start with a simple accounting software package (see Manager's Notebook, "Computerized Accounting Packages"). Another stellar piece of advice is to pay an accounting firm that specializes in small businesses to set up your accounting system. You don't have to use them for all of your accounting needs like payroll preparation, tax form preparation, and creation of monthly financial statements, although you could. Money would be well spent getting a system that will work for your business from the very beginning—as opposed to throwing all receipts, invoices, and paperwork into a shoebox and panicking when the time comes to file quarterly taxes. Do yourself and your business a favor, and get started correctly by using a professional.

accounting The system within a business for converting raw data from source documents (like invoices, sales receipts, bills, and checks) into information which will help a manager make business decisions.

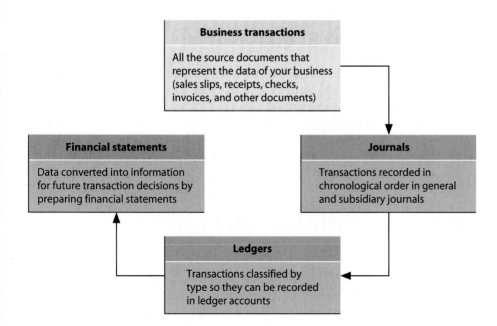

FIGURE 8.1

The Accounting Process

An accounting system works on a cycle to convert raw data into usable information for making decisions about how to run your small business.

How Important Are Financial Records?

Financial records are important to businesses for several reasons. Remember when we discussed the reasons for failure of small businesses in Chapter 1? Most of the mismanagement decisions that spell the doom of many small businesses are related to financial and accounting issues.

Too often, the last thing small business owners think of is careful accounting, but it should be the first. While you are plagued with a lot of worries—from making payroll to buying products to selling your services—you can put yourself at a competitive disadvantage by not being accounting oriented from the beginning. Many small business owners don't hire an accountant right away because they are afraid of the cost, but many accounting firms specialize in small business and are available at reasonable prices. It's like the advice you have probably heard your whole life: Getting things right the first time costs less than fixing mistakes the second or third time.

Accurate Information for Management

You need to have accurate financial information to know the financial health of your business. To make effective management decisions, you must know things like the value of your accounts receivable, the age of each account, how quickly your inventory is turning over, which items are not moving, how much your firm owes, when debts are due, and how much your business owes in taxes and FICA (social security taxes). Good records are needed to answer these and many other similar questions. Without good records, these questions would be impossible to answer. Accurate financial records also allow you to identify problems before they become threats to your business.

Banking and Tax Requirements

The information on your financial statements is needed to prepare your tax returns. If the Internal Revenue Service audits your business, you will be expected to produce the relevant accounting records and statements.

Bankers and investors use your financial statements to evaluate the condition of your business. If you need the services of either, you must not only produce statements, you must also be ready to explain and defend their contents.

Small Business Accounting Basics

The accounting system provides you with information for making decisions about your small business. To access this information, you need to understand the entry systems you can use and how accounting equations work. Your accounting system should be easy to use, accurate, timely, consistent, understandable, dependable, and complete.

Double- and Single-Entry Systems

Double-entry accounting systems revolve around three elements: assets, liabilities, and owner's equity. **Assets** are what your business owns. **Liabilities** are what your business owes. **Owner's equity** is what you (the owner) have invested in the business (it can also be called "capital" or "net worth").

As the name implies, with a double-entry system, all transactions are recorded in two ways—once as a *debit* to one account and again as a *credit* to another account. Every "plus" must be balanced by a "minus" so that each transaction shows how assets are affected on one side and how liabilities and owner's equity are affected on the other.

A double-entry accounting system increases the accuracy of your system and provides a self-checking audit. If you make a mistake in recording a transaction, your accounts will not balance, indicating to you that you need to go back over the books to find the error. Debits must always equal credits. To increase an asset, you debit the account. To increase a liability or equity, you credit the account.

A **single-entry accounting** system does exist and may be used by small sole proprietorships. With a single-entry system, you record the flow of income and expenses in a running log, basically like a checkbook. It allows you to produce a monthly statement but not to make a balance sheet, an income statement, or other financial records. The single-entry system is simple but not self-balancing, as a double-entry system is.

Popular computer programs like Quicken employ a single-entry accounting system. These programs provide attractive features like the ability to track expense categories, post amounts to those accounts, and print reports, but they are still pretty much electronic check registers. Many small, one-person businesses begin with them because of their simplicity and then graduate to more powerful, full-feature systems like the Peachtree or Great Plains accounting programs. There is no one-size-fits-all computer accounting program for your small business.[1] You may have to adjust as you grow.

On the subject of beginning simply: *Always* use separate checkbooks for your business and your personal life. Avoid the temptation to combine the two by thinking that "the business money and personal money is all mine—I'll just keep them together." At some point you will need to separate them, which can be very difficult to do later. Also, write checks instead of paying for items with cash. They serve as an accurate form of record keeping. Finally, reconcile your bank accounts monthly, and make sure all errors are corrected.

double-entry accounting An accounting system in which every business transaction is recorded in an asset account *and* a liability or owner's equity account in order for the system to balance.

asset Any resource that a business owns and expects to use to its benefit.

liability A debt owed by a business to another organization or individual.

owner's equity The amount of money the owner of a business would receive if all of the assets were sold and all of the liabilities were paid.

single-entry accounting An accounting system in which the flow of income and expenses is recorded in a running log, basically like a checkbook.

Accounting Equations

As stated earlier, numbers are the language of business. Three equations set the foundation for that language.

$$\text{Assets} = \text{Liabilities} + \text{Owner's equity}$$
$$\text{Profit} = \text{Revenue} - \text{Expenses}$$
$$\text{Cash flow} = \text{Receipts} - \text{Disbursements}$$

The first equation, Assets = Liabilities + Owner's equity, is the basis of the *balance sheet*. Any entry that you make on one side of the equation must also be entered on the other to maintain a balance. For example, say you have a good month

Computerized Accounting Packages

A computerized accounting information system can help a small business manager get accounting information efficiently and quickly. Some of the benefits of computerized accounting are

- Time saved by the structural methods of entering accounting data and generating accounting statements

- Better and more detailed information obtained than with manual systems

- Improved traceability of income and expenses (which could prove important for audits)

- Increased timeliness and frequency of accounting statements

However, selecting appropriate hardware and accounting software can be a major challenge. To make your decision easier, let's examine some of the better-known accounting packages.

Quickbooks Pro. The market leader for small accounting packages. Setup is straightforward and smooth. Over 100 customizable reports that can be exported to an Excel spreadsheet. Quickbooks Pro is a comprehensive package and an excellent choice for a small business. It will automate all money matters, including check writing, invoicing, billing, payroll, and receipts. Modules include an integrated merchant credit card service, electronic postal service, and web site creation using 250 templates.

Peachtree Complete Accounting. This powerful, comprehensive accounting package comes with payroll, inventory, job cost, and order entry functions to create an extensive array of reports, forms, and financial statements. Although Peachtree allows great versatility in creating accounting documents, the user needs a good understanding of debits, credits, and basic accounting principles. It's probably best suited for a well-established business wanting considerable sophistication in its accounting system and extensive flexibility in creating accounting reports. E-Peachtree is an application service provider product for tech-oriented small businesses.

MYOB Plus. Mind Your Own Business is another excellent general-purpose accounting program. It has more than 150 predefined reports and over 100 different custom charts of accounts. MYOB Plus lets you e-mail invoices, purchase orders, and reports. It will handle multiple currencies and multiple sales tax codes. Its strongest point is in inventory handling with support for multiple price matrixes and quantity discounts breaks. You can even include pictures of inventory items in their description.

Simply Accounting. This accounting package is aimed at the very small business market. It does not have all the features of other software discussed here but is a powerful package that is appropriately named.

Keep in mind that your choice of an accounting software package depends on the size of your business and its accounting needs. Generally speaking, the more features and customization options provided in the package, the more expensive it will be and the more complex to install and use. However, as you can see, there's a wide variety of packages to choose from. Be sure to get one that meets your particular needs.

Sources: John Hedtke, "Low-Cost High-Function Accounting," *Accounting Technology*, May 2000, 34–46; Cassandra Cavanah, "CyberCPAs," *Entrepreneur*, October 2000, 71–73; Brad Patten, "An Accounting App That Adds Up for Small Business," *Washington Business Journal*, 24 April 2000, 70; and Tracey Miller-Segarra, "Reaching the Small Business Accounting Market," *Accounting Technology*, July 2000, SR1–3.

and decide to pay off a $2,000 note you took out at the bank six months ago. You would credit your cash account (an asset) by $2,000 and debit your notes payable account (a liability) by $2,000. Your balance sheet remains in equilibrium. Of course, any equation can be rearranged if you understand it. For example:

$$\text{Owner's equity} = \text{Assets} - \text{Liabilities}$$

You can also think of it this way:

$$\text{What you have} = \text{What you own} - \text{What you owe}$$

The second equation, Profit = Revenue − Expenses, represents the activity of the *income statement*. In other words, the money you get to keep equals the money your business brings in minus what you have to spend.

The third equation, Cash flow = Receipts − Disbursements, is the basis of the *cash flow statement*. The money you have on hand at any given time equals the money you bring in minus what you have to pay out.

We will discuss the balance sheet, the income statement, and the cash flow statement in more detail later in this chapter.

Cash and Accrual Methods of Accounting

One decision you need to make in your accounting system is whether to use cash or accrual accounting. The difference between the two is how each shows the timing of your receipts and your disbursements.

Most businesses use the **accrual basis** method of accounting. In using this method, you report your income and expenses at the time they are earned or incurred, rather than when they are collected or paid. Sales you make on credit are recorded as accounts receivable that have not yet been collected. The accrual method also allows you to record payment of expenses over a period of time, even if the actual payment is made in a single installment. For example, you may pay for insurance once or twice a year, but you can record payment on a monthly basis.

With a **cash basis** method of accounting, you record transactions when cash is actually received and expenses are actually paid. The cash method is simpler to keep than the accrual method. Although it may be appropriate for very small businesses, for businesses with no inventory, or for businesses that deal strictly in cash, the cash method can distort financial results over time. You should not use the cash basis if your business extends credit, because credit sales would not be recorded as sales until you receive payment. Also, your accounts payable would not be recorded as an expense until the bill is paid.

accrual basis A method of accounting in which income and expenses are recorded at the time they are incurred, rather than when they are paid.

cash basis A method of accounting in which income and expenses are recorded at the time they are paid, rather than when they are incurred.

What Accounting Records Do You Need?

To turn data into management information, you need to follow certain guidelines or standards called **generally accepted accounting principles (GAAP)**. The group that monitors the appropriateness of these principles is the Financial Accounting Standards Board (FASB). These GAAP guidelines are intended to create financial statement formats that are uniform across industries. Because business is complex, flexibility in GAAP methods is acceptable as long as consistency is maintained within the business.

generally accepted accounting principles (GAAP) Standards established so that all businesses produce comparable financial statements.

journal A chronological record of all financial transactions of a business.

general ledger A record of all financial transactions divided into accounts and usually compiled at the end of each month.

JOURNALS AND LEDGERS. Your accounting actually begins when you record your raw data, from sources such as sales slips, purchase invoices, and check stubs, in journals. A **journal** is simply a place to write down the date of your transactions, the amounts, and the accounts to be debited and credited. You will have several journals, such as sales, purchases, cash receipts, and cash disbursements journals.

At some regular time interval (daily, weekly, or monthly), you will post the transactions recorded in all your journals in a general ledger. A **general ledger** is a summary book for recording all transactions and account balances. One of the advantages of using a computerized accounting system is that it can perform the monotonous task of posting electronically. To speed the posting process and to facilitate access to accounts, each account is assigned a two-digit number. The first digit indicates the class of the account (1 for assets, 2 for liabilities, 3 for capital, 4 for income, and 5 for expenses). The second digit is assigned to each account within the class. For example, your cash account could be assigned account number 11. The first 1 shows that the account is an asset, whereas the second means that it is your first asset listed. Your inventory could be assigned the account number 13, meaning that it is the third asset listed.

At the end of your accounting period or fiscal year, you will close and total each individual account in your general ledger. At this point, or at any time you wish if you are using a computerized accounting package, you can prepare your financial statements to see where your business stands financially. The three most important statements for providing financial information about your business are the income statement, the balance sheet, and the statement of cash flow.

income statement A financial statement which shows the revenue and expenses of a firm in order to calculate the profit or loss produced in a specific period of time.

INCOME STATEMENT. The **income statement,** also called the profit and loss (P&L) statement, summarizes the income and expenses that your company has totaled over a period of time (see Figure 8.2). The income statement illustrates the accounting equation Profit = Revenue − Expenses. Your income statement can generally be broken down into the following sections:

- Net sales
- Cost of goods sold
- Gross margin
- Expenses
- Net income (or loss)

common-size financial statement A financial statement that includes a percentage breakdown of each item.

Not only does the income statement show an itemization of your sales, cost of goods sold, and expenses, but it also allows you to calculate the percentage relationship of each item of expense to sales. Including these percentages on your financial statements produces what is known as a **common-size financial statement.** Common-size financial statements are valuable tools for checking the efficiency trends of your business by measuring and controlling individual expense items.

Consider the example of Stereo City, a retail company which sells home electronic equipment. Stereo City's net sales for the accounting period were $450,000. The business held a 40 percent gross profit (or margin), which means that, out of net sales, Stereo City had acquired $180,000 with which to cover its operating expenses. Total expenses were $157,250 (34.94 percent of sales). After adding interest income and deducting interest expenses and taxes, the company's net profit—the bottom line—was $4,830.

FIGURE 8.2
**Stereo City Income
Statement**

INCOME:		Percentage of Sales
Net Sales	$450,000	100.00
Cost of Goods Sold	270,00	60.00
GROSS PROFIT ON SALES	$180,00	40.00
EXPENSES:		
Selling Expense		
Advertising	$ 12,000	2.67
Delivery and Freight	10,000	2.22
Sales Salaries	25,000	5.56
Miscellaneous Selling Expenses	1,000	0.22
Administrative Expense		
Licenses	$150	0.03
Insurance	2,400	0.53
Nonsales Salaries	38,000	8.44
Payroll Taxes	6,300	1.40
Rent/Mortgage	12,400	2.76
Utilities	6,000	1.33
Legal Fees	1,500	0.33
Depreciation	42,000	9.33
Miscellaneous Administrative Expenses	500	0.11
TOTAL EXPENSES	$157,250	34.94
INCOME FROM OPERATIONS	$ 22,750	5.06
OTHER INCOME		
Interest Income	$300	0.07
OTHER EXPENSES		
Interest Expense	$ 15,000	3.33
NET PROFIT (LOSS) BEFORE TAXES	$ 8,050	1.79
INCOME TAXES	$ 3,220	0.72
NET PROFIT (LOSS) AFTER TAXES	$ 4,830	1.07
NOTE:		
Cash Flow from Operations Equals Net Profit or Loss After Taxes plus Depreciation	$ 46,830	

BALANCE SHEET. While the income statement shows the financial condition of your business over time, the **balance sheet** provides an instant "snapshot" of your business at any given moment (usually at the end of the month, quarter, or fiscal year; see Figure 8.3). A balance sheet has two main sections—one showing the assets of the business and one showing the liabilities and capital of the business. As explained previously under "Accounting Equations," these two sides must balance.

On Stereo City's sample balance sheet, you will see a column of percentages of total assets, liabilities, and capital. As with the common-size income statement, these percentages on the common-size balance sheet can indicate accounts and areas that are out of line compared to industry averages, such as those published by Financial Research Associates, Robert Morris Associates, or trade associations.

STATEMENT OF CASH FLOW. The **statement of cash flow** highlights the cash coming into and going out of your business. It is summarized by the accounting

balance sheet A financial statement that shows a firm's assets, liabilities, and owner's equity.

statement of cash flow A financial statement that shows the cash inflows and outflows of a business.

FIGURE 8.3

Stereo City Balance Sheet

ASSETS		Percentage of Total Assets
Current Assets:		
Cash	$ 3,500	1.08
Accounts Receivable	12,000	3.71
Inventory	125,000	38.64
Prepaid Expenses	5,000	1.55
Short-Term Investments	10,000	3.09
Total Current Assets	$155,500	48.07
Fixed Assets:		
Building	$150,000	46.37
Equipment	25,000	7.73
Leasehold Improvements	20,000	6.18
Other Fixed Assets	15,000	4.64
Gross Fixed Assets	$210,000	64.91
Less: Accumulated Depreciation	42,000	12.98
Net Fixed Assets	$168,000	51.93
Total Assets	$323,500	100.00

LIABILITIES AND OWNERS' EQUITY		Percentage of Liability and Equity
Current Liabilities:		
Accounts Payable	$ 75,000	23.18
Accruals	7,500	2.32
Current Portion of Long-Term Debt	17,500	5.41
Other Current Liabilities	5,000	1.55
Total Current Liabilities	$105,000	32.46
Long-Term Liabilities:		
Mortgage Loan	$ 93,000	28.75
Term Loan	39,500	12.21
Total Long-Term Liabilities	$132,500	40.96
Total Liabilities	$237,500	73.42
Owners' Equity		
Paid-in Capital	$ 75,000	23.18
Retained Earnings	11,000	3.40
Total Owners' Equity	$ 86,000	26.58
Total Liabilities and Owners' Equity	$323,500	100.00

equation Cash flow = Receipts – Disbursements (see Figure 8.4). The importance of tracking and forecasting your cash flow is difficult to overstate because it is often more critical to survival of the business than profits. Many businesses show considerable profit but have problems paying their bills—meaning that they have a cash flow problem.

It is common for new businesses to experience a situation in which more cash goes out than comes in, which is called a "negative cash flow." This condition is not too alarming if it happens when the business is very young or if it happens only occasionally. However, if you experience negative cash flow regularly, you may be undercapitalized, which is a serious problem.[2] More on managing your cash flow will be covered later in this chapter.

WHAT IF YOU ARE STARTING A NEW BUSINESS? If you are starting a new business, you don't have historical data to compile in financial statements. Still, you must estimate how much money you will need, what your expenses will be at differ-

	October	November	December	January	February	March	April	May	June	July	August	September	Total
Cash Receipts:													
Retail Receipts (a)	$46,875	$46,875	$46,875	$28,125	$28,125	$28,125	$37,500	$37,500	$37,500	$37,500	$37,500	$37,500	$450,000
Interest Income				100				100				100	300
Total Cash Receipts	$46,875	$46,875	$46,875	$28,225	$28,125	$28,125	$37,500	$37,600	$37,500	$37,500	$37,500	$37,600	$450,300
Cash Disbursements:													
Cost of Goods Sold (b)	$28,125	$28,125	$28,125	$16,875	$16,875	$16,875	$22,500	$22,500	$22,500	$22,500	$22,500	$22,500	$270,000
Sales Expenses	2,603	2,603	2,603	1,562	1,562	1,562	2,083	2,083	2,083	2,083	2,083	2,090	25,000
Advertising	1,000	1,000	1,000	1,000	1,000	1,000	1,000	1,000	1,000	1,000	1,000	1,000	12,000
Insurance	0	600	0	0	600	0	0	600	0	0	600	0	2,400
Legal and Accounting	0	0	375	0	0	375	0	375	375	0	0	375	1,500
Delivery Expenses	1,042	1,042	1,042	625	625	625	833	833	833	833	833	834	10,000
**Fixed Cash Disbursements	4,328	4,328	4,328	4,328	4,328	4,328	4,328	4,328	4,328	4,328	4,328	4,328	51,930
Mortgage (c)	1,033	1,033	1,033	1,033	1,033	1,033	1,033	1,033	1,033	1,033	1,033	1,037	12,400
Term Loan (d)	1,466	1,466	1,466	1,466	1,466	1,466	1,466	1,466	1,466	1,466	1,466	1,466	17,592
Total Cash Disbursements	$39,596	$40,197	$39,972	$26,889	$27,489	$27,264	$33,243	$33,843	$33,618	$33,243	$33,843	$33,630	$402,822
Net Cash Flow	$ 7,279	$ 6,679	$ 6,904	$ 1,337	$ 637	$ 862	$ 4,258	$ 3,758	$ 3,883	$ 4,258	$ 3,658	$ 3,971	$ 47,478
Cumulative Cash Flow	$ 7,279	$13,957	$20,861	$22,197	$22,834	$23,695	$27,953	$31,710	$35,593	$39,850	$43,508	$47,478	
FCD													
Fixed Cash Disbursements:													
Utilities	$ 6,000												
Non-sales Salaries	38,000												
Payroll Taxes and Benefits	6,300												
Licenses	150												
Misc. Selling Expenses	1,000												
Miscellaneous	480												
Total FCD	$51,930												
Avg FDC per month	$ 4,328												
Cash on Hand:													
Opening Balance	$ 3,500	$10,779	$17,457	$24,361	$25,697	$26,334	$27,195	$31,453	$35,210	$39,093	$43,350	$47,008	
– Cash Receipts	46,875	46,875	46,875	28,225	28,125	28,125	37,500	37,600	37,500	37,500	37,500	37,600	
– Cash Disbursements	(39,596)	(40,197)	(39,972)	(26,889)	(27,489)	(27,264)	(33,243)	(33,843)	(33,618)	(33,243)	(33,843)	(33,630)	
Total = New Cash Balance	$10,779	$17,457	$24,361	$25,697	$26,334	$27,195	$31,453	$35,210	$39,093	$43,350	$47,008	$50,978	

(a) This assumes that all sales are collected in the month the sale is made.

(b) This is just the Cost of Goods row from the monthly income projection worksheet. Cost of Goods is calculated as 60 percent of the estimated total sales for the month.

(c) The mortgage payments (including both principal and interest) are for a $93,000 15-year loan at 10.6 percent. You can use the spreadsheet function @PMT() to calculate this:
Payment = @PMT (loan amount, rate per month, number of months)
= @PMT (93,000, .106/12, 15*12)

(d) The loan is $39,500 for 2½ years at 8.5 percent. The amount shown includes both principal and interest and is calculated as follows: Payment = @PMT (39500, .85/12, 2.5*12)

(e) A typical strategy for established businesses with fairly predictable revenues and expenses is to open an account such as a "Money Market Deposit Account" with their bank. This account, which is interest earning, is used to store excess cash balances and cover cash shortages.

FIGURE 8.4

Stereo City Cash Flow

Financial Status Checklist

What should you know about the financial status of your business at any given time? According to SBA sources, you should know the following on a daily, weekly, and monthly basis:

Daily

1. Your cash balance on hand
2. Your bank balance
3. Daily summaries of sales and cash receipts
4. Any problems in your credit collections
5. A record of any money paid out

Weekly

1. *Cash flow.* Update a spreadsheet of regular receipts and disbursement entries. The discipline required will greatly help you see what is going on in your business.
2. *Accounts receivable.* Especially slow-paying accounts.
3. *Accounts payable.* Noting discounts offered.
4. *Payroll.* The accumulation of hours worked and total payroll owed.
5. *Taxes.* When tax items are due and which reports are required.

Monthly

1. If you use an outside accounting service, provide records of your receipts, disbursements, bank accounts, and journals to them.
2. Review income statement.
3. Review balance sheet.
4. Reconcile your business checking account.
5. Balance your petty cash account.
6. Review federal tax requirements and make deposits.
7. Review and age your accounts receivable.

Source: Recordkeeping in Small Business, U.S. Small Business Administration Management Development series.

ent sales levels, and how much money you can expect to make. Financial planning and budgeting are important parts of the business planning process. Making financial projections can even show you whether or not you should start the business. Are the financial risks you are about to take worth the *realistic* return you can expect?

In this case, you will need to produce pro forma financial statements for your business plan. **Pro forma financial statements** are either full or partial estimates, because you are making projections rather than recording actual transactions. (*Pro forma* is Latin for "provided in advance to prescribe form.") Because these state-

pro forma financial statements Financial statements that project what a firm's financial condition will be in the future.

Do You Have a Business or a Hobby?

If your sideline business produces revenue but consistently loses money, be careful—the IRS could consider your writing, woodwork, artwork, or crafts a hobby. If your business is classified as a hobby, you can't deduct the related expenses. Business expenses are fully deductible on Schedule C of your tax return. If your direct costs exceed your business income, you can use that loss to offset your other income on Form 1040.

Hobby expenses can't be used to offset income or losses, even if they exceed the income from your hobby. How does the IRS determine whether you have a business or a hobby? They presume that if you show a profit in three of the past five years, you have a business. If you fail the three-of-five-year test and can't demonstrate the following, you have a hobby. To classify as a business, you have to prove a profit motive. You can do that by

- Conducting activity in a businesslike manner.

- Demonstrating how much time and effort you devote to the activity.

- Demonstrating your expertise in the activity.

- Demonstrating that losses are due to circumstances beyond your control.

- Showing that you have tried to increase profitability by changing methods of operation.

- Demonstrating that you depend on income from the activity for your livelihood.

- Showing that you have made a profit in the past.

- Showing that the activity involves considerable activity that could not be considered "pleasurable." (such as cleaning animal stalls).

Source: Janet Attard, "Don't Get Caught By the Hobby Trap," www.businessknowhow.com. Reprinted by permission of Attard Communications, Inc.

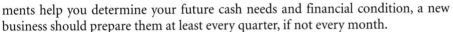

ments help you determine your future cash needs and financial condition, a new business should prepare them at least every quarter, if not every month.

In preparing pro forma statements, you need to state the assumptions you are making for your projections. How did you come up with the numbers? Did you grab them out of the air? Did the owner of a similar (but noncompeting) business share his actual numbers for you to use as a base? Are they based on industry averages, such as *Robert Morris Associates Annual Statement Summaries?*

Analyzing Financial Statements

Your ability to make sound financial decisions will depend on how well you can understand, interpret, and use the information contained in your company's financial statements. The purpose of this section is to give an overview of the most common form of financial analysis: ratio analysis.

Ratio Analysis

Suppose that two entrepreneurs are comparing how well their respective businesses performed last year. The first entrepreneur, Ms. Alpha, determines that her store made 50 percent more profits last year than the second entrepreneur, Mr. Beta's, store. Should Ms. Alpha feel proud? To answer this question, we need more information.

The profit figures tell us only part of the story. Although generating 50 percent more profits *seems* good, we need to see how profit relates to other aspects of each business. For example, what if Ms. Alpha's store is four times the size of Mr. Beta's store? Or what if Ms. Alpha's store made three times as many sales as Mr. Beta's store? Now does 50 percent more profits seem as good?

financial ratios Calculations that compare important financial aspects of a business.

The reality is that fair comparisons can be made only when we demonstrate the relationships between profit and other financial features of the businesses. The relationships that show the relative size of some financial quantity to another financial quantity of a firm are called **financial ratios.** Four important types of financial ratios are the liquidity, activity, leverage, and profitability ratios.[3]

Liquidity Ratios

liquidity ratios Financial ratios used to measure a firm's ability to meet its short-term obligations to creditors as they come due.

Liquidity ratios are used to measure a firm's ability to meet its short-term obligations to creditors as they come due. The financial data used to determine liquidity are the firm's current assets and current liabilities found on the balance sheet. There are two important liquidity ratios: the current ratio and the quick (or acid-test) ratio.

current ratio A financial ratio that measures the number of times the firm can cover its current liabilities with its current assets.

CURRENT RATIO. The **current ratio** measures the number of times the firm can cover its current liabilities with its current assets. The current ratio assumes that both accounts receivable and inventory can easily be converted to cash. Current ratios of 1.0 or less are considered low and indicative of financial difficulties. Current ratios of more than 2.0 often suggest excessive liquidity that may be adverse to the firm's profitability.

$$\text{Current ratio} = \text{Current assets/Current liabilities}$$

Using the data from Stereo City's balance sheet, the company's current ratio is computed as:

$$\$155,000/\$105,000 = 1.48$$

This means that Stereo City can cover its current liabilities 1.48 times with its current assets. Another way of looking at this is that the company has $1.48 of current assets for each dollar of current liabilities.

quick (acid-test) ratio A financial ratio that measures the firm's ability to meet current obligations with the most liquid of its current assets.

QUICK RATIO. The **quick (acid-test) ratio** measures the firm's ability to meet current obligations with the most liquid of its current assets. The quick ratio is computed as

$$\text{Quick ratio} = \text{Current assets} - \text{Inventory/Current liabilities}$$

With the data from Stereo City's balance sheet the quick ratio is:

$$\$155,000 - \$125,000/\$105,000 = 0.29$$

This means that Stereo City has only 29 cents in liquid assets (liquidity refers to how quickly an asset can be turned into cash—the quicker it can become cash, the more liquid it is said to be) for each dollar of current liabilities. The company obviously counts on making sales to pay its current obligations.

Activity Ratios

Activity ratios measure the speed with which various accounts are converted into sales or cash. These ratios are often used to measure how efficiently a firm uses its assets. There are four important activity ratios: inventory turnover, average collection period, fixed asset turnover, and total asset turnover.

INVENTORY TURNOVER. **Inventory turnover** measures the liquidity of the firm's inventory—how quickly goods are sold and replenished. The higher the inventory turnover, the more times the firm is selling, or "turning over," its inventory. A high inventory ratio generally implies efficient inventory management. Inventory turnover is computed as

$$\text{Inventory turnover} = \text{Cost of goods sold/Inventory}$$

Using data from Stereo City's income statement and balance sheet, the firm's inventory turnover is

$$\$270,000/\$125,000 = 2.16$$

This means that Stereo City restocked its inventory 2.16 times last year.

AVERAGE COLLECTION PERIOD. The **average collection period** is a measure of how long it takes a firm to convert a credit sale (internal store credit, not credit card sales) into a usable form (cash). All firms that extend credit must compute this ratio to determine the effectiveness of their credit-granting and collection policies. High average collection periods usually indicate many uncollectible receivables, whereas low average collection periods may indicate overly restrictive credit-granting policies. The average collection period is computed as

$$\text{Average collection period} = \text{Accounts receivable/Average sales per day}$$

Using the data from Stereo City's balance sheet and income statement, the average collection period is

$$\$12,000/\$450,000/365 = 9.93$$

This means that Stereo City collects its receivables in less than ten days.

FIXED ASSET TURNOVER. The **fixed asset turnover** ratio measures how efficiently the firm is using its assets to generate sales. The higher the ratio, the more effective the firm's asset utilization. A low ratio often indicates that marketing efforts are ineffective or that the firm's core business areas are not currently feasible. The fixed asset turnover ratio is calculated as

$$\text{Fixed asset turnover} = \text{Sales/Net fixed assets}$$

Using the data from Stereo City's income statement and balance sheet, the fixed asset turnover is

$$\$450,000/\$168,000 = 2.68$$

This means that Stereo City turns over its net fixed assets 2.68 times per year.

activity ratios Financial ratios that measure the speed with which various accounts are converted into sales or cash.

inventory turnover An activity ratio that measures the liquidity of the firm's inventory—how quickly goods are sold and replenished.

average collection period A measure of how long it takes a firm to convert a credit sale (internal store credit, not credit card sales) into a usable form (cash).

fixed asset turnover An activity ratio that measures how efficiently a firm is using its assets to generate sales.

total asset turnover An activity ratio that measures how efficiently the firm uses all of its assets to generate sales; a high ratio generally reflects good overall management.

TOTAL ASSET TURNOVER. The **total asset turnover** ratio measures how efficiently the firm uses all of its assets to generate sales, so a high ratio generally reflects good overall management. A low ratio may indicate flaws in the firm's overall strategy, poor marketing efforts, or improper capital expenditures. Total asset turnover is calculated as

$$\text{Total asset turnover} = \text{Sales/Total assets}$$

Using data from Stereo City's income statement and balance sheet, total asset turnover is

$$\$450,000/\$323,500 = 1.39$$

This means that Stereo City turns its assets over 1.39 times per year.

Leverage Ratios

leverage ratios Financial ratios that measure the extent to which a firm uses debt as a source of financing and its ability to service that debt.

Leverage ratios measure the extent to which a firm uses debt as a source of financing and its ability to service that debt. The term *leverage* refers to the magnification of risk and potential return that comes with using other people's money to generate profits. Think of the increased power that is gained when a fulcrum is moved under a simple lever. The farther the fulcrum is from the point where you are pushing on the lever, the more weight you can lift. The more debt a firm uses, the more financial leverage it has. Two important leverage ratios are the debt ratio and the times interest earned ratio.

debt ratio A leverage ratio that measures the proportion of a firm's total assets that is acquired with borrowed funds.

DEBT RATIO. The **debt ratio** measures the proportion of a firm's total assets that is acquired with borrowed funds. Total debt includes short-term debt, long-term debt, and long-term obligations such as leases. A high ratio indicates a more aggressive approach to financing and is evidence of a high-risk, high-expected-return strategy. A low ratio indicates a more conservative approach to financing. The debt ratio is calculated as

$$\text{Debt ratio} = \text{Total debt/Total assets}$$

Using the data from Stereo City's balance sheet, the debt ratio is

$$\$237,500/\$323,500 = 0.73$$

This means that the company has financed 73 percent of its assets with borrowed funds. Or, 73 cents out of every dollar of funding for Stereo City have come from debt.

times interest earned ratio A leverage ratio that calculates the firm's ability to meet its interest requirements.

TIMES INTEREST EARNED. The **times interest earned ratio** calculates the firm's ability to meet its interest requirements. It shows how far operating income can decline before the firm will likely have difficulties servicing its debt obligations. A high ratio indicates a low-risk situation but may also indicate an inefficient use of leverage. A low ratio indicates that immediate action should be taken to ensure that no debt payments will go into default status. Times interest earned is computed as

$$\text{Times interest earned} = \text{Operating income/Interest expense}$$

Using the data from Stereo City's income statement, times interest earned is

$$\$22,750/\$15,000 = 1.52$$

This means that the company has operating income 1.52 times its interest obligations.

Profitability Ratios

Profitability ratios are used to measure the ability of a company to turn sales into profits and to earn profits on assets committed. Additionally, profitability ratios allow some insight into the overall effectiveness of the management team. There are three important profitability ratios: net profit margin, return on assets, and return on equity.

NET PROFIT MARGIN. The **net profit margin** measures the percentage of each sales dollar that remains as profit after all expenses, including taxes, have been paid. This ratio is widely used as a gauge of management efficiency. Although net profit margins vary greatly by industry, a low ratio indicates that expenses are too high relative to sales. Net profit margin can be seen on a common-size income statement or computed with the formula:

$$\text{Net profit} = \text{Net income/Sales}$$

Using the data from Stereo City's income statement, the net profit margin is

$$\$4,830/\$450,000 = 0.0107$$

This means that the company actually generates 1.07 cents of after-tax profit for each dollar of sales.

RETURN ON ASSETS. Also known as **return on investment,** the **return on assets** ratio indicates the firm's effectiveness in generating profits from its available assets. The higher this ratio is, the better. A high ratio shows effective management and good chances for future growth. The return on assets is found with the formula

$$\text{Return on assets} = \text{Net profit after taxes/Total assets}$$

Using the data from Stereo City's income statement and balance sheet, return on assets is

$$\$4,830/\$323,500 = 0.0149$$

This means that the company generates approximately 1.5 cents of after-tax profit for each dollar of assets the company has at its disposal.

RETURN ON EQUITY. The **return on equity** measures the return the firm earned on its owner's investment in the firm. In general, the higher this ratio is, the better off the owner is. However, this ratio is highly affected by the amount of financial leverage (borrowed money) used by the firm and may not be an accurate measure of management effectiveness. The return on equity is calculated as

$$\text{Return on equity} = \text{Net profit after taxes/Owner's equity}$$

Using the data from Stereo City's income statement and balance sheet, return on equity is

$$\$4,830/\$86,000 = 0.0562$$

profitability ratios Financial ratios that are used to measure the ability of a company to turn sales into profits and to earn profits on assets committed.

net profit margin A profitability ratio that measures the percentage of each sales dollar that remains as profit after all expenses, including taxes, have been paid.

return on assets (return on investment) A profitability ratio that indicates the firm's effectiveness in generating profits from its available assets.

return on equity A profitability ratio that measures the return the firm earned on its owner's investment in the firm.

This means that the company generates a little more than 5.5 cents of after-tax profit for each dollar of owner's equity. This ratio tells a business owner if he is receiving enough return from invested money. In the Stereo City example, 5.5 percent return is not much for the risk involved. That $86,000 could be invested in a relatively safe investment like a corporate bond, earning a much higher return with less risk. This kind of information can tell a business owner if a business is a good investment compared with other alternative uses for his or her money.

The Use of Financial Ratios

cross-sectional analysis
Ratio comparison that compares different firms' financial ratios at the same point in time.

time series analysis Ratio comparison that compares a single firm's present performance with its own past performance.

Financial ratios by themselves tell us very little. For purposes of analysis, ratios are useful only when compared with other ratios. Two types of ratio comparisons can be made: **cross-sectional analysis,** which compares different firms' financial ratios at the same point in time, and **time series analysis,** which compares a single firm's present performance with its own past performance.

CROSS-SECTIONAL ANALYSIS. Cross-sectional analysis is often done by comparing an individual firm's ratios against the standard ratios for the firm's industry. Such industry ratios may be found in most college or large public libraries. Look for Robert Morris Associates' *RMA Annual Statement Studies* or Dun & Bradstreet's *Industry Norms and Key Business Ratios.* Another good source is *Financial Studies of the Small Business* from Financial Research Associates.[4]

Table 8.1 shows how some of Stereo City's ratios compare with the median ratios for stereo equipment retail stores with an asset size between $10,000 and $1,000,000. From the data we can conclude that Stereo City potentially has three major problems.

TABLE 8.1 **Comparing Company and Industry Ratios**		Stereo City	Industry
	Liquidity		
	Current Ratio	1.48	1.60
	Quick Ratio	0.29	0.50
	Activity		
	Average Collection	9.7	8.0
	Total Asset Turnover	1.4	4.2
	Leverage		
	Debt Ratio	73.0	61.5
	Times Interest Earned	1.5	6.1
	Profitability		
	Return on Assets*	2.5	6.2

* Uses pretax profits.
Source: Financial Studies of the Small Business, 17th ed. (Winter Haven, FL: Financial Research Associates, 1994).

First, Stereo City's quick ratio is only about half the industry average. This could mean that it has excessive amounts of inventory and faces the possibility of illiquidity if the inventory does not sell in a timely manner.

Second, Stereo City appears to have an excessive amount of debt in relation to its sales. The firm's times interest earned ratio is less than one-fourth the industry average, indicating a strong probability that the company will not be able to service its debt in the future.

Third, Stereo City's total asset turnover and return on asset ratios are both considerably below industry average. The likely cause of this is having insufficient sales to support the size of the business. The company must either downsize by selling off some assets or work harder to increase sales.

TIME SERIES ANALYSIS. Time series analysis is used to uncover trends in the firm's financial performance. If there is potential trouble in any of the four main areas of analysis (liquidity, activity, leverage, and profitability), managers will have time to correct these problems before the problems become overbearing. The key to potential solutions is found in the ratios themselves.

For example, if the time series analysis shows that the firm's liquidity is diminishing, the managers will want to take action to enhance the firm's liquidity position. By looking at the liquidity ratios, a number of possible solutions will become apparent.

Because ratio analysis has shown that Stereo City needs to increase its current assets (especially cash and short-term investments) without a commensurate increase in current liabilities, possible solutions are to borrow cash through a long-term loan, get a cash infusion from the firm's owner, or sell off some fixed assets for cash. An alternative approach would be to reduce current liabilities by restructuring short-term debt into long-term debt or using the proceeds of the sale of a fixed asset to retire some accounts payable. Any action that results in boosting the firm's liquidity helps to avoid the risk of Stereo City's becoming insolvent because of diminishing liquidity.

Reviewing financial ratios annually can help prevent difficult situations before they have the opportunity to occur. Thus ratio analysis allows small business owners and managers to become proactive directors of the financial aspects of their ventures.

Small businesses worldwide recognize that they must examine their financial ratios in order to determine how well they're doing. For instance, JCG Holdings Ltd., a Taiwanese-Japanese financial services company, makes loans to working-class people in Hong Kong. Its average loans range from $2,000 to $3,200 and typically mature in 12 months. The borrower pays an interest rate that runs about 30 percent on an annual basis. However, on its deposits, JCG pays an average interest rate of 6.5 percent. This spread has allowed the company to earn an incredible 12 percent return on assets. Compare this to the average U.S. financial services firm's ROA ratio of 1.5 percent. It doesn't take an accounting genius to recognize that JCG is doing well! However, JCG's managers wouldn't know this if they hadn't calculated and analyzed the financial ratios.[5]

If you find that you enjoy working with accounting information or creating accounting systems, you might even consider starting a small business to provide those services. Finding a unique accounting services niche can be profitable. Take, for instance, what Combined Resource Technology (CRT) of Baton Rouge, Louisiana, did. CRT started out as a real estate development company. However, when the oil and gas price crash battered Louisiana's economy, CRT found itself owing some $14 million to banks on loans it had taken out to buy a shopping center and apartment buildings. To avoid failure, CRT partners Darwyn Williams and Chris Moran had to do something quickly. Although their properties' values had plunged, they found that the tax assessor's property valuations hadn't changed. Thus out of desperation was born their new accounting services business, in which they peruse tax rolls to identify overassessed properties and contact the owners about getting the taxes reduced—for a fee, of course. They've since expanded their cost reduction services beyond taxes, to include utilities, waste disposal, freight, leases, and any other areas where they can help business owners reduce costs. CRT provides a unique accounting service that others have been willing to pay for.[6]

Managing Cash Flow

Each business day, approximately a dozen U.S. small businesses declare bankruptcy. The majority of these business failures are caused by poor cash flow management.[7] Companies from the smallest startups to the largest conglomerates all share the same need for positive cash flow. A company that does not effectively manage its cash is poised for collapse.

Cash Flow Defined

cash flow The sum of net income plus any noncash expenses, such as depreciation and amortization, or the difference between the actual amount of cash a company brings in and the actual amount of cash a company disburses in a given time period.

The accounting definition of **cash flow** is the sum of net income plus any noncash expenses, such as depreciation and amortization. This treatment of cash flow is largely misunderstood by many small business owners. A more "bottom-line" approach is to define cash flow as the difference between the actual amount of cash a company brings in and the actual amount of cash a company disburses in a given time period.

The most important aspects of this refined definition are the inclusion of the terms *actual cash* and *time period*. The goal of good cash flow management is to have enough cash on hand when you need it. It doesn't matter if your company will have a positive cash balance three months from now if your payroll, taxes, insurance, and suppliers all need to be paid today.

Cash flow management requires as much attention as developing new customers, perfecting products and services, and all other day-to-day operating activities. The basic strategy underlying cash flow management is to maximize your use of cash. This means not only ensuring consistent cash inflows, but also developing a disciplined approach to cash outflows.

Could your cash flow management system be computerized? As noted earlier in the chapter, there are single-entry general ledger accounting software packages that are easy to use. However, these packages can provide an unrealistic view of your business's *cash flow*. In a single-entry system, all cash coming into the business is put on the left-hand side of the ledger, and cash flowing out of the business is put on the right-hand side. However, if your business has accounts receivable or accounts payable, a single-entry system can fool you into thinking you have enough cash on hand to meet expenses or to use for business expansion.

Cash Flow Specialist

One reason that so many small businesses run into cash flow problems is that too often no one is put in charge of it. John Conroy, a cash flow expert from West Haven, Connecticut, offers an effective solution: "Appoint a cash flow specialist with the authority to cross department lines as he or she follows the trail of cash coming into—or failing to come into—the company."[8]

The idea of having one individual in a firm responsible for cash management is also endorsed by Leslie N. Masonson, president of Cash Management Resources and a leader of the American Management Association's corporate cash management course. He says that cash managers "should get help from financially savvy individuals, knowledgeable professionals, bankers, or colleagues in the financial profession. [They] should attend regional cash management seminars, read industry magazines, and read books on cash management."[9]

For most small businesses the responsibility of cash flow specialist will necessarily fall on the owner. Although this task may seem overwhelming, there are a few cash flow fundamentals that are not difficult to grasp and will help even the novice cash flow manager gain more control over this essential activity.

> *A company that does not effectively manage its cash flow—by balancing its income and expenses on a day-to-day basis—is poised for collapse.*

Cash Flow Fundamentals

The first step in cash flow management is to understand the purpose and nature of cash flow. Why do you need cash flow? How is cash flow generated? How do firms become insolvent even though they are profitable? To answer these questions we need to look at the motives for having cash, the cash-to-cash cycle, and the timing of cash inflows and outflows.

MOTIVES FOR HAVING CASH. Three reasons for which a firm needs cash are (1) to make transactions, (2) to protect against unanticipated problems, and (3) to invest in opportunities as they arise. Of these, the primary motive is to make transactions—the ability to pay the bills incurred by the business. If a business cannot meet its obligations, it is insolvent. Continued insolvency leads directly to bankruptcy.

Businesses, like individuals, occasionally run into unanticipated problems. Thefts, fires, floods, and other natural and man-made disasters affect businesses in the same way they affect individuals. Those businesses that have "saved for a rainy day" are able to withstand such setbacks. Those that have not planned ahead often suffer—and may even fail—as a result.

Finally, there are times when a business is presented with an opportunity to invest in a profitable venture. If the business has cash on hand to do so, it may reap significant rewards. If not, it has lost a chance to add to its cash flow in a way other than through normal operations.

Each of the three motives is important to understand, as they combine to create the proper mentality for the cash flow manager. Without proactively managing a firm's cash flow, the firm is exposed to many risks, each of which can spell disaster.

CASH-TO-CASH CYCLE. The **cash-to-cash cycle** of the firm, sometimes known as the *operating cycle,* tracks the way cash flows through the business. It identifies how long it takes from the time a firm makes a cash outlay for raw materials or in-

cash-to-cash cycle The period of time from when money is spent on raw materials until it is collected on the sale of a finished good.

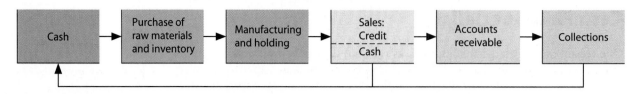

FIGURE 8.5

Cash-to-Cash Cycle

A chart of the cash-to-cash cycle of your small business shows the amount of time that passes between spending money for raw materials or inventory and collecting money on the sale of finished goods.

ventory until the cash is collected from the sale of the finished good. Figure 8.5 shows a typical cash-to-cash cycle.

The firm begins with cash that is used to purchase raw materials or inventory. The firm will normally take some time to manufacture or otherwise hold finished goods until they sell. As sales are made, cash is replenished immediately by cash sales, but accounts receivable are created by credit sales. Then the firm must collect the receivables in order to secure cash.

The cash flow process is continuous, with all activities occurring simultaneously. When the process is operating smoothly, cash flow is easy to monitor and control. However, for most firms, it is often erratic and subject to many complications, which makes cash flow management a challenge.

THE TIMING OF CASH FLOWS. The major complication to cash flow management is timing. While some cash inflows and outflows will transpire on a regular schedule (such as monthly interest income or payroll costs), other cash flows occur on no schedule whatsoever. For example, when a firm needs to make periodic purchases of capital equipment, which are not part of the daily cash-to-cash process, it will cause a major disruption in the firm's cash flow.

Even though a firm might send out all of its billings to credit customers at one time, you can be sure that these customers will not all pay at the same time. Uncollected receivables may count as revenue on an accrual-based income statement, but they are worthless from a cash flow standpoint until they turn into real money.

The small business owner needs to become well versed in the patterns of cash inflows and outflows of the firm. The nuances of timing become critical. There are a few tools that can assist in this process.

Cash Flow Management Tools

Once you have a good idea about the purpose and nature of cash flow, you are ready to take steps to manage it. Using cash budgets, aging schedules, and float to control the inflow and outflow of cash is paramount for effective management.

CASH BUDGETS. Cash budgets (also known as *cash forecasts*) allow the firm to plan its short-term cash needs, with particular attention to periods of surplus and shortage. Whenever the firm is likely to experience a cash surplus, it can plan to make a short-term investment. When the firm is expected to experience a cash shortage, it can plan to arrange for a short-term loan.

A cash budget typically covers a one-year period that is divided into smaller intervals. The number of intervals is dictated by the nature of the business. The more uncertain the firm's cash flows, the more intervals there need to be. Using monthly intervals is common, but some firms require daily cash budgets.

The cash budget requires the small business owner to determine all the known cash inflows and outflows that will occur during the year. Both the amount of cash involved and the cycle's length of time must be disclosed. This information is then put into a format, as shown in Table 8.2.

Table 8.2 lists some of the most common types of cash inflows and outflows experienced by a typical small business. Categories should be modified to fit the particulars of each individual business. The most important point is to include all relevant sources of and demands for cash.

	January	February	March	April	May	
Beginning Cash						**TABLE 8.2**
Plus Receipts:						**Cash Budget Format**
Cash Sales						
Receivable Collections						
Interest						
Owner Contributions						
Other Receipts						
Total Receipts						
Minus Disbursements:						
Cash Purchases						
Payment of Accounts Payable						
Wages and Salaries						
Payroll Taxes						
Advertising						
Office Supplies						
Rent/Mortgage						
Utilities						
Telephone						
Insurance						
Legal/Accounting						
Taxes and Licenses						
Interest Payments						
Loan Principal Payments						
Dues and Subscriptions						
Travel						
Miscellaneous Disbursements						
Total Disbursements						
Ending Cash (Beginning Cash + Receipts − Disbursements)						

Open-Book Management

At bulletin boards in the lobbies, conference rooms, and cafeterias of businesses across the country, employees are studying a type of information that had been off limits for years—the company's financial statements. The practice is called "open-book management," and it involves simply showing everyone in the business the numbers that are critical to the business's performance. When employees know and understand the numbers, they can measure their contribution to the company's bottom line and how their performance can make a difference in those numbers.

Open-book management gives logic and a rationale to many of today's management ideas, such as employee empowerment, total quality management, and self-directed work teams. Employees are more motivated to work harder when they can see that they have a direct stake in the company's ultimate success.

Open-book management is being used successfully by many small businesses. However, you cannot simply hand out income statements and expect employees to care about the information or understand how their efforts affect it. You must teach them what the numbers mean to them.

One of the first proponents of open-book management was Jack Stack, president and CEO of Springfield Remanufacturing Company. In the book Stack wrote on the topic, *The Great Game of Business,* he stated that for open-book management to work you need to teach employees the rules of the game, give them the information (the financials) they need to play the game, and make sure they share in the risks and rewards.

Stack draws an analogy between open-book management and a game of baseball. He asks, "Can you imagine taking a spectator to a baseball game and not explaining the rules, not showing them how they keep score, and not giving them a stake in the outcome? Can you imagine sitting in those stands trying to figure out why those crazy people are running around on that field and hitting this little ball with a stick? The same thing occurs every single day when someone goes to work. They aren't taught the rules, they don't know what business is all about. They're only taught a little circle, a little piece of the process. We tried to convert it into a game—move everybody from a spectator to a player."

Sources: "The Shift to Open-Book Management," *Financial Executive,* May/June 1998, 50–52; John Case, "The Open-Book Revolution," *Inc.,* June 1995, 26–43; David Whitford, "Before & After," *Inc.,* June 1995, 44–50; Michael Cronin, "Like Cookie, Like Company," *Inc.,* May 1994, 149; Chris Lee, "Open-Book Management," *Training,* July 1994, 21–27; "Managing by the (Open) Book," *Supervisory Management,* July 1995, 1–6; Nancy Austin, "When Honesty Is the Best Management Policy," *Working Woman,* May 1994, 25–26; and Catherine Romano, "When Money Talks," *Management Review,* November 1994, 44–47.

Many businesses find that adding a reconciliation component to the bottom of the cash budget is helpful. This reconciliation summarizes the total cash inflows and outflows for the period. When added to the beginning cash balance, you have the current cash status of the firm. Because there will be some minimum cash balance required to begin the next period, the ending cash figure is compared to this minimum figure. If there is a positive difference (ending cash minus minimum cash balance), the firm has cash to invest. If there is a negative difference, the firm must arrange for financing before beginning the new cycle.

By forecasting the inflows and outflows of cash, the small business owner will have a picture of when the firm will have cash surpluses and cash shortages. This knowledge allows the cash flow to be managed proactively rather than reactively.

Jack Stack has been a leader in the Open-Book Management field from his position as CEO of Springfield Remanufacturing Company

Cash budgeting is, however, not always easy to do. As noted earlier, there are always disruptions to the process. Unforeseen cash outflows and inconsistent cash inflows plague many small businesses. Another tool that helps reduce the uncertainty of the cash flow cycle is the aging schedule.

AGING SCHEDULES. **Aging schedules** are listings of a firm's accounts receivable according to the length of time they are outstanding. A **macro-aging schedule** simply lists categories of outstanding accounts with the percentage of accounts that falls within each category (see Table 8.3).

This schedule allows the small business owner to forecast the collection of receivables. Say, for instance, that the firm made credit sales of $10,000 three months ago, $12,000 two months ago, and $5,000 last month, and that it predicts it will make credit sales of $7,500 this month. Expected receivables collections for this month will be: $(0.25 \times \$7,500) + (0.5 \times \$5,000) + (0.2 \times \$12,000) + (0.05 \times \$10,000) = \$7,275$. This is the amount the cash flow manager will place in the Receivables Collection slot of the cash budget for that month.

aging schedule A listing of a firm's accounts receivable according to the length of time they are outstanding.

macro-aging schedule A list of accounts receivable by age category.

TABLE 8.3 **Macro-Aging Schedule**	Age of Receivables	Percentage
	0–30 days	25
	31–60 days	50
	61–90 days	20
	Over 90 days	5

TABLE 8.4
Micro-Aging Schedule

Customer	Amount	Current	Past Due Days 1–30	31–60	61–90	+90
Aardvark Supply	$1,500	$1,000	$200	$ 500		
Beaver Trucking	2,250				$2,250	
Canary Labs	1,000	500	500			
...						
Total	11,000	5,000	750	3,000	2,250	
Percentage	100	45	7	27	21	

micro-aging schedule A list of accounts receivable that shows each customer, the amount it owes, and the amount that is past due.

The **micro-aging schedule** offers another approach to showing receivables. This technique lists the status of each credit customer's account (usually in alphabetical order). This allows the small business owner to concentrate collection efforts on the specific companies that are delinquent in their payments (see Table 8.4).

Getting Paid Online

You've got your product perfected. You have your web site built and generating traffic. You have customers who want to buy. You have shipping arrangements made. But, first, how are you going to get paid for these online purchases? Because it is not possible (yet) to have customers stick dollar bills in the CD-ROM of their computer and have them come out of your machine, your best option is to use an e-payment system through a secure Internet gateway, such as PayStream, Paytrust, or PayPal. These sites use ECI (electronic commerce indicator) required of all e-commerce.

A serious problem of e-commerce is credit card fraud. Both Visa and MasterCard use a tool called AVS (address verification system) to help avoid credit card fraud. AVS is based on the assumption that a person attempting fraud with compromised credit card information will not have access to the legitimate cardholder's billing address. When a customer processes an order, the business will receive either a full match, a partial match, or a total mismatch response to authorize the purchase. If a partial or total mismatch between the card number and billing address occurs, your business will receive a pop-up screen that prompts you to ask the customer, "Did you move recently?" or "Is that your billing address?" If an incorrect address is entered again, the customer should be locked out and entered into your fraud avoidance file.

PayPal.com offers a way to send money securely via e-mail. Here is how it works.

- The customer logs in to his or her PayPal account.

- He or she registers a credit card and enters the amount to be sent and the recipient's e-mail address, and the money is sent. The recipient (your business) must be registered with PayPal. You may either receive a check directly from PayPal or have the amount directly deposited into your account

- The recipient receives an e-mail notifying you that money has been electronically transferred to you.

PayPal is a free, secure service and is not limited to businesses. For example, parents could use PayPal to send funds to college students for necessities like textbooks and pizza—just a thought!

Sources: www.paypal.com; David Shymkus, "E-Payment Systems Offer Secure Convenience," www .businessknowhow.com; and Mark Wilson, "E-Commerce Best Practices," www.businessknowhow.com

This aging schedule is invaluable for controlling receivables. Not only do you have the same information as shown in the macro schedule, but you also have specific information on each credit customer that will enable you to make future credit decisions.

FLOAT. The last cash flow management tool of note is called **float.** Float has two definitions. First, it is the difference between the company's checking account balance and the account balance shown in the bank. Second, it is the period of time between sending a check and when that check clears your bank.

As anyone with a checking account knows, float can be "played" to your advantage. By investing cash in interest-bearing accounts until the checks that have been written

float The difference between the balance in a checking account and the amount shown in the account, or the period of time between writing a check and the check clearing the account.

Turn Up the Tap on Your Cash Flow

Managing your accounts receivable is an important step in controlling your cash flow. You need a healthy stream of cash for your small business to succeed. The following tips can help you accelerate the flow:

- *Establish sound credit practices.* Never give credit until you are comfortable with a customer's ability to pay. You can get a credit report from Dun & Bradstreet to indicate a purchasing company's general financial health.

- *Process orders quickly.* Ensure that each order is handled on or before the date specified by the customer. Unnecessary delays can add days or weeks to customer payments.

- *Prepare the invoice the same day as the order is received.* Especially on large dollar amounts, don't wait until some "billing date" just because that's when you normally do it.

- *Mail the invoice the same day it is prepared.* The sooner the bill is in the mail, the sooner it is likely to be paid. When possible, send the invoice with the order.

- *Offer discounts for prompt payment.* Give customers an incentive to pay sooner. Trade discounts typically give 1 to 2 percent if paid within ten days.

- *Aggressively follow up on past due accounts.* Call the customer as soon as a bill becomes past due; ask when payment can be expected. Keep a record of conversations and customer responses, and follow up. For customers with genuine financial problems, try to get even a small amount each week.

- *Deposit payments promptly.* Accelerate receipt of checks by using a bank lockbox.

- *Negotiate better terms from suppliers and banks.* Improving cash flow also includes slowing money going out.

- *Keep a tight control on inventory.* Items sitting in inventory tie up money that could be used elsewhere. Be sure that deep discounts on volume purchases can be financially justified by the drain they will put on cash flow.

- *Review and reduce expenses.* Take a hard look at *all* expenses. What impact will an expense have on your bottom line?

- *Pay bills on time, but not before they are due.* Unless you receive enough trade discount incentive to pay early.

- *Be smart in designing your invoice.* Make sure that the amount due, due date, discount for early payment, and penalty for late payment are clearly laid out.

manager's **notebook**

Source: New York Society of CPAs, "10 Ways to Improve Small Business Cash Flow," *Journal of Accountancy* (March 2000): 14. Reprinted from *Journal of Accountancy,* March 2000.

are expected to clear, the business exploits the cash flow leverage of float. Many banks will do that for businesses using a service called the "zero-balance account."

With a zero-balance checking account, you sustain a zero balance and deposit money to cover checks on the account only when each check reaches the bank. Typically, the firm keeps deposits in an interest-bearing account at the bank, such as a money market deposit account, and simply transfers the exact amount of funds from this account into the checking account.

Float exists because of the delays caused by the mail system, the processing (recording and depositing) of checks by the recipient, and the bank clearing system. Float has been decreasing due to faster mail service and electronic transfers of funds, but opportunities still remain for those who play the float.

Strategies for Cash Flow Management

Once the small business owner understands some of the basic tools of cash flow management, he or she should develop a strategy for the firm. Which accounts should you concentrate on? At what intervals are cash budgets needed? What information is available or needs to be made available to track cash flow? Is the firm's bank providing services to assist in cash flow management? The answers to these questions, among others, help shape cash flow strategy.

ACCOUNTS RECEIVABLE. The first place to look for ways to improve cash flow is in accounts receivable. John Conroy, the West Haven, Connecticut, cash flow expert, maintains that the key to an effective cash flow management system is the "ability to collect receivables quickly."[10] If customers abuse your credit policies by paying slowly, any future sales to them will have to be COD (cash on delivery) until they prove that you will receive your money in reasonable time.

Receivables have inherent procedural problems in most small businesses. Information often gets lost or delayed between salespeople, shipping departments, and the accounting clerks who create the billing statements. Most firms bill only once a month and may delay that if busy with other activities.

INVENTORY. Inventory is another area that can drain cash flow. According to James Howard, chairman of the board of Asset Growth Partners, Inc., a New York City financial consulting firm for small businesses, inventory costs are often overlooked or understated by many small businesses. "A typical manufacturing company pays 25 to 30 percent of the value of the inventory for the cost of borrowed money, warehouse space, materials handling, staff, lift-truck expenses, and fixed costs."[11]

Cash flow determines how much inventory can safely be carried by a firm while still allowing sufficient cash for other operations. The inventory turnover ratio lends insight to this situation. If, for example, a firm has an inventory ratio of 12, it has to keep only a month's worth of projected sales in stock before enough cash returns to pay for the next month's worth of inventory.

However, if the firm has a ratio of 4, it must keep three months' worth of projected sales on the shelves. This ties up cash for as much as 90 days. In this case the firm should try to find suppliers that have terms extending to 90 days. Otherwise, it may have to borrow to meet current cash needs. The cash flow management goal is to commit just enough cash to inventory to meet demand.[12]

BANKS. Ideally, your bank should be your partner in cash flow management. The small business owner should request the firm's bank to provide an *account analysis.* This analysis shows the banking services the business used during the month, the bank's charge for each service, the balances maintained in all accounts during the month, and the minimum balances required by the bank to pay for the services.

A review of the account analysis will indicate whether any excess account balances are on deposit. These should immediately be removed and invested. Also, your firm may be better off removing all account balances that are earning little or no interest and reinvesting them at higher rates, even if it means having to pay fees for bank services.

Finally, determine how quickly checks that your firm deposits in the bank become available as cash. Banks normally require delays of up to two business days. Banks should have an availability schedule, and the small business owner needs to request one from each bank in the area to determine if his or her bank is competitive. Remember that the faster a deposited check becomes available as cash, the sooner your business has use of the money for other purposes.

OTHER AREAS OF CASH FLOW CONCERN. Although receivables, inventory, and bank services are the most likely places on which to concentrate cash flow management strategies, several other areas also deserve attention. They include

1. *Compensation.* Look for duplication of effort and lack of productivity within the firm's work force. Cut personnel hours in those areas to save on wage and payroll tax costs.
2. *Supplies.* Review all petty cash accounts. Show employees the cost of supplies by marking the cost of each item, such as tablets, on the boxes.
3. *Deliveries.* Keep track of local delivery costs to the business. It may be cheaper to hire a part-time worker to pick up supplies than to pay other companies to deliver items.
4. *Insurance.* Ask insurance carriers about ways to reduce premiums. One independent grocery store reduced premiums for its stock personnel by 15 percent simply by requiring them to wear supports while working.
5. *Borrowing.* Take the cost of borrowing into account when determining operational expenses. Even short-term loans can have a large impact on profit and cash flow.[13]

The process of cash flow management may be confusing to you in the beginning, buy you may find it relatively easy to monitor once everything is in place. Armed with a cash budget, aging schedules, and a set of feasible strategies, you can avoid cash flow problems and maximize your use of this precious resource.

SUMMARY

▬▬ The importance of financial records to a small business.

You need financial records so you can make managerial decisions on topics concerning how much money is owed to your business, how much money you owe, and how to identify financial problems before they become serious. Financial records are also needed to prepare your tax returns and to inform your banker and investors of your financial status. Without accurate financial records, you cannot exercise the kind of clear-sighted management control needed to survive in a competitive marketplace.

The accounting records needed for a small business.

The accounting records of your small business need to follow the standards of generally accepted accounting principles (GAAP). From your source documents, such as sales slips, purchase invoices, and check stubs, you record all the transactions in journals. Information from your journals will then be posted (transferred) into a general ledger. Financial statements like your balance sheet, income statement, and statement of cash flow are produced from the transactions in your general ledger.

Ratios used to analyze financial statements.

Ratio analysis is a way for you to compare the financial condition of your business to its performance in previous time periods or to similarly sized businesses within your industry. Four important types of financial ratios discussed in this chapter are liquidity, activity, leverage, and profitability ratios.

The importance of managing cash flow.

Cash flow is the difference between the amount of cash actually brought into your business and the actual amount paid out in a given period of time. Cash flow represents the lifeblood of your business because if you do not have enough money to pay for your operating expenses, you are out of business.

QUESTIONS FOR REVIEW & DISCUSSION

1. How can financial records allow you to identify problems in your business?

2. Assets = Liabilities + Owner's equity. How would you restate this equation if you wanted to know what your liabilities are? your owner's equity?

3. What purpose do GAAP and FASB serve for a small business owner?

4. Explain the difference between cash and accrual accounting.

5. Define the term *leverage* as it applies to accounting.

6. How can profitability ratios allow insight into the effectiveness of management? liquidity ratios? activity ratios? leverage ratios?

7. Why would a cash flow specialist be valuable to a small business?

8. Explain the difference between macro-aging and micro-aging accounts receivable schedules.

9. Cash flow is described as the lifeblood of a business. How would you explain this description to someone who does not understand business finance?

10. The sales projection for your retail business is $650,000. The industry average for the sales-to-inventory ratio is 5. How much inventory should you plan to stock?

QUESTIONS FOR **CRITICAL THINKING**

1. You need to write a business plan for a startup business. How do you come up with the numbers for your pro forma financial statements? Do you just guess and make them up? (*Hint:* The process starts with a sales forecast.)

2. Cash flow is more important than profit for a small business. Why is this statement true? If your income statement shows a profit at the end of the month, how can anything be more important?

Choose a type of small business that is of interest to you. Go to your library and find industry standard ratios in *Robert Morris Associates Annual Statement Studies* or Dun & Bradstreet's *Industry Norms and Key Business Ratios*. What do these standards tell you about the financial needs for this type of business? For example, is inventory turnover high or low in your chosen industry? Are profit margins tight or high?

Experience this...

WHAT WOULD **YOU** DO? | No. 1

The popularity of soccer as a participation sport attracted Leo Hernandez and Gil Ferguson to open an indoor soccer arena with retail shops selling soccer-related merchandise. Last year's financial statements for their business OnGoal are shown here. Leo and Gil are hoping to expand their business by opening another facility. However, before they approach banks or potential investors, they need to look closely at what the accounting statements show them.

OnGoal
Balance Sheet
December 31, 20——

Assets:
Current Assets:

Cash	$ 7,120	
Accounts Receivable	12,400	
Merchandise Inventory	18,200	
Prepaid Expenses	3,040	
Total Current Assets		$ 40,760

Fixed Assets:

Fixtures	$16,800	
Less Accumulated Depreciation	3,600	
Building	78,000	
Less Accumulated Depreciation	7,800	
Equipment	12,000	
Less Accumulated Depreciation	4,000	
Total Fixed Assets		$ 91,400
Total Assets		$132,160

Liabilities/Equity:

Current Liabilities:

Accounts Payable	$ 6,000	
Notes Payable	4,000	
Contracts Payable	8,000	
Total Current Liabilities		$ 18,000

Fixed Liabilities:

Long-Term Note Payable	$75,000	

Owners' Equity:

Shares held by Hernandez and Ferguson	$39,160	
Total Liabilities/Equity		$132,160

OnGoal
Income Statement
Year Ended December 31, 20—

Sales			$178,000
Cost of Goods Sold			
Beginning Inventory, January 1	$18,000		
Purchases during year	22,000		
Less Ending Inventory, December 31	(18,200)		
Cost of Goods Sold		$ 21,800	
Gross Margin			$156,200
Operating Expenses:			
Payment on building note	$34,000		
Salaries	68,000		
Supplies	7,460		
Advertising/promotion	3,000		
Insurance expense	18,000		
Utilities expense	10,000		
Miscellaneous expenses	4,000		
Total operating expenses		$144,460	
Net profit from operations			$ 11,740

QUESTIONS

1. Calculate liquidity, activity, leverage, and profitability ratios for OnGoal.

2. Pair off and compare your ratios. Discuss which of the ratios look weak and which look positive. Develop a one-page explanation of the company's ratios which you can show to potential lenders.

WHAT WOULD **YOU** DO?	No. 2

When Dan DaMann started his plastic injection-molding business, the numbers on the company's financial statements were simply a jumble of columns and rows. He thought only an expert could understand them. Then a friend explained accounting to him in a way he could understand and explain to his employees. He used a "bucket plan."

DaMann placed buckets (actually boxes) in the training room of his business to represent different areas of expense (taxes, rent, utilities, salaries, and so on) and one box for profit. As levels of revenue are reached, the boxes are filled with paper money (the play kind). This distribution of paper money enables employees to see literally where the company's revenues are going. Eventually, the money in the profit bucket (in real dollars) is distributed to employees. Each employee receives 5 percent of the profit bucket the first time it's filled and 2.5 percent of each succeeding bucket that month. If sales have increased by 25 percent at the time a bucket is filled, the bonus percentage is doubled.

QUESTIONS

1. What would a game like this teach employees about the business they work for? List five factors employees would learn and the benefit to the business.

2. Would you use such a game with a business you own? Why or why not?

CHAPTER CLOSING CASE	No. 8

The Pita Principle

Mark and Stacy Andrus believe in making every penny count. The only sign on their Randolph, Massachusetts, factory is a wooden slat and a sheet of paper with the company's name, Stacy's Pita Chip Co., taped to the door. Inside is spotless, but there's no lobby. Their offices, as founders and co-CEOs, have white cinder-block walls, a beige tile floor, folding tables, and décor that mixes Late College with Early Yard Sale.

The spartan surroundings reflect the CEOs' need to pay creditors and build the business. Mark, 36, still owes more than $100,000 in student loans for his doctorate in psychology. He and Stacy, also 36, owe about $370,000 in bank and SBA loans. They drive old cars, wear sweatshirts and jeans to work, and pay themselves what they call scavenger-level salaries. "Everything goes into the business," says Stacy.

It seems to be paying off. With sales in 37 states, Stacy's annual revenues hit $1.7 million recently, double those of a year earlier. Thanks largely to deals with big chains like Stop & Shop and Shaw's supermarkets, as well as private label business, Stacy's is now profitable.

Success Brings Problems   Stacy's began as a pushcart in Boston's Financial District. The couple was so successful at selling handmade pita-wrap sandwiches that they created a new problem: No matter how fast they worked, some people on line walked away. "We wanted to do something to make them wait," says Mark. Always frugal, he began to recycle the day's leftovers, taking extra pita bread, dusting it with cinnamon sugar or parmesan and garlic, chopping it into wedges, and baking it. The next day, he and Stacy handed out chips to people waiting in line. Soon customers started asking for the crispy, low-fat chips.

At that point, Mark and Stacy faced a decision: stick with sandwiches or switch to snacks? After poring over trade journals, quizzing industry brokers, and talking to other snack makers, they decided they could mass-produce and sell their snacks nationwide. "We thought we could get bigger faster with the chips," says Stacy.

Low-Tech, Low Budget Production   Initially, production was low-tech and low budget—except for what the founders spent on ingredients, an area where they've never scrimped. Orders came in on a home fax machine. They rented space cheaply at the Boston Pretzel Bakery, using it during the bakery's downtime. They cut, seasoned, baked, bagged, and labeled their chips entirely by hand. Their single piece of equipment was a heat sealer that resembled a pedal-driven 19th century sewing machine. With a top production rate of about seven cases per ten-hour day, revenues for that first year were barely $25,000. But as they grew more efficient and began investing in automated packaging equipment, sales grew.

When revenues reached $450,000, Mark and Stacy moved the business into its own headquarters inside a contracting company's warehouse. They cleaned, stripped, painted, and caulked the 10,000-square-foot factory themselves, using supplies they hauled from Home Depot. They shared the only existing office, and Stacy's brother, who had joined the company for $7 an hour and a share of the profits, built his own cubicle from plywood he salvaged from a shipping crate.

The Andruses initially made Stacy the majority owner so they'd be eligible for funding for female-owned companies. That paid off when they began buying automated packaging equipment and supplies and discovered that BankBoston (now Fleet) had a Small Business Administration-backed loan program to assist women entrepreneurs. Stacy applied for, and received, $60,000. Six months later she was able to borrow another $300,000. How? Stacy cites two ingredients: "I had a good, solid business plan. And we had demand."

Saving on Personnel Costs   They continued to plow the revenues and borrowed money into the company. When the business grew too brisk to hand-cut pita bread, they looked for an automatic slicer, but couldn't find one. Nor could they afford the $100,000 to have one custom-designed and built. They spent a year haunting used-equipment auctions before they found a carrot-cutting machine that had been owned by Campbell Soup for nearly 40 years. It had to be slowed and modified, but it now slices every Stacy's Pita Chip.

The penny-wise approach extends beyond capital expenses. Stacy's employs about 15 people, bringing in extras as needed to fill a big order. While they initially hired a few consultants, they now rely on the kindness of unofficial advisers and mentors in the industry for advice. They also negotiated an arrangement with Babson College to bring in summer interns who not only built the company's web site (*www.pitachips.com*) but maintain it as a class project. In exchange, Stacy frequently speaks on the business school's campus, 25 miles away.

"When we talked about starting our own business," says Mark, "we thought, if we don't do it now, we're going to someday look back and think, 'I wish I had.'"

Source: Adapted from "The Pita Principle" by Anne Stuart, from *Inc.: The Magazine for Growing Companies,* August 2001, 58–64. Copyright © 2001 by Goldhirsh Group/Inc Pubg. Reproduced with permission of Goldhirsh Group/Inc Pubg in the format textbook via Copyright Clearance Center.

QUESTIONS

1. How have Stacy and Mark created profit and a positive cash flow?

2. What cash flow problems have they faced at Stacy's Pita Chip Co., and how have they solved them?

3. Describe "Bootstrap Financing" in your own words. From this example of Stacy's Pita Chip Co., what bootstrapping principles could be applied to another small business?

9

Small Business Finance

After reading this chapter, you should be able to:

- Determine the financing needs of your business.

- Define basic financing terminology.

- Explain where to look for sources of funding.

LORI BONN GALLAGHER has a dilemma that many of us wouldn't mind having—how to best grow her already successful business. Lori started designing and manufacturing jewelry in 1991 with $1,000 of personal savings. She began factoring accounts receivable (selling her accounts receivable for less than their face value in order to get cash sooner) as soon as she had a customer base that included Nordstrom and Saks. In 1998, she switched her primary source of financing to a small community bank rather than factoring. She has been profitable since her first year of operation.

The situation she faces now is whether to continue growing at a steady pace, funded through internal cash flow and moderate bank debt, or to take on substantial loans to fuel growth. At the current pace, revenue could go from $3 million in 2000 to $10 million in five to seven years. Not bad, but Gallagher sees demand and the opportunity to grow much faster—if more capital were available. Even at current levels of operation, she can't make enough jewelry to keep up with sales.

The growth picture is complicated by the fact that Lori Bonn Design, Inc., needs some expensive things. Gallagher needs management help, especially financial management, so she can concentrate on what she does best—marketing and design. She wants to expand internationally with an aggressive campaign to increase name recognition and overseas suppliers. Finally, improvement can be made with inventory controls.

Currently, Lori owns 100 percent of the company stock and isn't completely comfortable with the idea of losing a chunk of that equity. What should Lori Bonn Gallagher do to finance her growth plans? See the advice that a group of investors gave her, at the end of this chapter.

Source: Jill Andresky Fraser, "Money Hunt—Plans for Growth," *Inc.,* March 2001, 49–57.

Although some entrepreneurs are well versed in determining their need for capital and knowing where to find it, the failure of many businesses can be traced to undercapitalization (see Reality Check, "The Evils of Undercapitalization"). A common approach is "not to worry about it" until the situation gets out of hand. However, every small business owner should understand how to define the amount of funding required to efficiently operate his or her business. Furthermore, the ability to be a proactive manager of the financing aspects of a business is paramount in a dynamic economy. As you've seen in earlier chapters, when circumstances change quickly, you must be prepared to adapt. This chapter covers issues of financing that every entrepreneur should understand before starting a business.

Because service businesses often require the purchase of fewer fixed assets at startup than do retailers or manufacturers, they can offer a good route to self-employment. And a survey by the national accounting and professional services firm Coopers & Lybrand found that many fast-growing companies now outsource certain service functions to outside providers. For small financial service firms, for instance, this means opportunity. How? This same survey found that the most commonly outsourced services were payroll services, tax compliance, employee benefits, and claims administration. It's a win-win situation for all parties involved. For the outsourcing firm, it's a way to reduce operating costs, because providers of a single type of service have a lower cost structure resulting from economies of scale. For the small service business, it's a prime market to exploit.[1]

■ Initial Capital Requirements

The fundamental financial building blocks for an entrepreneur are knowing what assets are required to open the business and how those assets will be financed. This knowledge has to do with *initial capital requirements*. Recall from Chapter 8 the importance of the balance sheet. The balance sheet lists the investment decisions of the business owner in the asset column and the financing decisions in the liabilities and owner's equity column. The financing necessary to acquire each asset required for the business must come from either owner-provided funds (equity) or borrowed funds (liabilities).

The process of determining initial capital requirements begins with identifying the short-term and long-term assets necessary to get the business started. Once you have this list of required assets, you must then determine how to pay for them.

Defining Required Assets

short-term assets Assets that will be converted into cash within one year.

long-term assets Assets that will not be converted into cash within one year.

Every business needs a set of short-term and long-term assets in place before the business ever opens its doors. **Typical short-term** assets include cash and inventory but may also include prepaid expenses (such as rent or insurance paid in advance) and a working capital (cash) reserve. Because many businesses are not profitable in the first year or so of operation, having a cash reserve with which to pay bills can help you avoid becoming insolvent.

The most common **long-term assets** are buildings and equipment, and may also include land, leasehold improvements, patents, and a host of other items. Each of these assets must be in the business *before* the enterprise earns its first dollar of sales. For this to happen, you must carefully evaluate your situation to determine exactly what *needs* to be in place in order for the business to effectively operate.

A useful exercise to help accomplish this task is to prepare a list of the assets the business would have if money were no object. Then review the list and determine the essential assets that are needed to operate the business on a "bare-bones" basis. Finally, try to determine the cost of these assets under each scenario.

For example, say you are an entrepreneur starting a restaurant and want seating for 100 people. If money were no object, you could choose brand new oak dining sets at a cost of $1,200 per six-place setting. On the other hand, at an auction of restaurant supplies and equipment, you could purchase used pine dining sets at a cost of $200 per six-place setting. Either choice will allow the seating requirement to be met.

By carefully completing this exercise for all assets, you end up with a list of assets with a minimum dollar investment and another list of assets needed for the dream business. Often your actual business will wind up somewhere in the middle of those two lists as you make final decisions.

With the final list of required assets and corresponding dollar costs in hand, you can then determine your financing requirements. Remember that each dollar of assets must be supported by a dollar of equity or liability funds. How much equity can you contribute personally to the enterprise? This contribution does not necessarily have to be all in cash.

For example, if your business requires a delivery vehicle and you already own a van with a market value of $12,000 that would be suitable for deliveries, the asset will be listed as "Delivery Vehicle—$12,000," and the balancing entry would be $12,000 of owner's equity. The total market value of the owner's assets used in the business plus all cash contributions from the owner to purchase assets or set up cash reserves is *owner's equity*.

The final step in the process is to subtract the total dollar value of owner's equity from the total dollar value of the required assets. Generally, this results in the dollar amount that must come from other sources. Sometimes there will be more owner's equity than needed to finance the required assets. In this situation, the entrepreneur can afford to invest in more assets or in more expensive assets—such as the new oak dining sets rather than the used pine dining sets for the restaurant mentioned earlier. More commonly, however, businesses will need additional capital to finance the required assets. This additional capital will come from one or more sources, which are most likely external to the business.[2]

It may not take as much initial startup money as you may think. Of the 2000 Inc. 500 (fastest-growing companies), the majority started with between $1,000 and $10,000 (see Figure 9.1).

> *Each business must have its assets in place—cash, inventory, patents, equipment, buildings, whatever it needs to operate—before it ever opens its doors.*

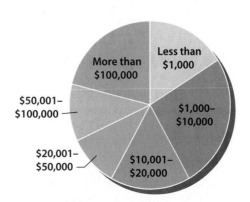

FIGURE 9.1

Start Me Up

Percentage of Inc. 500 companies that had differing amounts of initial startup capital.

Source: "The 2000 Inc. 500 Almanac Data Mine," 65.

The Evils of Undercapitalization

Let's say you had a marketable idea for a new venture, wrote a detailed business plan, secured some financing, and found a promising location. After two years the business was averaging $1,100 per day in revenues—a 40 percent jump from the first year's operations. Sounds pretty good, right?

Not so fast. This is the story of Rochelle Zabarkes, founder of Adriana's Bazaar, a specialty food shop in Manhattan. Despite being well organized and hard working, Zabarkes had a slight problem: she was broke—a victim of undercapitalization.

Undercapitalization means simply not having enough capital to effectively and efficiently run a business. Undercapitalization can happen for two reasons: (1) the combined miscalculation of overestimated revenues and underestimated costs, and (2) the owner's inability to secure adequate capital to cover cash shortages. The problem is one of the most common and serious facing entrepreneurs—to the point where it often leads to the failure of their venture.

In Zabarkes's case, she wound up with stacks of unpaid bills from her creditors, a default notice on her SBA loan, and an eviction threat from her landlord. She had to seek to arrange a new loan that would enable her to get out of the red with her suppliers and other lenders, while financing planned expansion.

Bernie Showman and Patricia Gauss wanted to serve a niche in the nursery and gardening business with hard-to-find tropicals like coconut and Christmas palms. The pair opened Tropical Exotics in St. Petersburg, Florida, and closed it 18 months later—another victim of small business undercapitalization.

Startup costs were higher than anticipated for items like a new truck and lawn mowers. It all added up fast. Then a drought forced the Southwest Florida Water Management District to issue an emergency order restricting outdoor use of water. People can't buy plants if they can't water them. Higher than expected costs + lower than expected revenue = classic case of undercapitalization.

Showman recommends having at least two years' salary in the bank before beginning a business. He also suggests having three years of advertising money in the bank. He states, "I think one of the hardest things was becoming known. It took more money for advertising than we ever anticipated."

The plights of these two businesses point out important lessons for all entrepreneurs. Zabarkes's problem of undercapitalization resulted in a cash flow bind, whereas Showman's problem could have been lack of profit as well as cash flow. According to the *Wall Street Journal,* "No matter how smart, industrious and experienced you are, if you miscalculate your costs, you might soon be headed for a going-out-of-business sale."

Sources: Sharon L. Bond, "Tropical Exotics to Close Sunday," *St. Petersburg Times,* 15 November 2000; Brent Bowers, "This Store Is a Hit But Somehow Cash Flow Is Missing," *Wall Street Journal,* 19 June 1994, B2; and Tom Knight, "Small Business Adviser: Grow Revenues But Retain Control," *Crain's Chicago Business,* 13 November 2000, SB17.

The Five Cs of Credit

When an entrepreneur decides to seek external financing, he or she must be able to prove creditworthiness to potential providers of funds. A traditional guideline used by many lenders is the five Cs of credit, each C representing a critical qualifying element. These elements include

1. *Capacity.* Capacity refers to the applicant's ability to repay the loan. Capacity is usually estimated by examining the amount of cash and marketable securities available, and both historical and projected cash flows of the business.

Unexpected costs and unforeseen circumstances can cause problems with undercapitalization as in the case of Tropical Exotics.

2. *Capital.* Capital is a function of the applicant's personal financial strength. The net worth of a business—the value of its assets minus the value of its liabilities—determines its capital.
3. *Collateral.* Assets owned by the applicant that can be pledged as security for the repayment of the loan are collateral. If the loan is not repaid, the lender can confiscate the pledged assets.
4. *Character.* The applicant's character is considered important in that it indicates his or her apparent willingness to repay the loan. Character is judged primarily on the basis of the applicant's past repayment patterns, but lenders may consider other factors, such as marital status, home ownership, and military service, when attributing character to an applicant. The lender's prior experience with applicant repayment patterns affects his choice of factors in evaluating the character of a new applicant.
5. *Conditions.* The general economic climate at the time of the loan application may affect the applicant's ability to repay the loan. Lenders will usually not extend credit in times of economic recession or business downturns.

Additional Considerations

In addition to the five Cs, potential investors will want to know more about you and your business. For startups, simply having a good idea will not be enough evidence to convince many investors to risk their capital in your business. You will need to show that you are a competent manager with a track record of prior business success. If possible, you should show an informal board of directors made up of the people whom you may contact for assistance. Potential members on such a board include bankers, attorneys, CPAs, and successful business owners.

Vintage Financing

What help is available to assist small business owners and managers in thoroughly estimating assets? Patrick and Peggy Duffeler, owners of Williamsburg Winery, a $2 million-a-year wine producer in Williamsburg, Virginia, utilized different means. First of all, they scoured industry data for information. They learned the rule of thumb among wine producers: For every $1 worth of revenues that one hopes to produce, an initial investment of $2 to $3 in land, grapes, barrels, and laboratory equipment needs to be made. However, the would-be vintners also need to take into consideration whether they intend to produce upscale wines (which producers anticipate will appreciate in value over time), plus the prospect of unpredictable weather conditions and the uncertainties of competition and consumer tastes.

The Duffelers spent their initial investment of $180,000 on 2,500 grape plants, production equipment rental fees, and a trial production run. The test "crush" was a good way for the couple to test their processes—and to determine whether their asset estimation was on target. The test run was so positive, from both angles, that they were able to raise the money to move the winery into full production.

Expanding also meant investing in 60 wine barrels that cost upwards of $500 each. Then the Duffelers had to plant new fields, buy fermenting equipment, and hire a wine specialist (viniculturist) and a wine maker to supervise the growing and producing processes. By carefully assessing their asset needs, the Duffelers have been able to build a successful small winery.

Source: Jill Andresky Fraser, "How to Finance Anything," *Inc.*, February 1994, 38–46.

If yours is a growing or emerging business, you will need to be ready to provide well-audited financial statements and show a solid record of earnings. It is difficult to attract investors without proven performance and a high likelihood of continued growth and success.

The old adage "You have to have money to make money" is largely true in the area of financing. However, it might be amended to say, "You have to show an ability to make money in order to attract money."

Basic Financial Vocabulary

Before an entrepreneur can begin looking for other sources of funds, two basic types of funds, as well as the terminology associated with them, must be understood.

Forms of Capital

leverage The ability to finance an investment through borrowed funds.

Two kinds of funds are potentially available to the entrepreneur: debt and equity. Debt funds (also known as liabilities) are borrowed from a creditor and, of course, must be repaid. Using debt to finance a business creates **leverage,** which is money you can borrow against the money you already have (see Chapter 8). Leverage can enable you to magnify the potential returns expected due to investing your equity in the business.

However, debt funding can also constrain the future cash flows generated by the business and can magnify losses as well. Debt creates the risk of becoming technically insolvent if the entrepreneur is unable to make each debt payment on time. Continued nonrepayment of debt will ultimately lead to the bankruptcy of the business. Debt as a funding source will be examined more closely in the next section.

Equity funds, by contrast, are supplied by investors in exchange for an ownership position in the business. They need not be repaid. Providers of equity funds forgo the opportunity to receive periodic repayments, in order to share in the profits of the business. As a result, equity financing does not create a constraint on the cash flows of the business.

However, equity providers usually demand a voice in the management of the business, thus reducing your autonomy to run the business as you would like. It is easy to see that the decision to seek outside funds is both critical and complex. Therefore, a more detailed view of each kind of financing is presented.

Figure 9.2 contains the results of a survey of the CEOs of some of the best-managed small businesses in the United States. In particular, the bar graph shows the sources of capital the CEOs use. Although a majority predicted having operating profits available for their use, a significant number expected to use short-term and long-term debt.

DEBT FINANCING. Three important parameters associated with **debt financing** are the amount of principal to be borrowed, the loan's interest rate, and the loan's length of maturity. Together they determine the size and extent of your obligation to the creditor. Until the debt is repaid, the creditor has a legal claim on a portion of the business's cash flows. Creditors can demand payment and, in the most severe case, force a business into bankruptcy because of overdue payments.

The **principal** of the loan is the original amount of money to be borrowed. You should try to minimize the size of the loan to reduce your financial risk. The pro forma balance sheet estimates the amount of funds needed (see Chapter 8). The amount you need to borrow is the difference between the total of pro forma assets and total owner's equity.

The **interest rate** of the loan determines the "price" of the borrowed funds. In most cases it will be based on the current prime rate of interest. In the past, the prime rate was defined as the rate of interest banks charge their "best" customers—

debt financing The use of borrowed funds to finance a business.

principal An amount of money borrowed from a lender.

interest rate The amount of money paid for the use of borrowed funds.

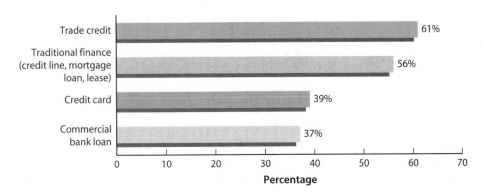

FIGURE 9.2

Where Capital Comes From

Responses to an SBA/Federal Reserve survey question regarding where small business owners intended to get their capital.

Source: "The Facts About Small Business 1999," www.sba.gov/ADVO

those with the lowest risk. More recently, it has also become a benchmark for determining many other rates of interest. Interest rates for small business loans are normally prime plus some additional percentage. For example, if the prime rate is 8.5 percent, a bank might offer small business loans at "prime plus four," or 12.5 percent. Additional factors, such as default risk and maturity, will also affect the cost of a loan.

The actual rate of interest the borrower will pay on a loan is called the *effective rate of interest.* It is often higher than the stated rate of interest for several reasons. A lender may require a *compensating balance,* meaning that the borrower is required to keep a minimum dollar balance (often as much as 10 percent of the principal) on deposit with the lender. This requirement reduces the amount of funds accessible to the borrower and increases the actual rate of interest because, over the life of the loan, the borrower pays the same amount of interest dollars for fewer available funds.

The frequency with which interest is compounded can also increase the cost of a loan. Compounding refers to the intervals at which you pay interest. Lenders may compound interest annually, semiannually, quarterly, monthly, weekly, daily, or even continuously. For example, quarterly compounding involves four compounding periods within a year—one-fourth of the stated interest rate is paid each quarter. The more compounding periods, the higher the effective rate. Financial institutions are required to inform borrowers of the effective rate of interest on all loans.

fixed-rate loan A loan with an interest rate that remains constant.

variable-rate loan A loan with an interest rate that changes over the life of the loan.

Whether a loan has a fixed rate or a variable rate of interest also affects its cost. A **fixed-rate loan** retains the same interest rate for the entire length of time for which the funds are borrowed. A **variable-rate loan** is one whose interest may fluctuate over time. Typically, the variable rate is tied to a benchmark such as the prime rate or federal funds rate. Every year (normally on the anniversary of the original loan date) a variable interest rate is adjusted according to changes in the benchmark.

A fixed-rate loan typically has a higher interest rate than the initial rate on a variable-rate loan. Therefore, the cost of a fixed-rate loan is higher in the first year (or longer). But because the variable interest rate could increase each year, it eventually might exceed the rate on the fixed loan by far. A variable-rate loan is much more of a gamble than a fixed-rate loan when borrowing for a long period of time.

Your goal is to find the lowest possible effective rate, given your current circumstances, by investigating different funding sources. For example, a particular bank may have excess funds available to lend and be willing to offer lower rates than its competitors. A startup business may want to consider a variable-rate loan to help offset its lower cash flows in the first year of operation.

maturity The length of time in which a loan must be repaid.

The **maturity** of a loan refers to the length of time for which a borrower obtains the use of the funds. A short-term loan must be repaid within one year, an intermediate-term loan must be repaid within one to ten years, and a long-term loan must be repaid within ten or more years. Typically, the purpose of the loan will determine the length of maturity chosen.

For example, you would use a short-term loan to purchase inventory that you expect to sell within one year, yielding the funds to repay the loan. For the purchase of a building, which presumably will serve the business for decades, a long-term loan is preferable. The maturity of the loan should essentially match the borrower's use of the loan proceeds.

The maturity of the loan also affects its interest rate. Ordinarily, the longer the maturity, the higher the rate of interest. The reason for this rule is that a lender must be compensated for the opportunity cost of not being able to use those loaned funds in other ways. Lenders will add a "premium" to the price that the borrower pays for a longer-maturity loan.

Your goal regarding loan maturity is to obtain as much flexibility as possible. On one hand, a shorter maturity will usually have a lower rate of interest but must be quickly repaid, thus affecting cash flow. On the other hand, a longer maturity, despite its higher rate, gives you more time to repay the loan, resulting in smaller payments and reduced constraints on your current cash flow. Flexibility is created by maximizing the maturity of a loan while retaining the option of repaying the loan sooner than the maturity date, if cash flows allow. Make sure that there is no penalty for early repayment.

Consider principal, effective rate of interest, and maturity very carefully when attempting to obtain debt financing. By ascertaining the proper amount of principal needed, comparing the effective rates of interest at your disposal, and matching the maturity of the loan with the projected availability of cash flows with which to make repayments, you will be able to make the greatest possible use of debt financing.

EQUITY FINANCING. As stated earlier, **equity financing** does not have to be repaid. There are no payments to constrain the cash flow of the business. There is no interest to be paid on the funds. Providers of equity capital wind up owing a portion of the business and are generally interested in (1) dividends, (2) increased value of the business (and thus their investment in it), and (3) a voice in the management of the business.

Dividends are payments based on the net profits of the business and made to the providers of equity capital. These payments often are made on either a quarterly, a semiannual, or an annual basis. Many small businesses keep net profits in the form of retained earnings to help finance future growth, and dividends are paid only when the business has profits above the amount necessary to fund projected new development.

Increased value of the business is a natural result of a successful business enterprise. As a successful business grows and prospers, the owners prosper as well. Because the providers of equity capital own a "piece of the action," the value of their investment increases in direct proportion with the increase in the value of the business. They are frequently not as concerned about dividends as they are about the business's long-term success. If the business is successful, the equity providers will have the opportunity to sell all or part of their investment for a considerable profit.

A voice in management is an additional consideration for providers of equity capital. The rationale underlying this concept is that, because the owners of a business have the most to lose if the business fails, they are entitled to have a say about how their money is being used. Not all equity providers are interested in running a business, but many can contribute important expertise along with their capital contributions. They can enhance your business's chances of success.

equity financing The sale of common stock or the use of retained earnings to provide long-term financing.

dividends Payments based on the net profits of the business and made to the providers of equity capital.

Other Loan Terminology

Two additional sets of terms that you will often encounter while searching for financing have to do with *loan security* and with *loan restrictions*. These terms can be of great importance and should be well understood.

LOAN SECURITY. **Loan security** refers to the borrower's assurance to lenders that loans will be repaid. If the entrepreneur's signature on a loan is not considered sufficient security by a lender, the lender will require another signature to guarantee the loan. Other individuals whose signatures appear on the loan are known as *endorsers*. Endorsers are contingently liable for the notes they sign. Two types of endorsers are *comakers* and *guarantors*.

loan security Assurance to a lender that a loan will be repaid.

Calvin and Hobbes

by Bill Watterson

CALVIN AND HOBBES Watterson. Reprinted with permission of UNIVERSAL PRESS SYNDICATE. All rights reserved.

Comakers create a joint liability with the borrower. The lender can collect from either the maker (original borrower) or the comaker. Guarantors ensure the repayment of a note by signing a guarantee commitment. Both private and government lenders often require guarantees from officers of corporations in order to ensure continuity of effective management.

LOAN RESTRICTIONS.   Sometimes called "covenants," loan restrictions spell out what the borrower cannot do *(negative covenants)* or what he or she must do *(positive covenants)*. These restrictions are built into each loan agreement and are generally negotiable—as long as you are aware of them.

Typical negative covenants will preclude the borrower from acquiring any additional debt without prior approval from the original lender or will prevent the borrower from issuing dividends in excess of the terms of the loan agreement.

Common positive covenants will require that the borrower maintain some minimum level of working capital until the loan is repaid, carry some type of insurance while the loan is in effect, or provide periodic financial statements to the lender.

By understanding that lenders will sometimes require the additional assurance of an endorser and will likely create covenants on loan agreements, you can be better prepared to negotiate during the search for financing. Doing your homework on loan terminology and processes improves your chances for successfully obtaining funds.[3]

How Can You Find Capital?

Once you determine how much capital is needed for the startup or expansion, you are ready to begin looking for capital sources. To prepare for this search, you need to be aware of what these sources will want to know about you and your business before they are willing to entrust their funds. You also need to understand the characteristics of each capital source and the process for obtaining funds from them.

The Loan Application Process

Typically, to determine creditworthiness, a lending institution will collect relevant information from financial statements supplied by the applicant and by external sources, such as local or regional credit associations, credit interchange bureaus, and the applicant's bank. This procedure is known as "credit scoring."

If the applicant meets or exceeds some minimal score (set by the lender) on key financial and credit characteristics, the institution will be willing to arrange a loan. Most lenders are hesitant to make loans to startup businesses, however, unless either a wealthy friend or a relative will cosign the loan or unless loan proceeds will be used to purchase assets that could be repossessed and easily resold in case of default.

Sources of Debt Financing

The wide array of credit options available confuses many entrepreneurs. A thorough understanding of the nature and characteristics of these debt sources will help ensure that you are successful in obtaining financing from the most favorable source possible.

Finding Financing Online

With the wide availability of information on the Internet, you shouldn't be surprised to discover that you can find financial assistance and investigate financing sources there as well. Let's look more closely at some Internet sites that you might find useful as you search for financial information.

Ebank.com has a strategy to become the prime bank for small businesses online. The board of directors is made up entrepreneurs who have started small businesses and have experience securing traditional bank loans. The small business loan process should be simplified by ebank.com through technology and straightforward criteria.

LiveCapital.com is an Internet borrower and lender matchmaking service that puts borrowers in touch with as many as 50 lenders—and borrowers can get instant credit decisions of up to $75,000 online.

At www.einet.net, Entrepreneurs on the Web, under the section on Business Information, you'll find links to other financial sites, including those that list businesses looking for startup or expansion capital.

At another site, Venture Information Network for Entrepreneurs, Inc. (VINE, at www.thevine.com), you'll find a virtual meeting place designed to bring together people in need of funding and people with available cash.

You might also want to check out FinanceHub (www.financehub.com), a site dedicated to helping entrepreneurs find financing.

Some other possible sites include:

The Small Business Resource Center: www.webcom.com/seaquest/sbrc/reports.html
The Corporate Finance Network: ww.corpfinet.com
The U.S. Small Business Administration: www.sba.gov

Sources: Richard Parlontieri, "Take a Look at These Play Books," *Community Banker,* January 2000, 24–27; and Miriam Leuchter, *USBanker,* September 2000, 24.

COMMERCIAL BANKS. Most people's first response to the question—Where would you borrow money?—is "a bank." Commercial banks are the backbone of the credit market, offering the widest assortment of loans to creditworthy small businesses.

Bank loans generally fall into two major categories: short-term loans (for purchasing inventory, overcoming cash flow problems, and meeting monthly expenditures) and long-term loans (for purchasing land, machinery, and buildings or renovating facilities).

unsecured loan A short-term loan for which collateral is not required.

Most short-term loans are **unsecured loans**—the bank does not require any collateral as long as the entrepreneur has a good credit standing. These loans are often self-liquidating, which means that the loan will be repaid directly with the revenues generated from the original purpose of the loan. For example, if an entrepreneur uses a short-term loan to purchase inventory, the loan is repaid as the inventory is sold. Types of short-term loans include lines of credit, demand notes, and floor planning.

line of credit An agreement that makes a specific amount of short-term funding available to a business as it is needed.

A **line of credit** is an agreement between a bank and a business, which specifies the amount of unsecured short-term funds the bank will make available to the business over a specific period of time—normally one year. The agreement allows the business to borrow and repay funds up to the maximum amount specified in the agreement throughout the year. The business pays interest only on the amount of funds actually borrowed but may be required to pay a setup or handling fee.

demand note A short-term loan that must be repaid (both principal and interest) in a lump sum at maturity.

A **demand note** is a loan made to a small business for a specific period of time, to be repaid in a lump sum at maturity. With this type of loan, the bank reserves the right to demand repayment of the loan at any time. For example, a bank might loan a business $50,000 for one year at 12 percent interest. The business would repay the loan by making one payment of $56,000 ($50,000 principal plus 0.12 × $50,000 interest) at the end of one year. The only reason a bank is likely to demand repayment sooner is if the business appears to be struggling and potentially unable to repay the loan in full at the end of the specified time period.

floor planning A type of business loan generally made for "big-ticket" items. The business holds the item in inventory and pays interest, but it is actually owned by the lender until the item is sold.

Floor planning is a special type of loan used particularly for financing high-priced inventory items, such as new automobiles, trucks, recreational vehicles, and boats. A business borrowing money for this purpose is allowed to display the inventory on its premises, but the inventory is actually owned by the bank. When the business sells one of the items, it will use the proceeds of the sale to repay the principal of the loan. The business is generally required to pay interest monthly on each item of inventory purchased with the loan proceeds. Therefore, the longer it takes the business to sell each item, the more the business pays in interest expenses. This is one instance in which the short-term loan is a **secured loan.** The assets purchased with the loan proceeds serve as collateral.

secured loan A loan that requires collateral as security for the lender.

installment loan A loan made to businesses for the purchase of fixed assets such as equipment and real estate.

Types of long-term bank loans include installment loans, balloon notes, and unsecured term loans. **Installment loans** are loans made to businesses for the purchase of fixed assets such as equipment and real estate. These loans are to be repaid in periodic payments that include accrued interest and part of the outstanding principal balance. In the case of many fixed assets, the maturity of the loan will equal the usable life of the asset, and the principal amount loaned will range from 65 to 80 percent of the asset's market value. For the purchase of real estate, banks will often allow a repayment schedule of 15 to 30 years and typically lend between 75 and 85 percent of the property's value. In every case, the bank will maintain a security interest in, or lien on, the asset until the loan is fully repaid.

balloon note A loan that requires the borrower to make small monthly payments (usually enough to cover the interest), with the balance of the loan due at maturity.

Balloon notes are loans made to businesses in which only small periodic payments are required over the life of the loan, with a large lump-sum payment at maturity. A typical balloon note requires monthly payments to cover accrued interest,

What to Do Before You Talk to Your Banker

One way to ensure that your business is getting the best rates and service from your bank is to nurture a strong relationship with your banker. The idea of meeting with a banker can be an intimidating process. To get your relationship off to a good start,

- Don't ask anyone else to do something you aren't willing to do. You have to put your own assets on the line to get a business loan.

- Start talking with your banker before you are in dire need. Bankers are naturally conservative because they have to protect their depositors' money.

- Don't surprise your banker. Don't go in on Thursday to say that you can't make your payroll on Friday.

- Have routine meetings with your banker to keep him or her up to date on how your business is progressing.

- Tell your banker in person when your business is having trouble and explain how you intend to overcome the problem.

- Take time to educate your banker about your business and industry. The better your banker understands your business, the better he or she can help you.

- Be timely with your payments and any financial information the bank may request from you.

- Give your banker all your business—both your personal and your firm's deposits. Use the bank's other services when appropriate.

- Refer potential customers to your banker.

- Keep a positive attitude. A banker asking for more documentation isn't necessarily looking for a reason to turn your loan down. More likely, you have provided inadequate information—the number one reason for loan delays. Your banker is looking for a reason to say "yes."

By sustaining a good relationship with your banker, you can enhance your chances of getting the best possible assistance from him. This is especially helpful in troubled times.

Sources: Julie Cripe, "Small Business Financing: What to Do Before You Talk to the Bank," *San Antonio Business Journal,* 8 October 2000, 2; and Frank Seffinger, "Maintain Good Relations with Your Banker," *Rocky Mountain News,* 25 January 1995, B1.

---

with the entire principal due at the end of the term of the loan. This allows you more flexibility with your cash flow over the life of the loan. If you are unable to make the final balloon payment, it is common for the bank to refinance the loan for a longer period of time, allowing you to continue making monthly payments.

Unsecured term loans are loans made to established businesses which have demonstrated a strong overall credit profile. Eligible businesses must show excellent creditworthiness and have an extremely high probability of repayment. These loans are usually made for very specific terms and may come with restrictions on the use of the loan proceeds. For example, a bank might agree to lend a business a sum of money for a three-year period at a given rate of interest. You must then ensure that the funds are used to finance some asset or activity that will generate enough revenue to repay the loan within the three-year time horizon.

unsecured term loan A loan made to established businesses which have demonstrated a strong overall credit profile.

Commercial banks remain a primary source of debt financing for small businesses. The type, maturity, and other terms of each loan, however, are uniquely a function of the financial strength or creditworthiness of the borrower.

COMMERCIAL FINANCE COMPANIES. Commercial finance companies extend short- and intermediate-term credit to firms that cannot easily obtain credit elsewhere. Because these companies are willing to take a bigger risk than commercial banks, their interest rates are often considerably higher. Commercial finance companies perform a valuable service to small businesses that have yet to establish their creditworthiness.

Among the most common types of loans provided by commercial finance companies are floor planning, leasing, and factoring accounts receivable.

FLOOR PLANNING. Finance company floor planning is similar to that offered by banks, with one important exception. The finance company can actually help generate retail sales by extending credit to the retail customers purchasing the floor-planned items. This in turn generates the need for more floor planning. Many small businesses seek finance companies that will finance both the wholesale (floor planning) and retail (customer purchases) aspects of their business.

LEASING. Leasing is a contract arrangement whereby a finance company purchases the durable goods needed by a small business and rents them to the small business for a specific period of time. The rent payment includes some amount of interest. Due to current tax laws, this activity is very lucrative for finance companies and often allows entrepreneurs to have the use of state-of-the-art equipment at a fraction of the cost.

factoring The practice of raising funds for a business through the sale of accounts receivable.

FACTORING ACCOUNTS RECEIVABLE. Another important type of loan available from commercial finance companies is accounts receivable **factoring.** Under this arrangement, a small business either sells its accounts receivable to a finance company outright or uses the receivables as collateral for a loan. The purchase price of the receivables (or the amount of the loan) is discounted from the face value of what the business is owed, in order to allow for potential losses (in the form of unpaid accounts) and for the fact that the finance company will not receive full repayment of the loan until sometime in the future.

Typically, the finance company will either purchase the receivables for or will lend the small business somewhere between 55 and 80 percent of the face value of the business's accounts receivable, based on their likelihood of being paid in a timely manner. If the finance company purchases the receivables outright, it will collect payments on them as they come due. If the small business uses its receivables as collateral for a loan, in a process known as "pledging," as the business collects these accounts due, the proceeds are forwarded to the finance company to repay the loan.

policy loan A loan made to a business by an insurance company, using the business's insurance policy as collateral.

INSURANCE COMPANIES. For some entrepreneurs, life insurance companies have become a principal source of debt financing. The most common type of loan is called a "policy loan." **Policy loans** are made to entrepreneurs based on the amount of money paid in premiums on an insurance policy that has a cash surrender value. Although each insurance company varies its methods for making these loans, a typical arrangement is for the insurance company to lend up to 95 percent of a policy's cash surrender value.

The collateral for the loan is the cash that the entrepreneur has already paid into the policy. In essence, the insurance company is lending the entrepreneur his or her own money. Because the default risk is virtually zero (defaulting on the loan merely reduces the cash surrender value of the policy), the rate of interest is often very favorable.

If an entrepreneur has been paying premiums into a whole-life, variable-life, or universal-life policy, it is likely that the option to borrow funds against it will be available. Term insurance policies, however, have no borrowing capacity. One caution about this type of borrowing is that the amount of insurance coverage is usually reduced by the amount of the loan.

FEDERAL LOAN PROGRAMS.   Government lending programs exist to stimulate economic activity. The underlying rationale for making these loans is that the borrowers will become profitable and create jobs, which in turn means more tax dollars in the coffers of government agencies providing the funds for the loans. The most active government lender is the Small Business Administration (SBA), a federal agency. **SBA loan** programs include guaranteed loans, direct loans, and the 504 loan program. For full descriptions of all SBA loan programs, see *www.sba.gov/finance* The majority of these loan funds go to service, retail, and manufacturing businesses (see Figure 9.3).

Guaranteed loans are generally known as the "7(a) program." Under this program, private lenders—usually commercial banks—make loans to entrepreneurs that are guaranteed up to 90 percent by the SBA. This means that the lender's risk exposure is reduced by the amount of the SBA guarantee. Since January 1, 1995, the SBA can guarantee as much as $500,000 per loan.

To be eligible for the 7(a) program, a business must be operated for profit and must fall within size standards set by the SBA (see Chapter 1). Loans cannot be made to businesses engaged in speculation or real estate rental. Existing businesses must provide, among other things, financial statements for the past three years and financial projections for the next three years. Startup businesses must provide three years of projected financial statements, a feasible business plan, and proof of adequate investment by the owners (generally about 20 to 30 percent equity).

SBA loan A loan made to a small business through a commercial bank, of which a portion is guaranteed by the Small Business Administration.

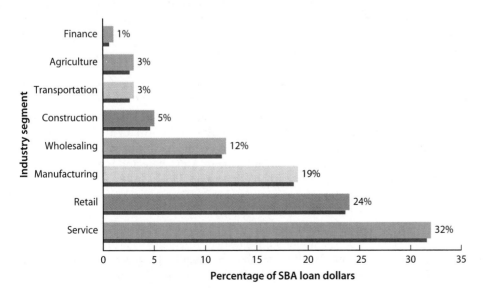

FIGURE 9.3

Who Gets SBA Loans?

The SBA guaranteed $10.5 billion in 7(a) business loans in 2000. The average loan was $250,656 with a maturity of 11.5 years; 21 percent of the loans went to businesses less than two years old.

Source: Small Business Administration, sba.gov

Government loan programs for small businesses are intended to help create jobs, prosperity, and tax revenues that make more loans available to other small businesses.

direct loan A loan made directly by the SBA to a small business, without the participation of a bank or other lender.

certified development company A nonprofit organization sponsored either by private interests or by state or local governments.

LowDoc program A relatively new loan program available through the SBA which simplifies the paperwork that has historically been required.

trade credit The purchase of goods from suppliers who do not demand payment immediately.

Successful applicants pay interest rates of up to 2.25 percent above the prime rate for loans with maturities of less than seven years and up to 2.75 percent above the prime rate for loans with maturities of seven years or longer. The borrower will repay the loan in monthly installments, which include both principal and interest. The first payment may be delayed up to six months, and the loans carry no balloon payments, prepayment penalties, or application fees.

Direct loans are those made directly by the SBA to a small business, without the participation of a bank or other lender. Most of these loans are made to special groups of individuals such as the Vietnam Veteran and Disabled Veterans Loan Program and the Handicapped Assistance Loan Program. Generally, these loans are limited to $150,000 and are made only when no other source of financing is available to the entrepreneur. These direct loan programs have come under some criticism because they have the highest default rate among all of the SBA's programs.

The 504 Loan Program provides small businesses with funding for fixed assets when conventional loans are not possible. These funds are distributed through a **certified development company,** which is a nonprofit organization sponsored by either private interests or by state or local governments. In a typical arrangement, a private lender will provide 50 percent of the total value of the loan, the borrower 10 percent, and the certified development company the remaining 40 percent of the necessary funds. Because the 504 portion of the funds—that contributed by the certified development company—is 100 percent guaranteed by the SBA, the private lender's risk exposure is significantly reduced. The maturity for 504 financing is 10 years for equipment purchases and 20 years for real estate.[4]

In addition to the preceding loan programs, the SBA offers loan programs to support small businesses engaged in international trade and rural development, those with women owners, and those with working capital needs. There is no doubt that the SBA plays a very significant role in providing debt financing for small businesses. However, the agency, like all other federal agencies, is subject to policy changes and budget cuts each year. The viability of the SBA in the future is dependent on its ability to effectively service the small business community.

One of the main criticisms of the SBA loan programs has been the amount of paperwork required, especially for relatively small loans. In response to this concern, the SBA recently created the **LowDoc program.**[5] Under this program, qualified small businesses can borrow up to $100,000 with a one-page application, although the lender may require additional information from the applicant. Additionally, there is a Micro-Loan Program for businesses needing loans of less than $50,000. Each of these programs has been very successful.

STATE AND LOCAL GOVERNMENT LENDERS. Many state and local governments lend money to entrepreneurs through various programs. As noted earlier, they can sponsor a certified development company to assist small businesses with the acquisition of fixed assets. Other loan programs are usually tied in with economic development—for instance, some loans are made contingent on the number of jobs that will be created by the small business. Most state and local government programs have lower interest rates than conventional loans, often with longer maturities. It is clearly to your advantage to find out if these programs would be available to you.

TRADE CREDIT. The last major source of debt financing we will cover is the use of **trade credit** or accounts payable. Recall from Chapter 8 that accounts payable are the amounts owed by a business to the creditors who have supplied goods or ser-

Plastic Finance—Tempting, But Risky

Credit cards for financing small business. Your loan officer will say, "Don't use it." Your SCORE counselor will say, "Don't even think about it." A lot of small business owners are using credit cards as a partial source of funding, but it isn't for the faint of heart.

Andy Jacob used credit cards to start his business called LoanGiant.com, but agrees that they should be a venue of last resort and that "only people that really believe in what they are doing should go in this direction." He didn't own a home or have experience in the mortgage lending industry, the business he and friends wanted to start. After a year of researching the industry and maxing out cards, he finally obtained investor finance. He now employs 155 people and generates $32 million of revenue.

Credit cards are enticing, because most offer an extremely low introductory rate—3.9 percent, 2.9 percent, even 0 percent—for a limited time. When those introductory rates end, the rate actually charged can jump as high as 22 percent APR within a matter of months. Think of it this way: If you aren't earning 22 percent on your equity, how can you afford to pay 22 percent for credit? Answer: You can't. Are you anxious to see how bankruptcy court works?

A recent survey of 500 small business owners by Arthur Andersen and National Small Business United revealed

- 50 percent use credit cards to finance their business, of which 20 percent use two or three cards, and 36 percent pay the bill in full each month.

- 64 percent of surveyed business owners use credit cards to cover day-to-day expenses.

- 46 percent use the cards to finance large capital outlays.

Gutsy move.

Sources: Brent Snavely, "Credit Card Financing: Tempting But Risky for Small Business," *Crain's Detroit Business*, 14 September 2000, 13; and Tara Teichgraeber, "Survey: Businesses Using More Plastic for Financing," *Phoenix Business Journal*, 7 July 2000, 8.

vices to the business. Although startups may find it difficult to obtain everything on credit right away, many manufacturers and wholesalers will ship goods at least 30 days before payment is required.

This 30-day grace period is essentially a loan to the small business. Because there is no interest charge for the first 30 days, the loan is "free." For this reason, you should take advantage of as much trade credit as possible. A survey of 300 small business owners by Dun & Bradstreet showed that 65 percent of the owners had used trade credit or lines of credit from vendors as their primary source of financing in the preceding 12-month period.[6]

Sources of Equity Financing

From our discussion of debt financing, you know that lenders will expect entrepreneurs to provide equity funds in the amount of *at least* 20 percent—and possibly 50 percent or more—of the business before approving a loan. The higher the risk the lender assumes, the more of your own money you must put into the business. The most common sources of equity financing are personal funds, family and friends, partners, venture capital firms, Small Business Investment Companies, angels, and various forms of stock offerings.

PERSONAL FUNDS. Most new businesses are originally financed with their creators' funds. The Department of Commerce estimates that nearly two-thirds of all startups are begun without borrowed funds. The first place most entrepreneurs find equity capital is in their personal assets. Cash, savings accounts, and checking accounts are the most obvious sources of equity funds. Additional sources are the sale of stocks, bonds, mutual funds, real estate, or other personal investments.

FAMILY AND FRIENDS. The National Federation of Independent Business reported that more than one-fourth of new businesses are at least partially funded by the family and friends of the entrepreneurs. Family and friends are more willing to risk capital in a venture owned by someone they know than in ventures about which they know little or nothing. This financing is viewed as equity as long as there is no set repayment schedule.

Financing a business with capital from family and friends, however, creates a type of risk not found with other funding sources. If the business is not successful and the funds cannot be repaid, relationships with family and friends can become strained. You should explain the potential risk of failure inherent in the venture before accepting any funds from family and friends.

Financing for your small business can come from some unusual sources. Dilip Barot, a native of India's Gujarat region, manages 2,000 public housing apartments in four states from Florida to Nevada. His Miami Beach–based company, Naimisha Group, utilized creative financing to get going. Barot tapped into the informal network of other successful Gujarati businesspeople—mostly doctors and engineers—and raised the financing he needed. He has used this "tried-and-true immigrant network" several times and has even gone back to India for help with financing if he found himself in a real bind.

Using whatever financing sources are open and available is smart business, as Barot has discovered. The Naimisha Group earns a nifty $10 million on revenues of $50 million.[7]

PARTNERS. Acquiring one or more partners is another way to secure equity capital (see Chapter 2). Approximately 10 percent of U.S. businesses are partnerships. Many partnerships are formed to take advantage of diverse skills or attributes that can be contributed to the new business. For example, one person may have the technical skills required to run the business, whereas another person may have the capital to finance it. Together they form a partnership to accomplish a common goal.

Partners may play an active role in the venture's operation or may choose to be "silent," providing funds only in exchange for an equity position. The addition of one or more partners expands not only the amount of equity capital available for the business, but also the ability of the business to borrow funds. This is due to the cumulative creditworthiness of the partners versus that of the entrepreneur alone.

VENTURE CAPITAL FIRMS. Venture capital firms are groups of individuals or companies that invest in new or expanding firms. Of the more than 600 venture capital firms operating in the United States, about 500 are private independent firms, about 65 are major corporations, and the rest are affiliated with banks. Obtaining capital from them is not easy.

Bootstrapping Your Way to Success

creating competitive advantage

When lenders say "no"—everybody from bankers to private investors—tough small business owners turn to themselves. They raise money from within by bootstrapping. Bootstrapping involves *saving*, rather than *borrowing*, money. It requires being as frugal as possible. You have to have discipline, determination, and a serious desire to succeed, so not everyone has the guts to bootstrap.

Tae Wan Cho and Young Suk, husband and wife business partners, provide an excellent example of how to succeed when bank financing isn't available. In 1982, Tae Wan Cho left his native South Korea for the United States seeking, as many immigrants do, more freedom and opportunity. Young Suk and the couple's two daughters remained in Korea until he could get a business started—although he had no idea what type of business or where it would be.

Upon arriving in the United States, Tae stayed with an American friend in Harrisonville, Missouri. After reading a trade magazine article about the strong growth in sales of hair care products for African Americans, he decided to open a store in St. Louis, an affordable metropolitan area. To get his business off the ground, Tae applied for a $10,000 loan from a local bank. Turned down by the bank, he borrowed $3,000 from his Harrisonville friend and another $2,000 from his landlord in St. Louis. His business, King's Beauty Supply, opened in a 500-square-foot space in a vacant downtown building. He sold $40 worth of merchandise his first day and $3,000 within the first month. However, because he couldn't afford to heat his shop that first winter, many of his products froze. Cash flow became such a severe problem that Tae could stock only two of many of his products.

Tae decided that everything he made would be reinvested in the business. He reminisced, "I spent no money on myself. I paid my bills before I ate. I had no radio, no television, no chair, no sofa, no bed. . . . All I had was a blanket and a ten-year-old Ford Pinto." For three years, Tae worked ten hours a day, seven days a week. When he finally was confident that the business would survive, Young Suk and their daughters made the move to St. Louis. Shortly afterward, they opened a second store, which Young Suk managed. Was all this hard work and sacrifice worth it?

Well, today, Tae Wan Cho and Young Suk operate nine retail stores in St. Louis and wholesale their products all over the United States, generating around $8 million in sales. King's Beauty Supply Distributor, Inc., now occupies a 30,000-square-foot warehouse. And the bank that first turned Tae down has extended the firm a $1 million line of credit. The lesson, learned by millions of native-born and naturalized Americans, is that, with initiative, focus, and sheer hard work, you *can* make it on your own.

Sources: Jenny C. McCune, "Bootstrapping: Cutting Corners and Pinching Pennies to Finance Your Business," March 2001, ZDNET.com – bankrate.com; and Cheryl Jarvis, "When Sacrifice Equals Success," *Nation's Business,* July 1994, 14–16.

Most venture capital firms have investment policies that outline their preferences relative to industry, geographic location, investment size, and investment maturity. These firms look for businesses with the potential for rapid growth and high profitability. They provide funds in exchange for an equity position, which they hope to sell out within five to ten years or less.

A recent study showed that the average sum invested by venture capital firms is between $1.5 and $2 million per business, with an overall range between $23,000 to more than $50 million. An excellent business plan is essential when approaching a venture capital firm, and a referral from a credible source—such as a banker or attorney familiar to the venture capital firm—may also be necessary. It takes an average of six to eight months to receive a potential investment decision. It has been estimated that less than 10 percent of the plans submitted to venture capital firms are ultimately funded.

Venture capital firms rarely invest in retail operations. They tend to focus on high-technology industries, growth industries, and essential services. Ventures within these fields with strong, experienced management teams have the best chance of being funded. *Pratt's Guide to Venture Capital Success* is a good source of information.

SMALL BUSINESS INVESTMENT COMPANIES. Small Business Investment Companies (SBICs) are venture capital firms licensed by the SBA to invest in small businesses. SBICs were authorized by Congress in 1958 to provide equity financing to qualified enterprises. In 1969, the SBA, in cooperation with the Department of Commerce, created Minority Enterprise Small Business Investment Companies (MESBICs) to provide equity financing to minority entrepreneurs. Any business that is more than 50 percent owned by African Americans, Hispanics, Native Americans, Eskimos, or socially and economically disadvantaged Americans is eligible for funding.

SBICs and MESBICs are formed by financial institutions, corporations, or individuals, although a few are publicly owned. These investment companies must be capitalized with at least $500,000 of private funds. Once capitalized, they can receive as much as $4 from the SBA for each private dollar invested.

SBICs and MESBICs are excellent sources of both startup and expansion capital. Like venture capital firms, however, they tend to have investment policies regarding geographic area and industry. There are about 300 SBICs and MESBICs currently in operation in the United States. They are listed in the *Directory of Operating Small Business Investment Companies* available from any SBA office.

angel A lender, usually a successful entrepreneur, who loans money to help new businesses.

ANGELS.   An **angel** is a wealthy, experienced individual who has a desire to assist startup or emerging businesses. Most angels are self-made entrepreneurs who want to help sustain the system that allowed them to become successful. Usually they are knowledgeable about the market and technology areas in which they invest.

According to a study on business angels, there are more than 250,000 such investors in the United States. A typical investment ranges from $20,000 to $50,000, although nearly one-fourth are for more than $50,000. An angel can add much more than money to a business. His or her business know-how and contacts can be far more valuable to the success of the business than the capital he invests.

Finding an angel is not easy. The best ways for an entrepreneur to locate an angel are to maintain business contacts with tax attorneys, bankers, and accountants in their closest metropolitan area, and to find out if a regional venture capital network exists.

STOCK OFFERINGS.   Selling company stock is another method of obtaining equity financing. The entrepreneur must consider this decision very carefully, however. The sale of stock results in the entrepreneur's losing a portion of the ownership of the business. Furthermore, certain state and federal laws govern the way stock offerings are made. Private placements and public offerings are the two types of stock sales.

PRIVATE PLACEMENTS.   A private placement involves the sale of stock to a selected group of individuals. This stock cannot be purchased by the general public.

Sales may be in any amount, but placements less than $500,000 confront fewer government-imposed restrictions and disclosure requirements than those over $500,000. If the company selling the stock is located and doing business in only one state, and stock is sold only to individuals within that same state, the sale is considered an *intrastate stock sale* subject only to that state's regulations.

If the sale involves more than one state, then the sale is an *interstate stock sale,* and the federal Securities and Exchange Commission's regulations will apply.

PUBLIC OFFERINGS. A public offering involves the sale of stock to the general public. These sales always are governed by Securities and Exchange Commission regulations. Complying with these regulations is both costly and time consuming. For public offerings of $400,000 to $1 million, the legal fees, underwriting fees, audits, printing, and other costs can easily exceed 15 percent.

The first time a company offers its stock to the general public is called an **initial public offering (IPO).** In order to be a viable candidate for an IPO, a company must be in good financial health and be able to attract an underwriter (typically a stock brokerage firm or investment banker) to help sell the stock offering. In addition, the market conditions must be favorable for selling equity securities.

There are three main reasons companies choose public offerings.

initial public offering (IPO)
The first sale of stock of a business made available to public investors.

1. When market conditions are favorable, more funds can be raised through public offerings than through other venture capital methods, without the repayment burdens of debt.
2. Having an established public price for the company's stock enhances its image.
3. The owner's wealth can be magnified greatly when owner-held shares are subsequently sold in the market.

One critical caution about public stock offerings is that they require companies to make financial disclosures to the public. If a company fails to live up to its self-reported expectations, shareholders can sue the company, charging that the company withheld or misrepresented important information.

Choosing a Lender or Investor

This chapter has described many sources of financing. The key decision facing entrepreneurs is determining which sources to pursue. Your choice will often be limited by the degree to which you meet the requirements of each lending or investing source. If you decide to pursue debt financing, you must have the minimum down payment or other capital requirements necessary to secure the loan. Assuming that these requirements can be met, you will have to determine which lending source to approach. Usually, the foremost criterion will be finding the lowest cost or interest rate available. However, other factors must also be considered.

According to small business expert G. B. Baty, other important lender selection criteria are

1. *Size.* The lender should be small enough to consider the entrepreneur an important customer, but large enough to service the entrepreneur's future needs.
2. *Desire.* The lender should exhibit a desire to work with startup and emerging businesses, rather than considering them too risky.

3. *Approach to problems.* The lender should be supportive of small businesses facing problems, offering constructive advice and financing alternatives.

4. *Industry experience.* The lender should have experience in the entrepreneur's industry, especially with startup or emerging ventures.[8]

These factors can help you make reasoned judgments about which lender to approach. The best guideline may be to seek the lenders with whom you feel the most comfortable. A loan relationship can last for a decade or more. Finding a lending source that is pleasant to work with is often as important as finding the lowest cost of debt.

If you decide to pursue equity financing, a number of different considerations emerge. Although the use of funds obtained from family members, friends, or partners is perhaps conceivable, none of these sources may be acceptable or feasible for personal reasons. For example, close personal relationships can become strained when money is involved.

Autonomy is another important consideration. Equity financing always requires that you give up a portion of ownership in the venture. If independence is critical to you, then think carefully about the source of equity you pursue.

The most important criterion in choosing investors should be matching the needs of the business with what the investors can offer. If the business requires only money, then you should attempt to find a "silent" partner—one who is willing to provide capital without playing an active role in the management of the business.

But if your business needs a particular type of expertise, in addition to money, then you should seek an investor who can provide management advice or other assistance along with needed capital. For example, a new business in a high-tech industry might pursue angel financing from a successful individual who has prospered in that industry.

Entrepreneurial guru Jeffry A. Timmons offers a few more cautions when choosing an investor. Each of the following "sand traps," he says, imposes a responsibility on the entrepreneur:

1. *Strategic circumference.* A fund-raising decision can affect future financing choices. Raising equity capital may reduce your freedom to choose additional financing sources in the future, due to the partial loss of ownership control that accompanies equity financing.

2. *Legal circumference.* Financing deals can place unwanted limitations and constraints on the unwary entrepreneur. It is imperative to read and understand the details of each financing document. Competent legal representation is recommended.

3. *Opportunity cost.* Entrepreneurs often overlook the time, effort, and creative energy required to locate and secure financing. A long search can exhaust the entrepreneur's personal funds before the business ever gets a chance to get off the ground.

4. *Attraction to status and size.* Many entrepreneurs seek financing from the most prestigious and high-profile firms. Often, a better fit is found with lesser-known firms that have firsthand experience with the type of business the entrepreneur is starting.

5. *Being too anxious.* If the entrepreneur has a sound business plan, there will often be multiple venture capital firms interested in investing in it. By accepting the first offer, the entrepreneur may overlook a better deal from another source.[9]

Clearly, choosing a lender or investor takes time and patience. The process is similar to finding a spouse. The relationship that is forged between the entrepreneur and the source of financing can be long lasting and should be mutually beneficial.

SUMMARY

▇▇▇ The financing needs of your business.

A straightforward process for determining financing need is to (1) list the assets required for your business to operate effectively; (2) determine the market value or cost of each asset; (3) identify how much capital you are able to provide; and (4) subtract the total of the owner-provided funds from the total of the assets required. This figure represents the minimum amount of financing required.

▒▒▒ Basic financing terminology.

To procure financing you must be able to understand basic financial vocabulary. Each major form of capital (debt and equity) has unique terminology that defines the details underlying financing agreements. Each form of capital has pros and cons that make it more or less desirable to the entrepreneur under given circumstances.

▒▒▒ Where to look for sources of funding.

The search for capital and the application process can be unsettling as you sort through the various sources of funds. Major sources of debt financing include commercial banks, finance companies, government lenders, and insurance companies. Sources of equity include partners, venture capital firms, angels, and stock offerings. Finding capital is one of the most important tasks you face in starting and managing a business. An understanding of this material will enhance your chances of finding the best source for your business.

QUESTIONS FOR REVIEW & DISCUSSION

1. Define "initial capital requirements." How can you determine these?

2. What are the 5 Cs of credit, and how do lenders use them?

3. What are the differences between debt funds and equity funds?

4. What kinds of businesses would depend on floor-plan financing?

5. What is "pledging accounts receivable"?

6. What are the advantages of borrowing through the SBA?

7. Why do suppliers extend trade credit to other businesses? What are the advantages and disadvantages of using trade credit?

8. How are private placements and public offerings different?

9. Discuss the types of interest that may apply to a loan.

10. What is the difference between a secured loan and an unsecured loan?

QUESTIONS FOR **CRITICAL THINKING**

1. *Inc.* magazine showed that, of the approximately 600,000 companies that started in the year 2000, only about 5,000 received funding from venture capitalists. If only such a small percentage received venture capital, then why do small business magazines print such a disproportionately large number of articles about venture capital?

2. How does a small business's capital structure change over time?

Experience this . . .

Make arrangements with your instructor to invite a commercial banker to speak to your class. Discuss what factors bankers find most important in making a small business loan. Do they *really* want to see a business plan? What should be included in it? Which section do they look at first? second? In what order of importance would they rank the five Cs of credit? Does their bank make SBA loans? What is different about them? What other options to direct loans does the bank offer—lines of credit? access to factoring? Does the bank make recommendations (and arrange meetings) to send a small business owner on to meet with angel investors or venture capitalists?

WHAT WOULD **YOU** DO?   No. 1

We're going to take a different approach in this What Would You Do? For once, *you* get to choose the type of small business you want to look at. So think long and hard, and select a hypothetical small business you'd like to start. Then answer the following questions.

QUESTIONS

1. Develop a listing of the assets that you'll need for this business. Be sure you're considering all the aspects of your business in determining these assets. Then write a short report describing the type of financing you're going to seek for your business.

2. It's time to role-play. Divide into teams. Each person will take a turn presenting his or her idea to the other members of the group, who are acting as potential investors. As the entrepreneur, be sure to provide information that you think the investors will want to know. As the investor group, be prepared to ask questions of the person requesting financing.

WHAT WOULD **YOU** DO? No. 2

Finding money to finance your small business can be a real challenge. You might look to the traditional avenues, such as using personal funds, tapping the resources of family and friends, or even relying on partners for financial backing. In the mid-1990s, however, a new approach to finding financing has emerged—one that utilizes the networking capability of the Internet. And that's what Pam Marrone of AgraQuest, Inc., tapped into when she needed additional financing.

Marrone's Davis, California, company develops and manufactures all-natural pesticides. She needed $2.5 million to pay the research, development, and production costs of two pest-control products. Marrone knew how to find money the old-fashioned way. After all, she had raised $300,000 in startup financing to launch her company. But when she began looking to expand her business's product line, she decided to experiment with a more direct link to potential investors via the Internet.

Marrone chose to list her business idea (at a minimal charge) with Venture Connect, a World Wide Web site designed to match investors and entrepreneurs. She also developed her own company home page, which included an extensive business summary and job postings, and promoted it through Yahoo!'s business directory. "This is a potential way to get directly to investors," Marrone said. "The responses have been fast." Marrone was confident that her unique search for financing would pay off, yet she was being just as cautious in her search for financing in this high-tech approach as if she had taken a more traditional approach. After all, we're still talking about money.

QUESTIONS

1. What are the advantages and disadvantages of financing via the Internet, as Marrone did?

2. Should Marrone use her Internet financing source exclusively, or should she maintain a relationship with her local bank commercial loan officer? Why or why not?

ANSWERS TO CHAPTER OPENER QUIZ

Experts' advice for Lori Bonn Gallagher:

Brett W. Kaplowitz, *vice president of Potomac Valley Bank:*
For financing the growth, I'd want to know how much money will she need, what will she need it for, and what will it accomplish? If she switches to a larger bank she should be able to explore a range of different options. There could be two loans, for example. A working-capital line of credit would be at a lower interest rate and could be collateralized through the company's assets—receivables. Banks don't like to lend against inventory or supplies that are easily movable, such as jewelry. A term loan for expansion would be a higher-risk component with a higher interest rate.

Kathy Elliot, *member of Renaissance Ventures, a group of angel investors interested in funding businesses owned by women:*

Revenues would have to exceed, at the very least, $50 million within five years to spark the interest of angel investors or VCs. That's unlikely in this case. This business doesn't appear to be a candidate for a private-equity investment. [This doesn't mean it's a bad business; it just doesn't generate enough revenue or growth to qualify for angel or VC funding.]

Bradley Pane, *director of Kurt Salmon Associates Capital Advisors, Inc.:*

I'd have to agree that this isn't a company that's likely to attract the private-equity community because of concerns about the size of the company and lack of depth in the management team. I'd recommend the transition to a bigger bank and attempt to increase her credit availability. Then she could concentrate on achieving some of her near-term goals such as building brand identity and broadening her distribution *before* trying to attract an angel or strategic partner. You know one thing that could help her? Maybe she could bring in a transitioning or retired retailing executive interested in pursuing a second career. Someone like that might be in a position to make a financial investment in return for a management role and equity stake. And that type of person could bring further credibility to the business.

CHAPTER CLOSING CASE   No. 9

A CFO's Persistence Pays Off

The management at PlasmaQuest, a $5 million company in Richardson, Texas, knows from experience that it takes time to win adequate financing. The company makes high-density plasmas used in the manufacture of semiconductors. Since its founding in 1987, the company has enjoyed impressive revenue growth, but in recent years its meager cash flow was inadequate to fund the production of $500,000 orders.

Zan Mengle joined the company nearly three years ago as chief financial officer, bringing a solid background in financial analysis and familiarity with the rules and priorities of the banking community. When she signed on, PlasmaQuest was limping along with a single $200,000 term loan. "We had just signed an international order for $300,000 worth of equipment, and soon after that, we got two more overseas orders for an additional $600,000. But we didn't have the working capital," Mengle recalls. Overseas customers were unwilling to make down payments, and they refused to comply with the payment terms PlasmaQuest's U.S. customers met.

Mengle started her search for financing with an investigation of local options. "There was a local export program back then, but it had only about $1 million in its kitty," she says. At the same time, the better-heeled local bankers didn't think PlasmaQuest qualified for what Mengle terms "purchase-order financing"—cash that covers corporate needs from the moment a sales order takes effect.

Eventually, Mengle's contacts put her in touch with a foreign banker who was interested in bankrolling the overseas activities of U.S. companies. That lender extended "a $1.5 million line of credit," says Mengle, "which was wonderful . . . except for one problem: Only $100,000 of it could be used on U.S. business. But it still helped, because it supported some foreign growth and ultimately helped give us credibility among U.S. bankers."

It took considerable determination and more time than Mengle had anticipated before she obtained the financing PlasmaQuest needed. "It was so ironic," the CFO recalls. "Dozens of bankers approached us, but they'd end up rejecting us when they saw the type of financing we needed."

Eventually, a local banker suggested that PlasmaQuest seek Small Business Administration backing for a purchase order–collateralized credit line. "With the help of a specialist who packaged us for the SBA approval process," says Mengle, "we finally worked out a deal that was right for us: a $1-million line of credit, 75 percent of which was guaranteed by SBA funds. We had to pay a 2 percent fee on that $750,000, but it was worth it—especially since we got to factor that cost into the overall size of the loan." And the interest rate on the loan is only 1 percent above prime, compared with the 2.5 percent above prime that PlasmaQuest pays its foreign bankers.

"When you're looking for bank financing," Mengle advises, "persistence is your strongest weapon. That and a willingness to provide every piece of financial information any banker could ever require."

Source: Adapted from "Anatomy of a Financing: A CFO's Persistence Pays Off" by Jill Andresky Fraser, from *Inc.: The Magazine for Growing Companies*, October 1995, 115. Copyright © 1995 by Goldhirsh Group/Inc Pubg. Reproduced with permission of Goldhirsh Group/Inc Pubg in the format textbook via Copyright Clearance Center.

QUESTIONS

1. Why would the local bankers not loan PlasmaQuest money even with a purchase order?

2. Describe why persistence is so important when small businesses look for bank financing.

10

The Legal Environment

After reading this chapter, you should be able to:

- Discuss laws and regulations that affect small business.

- List the types of bankruptcy.

- Describe the elements of a contract.

- Explain how to protect intellectual property.

IS YOUR SMALL business snooping on employees? If it is, you are in the majority. The American Management Association found that about 67 percent of the companies it surveyed practiced some form of electronic monitoring or surveillance. Although it might make good business sense, be careful—you could end up in legal trouble.

Videotaping work areas, tracking employees' computer use, keeping records of telephone numbers called and duration of calls are all part of surveillance tactics. If these represent some of the hows, what are the whys? Why would you want to watch employees at work? Isn't that crossing some Big Brother line? Well, yes, if you are monitoring locker rooms and restrooms, but monitoring can have some legitimate reasons. It can be a safety issue. Cameras can prevent violence from escalating, for example. The mere presence of cameras can prevent shoplifting (or worse).

Monitoring employees on the phone can be a valuable management tool. What better way to determine whether your customer service representatives are taking care of customers than to listen to conversations? If your company sells financial services, there are legal limitations to promises that your employees can make. Monitoring can provide you with a level of legal protection, because you can know immediately if your agents are making promises that they can't deliver.

How do you ensure that you are not violating your employees' privacy rights? You can keep yourself out of the courtroom, first of all, by letting employees know what you are doing—in writing. Distribute your workplace monitoring policy either separately or in the employee handbook, and have employees sign a consent decree that states they have read and understand it.

Where do your rights as an employer begin and employee rights end? This question underscores the importance of knowing where the legal line is drawn in all business situations and leads us into this chapter on the legal environment of small business. Tripping over those legal lines can be very expensive.

Sources: Adapted from Sheryl Nance-Nash, "I'll Be Watching You," *Fortune Small Business,* April 2001. © 2001 Time, Inc. All rights reserved.

■ Small Business and the Law

> *We need laws to ensure competition, enforce contracts, and protect our rights as consumers, workers, and property owners.*

Would you like to live in a place with no laws? You could drive as fast as you wanted. You could drink alcohol at any age. You could do whatever you wanted, and, just think, there would be no taxes to pay because there would be no government making up rules and regulations! Although such absolute freedom might sound exciting at first glance, you don't have to think about this scenario for long to realize that it also includes no protection for anyone or any groups—it would be chaos. Orderly, civilized societies are built on laws.

We need laws to ensure fair competition between businesses, to protect the rights of consumers and employees, to protect property, to enforce contracts and agreements, and to permit bankruptcy when things go bad. And we need tax laws to collect the money needed for government to provide these protections. The balance of how much or how little protection we need or we want changes over time. Through elections and open debate, our laws evolve to reflect the needs of and changes in society. But, as an old saying goes: It's a good thing that we don't get half the government we pay for.

One of the many problems facing small business owners is keeping up with the changes and understanding the laws and regulations by which they must abide. The wording of many laws and regulations is often baffling and easy to misunderstand. Another problem of regulations for small businesses is the enormous amount of paperwork required to generate reports and records. This paperwork imposes time and resource burdens on often-strapped business owners. A third problem is the cost (for administrative and actual expenses) and difficulty in complying with regulations.

Running a small business does not require a law degree, but you do need two things to avoid trouble. You need a working knowledge of legal basics, and you need a good lawyer. The best time to get a lawyer for your small business is when you are writing your business plan—not when you are already in trouble.

The weight of government regulations has become a serious burden to small businesses. A study by the National Federation of Independent Business showed that a majority of people who start businesses underestimate the degree of government regulations and red tape more than any other factor. Almost 60 percent were

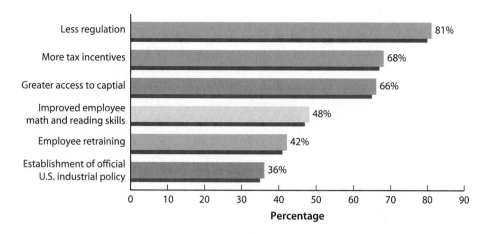

unprepared for the volume of regulations they faced.[1] The *Wall Street Journal* polled 250 top executives of small to midsize manufacturing companies on what would benefit their business. Figure 10.1 shows that "less regulation" was their top priority.

Regulations and the legal environment of small business cover a lot of ground. This chapter will discuss several major areas of business affected by the law: regulations, licenses, bankruptcy, contracts, and protection of intellectual property.

We need laws to ensure competition, to enforce contracts, and to protect our rights as consumers, workers, and property owners.

Laws to Promote Fair Business Competition

Competition between businesses lies at the heart of a free enterprise system (see Chapter 1). Healthy competition provides the balance needed to ensure that buyers and sellers are both satisfied. It decreases the need for government intervention in the market.

Antitrust laws like the Sherman Antitrust Act of 1890 and the Clayton Act of 1914 were written to prevent large businesses from forming trusts—large combinations of firms that can dominate an industry and stifle competition, preventing new or small businesses from participating. Under **antitrust laws,** any agreements or contracts that restrain trade are illegal and unenforceable. The Sherman Antitrust Act and the Clayton Act are two of the best-known antitrust laws and are still widely used in preventing business mergers and acquisitions judged to decrease competition.

The Federal Trade Commission Act of 1914 created the Federal Trade Commission (FTC), the agency that regulates competition in our economy. The FTC has the power to issue cease-and-desist orders, which prohibit offending companies from unfair or deceptive practices such as collusion (acting together to keep prices artificially high). The five-member commission has the power to conduct hearings, direct investigations, and issue cease-and-desist orders to violators, which are enforceable in federal court.

antitrust laws Legislation that prohibits firms from combining in a way that would stifle competition within that industry.

Sometimes You Can't Win

Laws, regulations, "special interests." Is it really necessary for the U.S. government to be so involved in business affairs? As owner of a business, for instance, would you expect to have the right to fire an employee without providing a specific reason? Until the late 1980s, you had that right in almost every state. But now courts have severely limited at-will powers in over 30 states, and even where it is allowed, the at-will doctrine is shaky and undermined by several other laws.

The pendulum of rights within the legal system has swung into dangerous territory for small business owners who lack resources to fight claims against them in court. Commercial litigator Joseph Ortego states that legal fees for defending an employer can cost $100,000 by the time a verdict is reached. All a disgruntled employee has to do to start the legal process is fill out a form, at little or no cost. Unfortunately, laws created to protect hard-working employees also open doors for unscrupulous individuals, who may file a costly suit—even if they don't have a legal case against the company. Whether or not more laws have increased the number of fraudulent claims, people are more comfortable contacting attorneys on the chance that they might have a case. Employees who may have little to lose can sue the business, or they can sue the owner personally. Small business owners have trouble defending themselves. Although many lawsuits against small businesses are legitimate, many more are not. Some examples of potential abuses include

- When a sweet little elderly lady asked the founder of a small woman's clothing manufacturer for a job "at any wage, just to finish my time," he hired her to clean desks. After exactly ten days of work, she asked for a leave of absence. Still sentimental, the business owner said, "Give a call when you are ready to come back." The sweet lady didn't call back, but her lawyer did. She was filing a suit against the company claiming that she had developed double carpal tunnel syndrome which prevented her from doing work of any kind—to the tune of $20,000 per wrist! Many months and many legal fees later, the owner ended up settling on the courthouse steps, even though he found that she had lined up her lawyer even before she applied at the business.

- According to witnesses, a worker laying shingles for a siding chain was not following prescribed safety procedures and, due to his own carelessness, fell from a scaffold. Workmen's compensation laws call for wages and medical payments to be paid to injured employees for up to 160 months (13.3 *years*)—no matter who is at fault. In this case, the siding company was faced with paying out $28,000 per year and protested the claim on the grounds that the worker was malingering. Because back injuries (the most common type of complaint) are difficult to prove, a doctor's statement convinced the judge to rule for the employee. Later, when the siding company had an opening for a management position, the injured worker applied. The company hired a person with management experience. The former employee sued for discrimination against the handicapped.

- A small Philadelphia equipment repair company had a problem with an employee who was habitually absent without prior notification. The company was tolerant past the number of absences allowed by its policy. The employee claimed that bursitis would flare up randomly, leaving his arm incapacitated. One day, a manager was driving by the employee's home and saw him vigorously polishing his car with the allegedly "bad" arm. When he came back to work, the employee was called into the manager's office for a little talk. When the door was shut, the employee did an immediate U-turn and left. The next day, the sheriff served both managers with criminal charges, including interference with the exercise of civil rights, assault and battery, stalking, and kidnapping. The employee claimed he was held in a locked room against his will, threatened, and injured permanently when the defendant pulled on his arm. Because it was a criminal rather than a civil trial, the company's liability insurance did not cover legal expenses. The defendant spent nothing.

What can you do if you are a small business owner facing such circumstances? Sometimes not much, but after reading this chapter, you will find some ways to protect yourself and your business.

Laws to Protect Consumers

Up until the past few decades, U.S. consumer laws were based on the rule of caveat emptor—"Let the buyer beware." Now laws have largely abandoned this precept to offer ever-increasing protection for consumers, administered by a wide variety of state and federal agencies. The most common practices that government protects consumers against involve extension of credit, deceptive trade practices, unsafe products, and unfair pricing.

The Federal Trade Commission, for instance, is involved in product labeling standards; banning hazardous products; ensuring consumer product safety; regulating the content and message of advertising ensuring truth-in-lending practices, equal credit access to consumers, and fair credit practices; and many other areas. Many laws that are intended to protect consumers fall under the jurisdiction of the FTC, including the Nutrition Labeling and Education Act of 1990, the Fair Debt Collection Practices Act of 1977, the Truth-in-Lending Act, and the Consumer Product Safety Act, to name but a few. The FTC is an agency of the federal government with broad and deep power when it comes to protecting consumers.

Laws to Protect People in the Workplace

A major thrust of federal employment legislation today is equal opportunity employment. This goal is based on the belief that an individual should be considered for employment on the basis of individual merit rather than with regard to race, color, religion, sex, age, national origin, or disability. The origin of this goal dates back to the U.S. Constitution, and it was fortified by the Fourteenth and Fifteenth Amendments in the 1860s. However, beginning in the early 1960s, in response to great social change and unrest, Congress acted to strengthen the enforcement of this belief, passing several comprehensive pieces of legislation, outlined here.

EQUAL PAY ACT OF 1963.   As an amendment to the 1938 Fair Labor Standards Act, this act requires businesses with two or more employees engaged in commerce or activities affecting commerce to pay men and women in the same organization who are performing equal work an equal wage. Equal work is defined in terms of skills, effort, job conditions, and responsibilities. The law does, however, permit wage differentials for reasons other than sex. These might include a bona fide seniority system, merit pay decisions, quantity and quality of production scales, and other practices, such as shift differentials.

Compliance is regulated by the Equal Employment Opportunity Commission (EEOC). Employers covered by the law must provide, on request, detailed records of compensation, including rates of pay, hours worked, overtime payments, deductions, and other related pay data. In addition, supporting documents, such as wage surveys, job descriptions, job evaluation studies, collective bargaining agreements, and the like, may also be requested.

CIVIL RIGHTS ACT OF 1964. The Civil Rights Act (CRA) of 1964 prevents discrimination on the basis of sex, race, color, religion, or national origin in any terms, conditions, or privileges of employment. Discrimination on the basis of pregnancy, childbirth, and related medical conditions is also prohibited as a result of a 1978 amendment. Title VII of this landmark legislation applies to all organizations with 15 or more employees working 20 or more weeks a year in commerce or in any industry or activity affecting commerce. As amended, state and local governments, labor unions, employment agencies, and educational institutions are also covered. However, religious organizations, private clubs, and places of employment connected with a Native American reservation are not covered by the act.

Provisions of the act are enforced by the Equal Employment Opportunity Commission. Private employers with 100 or more employees are required to file annually Form EEO-1, detailing the makeup of the company's work force. In addition, all employers are required to keep employment-related documents for at least six months from the time of their creation or, in the case of a personnel action such as a discharge, from the date of the action.

IMMIGRATION REFORM AND CONTROL ACT OF 1986. The Immigration Reform and Control Act (IRCA) was passed in 1986 with two intended goals. First, it seeks to discourage illegal immigration into the United States by denying employment to aliens who do not comply with the Immigration and Naturalization Service regulations. It achieves this goal by requiring employers to document worker eligibility. All U.S. employers must complete Form I-9 for new hires, for which the employee must provide documentation proving his or her identity and work authorization. Permissible documents include a birth certificate, U.S. passport, certificate of U.S. citizenship, certificate of naturalization, unexpired foreign passport, resident alien card, or a combination of documents attesting to identity and employment authorization as outlined on Form I-9.[2]

A second goal of the act was to strengthen the national origin provisions of Title VII of the 1964 Civil Rights Act by extending coverage to "foreign-sounding" and "foreign-looking" individuals, and to all employers with 4 or more employees (rather than the 15 or more established by the CRA). If found guilty of discrimination under the IRCA, you may be assessed back pay for up to two years and civil fines of up to $2,000 per violation and $10,000 for multiple violations.[3] Enforcement responsibilities were assigned to the Office of the Special Counsel for Immigration-related Unfair Employment Practices, a division of the Department of Justice.

AMERICANS WITH DISABILITIES ACT OF 1990. The 1990 Americans with Disabilities Act (ADA) was passed to guarantee individuals with disabilities the right to obtain and hold a job, to travel on public transportation, to enter and use public facilities, and to use telecommunication services. One or more of the act's provisions affects almost all businesses, regardless of size.

If you are a private employer with 15 or more employees (including part-time employees) working 20 or more calendar weeks a year, you are covered by Title 1, the employment discrimination provision. As such, you may not discriminate against qualified disabled individuals with regard to any employment practice or terms, conditions, and privileges of employment. Under the act, a disabled person is one who (1) has a physical or mental impairment that substantially limits one or more major life activities, (2) has a physical or mental impairment, or (3) is regarded as having such an impairment. Specifically included within this definition are recovering drug addicts, alcoholics, and individuals infected with HIV and AIDS. In turn, a qualified applicant is one who (1) meets the necessary prerequisites for the job, such as education, work experience, or training, and (2) can perform the essential functions of the job, with or without reasonable accommodation.

Once a set of effective accommodations has been identified—which might include restructuring a job, modifying work schedules, providing readers and interpreters, or obtaining and modifying equipment—you are free to select the one that is the least expensive or easiest to provide. Even then, you need make the accommodation only if it does not present an undue hardship on the operation of your business. An undue hardship is an action that is "excessively costly, extensive, substantial, or disruptive, or that would fundamentally alter the nature or operation of the business."[4] In determining undue hardship, you should consider the nature and cost of the accommodation in relation to your business's size, its financial resources (including available tax credits, as discussed later), the nature and structure of its operation, and the impact of the accommodation on its operation.

In addition to the issue of reasonable accommodation, you should also keep the following points in mind:

- Prior to a conditional offer of employment, inquiries of others about the applicant's disability, illness, and workmen's compensation history are prohibited.

- Required medical or physical examinations are prohibited prior to a conditional offer of employment. Drug tests may be given, however, at any point in the employment process, because such tests are not considered medical examinations under the law.

- Any selection or performance standards should be job related, be based on a thorough job analysis, and be prepared prior to advertising the position.

- Asking the applicant about the nature, origin, or severity of a known disability is prohibited. You may, however, question the applicant about his or her ability to perform the essential functions of the job and to describe or demonstrate how to perform such functions.

- An employer may not refuse to hire an individual simply because he or she might or will require accommodation under the act.

- All application materials and processes from the application form to the interview and beyond must be free of references to or inquiries about disabilities.

Under Title III of the ADA, virtually all businesses serving the public must make their facilities and services accessible to the disabled. This may require you to modify your operational policies, practices, and procedures; remove structural barriers; and provide auxiliary aids and services to the disabled. Technical standards for

Living with the ADA

The cost of compliance with government regulation can be high. For Wilma Staudinger and Sheri Drewry it was over $250,000.

Their story started with a simple letter. The mother-daughter team owns Wilma's Patio, a small restaurant on Balboa Island, just off the coast of Newport Beach, California. The letter they received was a form letter from a local lawyer informing them that they had discriminated against his client, a wheelchair-bound man they had never met. It stated that their facilities—doorways, tables, and bathrooms—were not compliant with the ADA. He threatened to take them to court if they did not make immediate accommodations—and pay him money—a lot of it. Like any small business owner, they were stunned and lost.

They soon found that the same attorney and plaintiff had sent identical letters and filed lawsuits against 50 other local businesses. Staudinger and Drewry had an independent audit of their 30-year-old building and found that, like any building of that age, some ADA violations existed. Their restaurant was too small to be modified to the lawsuit's demands (which may or may not have been proven to be reasonable accommodations), so a consultant told them that their only option was to move to a larger lot down the block. The building they owned would have to be gutted and sold at a loss.

Staudinger says, "I was ready to sell my home and fight him all the way." Escalating expenses forced them to settle out of court for more than $250,000. What hurt more than the money, though, was the feeling of violation they experienced from the written words of condemnation and the feeling of guilt from being accused of doing something horrible when they had no idea they had done anything wrong. In the decade since the ADA was passed, many small business owners have added ramps, widened doorways, and renovated restrooms, yet have no idea they are still violating one or more of the 618 prescribed access standards—until they get sued.

A disturbing fact is that litigation costing millions of dollars and driving many small businesses out of operation is not necessarily improving access to facilities. Some suits are filed by actual victims who have suffered legitimate damages. The real problem is known as "drive-by lawsuits." Drive-by lawsuits are filed by attorneys, sometimes against hundreds of businesses, some of which the plaintiff has not even visited. Although the ADA does not allow disabled plaintiffs to collect damages from businesses (except in California, where the ADA is tied to the state's civil rights law), it does allow attorneys to collect fees to the tune of $275 per hour.

Almost all businesses are forced to settle out of court when facing the astronomical judgments and legal costs of defending such suits. The restaurant industry estimates the out-of-pocket expenses to top $15,000. Another scary factor is that a settlement and attempts to fix problems are no guarantee that another suit won't be filed. Such lawsuits are locally concentrated now but may reach epidemic proportions.

The situation that happened to Staudinger and Drewry goes completely against the original intent of the ADA. The law was intended to allow the 54 million Americans who live with some form of disability reasonable access in their daily lives. What is happening is a relatively few lawyers trying to take advantage of some ambiguous wording to abuse a law and make a quick buck.

The point to remember as a small business owner is to know and understand (as difficult as that may be) the laws and regulations that pertain to his or her business. In the case of the ADA, go to: www.usdoj.gov/crt/ada/adahom1.htm or www.janweb.icdi.wvu.edu or www.sba.gov/ada or www.workforce.com/disabilities

Sources: Victor Wishna, "Caught in the Act," *Restaurant Business,* February 2001, 36–42; and Gail Dutton, "The ADA at 10," *Workforce,* December 2000, 41–46.

When Abilities Matter More Than Disabilities

Hiring disabled employees proved to be a winning formula for Exabyte, a manufacturer of computer storage tape drives located in Boulder, Colorado. When the company hired its first hearing-impaired employee to work in the assembly plant, supervisors' initial concerns soon dissolved. In fact, the excellent organizational skills and work habits of the new hire led the company to promote him to a position coordinating production in the assembly plant and to add more hearing-impaired employees to its payroll. The company's rapid growth created a demand for good, reliable workers, and Exabyte found its hearing-impaired employees to be a valuable addition to its human resources. Exabyte provides accommodations as needed—a translator for departmental meetings and sign language classes for other employees. In fact, one of the hearing-impaired employees who supervises five "hearing" employees has taught them sign language for phrases such as "Good!" and, more exotically, "Put on your antistatic jacket." As Exabyte has shown, what workers cannot do is less important than what they can do.

Gene Van Grevenhof drove a truck from coast to coast hauling meat for Decker Truck Lines for 23 years. While picking up a small, five-pound box, the 45-year-old broke his back. He went through two major surgeries and had a stabilizer bar inserted into his spine, effectively ending his driving career. After a year and a half off work, he started his own business, Eagle Communications, in Fort Dodge, Iowa, remanufacturing laser printer cartridges. Van Grevenhof understands the challenges that people with disabilities face and makes every effort to hire them in his own business.

HalfthePlanet.com has partnered with the Abilities Fund to provide disabled entrepreneurs with information, resources, venture capital, and online technical and financial assistance.

Sources: Jane Applegate, "Small Business Is Option for Disabled," *Chicago Sun-Times*, 8 August 2000, 44; Jennifer Reese, "If You Can Read This, You Can Get a Job," *Fortune*, 12 July 1993, 11; and John Williams, "Getting Answers on Hiring the Disabled," *Nation's Business*, November 1998, 44–48.

building and site elements, such as parking, ramps, doors, and elevators, have been set forth in the *ADA Accessibility Guidelines for New Construction and Alterations* handbook. The handbook is available from the Office of the Americans with Disabilities Act, U.S. Department of Justice.

Tax incentives are available to aid businesses with ADA compliance. The Disabled Access Credit for small businesses allows one-half the cost of eligible access expenditures that are more than $250 but less than $10,500 to be taken.[5] You may also qualify for tax deductions under the Architectural and Transportation Barrier Removal and Targeted Job Tax Credit provisions. You should contact your local IRS or vocational rehabilitation office for additional information.

CIVIL RIGHTS ACT OF 1991.   Congress passed the 1991 Civil Rights Act in reaction to several 1989 U.S. Supreme Court decisions which, it believed, unnecessarily shifted the focus of employment law in favor of U.S. business. The act amends Title VII and the ADA with the following provisions:

■ It prohibits **race norming,** the practice of using different cutoff test scores for different groups.

race norming An illegal activity of setting different test standards for divergent groups, for purposes of hiring or promotion.

Small business ownership provides opportunity for everyone.

■ It provides that, in cases where an otherwise neutral employment practice results in an underrepresentation of minorities (called "disparate impact cases"), employers must show that (1) the practice is job related; (2) the practice is consistent with a business necessity (that it exists in the best interest of the firm's employees and the general public); and (3) a less discriminatory practice does not exist.

■ In cases of intentional discrimination, it provides for both compensatory and punitive damages and allows for jury trials.

■ It places a cap on the amount of punitive and compensatory damages that may be awarded, depending on company size.

Company Size	Maximum Award
14 to 100 employees	$ 50,000
101 to 200 employees	100,000
201 to 500 employees	200,000
More than 500 employees	300,000

■ It provides that any reliance on a discriminatory factor in an employment decision is grounds for litigation.

The impact of the 1991 Civil Rights Act on small business owners is clear: The legitimacy of any employment practice or decision is yours to prove. If you are challenged and cannot prove that you did not intend to discriminate, you face the possibility of both compensatory and punitive damage awards. Therefore, you must be sure that any employment decision is based on a business need rather than on race, sex, color, religion, disability, or national origin.

The Civil Rights Act of 1991 also added teeth to EEOC guidelines on sexual harassment (see Chapter 3). The Civil Rights Act of 1991 provides victims of discrimination, including sexual harassment, access to trial by jury, compensatory damages for pain and suffering, and punitive damages if employers are proven to have acted with "malice or reckless indifference."

Small businesses are certainly not immune from sexual harassment. Unfortunately, such unwelcome behavior can occur in any company. Yet the penalties faced by small businesses are proportionately higher than those for large businesses. Limits vary from state to state, but consider the disparity in awards. A business with 15 employees could be assessed a maximum fine of $50,000 for a harassment conviction, or $3,333 per employee. A business with 500 employees could be fined $200,000, or $400 per employee. Which award do you think would have a greater impact on the business—$50,000 for a business of 15 or $200,000 for a business of 500?[6]

Because they can be held legally responsible not only for their own actions, but also for the actions of their managers and employees, small businesses must be prepared by setting policies and procedures. Employees and managers need to be trained, as do subcontractors, because the business can be held liable for both. For example, the owners of a Florida hotel were required to pay $420,670 to a former employee who was harassed by the president of the hotel management company.[7] A business owner should be ready to investigate any complaint in a timely manner. Finally, if the investigation finds that suspect behavior has occurred, the company should be ready to take appropriate action.[8]

FAMILY AND MEDICAL LEAVE ACT OF 1993. The Family and Medical Leave Act (FMLA) of 1993 requires private employers with 50 or more employees who work for 20 or more calendar weeks per year to make at least 12 weeks of unpaid leave available to eligible employees. To be eligible, an employee must have worked for a covered employer for at least 12 months, putting in at least 1,250 hours over the prior 12 months at a location where at least 50 employees work for the employer within a 75-mile radius.[9] Due in part to the 75-mile restriction, it is estimated that as many as 60 percent of U.S. workers and about 95 percent of all employers are not affected by the act.[10]

Eligible employees may take leave for one or more of the following reasons: for the birth or placement of a child for adoption or foster care, to care for an immediate family member with a serious health condition, or to take medical leave when the employee is unable to work because of a serious health condition. This leave may be taken during any 12-month period, in a block of time or intermittently through reduced work schedules. Within limitations, paid leave may be substituted for unpaid leave.

Covered employers are required to maintain group health insurance coverage for employees on FMLA leave and to provide equivalent job restoration upon completion of the leave. Employers are allowed to exempt "key" employees—employees who are among the highest-paid 10 percent of employees within 75 miles of the work site—from the restoration requirement. In addition, employers may require employees requesting FLMA leave to comply with certain notification and certification requirements, such as providing 30 days' advance notice when the leave is foreseeable, providing medical certification of serious health conditions, or requiring a fitness-for-duty certificate upon returning to work.

In addition to complying with FMLA leave requirements, employers must inform employees about their rights and responsibilities under the act. In response to specific notices of need, employers also must notify employees of the conditions under which the leave is being granted or denied. The Wage and Hour Division of the U.S. Department of Labor is responsible for enforcing the provisions of the act.

OCCUPATIONAL SAFETY AND HEALTH ADMINISTRATION (OSHA).

Congress passed the Occupational Safety and Health Act of 1970 to "assure, so far as possible, every working man and woman in the nation safe and healthful working conditions and to preserve our human resources."[11] The act created three federal agencies: the Occupational Safety and Health Administration (OSHA), the enforcement arm; the National Institute of Occupational Safety and Health (NIOSH), the research center; and the Occupational Safety and Health Review Commission (OSHRC), the enforcement review board.

As the enforcement agency, OSHA establishes and enforces occupational safety and health standards in all places of employment affecting commerce. OSHA compliance officers have a right to enter your workplace (you may require them to obtain a search warrant first); inspect part or all of your workplace (you should negotiate the scope and conditions before voluntarily permitting entry); issue citations for alleged violations; and propose penalties and abatement periods. Inspections are conducted to investigate a reported accident, injury, or fatality at a work site, an employee complaint alleging a violation, or as part of a regular or programmed schedule of inspections. If you as an employer are cited for a violation, you may either correct the alleged violation, seek a variance, or appeal the penalty.

When Harassment Comes from Outside

Sexual harassment is difficult to deal with when it occurs within a business, but what about when it comes from a customer, a supplier, or an advisor? What is the victim to do? What is the business to do?

Caryn Wilde owned a secretarial services business in Minnesota. For over a year, her largest client, Wilton Croonquist, head of a regional economic development agency, became increasingly aggressive in his advances toward her. When she refused, Croonquist implied that, if she took any action against him, he would take his business elsewhere. Because Croonquist's business represented 15 percent of Wilde's revenue, this was a serious threat.

As Croonquist continued to harass her, the normally gregarious Wilde became withdrawn, confiding only in her husband and a few close friends. Afraid of losing her business, she was also afraid of losing her health and her well-being. After 15 months, she filed a restraining order against Croonquist. Within minutes of receiving the order not to contact Wilde, Croonquist phoned her. She in turn called the police, who arrested Croonquist. Shortly afterward, Wilde's fears came true: Croonquist's agency canceled its agreement with Wilde's company.

Then things got even worse. Although Wilde had filed sexual harassment charges for workplace discrimination under Title VII of the Civil Rights Act of 1964, a loophole existed. The law was interpreted as applying only to employees, and Wilde was not Croonquist's employee. Therefore, "by law," she said, "I could not be sexually harassed."

When Wilde finally had her day in court, with a jury, Croonquist denied any wrongdoing. The jury awarded Wilde $113,100 directly from him and $36,900 from the agency. Unfortunately, the story does not end happily. Croonquist subsequently declared bankruptcy, leaving Wilde without her settlement. Shaken and denied her settlement, Wilde sold her house and put her business on the market, hoping to move as far away from the incident as possible. Third-party harassment will surely be the next battlefield in the fight against sexual harassment.

Source: Adapted from Frank Clancy, "When Customer Service Crosses the Line," *Working Woman,* December 1994, 36–39, 77–78.

OSHA requires most employers with 11 or more employees to keep records of occupational injuries and illnesses. Employers must also post an approved state or federal OSHA poster and any citations, which must be displayed at or near the site of the alleged violation for three days or until corrected, whichever is later.

As a small business owner, you may request information from one of ten regional OSHA offices or request a free on-site OSHA-supported consultation through your state's labor or health department. No citations are issued or penalties proposed, nor is the name of your firm or any information regarding your firm given to OSHA. However, you will be expected to correct any serious job safety and health hazards identified.

Licenses, Restrictions, and Permits

Because there are different requirements for licenses and permits at the federal, state, regional, county, and city government levels, a comprehensive list is not possible. But there are some general guidelines for finding information on regulations at each level.

Double-check license and permit rules. Check with the appropriate government agency directly—don't rely on real estate agents, sellers, or anyone else's opinion.

At the federal level, get an employer identification number for federal tax and social security withholdings. File Form 2553 if you are forming a corporation. Check with the appropriate agency for your specific type of business. For example, if you are starting a common-carrier trucking company, you should contact the Interstate Commerce Commission.

At the state level, professionals, such as lawyers, dentists, and architects, need professional licenses. You need to register for a state tax number with the Department of Revenue. You need an employer identification number for state tax withholding. Special licenses are usually needed for selling liquor, food, gasoline, or firearms.

At the regional level, several counties may form regional agencies that oversee environmental regulations and water usage.

At the local level, permits and licenses to comply with local and county requirements will vary from place to place.[12] You need answers from the local level—the local chamber of commerce and lawyers are good sources of information. Offices to check with would be

City or county clerk
City or county treasurer
Zoning department
Building department
Health department
Fire department
Police department
Public works department

If your business involves the sale or preparation of food, you will need not only a permit from a local health department, but also regular inspections. Local health departments may also be involved with environmental concerns, such as asbestos inspections, radon testing, and water purity testing.

ZONING LAWS. You need to be absolutely sure how a property is zoned before you sign a lease. If it is not zoned properly, you can sign the lease with a contingency clause that the property will be rezoned. You can also apply to the local zoning

zoning laws Local laws that control where and how businesses may operate.

commission to get a variance, which allows you to operate without complying with the regulation or the regulation's being changed.

Zoning laws control what a business can sell and where it can operate. They are typically used to control parking, waste disposal, and sign size and placement. You may not even be able to paint the building a certain color due to zoning restrictions. For example, a White Castle hamburger franchise in Overland Park, Kansas, was not allowed to paint the building white because a zoning ordinance prohibited white buildings.

How do zoning laws affect home-based businesses, the fastest-growing segment in business (see Chapter 7)? Technology is making it possible for you to be productive at work from the comfort of your own living room. Are zoning boards as comfortable with the idea? Although some zoning ordinances prohibit home businesses, most don't. Restrictions on what you can and can't do on the property are more common. Most are looking primarily to maintain the residential nature of the neighborhood.

You should check zoning laws before you start your business, whether or not it is home based. At the zoning department at city hall, find out not only about the written laws but also about the community attitudes of administrators, citizens, and the business community. Are other home-based businesses allowed? If you disagree with a zoning ruling, you may be able to appeal to a variance board, the city council, or local commissioners.

Bankruptcy Laws

bankruptcy A ruling granted by courts to release businesses or individuals from some or all of their debt.

Bankruptcy is a remedy for becoming insolvent. When an individual or a business gets into a financial condition in which there's no other way out, the courts administer the estate for the benefit of the creditors. The Bankruptcy Reform Act of 1978 established eight chapters for businesspeople seeking the protection of bankruptcy. Three of these chapters—Chapters 7, 11, and 13—apply to most small business situations:

Bankruptcy can accomplish two different objectives: liquidation, after which the business ceases to exist; and reorganization, which allows the business owner to file a plan with the court that offers protection from creditors until the debt is satisfied.

Chapter 7 Bankruptcy

Chapter 7 bankruptcy means that the business is liquidated. All of the assets of the business are sold by a trustee appointed by the court. After the sale, the trustee distributes the proceeds to the creditors, who usually receive a percentage of the original debt. If any money is left over, it is divided among shareholders. About three of every four bankruptcy filings are under Chapter 7.

Declaring bankruptcy does not necessarily leave you penniless and homeless. Most states have provisions that allow individuals to keep the equity in their homes, autos, and some personal property.

Other businesses that declare bankruptcy may provide an opportunity for you. For instance, imagine you are in business and one of your key suppliers goes bankrupt. What are your options? You could try to continue doing business with that firm for as long as possible. You could try to find a new supplier. Or you could use your knowledge of the bankrupt company and industry to your advantage, and buy the supplier at a bargain price, assuming you could operate the failed business more efficiently than the previous management.[13] Other strategic purchases could include buying a financially strapped competitor, to increase your market share, or buying a business that is a customer, to provide an outlet for your products.

Chapter 11 Bankruptcy

Chapter 11 provides a second chance for a business that is in financial trouble but still has potential for success. Chapter 11 can be either voluntary or involuntary. Once you file for Chapter 11 protection, you file a reorganization plan with the bankruptcy court. The plan includes a repayment schedule for current creditors (which may be less than 100 percent of amount owed), and how the business will operate more profitably in the future. Only about 3 percent of bankruptcy filings are under Chapter 11.

This reorganization protection keeps creditors from foreclosing on debts during the reorganization period. The business continues to operate under court direction. The court and the creditors must approve the plan. The reorganization plan also spells out a specific time period for the reorganization. If the business cannot turn operations (and profits) around, the likelihood of its switching to a Chapter 7 liquidation is great.

Michael Blair, the owner of a small Hollywood advertising and design studio called Blair Communications, learned about the dark side of federal laws and regulations the hard way. According to the Federal Bankruptcy Code, every person or company that has declared bankruptcy may, in certain circumstances, sue for the return of money paid out to others within three months of the bankruptcy filing. This section in the code applies when preferential payments were made to some creditors over others during that time period, in order to give all creditors an equitable distribution of assets. However, what's happened to Blair shows the downside of this supposed protection.

Blair was sued by a company for which he developed advertising—a company by the name of PC Brand Computers, a subsidiary of Tandon Corporation. Tandon had filed for Chapter 11 bankruptcy protection two months after its last payment to Blair. What happened next was, for Blair, like a nightmare gone out of control. Blair received a parcel by registered mail containing a mass of legal documents—the gist of which was that Tandon was suing him for the return of the previous payment. He was asked to send a check reimbursing the company for the full amount. Is that what the law's creators had in mind when they wrote this particular "preferential payments" section? Probably not. But this example illustrates how important it is for small businesses—especially for service businesses that deal in intangibles—to understand the legal environment.[14]

Chapter 13 Bankruptcy

Chapter 13 bankruptcy allows individuals, including small business owners, who owe less than $250,000 in unsecured debts and secured debts of less than $750,000 to pay back creditors over a three- to five-year period. As with Chapter 11, a repayment plan is submitted to a bankruptcy judge, who must approve the conditions of the plan. The plan must show how most types of your debt will be paid in full. Other types can be reduced or even eliminated by the court. About one-fourth of bankruptcies filed are under Chapter 13.

Although much of the negative stigma attached to declaring bankruptcy of any type has decreased, it is still absolutely not an "easy way out." Bankruptcy stays on your credit report for at least seven years. It is expensive and time-consuming. Chapters 11 and 13 may be better than liquidation, but they are not a solution to all of your problems.

▬▬ Contract Law for Small Business

contract An agreement between two or more parties that is enforceable by law.

A **contract** is basically a promise that is enforceable by law. Contract law comprises the body of laws that are intended to make sure that parties entering into contracts comply and provides remedies to those parties harmed if a contract is broken.

A contract does not have to be in writing to be enforceable. Although it is a good idea to get any important agreement in writing, to help settle future disputes, the only contracts that must be in writing are those that

■ Involve the sale of real estate.

■ Involve paying someone else's debt.

■ Take longer than one year to perform.

■ Involve the sale of goods valued at $500 or more.

Even contracts that are written do not have to be complicated, formal documents written by a lawyer. Although you may not want to rely on contracts that are too sketchy, a letter or memo that identifies the parties, the subject, and the terms and conditions of the sale can be recognized as a valid contract.

The Elements of a Contract

The four basic conditions or elements that a contract must meet to be binding are legality, agreement, consideration, and capacity.

LEGALITY. A contract has to be intended to accomplish a legal purpose. For instance, you can't make a contract that charges an interest rate higher than legal restrictions allow. At the same time, just because a deal is unfair, it is not necessarily illegal. You can't get out of a deal later if you offer to pay $1,500 for a used computer that is worth only $150.

AGREEMENT. A valid contract has to include a legitimate offer and a legitimate acceptance—called a "meeting of the minds." If a customer tells you his traveling circus will pay your print shop $600 to print 200 circus posters and you say, "It's a deal," you have a legally binding contract. In this case, it is an oral one, which is as legally binding as a written contract.

Finding Answers to Your Legal Questions Online

Looking for answers to legal questions? Although there is no substitute for a flesh-and-blood lawyer sometimes, they can be expensive. Here are some Internet sites to check first:

- The mother lode of business law web sites is 'Lectric Law Library (lectlaw.com). This is truly a one-stop shop to answer your small business legal questions. Start with the library tour, where you will find information in thousands of stacks, including the Reference Room, Forms Room, Book Store, Laypeople's Law Lounge, Legal Professional's Lounge, and (most important to you) the Law for Business Lounge. Every time you log on later, you can go the Rotunda and directly to the Business Lounge. This is a great source of information.

- Findlaw.com looks like a legal version of Yahoo! with more than 25,000 links. You will be most interested in the Small Business Toolbox (www.smallbiz.findlaw.com). Here you will find information on sample business plans, step-by-step checklists, downloadable legal forms, and documents. Findlaw is also a good resource for legal information on the online world, in its CyberSpace Law Center.

- FreeAdvice.com uses the slogan "The easy-to-use site for legal information." Not too catchy, but fairly accurate. You will find topics including bankruptcy, business law, employment, intellectual property, tax law, and small claims. In addition to details of these and other topics, you will find links to attorneys who specialize in that area.

- At Lawoffice.com, West Group has compiled a site to help "businesses, professionals, and consumers navigate through legal issues that affect their professional and personal lives." The lawoffice.com Law Pathfinders section includes a dictionary of over 5,000 legal terms and links to print publications and other sites arranged by topic. The site's Law Knowledgebase includes articles about legal issues written by law firms across the United States. The Law Tools section will give you advice about how to hire the right attorney for you and even how to understand lawyer's fees.

- Allaboutlaw.com offers over 1,200 generic legal forms and documents that you can download.

- Nolo.com comes from the publisher of many great self-help guides and books on legal topics. The web site features forms and documents to download, legal software, even an online legal encyclopedia, dictionary, and Q&A section.

CONSIDERATION. Something of value must be exchanged between the parties involved in the contract. Without consideration, the agreement is about a gift, not a contract. In the preceding example, the $600 and the 200 posters are the consideration. If the circus owner picks up the posters, pays you the $600, and says, "Wow, for doing such a great job, come to the circus and I'll give you a free elephant ride," can you legally demand to ride the elephant later? No, you got what you agreed to—the $600—but there was no consideration for the bonus.

CAPACITY. Not everyone has the capacity to legally enter into a contract. Minors and persons who are intoxicated or who have diminished mental ability cannot be bound by contracts. This is an important point to remember when running a small business. For example, if you sell a used car to a person under the age of 18, you could end up with a problem. The minor could take the car, run it without oil, smash it into a tree, and come to you to get his or her money back. You would be legally obligated to return the money because a contract with a minor is not binding.

Contractual Obligations

breach of contract A violation of one or more terms of a contract by a party involved in the contract.

compensatory damages Money awarded by the courts to a party of the contract who has suffered a loss due to the actions of another party.

What can you do if a party with whom you signed a contract doesn't hold up her end of the agreement? This is called **breach of contract,** and you have several remedies available. Usually either money or some specific performance is used to compensate the damaged party. With either remedy, the intent of litigation is to try to put you back to where you were before the agreement was made.

If the judge or arbitrator awards money, it is called **compensatory damages.** Go back to the circus poster example. If you were not able to complete the job as agreed and the circus owner had to pay someone else $800 to get the posters printed, you could be sued for $200 for breach of contract (probably in small claims court). Why $200? That amount represents the compensatory damages the circus owner suffered because you couldn't do the job for $600.

In some contract dispute cases, money alone is insufficient to put a person back to his or her original state. In these cases, a judge may order a specific performance by the damaging party to make sure justice is done. **Specific performance** requires one party to do exactly what he or she has agreed to do.

specific performance A non-monetary award granted by the courts to a party of the contract who has suffered a loss due to the actions of another party.

Consider buying an existing business for which the sales contract includes a noncompete covenant. This means that the previous business owner will not start or own a similar business within a specific geographic area for a certain amount of time. If the previous owner breaks the noncompete covenant and starts the same type of business, a single monetary award won't be enough. The judge can issue an **injunction,** which prohibits the previous owner from operating the new business for the duration of the agreement.

injunction A court order that prohibits certain activities.

Specific performance is awarded only if the item involved is unique and not substitutable. In this case, a judge will require the losing party to surrender the item in question.

DILBERT reprinted by permission of United Features Syndicate, Inc.

If Only I'd Thought of That . . .

Are you a potential inventor? Do you come up with ideas for new products that the world can't live without when you are in the shower or driving to work? Here are some products or services that have recently been patented. Keep thinking, and you may come up with a patentable product.

- Ted Schott, who invents games, has patented a "stress-reducing" board game that involves up to six players in pillow fights. He says it is a good way for children to use up excess energy.

- John Dahman, a mechanical engineer by trade, came up with a solution to one form of household drudgery—ironing. Dahman patented a process for drying cotton pants so that no ironing is needed, by using an ordinary hair dryer.

- Leroy Forney designs medical devices. His latest patented invention looks like a pacifier, but it keeps people from snoring. Unfortunately, at this writing, the FDA has not yet approved the product.

- Raymond and Hilde Smith wanted more room in their recreational vehicle, so they invented and patented a two-story RV. The second story slides down into the first while traveling and goes up to double your floor space when parked.

- Ellis Gordon invented and patented a computerized kitchen appliance that can be programmed to mix ingredients together, then prepare a meal by cooking or cooling.

- Is kitty litter a problem? Traditionally used sodium bentonite does not decompose. Theodore Kiebke patented a more environmentally friendly version made from wheat.

- Optometrist Sidney Slavin had dreamed of being able to show driver's education students the deadly effects of driving drunk, so he invented and patented eyeglasses that distort, rather than clarify, vision. The glasses simulate the effects of drugs or alcohol (without the side effects).

- William Holmes patented an insulated drinking bag that fits on bicycles. The rider does not have to remove his hands from the handlebars to search for a bottle, remove it, take a drink, and return the bottle to its holder. Holmes's invention's unique attribute is a tube that extends from the handlebar. Riders just lean over to take a drink.

- Not all inventors think on a small scale. Retired aerospace engineer George Neumayr patented a design for a flying machine that can take off and land straight up and down, even over water. The design looks like a flying saucer and can carry up to 800 people. Sorry, Trekkies, beaming up is not yet an option.

- With some products, you have to wonder, "Do we really need this product?" Who would invent something like synthetic human feces? Actually, Kimberly-Clark patented this invention, which it used as an odorless alternative in testing its diapers.

Sources: All adapted from the *New York Times* patent column (www.nytimes.com). "A Board Game to Inspire Fighting," 2 January 1995, A40; "Device to Aid Drying of Trousers," 9 January 1995, D2; "Anti-snoring Unit Resembles Pacifier," 9 January 1995, D2; "Recreation Vehicle with a 2nd Story," 2 January 1995, A40; "Patents," 26 December 1994, A56; "A New Cat Litter, Made from Wheat," 12 December 1994, D2; "Patents," 5 December 1994, D2; "A Pressurized Bag for Thirsty Cyclists," 21 November 1994, D2; "Patents," 7 November 1994, B14; and "An Odorless Way of Testing Diapers," 24 October 1994, D2.

■ Laws to Protect Intellectual Property

intellectual property Property that is created through the mental skills of a person.

Intellectual property is a broad term that refers to the product of some type of unique human thought. It begins as an idea that could be as simple as a new name or as complex as the invention of a new product. Intellectual property also includes symbols and slogans that describe your business or product and original expression, whether it takes the form of a collection of words (like a published book), an artistic interpretation (like a videotape of a concert performance), or a computer program. These products of human thought have some value in the marketplace. A body of laws determines how, and for how long, a person can capitalize on his idea.

The forms of legal protection for intellectual property that will be discussed in this section are patents, copyrights, and trademarks. Although commonly used, the term *protection* may be misleading when we are discussing intellectual property, because it implies defense. Actually, patents, copyrights, and trademarks give the owner more offensive rights than defensive protection. They provide a tool for you to use in protecting your property against infringers. Realistically, this means that patents and other protections do not stop others from infringing on your registered idea. You only have the right to prevent others from using your ideas by challenging them in court, but these challenges often do not prevail. In the United States, this right has been considered so essential a part of the country's economic functioning that it was written into the Constitution.[15]

> *Safeguarded by the U.S. Constitution, copyright protection encourages entrepreneurs to invent new ideas and products.*

Patents

patent A form of protection for intellectual property provided to an inventor for a period of 17 years.

A **patent** gives you the right to exclude someone else (or some other company) from making, using, or selling the property you have created and patented for a period of 17 years. To receive this protection, you have to file for a patent through the Patent Trademark Office (PTO). This requires paying filing fees and maintenance fees. Three maintenance fees must be paid 4, 8, and 12 years after the patent grant, or the patent will expire before 17 years.

Although it is commonly believed that you have to hire a patent attorney to file a patent application, this is not the case. Actually, regulations require the PTO to help individuals who do not use an attorney. Hundreds of patents are granted each year to inventors who go through the process alone. But just because you can complete the patent process without legal counsel, does that mean you should attempt it? It depends. Patent attorneys charge $3,000 to $5,000 to prepare a patent application. How many earth-changing widgets will you have to sell to cover that kind of overhead? If you are unsure of what the market for your widgets will be, books like *Patent It Yourself* by David Pressman contain all the instructions and forms you need to do it yourself.[16] Doing as much as you can yourself, while checking periodically with an attorney throughout the process, may be a reasonable compromise to offer you both expertise and cost savings.

Three types of patents exist. The most common type is the utility patent. This patent covers inventions that provide a unique or new use or function. If you could come up with a new way to keep shoes on people's feet without using laces, buckles, Velcro fasteners, zippers, or other ways currently used, you would need to file for a utility patent.

Whereas utility patents cover use, design patents protect unique or new forms or shapes. If the new shape also changes the function of the object, then you need to apply for a utility patent. If looks alone are different, you need a design patent. For example, if you were to design a ballpoint pen that looked like a fish, but which served no other function than that of a ballpoint pen, you would file a design patent for your invention.

The third patent type is a plant patent. This patent covers living plants, such as flowers, trees, or vegetables that can be grown or otherwise reproduced.

WHAT CAN BE PATENTED? The PTO reviews each application and decides whether or not to grant a patent by four tests, which come from the following questions:

- Does the invention fit a statutory class?

- Is the invention useful?

- Is it novel?

- Is it unobvious?

The invention must fit into one of the five statutory classes—which means that you must be able to call it a machine, process, manufacture, chemical composition, or combination of those terms.

The invention must provide some legal utility. It must be useful in some way. If the invention has some commercial value, this test shouldn't be difficult to pass. If it doesn't, you will have a hard time building your small business on it. The invention must be possible to build and be workable to be granted a patent. You have to be able to show the examiner that the invention will operate as you say it will.

The invention must be novel. It must be different from all other things that have previously been made or described anywhere else in the world (called "prior art"). Meeting this test can be a difficult and confusing one to everyone involved.

Three types of novelty that meet this requirement are those created by physical difference, by a new combination of existing parts, or by the invention of a new use.

The invention must be unobvious. Although this rule is also difficult to understand, it is an important one. It means that the difference between your invention and other developments (or prior art) must not be obvious to someone with common knowledge in that field. The novelty of your invention needs to produce new or unexpected results.

The flowchart in Figure 10.2 can help you visualize the tests your invention must pass to get a patent.

PATENT SEARCHES. Before you file a patent application, you should conduct a patent search to save time and money later. You can conduct a search yourself, or hire a patent agent or patent attorney. You are searching for existing patents for inventions that are or may be similar to yours.

Start by coming up with several key words that could be used in describing your invention. These key words will be run through the primary patent reference publication at the Patent and Trademark Office in Arlington, Virginia, the Index to the U.S. Patent Classification. If you can't go to the PTO, you can search a Patent Depository Library. In these libraries, you can use the Official Gazette of the U.S. Patent and Trademark Office.

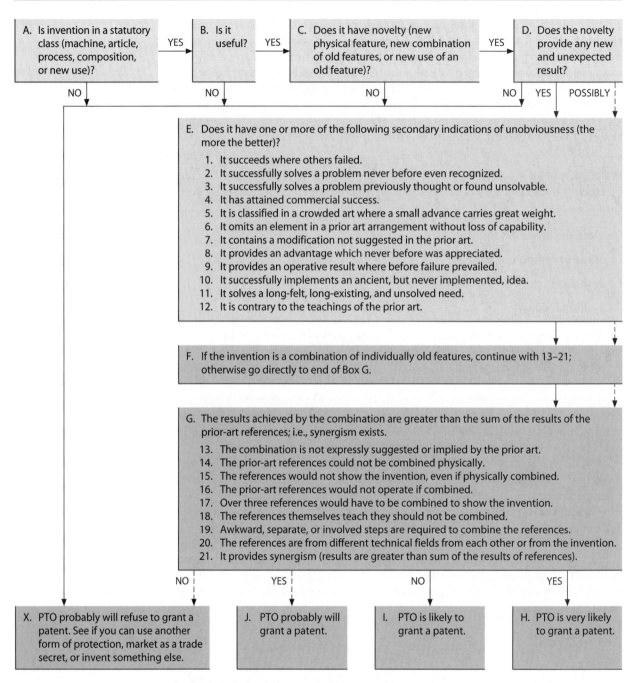

FIGURE 10.2

How Do You Get a Patent?

The steps needed to receive a patent on your product.

Source: "How Do You Get a Patent?" from *Patent It Yourself, 8/e* by David Pressman. Reprinted with permission from the publisher, Nolo.com. Copyright 2001. http://www.nolo.com.

You can also conduct a patent search by subject or by specific patent via the Internet. This is done through the Shadow Patent Office. For more information, visit the PTO home page at www.uspto.gov through the Internet.

PATENT APPLICATION. When submitting your patent application, you should include

1. A self-addressed postcard to show receipt of packet.
2. Payment of the filing fee.
3. A letter of transmittal.
4. Drawings of your invention.
5. Specifications, including
    a. The title or name of your invention.
    b. Cross-reference of similar inventions.
    c. A description of the field of your invention.
    d. Prior art.
    e. Features and advantages of your invention.
    f. Drawing descriptions.
    g. A description of how your invention works.
    h. A conclusion.
6. The claim, patent details that define the scope of your invention.
7. An abstract, summarizing the whole project.
8. A patent application declaration form, which says that you are the true inventor.
9. A statement that you have not transferred patent ownership to anyone else.
10. An information disclosure statement and a list of prior art.[17]

Your application will be reviewed by a PTO examiner in the order in which it is received, meaning that it could be months or years before the review begins. The examination process can take from one to three or more years with revisions and amendments.

If your patent is approved, you will be notified, and a copy of the application will be sent to the U.S. Government Printing Office.

Copyrights

A **copyright** is the protection of literary, musical, or artistic works. Copyright laws protect the expression of ideas, not the ideas themselves, because lawmakers want to encourage the dissemination of ideas while protecting the rights of the original owner.

The length of copyright protection is the life of the author plus 50 years. If your corporation is the owner of a book's copyright, it will continue as owner for 75 years after the first publication, or 100 years after creation.

You don't have to register your work to receive copyright protection, but it does strengthen your rights to do so. If registered, you don't have to prove actual damages to collect up to $500,000. The act of creating the work begins the copyright protection, whether or not it is published. If you do choose to register your work, all you need to do is complete the proper forms and send the fees to the Copyright Office along with a copy of your work.

copyright A form of protection for intellectual property provided to the creator of a literary, musical, or artistic work for a period of the creator's life plus 50 years.

Keeping a Trademark in Shape

When you've got a good thing, you want to keep it. That's why it's particularly important for small business owners to register ideas and products as soon as possible and to monitor for any misuse of your trademark. Designer Nancy Ganz introduced the Hipslip™ in 1988. It's a product she created from nylon and Du Pont's Lycra to provide extra support for the body-hugging garments that she designed. Today, her Manhattan-based company, Bodyslimmers™ By Nancy Ganz, ships more than 90,000 Hipslips a month and has annual sales of nearly $10 million.

Ganz recognized that new ideas and products are quickly imitated, so she registered Hipslip with the U.S. Patent and Trademark Office as soon as she coined the name. In addition, she feels that by keeping her company's name unique, she's been better able to protect her rights. For instance, instead of calling her company Bodyslimmers, which she felt was too generic, Ganz added her name and thus achieved both legal protection and added identity.

Ganz is also vigilant in her monitoring of any misuse of her registered trademark. How does she keep up? Ganz chose to hire a press-clipping service to track references to her company or products, including those in advertisements. This nationwide search costs her about $200 a month plus about $1.50 per clipping. And, as Ganz agrees, protecting your rights also means sometimes confronting the "bad guys."

When a problem does arise, Ganz has her lawyer send offending parties a letter notifying them of her trademark and position in the industry. In extreme instances, Ganz has had to take legal action to recover some of the proceeds that offenders have received using her trademarked name. Finally, Ganz feels it's important to get your name out and let people see it frequently. For instance, she often takes out full-page ads in trade publications. All of these actions help Nancy Ganz "protect" her good name.

Source: From "Protecting Your Good Name" by Nancy Ganz. Reprinted by permission, *Nation's Business*, September, 1995. Copyright 1995, U.S. Chamber of Commerce.

Many small businesses are involved in creating computer software. Should they seek a patent or a copyright for their creation? Actually, software could qualify for either or both, so which would be better? A patented computer program is difficult for competitors to simulate or design around and lasts for 17 years, but consider the disadvantages. Patents can be expensive, take a lot of work to apply for and search, and take several years to obtain. Windows of opportunity open and shut quickly in the software market. Your software may be obsolete before a patent can even be granted.

Copyrighting software is quick and inexpensive but doesn't provide the offensive punch of a patent. You can't copyright what a program does, only the specific way it is written. So competing small business programmers need only write the program for their software in a different manner to avoid copyright infringement.

So what's the answer for "protecting" your software? Frankly, neither patents nor copyrights do a thorough job. Protecting intellectual property for quickly changing industries and global markets is a serious problem which small businesses and regulators will have to face in the near future.

Trademarks

A **brand** is a name, term, symbol, design, or combination of these elements that clearly identifies and differentiates your products from those of your competitors. A **trademark** is a registered and protected brand. Therefore, all trademarks are brands, but not all brands are trademarks. A trademark can include a graphic as well as a brand name. For example, not only is the Coke name protected, the style of its script also makes it a trademark.

Trademark rights continue as long as you continue to use the trademark. This is an advantage over patents or copyrights. Trademarks are useful because they provide brand recognition for your product and are a good way to create an image in your customer's mind.

Because there are over a million trademarks in use in the United States, how do you find one that isn't already taken? As with the patent search, you can either do the search yourself or hire someone to do it for you. The problem gets even more complicated because a 1989 regulation change makes it possible to reserve a trademark before it is even put into use.

Several businesses specialize in trademark searches of registered and unregistered marks. They include Trademark Service Corporation, 747 Third Avenue, New York, NY 10017, (212) 421–5730; Thompson & Thompson, 500 Victory Road, North Quincy, MA 02171–2126, (800) 692–8833; and Compu-Mark U.S., 1333 F Street NW, Washington, DC 20004, (800) 421–7881. You can conduct a search yourself with *The Trademark Register of the U.S.,* available in many libraries, or a similar directory. You can file for a trademark with the Patent and Trademark Office, Washington, DC 20231 (www.uspto.gov) with an application and a $325 fee. You can also register your trademark in your state with the secretary of state at your state capitol.

Your trademark is worthless (and actually invalid) if you don't use it. Before your product is registered, use the symbol ™, and after it is registered, use ®.

brand A name, term, symbol, design, or combination of these elements that clearly identifies and differentiates your products from those of your competitors.

trademark A form of protection for intellectual property provided to the owner of a brand name or symbol.

Global Protection

Protecting intellectual property in other countries is difficult. Your patent, copyright, or trademark protection in the United States does not apply in most foreign markets. You need separate protection in each country, so you must check regulations and filing procedures for each market you intend to enter. Timing is critical. You should file before entering a foreign market, or you may lose the right to do so later.

Complications associated with protecting intellectual property in global markets are bound to arise because there is no single body of international copyright law. But what protection does a small business person have over intellectual property when expanding into global markets? Through a series of international treaties, almost all nations—the former Soviet Union countries and China are the major exceptions—have agreed to give each other's citizens the same copyright protection given to their own citizens. So, if you take the appropriate procedural steps, your copyright will be protected in virtually every global market.

The two most important and overlapping copyright treaties are the Berne Convention and the Universal Copyright Convention (UCC). International copyright protection for works by U.S. citizens and permanent residents depends largely on the rights granted by these two international treaties.

The Berne Convention is the most important international copyright treaty, affording the highest standards of protection. Every country that has signed the Berne Convention (which the United States did in 1989) must give citizens or permanent residents of other Berne countries at least the same copyright protection it gives its own nationals. Under the Berne Convention, no formalities such as notice and registration may be required for basic copyright protection. However, some countries will provide greater copyright protection if a copyright is registered or carries a particular type of notice. Other countries have certain procedural requirements that must be followed. It's important for the small business person to determine what these requirements are for each country in which he or she hopes to do business—and to follow them in order to protect his or her intellectual property rights.

The United States joined the Universal Copyright Convention (UCC) on September 16, 1995. The UCC is very similar to the Berne Convention, except that it allows member countries to establish and require some formalities. (When a country has signed both the Berne Convention and the UCC, the Berne Convention has priority over the UCC). Again, it's important that a small business person determine the copyright protection formalities that are required in each country.

What happens if you find that your intellectual property is being used improperly and illegally? It's important to consult with an experienced U.S. copyright attorney to help you through the maze of how, when, and whether to file a lawsuit. Although the United States has urged other foreign governments to take copyright infringement seriously, some countries still do not.

One of the newest challenges in the protection of intellectual property concerns the uncharted legal territories of cyberspace. The uncertainties and rapidly changing nature of linked global computer networks and the content that floats throughout these networks are creating their own sets of legal issues, which are still being discussed and developed. If electronic publishing and digital information is what your small business does, be sure to get good legal help to protect your hard-earned intellectual property.

SUMMARY

▆▆▆ Laws and regulations that affect small business.

Laws and regulations exist to protect competition, consumers, people in the workplace, and intellectual property; to allow bankruptcy; and to establish contracts. Specific laws that owners of small businesses should know include the Equal Pay Act, the Civil Rights Acts of 1964 and 1991, the Immigration Reform and Control Act, the Americans with Disabilities Act, the Family and Medical Leave Act, and the Occupational Safety and Health Act.

▆▆▆ Types of bankruptcy.

The U.S. Bankruptcy Code is made up of nine chapters, only three of which apply to many small businesses (Chapters 7, 11, and 13). Chapter 7 uses liquidation, meaning that the business ceases to exist in order to provide the debtor with a fresh start. Liquidation involves selling all of the business assets and nonexempt personal assets to distribute the proceeds among creditors. Chapters 11 and 13 allow the business owner to file a plan with the court that offers protection from creditors until the debt is satisfied.

The elements of a contract.

For a contract to be legally binding, it must be intended to accomplish a legal purpose. Both parties must come to an agreement including a legitimate offer and a legitimate acceptance. Consideration, or something of value, must be exchanged. Finally, all parties must have the capacity to enter a binding contract, meaning that they must not be underage, intoxicated, or of diminished mental ability.

Ways to protect intellectual property.

Patents, copyrights, and trademarks are legal ways to protect intellectual property. A patent grants an inventor the exclusive right to make, use, and sell an invention for a period of 17 years. A copyright provides legal protection against infringement of an author's literary, musical, or artistic works. Copyrights usually last for the author's life plus 50 years. A trademark is a legally protected name, term, symbol, design, or combination of these elements used to identify products or companies. Trademarks last for as long as they are in use.

QUESTIONS FOR REVIEW & DISCUSSION

1. Are the antitrust laws established in the late 1800s and early 1900s still pertinent in the twenty-first century? Why or why not?

2. What does the Federal Trade Commission do to protect consumers?

3. What rights does owning a patent protect? How do you get this protection?

4. What tests must an invention pass in order to receive a patent?

5. What is the difference between a copyright and a trademark? between a trademark and a brand?

6. Name and explain the four elements that a contract must have to be valid.

7. List and briefly explain the laws that protect people in the workplace.

8. How are liquidation and reorganization used as different approaches to bankruptcy? What chapters of bankruptcy law accomplish these objectives?

9. What licenses does the owner of a small business need in order to comply with regulations?

10. What risk does an inventor assume when filing for a patent for an invention?

QUESTIONS FOR CRITICAL THINKING

1. Because compliance with government regulations is such a big issue for small business owners, what can they (and you) do to effect change in laws and regulations that influence small business?

2. Think of transactions you have entered into in the past: who were you agreeing with, what was the agreement about, and what were the terms? When did you have a written contract? When was an oral contract in place? Use several examples to analyze: buying a car, accepting a job, ordering a pizza. What elements of contract law applied?

Experience this . . .

Tired of boring, in-the-box thinking? Do you think that the United States is becoming a nation of more Homer Simpsons than of Thomas Edisons? Well, there are people out there solving problems that we didn't even know existed. Did you know that mechanical bat wings to provide aerodynamic lift for in-line skaters have been patented? How about the BinoCap that builds binoculars onto the bill of a cap? Ted VanCleave has created a web site called Totally Absurd (www.totallyabsurd.com), complete with hilarious commentary on wacky inventions that have received U.S. patents. Of course, it can be easy to be funny when you're talking about toilet landing lights (they add "an almost mystical glow"), hair-braiding machines, hat tethers, and a diaper alarm. Visit this web page to lighten your day and stimulate your creativity.

WHAT WOULD YOU DO?   No. 1

The creativity of the human mind is often quite amazing. Read through the descriptions of the following entrepreneurial ideas, pick one that sounds interesting, and then answer the questions:

Harasser Flasher. This battery-operated pin enables wearers to "avoid harassment with the touch of a button." The red light and siren can be used against offensive come-ons. The yellow light can signal "You're pushing the limits." And the green light can reinforce acceptable actions and speech.

Alan's X-Tenda Fork. This fork telescopes from standard size to 23 inches so that users can sample tablemates' food.

File-A-Way Desk Bed. This 36-by-72-inch desk quickly converts to a standard-sized double bed. How's that for your home office?

Automatic Umpire. This high-tech home plate calls its own balls and strikes with the aid of embedded sensors and voice chips. Programmed phrases include "Ball," "Strike," "Take your base," and, of course, "You're out!"

Source: Springfield News Leader, 31 December 1995, 4E.

QUESTIONS

1. Draft a mock specification sheet (item 5 of Patent Application, page 319) for the patent application. Try to make your drawing as coherent and realistic as possible.

2. Those who have selected the same gadget are to divide into teams of six. Two students are to compose items 6 and 7 of Patent Application, page 319, each working on one item individually. The remaining four students are to review the specifications done by each member and select the best submission. Be prepared to make a presentation of your best submission in front of the class.

WHAT WOULD **YOU** DO?	No. 2

The stories of companies like KFC, Coca-Cola, and McDonald's guarding their recipes for batter, syrup, and hamburger sauce are legendary. Triple-locked safes, binding contractual agreements, spies, and counterspies are all involved. A company's trade secrets are worth significant (sometimes staggering) amounts of money. Like any good secret, they are known to only a handful of people.

Many assets, like chemical formulas, or specific designs are protected by patents. But in exchange for the legal protection afforded by a patent, the patent holder must surrender the leverage of secrecy. Part of the patent application process involves a full explanation of the process or product. The PTO (Patent and Trademark Office) publishes all patent applications within 18 months of their filing. Protecting a trade secret is complicated by the fact that, unlike patents, copyrights, and trademarks, trade secrets do not fall under federal jurisdiction. They are regulated by individual state laws. Trade secrets must be *proved* to be secret to qualify for protection. At the very minimum, the owner must prove that procedures were in place to protect the information prior to any legal challenge.

Source: Sabra Chartrand, "Patents," *New York Times,* 5 February 2001, C–14.

QUESTION

1. Imagine that you have developed a unique formula for a soft drink that, upon entering a person's mouth, analyzes the drinker's DNA to determine his or her favorite flavor, and then the drink instantly realigns its chemical composition to become that flavor. Write a two-page paper describing how you can best protect this trade secret. Will you patent it? Why or why not?

CHAPTER CLOSING CASE	No. 10

Knocking Off the SuperClip

Linda Froehlich dreamed up and patented a better paper clip, which she called the Super-Clip, but rather than beating a path to her door, the world knocked off her idea.

She and her husband Richard run Ace Wire Spring & Form Company in McKees Rocks, an industrial suburb of Pittsburgh. Linda's father, who founded Ace in 1939, sold the company to Linda and Richard when he retired. Ace's main business is manufacturing wire forms, such as bucket handles, paper racks, and springs that go into everything from screen doors to M–1 tanks. It employs 50 people and has annual sales of more than $5 million, but the SuperClip is the company's only office supply product.

Birth of the SuperClip   Linda developed the SuperClip 15 years ago, after a customer requested an oversize paper clip mounted on a wooden base as a paper holder. The SuperClip that evolved makes two uniqueness claims on its patent application:

1. The clip is made from high-carbon steel that springs back to its original shape.

2. The clip's "arms" are extended the length of the clip, so they won't tear the paper when removed.

One of Linda's early allies was Steven Meyer, who met her in 1987 and helped her with a promotion in which a SuperClip was folded into every copy of a local business journal. An office products distributor and the founder of a network of 100 office supply dealers, Meyer calls the SuperClip "a really functional product. People really wanted it." He adds that Linda "was not naïve, but what she didn't realize was that she was playing in the big leagues. I apprised her of the strength of the manufacturers and what it would mean to be dealing with the likes of Wal-Mart and Office Depot. I talked to her extensively about the possibility of someone knocking off the product."

Linda understood the risks but believed that, with the patent to protect her, "the road ahead would be smooth." Because she was aiming for "a big hit" in the mass market, she chose not to pursue a joint-marketing venture with Meyer.

Seeking Links with Major Players   Instead, she approached Acco USA, a $1 billion office products manufacturer and distributor, to see whether it wanted to acquire patent rights to the SuperClip. "Acco told me it was a novelty," says Linda. "They weren't interested." An Acco spokesperson says the company "has no record that we were contacted."

But then Linda made her first sale to Office Depot, a major player. Then Kmart tested the product and gave Ace an $85,000 order, and Target's West Coast stores began carrying the clip. Annual sales soon reached $400,000.

Now Acco had to take notice, but not the way Linda expected. Using its contacts in Taiwan, Acco produced a knockoff called the MegaClip, which, given Acco's marketing clout, it easily sold to Staples, Office Depot, and OfficeMax.

Acco says it was simply responding to customer demand. "We were approached by our customers to come out with a similar product. Of course, we put our spin on it through better manufacturing processes and better packaging. The product also has to meet a certain price point."

The price point, as established by the industry, appears to be 99 cents for a package of five. To meet it, other manufacturers go offshore, where wages are low and environmental laws lax. But Linda and Richard have "always thought of ourselves as an American manufacturer. We never thought about going offshore, because we wanted to keep control of the quality."

Made in America—For a While   Ace manufactured SuperClips in Pennsylvania from domestic steel. Because of tough Pennsylvania environmental laws, they were shipped out of state for plating, then back to Pittsburgh, where handicapped workers packaged them. To pay for Ace's quality, however, a package of five SuperClips retailed for $2.49—and as cheaper knockoffs appeared, orders for SuperClips evaporated.

In May 1996 Linda sent the SuperClip to Wal-Mart for inclusion in its "Support American Made" program. In mid-June, Wal-Mart wrote that the SuperClip had "commercial potential" and would be passed along to a buyer for further review. In December, Wal-Mart's buyer wrote, "I do not see a need for your product at this time . . . and I would like to bring the pricing of this product to your attention. I have received comparable products, and your cost is not in line with other manufacturers." Meanwhile, Wal-Mart had begun buying a knockoff from Taiwan in September.

Linda and Richard finally decided that they must have their SuperClips made in Taiwan. "We'll meet the competition's price, and our quality will be better," says Linda. Still, there's a hollow feeling about the decision. She and Richard have always prided themselves on being American manufacturers. Their Taiwanese supplier operates in a 2,000-square-foot space in what amounts to the ground floor of his apartment building. "It's not a factory as you or I would know it," says Linda.

Source: Adapted from "Clipped," by Edward O. Welles, from *Inc.: The Magazine for Growing Companies.* Copyright ©1997 by Goldhirsh Group/Inc Pubg. Reproduced with permission of Goldhirsh Group/Inc Pubg in the format textbook via Copyright Clearance Center.

QUESTIONS

1. Linda Froehlich believed that patenting her SuperClips would be all the legal protection she needed. Why did that turn out not to be the case?

2. Did Froehlich make a mistake in approaching Acco regarding the purchase of her patent rights?

3. How can a company prevent a patented product like the SuperClip from being knocked off?

4. Analyze Froehlich's initial decision to insist on making SuperClips in Pennsylvania, rather than moving production offshore as competitors had done.

5. What advice would you give Froehlich at this point?

Marketing the Product or Service

Marketing your small business involves more than just personal selling or writing newspaper ads. Marketing involves every form of customer contact—plus much more. The theme of this book is creating a sustainable competitive advantage. Topics in this section will be the basis for many of those advantages. You must understand how you serve your customers better than your competitors. Chapter 11 will explore small business marketing strategies and delve into bases for competitive advantage. Chapter 12 highlights factors related to the products you sell. Chapter 13 discusses location and layout. Chapter 14 is on pricing and promotion strategies.

11

Marketing for Competitive Advantage

After reading this chapter, you should be able to:

- Describe the importance of marketing to small businesses.

- Explain the process of developing a small business marketing strategy.

- Define competitive advantage, as well as its importance and benefits.

- Understand the purpose of the market research process and the steps involved in putting it into practice.

Small business is about taking risks and breaking away from the pack. A marketing strategy that little 25-employee Rachel's Gourmet Snacks has used to enhance its company image is sports sponsorship—specifically, backing the Indy car team with driver Eddie Cheever, who ended up winning the 1999 Indianapolis 500. After beating 30-to-1 odds and outlasting 32 other drivers, Cheever pulled into the checkered winner's circle with the "Rachel's" name across his fireproof driving suit and across his beautiful steel-blue car. Millions of fans saw that image.

Sponsorship at this level is not for the faint of heart among small business owners. It's a risky strategy for a financially struggling company to sign a three-year, multimillion-dollar sponsorship. But the image enhancement, visibility, and differentiation from competitors has been awesome for the Bloomington, Minnesota, potato chip producer. Right after the race, the phone started ringing with new customers, new distribution outlets started contacting them, and employees had an extra bounce of pride in their steps. Leo Short, executive vice president of sales and marketing, calls Cheever's win magic and compares the feeling to winning the Super Bowl.

Small businesses use marketing strategies and techniques to create and communicate their competitive advantage. Sponsorship is just one way (and it is most effective when used as part of a balanced marketing mix). Let's take a look at some others throughout the following chapters.

Source: Harvey Meyer, "And Now, Some Words About Sponsors," *Nation's Business,* March 1999, 38–39.

▬ Small Business Marketing

What do you think of when you hear the term *marketing?* Do you think of selling or advertising? Probably, but marketing is actually much more than just selling or advertising. Marketing involves all the activities needed to get a product from the producer to the ultimate consumer. Management guru Peter Drucker stated that businesses have two—and only two—basic functions: marketing and innovation. These are the only things a business does that produce results; everything else is really a "cost."[1] This is just as true for the one-person kiosk as it is for the largest corporate giant.

Of course, some selling will always be necessary, but the goal of marketing is to make selling superfluous.[2] A truly customer-driven company understands what consumers want in a product and provides it so that its products sell themselves. Of course, this is not easy. To paraphrase President Lyndon Johnson, doing the right thing is easy. Knowing the right thing to do is tough.

The Marketing Concept

marketing concept The philosophy of a business in which the wants and needs of customers are determined before goods and services are produced.

production concept The philosophy of a business that concentrates more on the product the business makes than on customer needs.

Many businesses operate today with a customer-driven philosophy. They want to find out what their customers want and then provide that good or service. This philosophy is called the **marketing concept.**

Businesses have not always concentrated their efforts on what the market wants. Before the Industrial Revolution and mass production, nearly all a business owner needed to be concerned about was making products. Demand exceeded supply for most goods like boots, clothing, or saddles. People had to have these products, so about all a business had to do was to make them. This philosophy in which companies concentrate their efforts on the product being made is now called the **production concept** of business.

After the mid-1800s, when mass production and mass distribution became possible for manufactured products, supply began to exceed demand. Some selling was needed, but the emphasis was still on producing goods. World War II temporarily shifted resources from consumer markets to the military. But after the war, when those resources were returned to the consumer market, businesses were producing at capacity, and many new businesses were started. Managers found that they could no longer wait for consumers to come to them in order to sell all they could make. Although these companies still emphasized making products, they now had to convince people to buy *their* products, which inaugurated the *selling concept* of business.

Early in the 1960s, many businesses began to adopt the marketing concept. According to this view, the customer is the center of a business's attention. It involves finding out what your customers want and need, and then offering products to satisfy those desires.

Scott MacHardy and Mark Lane exemplify entrepreneurs who understand the marketing concept. In the early 1990s, they purchased Coed Sportswear, the company that made T-shirts bearing the "Coed Naked" logo. They had seen the success the products enjoyed on their own campus and were sure that success could be duplicated elsewhere. MacHardy and Lane knew what their customers wanted and made a product to satisfy them. To keep their core target market of unpredictable teenagers happy, MacHardy and Lane are constantly looking for outrageous new slogans. The partners employ 60 young people who are encouraged to submit marketing or new product ideas. Recent additions include "I Own the Zone" and "Just Hafta."[3]

World-Class Marketing

If you take the marketing concept another step beyond production and apply it to the internal operation of a business, it is the basis of total quality management (TQM). TQM is defined as the process of meeting the wants and needs of internal and external customers by developing and providing them with high-quality, high-value, want-satisfying products.[4] Businesses of all sizes are facing increasingly tougher world-class competition, which calls for **world-class marketing (WCM)**. WCM combines the basics of TQM with the following best marketing practices:

> *The essence of the marketing concept is to first find out what customers want and then supply it. It is a practice of world-class businesses.*

world-class marketing (WCM) The practice of satisfying the internal and external customers of a business.

- *An external customer orientation.* Everyone in the organization concentrating on customer wants; the marketing concept.

- *An internal customer orientation.* Hiring, training, motivating, rewarding, and empowering employees to provide world-class service, including continuous training to maintain world-class standards.

- *A total quality orientation.* Putting the 14 points of TQM into practice (see Chapter 16).

- *A goal orientation.* Measuring results to ensure that the organization is meeting goals previously established.

- *A societal orientation.* Recognizing that your business has an impact on other stakeholders, such as suppliers, dealers, community leaders, government agencies, stockholders, and the environment.[5]

The role of marketing in small and large businesses continues to change. Marketing must be used not only to bring in customers but also to build alliances and long-term relationships with customers. Businesses that adopt this long-term view could be furthering the evolution of the marketing concept into what may become known as the *customer concept.*[6]

Marketing Strategies for Small Business ▬

Your **marketing strategy** should be decided in the early stages of operating your business. It should state *what* you intend to accomplish and *how* you intend to accomplish it. The marketing section of the business plan is a good place for the small business owner to identify marketing strategies. Any potential investor will carefully inspect how you have laid out the marketing action that will drive your business.

marketing strategy What the marketing efforts of a business are intended to accomplish and how the business will achieve its goals.

Global Small Business Marketing

It is just as important to craft an appropriate marketing strategy for global markets. And the number of small business owners and managers going global is surging. One small business that has made the leap is Preco Industries of Kansas City, Missouri, a manufacturer of automated die-cutting and stamping equipment. With annual sales of around $12 million, Preco sells 32 percent of its equipment overseas. It has been able to market overseas successfully by preparing thoroughly before entering any of its global markets, adapting to the country's culture, and making a firm commitment to its global ventures. It maintains its position by responding immediately to problems and challenges, being realistic about expectations, and nurturing relationships within the country.

Sources: Amy Barrett, "It's a Small (Business) World," *Business Week,* 17 April 1995, 96–101; Judith Ferlig, "Small World," *Ingram's,* June 1995, 53; and Norman Remich, "Advanced Technologies," *Appliance Manufacturer,* 1 March 2000, 76–77.

A good marketing strategy will help you to be proactive, not reactive, in running your business. You can enhance your marketing plan by

- Watching and understanding trends in your customers, suppliers, demographics, and technology.

- Having a vision that provides direction for your business.

- Having an adaptable, flexible organization.[7]

Small businesses in the service industries must pay special attention to marketing. When their service is one that customers could perform themselves, such as lawn mowing, a marketing strategy is critical. It is also often more difficult to differentiate or establish a brand image with services than with tangible products. Can the average car owner tell the difference between automatic transmissions that have been rebuilt by different shops? Probably not. A marketing strategy that communicates the benefits that consumers receive is crucial. However comprehensive or simple your marketing plan, it should include a description of your marketing objectives, sales forecast, target markets, and marketing mix.[8]

Setting Marketing Objectives

Your marketing objectives define the goals of your plans. They can be broken into two groups: marketing performance objectives and marketing support objectives.[9] *Marketing performance objectives* are specific, quantifiable outcomes, such as sales revenue, market share, and profit. For example, an objective of this type for a local insurance agency could be "to increase sales of homeowner's insurance by 10 percent for the next fiscal year." *Marketing support objectives* are what you must accomplish before your performance objectives can be accomplished, such as educating customers about your products, building awareness, and creating image.

Like any goal you want to accomplish in business, marketing objectives need to be (1) measurable, (2) action oriented by identifying what needs to be done, and (3) time specific by targeting a date or time for achievement.

Developing a Sales Forecast

Your marketing plan should include a **sales forecast,** in which you predict your future sales in dollars and in units—in other words, what your "top line" will be. If you are writing a business plan for a startup business, this sales forecast is one of the most important pieces of information you will gather. Why? Because that "top line" figure becomes the foundation for your pro forma income statements and cash flow statement. From your projected revenues you will subtract your expenses and disbursements to see if and when you will make a profit.

Forecasting is difficult, but it will help you establish more accurate goals and objectives. Your sales forecast will have an impact on all sections of your marketing plan, including appropriate channels of distribution, sales force requirements, advertising and sales promotion budgets, and the effects of price changes.

There are two basic ways to forecast sales: *build-up methods* and *break-down methods.* With a build-up method, you identify as many target markets as possible and predict the sales to each group. Then you combine the predictions for a total

sales forecast The quantity of products a business plans to sell during a future time period.

There *Is* a Difference

Brenda Laurel and her colleagues at Interval Research have been trying to piece together information about a gargantuan hole in a large market—kids' software and video games. They could see that 93 percent of the products in that market were targeted to boys, but why? To answer that, Laurel had to attack a question that many said could not be answered: How do boys and girls play differently? Results could open a gigantic market—computer software and video games targeted toward girls aged 7 to 12.

They started with many assumptions. Many assumed that girls just were less interested in computer technology. Many of Laurel's female researchers assumed that, because they had been girls, they knew all about the problem. But, being good researchers, they were determined to push through assumptions and treat their findings seriously, politically correct or not.

What girls told them was that they liked to go to a secret, quiet place to be alone. They were not especially interested in taking care of animals or anything else (an early assumption). If animals or plants were there and if they turned out to be magic, they would take care of the girl. Girls were looking for a place to be nurtured, rather than to nurture something else. Girls said the biggest reason they didn't play existing computer games was because they were boring, not because they were violent (another early assumption). They reviewed a game as "terrible" because a story could not be made up about a single character.

Interval Research's findings led to the creation of Purple Moon, one of the first companies to focus on computer and video games targeted to 7- to 12-year-old girls. Purple Moon created its Secret Paths series, in which girls would virtually meet characters their same age and invite them to a treehouse—a secret, magic place. Purple Moon's competitive advantage is that its products satisfy the specific needs of its target market by allowing girls to project themselves into the lives of characters.

Although Purple Moon correctly identified and (for a while) satisfied its target market, the software market is brutal. It was the first in the market but was soon overshadowed by Mattel's introduction of the Interactive Barbie Fashion Designer (and subsequent line extensions). Purple Moon was purchased by Mattel in June 1999.

Sources: Suzie Amer, "Girls Play Differently Than Boys," *Forbes ASAP Supplement,* 23 February 1998, 24–26; Bronwyn Fryer, "Where the Girls Are," *MC Technology Marketing Intelligence,* June 1998, 22–27; and David Futrelle, "Barbie Will Still Fall," *Upside,* June 1999, 40.

sales forecast. For example, if you plan to open an ice cream shop, can you estimate how many ice cream cones you will sell in a year? Not very easily or accurately without some research. But you can estimate with some degree of accuracy how much ice cream you could sell in one day—especially if you spend several days outside an existing ice cream shop observing how many people go in and out, and about how much they are buying. From that daily sales figure, you can project sales for the week, month, and year. Would you expect to sell the same amount per day in April? July? October? January? Probably not, so you come up with a daily sales projection at different times of the year to allow for seasonal fluctuations.

But with some types of products it is difficult to estimate daily sales. Then what? You may be able to use a break-down method. For this approach, you begin with an estimate of the total market potential for a specific product or an entire industry. This figure is broken down into forecasts of smaller units until you reach an estimate of how large a market you will reach and how many sales you will make. For example, if industry information from a trade association for a product you consider selling shows that 4 percent of a population will be in the market for your product at any given time, how many units and dollars of sales could you realistically generate? Do enough people live in your area, or can you reach enough market for your business to be profitable?

Identifying Target Markets

target market A group of people with a common want or need which your business can satisfy, who are able to purchase your product and who are more likely to buy from your business.

Market segmentation is the process of dividing the total market for a product into identifiable groups, or **target markets,** with a common want or need that your business can satisfy. These target markets are important to your business because they are the people who are more likely to be your customers. They are the people toward whom you direct your marketing efforts. Identifying and concentrating on target markets can help prevent you from getting caught in the trap of trying to be everything to everyone—you can't do it.[10]

When asked about their target markets, many small business owners will respond, "We don't have specific target markets; we will sell to anyone who comes in the door." Of course, you sell to anyone who wants your product, but that is not the point of segmenting target markets. A market for your business must have

1. A need that your products can satisfy.
2. Enough people to generate profit for your business.
3. Possession of, and willingness to spend, enough money to generate profit for your business.

segmentation variables Characteristics or ways to group people which make them more likely to purchase a product.

To identify the most attractive target markets for your business, you should look for characteristics that affect the buying behavior of the people. Does where they live influence whether or not they buy your product? Does income, gender, age, or lifestyle matter? Do they seek a different benefit from the product than other groups do? These differences, called **segmentation variables,** can be based on geographic, demographic, or psychographic differences, or on differences in benefits received. A small business owner should start (and occasionally revisit) the process of segmenting a market by committing to writing a description of "ideal" customers. For example, for a small accounting firm, that description could be "Entrepreneurs in their early thirties to early fifties; owners of retail, service, or manufacturing firms with sales of $500,000 to $3 million." Ideal customer purchasing patterns could include "When they are aware of a business need our accounting firm can solve, they want aggressive and innovative solutions. They don't have time to research solutions themselves. (This preference pattern shows that our accounting firm is segmenting on the basis of benefit received by customers)." What makes them ideal customers? They actively want the skills of our professional service and are willing and able to pay for them.

Not every way to segment a market is equally useful for every business. For example, if males and females react to the marketing efforts of your business in the same way, then segmenting by gender is not the best way to identify a target market for your business. When segmenting target markets, keep in mind that the reason for grouping people is to predict behavior—especially the behavior of buying from you.

A caveat for the future: Segmenting and targeting may not always be enough. The most common marketing strategy in the 1960s was **mass marketing,** or selling single products to large groups of people. Then, in the 1970s, **market segmentation** was used. Businesses took segmentation a step further in the 1980s with specialized **niche marketing,** which involves concentrating marketing efforts toward smaller target markets. The next step in market evolution for the 1990s was **individualized marketing,** or customizing each product to suit the needs of individual customers. These trends in marketing techniques do not mean that businesses need to throw out every technique that has been used in the past. Rather, these trends indicate that businesses may need to add another tool to their marketing toolbox.

Two factors leading to more individualized marketing are clutter and technology. Clutter in traditional media channels (newspaper, direct mail, television, radio) has reached a point where "shotgun" approaches—the same message directed to no one in particular—do not stand out. Consider that the average American household has access to 22 television channels and spends 50.8 per week watching them.[11] The American public has over 11,500 different magazines to choose from. Then add all the radio stations, the catalogues, and the direct mail consumers

mass marketing Treating entire populations of people as potential customers for specific products.

market segmentation Breaking down populations of people into groups, or target markets.

niche marketing Segmenting populations of people into smaller target markets.

individualized marketing Adjusting the marketing mix of a business to treat individual persons as separate target markets.

Who is the target for your products? Why are they more likely to buy? What other products may be attractive to them?

Target Markets of One

Several popular marketing terms, such as *database marketing, relationship marketing,* and *one-to-one marketing* are adding up to the same thing—collecting mountains of information on customers and storing it in a computer, using that information to predict how they are likely to buy, and customizing a marketing message to encourage them to do so. Database marketing can allow businesses to tailor their services to the point where each customer can comprise an individual target market. Big companies use database marketing to appear small. Small companies can use it to look big and well organized.

Beginning in 1984, Pizza Hut franchises have entered all of the phone orders they receive into a database, creating profiles of about 9 million customers. Now, each franchise in the chain can use those profiles to get a relevant message to the right customers. For instance, people who usually order thick-crust pizza are mailed coupons for thick-crust pizza. People who order their pizza Sicilian style get a coupon for that. When the company introduced the Big New Yorker, coupons were sent to people willing to try new foods. Customers who have not bought pizza for a while are offered big discounts. As a result of initiating these precision marketing techniques, Pizza Hut's earnings have increased 25 percent.

The cost of database marketing is dropping rapidly. Even a small business on a tight budget can creatively use databases to help individualize its service. For instance, with the purchase of the right computer equipment, a small business can track its own customers over time. Or to create or expand a list of potential customers, the business owner can purchase a database from an existing business in the same industry.

Pizza Hut has expanded its database marketing "across the pond," with data on 650,000 customers in London. Single 20- to 30-year-old Londoners received a packet in the mail containing several paper plates and coupons. The paper plates convey the message that delivery cuts down cooking and clean-up time and that Pizza Hut delivery is a sociable option when friends drop by.

Sources: Adapted from Amy Zuber, "Large Pizza Players Slice Growing Pie," *Nation's Restaurant News,* 28 June 1999, 124–128; "Direct Marketing: Pizza Hut," *Marketing,* 19 November 1998, 7; Susan Greco, "The Road to One-to-One Marketing," *Inc.,* October 1995, 56–66; Jonathan Berry, John Verity, Kathleen Kerwin, and Gail DeGeorge, "DataBase Marketing," *Business Week,* 5 September 1994, 56–62; and Zachary Schiller, "How to Get Close to Your Customers," *Business Week, Enterprise Edition 1993,* 42–45.

absorb daily, and you begin to understand how consumers are bombarded with advertising. An individualized message to segments in need of your product has a better chance of being heard above the noise.

Technology is also allowing us to conduct more individualized marketing by allowing us to track our customers with more precision.

Individualized marketing, if taken to an extreme, could mean treating each person as a separate market (offering different products, different advertising, and different channels to each). Although this may not be practical, technology has made it possible.

A good place for you to start in obtaining specific information about your target market is at the Small Business Administration home page (http://www.sbaonline .sba.gov). Here, under the category of Business Development/General Information and Publications, you'll find a couple of files worth reading. One is called "Knowing Your Market" and the other is "Marketing Strategies for the Growing Business." Each provides basic background information on marketing topics for small business managers and owners.

The Fine Art of Selling Junque

creating competitive advantage

Terry Watanabe, owner of Oriental Trading Company in Omaha, Nebraska, has made his money selling yo-yos, costumes, whoopee cushions, and other outrageous and amusing things. From the company's slick and colorful catalogue, you can purchase four dozen Groucho glasses (with big nose and mustache attached) for $4.80. Or you might settle on 144 two-inch plastic spiders for $1. Watanabe says, "What this company really comes down to is getting a package and opening a box of fun." But as fun as Oriental Trading Company's products might be, it takes its marketing very seriously. It's as sophisticated as a mail-order business can be. The company tracks its 4 million customers by what, when, where, and how much they bought, and mails future catalogues accordingly. For instance, if you ordered a dozen friendship bracelets with a religious saying imprinted on them, you'll get future catalogues with extra pages of religious and inspirational products. Or, if you once bought Oriental's nutty, cheap products but stopped, you'll get a catalogue from Terry's Village, a more expensive giftware catalogue (also part of Oriental Trading Company). Watanabe knows that, in order to provide good service to customers, the company needs to be great at marketing, too.

Sources: John R. Hayes, "Fun by the Gross," *Forbes,* 24 April 1995, 80–84; and Diane Cyr, "High Profits, Low Profile," *Catalog Age,* November 1996, 133–138.

When you're ready for more specific information on markets, check out the Census Bureau's web site (http://www.census.gov). Here you'll find specific information by state and county regarding county business patterns and census information for a specific county. So, as you're researching the viability of a target market, you can check for the number and types of businesses already operating and also the demographic characteristics of that location's population. The Census Bureau is also fine tuning its TIGER map service (http://tiger.census.gov), which provides census maps with street-level detail for the entire United States, counties and states for the entire United States, cartographic design, and many other features. However, be aware that this site can be slow in creating the maps because of the amount of data that must be transmitted.

Understanding Consumer Behavior

Whereas market segmentation and target marketing tell you *who* may buy your products, it is also essential to your small business marketing efforts to understand consumer behavior—*why* those people buy.

Information on consumer behavior comes from several fields, including psychology, sociology, biology, and other professions that try to explain why people do what they do. In running a small business, the behavior we are interested in is why people purchase products. We will start with a stimulus-response model of consumer behavior called the "black box model" (see Figure 11.1). This model is based on the work of psychologist Kurt Lewin, who studied how a person's behavior is determined or affected by the interactions of personal influences, such as inner needs, thoughts, and beliefs, and a variety of external environmental forces.

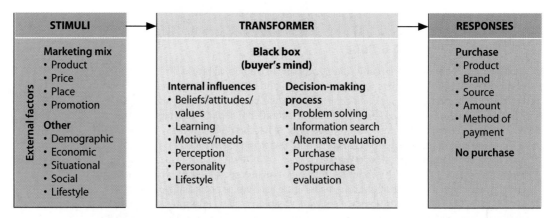

FIGURE 11.1
The Black Box Model of Consumer Behavior

Many internal and external factors influence consumer behavior.

Source: "The Black Box Model of Consumer Behavior," from *Marketing* by Warren Keegan et al. (Prentice Hall, 1992), 193. Reprinted by permission of Sandra Moriarty.

The title "black box" is appropriate because it represents what goes on in the customer's mind that remains hidden from businesspeople. We can see the external factors that go in and the responses that come out, but we can't see the internal influences or the decision-making process.

As a small business owner, closeness to your customers is an advantage in understanding the internal influences that are going on in customers' minds. Their beliefs, attitudes, values, and motives, as well as their perceptions of your products, are critical to your success.

A small business owner needs to be aware of the steps of the mental decision-making process that consumers use in satisfying their needs. We all use them, even if we are not conscious of every step. Most people do not usually buy products just for the sake of buying. What consumers buy is the solution to some problem or need in their lives. *Problem recognition* occurs when we are motivated to reduce a difference between our current and desired states of affairs. For example, consider a young couple expecting their first child, who realize they do not have a way to record events for future memories. They have recognized a problem. Now they begin the second step in the decision-making process: an *information search*. What products exist that can solve the problem identified in the first step? This search will usually lead consumers to read advertising, magazine articles, and ratings like *Consumer Reports*. They also talk with salespeople, friends, and family members to learn more about products that will satisfy their needs.

These information searches usually turn up several possible solutions, which lead the consumer to the third step: an *evaluation of alternatives*. The parents-to-be need a camera to capture little junior for posterity, but the choices of an analogue 35mm (SLR or point-and-shoot), a digital camera, or a camcorder (VHS, compact VHS, or 8mm) leave them with six alternatives to evaluate. As a small business owner, you enter the customers' decision-making process by being in their **evoked set** of brands or businesses that come to mind when considering a purchase. For example, if you need a pair of shoes, how many businesses that sell shoes come to mind quickly? Those stores are your evoked set for shoes. If your business does not come into customers' minds as a possible solution to their problem, you can't sell

evoked set The group of brands or businesses that come to a customer's mind when he or she thinks of a type of product.

Online Marketing

There is a new tool that many small business marketers now need in their toolbox of marketing tricks—creating a professional online catalogue. Thirty-five-year-old Dave Secunda lives in Boulder and, like most Coloradans, loves the outdoors. He wanted to create a specialty outdoors store online. His company PlanetOutdoors.com depends on an online catalogue format.

Secunda knows that online shoppers are savvy. If they see an unprofessional site, they will bolt before the opening screen loads, so he wanted to do his catalogue the right way from the beginning. He has experts from many different sports write product descriptions, he has a fashion photographer capture his product images, and he has a site structure that allows customers to navigate "aisles" by product, sport, or brand.

As with a print catalogue, organization of your online catalogue is critical. Shoppers have to be able to get to what they want quickly (two clicks, tops). Arrange items hierarchically, in well-thought-out categories, with full search capability. Use thumbnail photos of products arranged by category, with a brief description. Supply more detailed descriptions with larger photos when the customer clicks on the thumbnail. If you are selling a product that people are used to touching before purchase (like clothing), provide a close-up, detailed photo.

Secunda makes his catalogue interactive by asking customers to provide product reviews (which he posts) for every item. Whether you do this or not, be sure you don't just create an electronic version of your print catalogue, or you'll miss the features that people expect and the reasons why they shop online.

Another way to increase awareness of your business and enhance your image is to add an e-mail company newsletter to your promotional mix. You want your newsletter to have a consistent look, so that people recognize it as yours. Use a standard template for each issue. Start with your newsletter name, your company name, followed by your name and contact information.

Have regular sections, to make reading and writing easier, like "Expert Tips," "Success Stories," or "How To. . . ." Newsletters can be sent anywhere from every day to once a month. Include a privacy notice to assure receivers that you'll keep their e-mail address private. You can get a privacy statement from the Direct Marketing Association at www.the-dma.org/topframe/index7

How do you know whom to send your newsletter to? Start with your own customer database. From there, get involved with online discussion groups related to your type of product and interests. Most have rules about whether it is appropriate to contribute company newsletters. Also check www.dejanews.com for a searchable list of newsgroups— they exist for every topic imaginable. Commercial services like AOL have chat rooms, from which you can surely find people interested in your business and your professional advice.

Other resources for getting your newsletter online include

Listbot free and listbot gold (www.listbot.com) offer e-mail newsletter distribution. Coollist (www.coollist.com) and onelist (www.onelist.com) are free newsletter mailing list services.

Listserv (www.lsoft.com/listserv.stm) is a list management program.

Online Publishers is a discussion-based newsletter on creating e-mail newsletters. For a free subscription, send an e-mail with the word "subscribe" (without quotation marks) as the body of the message to op-request@listhost.net

Sources: Mark Henricks, "Page Turners," *Entrepreneur's Start-ups,* October 2000, 16; Gisela M. Pedroza, "Do or Die," *Entrepreneur's Start-ups,* October 2000, 17; and Shannon Kinnard, "They've Got Mail," *Entrepreneur's Start-ups,* October 1999, 45–49.

them anything. The purpose of most advertising (including small business advertising) is to get products into a customer's evoked set.

The most attractive alternative usually leads consumers to the fourth step, which is *purchase,* but many factors that you don't know about can alter this decision. For example, the attitudes of other people can influence the purchase decision. If the prospective parents intended to buy a specific camera and learned that friends had trouble with that model, their decision to purchase would probably be changed.

Finally, the *postpurchase evaluation* occurs when the consumer uses the product and decides about his or her level of satisfaction, which will affect your repeat sales. **Cognitive dissonance,** which is the internal conflict we feel after making a decision, is a normal part of the process. If the parents in our example purchased a 35mm SLR camera, you might expect them to later think about the motion and sound that they could have received from a camcorder. As a small business owner, you try to reduce cognitive dissonance with return policies, warranties, and assurance that the customer made the right choice.

cognitive dissonance The remorse that buyers feel after making a major purchase.

Competitive Advantage

If you were forced to condense the description of your business down to *one* thing that is most important; to count on *one* finger what makes you successful; to identify *one* factor that sets your business apart from all other similar businesses, you would recognize your **competitive advantage.**

competitive advantage The facet of a business that it does better than all of its competitors.

Definition of Competitive Advantage

A competitive advantage is the aspect of your business that gives you an edge over your competitors. Your strategic plan (discussed in Chapter 3) helps you to identify and establish a competitive advantage by analyzing different environments, studying your competition, and choosing appropriate strategies. Advantages you have over your competitors could include price, product features and functions, time of delivery (if speed is important to customers), place of business (if being located near customers is needed), and public perception (the positive image your business projects). Remember, a competitive advantage must be sustainable. If competitors can easily copy it, it is not a true competitive advantage.

Three core ideas are valuable in defining your competitive advantage. First, keep in mind that any advantage is relative, not absolute. What matters in customers' minds is not the absolute performance of your product or service, but its performance compared with competing products. For example, no toothpaste can make teeth turn pure white, but you could build an advantage if you developed a toothpaste that gets teeth noticeably whiter than competing toothpastes.

Second, you should strive for multiple types of competitive advantage. Doing more than one thing better than others will increase the chances that you can maintain an advantage over a longer period of time.

Third, remember that areas of competition change over time. Customers' tastes and priorities change as products and processes for making them evolve, as the availability of substitute products changes, and for a variety of other reasons which can affect your competitive advantage. For example, consumers used to compare watches on their ability to keep time accurately. But the introduction of the quartz watch changed customer priorities. The cheapest quartz watch in the display case kept time more accurately than the most expensive mechanical watch, so the differentiating factors for watches are now styles (types of watch faces) and features (built-in calculators, stopwatches, and television remote controls).[12]

> *Competitive advantage must be defined from the customer's perspective. A brand of tight-fitting jeans may prove popular among the young and slim, while losing market share among the not-so-young and not-so-slim.*

Five Basic Forces of Competition

One of the leading researchers and writers on the topic of competitive advantage is Michael Porter, professor at Harvard Business School. Porter identified five basic forces of competition that exist within every industry. Analyzing these forces for your chosen industry can help you determine the attractiveness of the industry and the prospects for earning a return on your investment (see Figure 11.2).

The *degree of rivalry among existing competitors* refers to how passively or aggressively the businesses within an industry compete with one another. If they consistently attack one another, the attractiveness of the industry is reduced because the potential to make a profit is decreased. For example, compare the airline industry, whose strong rivalries produce low profits, with the packaged consumer goods industry, where companies try to attract different groups of customers.

The *threat of new entrants* is a function of how easily other businesses can enter your market, which keeps prices and profits down. If a certain type of food, like Cajun bagels, becomes popular, very little prevents new bakeries from opening or converting to produce this popular item. Low barriers to entry reduce profitability for incumbents.

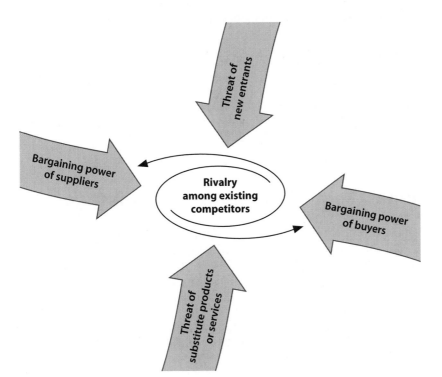

FIGURE 11.2

The Five Forces for Competition

The interplay of competitive forces helps to determine which products and companies succeed in the marketplace—and which don't.

Source: Michael Porter, "Know Your Place," *Inc.,* September 1991, 91. Reprinted from "The Five Forces for Competition" from "Know Your Place" by Porter, *Inc.,* September 1991.

The *bargaining power of suppliers* affects the price you will have to pay to produce your goods. If the supplies in question are commodities carried by several companies, suppliers will have little power to raise the prices they charge. If you only have one or two choices of vendors, or if you require very specialized goods, you may have to pay what the suppliers ask.

The *bargaining power of buyers* affects how much latitude you have in changing your prices. The more choices of substitutes your buyers have, the more power they have to influence your prices or the extent of services you must provide to keep their business.

The *threat of substitute products or services* is determined by the options your customers have when buying your product or service. The greater the number of substitutes available, the more your profit margin can be squeezed. Overnight delivery services must consider the threat of fax machines and e-mail, even though they are entirely different ways to transmit messages.

There are five fatal flaws associated with applying strategic thinking to specific competitive situations.

- *Misreading industry attractiveness.* The highest-tech, highest-glamour, fastest-growing field may not be the best for making a profit because of its attractiveness to competition.

- *Failure to identify a true competitive advantage.* Imitation can put you in the middle of the pack. Being different from competitors is both risky and hard.

- *Pursuing a competitive advantage that is not sustainable.* Porter recommends that, if small businesses cannot sustain an advantage, the owner should view the business as a short-term investment rather than an ongoing enterprise. This business philosophy might be stated as "Get in, grow, and get out."

- *Compromising a strategy in order to grow faster.* If you are fortunate enough to identify a significant competitive advantage, don't give it up in order to become more like your larger competitors. Remember what made you successful in the first place.

- *Not making your strategy explicit or not communicating it to your employees.* Writing your strategy down and discussing it with your key people sets up an atmosphere for everyone in your organization to move toward a common goal. Each of your employees makes decisions every day. If your overall strategy is to offer products at the lowest possible cost, decisions by everyone in your business need to reinforce that goal.[13]

Importance of Competitive Advantage

Having a competitive advantage is critical: Your business must do *something* better than others or it is not needed. In order to cope with a quickly changing competitive environment, small businesses need to be market driven.[14] Part of becoming market driven includes closely monitoring changing customer wants and needs, determining how those changes affect customer satisfaction, and developing strategies to gain an edge.

Competitive advantage as a core of small business strategy is critical because small businesses cannot rely on the inertia of the marketplace for their survival.[15]

Point, Click, and Drag a Can of Pork 'n Beans

Peapod Grocery was way ahead of the curve (and the competition) when it came to selling groceries via nontraditional means. Back in 1989, Peapod started as a phone and fax service, selling perishable and nonperishable groceries. Although it started in the Chicago area, it has expanded to eight U.S. metropolitan areas. Peapod offers same-day delivery for all types of grocery items and has extended lines into books, CDs, and software. Members pay a monthly fee and between 10 and 12 percent for delivery, depending on distance and amount of the total order.

Peapod was onto a big idea—it was the hottest thing in the grocery business since sliced bread. Sales grew to $70 million by fiscal year 1999. Although that staggering total represents only 2 percent of the total U.S. packaged goods retail market, it's a figure that brick-and-mortar grocery chains cannot ignore. A survey by Peapod shows that consumers rank grocery shopping as the chore they dislike most—with one exception: going to the dentist.

Seventy million in annual sales. But that was then. It lost $19 million in the first nine months of fiscal year 2000 and found itself fighting for survival. Peapod became synonymous with the dot-com downturn. Once Peapod was one of the hottest names on the web, then it had to be financially resuscitated by Dutch-owned Royal Ahold for $73 million and a 51 percent equity position.

Peapod paid extreme attention to the convenience of its web site. It tries to make ten improvements every quarter based on customer feedback. Customers choose from two links at the home page—one for members and one for new users—to get a feel and to browse the virtual aisles. No personal or payment information is requested until the first delivery is scheduled. Members skip preliminary steps and can even begin with a customized grocery list of regularly purchased items already in their cart. A running list and total are kept on a side window. Shoppers can click buttons to find an item, browse aisles, or view previous orders.

Peapod estimates that customers spend about 45 minutes shopping online compared with an hour at supermarkets. The average member buys $1,750 of groceries per year, but heavy users top $4,500. Of Peapod's 100,000 members, 20 percent are heavy users and account for half of its annual sales

Peapod's problems do not appear to be an indictment of all online grocers. They save customers time, but there just have not been enough customers to make the economy of scale work. Profitability comes down to making the math work. A 100,000-square-foot facility must generate $150 million annually, and none of the existing online grocers has figured out a way to pull that off. The key for now is to concentrate on urban areas, where you have population density, bringing less urban areas (with less density) online.

Peapod's story illustrates the importance of efficiency in new business models, even in a "new economy." Can it make its new model work?

Sources: Sami Lais, "Peapod Online Grocer Is Wilting," *Computerworld*, 27 March 2000, 46; "Grocery Sites Hungry for Prospects," *DSN Retailing Today,* 8 May 2000, 118; David Jastrow, "Reviving the Web Grocery," *Computer Reseller News,* 8 May 2000, 45–48; Cole Corbin, "Peapod's Peril Offers Lessons for Foodservice B2B Hopefuls," *Nation's Restaurant News,* 10 April 2000, 24; Tony Lisanti, "For a Lesson in E-tailing, Turn to Yahoo, Not Peapod," *DSN Retailing Today,* 17 April 2000, 13; Cecile Corral, "On-line Grocery Shopping Heats up Despite Concern over Big Issues," *Discount Store News,* 12 July 1999, 18–20; Barry Janoff, "Point, Click, Shop," *Progressive Grocer,* June 1999, 31–34; and Barbara Marsh, "Peapod's On-Line Grocery Service Checks Out Success," *Wall Street Journal,* 30 June 1994, B2.

When running a small business, you cannot solve problems by throwing money at them—you need to see your competitive environment with crystal clarity, then identify and secure a position you can defend.

In developing your competitive advantage, you will make decisions under conditions of uncertainty. This is the art, rather than the science, of marketing decision making. In his book *Marketing Mistakes,* Robert Hartley notes that we can seldom predict with any exactitude the reactions of consumers or the countermoves and retaliations of competitors.[16]

Although it may be easy to play Monday morning quarterback, or view mistakes with 20:20 hindsight, we can learn lessons from others' mistakes, especially when looking for a competitive advantage. It seems safe to say that no one ever set out to design a bad product or start a business that would fail. But what seems to be a good idea for a competitive advantage often may not be, for one reason or another.

The lack, or loss, of competitive advantage exists in every size of business. Apple Computer, which began small, has fought to maintain the competitive advantage of ease of use. In 1983, Apple tried to break into the business market for personal computers with the Lisa. Although that computer was easy to use and had nice graphics, its advantages were not noticed by the business community because of its limited software and expensive price tag ($10,000).[17] Similar problems (performance below customer expectations and high price) plagued Apple's Newton MessagePad when it came out in 1993. Occasionally, competitive advantages are gained well after a product is introduced. For instance, the unsuccessful Lisa evolved into the Macintosh, one of the world's most popular models.

In the late 1970s and early 1980s, videodisks tried to break into the fledgling videocassette market. Videocassettes quickly won the battle in the marketplace for one simple reason: their advantage of being able to record programs, even though recording accounts for a small percentage of VCR use.[18]

Just being the first product in the market may be all the competitive advantage that you need. Despite the advantages of being quicker and easier to use, the Dvorak keyboard has not made a dent in the traditional "QWERTY" keyboard market for typewriters and computers. The reason? Once people learn to type in one layout, they don't want to relearn how to type—even on a better keyboard.[19]

The list of products and businesses that have failed to gain a competitive advantage is long and distinguished. Entrants include Ford's Edsel (a car with lots of innovations—and lots more problems), DuPont's Corfam (synthetic leather), Nutrasweet's Simplesse (edible fat substitute), and R. J. Reynolds's Premier (cigarettes that didn't burn or smoke).[20]

Benefits of Competitive Advantage

Gaining a competitive advantage can help you establish a self-sustaining position in the marketplace. Whether your edge comes from external factors, such as luck or the failure of a competitor, or internal factors, such as exceptional skills or superior resources, it can set up a cycle of success (see Figure 11.3).[21]

Because of your competitive advantage, your customers will be more satisfied with your business than with your competitors'. You will therefore gain market share. Increased market share translates into larger sales and profits, which in turn give you more resources for improving your products, facilities, and human resources—all of which allow you to improve your competitive advantage. Businesses

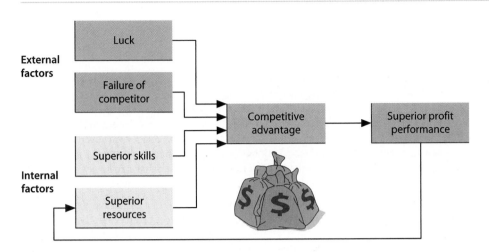

FIGURE 11.3
Competitive Advantage Cycle

However it is created, a competitive advantage will increase your profit margins, providing more resources for your small business to use to strengthen itself.

Source: "Competitive Advantage Cycle", from *Competitive Marketing Strategy,* Czepiel. Copyright ©1992. Reprinted by permission of Pearson Education, Inc.

that don't gain competitive advantage, therefore, lose out in this cycle. Their customers receive less value and are less satisfied. Their market share, sales volume, and profit fall. Without profits, they have fewer resources to reinvest in the business, so positioning is difficult to maintain. The gap between follower and leader grows wider.

How to Create Competitive Advantage

Three generic competitive strategies exist through which a business can gain a competitive advantage: lower cost, differentiation, and focus strategies.[22] Focus strategies mean aiming at a narrow segment of a market. By definition, all small businesses concentrate on niches or narrow market segments, so let's concentrate on the first two strategies.

You must find a way to lower costs if you intend to compete primarily on price. If you try to compete on price without obtaining a cost advantage, you are headed for trouble. This advantage can come from reduced labor costs, less expensive raw materials or supplies, more efficient distribution, or any number of other factors.

A competitive advantage based on differentiation means that your product or service is different from your competitors'. Its value is that you can show customers why your difference is *better,* not just cheaper. In this way, differentiation can effectively remove direct competition. For example, when a mass merchandiser like Walmart or Target enters a town, small retailers are not necessarily run out of business. Studies that measure the impact of Walmart on local retailers in Iowa have shown that, as long as the small retail stores stock different merchandise than Walmart, they actually benefit due to the increased number of shoppers coming into town. Small stores have to differentiate rather than try to compete head to head against the giants.[23]

An advantage does not have to be in the product itself. It can come from anything your business does—including distribution. In his autobiography *Iacocca,* Lee Iacocca stated, "The company with the best distribution system and the best service will win all the marbles—because you can't keep an advantage in other areas for long."[24]

Competing on Intangibles

Many businesses operating in today's information age are built on intangible services and assets, such as expertise in gathering, analyzing, and transmitting information. The competitive advantages of businesses that work in intangibles are inherently different from those of producers of tangible goods like automobiles, furniture, or typewriters. A few decades ago, when U.S. businesses were concerned primarily with manufacturing products, such advantages were easy to quantify. The success factors for businesses to compete in the twenty-first century are difficult (or impossible) to quantify, but just as important to have. Following are examples of ways for information-based businesses to create competitive advantages:

- *Generate passion.* A recent study showed that only 23 percent of U.S. workers surveyed were currently working to their full potential. About 44 percent stated that they put out only enough effort to keep their job. Three-fourths said they could do their job significantly more effectively than they do now. Think of the effect of these attitudes on productivity. What can you do to build a bond between your business and your employees, so that they care about what happens to the business and your customers? An orientation toward long-term outcomes rather than short-term actions is a start. Giving people a reason to feel pride in their work, that they are making a real contribution, and that the results of their efforts matter shows employees that they are important.

- *Constantly reinvent yourself.* If you want the people in your company to be innovative, you have to reward new ideas, rather than stifle them with politics and protocol. Creativity is important in maintaining a sustainable competitive advantage—and it must be nurtured. You will encourage more ideas by looking for the good in them rather than automatically shooting them down.

- *Build concentration and focus.* Everyone in your business should know the direction and priorities of your business. If your people don't know the mission of your business, don't expect them to be passionate enough about the company to make personal sacrifices when needed.

- *Devote yourself to service excellence.* Traditional accounting systems do not show the true costs or benefits of long-term customer relations that are developed through providing excellent service. For example, they do not show the cumulative cash flows that you build by doing business with the same customer over a long period of time. Each sale is not an isolated event; it is an investment in future business. You can develop a competitive advantage by treating customers well to encourage future business.

- *Adapt to change.* Rapidly increasing changes at work and home mean that advantages can be quickly lost without the ability to adapt. Change needs to become part of your and your employees' mind set. Be prepared to adjust your product offerings, the services you provide, or your organizational structure to take advantage of new opportunities.

Source: From "The Age of Intangibles" by Martha H. Peak. Copyright (c) 1994 by American Management Association (J). Reproduced with permission of American Management Association in the format textbook via Copyright Clearance Center.

To create a sustainable competitive advantage, your strategy needs a combination of methods to continuously differentiate your product and to improve it in areas that make a meaningful difference to your customers.[25] But how can you keep up with the changing tastes and preferences of your customers? There are so many questions about your customers you must try to answer. The products and services that people like and dislike at any particular time are shaped by hundreds of influences, many of which can't be identified. You need to gather facts about your markets in an objective and orderly manner. Market research is a way to answer questions about your customers' changing wants and needs, to help you create and hold onto your competitive advantage.

Small businesses can also find it difficult to compete against foreign competition, particularly when it comes to sales price. However, by developing a competitive advantage based on a variable other than price, you can overcome even this challenge. Take, for instance, Lyon's Designs of Salt Lake City, Utah, which designs, manufactures, and sells gifts and novelties. The retail gift industry is fickle and tricky to compete in. To survive, suppliers must constantly provide new designs at attractive prices. Paul Lyon, founder and owner of Lyon's Designs, knew that he couldn't compete with Taiwanese designers and manufacturers on price. It made more sense for him to work closely with foreign suppliers than to compete head on, so he decided to establish a close manufacturing relationship with a limited number of factory owners in the Far East. Most of Lyon's Designs' products now come from this region. To further cement his company's relationships, Lyon invited two Taiwanese factory owners to go camping in the Utah mountains. (When he asked a third Taiwanese to visit the United States, the man accepted but said, "Promise you won't take me camping!") Through its owner's ingenuity, Lyon's Designs has created a competitive advantage based on its global manufacturing relationships.[26]

Market Research ▬

One of the major advantages that small businesses have over large businesses is close customer contact. Although this closeness can help you maintain your competitive advantage, you will also need a certain amount of ongoing **market research** to stay closely tuned to your market. If you are starting a new business, you will need market research even more.

market research The process of gathering information that will link consumers to marketers in order to improve marketing efforts.

"Business is lousy. Maybe I should have done more market research first."

© 1997 Randy Glasbergen www.glasbergen.com

The American Marketing Association (AMA) defines market research as the function that links the consumer, customer, and public to the marketer through information. That information can be used to identify and define marketing opportunities and problems; to generate, refine, and evaluate marketing actions; to monitor marketing performance; and to improve understanding of marketing as a process.[27]

Not all market research conducted by small businesses is formal and intense. Most small business owners want to get information as quickly and as inexpensively as possible (see Figure 11.4). One survey showed that most spend between one and six months and less than $1,000 conducting market research on the last product or service they launched.

Market research can be as simple as trash and peanuts—literally. Owners of small restaurants often inspect outgoing waste to see what customers leave on their plates uneaten. Why? Because customers may order a dish like crayfish and pineapple pizza for the novelty, but if most don't actually eat it, it should be taken off the menu. One creative discount merchant conducted an in-store market research project using peanuts. During a three-day promotion, customers were given all the roasted peanuts in a shell they could eat while in the store. At the end of each day, the empty hulls on the floor provided information about traffic patterns of people moving through the store. Piles of shells in front of displays showed the merchandise that was attracting particular interest.[28]

This is one large factor for an increase in the amount of time and money small businesses should spend on market research: changing conditions. Because many markets and demographics change quickly, the businesses that emerge as winners are those that are *proactive* rather than *reactive*. Market research can give you information on what your customers are going to want as opposed to historical data that tell you what they used to want.

Small business owners who have been in business for more than, say, two days have learned two things about market research—they need it, and it's expensive. An in-depth survey constructed, administered, and analyzed by a professional market research firm can easily cost $40,000 to $50,000. Denver-based Market Perceptions does those, but it has also created an alternative for small business clients.

> *One creative merchant conducted a secret marketing survey by giving his customers roasted peanuts. The piles of empty hulls on the floor showed him how people had moved through the store—and which displays had attracted the most attention.*

FIGURE 11.4

Market Research Expenditures

Small businesses often spend less than $5,000 and less than six months gathering market research for new products.

Sources: Survey of 173 CEOs, 57 percent from companies with sales of $10 million or less, by *Inc.* and The Executive Committee, San Diego, 1992; and Susan Greco, "Sales & Marketing," *Inc.*, July 1992, 118.

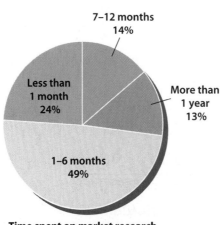

Time spent on market research before launching most recent new product or service

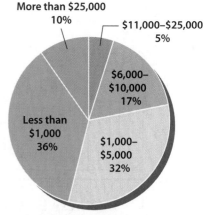

Out-of-pocket money spent on market research

Market Perceptions allows small businesses to participate in a "shared survey" called the Colorado Opinion Tracker. It runs a monthly poll of 500 people and, for a fee, a small business owner can add his or her own questions. Two questions cost $1,250, with $500 for each additional question. Small business owners get a 15 percent discount if questions need to run for more than one month. In addition to the small business owners' questions, Market Perceptions collects demographic information like age, gender, and residence to use as independent variables.

Fantastic Foods, of Petaluma, California, used ten questions in the Colorado Opinion Tracker to learn about Colorado eating habits and attitudes toward vegetarian meals. With this benchmark, they built a promotion encouraging people in the metropolitan Denver and Los Angeles areas to eat one vegetarian meal per week.

Now, at least in Colorado, small businesses can get the information they need at a price they can afford. Does a market research firm in your area conduct omnibus surveys?[29]

The Market Research Process

The market research process follows five basic steps: identifying the problem, developing a plan, collecting the data, analyzing the data, and drawing conclusions (see Figure 11.5).

IDENTIFY THE PROBLEM. The most difficult and most important part of the market research process is the first step—identifying the problem. You must have a clearly stated, concisely worded problem in order to generate usable information. Many people (novice and experienced researchers alike) have trouble with this step because they confuse problems with symptoms. If there is an underlying reason for what you have identified, it is a symptom and not the problem itself.

For example, if you go to a physician complaining of a fever, the physician could prescribe medication that would bring your fever down. But that would not cure you. There is an infection or other problem that is causing your fever to be high. Your physician will search until the problem is found and then fix it—not just mask the symptom. Would declining sales in your small business be a problem or a symptom? A drop in your sales revenue would be like the fever—it is a symptom.

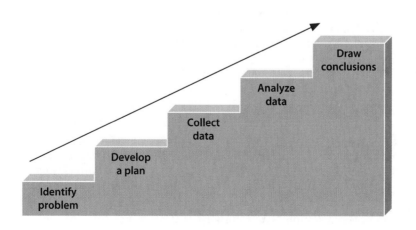

FIGURE 11.5

Market Research Process

Conducting research on your markets involves a logical five-step process.

Although the symptom itself is not pleasant to experience, there is an underlying reason causing it to occur. That is what you would want to try to uncover with your research. Has the competition increased? Do your salespeople need retraining? Have your customers' tastes changed?

Your marketing problem does not always have to be something that is wrong. You can use market research to find real problems or to identify new opportunities. Whatever your goal, your ability to complete this first step of the research process is important in guiding the rest of your research efforts.

PLANNING MARKET RESEARCH. Market research is often expensive, but a plan of how you will conduct your research project can help keep costs down. Before you start, you must separate what is "critical to know" from what would be "nice to know." Your next step is to design a way to address the problem or answer the question that you have identified concerning your business. You can do it yourself, and you should keep it as simple as possible.

In planning your market research project you need to

- Identify the types of information that you need.

- Identify primary and secondary sources of data.

- Select a sample that represents the population you are studying.

- Select a research method and measurement technique (phone survey, focus group, and so on) to answer your research question.

In conducting market research for your small business, you should choose a method that provides enough reliable data for you to make a decision with confidence. The method you choose must also use your limited time, money, and personnel efficiently.

COLLECTING DATA. After you have identified the research problem and laid out a plan, you are ready to gather data. Although it sounds simple, don't get this order reversed. A common research error is to begin the process by gathering data and then trying to figure out what the information means and where to go with it— putting the cart before the horse. Determine what you need, then go get it. There are two basic types of data you may seek: secondary and primary.[30]

secondary data Marketing data that have been gathered, tabulated, and made available by an outside source.

Secondary data are those that already exist, having been gathered for some other purpose. You should check secondary sources first, because they are less expensive than conducting your own study. You may be able to solve your problem without an extended primary search.

The good news about secondary data is that the amount of available data is considerable. The bad news, however, is that that mountain of information can be overwhelming.

A good place to begin your search of secondary data is your local library. Online databases like Lexis-Nexis or ABI-INFORM allow you to enter key terms into the program and immediately receive titles, abstracts, and entire articles from journals and periodicals. The *Government Printing Office Monthly Catalog* contains report references from many government agencies, such as the Department of Commerce and the Small Business Administration, which may help you. The Department of Commerce also publishes *Selected Publications to Aid Business and Industry.* Check the *Encyclopedia of Associations* for the thousands of trade, professional, technical, and industrial associations that exist. These associations compile information that can be very relevant to your business.

You can get data on your personal computer from online computer services such as Dun & Bradstreet's home page, Yahoo!, or Dow Jones, publisher of the *Wall Street Journal,* which offers Dow Jones News/Retrieval®. This service can help you scan the newspaper's daily Enterprise column, which is devoted to topics on small business. The SBA provides 24-hour access to information on services it provides, publications, training, trade fairs, and other programs, through its electronic bulletin board *SBA On-line* at sba.gov

If you have an aversion to libraries or a computer phobia, there is an alternative to aid your research. *Information brokers* are companies that are expert gatherers of competitive information.[31] Rates and specialties of these businesses vary. To find an information broker near you, contact the Association of Independent Information Professionals (AIIP) or the *Burkwell Directory of Information Brokers.*[32]

Potential problems with secondary data are that they may not be specific or detailed enough for your purpose or that they may be obsolete. In either case, you will need to gather your own primary data.

Primary data are qualitative or quantitative data that you collect yourself for your specific purpose. Both types of data have their advocates and critics, but either type can provide valuable information if collected and analyzed correctly.

primary data Marketing data that a business collects for its own specific purposes.

Qualitative data refer to research findings that cannot be analyzed statistically. Qualitative data are useful if you are looking for open-minded responses to probing questions, not yes-or-no answers.[33] These can be obtained through personal interviews or focus groups (groups of six to ten people), which provide considerable depth of information from each person. Qualitative data do not lend themselves to statistical analysis. They help you look for trends in answers or obtain specific or detailed responses to your questions.

Quantitative data are structured to analyze and report numbers, to help you see relationships between variables and frequency of occurrences. Quantitative data are useful in providing information on large groups of people. Their less-probing questions yield results that can be analyzed statistically to show causation.

Telephone interviews, personal interviews, and mail surveys are common methods small businesses use to gather both types of primary data. Because the questionnaire is such a common small business research tool, the following advice is offered to increase its usefulness and the readers' response rate:

- Try to make the questionnaire visually attractive and fun to answer. This will help keep it from ending up in the recipient's wastebasket.

- Try to structure possible responses. Instead of asking, "What do you think of our product?" list answers like reliability, quality, and price for respondents to check off.

- Don't ask for more than most people remember. Annoying questions, like asking for the number of light bulbs a business uses in a year, can end the response.

- Don't have more than 20 words per question. People lose interest quickly if questions are too long.

- Be as specific and unambiguous as possible.

- Include a cover letter explaining the reason for the questionnaire. Say "thank you."

- Include a self-addressed, stamped return envelope to increase the response rate.

- Include a return date. A reasonable deadline will increase the number of responses and will let you know how long to wait before tallying the results.[34]

Other techniques of primary data collection for small businesses are limited only by your imagination. The automobile license plates of many states show the county where the vehicle is registered. You can get an idea of where your customers live by taking note of the license plates in your parking lot. This information can help you determine where to aim your advertising. You can use the same technique by spending some time in your competitors' parking lots. Telephone numbers can also tell you where customers live. You can get this information from sales slips, credit slips, or checks.

By running "lucky draw" contests, you can get a lot of information about your customers. Have customers fill out cards with name and address to win a prize if their name is drawn from the box. You can plot these addresses on a local map to see your trade area for the price of a small giveaway prize.[35]

Advertisements that provide coded coupons or phrases in your broadcast advertising that customers can use to get a discount can help you determine the effectiveness and reach of your ads.

DATA ANALYSIS. Basically, data analysis is the process of determining what the responses to your research mean. Once data have been collected, they must be analyzed and translated into usable information. Your first step is to clean the data. This includes removing all questionnaires or other forms that are unusable because they are incomplete or unreadable. Depending on the instrument or methodology used to gather data, you need to code and examine the data to identify trends and develop insights. (An exhaustive description of data analysis is not appropriate for this text. For details of this process, refer to a source such as a market research text.)

If you collected quantitative data, several software programs exist to aid you in number crunching and transforming data into charts and graphs to make interpretation easier.

PRESENTING THE DATA AND MAKING DECISIONS. Market research that does not lead to some type of action is useless. Your research needs to aid you in making management decisions. Should you expand into a new geographic area? Should you change your product line? Should you change your business hours?

Conclusions based on your data analysis may be obvious. Data may fall out in such a way that you can see exactly what you need to do next to answer the research problem identified in step 1.

Market research can provide you with information that will allow you to be proactive. This is important because, as a small business owner, deciding what you need to do in the future is much more important than knowing what has happened in the past.

Limitations of Market Research

As important as market research can be for small businesses, it should be used with caution. Market research can provide you with a picture of what people currently know and expect from products or services, but it has limited ability to indicate what people will want in the future. Relying on market research exclusively for your marketing strategy and new product ideas is like driving a car while watching only the rear-view mirror.[36]

As noted in Chapter 1, small businesses provide many of the most innovative products that we use. Our economy and consumers depend on a stream of such innovations as fax machines, CD-ROMs, and minivans, but innovation does not

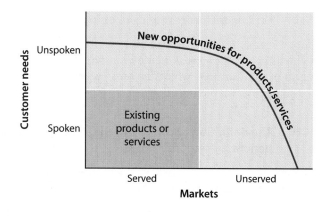

FIGURE 11.6

Matrix of Customer Needs and Types

Market research is most effective when used to evaluate existing products that satisfy known needs that customers can talk about.

Source: Material adapted from "Seeing the Future First," Hameland and Prahaled, from *Competing for the Future.* Copyright ©1994 by the Harvard Business School Publishing Corporation. All rights reserved.

come from market research. Peter Drucker notes that, although the fax machine was designed and developed by U.S. companies, no U.S. companies began producing fax machines for domestic consumption because market research indicated that there would be no demand for such a product.

When asking about a product that does not yet exist, Drucker says that all you can do is ask people, "Would you buy a telephone accessory that costs upwards of $1,500 and enables you to send, for one dollar a page, the same letter the post office delivers for 25 cents?" The average consumer would predictably say "no."[37] Hal Sperlich designed the concept of the minivan while he was working for Ford, but when Ford didn't believe a market existed for such a vehicle (based on its historical market research), he switched to Chrysler. Sperlich says, "In ten years of developing the minivan, we never once got a letter from a housewife asking us to invent one." To the skeptics, that proved there wasn't a market out there.[38]

Although market research is good for fine-tuning concepts for known products, customers don't have the foresight to ask for what they don't know about or don't know they need. As one axis of Figure 11.6 shows, there are two types of customer needs: those that they can tell you about and those that they have without realizing they have them. How many people were asking for cellular telephones, MTV, or compact disk players ten years ago? The other axis of Figure 11.6 shows that there are two types of markets or customers for any given business: those served by the company's existing products and those not yet served—the company's potential customers. Market research can tell us the most about the spoken needs of a served market, but there is a lot of room for growth in exploring the three other sectors. When you are driving a car, you need to check the rear-view mirror occasionally, just as you should check your current and past markets with market research. But the ideal is to concentrate on defining markets rather than reacting to them. An entrepreneur must go beyond what market research can tell.

> *"In ten years of developing the minivan, we never once got a letter from a housewife asking us to invent one."*

SUMMARY

▬▬▬ Describe the importance of marketing to small businesses.

Marketing involves all the points of contact between your small business and your customers. Marketing is how you find out what they want and need; it is how they are treated by you and everyone in your business; it is how you communicate with them through selling and advertising. What could be more important?

Explain the process of developing a small business marketing strategy.

Market segmentation is needed because no business can be everything to everyone. Segmenting involves breaking down a population into target markets that have a common want or need which the business can satisfy. Target markets are the focus of a company's marketing efforts.

The definition of competitive advantage, as well as its importance and benefits.

A competitive advantage is what a business does better than all of its competitors. It can be built on any facet of a business, including price, location of the business, product features, or customer perception of the business. A competitive advantage must be sustainable. Competitive advantages are relative, not absolute. Having more than one base for your competitive advantage increases your chances for success. Bases for competition, along with customer tastes and preferences, change over time.

If a business does not have a competitive advantage—if it does not do something better than competitors—that business is not needed and will not survive. Having a competitive advantage can set up a self-sustaining cycle of success, in which higher profit margins are generated that can provide you with superior resources and allow you to increase your competitive advantage. A business can build a competitive advantage by using a low-cost, a differentiation, or a focus strategy. The only way for a business to successfully compete on price is to adopt a low-cost strategy. Differentiation builds competitive advantage by showing customers important differences, benefits, and product uses among competing products. Differentiation is the way businesses avoid competing on price alone. Focus strategies involve concentrating on narrow segments of a market, which provides an advantage for all small businesses.

The purpose of the market research process and the steps involved in putting it into practice.

Market research provides information about the people who are buying the products of a business. Conditions change, and the owner of a business must know about those changes in order to be proactive and maintain a competitive advantage. The steps of the market research process include problem identification, development of a plan, data collection, data analysis, and drawing conclusions. Market research can provide valuable information regarding people's current tastes, preferences, and expectations. It is useful in fine-tuning products that already exist for markets that are already known. Market research is of limited use for markets that do not exist yet or for needs that customers do not realize they have.

QUESTIONS FOR REVIEW & DISCUSSION

1. Why is competitive advantage such an important concept for the small business owner to understand? Define competitive advantage and how it relates to the strategic plan for the business.

2. Explain Porter's concept of the forces of competition. What does Porter mean when he says that small businesses can't rely on the inertia of the marketplace? Why is that important?

3. Define and elaborate on the five fatal flaws that can occur when strategic thinking is applied to specific competitive situations.

4. How does the entrepreneur create competitive advantage, and how is it measured?

5. The lack or loss of competitive advantage is not limited to small businesses. Elaborate on some failures that have been produced by large corporations. Give your opinion as to why the products failed to gain a competitive advantage.

6. What is the significance of market research to the small business owner? How is market research defined, and what degree of complexity is necessary in the research plan for it to be valid?

7. Explain the market research process from a small business owner's perspective when he or she is trying to assess competitive advantage.

8. What types of data should be collected and analyzed in order to get a clear picture of the market for the good or service being produced?

9. Name some sources of information that are valuable to the entrepreneur who is designing a market research plan to analyze competitive advantage.

10. What are some of the limitations of the process of market research? What can the entrepreneur do to offset these limitations?

QUESTIONS FOR **CRITICAL THINKING**

1. Segmentation is the process of breaking a population down into smaller groups to market to. Is it possible for a small business to oversegment? How would that be dangerous?

2. What do you think is the biggest limitation for small businesses conducting market research?

You decide that you need to create a survey to get customer feedback on a new product you have developed, when you realize, "Oh, no! I've never created and administered a real survey before!" Go to your favorite search engine and conduct a search for "small business" and "market research." From your findings, create a bullet-point list of 10 factors you should keep in mind when writing survey questions.

Experience
this...

WHAT WOULD **YOU** DO?	No. 1

Market research is an important tool for small business owners and managers. Knowing what to ask and how to ask it are important skills. The three businesses described here all need help in terms of performing market research. Read through the scenarios and then answer the questions.

Vitalink.   During the late 1980s, the federal government proposed more stringent controls of drugs in nursing homes. Sensing an opportunity, Donna DeNardo established Vitalink to provide this service. She describes her company as "basically a hospital pharmacy, but we're not in the hospital basement." The company provides drugs and record-keeping services to nursing homes. As the population of the United States continues to age, you'd think that Vitalink's revenues would be increasing. However, revenues have not increased as fast as DeNardo would like. She'd like to find out possible reasons for this situation.

Klutz Press.   This company isn't anything like its name implies. Klutz Press is a successful publisher of interactive multimedia children's books, covering diverse topics from clay modeling to knot tying to map reading. The company has published 45 titles and sells nearly 5 million books a year to the tune of $25 million. Its books are unique because, in addition to their durable cardboard pages, they are accompanied by "equipment" that lets readers experience what they read. For instance, the company's *Braids and Bows* book comes with the hair ribbons and ties to actually make braids and bows. The *Cat's Cradle* book comes with a tie-dyed loop of string, so that kids can try out the string figures illustrated in the book. But Klutz Press wants to expand into Europe. Market research could help answer its questions about that move.

Westec Security.   Westec Security Inc. is one of the largest full-service security firms in the United States, with more than 60,000 monitored clients and revenues of around $80 million. The company provides clients with an in-house security system and employees who patrol clients' neighborhoods. Because excellent service is extremely important for getting and keeping customers in this type of industry, Westec wants to survey its customers to get their feedback about the service being provided.

Sources: Nancy Rotenier, "Drug Runner," *Forbes*, 23 October 1995, 332; Steven B. Kaufman, "A 'Klutz' Who Knows Kids," *Nation's Business*, May 1995, 14–15; and Thomas Rollins and Dennis Buster, "Westec Guards Its Competitive Edge," *Personnel Journal*, August 1995, 84–88.

QUESTIONS

1. Select one of the three businesses described. State what you think the research problem is. Then develop five survey questions that you think would help answer the question posed in the research problem.

2. Divide into student groups with others in the class who selected the same business you did. (Aim for five to eight people per group.) After discussing your proposed research problems, select the five survey questions that you think would best answer the research problem. Be prepared to present your group's work to the class.

The bigger and stronger the competition is, the better a small business's marketing strategy needs to be. In that case, Amilya Antonetti may need *your* help with a marketing strategy. Antonetti is starting a business to break into the $4.7 billion U.S. laundry detergent market, competing directly with the likes of Procter & Gamble. The niche of the detergent market that she is filling is hypoallergenic cleaning products, because her infant son had health problems aggravated by chemicals in standard brands. She started her company SoapWorks after conducting market research, primarily from other mothers of infants, and finding that many other families faced similar problems. Her annual advertising budget is limited to $60,000 (about what her huge competitors spend on one 30-second prime-time network TV ad), so she had to find different ways to let people know what SoapWorks would do for them.

Source: D. M. Osborne, "Taking on Procter & Gamble," *Inc.*, October 2000, 66–73.

QUESTIONS

1. If you were in Amilya Antonetti's place starting SoapWorks, what marketing strategy would you use to compete with Procter & Gamble and Clorox? How would you reach your target markets? How and where would you advertise? We talk about the power of word of mouth among our customers—how do you use it to your advantage as a small business marketer?

2. One of the biggest challenges SoapWorks faced was getting its products on the shelves of grocery stores. By 1999, they were in 2,500 stores from California to Florida with revenues of $5 million. How would you create such market penetration?

CHAPTER CLOSING CASE   No. 11

Computers for the Blind

Situation Summary   Dr. Roman Gouzman and Dr. Igor Karasin, both entrepreneurs, had developed a system to enable blind people to use a computer to feel representations, including maps and fine art. They called their innovation the Virtual Touch System for the blind, and they applied to the U.S. Patent Office for a patent. The patent was issued in June 1999. The commercialization of the invention, however, was quite complex.

The Firm   VirTouch Ltd. was created by Gouzman and Karasin in 1996 to market their Virtual Touch System. The firm was established in the framework of the Jerusalem Software Incubator, and in 1998 VirTouch became a full-fledged high-tech new venture. It built its reputation as a beta-site (testing ground) for Microsoft technology development. In Jerusalem, the capital city of Israel, the Chief Scientist of the Israel Ministry of Industry and Trade approved the firm to operate in Israel.

The Environment for Enterprise in Israel   With more than 80 venture capital firms in Israel, finance is seldom a problem. Furthermore, special financial incentives are available for firms that contribute to employment or exports.

The state offers tax-free investment grants, and a variety of research-and-development (R&D) grants. Among these are R&D grants for the development of innovative products (50 percent of approved expenditures) and R&D grants for new ventures (66 percent of approved expenditures). In addition, assistance is available to train employees and to reduce the cost of rent. The government also provides market research grants and subsidies toward the preparation of business plans. The Marketing Encouragement Fund, for instance, gives financial support to enterprises seeking to enlarge their international marketing efforts.

Complementing the many grants, loans are also readily available. There are several loan funds in Israel, totaling $150 million. These include government, philanthropic, and private loan funds.

Israel is the only country to have free trade agreements with Canada, the European Union, Turkey, and the United States. On March 6, 2000, Israel signed a free trade agreement with Mexico. Israel also has preferential customs agreements and agreements avoiding double taxation with other countries.

The Product   The Virtual Touch System includes a device that functions as a tactile display and provides resolution close to the maximum limit of a finger's perception. Three dimensions also allow for the representation of colors. The system displays Braille and easy-to-feel Latin characters.

The system helps develop spatial awareness and related motor skills. The user can navigate the cursor to transform images, caption illustrations, and play computer games. For the blind it makes possible career options in virtual arts as well as computer science.

The Virtual Touch System includes educational materials to teach algebra, astronomy, chemistry, geography, and geometry. A special program allows the user to learn specific routes (e.g., how to walk from home to the post office).

The Market   The Virtual Touch System was introduced at the July 1998 National Federation of the Blind Convention in Dallas, Texas. Later that year, the system was demonstrated at a convention in Minneapolis, Minnesota, and in 1999 at California State University. Potential users expressed enthusiasm for the system and prospects for sales seemed promising.

Furthermore, there was a large potential market for the system. There were 17 million visually impaired people in the industrialized world. In the United States, half a million of these were already computer users. It was felt that a large demand could arise for the Virtual Touch System worldwide.

Just as Louis Braille introduced in 1829 a tactile system of reading and writing for the blind, the inventors of the Virtual Touch System intended to open the computer graphic world to the visually impaired, enhancing the spatial awareness of users.

Source: Leo Paul Dana (University of Canterbury) and Joan Winn (University of Denver). Reprinted by permission of the authors. To read the entire case, visit the *Small Business Management: Entrepreneurship and Beyond* website at http://business.college.hmco.com/students.

QUESTIONS

1. Serve as consultant for the Virtual Touch System. What do you see as this system's competitive advantage?

2. What are your recommendations for pricing, promotion, and distribution of the product?

12

Small Business Marketing: Product

After reading this chapter, you should be able to:

- Define the term *marketing mix*.

- Discuss the different forms a product can take, and identify the five levels of product satisfaction.

- Outline the importance of purchasing and its procedures.

- Discuss the main concerns in selecting a supplier.

- Calculate how much inventory you need and when.

- Describe seven methods of inventory control.

INVENTORY REPRESENTS MONEY stacked on a shelf. Until it is sold, it does not generate cash—in fact, it ties up cash. Many small business owners fail to realize the direct impact that inventory has on cash flow. Lose track of your inventory and your checkbook balance can hit zero in a hurry.

Todd Heim, who owns Future Cure, Inc., of North Olmsted, Ohio, realizes how important inventory control is. Future Cure manufactures automotive paint spray booths. A typical booth contains more than 300 parts (some of which are big and expensive), so Heim has to manage inventory effectively.

Heim installed a state-of-the-art automated financial system which included a component to track inventory in detail. That detail allowed him to cut the inventory the company held in stock by 25 percent in a matter of months. On top of decreasing inventory, better tracking has also led to better stock selection, so parts are on hand when needed. Overnight shipping costs have dropped. That 25 percent decrease was almost exclusively dead stock, so employees spend less time scrambling and digging to find the parts they need.

Before his automated inventory control, Heim would have a year's supply of some parts and be completely out of others. Inventory control means tracking individual items as well as the total.

Source: J. Tol Broome, Jr., "The Benefits of Smart Inventory Management," *Nation's Business*, June 1999, 18–19.

Using Your Marketing Mix

marketing mix The factors that a business can change in selling products to customers—product, place, price, and promotion.

Marketing involves *all* the activities that occur from the time your product is made until it reaches the consumer. Your **marketing mix** consists of the variables that you can control in bringing your product or service to your target market. Think of them as the tools your small business has available to use. The marketing mix is also referred to as the "Four Ps": product, place, price, and promotion. You must offer the right *product* (including goods and services) that your target market wants or needs. *Place* refers to channels of distribution you choose to use, as well as the location and layout of your small business. Your *price* must make your product attractive and still allow you to make a profit. *Promotion* is the means you use to communicate with your target market. This chapter and the following two chapters will cover your use of the marketing mix to build and run your business.

Product: The Heart of the Marketing Mix

product A tangible good, an intangible service, or a combination of these.

The product is at the heart of your marketing mix. Remember that **product** means tangible goods, intangible services, or a combination of these (see Figure 12.1). Hiring someone to mow your lawn is an example of the service end of the goods and services spectrum. Here you don't receive a tangible good. A tangible good would be the purchase of a chair that is finished and assembled, but not delivered. Thus no services were purchased. Many businesses offer a combination of goods and services. Restaurants, for instance, provide both goods (food and drink) and services (preparation and delivery).

When determining your product strategy, it is useful to think about different levels of product satisfaction. Products are the "bundle of satisfaction" that consumers receive in exchange for their money (see Figure 12.2).

The most basic level of product satisfaction is its *core benefit*. The core benefit is the fundamental reason why people buy products. For an automobile, the core ben-

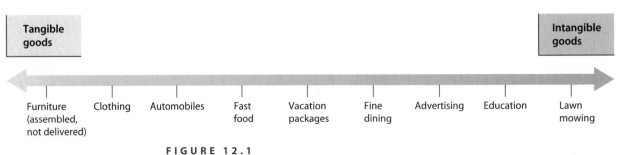

FIGURE 12.1

Spectrum of Goods and Services

What most small businesses sell is a combination of goods *and* services.

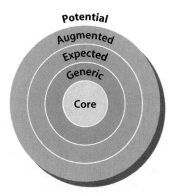

F I G U R E   1 2 . 2
Levels of Products

The benefits that consumers receive from products are represented by different product levels.

efit that customers purchase is transportation from point A to point B. With a hotel room, the core benefit is a night's sleep. People don't buy drills—what they really buy is holes.

The next level of product satisfaction is the *generic product*. For an automobile, the generic product is the steel, plastic, and glass. For the hotel, the building, the front desk, and the rooms represent the generic product.

The third level of product satisfaction is the *expected product,* which includes the set of attributes and conditions that consumers assume will be present. U.S. consumers expect comfortable seats, responsive handling, and easy starting from their cars. A hotel guest expects clean sheets, soap, towels, relative quiet, and indoor plumbing.

The *augmented product,* the fourth level of product satisfaction, is all the additional services and benefits that can distinguish your business. For example, night vision built into windshields, satellite-linked navigational systems in autos, and express checkout and health club facilities in hotels are product augmentations. Augmentations represent the sizzle that you sell along with the steak. The problem with product augmentations is that they soon become expected. When you have raised your costs and prices by adding augmentations, you open the door for competitors to come in and offer more of a generic product at a lower price. That's how the Motel 6 franchises became so successful—by offering a plain room for a low price when competitors were adding amenities which raised their cost structure and prices.

The fifth and final level is the *potential product.* This includes product evolutions to come. Not long ago, CD-ROM was a potential product for personal computers. It soon became a product augmentation and, quickly after that, expected.

Recognizing a customer need for new service products and acting on it can be the impetus to starting a new small business. Tom Christopher first spotted a demand for same-day delivery services while employed at a large transportation company. A customer came in asking to rush a package from Nashville, Tennessee, to Arlington, Texas. When his boss refused, Christopher volunteered to make the delivery on his own time for the price of a tank of gas for his Cessna 310 airplane. Eventually, Christopher decided to go into business himself to offer the service. His business, Kitty Hawk Group, Inc., has since grown from being just a freight forwarder to a full-fledged air freight carrier. In fact, his freight service company now has a fleet of 21 planes to service customer needs.[1]

Big-Time Products for Small Niches

You could call it narrow-minded. You could call it focused. What it really is, is getting big by thinking small and targeting Internet products to niche markets. But nicheing is nothing new to small businesses who have been banging heads with mass merchandisers like Wal-mart, category killers like Home Depot, and merger maniacs like Citigroup.

Matthew Cole saw a crowded market in selling wine to consumers via the net, so he decided "on a strategy to go deep, not broad." Cole created B2BWine.com by selling wines and services to the $111 billion wine industry's wholesalers, distributors, and retailers, or business to business (B2B). By nicheing in the business market, he does not have to spend a bundle on nationwide advertising. He can go to trade shows and advertise in cheaper trade magazines and newsletters.

Check out B2BWine.com's web site; then identify the five levels of their product (Figure 12.2).

Source: Arlyn Tobias Gajilan, "Wish I'd Thought of That," *Fortune Small Business*, May/June 2000, 56–62.

Developing New Products

Part of a marketer's job is managing products through the stages of their life cycle (see Figure 7.2, page 210). Trends like increased global competition and quickly changing customer needs have shortened product life cycles and increased the need for new products.[2]

As a company's current products enter the stages of late maturity and decline, they need to be replaced with new ones in demand. What is new? Good question. Marketing consultants Booz, Allen & Hamilton group new products into six categories

1. *New-to-the-world products.* Products that have not been seen before, which result in entirely new markets. Ken Fischer developed and patented a marine paint that the U.S. Navy uses to keep its ships free of barnacles. The paint is made from a mixture of epoxy and cayenne pepper. Fischer came up with the idea for the paint after blistering his mouth on a Tabasco-covered deviled egg. He decided that animals would react the same way. He was right.[3]

2. *New product lines.* Products that exist but are new to your type of business. For example, the addition of a coffee bar to your bookstore would be taking on a new product line.

3. *Additions to existing product lines.* Products that are extensions of what you already sell. For example, creating Jell-O Gelatin Pops from existing Jell-O Pudding Pops.

4. *Improvements in, revisions of, or new uses for existing products.* Increase the value or satisfaction of your current product. Take the example of WD–40 spray lubricant. Although it was originally developed to prevent rust by displacing water, so many new uses have been found for it that the WD–40 Company holds an annual "Invent Your Own Use" contest. Besides quieting squeaky hinges and freeing zippers, the product also removes gum stuck in

hair or carpet, and sticky labels from glass, plastic, and metal. The Denver Fire Department even used WD–40 to free a nude burglary suspect who got stuck while attempting to enter a restaurant through an exhaust vent.

5. *Repositioning.* Changing the perception that customers have of your product rather than changing the product. John Sundet, owner of SnowRunner, makes recreational snow skates, which are like ski boots with short runners attached. Sundet wanted a new image for his three-year-old company. A Minneapolis-based consulting firm, Nametag, helped him come up with the name Sled Dogs™, because *dogs* is a slang term for feet and sleds are fun in the snow. The new name has created a new image for the product by opening up promotional phrases like "Unleash Yourself," "Join the Pack," "You're Not an Indoor Animal," and "Sled Dogs Obey Your Every Command."[4]

6. *Cost reductions.* Products that provide value and performance similar to those of existing products but at a lower cost. For example, food stands that sell hamburgers and hot dogs offer products similar to the big-name fast-food franchises but at a lower price, thus enticing customers with their cost advantage.

Of course, there is increased risk in new products. How many new products can you remember seeing on the shelves at the grocery store in the last year? 10? 50? 100? Now think of how many of those you chose to adopt. However many you remember, it was surely far below the 20,000 new food products and 5,000 nonfood items introduced in 1996.[5] Many of those new products did not survive. Despite the risk, innovation is the key to success. Innovation is part of being proactive in the marketplace.

"I like it. Let's build a few million and see if anyone else likes it."

Ted Goff Cartoons, po Box 22679, Kansas City, MO 64113

Slotting Fees: Ripping Off Small Businesses?

Did you pick up some of the great flavors of Lee's Ice Cream the last time you were in a grocery store? It's great stuff. It must be; the ice cream store in Baltimore has the highest gross sales per square foot of any ice cream stand in America. Sorry, but you couldn't buy it in any grocery store because of slotting fees.

What are slotting fees? They are a payment or a fee paid by a manufacturer to ensure that a retailer places its products on store shelves. The practice of paying slotting fees has been around for about 20 years, mainly in the grocery business, but it has not been widely publicized. Manufacturers of all types have complained about slotting fees for years, but they complain to themselves for fear of retailer reprisal. Some companies, like Pacific Valley Foods of Bellevue, Washington, are going public in saying that slotting destroyed 70 percent of its business.

Large grocery chains justify the practice by saying that the fees offset the expense and risk of putting new products on their shelves in place of proven products, and that they discourage random and poorly researched new products—in short, that they are a tool for improving distribution efficiency. Manufacturers say that slotting discourages product innovation, damages competition, destroys small food processors, and severely restricts product choices for consumers. With the slim margins of commodities in the food industry, the pay-out period can be stretched up to five to seven years. Large food manufacturers can spread the fees (which can run as high as $50,000 per shop-keeping unit (SKU) per store in a chain) over many existing products, with a slight price increase that is not noticed. Because small producers have to include slotting fees in the price of their new products, they often can't afford to get their foot in the door (or products on the shelf).

Are slotting fees a way for grocery stores to shift the financial risk of new grocery products (80 percent of which fail) from the retailer to the manufacturer? Or are they a competition-stifling practice that unfairly punishes the smallest, most innovative companies?

Sources: Richard Merli, "Slotting Just About Killed Us," *Frozen Food Age,* April 2000, 1, 12; Paul Bloom, Gregory Gundlach, and Joseph Cannon, "Slotting Allowances and Fees: Schools of Thought and the Views of Practicing Managers," *Journal of Marketing* (April 2000): 92–108; Kent Hoover, "Small Manufacturers Say Slotting Prices Them Out of the Market," *San Antonio Business Journal,* 14 September 1999, 38; Warren Thayer, "Slots to Get FTC Scrutiny," *Frozen Food Age,* May 2000, 1, 18; and Chris White and Lisa Gerlich, "The Role of Slotting Fees and Introductory Allowances in Retail Buyers' New-Product Acceptance Decisions," *Academy of Marketing Science* (Spring 2000): 291–298.

Packaging

If you are selling a packaged consumer product, think of packaging as your last chance to catch customers' attention—kind of like the last five seconds of marketing. But packaging provides more than just a wrapper around your product; it can add value that benefits both you and your customers. Good packaging can make handling or storage more convenient. It can reduce spoilage or damage. Packaging can be beneficial to your customers by making the product more identifiable and therefore easier to find on a crowded shelf.

Packaging can help create a new product or market. Chesebrough-Ponds didn't change the formula of nail polish with its Polishing Pen, but the changed packaging has made the product very successful. Inspired by the Magic Marker, Chesebrough-Ponds developed what amounts to nail polish in a pen.[6]

Good Product, But Who Knows?

Paul Gallant faced a problem common to innovative startup companies like his Wrebbit, Inc., of St-Laurent, Quebec, Canada. He knew that he could sell millions of his three-dimensional puzzles that modeled structures like the Eiffel Tower and the Empire State Building—but only if people knew about them. Gallant spent $250,000 on a prototype and a factor, so he had little money left for marketing.

Gallant decided that the least expensive way to get the word out about his products would be to leverage media coverage via publicity. He was banking on the "gee whiz" factor of his puzzles catching the eye of journalists. He made some key media contacts at an international toy fair. He put together a press kit that he distributed widely across Canada and the United States, along with sample puzzles for journalists to put together. Soon after articles on Wrebbit's 3-D puzzles ran in the *New York Times* and the *Washington Post,* invitations came in for Gallant to appear on radio and TV talk shows, all of which created a flood of calls from stores wanting to stock the puzzles. Total cost of the PR campaign: $15,000—a very small amount to increase sales from $1.3 million to $5.7 million in only one year.

Growth spurts that large catch the attention of large competitors. Toy giant Hasbro approached Wrebbit and ended up forming a partnership. Together they have sold 20 million Wrebbit puzzles worldwide, with 1997 sales of $135 million. Gallant was correct from the beginning—his small business could sell millions of his product if he could get the word out.

Source: Bruce Livesey, "Great Moments in Marketing," *Profit,* March 1998, 34. Reprinted from "Great Moments in Marketing" by Bruce Livesey, as appeared in *Profit,* March 1998.

Paul Gallant used creativity in marketing his awesome Wrebbit's 3-D puzzles.

■ Purchasing for Small Business

Your ability to offer quality goods at competitive prices depends on your purchasing skills. You need to seek the best value—the highest quality for the best price—for the goods, services, and equipment you purchase, because that is exactly what your customers will be expecting when they purchase your products. Price is therefore only one of many factors to consider. You should also consider the consistency of your suppliers' quality, their reliability in meeting delivery schedules, the payment terms available, product guarantees, merchandising assistance, emergency delivery and return policies, and other factors.

Purchasing Guidelines

Your purchasing skills greatly affect your company's profitability, yet price is only one of many factors you must consider.

The following questions provide guidelines for evaluating your small business purchasing and inventory control:

■ Are you using the proper sources of supply?

■ Are you taking advantage of all purchase discounts?

■ How do you determine minimum inventories and reorder points?

■ Have you run out of raw materials or finished goods?

■ What is the record of your current suppliers for quality, service, and price?

■ Are you using minimum quantities or economic ordering quantities?

■ What are your inventory holding costs?

■ Do you know your optimum average inventory? Does it guide your purchasing policy?

■ Could you improve your purchasing to increase profits?

■ What is your inventory turnover ratio? How does it compare with the industry average?[7]

To illustrate the importance of purchasing to the profit of your small business, suppose your business spends $500,000 annually, has yearly sales of $1 million, and enjoys a profit margin of 10 percent or $100,000. If you were able to decrease the costs of your purchases by 3 percent, you would save $15,000—increasing your profits by 15 percent. To see the same profit increase through sales revenue, you would have to generate $150,000 additional sales, or a 15 percent increase. This means that a 3 percent savings on the cost of purchased items has the same impact on your bottom line as a 15 percent increase in sales.

Purchasing Basics

Whether you're purchasing inexpensive toilet paper for the employee bathroom or expensive components for your manufacturing process, you want to make good purchasing decisions—decisions that will get you the best possible product at the best possible price. To make your decisions wisely, it helps to know how the purchasing process *should* work. Let's look more closely at the steps in the purchasing process.

What the Best Companies Do

creating competitive advantage

Few would argue that the length of time many products have before they become obsolete has decreased rapidly over the past few years. Factors like new technologies, an increasing number of substitute products, quickly changing consumer tastes and preferences, and shifting consumption patterns all play a large role. Small businesses are more vulnerable to product obsolescence because they typically depend on fewer key products and have fewer resources to develop new ones. The small niche markets that small businesses serve can dry up or be lured away by a larger, low-cost competitor. The optimum scenario has a steady stream of new products being developed to replace existing ones as they pass through the product life cycle.

Sorry, but none of us actually *run* businesses that operate within optimum scenarios, so the best most of us can do is look at what other successful small businesses do. A recent study illustrated some fundamental practices for small businesses to create and retain a competitive advantage.

First, successful firms maintain focus on specialized products serving niche markets and rely on their existing core competitive advantage to new markets. A sustainable competitive advantage is based on something that firm does better than others—a core competence. In order to be classified as a core competence, a factor should:

1. Be applicable across a range of products,

2. Be difficult for competitors to duplicate, and

3. Provide a fundamental and valuable benefit to customers.

Assuming that core competencies are intact, some common characteristics—best practices—that successful companies share include:

- **Leveraging existing capabilities** Understand what you do well and use those skills to enter new markets.

- **Entering growth markets** Avoid cutthroat price competition and zero-sum games by entering markets that are growing rapidly.

- **Targeting niche markets** By definition, niche markets are less crowded with competitors than mass markets and customers are willing to pay premiums for specialized products.

- **Diversification strategy** To spread risk, don't put all your eggs in one basket.

- **Adding new capabilities** Build some set of skills, such as technology, marketing, or distribution.

- **Strong top management leadership** Aggressive small business owners lead diversification efforts. They take the risks necessary to reposition their organizations.

- **Skilled work force** Successful small companies have employees who are skilled, flexible, and self-motivated.

- **High employee productivity** Without adding employees, overhead costs are lowered and product output is increased.

- **Low overhead** All companies in the study had a lean management structure and avoided major new investments in buildings and equipment by adding extra shifts and overtime.

- **Tenacity** Most small companies have three choices—diversify, shrink, or go out of business.

Source: Sandvig, Christopher J., and Coakley, Lori, "Best Practices in Small Firm Diversification," *Business Horizons,* May/June 1998, 33–40.

1. *Recognize, describe, and transmit the need.* If you're the only employee in your business, you'll have to rely on your own knowledge of your work processes to know *what* needs to be ordered and *when*. However, if your small business has other employees, you should train them to alert the person in charge of purchasing (yourself or another person whom you designate) of any needs. You'll probably want to use a purchase requisition form to standardize this process. A *purchase requisition* is simply a form that lists and describes the materials, supplies, and equipment that are needed. In addition, the purchase requisition should list the quantity needed, date required, estimated unit cost, budget account to be charged, and an authorized signature. This form should also have at least two carbons: one for the person who does the purchasing and the other for the person requesting the items.

2. *Investigate and select suppliers and prepare a purchase order.* Once you know what's needed, you can begin to look for the best possible sources for obtaining the desired products. Because the text describes the factors you need to examine in selecting a supplier, let's concentrate on describing the purchase order.

    Once you've selected a supplier, you should prepare a serially numbered purchase order. In most instances, the *purchase order* becomes a legal contract document between you and the supplier, so you want to make sure you prepare it carefully. Be sure to specify quantity requirements, price, and delivery and shipping requirements accurately. If you have any quality specifications, these should also be described precisely. If you have any product drawings or other documents that relate to the order, these should be included as well. If it's necessary for you to inspect sample products before an order is completed, be sure to specify what, when, and how much you want to sample. In other words, be sure to include all the data on your purchase order and word it so that it's clear to both you and the supplier what the specifications and expectations are.

    You'll probably want to use a multipart purchase order form so that you and the supplier can keep track of the order coming in and being fulfilled. In fact, purchasing experts say that *seven* is the minimum number of copies you'd want on a purchase order form. Although you may consider this to be extreme, be sure that your purchase order form has enough copies so that both you and your supplier can keep track of the order.

3. *Follow up on the order.* Although the purchase order represents a legal offer to buy, no purchase contract exists until the seller accepts the buyer's offer. The supplier accepts by either filling the order or at the very least notifying the purchaser that the order is being filled. By *following up* on the order by mail, e-mail, fax, or phone call, you can keep on top of the status of your orders. If the goods you ordered are critically needed, the followup can be doubly important. (For important orders, you'll want to get written verification that your order was accepted.) Besides being a good way to keep on top of your purchasing activities, the followup also lets you maintain good relations with your suppliers.

4. *Receiving and inspecting the order.* Once the order is received, you should inspect it immediately to see if it's correct. The supplier should have enclosed a *packing slip* with the order that you can use to compare against your copy of the purchase order. You should check for quantity as well as quality of the goods. If you have someone other than yourself checking orders, you'll probably want to use a *receiving report form* that indicates what's included in the order—quantity and quality. And, in fact, even if you're the person who checks the order, it would be smart to have some way of noting the condition of the shipment, just in case you need this information in the future. If the order is correct, it's ready to go into inventory or into use. However, if

there's a problem with the order, you should contact the supplier immediately. Let the supplier know what the problem is and follow up with written *documentation* describing the problem. The supplier will let you know the procedure for handling the incorrect order.

5. *Completing the order.* The order isn't complete until you've paid the *invoice*—a bill that should be included with the order or may even be sent later by the supplier—and prepared whatever accounting documents you need. Once you've done this, the purchasing process is complete.

Although the purchasing process as outlined here may seem burdensome and time consuming, keep in mind that being an effective and efficient purchaser makes an important difference in your small business.[8]

Selecting Suppliers ▬▬

Whom you buy from can be as important as what you buy. At the very least, supplier (or vendor) selection should be based on systematic analysis, not on guesswork or habit. Vendors are an important component of your operation.

Make-or-Buy Decision

A decision you must make in running your small manufacturing business is whether to produce your own parts and components or buy them from an outside source. It is called a **make-or-buy decision.** Much of the decision rests on the availability and quality of suppliers.

The more specialized your needs or the more you need to hide design features, the more you may need to make your own parts. Standardized parts like bolts or standardized components like blower fans are generally better to buy than to make.

The make-or-buy decision is not limited to manufacturing operations or functions. Service and retail businesses need to consider whether or not to outsource such functions as janitorial or payroll services. You could hire either your own personnel for those services or another specialized business to produce them for you.

make-or-buy decision The choice of whether to purchase parts and components or to produce them.

Investigating Potential Suppliers

Because the products you purchase become the products you sell, you want to be sure that you are dealing with the best suppliers available. But how do you do that? Tom Thornbury, CEO of Softub, a hot tub builder in California, asked that very question after his company had been burned by some bad vendors. His answer was to create a vendor audit team made up of ten employees from several areas of the business. The team spends from two hours to two days visiting and investigating the potential supplier.

Such thorough investigation is justified because companies like Softub are viewing their relationship with vendors as a long-term partnership. Since developing the audit team, product defects have dropped, and vendor turnover has been cut in half. To help the audit team remember everything it wants to look for, Softub developed a checklist (see Figure 12.3).[9]

SOFTUB'S MANAGERS POINT OUT THE VIRTUES OF THEIR VENDOR CHECKLIST

"We want to make sure a supplier's sales manager will work with its manufacturing people to meet our needs. When we hit a problem, the sales manager is our liaison. Does he have the influence to change schedules on the production line? Also, the vendor's ability to turn out a quality product is often reflected by the quality-control manager's experience. We want to know all about that."

"We check how busy vendors are in relation to their size. Say they're using only an eighth of a building's footage. Why is it empty? Did they lose business? The ones we'll end up doing business with can answer easily. And if you notice they don't have the proper space, you'll want to know where they keep their material. Will they have to leave it outside in the rain? They might show you a fancy brochure, and you find they're operating out of five garages."

"Once we went into a place where they said they made circuit boards, but they really specialized in making custom boards in very small volumes. We needed someone who could make thousands a month."

"When we get back to the office, we always check with other customers to ask if the supplier delivers on time or has quality problems."

"We don't have the expertise, the manpower, or the time to look into every procedure. If a large company (or the military) has done an audit on the supplier and given it a rating, it gives us a good idea if the supplier has sound systems and procedures in place. Why not let the big company do the work for us?"

"Our impression of this supplier was really favorable, and we've learned from it, too. During our audit, we saw illustrated work instructions hanging in front of every station on the line. Each sheet had a checklist of things the operator was supposed to do. We started using similar instructions here. We asked the supplier to send one of its engineers to help us do it."

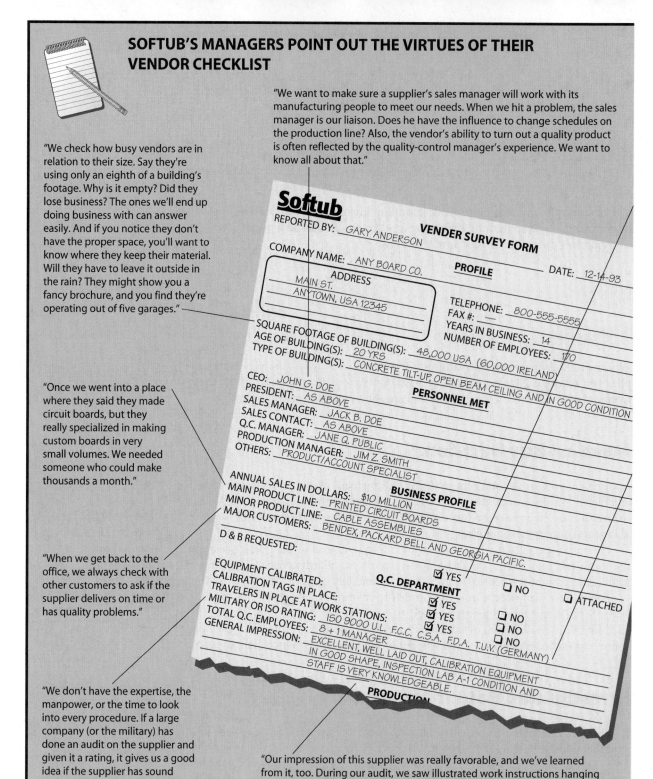

Softub

VENDER SURVEY FORM

REPORTED BY: GARY ANDERSON

COMPANY NAME: ANY BOARD CO.

PROFILE DATE: 12-14-93

ADDRESS
MAIN ST.
ANYTOWN, USA 12345

TELEPHONE: 800-555-5555
FAX #: —
YEARS IN BUSINESS: 14
NUMBER OF EMPLOYEES: 170

SQUARE FOOTAGE OF BUILDING(S): 48,000 USA (60,000 IRELAND)
AGE OF BUILDING(S): 20 YRS
TYPE OF BUILDING(S): CONCRETE TILT-UP, OPEN BEAM CEILING AND IN GOOD CONDITION

PERSONNEL MET
CEO: JOHN G. DOE
PRESIDENT: AS ABOVE
SALES MANAGER: JACK B. DOE
SALES CONTACT: AS ABOVE
Q.C. MANAGER: JANE Q. PUBLIC
PRODUCTION MANAGER: JIM Z. SMITH
OTHERS: PRODUCT/ACCOUNT SPECIALIST

BUSINESS PROFILE
ANNUAL SALES IN DOLLARS: $10 MILLION
MAIN PRODUCT LINE: PRINTED CIRCUIT BOARDS
MINOR PRODUCT LINE: CABLE ASSEMBLIES
MAJOR CUSTOMERS: BENDEX, PACKARD BELL AND GEORGIA PACIFIC.
D & B REQUESTED:

Q.C. DEPARTMENT
EQUIPMENT CALIBRATED: ☑ YES ☐ NO ☐ ATTACHED
CALIBRATION TAGS IN PLACE:
TRAVELERS IN PLACE AT WORK STATIONS: ☑ YES ☐ NO
MILITARY OR ISO RATING: ISO 9000 U.L. ☑ YES ☐ NO
TOTAL Q.C. EMPLOYEES: 8 + 1 MANAGER ☑ YES ☐ NO
GENERAL IMPRESSION: F.C.C. C.S.A. F.D.A. T.U.V. (GERMANY) ☐ NO
EXCELLENT, WELL LAID OUT, CALIBRATION EQUIPMENT
IN GOOD SHAPE, INSPECTION LAB A-1 CONDITION AND
STAFF IS VERY KNOWLEDGEABLE.

PRODUCTION

FIGURE 12.3

Vendor Audit Checklist

Sample checklist, which Softub uses to analyze potential suppliers.

Source: From "The Smart Vendor-Audit Checklist", by Stephanie Gruner, from *Inc.: The Magazine for Growing Companies,* April 1995, 93–95. Copyright © 1995 by Goldhirsh Group/Inc Pubg. Reproduced with permission of Goldhirsh Group/Inc Pubg in the format textbook via Copyright Clearance Center.

"We always request a Dun & Bradstreet report unless it's a mom-and-pop shop. Our chief financial officer also looks at the report. We want to know if the company owes more than it's worth. If it does, our finance department will call their finance people and ask more detailed questions."

"This company has the resources to make our product. But the 50% capacity would trigger us to check its financials and talk to its management, because it should be a little busier. We'd also ask how many shifts it's running, how many hours a day it's using certain machines, how many people it has now, and how many people it's had there before."

"If the place is messy and dirty, that's an indicator of the kind of service and product you're going to get. But if we see a board with tools hanging there so that when a tool is in use you see a black silhouette, that's a pretty good sign. It means people aren't wasting time looking for things, and they're probably not going to ship us a product with tie wraps in places where they don't belong."

"One big accident and a company can get sued and be out of business. Are first-aid charts posted on the walls? Are people wearing safety glasses? We want to know what a vendor is doing to prevent accidents. It's also a good indication of its management philosophy.

"International ratings are important because we sell our product overseas. If a vendor is already certified to sell in that country, we feel more confident that its product will pass inspection."

CLEANLINESS: EXCELLENT
ORGANIZED: EXCELLENT
SQ. FOOTAGE: 43,000 APPROX.
CAPACITY PERCENTAGE OF TOTAL PRODUCTION: 50%
SAFETY DEVICES IN PLACE: ☑ GOOD
GENERAL SAFETY CONDITION: ☑ GOOD
GENERAL EMPLOYEE DEMEANOR: ☑ GOOD
EQUIPMENT CONDITION: ☑ YES
REGULAR MAINTENANCE SCHEDULES MAINTAINED: ☑ YES
DOES THE FACTORY APPEAR BUSY?: ☑ YES
IS THE EQUIPMENT RUNNING?: ☑ YES
ARE THERE STOCK PILES OF RAW MATERIAL?: ☑ YES
ARE THERE STOCK PILES OF FURNISHED GOODS?: ☑ YES
IS THE SHIPPING DOCK BUSY?: ☑ YES

☐ NO
☐ POOR
☐ AVERAGE / ☐ POOR
☐ AVERAGE / ☐ POOR
☐ AVERAGE / ☐ NO
☐ NO
☐ NO
☐ NO
☐ NO
☐ NO

SUMMARY

HOW DOES VENDOR INTEND TO MEET OUR REQUIREMENTS?: THEY WILL RAMP UP TO MEET OUR REQUIREMENTS, 3 NEW EMPLOYEES AND 1 NEW FLOW SOLDER MACHINE.

OVERALL IMPRESSION: ☑ EXCELLENT ☐ GOOD ☐ AVERAGE ☐ POOR

SHOULD SOFTUB DO BUSINESS WITH THIS COMPANY?: YES! NOTES: 1) REVIEW D & B WITH FINANCE 2) REVIEW WITH MANAGEMENT AND HAVE THEM VISIT ALSO 3) MAKE FINAL DECISIONS AFTER REFERENCE CHECKS.

VENDOR RATING
PLEASE CIRCLE ONE

1 – SHOULD NOT DO BUSINESS WITH
2 – CAUTION RATING
3 – AVERAGE
4 – GOOD RATING
⑤ – WORLD CLASS RATING

WHITE – PURCHASING   CANARY – Q.C.   PINK – OPERATIONS

"If a vendor is doing preventive maintenance, there are records we can see. If machines are down, it could cost a company hundreds of thousands of dollars a day. Good companies will monitor their machines religiously."

"The pink copy goes to operations. If the supplier is ISO 9000 certified or doing business with a *Fortune* 500 company, we'll request a copy of its quality manual."

Perhaps you could develop a checklist to evaluate your vendors. Factors you need to consider would include product quality, location, services provided, and credit terms.

A serious question that a small business owner must answer is whether to use one supplier or multiple suppliers. It takes time to investigate and analyze several potential suppliers, so many businesses are working toward building long-term relationships with fewer suppliers and vendors. An advantage for buyer and seller when using a single source comes from a mutual dependence that benefits both companies. Another benefit of using a single source is the savings in paperwork from dealing with only one other business.[10]

An advantage of multiple-source purchasing is the competition between vendors to decrease prices and improve services offered. A lack of this competition can be a disadvantage of single-source purchasing if your one supplier becomes complacent or is unable to provide the goods you need when you need them.

▬ Managing Inventory

inventory Goods a business owns for the completion of future sales. Also the act of counting the goods held in stock.

Before considering how much inventory is needed, we should investigate the meanings of the term **inventory.** Depending on the context, there are four common meanings of the term.

1. The monetary value of goods owned by a business at a given time. "We carry a $500,000 inventory."
2. The number of units on hand at a given time. "We have 1,000 yo-yos in inventory."
3. The process of measuring or counting goods. "We inventory the office supplies every month."
4. The detailed list of goods. "I need to look at the inventory on the computer."

How Much Inventory Do You Need?

Managing inventory is like performing a balancing act. On one side of the scale, you have to keep an adequate supply of goods on hand. You don't want to shut down operations because you ran out of a needed part, and you don't want to lose a sale because customers find an empty shelf where they expected to find a product. On the other side of the scale, inventory represents money sitting idly on the shelf. And to complicate things, the more you try to decrease the risk of running out of more obscure items, the more you increase the risk that some items will become obsolete.

RETAIL BUSINESS. An important factor in considering the inventory needs of many small retail businesses is the time needed to get fresh inventory in and how much reordering will cost. If you can replace inventory quickly at a reasonable price, you can hold down your inventory costs by keeping fewer items yourself.

Retailers should be aware of the 80–20 principle, also called the "Pareto rule." According to this rule, about 80 percent of the firm's revenue will come from about

20 percent of the inventory. What this principle does for the small retailer is that it reminds him or her to concentrate on the "vital few" rather than on the "trivial many."

SERVICE INDUSTRY. Even service businesses that aren't retail based must consider their inventory needs. For instance, a restaurant needs appropriate food and beverages, cleaning fluids, table service equipment, and miscellaneous supplies, such as menus, toothpicks, cash register tape, and check slips. Financial service firms need adequate supplies of paper, pencils, accounting forms, and other types of office supplies. They might even need to have a supply of cash on hand to meet certain customer needs. Security firms need to keep items such as flashlights, mace or pepper spray, whistles or alarms, and, of course, office materials and supplies in their inventories. Auto repair shops must stock tires, batteries, wrenches, engine oil, grease, cleaning supplies, and other items. There are many other types of service businesses not mentioned here. The point is that small service business managers should pay just as much attention to inventory control as their counterparts in manufacturing and retail.

MANUFACTURING BUSINESS. Inventory needs for a small manufacturer are different from those of retailers. Manufacturers' needs are based on production rate, lead time required to get in new stock, and the order amount that delivers the optimum economic quantity. Common techniques of manufacturers include just-in-time (JIT) inventory control and materials requirement planning (MRP), considered later in this chapter.

Costs of Carrying Inventory

There are several obvious and not-so-obvious costs of carrying inventory of any type. Financing is the most apparent cost of inventory. Because inventory is an asset, it must be offset by a liability—the cost of borrowing money or diverting your own cash from other uses. If you can sell merchandise and collect payment before you have to pay the supplier who provided you with that merchandise, you can avoid direct finance costs. Because that usually isn't the case, most inventory has a cash cost to the business.

Inventory **shrinkage** is another cost to your business. Shrinkage can come from theft or spoilage. Employee theft and shoplifting by customers result in inventory that you had to pay for that is not available for sale. Spoilage is inventory you have purchased that is not fit for sale because of damage or deterioration.

Obsolescence, in which products become outdated or out of fashion, produces the same effect as spoilage: unrecoverable inventory costs caused by merchandise you can't sell. Such merchandise is known as "dead stock." Obsolescence is a problem for a wide variety of businesses, especially those in which styles, tastes, or technology change quickly, such as clothing, automobile parts, and computer parts and accessories. You may be able to salvage some money from inventory that is obsolete (or on its way) through price reductions or recycling, but dead stock is still a major cost.

Holding costs are what you incur for keeping extra goods on hand—warehouse building expenses (either purchase and upkeep or rent), added utilities, insurance, and taxes on the building. Then there is insurance on the value of the inventory and

shrinkage The loss of goods held in inventory due to theft or spoilage.

obsolescence When products become outdated or out of fashion.

holding costs Expenses related to keeping inventory on hand.

taxes on the inventory. Merchandise that spoils, becomes obsolete, depreciates, or is pilfered is part of holding costs. Finally, you have interest expenses if you borrow money to pay for the goods.

ordering costs Expenses related to procuring inventory.

Ordering costs are the expenses you incur in either ordering or producing inventory. Ordering costs tend to be fixed, meaning that they cost about the same no matter what quantity of goods you order. They include all the clerical expenses of preparing purchase orders, processing orders and invoices, analyzing vendors, and receiving and handling incoming products.

If holding costs were your only inventory expense, you would want to order as few items at a time as possible to minimize your cost of holding on to inventory. Ordering one part at a time would cut down on your storage expenses, but think of the cost in time, paper, and people needed to process that many order forms and receive goods one at a time; your total costs would go through the roof. Likewise, if ordering costs were your only inventory expense, you would want to send for as many goods as possible at one time to minimize your costs of ordering. Although your clerical needs would be cut by making out just one order, think of the size of the storage facility you would need and the cash flow problems created by having all your money tied up in inventory.

In the real world, every business incurs both holding and ordering costs. Striving to maintain a balance between them is part of the difficult job of controlling inventory.

■ Controlling Inventory

Inventory, like cash flow, can make or break your business. Because you may invest up to 80 percent of your company's capital in inventory, you must manage it wisely.

Because inventory is such a significant expense, most businesses look carefully for ways to determine the right levels of and control for their inventory. Inventory control is the process of establishing and maintaining the supply of goods you need to keep on hand. Inventory control is important because inventory represents about 25 percent of a manufacturing firm's capital and up to 80 percent of a retailer's. There are many techniques used to control inventory, depending on the type of business and the kind of inventory. Several techniques are described in this section.

Reorder Point and Quantity

Controlling your inventory begins with determining when you need to restock inventory and how much you need to reorder. These are called *reorder point* and *reorder quantity*. The time period that begins when an item is at its highest desired stocking level, continues as the item is used or sold, and ends when it is replenished is called an **inventory cycle.**

inventory cycle The period of time from the point when inventory is at its highest until it is replenished.

lead time The period of time from order placement until the goods are received.

For example, say that you are a retailer who sells a certain product—such as Elvis Presley statuettes—with an average weekly demand of ten units (see Figure 12.4). The **lead time** (time from order placement until delivery) is three weeks. You would need to reorder when inventory drops to 30 Elvises so that you don't completely run out before the ordered items arrive. The reorder quantity would be 100 statuettes, so you would have a ten-week supply of goods on hand at your highest desired stocking level.

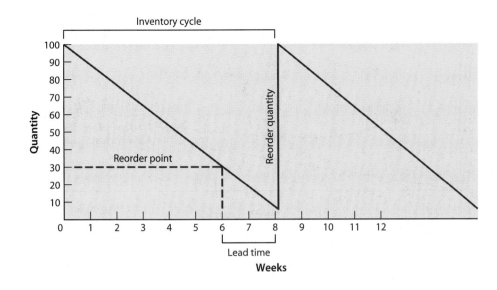

FIGURE 12.4
Inventory Cycles

An inventory cycle lasts from the time the goods are used or sold until they are replenished. The reorder point indicates when you need to order goods. The reorder quantity is how many items you wish to put back in stock.

Visual Control

Many small businesses operate without a formal or complex inventory control system. If you run a one- or two-person business that sells a relatively narrow selection of items, visual control may be the only inventory system you need. Visual inventory control means that you look at the goods you have on hand and reorder when you appear to be running low on items. It depends on your being in the business during most business hours and your knowledge of usage rate and reorder time needed.

Economic Order Quantity (EOQ)

Economic order quantity (EOQ) is a traditional method of controlling inventory which minimizes total inventory costs by balancing annual ordering costs with annual holding costs for an item.

EOQ balances these two types of costs to minimize your total costs (see Figure 12.5). Several models exist for the EOQ approach which go beyond the scope of this book, so in practice you simply need to find a model that fits the cost structure of your business and use it. The basic model of EOQ assumes that (1) you can't take advantage of volume discounts; (2) you can accurately predict annual demand; and (3) your average inventory level is equal to your maximum level minus your minimum level divided by 2. If your business meets these assumptions, you can use the following formula:

$$EOQ = \sqrt{\frac{2DO}{C}}$$

where

D = annual demand for the product (in units)
O = average ordering cost for the product (in dollars per year)
C = average holding cost for one of the products (in dollars per year)

economic order quantity (EOQ) A traditional method of controlling inventory which minimizes total inventory costs by balancing annual ordering costs with annual holding costs for an item.

FIGURE 12.5
Economic Order Quantity

Economic order quantity (EOQ) is a way to minimize total inventory expenses by balancing holding costs and ordering costs.

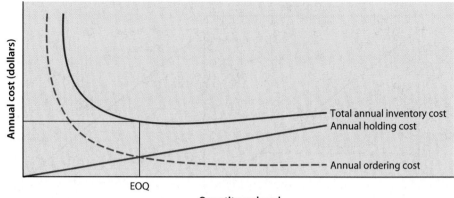

To illustrate, imagine a sporting goods store that meets the assumptions stated previously. This sporting goods store usually sells 12,000 pairs of hiking boots per year. The ordering costs are $10 per order. The holding costs run $0.96 per pair per year. The EOQ for hiking boots for this store would be 500.

$$EOQ = \sqrt{\frac{2 \times 12,000 \times 10}{0.96}}$$
$$= 500$$

This tells us that to minimize total inventory costs and balance ordering and holding costs, the sporting goods store would need to order 500 pairs of hiking boots at a time. That means that, in selling 12,000 pairs of boots and ordering 500 pairs each time, the store would need to make 24 orders of hiking boots per year.

$$\text{Orders per year} = \frac{D}{EOQ}$$
$$24 = \frac{12,000}{500}$$

ABC Classification

In the process of handling many types of goods, some can get misallocated. A reason for misallocation can be that the person in charge of inventory is spending as much attention on an item that costs $5 and is sold twice a year as on items that cost $500 and are sold many times a month.

An inventory system that helps to allocate more appropriate time and attention to items is **ABC classification.** This system classifies items based on the total dollar volume of sales each generates. To calculate the total dollar volume, multiply the cost of an item by the number of units sold annually. The greater the weighted dollar volume generated by an item, the more attention you will want to give it in your inventory control.

Items that generate high dollar volume will be classified in the A category and will receive the highest priority. Proportionately less attention will be given to the moderate-dollar-volume goods in the B category, and low-dollar-volume items in the C category. A rule of thumb for percentage allocation for each group is shown in Table 12.1.

ABC classification An inventory control system that classifies items based on the total dollar volume of sales each generates.

TABLE 12.1 ABC Inventory Investment Classification	Classification	Percentage of Total Inventory Investment
	A. High dollar volume	60–80
	B. Moderate dollar volume	10–40
	C. Low dollar volume	5–15

The use of a computer database in your inventory control makes monitoring your ABC classification system relatively quick and easy to adjust if necessary.

Electronic Data Interchange (EDI)

Electronic data interchange (EDI) is an electronic means of inventory control. It is made possible through the use of bar coding, the black-and-white parallel bars on packaged goods. When goods are scanned into your inventory system by employees receiving them in a shipment or ringing them up as a sale at the cash register, the transactions are updated in the company's computer inventory program. By using this technology, you can track sales, determine what needs to be ordered, and transmit the inventory data to your suppliers through the same EDI system. EDI is one type of **perpetual inventory system** which allows you to know how many items you have in stock at any given time.

There are a number of software programs you can use to help you better control your inventory. Peachtree Complete Accounting and Peachtree Accounting (Peachtree Software) are particularly good programs for tracking inventories and accounts receivable. You can also customize these packages to your unique inventory needs. Intuit Corporation's QuickBooks Pro is another popular software package that you can use to track inventory. These software packages are relatively inexpensive, ranging from $99 to $199.

However, you might decide to invest a little more in a more extensive software/hardware package called SellWise from CAP Automation (www.capauto .com). This program (list price of about $1,500) handles sales, tracks customers, produces reports, orders, receives, controls inventory, and creates tags (bar codes). This package is particularly good for small retail businesses. Finally, one of the newest software programs to come out is called Big Business (www.bigsoftware .com; list price about $350 for single user or $750 for multiple users on a network version). This program is ideal for many different small business applications because it integrates four critical business functions: sales, marketing, inventory, and finance. Its creators say that it's perfect for individuals who have limited accounting knowledge. This program may be just the ticket for helping you control your inventory.

Regardless of the specific software that you choose to help you manage your inventory, be sure to select one that you'll *use*. After all, this is one area of your business that you *can* control so why not be effective and efficient at it?[11]

EDI can be beneficial to both supplier and customer. But what if the supplier is domestic and the customer is in a different country? And what if the cost of implementing an EDI system is just too expensive for a small business? Well, some indus-

perpetual inventory system An inventory system that indicates how many units of an item are on hand at any given time.

try trade associations are taking the lead by helping their members garner the benefits of EDI and be able to compete globally. They're doing this by creating networking collaborations among small businesses in a certain location. For instance, the National Tooling and Machining Association helped Kansas Manufacturers, Inc., in Wichita, a consortium of approximately 20 job shops, none with annual sales revenues over $4.5 million, by providing seed money for EDI links. This networking capability helped the Kansas job shops capture a $1.7 million order for auto parts from a Swedish corporation.[12]

The benefits to be gained from conducting business online can be numerous. However, you should also be alert to some of the security concerns that arise from electronic commerce. The Internet's accessibility is one of the biggest advantages—and one of its biggest liabilities. The free-flow exchange of information among millions of users creates the possibility of a scenario in which your transactions or even the personal files on your PC are susceptible to outsider tampering. But there are ways to protect yourself.

If you've got a web page, it's probably worth the time and expense to install a "firewall." The firewall guards your PCs and your web site, and includes both hardware and software to detect break-ins. If unauthorized activity is taking place, your firewall will automatically shut your system down before any damage be done. Unless you have a solid knowledge of computers and software, you'll probably want to pay a consultant to help you erect this safety feature. If you're going to be doing a lot of business via the Internet, it's a wise investment.

Another protection to help secure confidential transactions (such as those taking place in EDI) is to use encryption software. Encryption software scrambles a message so that only the intended receiver can decode it. Both Netscape and Open Market (Internet firms with popular web browsers) have built-in encryption software. Or you can use software programs like IStore, Merchant Solution, or Web-Trader to help you secure your transactions. However, if the security of financial transactions on the Internet still concerns you, you can always print a toll-free number on your home page and let customers contact you by phone or fax. [13]

Just-in-Time (JIT)

just-in-time (JIT) A
Japanese approach to inventory management that aims to reduce order sizes and time orders so that goods arrive as close to the time they are needed as possible.

A Japanese approach to inventory management that has received a lot of attention in the last few years is called **just-in-time (JIT).** The basic idea of JIT is to reduce order sizes and time orders so that goods arrive as close to the time they are needed as possible. The intent is to minimize a business's dependence on inventory and cut the costs of moving and storing goods. JIT is used more by producers than by retailers.

There are notable differences between a JIT approach and a more traditional approach (which you could think of as "just-in-case"). Table 12.2 highlights some of these differences.[14]

JIT is based on a *kanban* (pronounced KAHN-bahn) system, which translates roughly as "card." Kanban was developed by Toyota, which used cards to initiate and authorize many activities within the business, such as production, purchasing, and moving goods.

JIT is most effective when it is part of an overall philosophy. For example, American Standard, Inc., producer of bathroom fixtures, calls its JIT system "demand-flow manufacturing" and considers it to be part of its overall TQM philosophy. By concentrating on keeping the product moving continuously and eliminating dead

JIT Inventory	Traditional Inventory	
Small orders and frequent deliveries	Large orders and infrequent deliveries	**TABLE 12.2** **JIT and Traditional Inventory Comparison**
Single-source supplier for a given part with long-term contract	Multiple sources of suppliers for same part with partial or short-term contracts	
Suppliers expected to deliver product quality, delivery performance, and price; no rejects acceptable	Suppliers expected to deliver acceptable level of product quality, delivery performance, and price	
Objective of bidding is to secure highest-quality product through long-term contract	Objective of bidding is to find lowest possible price	
Less emphasis on paperwork	Requires more time and formal paperwork	
Delivery time and quantity can be changed with direct communication	Changes in delivery time and quantity require new purchase orders	

time, everyone is looking for adjustments that need to be made to free up bottlenecks. With this mindset, continuous improvement, which is the overall goal of TQM, becomes automatic. At American Standard, efficiency has improved 20 percent, its cycle time to produce a toilet has decreased from 180 hours to about four hours, and inventory has been cut drastically.[15]

JIT works best in situations that allow accurate forecasting of both demand and production. Since JIT is based on actual rather than projected demand, a small business may have to be in operation for a while before it can take advantage of it, as a company called Lifeline Systems learned. When Lifeline first began making its voice-activated personal response devices, which allow people to call for help in an emergency, production lead time was 30 days from order to shipment.

After adopting JIT, TQM, and manufacturing resource planning, that figure has dropped to four days. John Giannetto, corporate manager of materials and purchasing, stated, "What comes in the back door [in parts and materials] is gone four days after it gets here."[16] Keeping in line with JIT philosophies, Lifeline has cut the number of suppliers from 300 to 75, 85 percent of whom offer service and quality at a level that makes inspection unnecessary.

One caveat of JIT is that everyone involved *must* be able to do what they say they can, when they say they can do it. If you are operating with enough inventory to support one day's production, which is common with JIT, one unexpected trucking strike, breakdown, or shortage can shut down your entire operation. Just-about-in-time or almost-in-time won't cut it.

Materials Requirements Planning (MRP)

Another new inventory control method for producers is materials requirements planning. **Materials requirements planning** (MRP) depends on computers to coordinate product orders, raw materials in stock, and the sequence of production. A master schedule ensures that goods are available at the time they are needed in the production cycle.

materials requirements planning (MRP) Inventory control system that depends on computers to coordinate product orders, raw materials in stock, and the sequence of production.

Whereas JIT is a pull system, based on actual customer demand, MRP relies on the push of estimated demand. MRP is an inventory management technique for use when demand for some materials depends on the demand for others. For example, if your business makes customized mountain bikes, and you anticipate sales of 1,000 bikes next month, you know how many components you will need. You need 1,000 frames, 2,000 pedals, 4,000 wheel nuts, and so on. The demand for each of these items depends on the demand for bikes. Rather than keep all of those supplies in stock, as with EOQ, MRP is a process for determining the number of components and subassemblies needed and coordinating their ordering and delivery.

A more advanced control system that has evolved from MRP is *manufacturing resource planning II (MRPII).* MRPII coordinates inventory management with all other functions of a business, such as marketing, accounting, financial planning, cash flow, and engineering. Because it is more complex and expensive, it is used mainly in large businesses but is worth noting here because techniques and processes often find their ways into small businesses after a period of time.

SUMMARY

▬▬ What is the marketing mix?

Your marketing mix consists of the variables that you can control in bringing your product or service to your target market. Also referred to as the "Four Ps" (product, place, price, and promotion), it includes the *product* (including goods and services) that your target market wants or needs; *place,* or the channels of distribution you choose to use, as well as the location and layout of your small business; the *price* that makes your product attractive and still allows you to make a profit; and the methods of *promotion* you use to communicate with your target market.

The different forms a product can take and the five levels of product satisfaction.

Products are tangible goods, intangible services, or a combination of these. The five levels of product satisfaction are the core benefit, the generic product, the expected product, the augmented product, and the potential product. The core benefit represents the value a customer gets from a product. The generic product is the simplest components from which a product is made. The expected product represents the characteristics that customers expect to find in a product. The augmented product contains the characteristics of a product that are over and above what customers expect to find.

The importance of purchasing and its procedures.

Purchasing is an important part of a small business because the goods or raw materials that you bring into your business become the products you will in turn have available to sell to your customers. A savings gained from the cost of purchased items has a larger impact on your profit level than an increase in sales revenue.

Considerations for selecting suppliers.

Small manufacturers must first decide whether to make parts needed in their production or to purchase components from another business. Retailers must decide whether to hire personnel or to outsource needed services. Both of these are examples of the make-or-buy decision. Factors such as product quality, location of supplier, services that suppliers offer, and credit terms available need to be considered when selecting suppliers.

How to determine inventory needs.

If your small business requires inventory, you must maintain a balance between having enough goods on hand to prevent lost sales due to items being out of stock and having inventory dollars lying idle on a shelf. Retailers and manufacturers need to heed the Pareto rule by paying attention to the "vital few" rather than the "trivial many" items in inventory. Shrinkage, obsolescence, holding costs, and ordering costs are factors to be considered in determining the inventory needs of your business.

Procedures for different types of inventory control.

To control your inventory, you must begin by determining your reorder point (when you need to reorder) and your reorder quantity (how much you need to reorder). Many small businesses depend on visual control to maintain inventory. Economic order quantity, ABC classification, electronic data interchange, just-in-time, and materials requirements planning are common tools for controlling inventory.

QUESTIONS FOR **REVIEW & DISCUSSION**

1. What factors should be considered when purchasing for a small business?

2. Explain how the Pareto rule is important to a small business owner.

3. What impact can shrinkage have on an inventory system?

4. Assume that you are the owner of the sporting goods store used in the example of economic order quantity inventory control on page 379. You typically sell 14,500 sweatshirts per year. Your ordering costs are still $10 per order. Holding costs are $0.60 per sweatshirt per year. What is your EOQ for sweatshirts? How many sweatshirt orders would you place per year?

5. When would an ABC inventory system be appropriate?

6. Aside from reducing inventory levels, what does the just-in-time philosophy promote?

7. What is the difference between a pull system and a push system of inventory control?

8. Consider the make-or-buy decision. Give three examples of situations in which a business should make, rather than buy. Give three examples of situations in which a business should buy, rather than make.

QUESTIONS FOR **CRITICAL THINKING**

1. Many small businesses are built around one product. What risks does this pose? What should small business owners do to minimize those risks? How can a small business develop new products?

2. Purchasing products or materials is obviously an important part of running a small business. What are the pros and cons of developing a relationship with a single vendor from whom to purchase most of your products versus using multiple vendors and not depending on one other company?

Experience this...

Arrange with your instructor for your class to visit a local business (preferably a larger retail store, but still a small business or some type of manufacturing business that uses multiple materials or components). Check out their inventory system. How are items brought in (physically and paperworkwise); how is inventory stored and tracked; how are vendors selected and evaluated; how are products chosen for the business to sell?

Costume Specialists, Inc. Storybook characters like Madeline, Babar the Elephant, and even Stinky Cheese Man come alive under the watchful eye of Wendy Goldstein of Columbus, Ohio. Her company, Costume Specialists, Inc., fashions the complicated costumes from scratch and sells the creations to book publishers and bookstore chains. Each costume takes about 60 to 80 hours of artistic effort and costs up to $3,000 in materials and labor to produce. Goldstein's business brings in $600,000 annually.

Catch the Wave. Catch the Wave is a marketing information and graphics design firm located in Minneapolis. The firm designs web pages for clients wanting to get on the Internet. The firm's 20 employees have varied experience in design, advertising, writing, photography, and computer graphics. Prices charged clients depend on the desired sophistication and interactivity of their web site. The popularity of the Internet and World Wide Web has sent the company's annual revenues soaring to $7 million. And this figure is expected to continue to rise, as more and more clients want to "catch the wave."

Margaritaville Store. Of course, it has to be in Key West! Where else to find Jimmy Buffett's 400-square-foot shop, Margaritaville Store. And what else would you expect to find there but T-shirts and other beach paraphernalia? The first store did so well that Buffett expanded the retail store and even added a café in New Orleans. Total annual sales revenues for Jimmy Buffett's empire exceed $50 million. That's a lot of CDs, tapes, books, T-shirts, trinkets, and food—even in Margaritaville!

QUESTIONS

1. Select one of the companies described and write a short paper (no more than two pages) about the type of inventory control techniques that the business should use. Explain what you think would be an appropriate number of suppliers for this company and why.

2. Effective inventory management also means being ready to cope with problems. Divide into groups according to the companies you selected, and then discuss how you could design an inventory system that would adapt to such "shocks." (Read on for additional information.)

Costume Specialists, Inc. You just found out that your long-time supplier of flexible costume mouthpieces has been purchased by a Japanese conglomerate that has strict purchasing guidelines and wants you to go EDI.

Catch the Wave. You were hoping it would never happen, but now it has. A computer virus has wiped out all but two of your firm's computers.

Margaritaville Store. Trouble in paradise comes in the form of hurricanes. Even though you've been lucky so far, the 2001 hurricane season came a little too close for comfort.

Digiscents. Biologist Joel Lloyd Bellenson and industrial engineer Dexster Smith were relaxing on the beaches of southern Florida when they noticed all the different, exotic smells—sea mist, tropical plants (and drinks). Their analytical nature led them to realize that scents are all biochemical reactions that could be represented mathematically. They set out to find a way to digitize scents and send them via computer. iSmell is the device they created to attach to a PC. It's about the size of a pencil sharpener and contains a cartridge with 64 scents of natural and synthetic oils. When you visit a web site that has signed up with Digiscents, an atomizer sprays vapor into the air.

Source: Lee Smith, "The Innovators," *Fortune Small Business,* May 2001, 44–64.

QUESTIONS

1. Use Figure 12.1 to identify and describe each of the five levels of this product (core, generic, expected, augmented, and potential).

2. What types of companies would find such technology useful?

CHAPTER CLOSING CASE No. 12

Sheep Farm in the Pyrenees

During the late 1990s, Aline Alègre and Pascal Blanchard were looking for ways to improve the profitability of their sheep farm in the French Pyrenees.

The farm is based in Aulon, a small village in the Vallée d'Aure in southwest France, close to the Spanish border and about 1,200 meters above sea level. Before Aline and Pascal established their farm in 1991, Pascal made a living shearing sheep for area farmers.

By the mid-1990s, Aline and Pascal owned 170 sheep, each of which produced 1.5 kilograms of wool annually. Because the price of wool in France had dropped from 9FF per kilogram in 1987 to 2FF in 1993 before recovering slightly to 3FF in 1995, French farmers had found that raising sheep for fleece was not a profitable business. (Given these figures, Aline and Pascal would earn only 765FF annually from their wool—and that assumed they would not have to pay a worker the standard 8FF per head to shear sheep.)

Aline and Pascal made some money by selling one-month-old lambs, which are usually born in November, for around 250 FF a head. When a ewe reached 8 years old and became less productive, they sold it at market value. Sheep generally have a natural life span of approximately 15 years. Every two years, Aline and Pascal also sold rams at market value (for considerably more than ewes bring) to prevent them from mating with their own offspring.

Selling Sheep's-Milk Cheese   The farm's primary source of income was the sale of cheese. The owners had started the cheese venture with mold from existing cheese. The enterprise was completely self-sufficient with milk Aline and Pascal took from their own sheep. They milked the sheep twice daily from December 1 to June 30.

At the end of June, dry females were sent up to pasture in the highlands and at the end of September they were brought back down to the valley. During these three months, somebody would have to check the flock every Tuesday and Friday, give the animals salt blocks to lick, and treat wounded sheep. Often Aline and Pascal would find that a ewe had fallen and hurt itself; flies were attracted to the wounds and then caused serious infection.

Aline and Pascal did not send their rams to graze at higher elevations, both because they were so much more valuable than the females and because they tended to be frailer and more prone to injury than ewes. While at the farm, each animal ate about 2.5 kilograms of hay per day.

Each female sheep produced 150 liters of milk annually. Each kilogram of cheese that Aline and Pascal produced required 6 liters of sheep's milk, which was not pasteurized. Given that 1-kilogram cheeses would dry too rapidly for proper aging, Aline and Pascal manufactured only 2.5- and 5-kilogram heads of cheese. Curing and ripening took place over a period of three months in a cellar, with the temperature controlled at a constant 12 degrees Celsius. Each head of cheese had to be turned over every day.

Possibilities for Expansion Aline and Pascal sold their cheese cut from the head for 98FF per kilogram. Their second product consisted of tidbits of cheese, with olive oil and local herbs, packed in small jars. Aline sold their cheeses in the Aulon and Saint-Lary markets on weekends and had recently begun selling at Arreau's Thursday market. They were the only farmers producing cheese from sheep milk in the Vallée d'Aure.

To expand their business, Pascal suggested that exporting their meat and cheese to Canada might be an attractive possibility. He also thought that, for logistical reasons, it might be more sensible to export to Spain, about 100 kilometers away. Another option was to focus on marketing to tourists visiting their area.

The Advantages of Goats Yet another possibility was adding goats to their existing flock of sheep. Goats and sheep are similar in estrous cycle (19 to 20 days) and gestation period (approximately 140 days). They are both most fertile in the autumn, and both are easily handled. Compared with sheep, goats have substantially higher weaning rates and fewer problems with kidding. In addition, goats are attractive because they are browsers—they eat weeds and thistles, making them highly compatible with sheep and cattle, both of which avoid weeds. One problem with goats, however, is that they require more expensive, stockproof fencing.

Like sheep, goats are raised for fiber, meat, and milk. Goats are also valued for cashmere, which is their winter underhair. However, the French goat industry has remained relatively small due to the time it takes to learn to successfully raise the animals and due to the capital costs of fencing and the like. As they considered their various product options, Aline and Pascal were uncertain which might be the most promising.

Source: Summarized from Leo Paul Dana, "Sheep-Farm in the Pyrenees," 1998. To read the entire case, visit the *Small Business Management: Entrepreneurship and Beyond* web site at http://business.college.hmco .com/students.

QUESTIONS

1. What products are available for Aline and Pascal to sell?

2. Assume that the jars of cheese tidbits are more profitable than cheese cut from the head. How can Aline and Pascal sell more of the jarred product?

3. If Aline and Pascal added goats to their farm, what additional products could they consider marketing as a result? Identify the advantages and disadvantages of marketing these new products.

13

Small Business Marketing: Place

ENTREPRENEURS ARE RAPIDLY discovering a new competitive advantage based on location at points surprising to some—inner cities. Proximity to customers and transportation infrastructure are key strengths to being downtown in major cities. These two strengths become more significant as the speed of business accelerates. Business and customer expectations are for just-in-time service, so inner-city locations are turning into prime real estate after decades of exodus and industrial restructuring. Inner cities are not geographically just the hub of cities, but also the hub of regions. From their head-quarters in downtown Indianapolis, Pac-Van is within a day's drive of 60 percent of the total U.S. market.

Pac-Van sells and leases mobile offices, modular buildings, and storage trailers. Pac-Van was started and is run by the Claymon brothers, Scott, Brent, and Matthew. They started the business out of their father's Roto-Rooter franchise—cramped quarters for a business that hit $6 million annual revenue in their third year of operation. The Claymon brothers realized that they needed to move, but where? Given a five-year growth rate of more than an astonishing 19,000 percent, which put them on top of *Inc.* magazine's first 100 fastest-growing inner-city businesses, they could go anywhere they wanted. Their choice? They decided to stay in familiar territory, inner-city Indianapolis, with access to highways (two miles to I–465 and I–70), lots of parking for their large vehicles, flexible zoning, and cheap land.

Pac-Van's fifth year of existence saw 1998 revenues reach $15 million, and the Clay-mons expect growth to continue at 60 percent per year. Success and growth like this comes from a serious competitive advantage. In the case of Pac-Van, location plays a big part.

Sources: Michael Porter and Anne Habiby, "A Window on the New Economy," *Inc.*, May 1999, 49–50; and Mike Hofman, "Empire of the Sons," *Inc.*, May 1999, 55–56.

In this chapter, we will explore the role of product distribution, business location, and layout of your small business. In marketing terms, these functions are categorized as *place*.

Small Business Distribution

distribution channel The series of intermediaries a product passes through when going from producer to consumer.

Of the Four Ps of the marketing mix, place (or distribution), is especially significant for your small business because an effective distribution system can make or save a small business just as much money as a hot advertising campaign can generate. In fact, distribution is about the last real bastion for cost savings—as techniques for tracking and individualizing promotion improve, as manufacturing becomes more and more efficient, and as employee productivity rises. Your choice of **distribution channel** is especially important when entering international markets, where you are not likely to have as many options for distribution as in the U.S. market.

In marketing, distribution has two meanings: the physical transportation of products from one place to the next, and the relationships between intermediaries who move the products—otherwise called the channels of distribution.

direct channel A distribution channel in which products and services go directly from the producer to the consumer.

There are two types of distribution channels: direct and indirect (see Figure 13.1). With a **direct channel,** products and services go directly from the producer to the consumer. For example, when you buy sweet potatoes and corn at a farmer's market, or a pair of sandals directly from the artisan who made them, those are examples of sales through a direct channel. Other examples are buying seconds and overruns from factory outlets or through catalogue sales managed by the manufacturer. **Indirect channels** are so called because the products pass through various intermediaries before reaching the consumer. Small businesses that use more than one channel (such as a swimsuit producer selling to an intermediary like a retail chain and directly to consumers via catalogue sales) are said to use **dual distribution.**

indirect channel A distribution channel in which the products pass through various intermediaries before reaching the consumer.

Intermediaries include the following:

Agents. **Agents** bring buyers and sellers together and facilitate the exchange. They may be called manufacturer's agents, selling agents, or sales representatives.

agent An intermediary who brings buyers and sellers together and facilitates the exchange.

Brokers. **Brokers** represent clients who buy or sell specialized goods or seasonal products. Neither brokers nor agents take title to the goods sold.

Wholesalers. **Wholesalers** buy products in bulk from producers in order to resell them to other wholesalers or to retailers. Wholesalers take title to goods and usually take possession.

broker An intermediary who represents clients who buy or sell specialized goods or seasonal products.

Retailers. **Retailers** sell products to the ultimate consumer. Retailers take title and possession of the goods they distribute.

wholesaler An intermediary who buys products in bulk from producers in order to resell them to other wholesalers or to retailers.

The key word for evaluating a channel of distribution is *efficiency*—getting products to target markets in the fastest, least expensive way possible. Did you realize that about three-fourths of the money spent on food goes to distribution?

retailer An intermediary who sells products to the ultimate consumer.

Does adding intermediaries to the channel of distribution increase the cost of getting the product to the consumer? Or does "doing away with the middleman" always mean savings to consumers? Although the latter has become a marketing cliché, it is not always true. Adding intermediaries can *decrease* the price to the consumer if each intermediary increases the efficiency of the channel. You can do away with the middleman, but you can't replace his function. *Someone* still has to do the job.

CONSUMER PRODUCTS

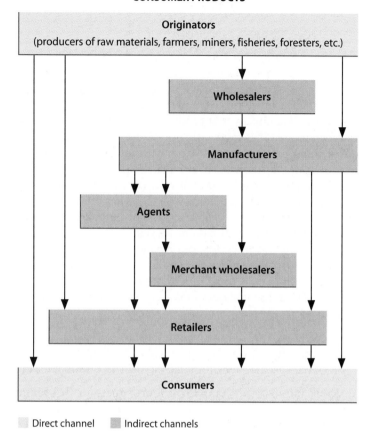

FIGURE 13.1
The Channels of Distribution

Channels of distribution are systems through which products flow from producers to consumers.

For example, if your business needs half a truckload of supplies every month from your main supplier 400 miles away, should you buy your own truck or have the supplies shipped via a common carrier (a trucking company that hauls products for hire)? If that were the only time you needed a truck, of course it would be cheaper to have the supplies shipped, even though it adds an intermediary to your channel of distribution. If you do away with the middleman—in this case, the trucking company—you must replace its function by buying your own truck, paying a driver, maintaining the vehicle, filing paperwork, and so on. The question here is not *whether* the functions of an intermediary are performed; the question is *who* performs them.

You need to be prepared to revise the way you get your products to consumers because the efficiency of channels can change. Currently the fastest-growing distribution systems involve nonstore marketing, including vending machines, telemarketing, and direct mail. Sometimes a break from the industry norm can create a competitive advantage for your business. When Michael Dell started Dell Computer, he eliminated all the usual intermediaries found in the personal computer market. Dell advertised and sold directly to consumers. This distribution strategy shot Dell Computer into the Fortune 500.

Efficiencies in channels of distribution not only allow small businesses to offer goods more efficiently (and therefore more profitably), they also provide opportunities for starting new businesses. If you establish a firm that will increase the efficiency of an existing channel, you are providing a needed service, which is the basis for a good business.

Locating for the Long Run

Selecting a location for your business is one of the most important decisions you will make as a small business owner. Although not every business depends on foot traffic for its customers, just about any business can pick a poor location for one reason or another. For example, retail businesses need to be easily accessible to their consumers. A company that produces concrete blocks for construction must be located in an area that frequently uses that type of building material, if it is to keep down transportation costs. Manufacturing businesses need to consider locating near their workers, sources of raw materials, and transportation outlets.

People do not tend to go out of their way to find a business. Although Ralph Waldo Emerson had great literary success when he wrote, "If a man can make a better mousetrap than his neighbor, though he builds his house in the woods, the world will make a beaten path to his door," it's best not to take his advice literally when selecting a location for your business.

This chapter will follow the building location process from the broadest decisions (selecting a state or region) to the narrowest (designing a layout of your facilities). The four essential questions you need to ask are

1. What region of the country would be best for your business?
2. What state within that region satisfies your needs?
3. What city within that region will best suit you?
4. What specific site within that city will accommodate your business?

Don't automatically jump to the fourth question. By beginning the site selection process broadly and then narrowing your choices down, you can choose a location that meets the needs of your target market and is near other businesses that are complementary to yours (see Figure 13.2).

To analyze a potential location for your business, you will want to consider the specific needs of your business in conjunction with your personal preferences. First establish the criteria that are essential to your success. Then list those that are desirable but not mandatory. Examples of criteria include

- Price and availability of land and water.

- Quality and quantity of labor pool.

- Access to your customers.

- Proximity of suppliers.

- Access to transportation (air, highway, rail).

- Location of competition.

- Public attitudes toward new businesses.

- Laws, regulations, and taxes.

- Your personal preference of where to live.

- Financial incentives provided (tax breaks, bond issues, guaranteed loans).

- Quality of schools.

- Quality of life (crime rate, recreation opportunities, housing, cost of living, cultural activities).

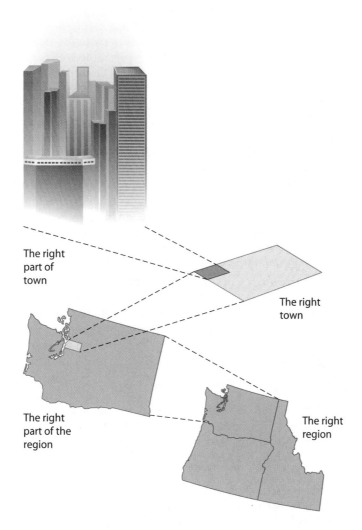

FIGURE 13.2

Identification of Regional and Local Markets

Choosing the right location for your business may be a process of narrowing down the region, state, city, and neighborhood that are right for you.

The right part of town

The right town

The right part of the region

The right region

State Selection

Most small business owners start and operate their business in the area where they currently live. However, there are people who are anxious to relocate to another part of the country (or world) to run their small business.

The United States is a collection of local and regional markets rather than one big market. Business conditions vary from place to place. Economic booms and recessions vary from region to region.[1] Markets and people's tastes vary from region to region as well, and these regional differences may have an impact on where you should locate your business. For example, your recipe for deep pan pizza may not set your business apart from the competition in Chicago, where that style of pizza is very popular. But it may make your business unique in Flagstaff, Arizona, or Biloxi, Mississippi.

Where do you find information to compare and contrast the economic performance of regions, states, and cities? Several sources are available. Every year, *Inc.*

magazine publishes its annual Metro Report, which ranks job growth, population growth, business starts, growth in personal earnings, and employment pool data. *Fortune* magazine regularly includes information on regional and state economies in its *Fortune* Forecast. *Business Week, Forbes,* the *Wall Street Journal, Entrepreneur,* and *USA Today* all publish regular accounts of current regional and national information. The U.S. Census Bureau gathers data by geographic region every ten years and maintains an extensive database. Census data are reported by several sources, including the *Survey of Buying Power,* which is published annually by *Sales and Marketing Management (SMM).*

The *SMM Survey of Buying Power* combines data on population, income, and retail sales for nine regions within the United States. The survey assigns a weight to each factor to calculate a buying power index (BPI), so that different markets can be compared. See Table 13.1 for an example of BPI by region, plus all the additional data available and further broken down to state, county, and city levels. The BPI allows you to compare any city, county, or state to the United States as a whole (U.S .= 100).[2]

effective buying index (EBI) The amount of personal income after taxes and deductions made by people in a specific geographic area.

Another figure useful in helping you determine a location for your business is the **effective buying index (EBI).** The EBI takes the census's figures for personal income and subtracts all personal taxes and deductions that are charged in each area. This shows what is known as *disposable personal income*, or money that people have left over after taxes. This figure is especially useful if your business is based on a product or service that is more of a luxury than a necessity. You would want to locate a business that sells luxury goods in an area with a high EBI, because a higher disposable income means that more people in that area are available to buy your goods.

Your location decision will depend on criteria that you establish yourself. However, some trends among entrepreneurs are noticeable. Economic consultant David Birch has noticed that fast-growing companies tend to locate in "nice places to live," such as Hawaii, Nevada, Georgia, Utah, and North Carolina—even if the cost is higher.[3]

The six-state Rocky Mountain region—Colorado, Idaho, Montana, Nevada, Utah, and Wyoming—has grown economically much faster than the economy of the United States as a whole.[4] All six states rank among the top 11 states for employment growth. Attractive tax rates, reasonable government regulations and cost of living, high quality of life, and available telecommunications combine to make this the fastest-growing economic area of the country.

Once again, be warned to do your homework in advance. Do not assume that every state is looking for economic expansion and new businesses. For instance, while Utah actively pursues businesses to locate there, neighboring New Mexico is much less interested in rapid growth.[5]

■ City Selection

To most business owners, what is going on in our city or state is more important to us than what goes on in the $8.5 trillion U.S. economy.[6] The economic condition of a particular city, state, or region is often much different than the national situation. Check out *Entrepreneur* magazine's annual rankings of top U.S. cities for small business.

REGIONAL & U.S. TOTALS

1999 Totals of U.S. Population by Age Group

Region	Total Population (000s)	% Of U.S.	Population by Age Group (000s) 0-17 years	18-24 years	25-34 years	35-49 years	50 & over	Total Households (000s)	% Of U.S.
New England	13,471.7	4.9249	3,137.8	1,283.7	1,996.9	3,236.1	3,817.3	5,101.2	5.0227
Middle Atlantic	38,415.1	14.0439	9,066.8	3,431.8	5,434.5	9,057.4	11,424.8	14,240.4	14.0212
East North Central	44,410.1	16.2354	11,623.5	3,986.3	6,232.1	10,312.7	12,255.5	16,653.7	16.3974
West North Central	18,760.4	6.8584	4,972.8	1,616.3	2,603.4	4,234.1	5,333.8	7,196.4	7.0857
South Atlantic	49,605.4	18.1347	12,051.6	4,500.8	7,155.9	11,738.4	14,158.7	18,955.4	18.6638
East South Central	16,571.9	6.0583	4,349.5	1,535.5	2,239.7	3,808.6	4,638.5	6,293.1	6.1963
West South Central	30,274.2	11.0678	8,601.8	2,791.3	4,418.3	6,915.7	7,547.1	10,995.5	10.8262
Mountain	17,243.5	6.3039	4,911.1	1,492.5	2,477.2	4,050.4	4,312.3	6,438.9	6.3400
Pacific	44,785.4	16.3727	11,825.4	4,185.3	6,963.6	10,822.1	10,989.0	15,688.1	15.4467
TOTAL UNITED STATES	273,537.8	100.0000	70,540.3	24,823.6	39,521.5	64,175.5	74,476.8	101,562.7	100.0000

REGIONAL & U.S. TOTALS

1999 U.S. Totals of Effective Buying Income

Region	1998 Total EBI ($000)	% Of U.S.	Per Capita EBI ($)	Average Household EBI ($)	Median Household EBI ($)	EBI by Income Group (000s) $20,000–$34,999	$35,000–$49,999	$50,000 & Over
New England	268,347,466	5.8064	19,919	52,605	42,203	974.3	908.0	2,085.6
Middle Atlantic	715,613,936	15.4844	18,628	50,252	38,906	2,888.5	2,489.6	5,313.3
East North Central	762,785,932	16.5051	17,176	45,803	36,972	3,602.2	3,084.0	5,668.7
West North Central	310,162,727	6.7114	16,533	43,100	34,278	1,690.3	1,345.2	2,176.8
South Atlantic	827,665,043	17.9093	16,685	43,664	33,847	4,461.6	3,454.7	5,704.2
East South Central	246,760,477	5.3393	14,890	39,211	29,744	1,434.6	1,052.1	1,637.1
West South Central	472,677,475	10.2278	15,613	42,988	31,955	2,472.8	1,815.3	3,226.5
Mountain	267,604,563	5.7905	15,519	41,561	32,655	1,578.1	1,187.5	1,805.2
Pacific	749,874,119	16.2258	16,744	47,799	37,339	3,438.9	2,855.5	5,464.3
TOTAL UNITED STATES	4,621,491.73	100.0000	16,895	45,504	35,377	22,541.3	18,191.9	33,061.7

TABLE 13.1

Regional Summaries of Population, Effective Buying Income, and Retail Sales

Source: From "1999 Survey of Buying Power," *Sales and Marketing Management* (September 1999), 58. Copyright © 1999 by VNU Business Publications USA. Reproduced with permission of VNU Business Publications USA in the format textbook via Copyright Clearance Center.

REGIONAL & U.S. TOTALS

1999 U.S. Totals of Retail Sales

Region	1998 Total Retail Sales ($000)	% Of U.S.	Per Household Retail Sales	Retail Sales by Store Group					Sales/Advertising Indexes		
				Food ($000)	Eating & Drinking Places ($000)	General Merchandise ($000)	Furniture/ Home Furnish. Appliance ($000)	Automotive ($000)	Sales Activity	Buying Power	Quality
New England	141,603,716	5.2526	27,759	27,074,932	11,741,696	13,870,291	6,542,928	30,645,258	107	5.4637	111
Middle Atlantic	352,021,564	13.0580	24,720	59,006,798	29,723,913	34,157,825	19,397,081	85,413,547	93	14.4687	103
East North Central	455,734,241	16.9051	27,365	64,285,603	46,103,974	60,982,034	28,306,560	121,021,105	104	16.5713	102
West North Central	196,101,659	7.2743	27,250	32,905,514	17,906,833	26,710,063	9,926,365	52,098,910	106	6.9097	101
South Atlantic	525,813,965	19.5046	27,740	89,863,162	52,910,217	63,847,992	32,380,971	130,921,432	106	18.4327	102
East South Central	154,423,470	5.7281	24,539	26,120,103	13,463,388	24,504,557	6,474,617	40,153,813	95	5.5999	92
West South Central	284,461,833	10.5519	25,871	47,722,445	26,950,565	40,726,737	13,370,165	79,951,521	95	10.4930	95
Mountain	179,862,935	6.6716	27,934	33,241,969	22,222,074	21,583,363	11,053,707	43,070,771	106	6.1575	98
Pacific	405,829,046	15.0538	25,869	68,041,450	38,685,203	53,342,073	25,800,381	94,725,700	92	15.9035	97
TOTAL UNITED STATES	2,695,852,429	100.0000	26,544	448,261,976	259,709,863	339,724,935	153,252,775	678,002,057	100	100.0000	100

TABLE 13.1
Regional Summaries of Population, Effective Buying Income, and Retail Sales (continued)

Let's look at the Fort Collins–Loveland metropolitan area of Colorado as an example of the specific demographic information available from the annual *SMM Survey of Buying Power* (see Table 13.2). You can compare population by age groups, retail sales by type of store, and percentages of effective buying income to those of other cities that you are also considering for your business location.

A Canadian company that makes city buses, New Flyer Industries Ltd., built a new plant outside of Oakland, California, to be near a major customer.[7] But productivity at the plant was not what the company had hoped, and the expense of transporting its finished buses became a problem as its customer base increased. Admitting that the California location had been a mistake, New Flyer decided to close the plant and set up operations elsewhere. The company selected Grand Forks, North Dakota, where rent cost them $7,000 per month compared to $23,000 per month in Oakland, and where average wages were just under $8 per hour instead of the $12 to $13 per hour paid in California. Company president Guy Johnson stated that employee attitude was one of the largest benefits of the move, with a productivity increase of 25 percent.

If your business is involved in retail or service sales, a technique for comparing different locations based on residents' ability to convert personal income into retail purchases is the sales conversion index (SCI).[8] This index allows small business managers to analyze a market area in relation to a benchmark area with similar income and nonretail spending characteristics. You can even examine specific categories of retail activity. The SCI measures the strength of the retail sector by calculating **inshopping,** which occurs when consumers come from outside the local market area to shop. A city with a weaker retail sector experiences **outshopping,** or consumers' going outside the community to shop.

inshopping The effect of more consumers' coming into a town to purchase goods than leaving it to buy the same product.

outshopping The effect of more consumers' leaving a town to purchase goods than entering it to buy the same product.

Because it takes only a simple calculation of readily available secondary data, any business can use the SCI. The data can be found in *Sales and Marketing Management's Survey of Buying Power* (see Table 13.2). To make the calculation, you need to begin with the following data:

- Total retail sales from the retail trade areas being examined (called the *subject area*).

- Retail sales for an appropriate *benchmark* unit.

- Retail sales for the subject and benchmark areas in each of the product categories.

- Effective buying income (EBI) for the subject and benchmark areas. EBI is personal income minus personal tax and nontax payments.

Calculating the SCI takes five steps:

1. Determine the metropolitan area, city in metropolitan area, or county to be examined (the subject area).
2. Establish the benchmark area to use for comparison.
3. Divide retail sales by the EBI for both the trade area and the benchmark area. This provides conversion factors.
4. Divide the subject area's conversion factor by the benchmark area's conversion factor after both are expressed as a percentage of EBI. The figure is the sales conversion index (SCI).
5. Calculate SCI for each of the retail categories from the *Survey of Buying Power:* food, eating and drinking places, general merchandise, automotive, drugs, and furniture, furnishings, and appliances.

Retail Sales (in $000)	Fort Collins	Conversion Factor	SCI	Pueblo	Conversion Factor	SCI
Total retail sales	$2,049,038	1.12	83.58	$1,618,533	1.34	119.64
Food	297,362	.16	69.57	274,006	.23	143.75
Eating/drinking places	230,136	.13	86.67	177,150	.15	115.38
General merchandise	312,162	.17	73.91	272,906	.23	135.29
Furniture/appliances	184,275	.10	166.67	71,467	.06	60.00
Automotive	412,627	.23	100.0	272,686	.23	100.00
Total EBI (in $000)	$1,831,934			$1,209,826		
Buying Power Index	.0508			.0349		

TABLE 13.2
Retail Sales by Store Group and EBI to Calculate SCI

An SCI above 100 indicates inshopping. The higher the SCI, the more desirable the location. An SCI below 100 suggests outshopping. The lower the number, the less desirable the location.

Using the data from Table 13.2, let's calculate the SCIs for Fort Collins, Colorado, and Pueblo, Colorado.

$$\text{Fort Collins conversion factor} = \frac{2,049,038}{1,831,934} = 1.12$$

$$\text{Pueblo conversion factor} = \frac{1,618,533}{1,209,826} = 1.34$$

$$\text{Fort Collins SCI} = \frac{1.12}{1.34} = .8358 \times 100 = 83.58$$

$$\text{Pueblo SCI} = \frac{1.34}{1.12} = 1.1964 \times 100 = 119.64$$

Because the sales conversion index for Fort Collins is well below 100, at 83.58, you can conclude that the city experiences substantial outshopping compared with Pueblo. Conversely, Pueblo, with its 119.64 SCI, enjoys considerable inshopping compared with Fort Collins.

When Pueblo is used as the benchmark, the only Fort Collins store category that indicates inshopping is "Furniture/appliances," with an SCI of 166.67 (see Table 13.2). This would be a very interesting piece of information for you to know if you considered starting a furniture store and were trying to decide which city to locate it in. Calculation of SCI is not a difficult process when you consider the importance and permanence of locating your business.

Site Selection

Whereas the total makeup of the U.S. marketplace is diverse and complex, neighborhoods tend to be just the opposite. People are generally more comfortable in areas where people like themselves live. The cliché "opposites attract" doesn't usually hold true in neighborhoods, where residents tend to be very much alike. The reasons for this demographic fact can be a matter of practicality as much as of preference. People of similar income can afford similarly priced houses, which are generally built in the same area. Neighborhoods also tend to contain clusters of similar age groups, religious groups, families, and cultural groups. These factors distinguish one neighborhood from another. They are therefore important to consider in locating your business.

To distinguish different neighborhood types, Claritas Corporation has created a database program called PRIZM™ (Potential Rating Index for Zip Marketers).[9] For a neighborhood to be classified by the PRIZM program, it must be different enough from all others to be a separate segment, and it must contain enough people to be worthwhile to businesses. By using the ZIP + 4 codes combined with demographic data from the census, nationwide consumer surveys, and hundreds of interviews, PRIZM creates an accurate geodemographic segmentation system. Each of the 62 neighborhood types is ranked in socioeconomic order and is identified by a group identifier, an ID number, and a nickname. Check out www.claritas.com for a sample of its demographic data and projections.

Site Questions

Choosing the correct site involves answering many questions about each location being considered. You must find the right kind of site for your business. It must be accessible to your customers and vendors, and it must satisfy all legal requirements and economic needs of your business.

Type of site

- Is the site located near target markets?
- Is the type of building appropriate for your business?
- What is the site's age and condition?
- How large is the trade area?
- Will adjacent businesses complement or compete with your firm?

Accessibility

- How are road patterns and conditions?
- Do any natural or artificial barriers obstruct access to the site?
- Does the site have good visibility?
- Is traffic flow too high or too low?
- Is the entrance or exit to parking convenient?
- Is parking adequate?
- Is the site accessible by mass transit?
- Can vendor deliveries be made easily?

Talk About a *Small* Business

Geoff and Sara Gardner found a way to make a coffee shop better—make it so small that no customers can get in, take out all tables and chairs, and put it in the middle of a parking lot. Actually, Java Joe's Espresso to Go offers gourmet coffees only via two drive-up windows and one walk-up window from a booth in a Cleveland mall parking lot.

Some people are taking a little while to learn their business concept. Drivers still pull up to the window and try to hand them a roll of film, apparently thinking of those parking-lot photo-developing companies.

The Gardners have created a competitive advantage by identifying and serving a target market of customers (primarily parents running errands with kids in tow), who want a higher grade of coffee than available through typical fast-food restaurants but don't have time to lounge around a Starbucks or Arabica.

The biggest challenge they faced was finding a high-traffic shopping center that would allow a drive-through coffee shop in its parking lot. Many were concerned about disrupting traffic flows and blocking views of existing stores. After a year of location shopping, they finally landed a spot in suburban Parma Hills.

Source: Scott Suttell, "Plunging into a Novel Niche," *Crain's Cleveland Business*, 11 May 1998, 25.

Legal considerations

■ Is zoning compatible with your firm?

■ Does the building meet building codes?

■ Will your external signs be compatible with zoning ordinances?

■ Can you get any special licenses you will need (such as a liquor license)?

Economic factors

■ How much are occupancy costs?

■ Are amenities worth the cost?

■ How much will leasehold improvements and other one-time costs be?

Traffic Flow

The volume of automobile and foot traffic, the speed of vehicles, and the presence of turn lanes and parking are factors to consider when choosing a location for a retail or service business.

The number of cars and pedestrians passing a site strongly affects its potential retail sales. If you are a retailer, you need to determine whether the type and amount of traffic are sufficient for your business. Fast-food franchises have precise specifications for number counts of vehicles traveling at specified speeds in each direction as part of their location analysis. State highway departments can usually provide statistics on traffic counts for most public roads.

Type of traffic is important, because you don't receive any particular benefit if the people passing your business are not likely to stop. For example, suppose you are comparing two locations for your upscale jewelry store—one in a central busi-

The location of your small business may be your biggest primary competitive advantage.

ness district and the other in a small shopping center with other specialty stores in an exclusive neighborhood. Total volume of traffic by the central business district location will be higher, but you will enjoy more of the right type of traffic for your store at the small shopping center.

Other businesses in the area will affect the type of traffic. This explains why you often see automobile dealerships clustered together. The synergy created from several similar businesses located together can be very beneficial, with customers coming to a specific area to "shop around" before buying. Your chances of attracting customers in the market for an auto will be much greater in a location with complementary competition than if your location is isolated.

People Who Need People: Mapping Out Success

Geographic Information Systems (GIS). The business community is turning more and more to geographic information systems (GIS) to analyze the demographics of target markets, choose new retail site locations, and optimize distribution routes.

GIS enthusiasts predict that the use of digital mapping (in which maps are recorded on computer disks) will increase as companies recognize the importance of visualizing information in accurate, flexible ways. There is a variety of geodemographic segmentation systems on the market, in various price ranges. Geodemographic segmentation systems start with millions of raw statistics on individuals and then, on the basis of these statistics, divide the nation's households into groups based on similarities. (The process is much like biologists' dividing things into orders, families, genuses, and so on.) The various systems differ in the data they use, the number of segments they can configure, the base level of geography on which they're built, and the way they describe or name segments.

What are some of the more commonly used geodemographic segmentation systems? One desktop mapping and GIS program, ArcView, integrates map data, spreadsheets, business graphics, multimedia, large relational databases, and word processing in a single program. It allows you to see neighborhoods on a map and the concentration of demographic characteristics (age, income, and so on) of your target markets within each neighborhood. ACORN is available from CACI Marketing Systems of Arlington, Virginia. It divides over 220,000 census block groups into 40 clusters based on 61 characteristics (such as income, age, household type, types of cars owned, home value, and preferred radio formats). Another of these systems is ClusterPLUS 2000 from Strategic Mapping, Inc., of Stamford, Connecticut.

ClusterPLUS identifies a larger number of clusters (60 broad ones and 450 very specific ones). The PRIZM system (see page 401), available from Claritas of Alexandria, Virginia, classifies every U.S. neighborhood into one of 62 different types of clusters.

Most GIS applications are available on CD-ROM from many vendors, including the U.S. government's Topographically Integrated Geographic Encoding and Referencing (TIGER), which includes precise maps down to individual streets for any town in the United States.

Large companies like Levi Strauss make the most of geodemographic data (such as that generated by the PRIZM™ software) by comparing it to the company's own shipment data. This market analysis helps Levi's managers to determine the best merchandise mix for stores in specific areas.

Because all these systems provide a vast amount of information, they're not cheap. A complete geodemographic system can cost from $30,000 to $75,000 on an annual basis with data upgrades—an amount undoubtedly beyond the financial resources of most small businesses. But there are less expensive alternatives available that let you manipulate data from your personal computer and that will provide you with basic site information that you can use. One is called First Street, which has a list price of $1,995 and is available from Wessex, Inc., of Winnetka, Illinois. First Street consists of 17 CD-ROM disks. Eleven of these disks contain the U.S. Census Bureau's TIGER 92 files. The remaining six CDs hold 3,000 demographic variables which are broken down at the block-group level. Essentially, First Street provides the same type of information available in the more expensive geodemographic systems, but you have to manipulate the data yourself instead of paying for that to be done.

Another option would be the $395 Maptitude 3.0 by Caliper Corporation of Newton, Massachusetts. This package contains mapping software, a geographic information system, analysis tools, and a geographic and demographic database. Finally, MapInfo Corporation's MapInfo is another choice. This product is priced higher than Maptitude, but it's one of the best-selling geographic mapping software programs on the market. It provides many of the same features as First Street. However, a key factor to remember about any of these software tools, costly or inexpensive, is that they are just that—tools. You'll still have to correctly interpret and use the information in planning your location.

Sources: Susan Mitchell, "Birds of a Feather," *American Demographics,* February 1995, 40–48; Jon Goss, "We Know Who You Are and We Know Where You Live . . . ," *Economic Geography,* April 1995, 171–198; John Taschek, "First St. Helps Users Map out Business Plan," *PC Week,* 1 May 1995, 69; Bruce Brown, "First St.: The Road to Demographics," *PC Magazine,* July 1995, 48; Evelyn Gilbert, "Desktop Mapping Software Gaining Popularity," *National Underwriter,* 28 August 1995, 8ff.; Bruce Brown, "Maptitude: Mapping Software with Low Hurdles," *PC Magazine,* 12 September 1995, 56; and Maryfran Johnson, "GIS Popularity Growing," *Computer World,* 22 March 1993, 41–42.

Coffee, Tea—or How 'bout a Crab Ashtray?

It sounded like a dream come true: a new retail store in a prime location with nonstop customer traffic. And for Melissa Fulton, president and CEO of Celebrate Maryland! that dream became reality. Fulton was already operating two thriving stores in historic Maryland towns—their merchandise includes state souvenirs—when the opportunity came for her to establish a new location at the busy airport. She opened a 700-square-foot store in the Baltimore-Washington International Airport in September 1995. This location, although desirable, has meant some additional challenges. One is that her employees have needed to be superefficient in stocking merchandise and ringing up sales because most airport customers are in a hurry. But, Fulton says, she wouldn't dream of giving up this location.

Source: Roberta Maynard, "The Lure of Locating in the Fast Lane," *Nation's Business,* December 1995, 12.

Going Global

If you are considering expanding your operations into another country, you need information on the location of your foreign project. You can get background information and opinions on foreign locations from magazines and newspapers at your local library. Keep in mind that all local chambers of commerce and economic development groups exist to promote their area, not to criticize it, if you receive information from them. The American Management Association and the American Marketing Association (and other organizations) sponsor seminars on opportunities and problems in foreign operations.[10] The U.S. Department of State can be very helpful in telling you about political developments, local customs and differences, and economic issues in specific countries.

In addition to doing your research, it is very important that you get to know the area personally before you establish operations abroad. Visit potential sites, meet with others in business there, and locate your distribution sources before you consider setting up business in another country.

Finding information on the Internet to help you make intelligent location decisions about global markets is fairly easy. The U.S. government has created web sites for various government agencies that can provide the small businessperson with appropriate information. For instance, the Central Intelligence Agency server provides access to the latest edition of the *CIA World Factbook,* which includes information about every country in the world, with details such as geography, climate, terrain, natural resources, religions, languages, and so forth. The web address for the Central Intelligence Agency is http://www.odci.gov

In addition, there are some web sites devoted to specific geographic locations which you might want to access once you've narrowed your selection decision. For instance, you can access information about Vietnam, Latin America, China, the European Union, and Russia and Eastern Europe at the following addresses:

Vietnam. http://www.govietnam.com
Latin America. http://lanic.utexas.edu/
China. http://www.yahoo.com/Regional/Countries/China/Business
European Union. http://europa.eu.int/index.htm
Russia/Eastern Europe. http://www.pitt.edu/~cjp/rees.html

"We want to see a lot of hoopla about our new product line. In the Asian market, we'll need a lot more hoop and a bit less la. But in Europe, lighten up on the hoop and go heavy on the la."

© 1999 Randy Glasbergen www.glasbergen.com

Rostislav Ordovsky-Tanaevsky Blanco, a native of Venezuela, chose his father's homeland, the former Soviet Union, as the location for his chain of photo retail stores and restaurants. He's been called crazy by others, but Ordovsky-Tanaevsky has had the last laugh on those naysayers. His business, Rostik International, quickly grew revenues in excess of $100 million and employed about 6,000 people. He's become Moscow's leading restaurateur, with a number of hamburger joints, pizzerias, New York–style delis, and theme restaurants. Achieving this level of success hasn't been easy. Site selection of any type is fraught with risks. But when you add in the uncertainties of a newly democratized society, you've increased the challenges. However, Ordovsky-Tanaevsky is a perfect example of how a global small business owner can bridge the uncertainties and develop successful businesses in locations where others fear to tread.[11]

■ Location Types

Service and retail businesses have three basic choices for types of locations: central business districts (CBDs), shopping centers, and stand-alone locations. Let's look at them now.

Central Business Districts

The central business district (CBD) is usually the oldest section of a city. Although urban blight caused many businesses to desert CBDs in favor of the suburbs, many

Goin' Downtown

creating competitive advantage

When *Inc.* magazine and the Initiative for a Competitive Inner City (ICIC) compiled the Inner City 100 to look into a window of the new U.S. economy, they were surprised at what they saw. The 100 companies had an average annual compound growth rate of 44 percent, and collectively they created 4,695 jobs between 1993 and 1997.

Although many people assume that little economic activity occurs in inner-city neighborhoods well known for problems, the opposite is actually true. Inner cities are a hotbed of entrepreneurship. What competitive advantages could draw businesses to these areas? Michael Porter and Anne Habiby identified four principal competitive advantages:

1. *A strategic location at the core of major urban areas, highways, and communication nodes with potent logistical advantages.* Inner-city businesses are logistics-savvy, understanding the proximity to customers and to transportation infrastructure as their key advantages.

2. *An underutilized work force with high retention amid a tight overall national labor market.* For the past few decades, the most pressing human resource issue facing the U.S. economy has been the creation of jobs. Finding workers will be the critical issue for the next decade. Fueling the new economy with labor will come largely from the available and growing inner-city work force. More than 54 percent of the work force will come from minority communities, many of which are concentrated in cities and inner cities. The challenge will be to attract, train, and retain this mix of workers.

3. *An underserved local market with substantial purchasing power that can support many more retail and service businesses than it now has.* As standards of living improve in inner-city neighborhoods, the quantity of goods and services demanded in those areas will increase. The real opportunity to create self-sustaining income and wealth for inner-city residents is ultimately through the private sector—not through more expensive and failed government programs. If just 100 inner-city businesses created 4,695 jobs between 1995 and 1997, what could a concerted effort to foster entrepreneurship produce?

4. *Opportunities for companies to link up with and provide outsourcing for competitive clusters (for example, health care and tourism) in the regional economy.*

Source: Michael Porter and Anne Habiby, "A Window on the New Economy," *Inc.,* May 1999, 49–50.

---

other CBDs have undergone a gentrification process. This means that old buildings have been restored or razed and replaced with new offices, retail shops, or housing. This planning and development, such as Denver's Larimer Square and Chicago's Water Tower Place, has re-created some of the best and most expensive locations for many types of retailers.

The advantages of locating in a CBD are that your customers generally will have access to public transportation; to a variety of images, prices, and services; and to many other businesses. The disadvantages can include parking availability, which is usually very tight and expensive; traffic congestion; possible high crime rate; older buildings; and disparity between neighborhoods, in which one block can be upscale while the next is run down.

Shopping Centers

Although concentrated shopping areas have existed for centuries, the last four decades have witnessed the "malling of America." Shopping centers and malls are centrally owned or managed, have balanced store offerings, and have their own parking facilities. **Anchor stores** are major department stores that draw people into the shopping center.

anchor store A large retail store that attracts people to shop at malls.

Over the last several decades, shoppers have come to demand the convenience of shopping centers. People living in the suburbs want to be able to drive to a location where they can park easily and find a wide variety of goods and services. Shopping centers have also gone through an evolutionary process, tending toward larger centers offering more variety, wider selections, and more entertainment. Have megamalls like the West Edmonton Mall or the Mall of America gone too far in this evolutionary process? Have they reached the point of being "too big"? Ultimately, the consumer market will decide.

Advantages that shopping centers can offer to your business, compared to a CBD, include heavy traffic drawn by the wide variety of products available, closeness to population centers, cooperative planning and cost sharing, access to highways, ample parking, lower crime rate, and a clean, neat environment.

A disadvantage of locating within a shopping center is the inflexibility of your store hours. If the center is open from 9 A.M. to 10 P.M., you can't open your store from noon until midnight. Your rent is often higher than in an outside location. The central management of the shopping center may restrict the merchandise you sell. Your operations are limited, membership is required in the center's merchant organization, and you face the possibility of having too much competition. Smaller stores may be dominated by anchor stores.

Shopping centers will continue to evolve rapidly. Aging centers are being renovated. As shoppers become more dependent on malls and shopping centers to supply their needs, more service-oriented businesses, such as banks, health clinics, day care centers, and insurance offices, will be located in malls.

Stand-Alone Locations

Drawing in and keeping customers are difficult tasks, especially if you choose a freestanding, or stand-alone, location. With a freestanding location, your business must be the customers' destination point. Therefore, your competitive advantage must be made very clear to them. You must have unique merchandise, large selections, low prices, exceptional service, or special promotions to get them in.

Some advantages of stand-alone locations include the freedom to set your own hours and operate the way you choose. You may have no direct competition nearby. More parking may be available, and rent may be lower than what you would pay at a shopping center.

The disadvantages of having your business in a stand-alone location include the loss of synergy that can be created when the right combination of businesses is located together. You have to increase your advertising and promotional spending to get customers in your door. You can't share operating costs with other businesses. You may have to build rather than rent.

If the goods or services that you offer are destination-oriented products (like health clubs, convenience stores, or wholesale clubs), a freestanding location may be the right choice for your business.

Site-Seeing Help

What are the three most important aspects of real estate? Location, location, and location! That oft-repeated adage is especially true in choosing a site for your retail business. In an age of specialization, site selection specialists are now available to assist in the process. Sexter Marston, owner of Retail Site Selectors of Minneapolis, helps store owners find, evaluate, and negotiate the best deal possible for the best site possible.

A good site selection specialist is attuned to the real estate market in your area, possesses sharp negotiating skills, and knows the legal ins and outs of real estate contracts. He or she should also be able to evaluate market data based on your needs. If you decide to hire a site selection expert, be sure that he or she understands the intricacies of your particular business and industry. "Selecting a consultant is like hiring an employee," Marston suggests. "Don't be afraid to check references and interview the prospective site selection consultant to ensure that he or she will save you, not cost you, money."

Location can be your competitive advantage—you may just need a little help finding it.

Source: Adapted from Richard Maturi, "Site-seers," *Entrepreneur,* January 1994, 282–284.

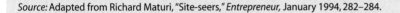

Service Locations

With some exceptions, the location decision for service businesses is just as important as it is to businesses selling tangible products. If your service business is visited by the customer, location is critical. Services tend to be hard to differentiate—to show how one is different from another. People will certainly not go out of their way if they think there is very little difference between services, so car washes, video rental stores, dry cleaners, and similar services must be *very* careful about the convenience of their locations. With service businesses that visit the customer (like plumbers, landscapers, and carpet cleaners), location is not critical.

Incubators

In the early 1980s, government agencies, universities, and private business groups began creating business incubators to help new businesses get started in their area. Today, there are several hundred incubators operating in the United States, and the number is growing. Incubators offer entrepreneurs rent below market prices, along with services and equipment that are difficult for startup businesses to provide on their own. Incubators encourage entrepreneurship, which contributes to economic development. Businesses are not allowed to take advantage of these benefits indefinitely, and they must "graduate" to outside locations as they grow.

Choosing an incubator as your starting location can help you through the first months when your new business is the most fragile. A major advantage of incubators is that they charge lower than market rent. Other benefits follow.

SUPPORT SERVICES Incubators typically make copy machines, computers, fax machines, and other equipment available for their tenants to share. These items can improve your productivity as a young business, but they would cost a lot of money

An incubator is an attractive place to start a new small business. It offers support services and such equipment as photocopiers, fax machines, and computers, which young businesses often cannot afford by themselves.

Incubation on the Internet

New ideas begat new ideas. As dot-com businesses grew in number and popularity, new forms of "help" popped up to be of assistance and to cash in on profit for themselves. Most notable was the Internet incubator. Internet incubators are related to traditional business incubators, which are usually nonprofit and associated with a municipality or a university. You can call them accelerators or startup rockets. Both traditional and Internet incubators provide business advice, connections to financing, and management and infrastructure services.

For-profit Internet incubators usually provide seed capital—sometimes a lot of it. In exchange, the incubator gets an equity position in the startup company—30 percent is common, but it may run much higher. The question for a cash-strapped, time-crunched Internet entrepreneur with little more than an idea is a tough one: Is incubating worth it? Robert Adelman and Stephen Knight, founders of Veritas Medicine, gave up over 51 percent equity in their business to locate in the Cambridge, Massachusetts, Incubator.

Veritas Medicine is based on a pretty straightforward idea—to compile a web-based database of pharmaceutical companies' new drug trials. This information would be useful in informing patients of trials in which they could participate and possibly benefit from new medication. At the same time, attracting patients would fill pharmaceutical company trials faster and save millions of dollars by getting drugs approved and on the market sooner. The benefits Veritas receives from the incubator, like office space, a T1 line, and access to management advice and venture capital, come at a price. A high one. Veritas has had to pay as much as $19,000 a month in fees.

Sure, the Internet is still a risky place and starting out is scary. That's where incubators come in handy. The National Business Incubator Association estimates that more that 800 incubators existed in 2000, and 87 percent of "graduated" businesses are still in operation. An important difference between traditional and Internet incubators is speed to market. While traditional companies stay in the safer confines of an incubator for an average of two and a half years, Internet startups are up and out in six to nine months.

The question arises: Is an incubator that takes over majority ownership of a startup simply providing an environment and resources to grow, or is it a cofounder? As an Internet entrepreneur, how would you approach starting in an incubator?

Sources: Thea Singer, "Inside an Internet Incubator," *Inc.,* July 2000, 92–100; Connie Guglielmo, "Bringing Up Baby," *Upside,* October 2000, 236–244; Chris Blackhurst, "Incubators Could Solve Your Catch-22 Problem," *Management Today,* October 2000, 118–123; Chris Murphy, "The Value of Incubators," *Informationweek,* 29 May 2000, RB14–RB22.

if you had to buy them. In an incubator, you can have access to such equipment and pay only when and if you use it. Receptionists, secretarial support, and shipping and receiving services are also available on a shared basis, so you don't have to add to your payroll.

PROFESSIONAL ASSISTANCE Incubators often negotiate reduced rates with needed professionals like accountants and lawyers. Incubators also offer training in cash flow management, marketing practices, obtaining financing, and other areas.

NETWORKING Incubators can put you in contact with other local businesses. A "family" atmosphere often develops between businesses located in incubators, because all are at about the same stage of development. This atmosphere usually leads to an esprit de corps among tenants.

FINANCING Incubators often have financial assistance available or access to other funding sources like revolving loan funds, which can provide loans at lower than market rates.[12]

Layout and Design ▰

After you have selected a site, you need to lay out the interior of your business. If yours is a type of business that customers visit, most of your management decisions will be directed toward getting customers into your business to spend money. No matter what type of business you run, this is where the activity happens. How your location is laid out and designed is important, because it affects the image and productivity of your business.

Legal Requirements

The Americans with Disabilities Act (ADA) of 1990 requires businesses to be accessible to disabled customers and employees, with businesses with over 14 employees required to accommodate disabled job candidates in hiring. This law affects the way every business operates. Buildings constructed after January 26, 1993, must meet stricter requirements than those built earlier.

Some ADA requirements for customer accommodation include the following:

- Access ramps must be built where the floor level changes more than half an inch.
- Elevators are required in buildings of three stories or more and in buildings with more than 3,000 square feet of floor space per story.
- Checkout aisles must be at least 36 inches wide.
- Carpets of accessible routes must be less than one-half inch in pile.
- Toilet facilities, water fountains, and telephones must be accessible to people in wheelchairs.
- Self-service shelves, counters, and bars must be accessible to people in wheelchairs and to the visually impaired.[13]

Retail

The layout of your retail store helps create the image that people have of your business. It is important to display merchandise in an attractive, logical arrangement to maximize your sales and to make shopping as convenient as possible for your customers.

Three types of layouts are commonly used in retail stores in various combinations. The simplest type is the **free-flow layout,** which works well with smaller stores such as boutiques that sell only one type of merchandise (see Figure 13.3). As there is no established traffic pattern, customers are encouraged to browse.

free-flow layout A type of layout used by small retail stores which encourages customers to wander and browse through the store.

FIGURE 13.3
The Free-Flow Layout

The free-flow layout encourages shoppers to browse.

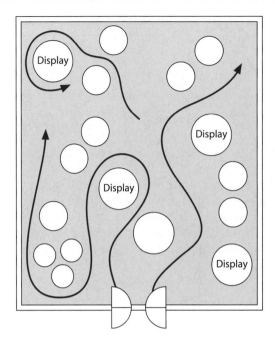

grid layout A type of layout used by retail stores to move customers past merchandise arranged on rows of shelves or fixtures.

loop layout A type of retail layout with a predominant aisle running through the store which quickly leads customers to their desired department.

A **grid layout** establishes a geometric grid by placing counters and fixtures at right angles in long rows (see Figure 13.4). It effectively displays a large amount of merchandise with tall shelves and many shelf facings. Supermarkets and drugstores tend to be set up with this layout, because it suits customers who wish to shop the entire store by moving up and down alternate aisles. But if customers can't see over fixtures or if they want only one or two specific items, they may find this layout frustrating.

The **loop layout** has gained popularity since the early 1980s as a tool for increasing retail sales productivity (see Figure 13.5). The loop sets up a major aisle that leads customers from the entrance, through the store, and back to the checkout counter. Customers are led efficiently through the store in order to expose them to the greatest amount of merchandise. Yet they still have the freedom to browse or cross-shop. This layout is especially good for businesses that sell a wide variety of merchandise, because customers can be routed quickly from one department of merchandise to another.

FIGURE 13.4
The Grid Layout

The grid layout routes customers up and down aisles to expose them to a large quantity of merchandise.

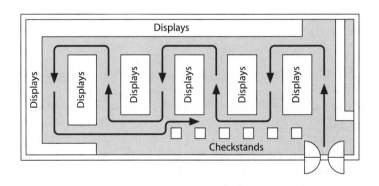

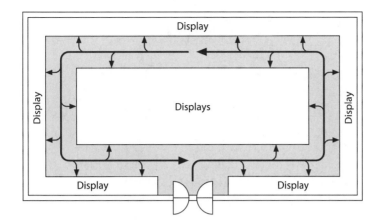

FIGURE 13.5
The Loop Layout

The loop layout allows customers quick access to any department in the store.

Service

Service businesses that customers visit, such as beauty shops and restaurants, need to be concerned about how their layout affects their customers' convenience and the business's work flow. The image of these service businesses is just as affected by layout as the image of retail stores is. Speed of service becomes more critical every year. Consider the decreasing amount of time needed for photo finishing—from one week, to two days, to one hour, to while you wait. Layout is critical to maintaining the speed and efficiency of service providers.

Manufacturing

The layout of a manufacturing business is arranged to provide a smooth flow of work. The specific layout of your plant will depend on the type of product you make, the type of production process you use, the space you have available, and other factors, such as volume of goods and amount of worker interaction needed. There are three basic types of manufacturing layouts, which may be combined as needed.

PROCESS LAYOUT With the **process layout,** all similar equipment and workers are grouped together so that the goods being produced move around the plant (see Figure 13.6). This layout is common in small manufacturers because of the flexibility it allows. The product being made can be changed quickly. An example of the process layout can be seen in a small machine shop, in which all the grinders would be in one area, all the drills would be in another, and all the lathes would be in a third. Restaurant kitchens commonly use this type of layout also, with the refrigerators in one place, the ovens in another, and a food preparation area elsewhere.

Another advantage of the process layout is that it minimizes the amount of tools or equipment needed. For example, an assembly line (which uses a product layout) might require a company to purchase several grinding machines, one for each point where it is used on the assembly line. With a process layout, by contrast, only one or two grinders need be purchased, and all can be used in one area. Because the machines operate independently, a breakdown in one does not shut down operations.

process layout A way to arrange a manufacturing business by placing all comparable equipment together in the same area.

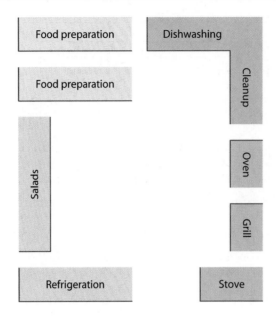

FIGURE 13.6
Process Layout in a Restaurant Kitchen

In a process layout, similar equipment is grouped together in areas to complete specified tasks.

A disadvantage of the process layout is that, when equipment is grouped together, increased handling is needed to move the product from one station to another when more than one task is performed. This can require additional employees. Because this layout is more general in nature, producing long runs of the same product would be less efficient than in the product layout.

product layout A way to arrange a manufacturing business by placing equipment in an assembly line.

PRODUCT LAYOUT With a **product layout,** you arrange workers, equipment, and activities needed to produce a single product in a particular sequence of steps (see Figure 13.7). Using a product layout is best when you are producing many standardized products or using specialized equipment. Auto assembly lines, textile mills, and other continuous-flow assembly lines in which raw material enters one

FIGURE 13.7
Product Layout in a Pizza Kitchen

In a product layout, workers, equipment, and activities are laid out according to the sequence of steps needed to make the product.

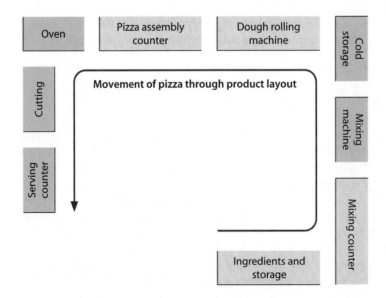

end of the line and finished products exit the other end are examples of a product layout. Material handling costs can be decreased and tasks can often be mechanically simplified so that skilled labor is not needed.

A restaurant that specializes in a product like bagels, pizzas, or cookies can make use of the product layout by moving through a sequence of steps to prepare the finished product. The kitchen can be arranged to store ingredients and mix the dough at one end of the counter before it is all moved to cold storage. Then batches can be removed and processed through a dough-rolling machine; prepared and mixed with other ingredients; and cooked, cut, and served in an assembly-line fashion. The layout works fine for making that one product, but what if you want to diversify your menu to offer other food items like hamburgers, French fries, or tacos? You would have to set up separate product lines with new ovens, stoves, and counters for each new product—an expensive way to expand a menu.

Product layout is inflexible because it is costly and difficult to change the product that is being made. It is usually more expensive to set up than a process layout because more specialized machinery is needed. A breakdown anywhere along the line can shut down the entire operation. The specialization needed for product layout eliminates most small businesses for cost reasons.

FIXED LAYOUT In a **fixed layout,** the product stays in one spot to which equipment, material, and labor are brought as needed for assembly. Types of businesses using this layout are building construction, aircraft and shipbuilding, and other large, immovable product production.

fixed layout A type of layout for a manufacturing business in which the product stays stationary while workers and equipment are brought to it.

Home Office

Is a home-based business right for you? It is becoming a popular option for business owners. Let's look at some advantages and disadvantages.

Advantages

- *Flexibility in scheduling personal, family, and business obligations.*

- *Low overhead expenses.* You are already paying for the space you live in and utilities.

- *No commute time.* Although that walk from the kitchen to the office can seem like a long one if you don't really feel like working.

- *Independence.* You can be your own boss and your own landlord. You have some degree of control over what work you schedule when.

- *No office distractions.* A lot of time can be wasted in office settings chatting with people who "pop in."

Disadvantages

- *Interruptions.* It's hard for family and friends to understand that you really do have work to do.

- *Isolation.* Much of the social aspect of work can be lost without contact with others. A house can get very quiet and lonely.

- *Credibility.* Although home-based businesses are much more accepted now, being taken as a serious business can be a challenge. This isn't a hobby, and you are not unemployed.

- *Work space.* Your working area may be cramped and not too private.

- *Zoning issues.* Be sure to check if it is legal for you to operate a business out of your home.

Thirteen-year-old Zachary Durst and his ten-year-old sister Laura know that a red scarf on mom's home office door means "Mom is on the phone. Do not interrupt unless one of you needs a tourniquet." Christine Durst (Mom) runs Staffcentrix from her home. She organizes an online network of "virtual assistants" who provide business support services. Durst loves the way she can manage a family and a business from her home. Her children are less resentful of her business and her time away if they are involved and understand the business. They help out by doing jobs like running the postage meter to feel as if they are part of the action. Durst is an example of a home-based business owner who takes a multitasking approach, rather than strictly separating her personal and professional roles. The approaches to running a home business are as varied as the millions of entrepreneurs who own them. Equipment needs vary almost as much. The essential home office equipment that Christine Durst needs is

- *Office.* Dell computer, $2,000; used HP laser printer, $250; Xerox printer/copier/fax machine, $400. A "Congragulations" (in third-gradeese) from her daughter's class.

- *Telecommunications.* A GE two-line phone with hold, mute, and conferencing, $100; Telco voice mail, $6.50/month.

- *Internet.* Two dial-up accounts (one as backup in case the other goes down), $20/month each.

- *Outsourcing.* Web site hosting from Interland, $850/quarter.[14]

Home-based businesses are becoming increasingly common as more people set up operations in their homes. The primary layout consideration for designing this type of space is to be sure that it is separate from all other home functions. If you don't do this, the IRS will not allow deductions for home-office expenses.[15] A home office may not also be used as a den or a guest bedroom if it is to be considered as a tax deduction.

You must make sure that it is legal to operate a home-based business where you live. Some communities have adopted tough restrictions, such as not allowing a home office even for work you bring home from your "real" office. More typical concerns involve complying with zoning regulations that govern parking, signage, and types of businesses allowed in residential areas. Check with your local zoning board.

Lease, Buy, or Build?

You have three choices of ownership for your location: leasing a facility, purchasing an existing building, or building your own. In this section, we will discuss the relative advantages of leasing or purchasing your building.

Leasing

A lease is basically a long-term agreement to rent a building, equipment, or other asset. The biggest advantage of leasing is the amount of cash you free up for other purposes. Not only do you avoid a large initial cash outlay through leasing; you also reduce your risk during the startup period. Once your business is established, your needs may change. A lease can give you the flexibility to move to a bigger, better, or more suitable location in the future.

A disadvantage of a lease is that it may prevent you from altering a building to fit your needs. You also do not have long-term assurance that you can stay in a location. The owner may decide not to renew your lease at the end of the term or may increase your rent payments. Leased space in shopping centers commonly requires a monthly fee based on square feet, plus a percentage of gross sales.

Review any lease with your lawyer before signing it. This is true of any legal document, but with a lease there is a tendency to think, "These forms are pretty much standard." Remember who drew up the document—the lessor. Whom do you think the conditions of the lease will favor? Not you, as the lessee. You may need to negotiate the provisions of the lease, or *escape clauses.* These can allow you to terminate the lease if your circumstances change drastically. You will also want to consider the lease's renewal options. Will it allow you to remain in the same location at the end of the lease period?

Leasehold improvements are important considerations to negotiate. These are the improvements you make to the property, such as upgrading lighting or plumbing, installing drop ceilings, building walls, and making other changes to the property. Of course, you cannot take these improvements with you when you leave, so try to negotiate rent payments in exchange for them. These are just a few factors you need to negotiate *before* signing a lease. Get all agreements in writing.

The best way to avoid disputes between landlords and tenants is for both parties to understand the lease agreement *before* it is signed. Because a lease will legally bind you for a long period of time, you should have the following questions answered to your satisfaction when you enter the deal:

1. *How long will the lease run?* The length of most leases is negotiable, with three to ten years being typical. In the past, landlords wanted the lease term to be as long as possible to hold down their vacancy rates. Now, in areas where vacant office space is at a premium, many businesses often want long leases as a hedge against rising prices. For example, in New York City, an office tower charges $60 per square foot for rent, whereas only five years earlier, the same offices rented for $16 per square foot.

2. *How much is the rent?* Be sure you know the dollar amount per square foot of space that the rent is based on for any location you consider. Be sure you know how much you are paying for different kinds of space—you don't want to pay the same dollar amount for productive office space as you do for space like lobbies, hallways, mechanical areas, and bathrooms.

    There are at least five types of leases, which calculate rent differently, though they are all based on square feet. The first is called a **gross lease,** which is a flat monthly amount paid by the tenant. The landlord pays all building operating expenses like taxes, insurance, and repairs. Utility bills may or may not be included. The second type is called a **net lease,** in which the tenant pays some or all real estate taxes above the base rent. The **net-net lease** includes insurance on top of base rent and taxes. The fourth type is called the *net-net-net,* or **triple net, lease.** It requires tenants to pay not only

leasehold improvements
Changes that make a property more valuable, such as painting, adding shelves, or new lighting.

gross lease A lease in which the monthly payment made by the tenant remains the same and the landlord pays the operating expenses of the building.

net lease A lease in which the tenant pays a base monthly rent plus some or all real estate taxes of the building.

net-net lease A lease in which the tenant pays a base monthly rent plus real estate taxes and insurance on the building.

triple net lease A lease in which the tenant pays a base monthly rent plus real estate taxes, insurance, and any other operating expenses incurred for the building.

the base rent, taxes, and insurance, but also to pay other operating expenses related to the building, such as repairs and maintenance. The final type is called a **percentage lease.** Common in shopping centers or other buildings that include many different businesses, it requires tenants to pay a base rent plus a percentage of gross income.

3. *How much will the rent go up?* To protect against inflation, most landlords include an **escalation clause** in leases, which allows them to adjust rent according to the consumer price index (CPI) or some other scale. You should not agree to pay the full CPI increase, especially if you are already paying part of the building operating expenses.

4. *Can you sublease?* There are many reasons why you might not be able to stay in a location for the stated duration of the lease, including at the extremes a failure of your business or being so successful that you need to move to a larger space. If you must move, can you rent your space to another tenant who meets the same standards the landlord applies to all other tenants?

5. *Can you renew?* Unless a clause is written into your lease that guarantees you the first right to your space at the end of the lease term, the landlord has no legal obligation to continue it. A formula for determining the new rent payment may be included in the renewal clause, or you may pay current market rate.

6. *What happens if your landlord goes broke?* A *recognition* or *nondisturbance clause* can protect you from being forced out or into a new lease should the property change ownership.

7. *Who is responsible for insurance?* Landlords should be expected to carry a comprehensive policy on the building which includes casualty insurance on the structure and liability coverage for all public areas like hallways and elevators. Building owners can require tenants to buy liability and content insurance.

8. *What building services do you get?* Your lease should state the specific services you can expect to receive, including any electricity use limits, cleaning schedules, and heating, ventilation, and air conditioning (HVAC). Note that, unlike residential rents, commercial space does not usually come with 24-hour HVAC service. (Monday through Friday from 8 A.M. to 5 P.M. and Saturday from 8 A.M. to 1 P.M. are normal.) This could produce some hot or cold working conditions if you work at other hours.

9. *Who else can move in?* Clauses can be written into leases that restrict direct competitors, or businesses that are exceptionally noisy or otherwise disruptive to others, from locating in adjoining spaces. Remember that such restrictions can become a problem to you if you need to sublease.

10. *Who pays for improvements?* Construction and remodeling become expensive quickly. Although you are usually allowed to make leasehold improvements, the building owner does not always have to pay for them. Improvements are an area wide open to negotiation in leases—make sure agreements are in writing.[16]

Purchasing

The decision to buy a building can be a difficult one. Ownership increases your upfront expenses and the amount of capital you need. The major expense of purchasing and remodeling can drain already stretched resources from other business needs.

With ownership, you gain the freedom of customizing the property any way you want. You know what your payments will be. At the same time, you are tied down to that location much more if you own rather than rent the property. Tax considerations enter the picture. Although lease payments are deductible business expenses, only depreciation on the building is deductible if you own it. Finally, the value of your investment is subject to the whims of the local real estate market. The value may appreciate or depreciate for reasons that have nothing to do with your own efforts. In the end, the choice comes down to economics and flexibility. Because most entrepreneurs are in business because of what they make or sell and not in the "brick-and-mortar" business of real estate speculation, a majority will choose leasing.

Building

Building a new facility to meet your own specifications may be necessary if your business has unique needs or if existing facilities are not located where you need them, which may be the case in some high-growth areas.

As with buying an existing property, building greatly increases your fixed expenses. Will your revenue increase enough to cover these additional expenses? Building a new facility may enable you to incorporate new technology or features that will lower your operating costs compared to using an older, existing building. Look at your *total* costs over the long term in making this decision.

SUMMARY

Small business distribution and how "efficiencies" affect channels of distribution.

The purpose of a channel of distribution is to get a product from a producer to consumers as quickly and cheaply as possible. Because distribution represents such a large portion of the price of many products, the channel that is most efficient will help keep costs down.

How the location of your business can be your competitive advantage.

Competitive advantages can be built on many factors. If the location choice of your business makes your product, good, or service more accessible to your customers, to the point where they buy from you rather than other sources, then location is your competitive advantage.

The crucial factors important in selecting a state in which to locate your business.

In deciding where to locate your business, you should consider the price and availability of land and water, the labor pool you can hire from, accessibility to customers and suppliers, closeness of competition, adequacy of transportation, public attitude toward new businesses, taxes and regulations, your personal preference about where you want to live, financial incentives offered, and the quality of life available.

▭ How to select a city and compare location sites for a business.

A city's sales conversion index (SCI) is calculated from *Survey of Buying Power* data to determine the amount of inshopping for a city compared to another benchmark location. Begin by determining a conversion factor for the considered city and the benchmark area by dividing total retail sales by the effective buying income for each place. Then divide the chosen city's conversion factor by the benchmark conversion factor. An SCI above 100 indicates inshopping, or that more people come to that town to buy your type of product than go elsewhere.

▭ The central issues in choosing a particular site.

The correct site for your business comes from answering specific questions related to matching the needs of your business with the type of site, accessibility, legal considerations, and economic factors.

▭ The three basic types of locations.

The three types of locations you may choose are central business districts, shopping centers, and stand-alone locations. The central business district for most cities and towns includes the original "downtown" area, so it is usually the oldest section of the area. Shopping centers can range from small, ten-store strip malls which serve a neighborhood to very large regional malls which draw customers from hundreds of miles. A stand-alone location places your business apart from other businesses.

▭ The types of layout you may choose.

For retail businesses, a free-flow layout encourages customers to wander and browse through the store. A grid layout moves customers up and down rows of shelves and fixtures. A loop layout features a wide central aisle which leads customers quickly from one department to another. For manufacturing businesses, a process layout groups all similar equipment and jobs together. A process layout provides flexibility needed by many small manufacturers. A product layout arranges equipment and workers in a series to produce products in a continuous flow. With a fixed layout, the product being made stays in one place, while equipment, materials, and labor are brought to it.

▭ Circumstances that make leasing or buying a building appropriate choices.

When deciding whether to lease or buy a building, you need to consider how long the building will be suitable for your business and whether you can afford to tie up your capital which could be used for other purposes. Before leasing, you need to carefully examine the terms and conditions of the lease before signing it.

QUESTIONS FOR REVIEW & DISCUSSION

1. How can a small business owner create competitive advantage with a channel of distribution?

2. Why should the small business owner consider the demographics of an area when choosing a location for opening a new business? Name some sources of demographic information that are valuable tools to use in this evaluation.

3. When choosing a location for a new business, what are the most important criteria for the entrepreneur to consider? Explain the connection between type of business and location.

4. Why would a small business flourish in one area of the United States but fail in another region?

5. What is the sales conversion index (SCI), and why should the small business owner become familiar with the way it is calculated and the information to be obtained from it?

6. Explain the importance of knowing the legal requirements of an area before attempting to open a small business.

7. What are some considerations that the entrepreneur should take into account if business is to be conducted in a foreign market?

8. What are the three location types and their subcategories? Give an example of a type of small business that would have the greatest chance of succeeding in each location type. State your reason for selecting that particular business type by giving specific advantages.

9. What is the ADA, and what is its impact on the small business owner's site layout and design plan?

10. What are the main types of layout plans, and what should the entrepreneur focus on when designing the layout plan for a new business?

11. Compare and contrast the advantages and disadvantages of buying, building, or leasing space for a small business.

QUESTIONS FOR CRITICAL THINKING

1. How can the location affect customers' image and perception of your business?

2. The old adage of the importance of "location, location, location" applies as well in cyberspace as it does for brick-and-mortar businesses. How does an Internet-based business influence its "location"? Which of the principles of location discussed in this chapter apply to e-businesses? What other factors do they have to deal with?

Choose a business you would like to start or own. If you are writing a business plan for this course, use this assignment in your business plan. Using graph paper (or simple architectural software if you have access), draw to scale the layout for your business. Include all office space, storage, restrooms, delivery, and so on, in addition to merchandise selling and working areas. Also include the exterior elevation, showing parking and customer entrances. Review Figures 13.3 through 13.7; in your layout you need to label what merchandise or work will be done in each area. Include a written description of why you are using your chosen layout.

WHAT WOULD **YOU** DO?   No. 1

Once you have chosen your location site, designing an effective and efficient layout for your business is the next important step. And it's important to keep in mind the legal requirements, as well as what is the best flow for your business. Read through the following descriptions of three small businesses and answer the questions at the end:

Sam's Suitables. Sam's Suitables is a specialty retail shop that will be selling suits, sport coats, shirts, slacks, and clothing accessories for big and tall men. Sam has found an ideal location in a strip shopping mall that has heavy traffic flow. The only challenge is that the store is fairly small (1,500 square feet), and Sam must provide display areas, dressing rooms, a cash register checkout, storage, and other back-store areas, in addition to an attractively designed front window to draw customers.

Diane's Delectables. Ahhhh . . . the fresh aroma of bread, cookies, and other pastries being baked. Diane's Delectables is opening a store that will make and bake the goodies as well as sell them to the public. In addition, Diane wants to have a limited number of tables and chairs so that customers can sit and enjoy pastries and beverages (coffee, juice, and soda) before taking a bagful of goodies to go. The bake shop has 900 square feet and is located on a busy downtown street with numerous office buildings.

Cathy's Crafts. Cathy's Crafts is a highly successful wood crafts business. Cathy has "carved" a lucrative niche for her hand-wrought products, which include items such as small shelves, picture frames, and wood cutouts (bunnies, Santa Clauses, roosters, cows, and so on). Each product in these lines is carefully cut (using state-of-the-art wood-cutting machines), meticulously sanded, and then either stained or painted. Then the finished products are ready to be prepared for shipping. Cathy's business has outgrown its present location, and she's found an ideal building (5,000 square feet of space) that's close to other light manufacturers.

QUESTIONS

1. Choose one of the businesses and draw a layout for it that you think would be efficient and effective. Think of the legal requirements that might affect the business. As part of your drawing, be sure to include a listing of the necessary equipment.

2. Divide into teams of two to three students, and make a list of the important factors that would influence the layout for one of these businesses. Then, keeping those factors in mind, discuss sites in your community that would be appropriate for it. (If you happen to be in a large city, narrow your site selection to a radius of five miles from your campus.)

WHAT WOULD **YOU** DO?	No. 2

Jodi has a problem. She has decided to go into business for herself selling used books, videos, music CDs, and DVDs. She lives in a community of about 200,000 in the northeast part of the United States. No other stores in the area specialize in the used products she will sell. Her community has a large regional shopping center with four anchor stores. Two sites the size she needs (approximately 2,000 square feet) are currently vacant in the mall. The central business district is thriving, primarily with small, boutique-type stores. The atmosphere is pleasant, with many trees, flowerbeds, and artistic sculptures lining the streets. The Downtown Business Association does a good job arranging events like parades and music festivals to draw people to the central business district. One site with 2,500 square feet is available. The community has two primary traffic arteries lined with stand-alone commercial businesses. One site is available that has ample parking and a traffic count of approximately 80,000 cars per day passing at 35 mph. This site is the right size, but it is not available to lease; she would have to buy the building. Foot traffic in the mall is the highest, but restrictions and lease payments are by far higher than in the other locations. Not as many people pass by the downtown location, but rent is much cheaper as well.

QUESTIONS

1. From the information you have been provided and from the advantages and disadvantages of the different types of locations in the chapter, where would you recommend that Jodi locate? Provide justifications for your recommendation.

2. What additional information would you want to have to make this location decision?

CHAPTER CLOSING CASE	No. 13

Pasta Perfect's Future Is Problematic

After four years in business, the Pasta Perfect chain of fresh pasta specialty shops seems to have come to a fork in the fettuccini: Should it continue with retailing or change strategies?

Founder Tom Walker, 42, had a background in specialty apparel retailing and was looking for an opportunity to build his own retail business in St. Louis. "When we lived on the East Coast, there was a fresh pasta store that my wife and I frequented at least once a week," he says. "Since fresh pasta cooks in two minutes, we could have a gourmet meal on the table in ten minutes when we got home from work."

With the growth he saw in the pasta market (sales of refrigerated fresh pasta had been rising 30 percent a year), consumer interest in fitness and nutrition, and his retailing background, Tom recognized a good opportunity. He decided to locate small, attractive shops in high-traffic areas and target upscale consumers who wanted a fresh, high-quality meal that they could prepare quickly and conveniently at home. He wrote a business plan, found partners with time and money to invest, and eventually went public to raise enough cash to launch Pasta Perfect.

Cluster Stores for Economies of Scale   Within three and a half years, Tom had ten St. Louis stores and four Chicago stores. He clustered groups of stores in large metropolitan areas to provide economies of scale in production (a central commissary prepared and delivered most Pasta Perfect products daily), as well as in advertising and store supervision.

Pasta Perfect's St. Louis stores are located in strip shopping centers anchored by major supermarket chains. The seven larger shops offer limited seating and a light lunch menu. Because fresh pasta sells at a premium over conventional dried pasta, it is important that the stores look attractive and inviting.

The company delivers fresh pasta to its stores in sheets that are cut to order for each customer. The stores also sell Pasta Perfect sauces, fresh and frozen specialty products (salads, ravioli, manicotti, and lasagna), bread, imported and domestic food products, Italian cookbooks, and utensils. Sauces and other products are shipped to the Chicago stores via refrigerated common carrier.

Only One Solidly Profitable Store   Unfortunately, after four years, only one St. Louis store is solidly profitable. To cut costs, Tom has made a number of productivity enhancements and personnel changes at Pasta Perfect's St. Louis commissary. The firm has also developed new flavors to feature on a rotating basis, so that customers will return more frequently. A radio advertising campaign improved consumer awareness in St. Louis but boosted sales only slightly; in the end, the campaign contributed to that year's operating loss.

The Chicago stores are located in busy, upscale neighborhoods, and the average store's sales are 75 percent higher than in St. Louis. On the other hand, rents are dramatically higher in Chicago, competent store managers command higher salaries, and shipping costs are higher. In addition, gross margins are lower because the Chicago stores cannot obtain the same economies of scale. Opening two or three new Chicago stores would improve margins but would leave Pasta Perfect perilously low on cash.

Sell Through Supermarkets?   Because he doubts the existing retail business can be turned around quickly, Tom is considering closing the stores and selling his products through supermarkets. Although Contadina (a Carnation brand) is selling refrigerated fresh pasta in St. Louis supermarkets, there are no well-established competitors, and the market is projected to grow rapidly.

To enter the supermarket channel, Pasta Perfect would have to install and learn to use specialized packaging equipment. Another option is to contract, at least at the beginning, with either of two factories in Alabama and Iowa that already manufacture and package fresh pasta. Tom feels that Pasta Perfect's reputation might help it secure St. Louis supermarket shelf space. However, heavy promotional costs and probable inefficiencies while Pasta Perfect implements new packaging technology could reduce margins to as little as 20 percent of sales. Outsourcing production would also mean lower margins.

Tom has other concerns. His skill and experience are in retailing. He and his executives know relatively little about marketing to supermarkets. Also, none of the managers has any previous manufacturing experience, yet manufacturing would be key to a successful super-market strategy. Moreover, many supermarket chains require promotional allowances and introductory deals before they will stock a new product. And, even if Pasta Perfect closes its stores, it will still owe rent and equipment payments until its leases expire.

Finally, the prospectus for the last round of funding said that the company would use the proceeds to expand its retail chain. If Pasta Perfect uses the money in another way, shareholders might feel misled and sue the company. Meanwhile, the specialty stores are losing money. Unless they become profitable, Pasta Perfect's shareholders will probably lose their entire investment.

Source: "Pasta Perfect's Future Is Problematic", adapted from "Pasta Perfect, Inc.", by Joan Winn and John W. Mullins, University of Denver. Copyright 1994. Reprinted by permission of Joan Winn. To read the entire case, visit the *Small Business Management: Entrepreneurship and Beyond* web site at http://business .college.hmco.com/students.

QUESTIONS

1. What location types are being used by Pasta Perfect?

2. What factors would influence the location of a business specializing in fresh pasta?

3. Would you advise Pasta Perfect to continue using specialty stores in strip malls or to begin selling through intermediaries like supermarkets? Justify your answer. What risks are involved with either alternative?

14

Small Business Marketing: Price and Promotion

After reading this chapter, you should be able to:

Establish the three main considerations in setting a price for a product.

Explain breakeven analysis and why it is important for pricing in a small business.

Present examples of customer-oriented and internal-oriented pricing.

Describe why and how small businesses extend credit.

Describe the advertising, personal selling, public relations, and sales promotions tools that a small business owner uses to compile a promotional mix.

THOMAS LAM UNDERSTANDS how important it is for a small business to balance pricing and demand. After immigrating to the United States from Hong Kong in 1969, Lam's first job—picking cucumbers in Oxnard, California—enabled him to learn the business side of growing and selling vegetables from older Asian growers. After attending college, Lam became the sales manager for an Oxnard vegetable wholesaler, Seaboard Produce, selling vegetables to Chinatown wholesalers in New York City.

A telephone call one night from a regular customer who had a problem got Lam thinking about the way his company's vegetables were packaged and priced. "We used to ship the broccoli whole, bound in rubber bands, but Chinese restaurants use only the tops. Send them ten boxes of broccoli, ten boxes of garbage go on the street," Lam said. And hauling away garbage is expensive, especially in New York. Lam's brainstorm was for Seaboard to ship only the broccoli crowns (the edible top part, without the stem) at a higher price than for the whole plant. Lam discovered that he could charge about 30 percent more for a box of broccoli crowns than for a box of whole broccoli.

In 1986, Lam left Seaboard to start his own company growing and wholesaling his own brand of fresh vegetables—Ho Choy, meaning "Good Luck." His business grew quickly, and Lam soon had to establish contracts with other vegetable packers to ship broccoli crowns. However, Lam soon learned another important lesson in pricing: Greater volume isn't always profitable. At Ho Choy's sales peak of $25 million, Lam was losing money as competition increased and as costs outstripped profits. So Lam cut back by cutting his sales staff in half. He decreased his reliance on mass-market vegetables like broccoli and began experimenting with more specialized crops like choy sum and yu choi, which faced less competition from the big growers. Despite the reduced sales volume, profits have grown. How much? "At $25 million a year, I lost money," Lam noted. "This year, at $11 million to $13 million, we'll be profitable."

Lam's experience illustrates that pricing and quantity are important parts of the marketing mix. Establishing the right price for your goods or services at an appropriate level of production is critical. In this chapter, we'll describe the factors that should be considered in setting prices, as well as how to establish credit policies.

Sources: Steve Kichen et al., "The Best Small Companies," *Forbes,* 6 November 1995, 237–238; and Joel Millman, "Imported Entrepreneurs," *Forbes,* 6 November 1995, 232–239.

In the previous chapters, we discussed two Ps of the marketing mix (product and place). In this chapter, we will investigate the third and fourth components of your marketing mix: price and promotion. We will consider why price is one of the most flexible components of a business's marketing mix, factors that must be considered in setting prices, strategies related to pricing, the use of credit in buying and selling, and how to use a multitude of media in communicating with your customers.

We deal with prices every day. The coins you exchanged for a cup of coffee on the way to class, the tuition you paid for the semester, and the money you earn from a job all represent a form of price for goods and services.

▬▬ The Economics of Pricing

Price is the amount of money charged for a product. It represents what the consumer considers the *value* of the product to be. The value of a product depends on the benefits received compared with the monetary cost. People actually buy benefits—they buy what a product will do for them. If consumers bought on price alone, then no Cadillac convertibles, Curtis Mathis televisions, or Godiva chocolates would ever be sold, because less expensive substitutes exist. People buy premium products like these because they perceive higher benefits and increased quality that delivers value despite the higher cost. Typical consumers do not want the *cheapest* product available—they want the *best* product for the most reasonable price.

Price is different from the other three components of the marketing mix because the product, place, and promotion all add value to the customer and costs to your business. Pricing lets you recover those costs. Although the "right" price is actually more of a range between what the market would bear and what the product costs, many elements enter into the pricing decision. For example, the image of your business or product has an impact on the price you can charge.

Your total costs *represent the minimum price you can charge for your goods or services. If you cannot cover your costs and make a profit, you will not stay in business.*

Even though the pricing decision is critical to the success of a business, many small business owners make pricing decisions poorly. Total reliance on "gut feeling" is inappropriate, but so is complete reliance on accounting costs that ignore what is going on in the marketplace—what the competition is doing and what customers demand.

Three important economic factors have an impact on what you can charge for your products: competition, customer demand, and costs. Let's take a closer look at how these forces can affect your small business.

Competition

Your competitors will play a big part in determining the success of your pricing strategy. The number of competitors and their proximity to your business influence what you can charge for your products, because they represent substitute choices to your customers. The more direct competition your business faces, the less control you have over your prices. Direct competition makes product differentiation necessary, in order to compete on points other than price.

Proximity of competition can be a factor in pricing for many small businesses. The closer the competition, the more influence it will have on your pricing. For example, if two service stations located across the street from each other had a price difference of 10 cents per gallon of gasoline, to which one would customers go? The same price difference between stations several miles apart may not have as dramatic an impact.

The type of products sold will also have an impact on price competition. If you run a video rental business, then other video rental places are not your only competition. So are movie theaters, athletic events, and even the opera. Don't think of being in the video rental business—think of being in the entertainment business, because you are competing for entertainment dollars. Therefore, you should monitor not only what other video rental places are charging, but also what indirect, or alternative, entertainment charges.

More small businesses are facing competition from large chains like Walmart and Kmart coming to town. Can small businesses compete with gigantic discount stores? Of course they can. The key is flexibility. In this situation, you probably can't compete on price for identical items. The discounters have economy-of-scale advantages from mass purchasing and distribution that can knock you out of a head-to-head price war over identical products.

Walmart is a formidable opponent to many small businesses. Its distribution system is state of the art in efficiency, linking manufacturers directly to individual stores. Its shrinkage (loss from theft and damaged goods) target is 1 percent.[1] Most retailers average 3 percent to 5 percent. Walmart spends only about 0.5 percent of sales on advertising, relying mainly on word of mouth, compared with major competitors, which spend about 2 percent on advertising. Walmart's success is directly related to its efficiency, which goes straight to the bottom line. Walmart holds a gross margin of 22 percent, compared with Sears's 30 percent. But Walmart yielded a 4 percent net profit margin—nearly double Sears's. Tough competition, but you *can* compete.

Ken Stone, professor of economics at Iowa State University, has studied the impact of Walmart on rural economies and small businesses. For a small business to compete with Walmart (and other major retailers), Stone recommends

- Don't compete directly—differentiate.

- Specialize—carry harder-to-get and better-quality goods.

- Emphasize customer service.

- Extend your hours.

- Advertise more—not just products, but also your business.

- Work together with other small businesses.[2]

In preparation for Walmart's move to Bath, Maine, Jayne Palmer took steps to ready her business, Gediman's Appliance. She increased advertising by 30 percent.

To survive in an industry dominated by giants, don't compete directly—differentiate. Offer your customers value—the best quality and service for their money.

She added a computer to track her inventory and linked it into General Electric Credit so that she could order directly with better credit terms. She extended the store's hours. She offered more credit to her customers. She built a television viewing room with space for children to play on the floor. Finally, she cut the low-end appliances from her inventory to avoid competing directly with Walmart on those items.

Although it seems as if the big retailers have all the ammunition for competing in the marketplace, small business owners and managers are finding that they *can* fight back. For instance, look at what's happened in the gardening industry. As sales revenues have "blossomed," competition in the gardening industry has intensified. Although large discount chains like Walmart and home improvement centers like Lowes and Home Depot may have lured away many customers with low prices, small nurseries like John Darin's English Gardens in Detroit have prospered by offering high quality, a wide selection of products, and specialized advice. In fact, Darin has been able to turn his exceptional customer service into a profitable sideline. Customers who want more than a few words of advice and a wide variety of unusual plants can hire his landscaping service to tackle any gardening or landscaping project. English Gardens' annual revenues now exceed $15 million. It is definitely possible for a small business to prosper even in an intensely competitive market—you just have to know your advantage.[3]

Demand

The second economic factor that affects the price you can charge for your products is demand—how many people want to buy how much of your product. Each price you may choose for a product will be accompanied by a different level of demand. The number of units people will buy at different prices is called the **demand curve** (even though in economic terms a curve is often a straight line, as in Figure 14.1). The slope of that curve is called the *elasticity of demand.*

Price elasticity is the effect that price changes have on sales. The elasticity of demand for a product indicates how price sensitive the market is. **Price elastic** demand means a *price-sensitive* market. **Price inelastic** demand means that the market is *not price sensitive.*

If sales rise or fall more than prices rise or fall in percentage terms, demand for your product is price elastic. For example, assume that the demand for your computer software is elastic (see Figure 14.1). If you drop your price by 5 percent, you would expect sales to increase by more than 5 percent. Restaurant usage, personal computers, and airline travel all tend to have elastic demand. Price elasticity is far from absolute; products and segments vary in the degree of elasticity depending on how consumers perceive their need for the product.

If sales rise or fall less than prices rise or fall in percentage terms, demand for your product is price inelastic. You would expect the change in demand to be small after a change in your price (see Figure 14.1). A physician who increases the price of a medical procedure by 10 percent can expect the demand for that procedure to change by less than 10 percent. Health care is price inelastic (at least without government intervention). Both staple necessities and luxury goods tend to have inelastic demand. If you absolutely have to have a product or service, you are less sensitive to price. If a product is truly a luxury, price becomes less of a concern.

demand curve The number of units of a product that people would be willing to purchase at different price levels.

price elastic Products for which customers are price sensitive.

price inelastic Products for which customers are not sensitive about the price.

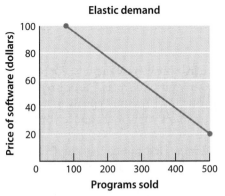

When demand for a product is elastic, as with computer software, a decrease in price will cause an increase in demand.

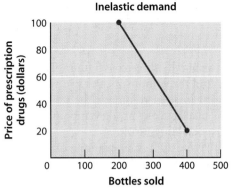

When demand for a product is inelastic, as with prescription drugs, a change in price will have little effect on the quantity demanded.

FIGURE 14.1

Demand Curves

When demand for a product is elastic, as with computer software, a decrease in price will cause an increase in demand.

When demand for a product is inelastic, as with prescription drugs, a change in price will have little effect on the quantity demanded.

Three factors influence the price elasticity of demand for a product.

1. *Product substitutes.* The more alternatives that exist, the more price elastic a product tends to be.
2. *Necessity of the product.* Necessary and luxury goods tend to be price inelastic.
3. *The significance of the purchase to the consumer's total budget.* Cars and houses are elastic. Food and clothing are more inelastic.[4]

The theory of the elasticity of demand is important to small business owners because it shows how price sensitive their customers are when setting prices. How easily your customers can do without your product or use something else in its place will affect what you can charge. Market research can tell you about the demand and elasticity for your product.

Costs

Earlier we stated that the "right" price is actually a range of possible prices. What your competition charges and what consumers are willing to pay set the ceiling of your price range. Your costs establish the floor of your price range. If you cannot cover your costs and make a profit, you will not stay in business.

Your total costs fall into two general categories: fixed costs and variable costs.

$$\text{Total costs} = \text{Fixed costs} + \text{Variable costs}$$

Fixed costs remain constant no matter how many goods you sell. In the short run, your fixed costs are the same whether you sell a million units or none at all. Costs like rent, property taxes, and utilities are fixed. **Variable costs** rise and fall in direct proportion to sales. Sales commissions, material, and labor tend to be variable costs.

fixed costs Costs that do not change with the number of sales made.

variable costs Costs that change in direct proportion to sales.

■ Breakeven Analysis

breakeven point The point at which total costs equal total revenue and the business neither makes nor loses money.

By using the three cost figures discussed above in a breakeven analysis, you can try to find the volume of sales you will need to cover your total costs.[5] Your **breakeven point** in sales volume is the point at which your total revenue equals total costs. Calculating your breakeven point will allow you to set your prices above your total costs, creating profit.

Figure 14.2 is an example of a breakeven graph. First notice that the fixed cost line runs horizontally because fixed costs don't change with sales volume. The total cost line begins where the fixed cost line meets the *y*-axis of the graph, showing that your total costs are your fixed costs when you haven't sold anything. Total costs rise from that point at an angle, as variable costs and sales increase. The area between the total cost line and the fixed cost line represents your variable costs. The revenue line represents the number of units you will sell at any given price level—the demand curve for your product. The point at which the revenue line meets the total cost line is your breakeven point (BEP). The area above the BEP between the revenue and total cost lines shows profit. The area below the BEP between the revenue and total cost lines represents loss.

The slope and shape of the revenue line for your business will vary depending on your customer demand. The information to draw this line can come either from sales history or, if hard data are not available, from your personal best "guesstimate" of how much people will buy. You can also plot other revenue lines based on different selling prices. The revenue line in Figure 14.2 is based on product sales. Let's use the example of compact disks (CDs) selling for $13 each. You can also find your BEP for units with the following formula:

$$\text{BEP (units)} = \frac{\text{Total fixed costs}}{\text{Unit price} - \text{Average variable cost}}$$

where average variable cost equals total variable cost divided by quantity.

FIGURE 14.2
Breakeven Analysis

When the price of a compact disk is $13, the breakeven point would be reached when 50 CDs are sold and $650 of revenue generated.

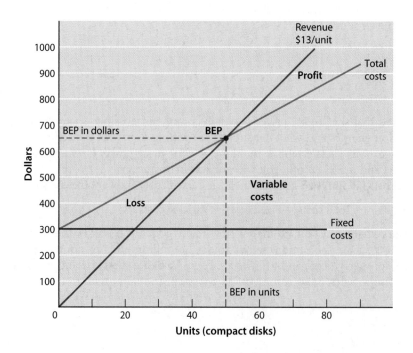

Using the data from Figure 14.2, we could calculate the breakeven point in units for a new CD of Christmas songs from Hatten and His Yodeling Goats. Total fixed costs to produce this musical masterpiece are $300. Variable costs run $7 per unit. Charging $13 per CD, we would have to sell 50 CDs to break even on the venture. (Would 50 people pay $13 to hear yodeling goats, or should Hatten keep his day job?)

$$\text{BEP (units)} = \frac{300}{13 - 7} = 50$$

In order to calculate our breakeven point in dollars, we need to find the average variable cost of our product. This is done by taking the total variable cost (350) and dividing by the quantity (50). The following formula is used to calculate the BEP in dollars:

$$\text{BEP (dollars)} = \frac{\text{Total fixed costs}}{1 - \dfrac{\text{Average variable costs}}{\text{Unit price}}}$$

To find the BEP in dollars for our struggling musician's CD, we would find that at $13 per CD, the breakeven point would be $650.

$$\text{BEP (dollars)} = \frac{300}{1 - \dfrac{7}{13}} = 650$$

What would happen to our BEP in dollars and our BEP in units if we changed the selling price to $20 each or $11 each? At $20 per CD, we would break even at only $400 in sales. At $11 per CD, we would break even at $880. Figure 14.3 illustrates what happens at different price levels. Breakeven analysis is a useful tool in giving you a guideline for price setting. It can help you see how different volume

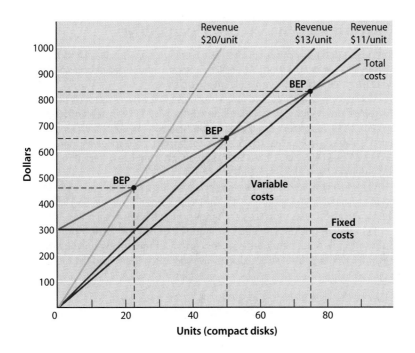

FIGURE 14.3

How Price Changes Affect the Breakeven Point

When the price of a compact disk is changed to $11 or $20, the breakeven point also changes.

levels will affect costs and profits. But in reality, lines rarely run perfectly straight indefinitely. The usefulness of your analysis depends on the quality of your data. The most valuable information for figuring your BEP is the demand for your products at each price level, which is difficult to predict with precision.

Another use for breakeven analysis is to tell you how many units you need to sell to earn your desired return. If Hatten and His Yodeling Goats wanted a return of $1,000, how many units would need to be sold?

$$\text{Target Return} = \frac{\text{Total fixed cost} + \text{Desired profit}}{\text{Unit price} - \text{Average variable cost}}$$

$$\$1,000 \text{ return} = \frac{300 + 1,000}{13 - 7} = 217 \text{ units}$$

When the sales price is $13 per CD, 217 CDs would have to be sold to generate a return of $1,000.

Price-Setting Techniques

After taking competition, consumer demand, and your costs into consideration, you have made a start toward establishing your "right" price. You have a feel for what the price floor and price ceiling might be, but the price you finally choose will depend on the objectives and strategies you choose to pursue—what you are trying to accomplish in your business. Pricing strategies fall into two broad categories: customer oriented and internal oriented.

Don't Give Away the Farm with Special Offers

Businesses with new products often use *seeding,* or giving away products to select people so they will spread the word. Approach Software influenced people to try its database software program without completely giving up sales.

Competing databases sold for as much as $799 when Approach brought out Approach 1.0 for Windows with a $149 limited time offer. Why $149, instead of $99, or even $49? Wouldn't a lower price reach more people? Research by Approach's marketing director Jaleh Bisharat showed that it is possible for prices to be *too* low. Bisharat tested price points of $99, $129, $149, and $199 to 50,000 prospects from five different mailing lists. Surprisingly, demand was almost as high at $149 as at $129.

CEO Kevin Harvey said, "We never could have guessed the price sensitivity curve if we hadn't tested it." Why sell for $20 below the price people are willing to pay? After the introductory period, it was much easier to move up to the full retail price.

Penetration pricing is a good technique for introducing a new product, but Approach Software shows that penetration prices can be set too low. When you have a competitive advantage, charge for it so you don't leave too much money on the table.

Source: Susan Greco, "Smart Use of 'Special Offers,'" *Inc.,* February 1993, 23.

Cost-Cutting Strategies

To run a profitable small business, cutting costs is as important as increasing sales, especially during difficult economic times like recessions. Cost reduction is often a matter of making many little cuts rather than one or two major ones. Strategies for trimming fat from your company include

- *Trim your payroll.* Laying off employees is no one's favorite activity, but sometimes it must be done. Labor costs can represent 20 to 30 percent of a small business's total expenses.

- *Evaluate attrition.* As workers leave your business, evaluate whether you need to hire a replacement or whether the job can be restructured so that someone else in the company can assume the duties. Some employees are made happier by adding more variety to their jobs.

- *Watch supplies and inventory.* These two areas can almost always be a source of savings. Don't reorder items that haven't sold quickly enough. You don't have to go so far as rationing pens and pencils, but you probably can cut supplies.

- *Shop around for suppliers.* Get competitive bids for merchandise. By letting your current suppliers know that you will be shopping for bids, you can probably sit down and negotiate new terms.

- *Do things really have to be there overnight?* Sending items via express mail is expensive—there is a large difference between first-class mail (34¢) and overnight delivery ($20). Use express mail as a last resort.

- *Make sure your advertising works.* Ask customers where they learned about your business. Cut back on advertising that isn't bringing in customers. Maybe you need just one Yellow Pages listing rather than multiple listings.

- *Set limits on travel and entertainment.* Authorize only those trips that bring in money. Stipulate that you and employees must travel coach, and take advantage of airline discounts for weekend stays. Rent compact or subcompact cars.

Source: From "Trimming the Fat" by Michelle Singletar, in *Black Enterprise* (June 1991), 246–250. Copyright © 1991 by Earl G. Graves Publishing Company. Reproduced with permission of Earl G. Graves Publishing Company in the format textbook via Copyright Clearance Center.

Customer-Oriented Pricing Strategies

Customer-oriented pricing strategies focus on target markets and factors that affect the demand for products. Strategies that are consumer oriented include penetration, skimming, and psychological pricing.

Your pricing objectives may be to

- Increase sales.

- Increase traffic in your store.

- Discourage competitors from entering your market.

To accomplish these objectives and gain rapid market share, **penetration pricing** is the most appropriate strategy. Penetration pricing is setting prices below what you might expect in order to encourage customers to initially try your product.

penetration pricing Setting the price of a new product lower than expected in order to gain fast market share.

This strategy is effective in keeping competition from entering the market for your product. Thus, by making less profit on each unit and removing the incentive for competition to enter, you are building a long-term position in the market.

Your pricing objectives may be to

- Maximize short- or long-run profit.
- Recover product development costs quickly.

price skimming Setting the price of a new product higher than expected in order to recover development costs.

If these are your objectives and if you have a truly unique product, a strategy of **price skimming** may be appropriate. Price skimming is setting your price high when you feel that customers are relatively price insensitive or when there is little competition for consumers to compare prices against. Skimming helps recover high development costs, so businesses with new-to-the-world inventions often use this strategy. Home electronics are often introduced using a skimming strategy. Think of the price declines in personal computers, cellular phones, and VCRs. These products usually have high development costs and have unit costs that fall as production increases. Of course, consumers have to be willing to pay a premium to be one of the first to own these new products. Skimming is not a long-term strategy. Eventually, competition forces prices down.

Your pricing objectives may be to

- Stabilize market prices.
- Establish your company's position in the market.
- Build an image for your business or product.
- Develop a reputation for being fair with suppliers and customers.

psychological pricing Setting the price of a product in a way that will alter its perception by customers.

To accomplish these objectives, you may employ one of the **psychological pricing** strategies. Psychological pricing aims to influence the consumer's reaction toward prices of products. Several strategies are included under psychological pricing: prestige pricing, odd pricing, and reference pricing.

prestige pricing Psychological pricing strategy used with goods whose quality is difficult to determine by inspection or for products about which consumers have little solid information.

People often equate quality with price, a belief that has led to a practice called **prestige pricing.** Prestige pricing is especially effective with goods whose quality is difficult to determine by inspection or for products that consumers have little solid information about. Products as diverse as jewelry, perfume, beer, and smoke detectors, or the services of law firms, can all be prestige priced.

In an experiment at Stanford University, graduate students were given three unmarked bottles of beer. One bottle had a dime taped to it, one had nothing, and the third required payment of a dime. The students did not know that the beer in all three bottles was identical. The "premium" beer (the one that cost a dime) won the taste test. Some students even said the "discount" beer made them ill. Price does affect the image of a product.

odd pricing Psychological pricing strategy in which goods are priced at, say, $9.99 rather than $10.00.

We are more likely to see goods priced at $4.98, $17.89, or $49.95 than at $5.00, $18.00, or $50.00—this is **odd pricing.** Research has yet to prove a positive effect of odd pricing, but proponents believe that consumers see $99.99 as a better deal than $100.00. Sales of some products seem to benefit from *even pricing* if you are trying to convey the image of quality. For example, pricing a diamond ring at $18,000 gives the appearance of being above squabbling over loose change.

reference pricing Psychological pricing strategy common in retailing goods for which consumers have an idea of what the price "should be."

Reference pricing is common in retailing goods about which consumers have an idea of what the price "should be" and have a "usual" price for that item in mind.

price lining Grouping product prices into ranges, such as low-, medium-, and high-priced items.

If your customers are price sensitive to comparison prices of competing items, you may choose to use **price lining.** An example of price lining would be a men's clothing store that has ties at three different price points, such as $24.95, $33.95, and $44.95.

Internal-Oriented Pricing Strategies

Pricing strategies that are internal oriented are based on your business's financial needs and costs rather than on the needs or wants of your target markets. Be careful if you use these strategies that you don't price your products out of the marketplace. Remember that consumers don't care what your costs are; they care about the value they receive. Internal-oriented strategies include cost-plus pricing and target-return pricing.

COST-PLUS PRICING Probably the most common form of pricing is adding a specified percentage, a fixed fee, or **markup,** to the cost of the item. Although this type of pricing has always been common in retailing and wholesaling, manufacturers also use this relatively simple approach. Markup can be based on either *selling price* or *cost,* and it is important to distinguish between the two.

markup The amount added to the cost of a product in setting the final price. It can be based on selling price or on cost.

For example, if an item cost $1.00 and the selling price is $1.50, the markup on selling price is 33.3 percent. Fifty cents is one-third of $1.50. However, using the same figures, the markup on cost is 50 percent. Fifty cents is one-half of $1.00. Markup based on cost makes your markup appear higher, even though the amounts are exactly the same. Most businesses base markup on selling price.

Effective use of markup depends on your ability to calculate the *profit margin* you need to cover costs. Formulas useful in calculating markup include

$$\text{Selling price} = \text{Cost} + \text{Markup}$$
$$\text{Markup} = \text{Selling price} - \text{Cost}$$
$$\text{Cost} = \text{Selling price} - \text{Markup}$$

TARGET-RETURN PRICING If you have accurate information on how many units you will sell and what your fixed and variable costs will be, target-return pricing will allow you to set your selling price to produce a given rate of return. To calculate a target-return price, add your fixed costs and the dollar amount you wish to make, divide by the number of units you intend to sell, and then add the variable cost of your product.

$$\text{Target return price} = [\text{Fixed costs} + \text{Target return over Unit sales}] + \text{Variable cost}$$

For example, say demand for your product is 5,000 units. To meet this demand, you need a target return of $100,000, while your fixed costs are $200,000 and your variable costs run $50 per unit. Using this strategy, your price would be:

$$\frac{\$200,00 + \$100,000}{5,000} + 50 = \$60 + \$50$$
$$= \$110 = \text{Your selling price}$$

Creativity in Pricing

The importance of being proactive and creative in running your business is a theme that runs throughout this book. The need for creativity may apply to pricing also. The key to creativity is breaking out of thought processes that keep you in ruts like

"That's not the way it's done in my type of business." To be creative in your pricing, look at techniques and practices of pricing used in different types of businesses and ask yourself, "How can that be applied to my business?" To begin this process, look at Table 14.1, the "Creative Pricing Primer" compiled by Michael Mondello of Celestial Seasonings.[6] Take note of how each approach could apply to your business.

TABLE 14.1
Creative Pricing Primer

Pricing Approach	How It Works	Example
1. Bundling or unbundling	Sell products or services together as packages or break them apart and price accordingly.	Season tickets; stereo equipment; car rentals charging for air conditioning
2. Time-period pricing	Adjust price up or down during specific times to spur or acknowledge changes in demand.	Off-season travel fares (to build demand); peak-period fees on bank ATMs (to shift demand)
3. Trial pricing	Make it easy and lower the risk for a customer to try out what you sell.	Three-month health club starter memberships; low, nonrefundable "pre-view fees" on training videos
4. Image pricing	Sometimes the customer wants to pay more, so you price accordingly.	Most expensive hotel room in a city; a private-label vitamin's raise in price to increase unit sales by signaling quality to shoppers
5. Accounting-system pricing	Structure price to make it more salable within a business's buying systems.	Bill in phases so no single invoice exceeds an authorization threshold; classify elements so pieces get charged to other line items.
6. Value-added price packages	Include free "value-added" services to appeal to bargain shoppers, without lowering price.	A magazine's offering advertisers free merchandising tie-ins when they buy ad space at rate-card prices
7. Pay-one-price	Unlimited use of a service or product, for one set fee	Amusement parks; office-copier service contracts; salad bars
8. Constant promotional	Although a "regular" price exists, no one ever pays it.	Consumer electronics retailers' pricing always matching "lowest price" in town; always offering one pizza free when customer buys one at regular price
9. Price = performance	Amount customers pay is determined by the performance or value they receive.	Money managers' being paid profits; offering a career-transition guide for $80 and allowing buyers to ask for any amount refunded after use

Pricing Approach	How It Works	Example	
10. Change the standard	Rather than adjust price, adjust the standard to make your price seem different (and better).	A magazine clearinghouse's selling a $20 subscription for "four payments of only $4.99"	**TABLE 14.1** **Creative Pricing Primer (continued)**
11. Shift costs to your customer	Pass on ancillary costs directly to your customer, and do not include those costs in your price.	A consulting firm's charging a fee and then rebilling all mail, phone, and travel costs directly to client	
12. Variable pricing tied to a creative variable	Set up a "price per" pricing schedule tied to a related variable.	Children's haircuts at 10 cents per inch of the child's height; marina space billed at $25 per foot for a boat	
13. Different names for different price segments	Sell essentially the same product, under different names, to appeal to different price segments.	Separate model numbers or variations of the same TV for discounters, department stores, and electronics stores	
14. Captive pricing	Lock in your customer by selling the system cheap, and then profit by selling high-margin consumables.	The classic example: selling razors at cost, with all the margin made on razor blade sales	
15. Product-line pricing	Establish a range of price points within your line. Structure the prices to encourage customers to buy your highest-profit product or service.	Luxury-car lines (high-end models enhance prestige of entire line but are priced to encourage sale of more profitable low end)	
16. Differential pricing	Charge each customer or each customer segment what each will pay.	In new-car sales, a deal for every buyer; Colorado lift tickets sold locally at a discount, at full price for fly-ins	
17. Quality discount	Set up a standard pricing practice, which can be done several ways.	Per-unit discount on all units, as with article reprints; discounts only on the units above a certain level, as with record clubs	
18. Fixed, then variable	Institute a "just-to-get-started" charge, followed by a variable charge.	Taxi fares; phone services tied to usage	
19. "Don't break that price point!"	Price just below important thresholds for the buyer, to give a perception of lower price.	Charging $499 for a suit; $195,000 instead of $200,000 for a design project	

Note: Once you've been creative, make sure you're covered. The most important aspect of any pricing approach is that it be legal and ethical. Check with counsel.

■ Credit Policies

After establishing your pricing practices comes an even more important task: deciding how you will get customers to pay for their purchases. Payment methods include cash, check, or credit.

Of course, accepting only cash really cuts down on those bad debts. But the trend is toward consumers' carrying *less* cash, not more, so a cash-only policy will probably keep many customers who would like to purchase with another form of payment from buying. Most small businesses accept checks with adequate identification, such as a phone number and driver's license number, in case the bank returns the check for insufficient funds. For bookkeeping purposes, checks are treated the same as cash and actually make bank deposits easier.

The main reasons for your small business to extend credit are to make sales that you would not have otherwise made and to increase the volume and frequency of sales to existing customers.

Types of Credit

consumer credit Credit extended to customers for the purchase of products.

trade credit Credit extended from one business to another.

Credit is broken down into two basic categories: **consumer credit,** offered to the ultimate consumers by retailers in exchange for goods and services, and **trade credit,** which is the sales terms that one business extends to another for purchasing goods.

Should you extend credit to your customers? Good question. Do your competitors? Will your sales increase enough to pay finance charges? Will sales increase enough to cover the bad debts you will incur? Can you extend credit and still maintain a positive cash flow? Will credit sales smooth out fluctuations in sales volume?

CONSUMER CREDIT You have several choices of ways to extend credit to your customers. You can carry the debt yourself, you can rely on a financial institution like a bank to loan money to your customers, or you can accept credit cards.

If you wish to carry the debt yourself, you can set up an open charge account for customers. Customers take possession of the goods, and you bill them. Invoices are usually sent out to customers monthly. You can encourage them to pay early by offering cash discounts or punish late payment with finance charges. Open accounts must be managed carefully. As we saw in Chapter 8, open accounts can absolutely kill cash flow and drain the life out of your business.

An installment account is frequently offered to customers purchasing big-ticket items (like autos, boats, and appliances). Customers rarely have the cash up front to pay for such items. With an installment account, consumers make a down payment and then make monthly payments on the unpaid balance plus interest for an extended period of time. This type of financing is not quite as dangerous as the open account, because you usually have the product to use for collateral. Generally, small businesses exist to sell their products, and financial institutions are in business to sell money—let them handle installment loans.

You may extend a line of credit to your customers. This operates like a revolving credit account: You approve credit purchases for your customer up to a certain dollar limit. Lines of credit allow customers to buy goods without a new credit check for each purchase. Finance charges are paid on the unpaid balance monthly. Extending lines of credit can simplify the amount of paper in your credit application process, because a new application is not required for each purchase. This type of financing allows you to control the total amount of credit you extend.

To avoid the expense and inconvenience of maintaining your own accounts receivable, you can rely on credit cards as your source of consumer credit. Consumers' use of cash and checks is decreasing as a percentage of total consumer spending, whereas the use of credit and debit cards is skyrocketing. Consumers still use cash and checks for about 67 percent of all payments made outside the home.[7] In the year 2000, the amount of purchases Americans charged on credit cards topped $1 trillion.[8] Check out www.cardweb.com for more information on accepting credit cards in your small business. Credit card use accounts for 50 percent of all transactions (see Figure 14.4).

In development now are plastic cards called Smart Cards, with microchips that handle purchasing transactions. They could have the effect of putting a personal computer in consumers' pockets. Other changes in plastic money include more use of debit cards, which electronically deduct purchases directly from checking accounts.[9] Increased use of debit cards can be good news for the small business owner, because the fees that businesses pay for accepting debit cards are usually lower than for credit cards.

New types of money transactions are changing the way we do business. The cafeteria and vending machines at the Chase Manhattan Bank Metrotech Center in Brooklyn, New York, take only prepaid cards. You can't pay with cash.

Convenience for customers comes at a price, however. Businesses have to pay a percentage of each sale to the credit card company handling the sale. Although card companies offer discount rates for small businesses, transaction and statement fees increase the amount you will pay. The percentage most small businesses pay to MasterCard and Visa varies according to the number of transactions made, but most small businesses are charged between 1.5 percent and 3 percent.[10] The Discover card's stated rates are 1 percent to 2.5 percent, whereas American Express discounts small business rates to 3.5 percent. Total fees, including sales percentages and transaction and statement fees, can run as high as 6 percent.

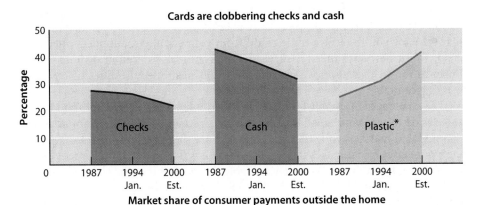

Cards are clobbering checks and cash

Market share of consumer payments outside the home

*Credit and debit cards

FIGURE 14.4

How Do Consumers Pay?

Consumers are using more credit cards than cash or checks to purchase products.

Source: "How Do Customers Pay?" Reprinted from February 14, 1994 issue of *Business Week,* (p. 105) by special permission. Copyright © 1994 by The McGraw-Hill Companies, Inc.

ONLINE CREDIT CHECKS It's a snap to find information about the creditworthiness of customers and suppliers on the Internet and through computer and other services. However, before trying this, you might want to use the net to do some background reading about effective pricing and credit decisions. The U.S. Small Business Administration's site is a good place to start, especially in the General Information and Publications section. There you'll find a file on "How to Price Your Products and Services" and another on "Pricing Your Products." In addition, you might find useful information in "Financial Management for the Growing Business" and "Cash Flow Analysis."

Once you're familiar with the ins and outs of pricing and credit, you're ready to begin conducting your credit checks. Where to start? Databases are available to help you look into a customer's financial past to determine the would-be customers who might have trouble paying you. You can instantly find out about any tax liens, bankruptcies, court judgments, payment history, financial data and analysis, company background, public filings, and other information. Data are available for each geographic zone in the country.

For business credit requests, the Yahoo! web search site lists several merchant credit services that you can access through the web links capability. Just point your mouse to the one you want to investigate and click. In addition, Dun & Bradstreet provides a free search of millions of U.S. companies. Then, for a nominal fee, you can receive a Business Background Report that lists important credit information about the company you're investigating.

For about $300 per year, you can join the National Association of Credit Management, a membership organization that researches and reports on many small firms that are often overlooked by larger credit agencies. As a member, you can get a comprehensive report on a particular firm from the database, which includes about 6.5 million firms.

TRADE CREDIT If you can purchase goods and services and are allowed to take 30, 60, or 90 days to pay for them, you have essentially obtained a loan of 30 to 90 days. Many new businesses can take advantage of trade credit even when no other form of financing is available. Be warned, however, that habitual late payment or nonpayment may cause your suppliers to cut off your trade credit and place your business on COD—cash on delivery.

Trade credit can be offered in several forms: extended payment periods and terms, goods offered on consignment, payment not required until sold, or seasonal dating, which means that suppliers ship goods before the purchaser's peak selling season and do not require payment until after the peak season. Credit lines are popular ways for you to receive trade credit from your suppliers. Suppliers offer trade credit to get new customers. A survey by the National Federation of Independent Business found that about 75 percent of small businesses use lines of credit for working capital.[11]

The challenges of establishing viable credit policies are magnified if and when you decide to take your small business global. Even with the vast economic potential of global markets, you still need to make sure that your customers can pay for their purchases. What makes the process difficult is that credit and payment history information typically isn't as widely available abroad as it is in the United States. For instance, Brian Nimbler, a law partner in a San Francisco law firm, tells of one of his small business clients who entered into a joint venture with a Russian partner and found out, much to his surprise, that the partner was part of the Russian Mafia.

Even though detailed credit checks and other payment investigations can be difficult to obtain, a small business owner can, with a little effort, find information to evaluate the creditworthiness of potential customers. A good place to start is to check with the U.S. Department of Commerce. For instance, if your business is looking at the Russian market, the department has a service called the Business Information Service for the Newly Independent States (BISNIS), which offers broad advice for doing business in Russia. Other possibilities include contacting industry trade associations or your local chamber of commerce for assistance and advice.[12]

Controlling Credit Accounts

If you don't collect on sales, they aren't sales. If you extend credit to customers, you need an accounts receivable system to keep cash flowing into your business. A very easy trap that growing new businesses fall into is the thought "Get the sales now, work on improving profit margins later."[13] This trap is especially serious for service businesses, whose largest expense is labor, which must be paid when the service is provided. Manufacturers also suffer from slow collection due to the long time lag between purchasing raw materials, labor, and inventory and the actual sale of the product.

Western Machine & Chrome, Inc., was a small machine shop that was at risk in 1989 when its overdue accounts stretched from 90 to 120 days.[14] CEO Alvin Bennett and bookkeeper JoAnne Wheeler revised the old collection system into one that identifies bills deserving immediate attention. Western Machine has so many different kinds of customers over a wide geographic area that the system had to be simple and concise. They produce one report for every different industry, showing details about customer invoices. The system allows them to manage time and money by asking the right questions: Which invoices present the biggest cash flow problems? Which aging bills are really not problems? Which present the biggest risk of not being paid? (See Figure 14.5.)

How can you make the arduous and often unpleasant task of collecting overdue bills more manageable? Help is as close as your nearest computer keyboard—*if* you have a good billing software program. Identifying overdue bills and following up to get payment as soon as possible can be automated using billing software that is relatively easy to use. One program packed with features is M.Y.O.B. Accounting (its initials stand for Mind Your Own Business). It's easy to set up and use and comes with more than 100 templates for different types of businesses. This program uses flowcharts for entering invoices and customer payments. However, it's designed more as a total accounting package rather than simply as billing software.

What are some stand-alone billing software programs? One is The Invoice Store, which is primarily for product-based, not service, businesses. It focuses on inventory management and shipping records and can create customized reports to track a customer's payment history. Another popular program is MyAdvancedInvoices & Estimates (Windows and Macintosh versions) by MySoftware Company. This program is easy to use and focuses specifically on invoicing and payment tracking. Another billing program designed for Macintosh users is OnAccount. This program lets users dress up invoices with artwork, but it uses balance-forward accounting— in which payments are recorded against client account totals. This approach means that you won't be able to match payments to individual invoices.

JoAnne Wheeler explains how the system works:

REPORT TYPE
This report is a sample of the type that my assistants—two full-timers and one part-timer—and I use. I've designed it specially to make it easy for each clerk to keep track of his or her collection responsibilities. It also helps me to evaluate each person's collection performance. There's a second type of report that I compile to keep the rest of our employees aware of every overdue account.

CLIENT TYPE
This page covers only our lumber clients. We follow different collection strategies with each sector. With municipalities, for example, we concentrate on making sure our paperwork is in order. We don't hound government agencies. They'll pay eventually—we just don't know when. But we aggressively pursue overdue lumber accounts, concentrating on the biggest amounts first because those have the largest effect on our cash flow. Farmers' invoices are generally smaller, so we go after the oldest bills first. They're the toughest to collect.

CLIENT
I don't alphabetize client names or list them numerically. I list customers with the largest and oldest outstanding balances at the top of each page, and those with the smallest and newest unpaid bills at the bottom. There's no confusion about which ones are most important to keep after.

INTEREST
It really pays to stay on top of your interest charges, and every month I mail our late payers separate invoices for interest fees. Collection clerks sometimes want to offer an incentive to get a very old bill paid. They can use the interest assessment listed on the form to help make a deal. And, if a case goes to court, we have complete records of our activities to support our claim.

SECURITY INDICATORS
An effective accounts-receivable form reports the good as well as the bad. We include the security-indicators column to show clerks which accounts have an additional measure of security, such as a personal guarantee, a letter of credit, a standby letter of credit, or collateral. I flag an unusually good relationship with a company's accounts-payable clerks, too. If we have no reason to worry about a particular bill, that helps our clerks decide whether to devote their collection efforts elsewhere.

LAST ACTION
I wish we had more room to record a description of the last action, because there are often so many details to keep track of. But to expand this colomn, I would have had to switch to a larger piece of paper, instead of using one that's 8¹/2 x 11 inches, and that would have taken up too much desk space and been more difficult to manage. So we simply use the back of the form when our follow-up activities get complicated.

PROBLEM INDICATORS
I've designed a code to highlight possible danger signs. These are the problem indicators: *P* stands for *past problems*. *I* indicates *invoices paid out of order*. *B* means *broke agreement*. *C* is *changes in payment practices*. *M* indicates *changes in major managment or other critical personnel*. *L*, the biggie, means *total due is at or exceeds credit limit*. These codes tell us which bills are crucial for us to collect quickly.

CLERK'S INITIALS
No accounts-receivable clerk wants the recognition of having the worst or the most outstanding accounts!

TOTALS AND PERCENTAGES
Calculating the dollar totals and the percentages is the most time-consuming part of preparing the forms every week, but it's so valuable. It reminds us that credit and collections are an aggregate issue. We have to keep track of the larger picture, even while we're pursuing individual accounts. These figures provide a fast and easy measure of improvement.

TOTAL DUE
Most accounts-receivable forms list this number on the right side of the page, but I'm convinced that people pay the most attention to details listed on the left. So I emphasize the total due and the oldest invoices. If the "current" column gets overlooked, because of its position on the page, that's much less worrisome than if the "over 120 days" number gets skipped.

FIGURE 14.5

Bill Collection System

Collecting Overdue Bills

Bill collecting is never fun, but it is critical for small businesses. Paul Mignini, Jr., president of the National Association of Credit Management, says that you will often hear customers' excuses like "Times are tough, we're having a hard time making it." You should acknowledge their difficulty by saying, "I know times are tough. Let's get this settled before other bills get in the way." The longer bills go unpaid, the lower your chances are of collecting (see Figure 14.6).

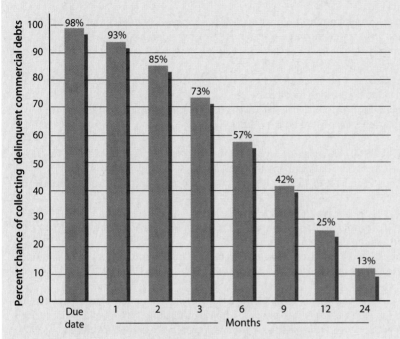

FIGURE 14.6
Show Me the Money

Begin your collection process by telephone if you don't receive a check after 30 days. Create a sense of urgency that the bill must be paid. Try to get a commitment for a certain amount by a specific day, like $100 by the 25th. That puts the burden on the customer. If repeated calls lead you to believe that the customer is playing games, with little intention of paying what he or she owes, you have five choices: a letter service, an attorney, small claims court, a collection agency, or writing it off. Always remain professional and try to stay on friendly terms. You can say something like, "I really busted my tail to get the delivery to you on time. Will you please help us serve other customers by sending a check?"

To help collections, pay attention to your invoices and credit applications. Always print your late service charges on your invoices. Include a venue provision on your invoices if you are selling goods out of state so that any court case concerning the sale will be heard in a court of your choice. State the specific number of days a customer has to notify you of any problems with the shipment.

On your credit application form, ask customers to sign a release that authorizes creditors to disclose relevant information. This will help you to spot credit problems in advance.

Sources: Adapted from Jill Andresky Fraser, "Improve Invoices and Credit Forms," *Inc.*, November 1992, 139; Eugene Carlson, "Collecting Overdue Bills Involves Walking Delicate Line," *Wall Street Journal*, 10 October 1990, B2; and from "Never Say Die" by Jill Andresky Fraser, from *Inc.: The Magazine for Growing Companies,* October 1993, 44. Copyright © 1993 by Goldhirsh Group/Inc Pubg. Reproduced with permission of Goldhirsh Group/Inc Pubg in the format textbook via Copyright Clearance Center.

Which Advertising Medium Should You Use?

Each section below shows the percentage of total media dollars spent by each medium.

Newspaper (23.2%) *Advantages.* Flexible; timely; covers local markets well; believable (because people read newspapers to get information); relatively inexpensive; can use color, coupons, or inserts
　　Limitations. Short life of ad; number of ads per newspaper causes clutter; poor photo reproduction; low pass-along value (meaning that newspapers are rarely read by more than one person)

Television (22.2%) *Advantages.* Reaches large audience; combines sight, sound, and motion; perceived to be prestige medium
　　Limitations. High absolute cost; several ads run together increases clutter and decreases impact; short exposure time

Direct Mail (19.8%) *Advantages.* Can be targeted very specifically; message can be personalized; less space limitations than other media
　　Limitations. Perceived as "junk mail"; relative high cost; mailing lists expensive and often inaccurate

Radio (6.9%) *Advantages.* Can be targeted to specific audience; low relative cost; short lead time so ads can be developed quickly
　　Limitations. People are often involved with other activities and do not pay full attention to ad; people cannot refer back to ad; competition for best time slots

Magazine (5.3%) *Advantages.* Target markets can be selected geographically and demographically; long life because magazines are often passed along; high-quality reproduction
　　Limitations. Long lead time needed in purchasing ad; no guarantee of placement within magazine; higher relative cost than other print media

Outdoor (0.8%) *Advantages.* High repeat exposure; low cost; little competition
　　Limitations. Limited amount of message due to exposure time to ad; little selectivity of target market

Yellow Pages *Advantages.* People viewing ad are likely to be interested buyers; relatively inexpensive; effectiveness of ad easy to measure
　　Limitations. All your competitors listed in same place; easy to ignore small ads; may need to be listed in several sections

Internet Banners *Advantages.* Good selectivity of target markets; inexpensive
　　Limitations. Often negative reaction to advertising on computer networks; uncertainty of number of people reached

Source: Alexander Hiam and Charles Schewe, *The Portable MBA in Marketing* (New York: Wiley, 1992), 365.

As with any software program, the key is to identify your needs and then find the best software to address those needs. With the wide variety of programs available, keeping on top of overdue accounts doesn't have to be a dreaded task.

Promotion ▬

The goal of a company's promotional efforts is to communicate with target markets. There are four major tools to use in developing a *promotional mix:* advertising, personal selling, public relations, and sales promotions. The weight you choose to place on each of these tools will depend on your type of business.

Advertising

Advertising is a way to bring attention to your product or business by publishing or broadcasting a message to the public through various media. Your choices of media include

Print media. Newspapers, magazines, direct mail, Yellow Pages
Broadcast media. Radio, television, or computer billboards
Outdoor. Billboards, or posters placed on public and other transportation

The habits of your target market will affect your choice of advertising media. For example, if your target market is teenagers, radio and television would be the most appropriate choices. The nature of your product will also help to determine the media. Does advertising for your product need to include color, sound, or motion to make it more attractive? The cost of your advertising is another important factor in choosing media. You should look at the total dollar amount an ad costs and the cost per thousand people exposed to the message.

Advertising is critical, but there are some real downsides to it, including slow feedback, expense, difficulty cutting through clutter, and difficulty creating a personalized message. Choosing the medium for your message is important (see the Manager's Notebook, page 446, for the advantages and disadvantages of each medium).

Many small businesses determine how much to spend on advertising by allocating a percentage of their total sales revenues. This percentage varies considerably by type of business (see Table 14.2).

ADVERTISING OBJECTIVES   Different types of advertisements help to accomplish different objectives. You may be trying to

- *Inform* your audience of the existence of your business, your competitive advantage, or product features and benefits.

- *Persuade* people to take an immediate action—such as buying your product.

- *Remind people* that your business or product still exists. Get them to remember what they received from your business in the past so that it remains in their evoked set.

- *Change perception* of your business rather than trying to sell specific products. This is generally called "institutional advertising," and it aims to build goodwill rather than to make an immediate sale.

These are broad objectives that you may try to achieve with your advertising, but creating effective advertisements is both a science and an art. Creativity, humor, and excitement can help break through the clutter or crowding of media. These traits,

TABLE 14.2		
Ad Dollars Spent by Business Type	Industry	Ad Dollars as Percent of Sales*
	Air-conditioning, heating, refrigerator equipment	1.5
	Air transport, scheduled	1.8
	Apparel and other finished products	2.9
	Beverages	9.5
	Bolts, nuts, screws, rivets, washers	0.9
	Bottled and canned soft drinks, water	2.9
	Canned/frozen/preserved fruit, vegetables	6.9
	Carpets and rugs	0.7
	Catalogue, mail-order houses	5.7
	Computer and office equipment	1.2
	Cutlery, hand tools, general hardware	10.9
	Educational services	5.0
	Electronic computers	5.1
	Games, toys, child vehicles—except dolls	14.2
	Groceries and related products—wholesale	1.5
	Grocery stores	1.3
	Guided missiles and space vehicles	5.3
	Hospitals	5.0
	Industrial inorganic chemicals	16.5
	Investment advice	8.6
	Iron and steel foundries	1.2
	Lawn, garden tractors, equipment	4.0
	Lumber and other building material—retail	1.8
	Membership sport and recreation clubs	11.0
	Motion picture, videotape distributors	13.0
	Perfume, cosmetics	10.4
	Phonograph records, audiotape, disc	8.3
	Prepackaged software	4.8
	Radio, TV consumer electronic stores	5.3
	Retail stores, all	5.8
	Security brokers and dealers	3.1
	Sugar and confectionery products	10.6
	Women's clothing stores	2.7

*Ad dollars as percentage of sales = Ad expenditures/Net sales.
Source: "Ad Dollars Spent by Business Type", from Hiame and Schewe, THE PORTABLE MBA IN MARKETING (p. 365), John Wiley & Sons, 1992. Reprinted by permission of Schonfeld & Associates, Inc., 2830 Blackthorn Road, Riverwoods, IL 60015.

however, can also hide the real message of your ad. Communicating your message clearly while catching the viewer's attention is a tough balance to achieve. Common strategies that you might choose to achieve your advertising objectives include

- *Testimonials.* Using an authority to present your message. Athletes and movie stars attract attention, but their public image can change rapidly and must be consistent with that of your business.

- *Humor.* Humor can get attention, but be careful who the brunt of the humor is or you could offend some group and generate negative publicity for your business. Advertising history is also full of some very funny ads that did not generate a single dollar of additional revenue.

- *Sensual or sexual messages.* A common cliché says, "Sex sells." Sex is certainly used in a lot of ads, but research shows that it is not an effective way to get a message across. Like humor, using sex to get attention is worthless if people don't get what you are trying to say.

- *Comparative messages.* Naming competitors in your advertising is legal and quite common. It can be a very powerful way to position your product in the customer's mind against another known entity. This gives the potential customer a reference point, but it also gives your competitor free exposure.

- *Slice-of-life messages.* These messages may use a popular song or a brief scene from life to position your product. Music is a great way to transport people mentally back to another time in their life. Nostalgia can help create a brand identity for your product.

- *Fantasy messages.* These messages stress the ideal self-image of the buyer. What you are trying to do is link a product with a desirable person or situation. This is what almost every beer or soft drink commercial is attempting. The message is "Drink this liquid and you will be beautiful, popular, and desirable." Right.

How do you tell if your advertising works? A common complaint among advertisers runs, "I know that half of my advertising dollars are wasted, I just don't know which half." Measuring the effectiveness of your advertising is difficult. Is the cost of producing and running the ad justified by increased sales and profit? A few techniques might help you find out.

- *Response tracking.* Coded or dated coupons can let you compare different media, such as redemption rate of coupons in newspapers compared with flyers handed out on the street.

- *Split ads.* Another way to compare the effectiveness of various media is to use split ads. You can code two different ads, different media, or broadcast times to see which produces a greater response.

- *In-store opinions.* You can ask in-store customers where they heard of your business, what they think, what you are doing right, and why they buy from you rather than from a competitor.

- *Telephone surveys.* Make random phone calls with numbers from customer files. Ask customers if they have seen your advertising and what they think of it.

- *Statement questionnaires.* Drop a brief questionnaire in the monthly bills you send out to ask customers if they are satisfied with the product or service and how they found out about it.

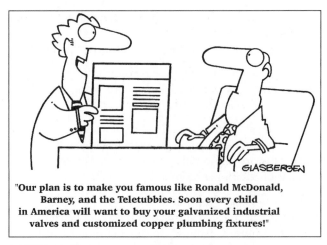

"Our plan is to make you famous like Ronald McDonald,
Barney, and the Teletubbies. Soon every child
in America will want to buy your galvanized industrial
valves and customized copper plumbing fixtures!"

© 1999 Randy Glasbergen www.glasbergen.com

With the wide range of hardware and software available today, you can turn out advertising and marketing materials like a pro. Desktop publishing is just what it says it is. It allows you to publish professional-looking materials from your own personal computer and printer. Whether you're using an Apple or an IBM-compatible computer, there are a variety of software programs that can help you get great-looking results.

Although some integrated software packages like Microsoft Office allow you to create attractively designed documents, specific desktop publishing software helps you produce documents with impressive layouts and graphics, giving you many more options than simple word processing software offers. It helps you publish materials that incorporate text, graphics, clip art, pagination, and background grids, among other elements.

One of the most popular desktop publishing software programs is Microsoft's Publisher. Publisher is an inexpensive option (with a suggested retail price of $99.95) which lets you create simple brochures, product flyers, business cards, labels, calendars, and newsletters. It is easy to insert text and graphics into the program's ready-made templates. Publisher walks users through the process, using "Page Wizards" (visual cues on screen) which ask you to "fill in the blank"—it's that simple. You can also couple it with Microsoft Picture It to add photos.

If you want to invest a little more in your desktop publishing system, or if you think that you might be creating marketing materials (such as flyers, newsletters, and product information sheets) that are longer than ten pages, you can consider higher-end desktop publishing software. QuarkXPress and Adobe PageMaker Plus, for instance, feature a design layout program, Adobe Photoshop provides a photo manager and is especially powerful when coupled with Adobe Illustrator, and Macromedia Flash/FreeHand Studio allows you to create special graphics or icons. However, these programs aren't inexpensive, and they aren't recommended for a desktop publishing novice.

Keep in mind that you can hire graphic design firms to do this type of work if you lack the time or desire to do it yourself. But if you're willing to give desktop publishing a try, you might look for courses that are offered on the topic.

ADVERTISING DEVELOPMENT   Most small business owners plan their own advertising programs, which is usually more appropriate for them than hiring a professional producer. Even if you choose to use an advertising agency, you should still be in active control of your advertising campaign. Remember, you cannot afford to buy a solution to every problem you will face. This is true with your advertising. Spending money will not automatically get you better advertising. As Paul Hawkin said, "The major problem affecting businesses, large or small, is a lack of *imagination,* not a lack of capital."[15] Don't let money replace creativity.

When Ben Cohen and Jerry Greenfield started Ben & Jerry's Ice Cream, they couldn't afford to buy an image, as Häagen-Dazs and its knockoff, Frusen Glädjé, did. Their message was unpretentious and "down home." That image became their biggest asset. Their packaging and advertising with their pictures on the top and a Vermont cow on the side represented their product—natural and honest.

A common problem among self-produced advertisements is that business owners try to cram too much into them. Their reasoning is "This space costs a lot of money, so I am going to use every minuscule part of it." The result is usually an ad that is busy, unattractive, and uninteresting. Simplicity should be the rule here. White space draws the reader's attention. The same principle applies to package design: It doesn't have to tell the consumer everything.

Even though self-produced ads are appropriate for many small businesses, owners should at least investigate the options and promotions that outside professional advertising services make available.

ADVERTISING AGENCIES   To mount an effective campaign, you may want to consider consulting an advertising agency. These businesses can help you by conducting preliminary studies, developing an advertising plan, creating advertisements, selecting the appropriate media, evaluating the effectiveness of the advertising, and conducting ad followup.

A small agency that specializes in and understands your type of business may be a better choice for a small business than a large agency.[16] Ask your friends and colleagues for recommendations, and get samples of the agency's work before signing a contract. Remember that fees are often negotiable, so the agency's fees may be flexible.

MEDIA AGENCIES   You can create your own advertising and hire a media buyer to coordinate the purchase of print space or broadcast time for your ads. Why would you choose to use a media buyer? If you have identified your specific target market, a media buyer can help coordinate your media mix to reach that market. Suppose you designed a new line of blue jeans targeted to urban females from 13 to 17 years old. A media buyer can tell you in which magazine, on which radio station, or on which television show to advertise.

ART AND GRAPHIC DESIGN SERVICES   If you design your own ads and write your own copy but lack the artistic skills needed to produce the final piece of art or film, an art service can do this for you. Like the art director in an advertising agency, this service needs to work closely with the person writing your copy to coordinate the message.

OTHER SOURCES   Radio and television studios, newspapers, and magazines with whom you contract to run your advertising can also produce ads for you. Their services generally cost less than those of an advertising agency.

creating **competitive** advantage

Guppy in a Shark Tank: Small Business, Big Trade Shows

The 1.3 million-square-foot McCormick Place convention center in Chicago can seem like a *very* large place if you are a small business owner setting up for a trade show. Giant competitors set up booths that dwarf the displays of small businesses. But trade shows can generate big deals for small businesses.

Gregory Perkins uses bright lights, bold, colorful graphics, and ten-foot-tall displays to catch the attention of the 20,000 people attending the Book Expo America. Perkins's business, Magic Image, sells African-American greeting cards, calendars, and pocket planners. He does about a dozen shows a year, and they generate most of his $500,000 annual sales. At the 1998 Book Expo, Perkins caught a big fish of a deal when Target Stores agreed to a $30,000 order on the spot.

Trade shows are a chance to bring prospects or current clients together without traveling all over the country a dozen times. Lou Kahn has a small 20-by-15-foot booth at the International Housewares show, also at the McCormick Center, for his Bakertowne Company, an exporter and distributor of housewares. Kahn estimates that about 15 percent of the contacts he makes at a show develop into new business. But measuring results precisely is difficult, because sometimes months pass after a show before a lead finally makes contact.

Research shows that trade shows can be more effective at generating sales than direct mail, telemarketing, or other sales strategies—but you have to develop some trade show savvy. To improve your odds of success at trade shows try the following:

- *Choose the right show.* Trade shows specialize by industry, market, or product. Size, draw, and cost vary widely. Find shows that offer the right mix of audience, location, industry, and price.

- *Plan ahead.* E-mail, snail mail a letter or postcard, fax, or phone the customers you want to pitch at the show. Let them know where your booth will be and how to reach you at the hotel. Don't just sit back and wait for people to approach you. Put forethought into your display. If you bought a ten-by-ten-foot space, re-create that size before you go to the show to make sure all the products you want to take will fit and how you want to display them.

- *Get a good spot.* You want a steady flow of foot traffic, so try to get an island location. Your chances of getting a good spot increase by registering early. You may have to pay a premium to be near the entrance or in a corner.

- *Pool resources with others.* Locating next to businesses with products that complement yours can build synergy. Gregory Perkins and five other business owners had their booths adjoin each other to strategically have a bigger presence of African-American products. Each paid for his own space, but the combination made an impressive display for bookstores looking for their products.

- *Use the right stuff.* Your sales tactics will have to be different than when you are on the floor or on the phone. You have only about 45 seconds to draw someone into your booth. You have to be quick, concise, and use the right buzzwords. Don't concentrate on talking to one customer at the expense of ignoring new people who wander in.

- *Follow up on leads.* Remember that your intent is to turn contacts into sales contracts. Although you may close some deals in the booth, more will take persistence and patience. Stay in touch via your company newsletters to keep potential customers informed about your business.

Sources: Michelle Wirth Fellman, "Small Booth, Big Show, Big ROI," *Marketing News,* 1 February 1999, 1; and Karen Gutloff, "Show and Sell," *Black Enterprise,* July 1998, 105.

Trade shows can be great places to pick up new product lines, suppliers, customers, and ideas.

Personal Selling

Personal selling involves a personal presentation by a salesperson for the purpose of making sales and building relationships with customers. There are many products not large enough, complex enough, or differentiated enough to need personal selling, but for those products that are, it is the best way to complete the purchase (close the deal).[17] Through personal selling, you are trying to accomplish three things: identify customer needs, match those needs with your products, and show the customers the match between their need and your product.

Cost is the biggest drawback to personal selling. When you calculate what it costs for a salesperson to contact each prospect, it is much more expensive than the cost per person for advertising. The average cost of a sales call is over $225.[18] Salespeople have gained a poor reputation because of the high-pressure tactics and questionable ethics of a few of them. The biggest advantage of using personal selling is the flexibility of the presentation that is possible. A trained salesperson can tailor a presentation to the prospect around

Features. What the product is.
Advantages. Why the product is better than alternatives.
Benefits. What the product will do for the customer.

Customer expectations are rising. A good product at a fair price, offered by a well-trained sales staff, backed by a responsive customer service department, is just the

Personal selling, though costly, can be closely tailored to customer needs—making it an effective way to close a sale.

starting point in a competitive marketplace. For your business to stand out, its products need to be tailored to the particular needs of your customers. George Robinson, CEO of Robinson Brick Company in Denver, Colorado, said, "A lot of competitors still think they're selling just bricks. We hope they keep thinking that way." Robinson Brick has changed its way of thinking about bricks—not as commodities, but as unique products. It offers extras that are unexpected in brick production, such as 68 colors; state-of-the-art, same-day delivery; and responsive field service.[19]

The steps in the personal selling process are as follows:

Preapproach. Before meeting with the prospective customer, a salesperson must acquire knowledge about the product and perhaps about the customer and his or her business.

Approach. Upon first meeting the customer, the salesperson tries to establish a rapport with him or her. People seldom buy from someone they don't trust, so a successful salesperson must first earn a customer's trust.

Questioning. To find out what is important to the customer, the salesperson will try to define his or her needs as early in the process as possible.

Demonstration. The salesperson shows how the product will solve the customer's problem and meet his or her needs.

Handling objections. An effective salesperson will listen to what the customer is really saying. An objection shows that the customer is interested but needs more information. Would you raise objections to a salesperson if you were not really interested in a product? No, you would probably just walk away.

manager's notebook

Road Warriors

Personal selling is an effective way to move products. It is also expensive and time consuming. Bob Crawford, CEO of Brook Furniture Rental, spends 50 percent of his time on the road with salespeople, going to conferences, chamber of commerce meetings, and showrooms.

Crawford is emphatic about the importance of business travel. "It's real hard to listen and get the full content, unless you see the person, feel his or her presence," he says. "A telephone gives you only diluted communications with customers."

To make the best use of your time on the road gathering useful information and capitalizing on it at home, Crawford recommends:

- Make sure the office can do without you. You must delegate tasks and invest in hiring and training team members.

- Commit to the time needed. Scheduling takes discipline.

- Let others tell you where you're needed. Crawford gets input from regional managers about traveling with salespeople.

- Talk about your objectives with your salespeople.

- Pump every meeting for industry information. People at most meetings become obsessed with getting their own messages out. Listen to what is going on elsewhere.

Crawford understands that the competitive advantage of his business is based on contacts—his contact with his salespeople and their contact with customers.

Closing the deal. When he or she senses that the customer is ready to buy, the salesperson should ask for the sale. Many sales are lost when a customer is ready to buy, but the salesperson continues to sell.

Suggestion selling and followup. Suggestion selling means recommending products that are complementary to those just sold. Following up with a phone call after the sale builds on the rapport established in the approach and works toward a long-term relationship between the customer and the business.

Public Relations (PR)

Public relations involves promotional activities designed to build and sustain goodwill between a business and its customers, employees, suppliers, investors, government agencies, and the general public.[20] **Publicity** is an aspect of PR consisting of any message about your company communicated through the mass media that you do *not* pay for. Generally, PR works by generating publicity.

Public relations involves a variety of communication formats, including company publications such as newsletters, annual reports and bulletins; public speaking; lobbying; and the mass media. Each format can have an appropriate use and benefit for your company's marketing effort. Table 14.3 shows some PR activities, their target audience, and their impact on your business.

publicity An aspect of public relations consisting of any message about your company communicated through the mass media that you do *not* pay for.

Sales Promotions

Any activity that stimulates sales and is not strictly advertising or personal selling is called a sales promotion. Special in-store displays, free samples, contests, trade show booths, and the distribution of coupons, premiums, and rebates are examples of sales promotions. These activities enhance but do not replace your advertising or personal selling efforts.[21] They are most effective when used in intervals, because customer response decreases over time as customers become familiar with the promotions.

Target	PR Activities	Benefits to Marketing
Customers	Press releases	Increase name awareness
	Event sponsorship	Increase credibility
Employees	Newsletters	Improve communications
	Social activities	Decrease absenteeism and product defects
		Increase morale
Suppliers	Articles in trade publications	Improve image
	Promotional incentives	Improve delivery schedule
General public	News releases	Attract better employees
	Plant tours	Improve image to customers
	Support for community activities	Improve local relations
Government	Lobbying	Favorable legislation
	Direct mail	Less regulation
	Personal calls	

TABLE 14.3

The Relationship Between Marketing and Public Relations

Wadda Ya Lookin' At?

You put a lot of effort, time, and money into creating your business web page. You try to make your web page an integral part of your promotional efforts. You have your dubya, dubya, dubya, dot all over the place for people to see. You know that if people don't find what they want on a web page quickly, they move on. But what do people see when they come to your site? Try looking through their eyes—literally. A company called eyetracking.com lets you do just that.

Eyetracking.com uses state-of-the-art technology to measure what web page visitors see first, what they stop longest to look at, and how easily they find what they want. Testers wear three head-mounted cameras, mounted to a headset shaped like a bike helmet, which follow the eye at 250 observations per second. A technician tracks eye movements across a web site and measures pupil dilation, which correlates with cognitive effort.

Analysis of these eye patterns and physical responses are used to create GazeStats, GazeTraces, and GazeTransitions to indicate site usability. GazeTransitions create a diagram that shows the order and progression with which the person being tested looks at web page items. GazeStat shows the percentage of time testers' eyes spend looking at each location over a prescribed time. Go to www.eyetracking.com to see what draws, attracts, and keeps our eyes engaged on web pages.

A typical one-day usability test requires between 8 and 12 subjects and costs between $10,000 and $15,000. This may sound like a lot at first glance, but not when you consider the value of the usability and sales potential of your web site. You may have problems too big to ignore.

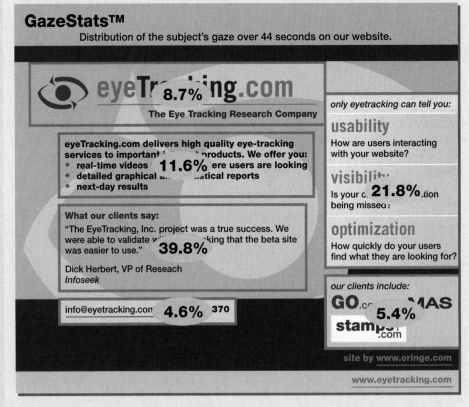

Screen shot of "GazeStats TM. Distribution of the subject's gaze over 44 seconds …" from www.eyetracking.com. Reprinted with permission of EyeTracking, Inc. © 2001.

Sources: Jason Toates, "What Makes Customers Click," *Ziff Davis Smart Business,* June 2000, 152; "Eyes Provide More Accurate MR with Improved, Proprietary Technology," *Research Department Report*, April 2000; and Tessa Romita, "The Eyes Have It," *Business 2.0,* November 2000.

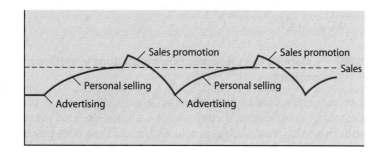

FIGURE 14.7
Short-Term Ratchet Effect of Sales Promotion

When used with advertising and personal selling, sales promotion can give a short-term boost to sales.

Advertising and personal selling are used on a continuous basis, whereas sales promotions are intermittent. A strategy that combines all three can produce a *ratchet effect* on sales (see Figure 14.7). Advertising is used to increase customer interest, whereas personal selling is used to increase sales. Sales promotions at the point of purchase are usually used to increase sales over a short period of time.

An important image builder that is the often overlooked and taken for granted is a $3^1/_2$-by-2-inch white rectangle—the business card. If done correctly and creatively, a business card not only provides information about your small business; it also becomes hand-to-hand advertising.

When asked how small businesses can get noticed, David Avrin of Avrin Public Relations Group says "to shout a little bit louder, do a little better job and be a little more impressive than established companies who get by on reputation alone." Business cards are a good way for a small business to differentiate itself.[22]

Senior Moves, a Boulder, Colorado, company that specializes in moving services for senior citizens, sets its cards apart by using a different shape than normal. Rather than the standard rectangle, Senior Moves cards are in the shape of Rolodex cards imprinted with its logo of a house on wheels. Co-owners Sarah Dillon and Michael Lackey pass out about 200 cards a month. At $22 for 500 cards, that's cheap advertising.

Don't make the common mistake of trying to include everything there is to know about your business on the card. You don't have to have *every* phone, fax, and cell number the business owns. You do, however, need to include your web page and e-mail addresses because your web site provides a wealth of business information (doesn't it?).

The Promotional Mix

In deciding how to combine each of your four tools into a promotional mix, you need to consider when each type of promotion may be appropriate. On one hand, advertising reaches so many people that it is good for creating awareness, but its power to stimulate action decreases quickly. Personal selling, on the other hand, is the most effective tool for building customer desire for the product and prompting customers to take action. But because it requires one-on-one contact, it is less useful in creating awareness. Sales promotions are most effective with customers who are already interested in the product, but who may need prompting to make the purchase. Public relations builds awareness, although it results in few immediate sales.

SUMMARY

Establish the three main considerations in setting a price for a product.

The economic factors that have the largest influence on pricing are the prices charged by competitors, the amount of customer demand for your product, and the costs incurred in producing, purchasing, and selling your products.

Explain breakeven analysis and why it is important for pricing in a small business.

The value of breakeven analysis is ensuring that your prices are set above total costs in order to make a profit. Breakeven analysis is also useful in estimating what demand for a product is likely to be at different price levels. Finally, breakeven analysis is useful to show how many units need to be sold to generate a target dollar return.

Present examples of customer-oriented and internal-oriented pricing.

Customer-oriented price strategies, such as penetration pricing, skimming, and psychological pricing, are based on the wants and needs of your target customers and how many units of your product they will buy. Internal-oriented pricing involves setting your prices according to the financial needs of your business, with less regard for customer reaction.

Describe why and how small businesses extend credit.

Small businesses extend credit to their customers in order to increase sales that would not have been made without credit, and to increase the volume and frequency of sales to existing customers. Credit is extended through open charge accounts, installment accounts, lines of credit, and acceptance of credit cards.

Describe the tools a small business owner uses to compile a promotional mix.

A promotional mix is the combination of advertising, personal selling, sales promotions, and public relations that best communicate the message of a small business to its customers.

QUESTIONS FOR REVIEW & DISCUSSION

1. What strategies should be considered if a small business is setting prices for a product that is to be exported? How are these strategies different from those used in a domestic market?

2. What advantages and disadvantages are involved for a small business offering sales on credit?

3. Discuss the different impressions a consumer has of a product that is "inexpensive" and one that is "cheap."

4. As the owner of a small, hometown drugstore, how would you prepare for a Walmart being built in your area?

5. Does demand for the following products tend to be elastic or inelastic?

   Guess? jeans

   generic corn flakes

   used Dodge Caravan

   new Dodge Caravan

   filling a cavity in a tooth

   automobile insurance

   automobile oil change

   health club membership

   haircut

6. What can happen if the price of a product does not fit with the three other Ps of the marketing mix?

7. Nestlé gave away candy bars on college campuses and issued coupons for free candy bars in newspapers to launch its new Lion bar. How could these practices affect the price strategy of the new candy bar?

8. Should a small business owner's judgment be used to determine prices, if so many mathematical techniques have been developed for that purpose?

9. Discuss the difference between price and value.

10. Discuss the importance of remaining professional and friendly when trying to collect an unpaid bill.

11. What factors should be considered when a small business owner decides to advertise?

12. How has television affected the marketing concept? How has the Internet?

13. Discuss the personality traits that a good salesperson should have. What traits would detract from the personal selling process?

14. Explain the ratchet effect on sales.

15. How would promotional mix decisions change for a small business expanding to a foreign market?

QUESTIONS FOR **CRITICAL THINKING**

1. A lot of self-produced small business advertising is weak. Think of an example of a local small business that uses especially effective advertising. Why is it successful at communicating with its target market when so many are not?

2. Of the pricing techniques described in this chapter, which one do you think is most commonly used by small businesses? Why?

Experience this...

In this exercise we will walk through the steps of creating a print advertisement.

Step 1: Choose a Concept. The following words commonly appear in advertising copy. Choose three or four words that will convey the message you want to send.

act	hurry	now	save
advantage	imagine	opportunity	thanks
benefit	invite	protect	today
convenient	know	proven	unique
discover	learn	results	valuable
exciting	limited time	reward	win
free	new	satisfaction	

Step 2: Work Up the Copy. Take the words you chose in step 1, and write several sentences to describe or promote your business, product, or idea. Your ad copy should answer five basic questions.

1. Who are you (and why should you be believed)?

2. What is your product?

3. How will it benefit the customer?

4. What do you want the customer to do?

5. Where can customers find or contact your business?

Analyze your sentences. Is your tone conversational? (It should be.) Are you targeting a specific market? Do you communicate your features, advantages, and benefits? Is your copy specific or general? (Specific is better.) Do you address your business's competitive advantage? How can the copy be shortened?

Step 3: Artwork. Not every print ad needs artwork, but based on the copy you have written in step 2, could a photo or drawing help customers visualize the point or the benefit you are providing? Sketch out your artwork.

Step 4: Headline. Now you need to grab your potential customer's attention. A good headline can

- Ask a question. (Are you tired of scrubbing tile and grout?)

- Offer a benefit. (Cut your yard work in half.)

- Make a promise. (No need to ever change filters again.)

- Identify a problem. (Using harsh chemicals can be dangerous.)

- Set a scenario. ("They laughed when I sat down at the piano, until. . . .")

Write some headlines that attract attention and engage the reader to continue reading the copy. Make sure the headline meaning is clear.

Step 5: Pull It All Together. Combine all the elements you created in the first four steps. Be sure you don't crowd too much in; white space draws attention. How does the finished product look?

WHAT WOULD YOU DO?   No. 1

Kadali Brothers Coffee Company. Mark Overly's Kadali Brothers Coffee has been voted as having the best espresso in Alaska. Based in Anchorage, Alaska, Overly has built the once-tiny coffee roasting and supply business into a multimillion-dollar venture. Kadali Brothers had projected sales of $4.2 million in 1995. Overly traces his company's success to the quality of his product and service.

Tenth Planet. With a name like Tenth Planet, you're sure to get attention. CEO Cheryl Vedoe has just seen her company's first product go on sale—a set of books, blocks, and CD-ROMs designed to acquaint schoolchildren in kindergarten through second grade with the basics of geometry. But how can a company make money supplying a product to cash-short schools? Because most public schools have invested in computers, Vedoe's company is confident that it can persuade these schools to buy its products and put those computers to good use.

QUESTIONS

1. Working in teams of no more than three, use Table 14.1 to propose at least three alternative pricing strategies for each of the small businesses just described. Think carefully about your suggestions.

2. Develop an appropriate credit policy for each of these small businesses. Be specific in defining what factors you're going to use in your decision about whether or not to extend credit.

WHAT WOULD YOU DO?   No. 2

Developing an effective marketing strategy can be tough. But without it, a small business will be fighting for survival. Read through the following two examples and answer the questions at the end.

DAPAT Pharmaceuticals. DAPAT is a small manufacturer of external analgesics (pain relievers) based in Nashville, Tennessee. Its main product, called Dr.'s Cream, faced this marketing challenge: In competition with much larger makers of over-the-counter remedies (such as Ben Gay), it had to find some ways to attract customers despite a small advertising budget.

Macromedia, Inc. Macromedia, Inc., is also in a highly competitive field—software publishing. The company makes graphic arts software tools for graphic designers, CD-ROM developers, and people who need to make "flashy" presentations. Macromedia's products are full of technical "bells and whistles." Yes, creating computerized dancing mice can be cool, but technology alone won't sell the product.

QUESTIONS

1. Working in teams of no more than three, choose one of the two examples to work on. Develop an outline for a comprehensive marketing strategy for the company and the product. Be specific in defining the product, place, price, and promotion aspects.

2. Once your team has developed its marketing strategy, find another team in the class that has worked on the same example. Take turns presenting your information to each other.

CHAPTER CLOSING CASE   No. 14

Reborn to Be Wild

Can Dave and Dan Hanlon ride off with a chunk of Harley-Davidson's business? As the co-founders of the Excelsior-Henderson Motorcycle Manufacturing Company in Belle Plaine, Minnesota, they are planning volume production of the first Excelsior heavyweight cruising cycle, the Super X model, in 60 years.

Offering Another Choice   In 1993 Dan, 41, had sold his biodegradable-packaging-materials company and was looking to do something different with his life. His brother Dave, 44, had worked for 17 years in the trucking business and was feeling bored. They have both owned and ridden motorcycles since they were teenagers. Says Dave, "Motorcycles are my release. I love to ride 'em, fix 'em, beautify 'em, and just have fun with them." Dave agrees, "Biking is a kind of cleansing of the soul."

That August they again rode their Harley-Davidsons to the biggest unofficial Harley party in the country, the Sturgis Rally and Races in South Dakota. They noticed that nearly everyone owned a Harley or a Harley knockoff, which was no surprise because Harley dominates the $2.1 billion U.S. street bike market, with a 39 percent share. (Nearest competitor Honda has a 22 percent share.) Harley has a 52 percent share of the cruising bike market and a 58 percent share of the touring bike market. Some dealers have waiting lists up to two years long for popular Harley models.

"Many Harley riders go out and buy the clothes, join the Harley Owners' Group—HOG—and put the patch on their backs," says Scott McCool, associate editor of *Easyriders* magazine. "I've yet to see a Kawasaki tattoo anywhere, but I've seen thousands of Harleys."

The Harley dominance gave the brothers an idea. "We decided to offer another choice," Dave recalls.

Finding the Right Name   Back home, they created a business plan, incorporated, kicked in seed money, and began to look for a name. Thinking that nostalgia sells, they wanted a historic name that would resonate with the biking community. They found hundreds of vanished names, but none resonated until they reached Excelsior.

Founded in 1876 as a bicycle company, Excelsior Supply was bought by Ignatz Schwinn in 1911, who later acquired the Henderson Motorcycle Company and merged the two. Charles Lindbergh and Henry Ford owned Excelsior motorcycles. Excelsior's Big X was the first cycle to go more than 100 miles per hour, but the depression forced Schwinn to close Excelsior forever in 1931.

Schwinn's trademark on the name had lapsed, and Dan and Dave leaped on it. "The Excelsior's reputation fit into what we wanted our motorcycle to represent," says Dave. "People want a machine that embodies the history of American motorcycling." They officially adopted the company name of Excelsior-Henderson Motorcycle Manufacturing Company.

Dan and Dave spent the next year raising money and attracting executives to their venture. These included Allan Hurd, then production engineering manager at England's Triumph Motorcycles; Neil Wright, another Triumph alum, who is designing the new bike's engine; Dave Auringer, who built a dealership network for Sea-Doo Watercraft; and Tom Rootness, who has 30 years of accounting experience.

Being Different Becomes a Competitive Advantage   Though the brothers do not claim to be going after Harley's market, their strategy is clearly to attract bikers who value a made-in-America heavyweight heritage cruiser. They believe the Excelsior Super X will succeed, in part, because it's not a Harley. "Our competitive advantage is that we're different," says Dan. "Our name is different. Our history is different. Everything's different."

The Super X will feature a sophisticated V-twin engine, dual overhead cams, and electronic fuel injection. This craftsmanship comes at a price. In fact, the projected retail price of $17,500 will slightly exceed that of a comparable Harley.

"People always think we're going to sell for less, like we've got to do that to get the sale," says CFO Rootness. "As a marketing strategy, we're saying, 'No, no, no. Ours is a higher technology. It's got a better engine, better brakes, and a better suspension. It will be a premium-priced bike.'"

Dan and Dave are riding Super X bikes to rallies and setting up an Excelsior-Henderson tent where prospects can examine the bike and buy Excelsior accessories—leather jackets, T-shirts, and vests. During a recent Sturgis rally, more than 25,000 people visited the tent and bought $45,000 worth of merchandise. In search of exposure, the brothers had gone to Sturgis the year before with the prototype Excelsior Super X, says Dave, "and we obtained that. This year we came for acceptance, for people to walk up to us and tell us they like our product. That's what we left town with—acceptance."

Bikers love to talk. If they talk favorably about the Super X, it will presumably translate into sales. Says Dan, "When you purchase an Excelsior-Henderson, you're buying a piece of American history, a piece of the frontier, a piece of freedom, and a piece of individuality."

Source: Adapted from "Born to Be Wild", by Marc Ballon, from *Inc.: The Magazine for Growing Companies,* November 1997, 42–53. Copyright 1997 by Goldhirsch Group/Inc. Pubg. Reproduced with permission of Goldhirsh Group/Inc Pubg in the format textbook via Copyright Clearance Center.

QUESTIONS

1. Analyze and discuss Excelsior's pricing strategy of making its motorcycles more expensive than the primary competitor, Harley-Davidson. Do you think this is a good strategy for a startup company competing against an established one?

2. Harley-Davidson is an American icon. If a motorcycle is shown on TV or movies, it's usually a Harley. Consumer passion runs strong for Harleys—how many other company names are tattooed on customers? How can Excelsior compete against that? Suggest ways the Hanlons can create a promotional campaign that will convince people that an Excelsior is more attractive than a Harley.

PART SIX

Managing Small Business

In this section we will bring together all the phases of running your own business. Visualize yourself making the decisions needed to make it all happen as you read these chapters. Are there opportunities for your business in other countries? Many small businesses find that there are, especially via e-commerce. Foreign sales can be an excellent way to generate growth. **Chapter 15** will explore those possibilities. **Chapter 16** explains professionally managing your business through the stages of growth it will experience. **Chapter 17** looks at managing your most valuable resource—people. **Chapter 18** covers the management of service and manufacturing operations.

15

International Small Business

After reading this chapter, you should be able to:

- List the factors to consider when preparing an international business plan.

- Enumerate the five ways for small businesses to conduct international trade.

- Analyze the advantages and disadvantages of exporting for small businesses.

- Discuss the factors to consider when importing products and materials.

- Explain how small businesses can manage their finances in international trade.

- Articulate the cultural and economic challenges of international small business activity.

IN 1973, TONY AND MAUREEN WHEELER went on their honeymoon. And this wasn't just a weekend at Niagara Falls. Tony had just received his master's degree from the London Business School, and Ford Motor Company had just offered him a job, but he deferred accepting for a year. They took a year-long trip to try to get the wanderlust out of their systems before "settling down." They bought a very used Austin minivan for $150 and still had $1,400 in savings. They drove across Europe and the Middle East to Afghanistan. There they sold the Austin and continued across Asia via train, bus, rickshaw, and boat, eventually ending up in Sydney, Australia, after spending a mere $6 per day. On this trip they kept a journal. Tony noted specific details. Maureen mused romantically. Their 96-page travel notebook became the foundation of a travel guide empire called Lonely Planet.

When they returned to Australia flat broke, they were surprised to find people whom they knew and met asking them repeatedly, "How did you do that?" So they wrote a travel guide entitled *Asia on the Cheap* to tell adventurous, unconventional people just that—how they did it. They set up a tiny office in Melbourne, where they returned from far-flung expeditions to compile their notes in another book. Since the 1970s, they have compiled over 400 guides touching every continent.

Like most small businesses starting out, they kept overhead to a minimum. Maureen organized layouts and set the type herself. Tony packed shipping cartons and wrote. They both did it all. Their traveling and their business were done on a shoestring, which became the competitive advantage of their guides. People wanted to learn how to travel on the cheap and were willing to pay for it. The Wheelers loved to travel and write about their experiences.

South-East Asia on a Shoestring, which sold 15,000 copies at $1.95, was followed by more shoestring guides for Hong Kong, Australia, Nepal, and Africa. They thought they were over their heads with the India guide, because it was twice the length (700 pages) and twice the price ($10) than their other products, but it sold over 100,000 copies in its first edition.

In 1980, they decided to get serious about their international business after the birth of their first child. They opened an office in Oakland, California, and one in London six years later. Lonely Planet was turning into a real business, gradually expanding its staff to 12 people.

Today, Lonely Planet has gone high tech. Lonelyplanet.com supports the guidebooks with message boards, printable updates to the publications, and medical advice. The web site receives over 350,000 hits per day, has developed a reputation as one of the best travel sites around, and is run by just three staffers. The company recently began to produce city guides specifically for travelers' Palm Pilots as part of its evolution.

Although their company has certainly changed over their 30-plus years, the Wheelers' mission has not changed—getting unique information to travelers as quickly and accurately as possible. They love books as a way to carry around information but are fluid to the idea of changing formats. Maureen says that, whatever way travelers learn about new places, they hope it will be from Lonely Planet.

Sources: Maggie Overfelt, "Wanderpreneurs," *Fortune Small Business,* 21 April 2000, fsb.com; "Roughing It," *Fortune Technology Guide,* Summer 2000, 257; Michael Schuman, "The Not-So-Lonely Planet," *Forbes,* 22 May 1995, 104–108; and Cade Metz, "How They Built It," *PC Magazine,* 8 February 2000, 147.

■ Preparing to Go International

The size of a business does not determine its ability to enter global markets, but it may influence the number and scale of markets a business can enter.

When most people think of international business, they envision large, multinational corporations with operations all over the globe. A common conclusion is that small and medium-sized businesses are at a disadvantage in their ability to compete internationally. Actually, research shows that the size of a business is not a barrier to entry into international markets; it only limits the number of markets you can serve.[1] Having improper strategies, negative attitudes toward expansion abroad, or lack of experience may keep businesses out of the international game, but size does not have to be a factor. In fact, the same competitive advantages—your unique skills, talents, and products—that have made your business successful in local markets may create the same advantage in foreign markets.

Growth of Small Business

Not only can small businesses compete successfully in other countries, they are increasing their export rate much faster than large businesses. An SBA study showed that 11 percent of small businesses exported goods and services to other countries in 1992. By 1994, 20 percent were exporting, and by 2000, over one-third of all U.S. small businesses were exporting.[2] Small businesses are major players in international business (see Figure 15.1).

"The bigger the world economy, the more powerful its smallest players," stated John Naisbitt, author of *Megatrends* and *Global Paradox.*[3] The world is integrating

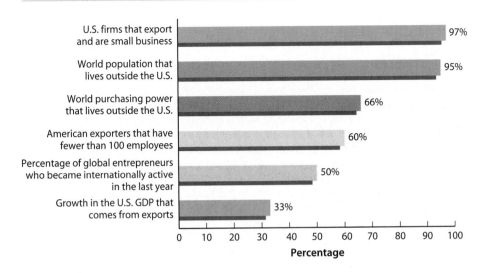

FIGURE 15.1
Small Business Globalization by the Numbers

Source: Allbusiness.com/Focus-Magazine/GoingGlobal, U.S. Department of Commerce, and SBA Office of Advocacy.

economically, and as it does, there will be more and smaller component parts. Market niches will become smaller, and this is good news for small businesses. "Success in seizing market niches has to do with swiftness to market and innovation, which small companies can do so well," added Naisbitt.[4]

International Business Plan

To navigate these shifting international tides, you will, of course, need a business plan. As we discussed in Chapter 4, a solid business plan is behind most successful small businesses.

So, what do you need in an international business plan? Begin with everything that is included in a domestic plan. You have to have a market (or preferably multiple markets) for your product, you have to have a unique product, you have to have the managerial skills to take advantage of the opportunity you have identified, and you have to have the financial capability to do the deal. In addition to the business plan content and analysis described in Chapter 4, the following information, at a minimum, will help you analyze your ability to go international and chart the course to follow:

- Your commitment to international trade
- Your export pricing strategy
- Your reason for exporting
- The most attractive potential export markets and customers
- Your methods of entering foreign markets
- Exporting costs and projected revenues
- Your financing alternatives to allow you to export
- Any legal requirements you need to meet
- The transportation method that would be most appropriate
- Any overseas partnership contacts and foreign investment capabilities[5]

Just Do It

You hear a lot about barriers that keep small businesses with few resources from entering foreign markets. Jeffrey Ake, vice president of sales and marketing at Electronic Liquid Fillers (ELF), which makes liquid-packaging equipment, thinks the biggest barrier is not expertise, finance, or culture—it's psychology. Ake says that, once you have made the decision that you want to sell in overseas markets, everything else will fall into place.

ELF had the typical problems that most small businesses face when considering international expansion—no expertise, no line of credit, and a location in the industrially depressed Rustbelt. But ELF's sales rose from $150,000 in 1988 to $6 million in 1992 due to entering international markets. This gain represented half of its total sales and all of its growth. Here's the advice Ake gives on getting started:

- Name someone—probably yourself, but maybe your top sales or marketing person—to be the international tiger.

- Announce to the world that your company's products exist and are available for purchase.

- Get yourself over there and sell.

- Stick to what you know works.

- Strongly consider raising your prices.

- Let the experts lead you through the details of processing the order.

- Once you get an order, service it.

- Keep your initial market-entry costs low, low, low.

Source: Jeffrey Ake, "Easier Done Than Said," *Inc.,* February 1993, 96–99.

One expert recommends that an international business plan should include both market entrance and exit approaches, because markets that are hard to leave can drain export sales profits.[6]

If you conclude from your planning that you should proceed with your expansion into other countries, you have five basic choices: exporting, importing, licensing your product, establishing a joint venture, or setting up operations in the other country. Each of these options represents an increased level of commitment on your part, so let's look at your options in that order.

Take the Global Test

Taking your small business across national borders can be a good move. You've heard stories of others striking gold that's out there just over the horizon—but it's not easy. You can bet you will build competitive advantage if you can pass this 10-part test.

1. *The "good reason" test.* If exporting is not part of your core business strategy, don't bother. A one-shot deal, even a big one, may not be worth the trouble. Software company Blue Pumpkin has been international since its beginning in 1996. Because Blue Pumpkin provides customer service software to many Fortune 1000 firms who want to use it all over the world, it has to be global.

2. *Do you have the right stuff to pull this off?* To be taken seriously by foreign buyers, your business needs a certain degree of success at home. Depending on your industry, this could be measured by market share, technical expertise, or brand awareness. In selling fishing lures, for example, brand awareness is key, so Kendall Banks makes sure that T-shirts for his Silver Buddy lures cover the BassMasters trade show in New Orleans for the benefit of foreign buyers.

3. *Can you identify a market?* Every country provides different sets of problems and customers. Forget about trying to enter more than one at a time. Randy Reichenbach has trouble competing in the Middle East against a competitor from Trieste, Italy, selling reconditioned surgery tables. Randy's American tables are top of the line, but the Italian models are great, too, and the weak Euro makes their prices low. Not good news for Randy.

4. *Are you flexible?* With few exceptions, product modifications will need to be made. Carroll Mixon's Kelley Manufacturing makes digger shaker inverters for planting peanuts in Georgia (the U.S. state, not the Eastern European country). South Africa uses different row spacing that required product changes. Is the expense of modifying your product for export worth it? It can be, if it's part of your overall strategy (see number 1).

5. *Can you find a good distributor?* Getting your products into the hands of end users in other countries is especially challenging for small businesses. Export managers and foreign distributors can be very helpful in preparing you for the twists and turns in reaching markets, but they may also change the way you want your product to be perceived by customers.

6. *Can you cope with all the complexity?* Jim Hunt, president of Kabobs, makes frozen hors d'oeuvres for ritzy hotels. He says that "every shipment to Canada requires 40 pieces of paper and you have to save all paperwork for at least three years." Another complexity is that, if one of his appetizers is, say, 25 percent chicken, does it fall under Canada's chicken import quota? You get the idea.

7. *Can you brave the, shall we say, nonlegal barriers?* Roger Berkeley wanted his textiles from Weave Corporation to reach buyers in Italy. The problem is that Americans were banned from the annual trade show in Como, Italy. Berkeley fought through the problem by laying out his goods at a nearby villa and picking customers up directly at the trade show to drive them to his goods. Someone, he alleges, got his drivers arrested. That was enough, so he now focuses on a friendlier show in Belgium.

8. *Are you willing to extend credit or deal with currency turmoil?* Sure, you would prefer to be paid up front and in U.S. dollars, but that option is not always available. You are more likely to receive a bankable letter of credit, which slows your ever-critical cash flow. Then you face the volatility of currency exchange rates. Weave Corporation saw its sales plunge with the decline in value of the Euro relative to the U.S. dollar because European rivals then had a price advantage.

9. *Are you ready to run a much different kind of company?* Get real with this; exporting will change your company—and your life. Changes may be as simple as going in to the office at 4 A.M. for a foreign conference call to deal with time zone differences.

10. *Do the rewards outweigh the costs?* This will be a personal decision that depends on what you want to get from the business. It may be a question whose answer changes from time to time. Many small business owners involved in international trade ask themselves, "What have I gotten myself into this time?" But there are times when sales are growing through the roof and you feel, you could say, on top of the world.

Source: Adapted from Kenneth Kale, "Going Global?" *Fortune Small Business*, March 2001, 98–103.

■ Establishing Business in Another Country

A vast majority of small business activity in the international market will be conducted via importing and exporting. Still, for the experienced, visionary, and adventurous businessperson, other options exist which represent an even greater commitment to global trade. Small businesses can license their products or services, form joint ventures or strategic alliances, or even set up their own operations to conduct business in other countries.

Exporting

exporting Selling goods or services in a foreign country.

The primary mechanism for small businesses to engage in international business is **exporting**, or sending the products they make to another country. Because of the importance of this option for establishing business in another country, we will cover direct and indirect exporting in more detail later in this chapter.

Importing

Many small business owners recognize that not only do markets for their products exist in other countries, but their domestic markets can also be served by bringing in products from other countries via importing. Importing represents such a viable option for small business that we will discuss it in more detail later in this chapter.

International Licensing

licensing The agreement that allows one business to sell the rights to use a business process or product to another business in a foreign country.

As an exporter, you can stop exporting at anytime you wish. However, other forms of international business represent a larger commitment on your part. The next level of commitment above exporting in international business is **licensing.** As a licenser you are contractually obligated to another business for a period of time.

Licensing is a way to enter foreign markets by assigning the rights to your patents, trademarks, copyrights, processes, or products to another company in exchange for a fee or royalty. The two biggest advantages of licensing are speed of entry and cost. You can enter a foreign market quickly for virtually no capital. Licensing is similar to franchising domestically. Licensing agreements are generally written to endure for a specified period of time. A disadvantage of licensing is that your licensee may become your competitor after the agreement expires, if it continues to use your licensed process without paying you for it.

International Joint Ventures and Strategic Alliances

A foreign **joint venture** is a partnership between your business and a business in another country. As with any partnership, choosing the right partner is critical to the success of the venture. Each of you needs to bring something (products, knowledge, channel of distribution, access to a market, or other quality) to the venture that the other would not have alone.[7]

Partnerships of *any* type can be difficult (see Chapter 2). Joint ventures are often costly failures. A study by Columbia University shows a success rate of only 43 percent, with an average life span of 3.5 years.[8] Despite the difficulties, joint ventures and strategic alliances are and will be needed to be competitive globally. Finding a local partner is the only way to enter some countries.

Following are seven advantages that often work in combination to improve your chances of forming a successful joint venture:

1. Penetrating protected markets
2. Entering heavily concentrated industries
3. Lowering production costs
4. Sharing risks and high R&D costs
5. Preventing competitive alliances
6. Maximizing marketing and distribution channels
7. Gaining leverage over a supplier and strategic knowledge of a supplier's products[9]

Strategic alliances are not exactly the same as joint ventures.[10] Lorraine Segil of the Lared Group specializes in establishing strategic alliances, helping to match small organizations with large ones through a chain of contacts in the United States, Europe, the United Kingdom, and Australia. The match is often made with a large, well-established company abroad that needs fresh ideas and products. Because many entrepreneurial firms have just that, but only limited capital, the result is often a profitable alliance for both.

> **joint venture** An agreement in which two businesses form a temporary partnership to produce a product or service in a market that neither could satisfy alone.

> **strategic alliance** A partnership between two businesses (often in different countries) that is more informal than a joint venture.

Direct Investment

Once you have established your international operations, you may choose to set up a permanent location in another country. Opening an office, factory, or store in a foreign land is the highest level of international commitment you can make. Of course you are making a significant financial investment that costs you money, but what other risk is involved with direct investment? Think about what would happen if you set up operations in a country experiencing political instability. What if a new political regime takes power? Will you be allowed to operate as you did before? Will you even be allowed to keep the assets you have invested in there? Maybe not on either count. Small businesses rarely start out their global experience this way. Exporting, licensing, or joint ventures are much more common vehicles.

■ Exporting

Exporting is defined as selling in another country the goods or services that you offer domestically. It is the most common way for small businesses to operate in other countries.[11] Of all the ways to conduct business internationally that we are considering in this chapter, exporting provides the lowest levels of risk and investment, increasing your chances of being profitable.

The Small Business Administration (SBA) has identified advantages and disadvantages of exporting. Advantages of exporting include

- Increased total sales and profits.
- Access to a share of the global market.
- Reduced dependence on your existing markets.
- Enhanced domestic competitiveness.
- A chance to exploit your technology and know-how in places where they are needed.
- Realization of the sales potential of existing products and extension of the product life cycle.
- Stabilization of seasonal market fluctuations.
- Opportunity to sell excess production capacity.
- Chance to gain information about foreign competition.[12]

Disadvantages to exporting revolve around the additional responsibilities and obligations your business may incur. You may be required to

- Develop new promotional material suitable for foreign customers.
- Forgo short-term profits in the interest of long-term gains.
- Incur added administrative costs.
- Allocate funds and personnel for travel.
- Wait longer for payments than with your domestic accounts.
- Modify your product or packaging.
- Acquire additional financing.
- Obtain special export licenses.[13]

Only you can decide if the disadvantages of global expansion outweigh the advantages. The timing of entering a foreign market may not be right, or you may be short on cash to fund the expansion at this point. But there are no solid rules of international expansion. Some businesses go abroad before selling *anything* at home. For instance, Ray Ciliv and Robin Hillyard, founders of NovaSoft Systems software company, were down to their last $250 when the stock market crashed in 1987. The only thing they had going for them was their company's product—the latest technology in computer-based engineering document management systems. Without the resources for marketing in the United States and no chance of attracting outside capital, their next step was unique—they decided to sell their software overseas to prove it was good and then let sales momentum bring it back to the United States. They started in Italy, then Germany, Venezuela, Belgium, Israel, and Japan—all *before* beginning distribution in the United States.[14]

If you decide that exporting is right for your business, you have two methods that you can use: indirect and direct exporting. Whether you choose to use intermediaries is the primary difference between the two.

Indirect Exporting

The simplest and perhaps most cost-effective way for a small business to export is to hire an export service company to market products abroad.[15] This method minimizes the financial and personnel resources needed to promote international sales. Using an intermediary reduces your risks and can help you learn the exporting process. Even if you start using indirect exporting, you may choose to set up an international sales staff once you develop the capital and expertise.

Of course, the fee charged by an export service company will reduce your profit margin, but the increased sales should offset this disadvantage. A more dangerous disadvantage is that you lose control by operating through an intermediary. Your company name and image are in the hands of the exporting intermediary. Finally, the price the ultimate consumer pays may be increased by using intermediaries. You should negotiate what all costs, fees, and the final price will be up front in the contract.

There are several kinds of intermediaries for you to consider. Agents and brokers, export management companies (EMCs) and export trade companies (ETCs), ETC cooperatives, foreign trade companies, and piggyback exporting are all domestic-based intermediaries. Foreign-based intermediaries include foreign distributors and foreign agents.

AGENTS AND BROKERS. Both agents and brokers will put your company in touch with foreign buyers. They set up the deal, but they don't buy the products from you. They can also provide consultation on shipping, packaging, and documentation.

EXPORT MANAGEMENT COMPANIES (EMCS). EMCs provide a much fuller range of services than agents or brokers, but they still do not take title to your goods. EMCs act as your own export department, conducting marketing research, arranging financing and distribution channels, attending trade shows, and handling logistics. EMCs will even use your company letterhead in all correspondence and provide customer support after a sale. EMCs are a good option for small businesses new to international trade.

EXPORT TRADE COMPANIES (ETCS). ETCs perform many of the same functions as export management companies, but they generally take title of your goods and pay you directly. ETCs operate individually and also join together to form cooperative groups of companies selling similar products.

PIGGYBACK EXPORTING. If you can find another company that is already exporting, you may be able to make a piggyback arrangement to take advantage of the international connections the other company has already established. If your products do not directly compete with the other company's products, it may simply add your product line to its own.

FOREIGN-BASED DISTRIBUTORS AND AGENTS. Using a distributor or an agent that is based in the foreign country, rather than one based in the United States, can provide the advantage of cultural and local knowledge that you may not be able to get elsewhere.

George Grumbles, president of Universal Data Systems, has been exporting electronic equipment for over 25 years. He believes in building groups of local distributors in his foreign markets. Grumbles says, "You have to work through nationals [residents of the foreign country]. If you send U.S. folks into a foreign country, you have to expect it will take a couple of years for them to find their way around. Instead, you should find people who are embedded in the local economy."[16]

Foreign agents do the same jobs overseas that manufacturer's representatives do in the United States. Agents work on commission within their sales region of specific countries. Local laws and customs vary greatly between countries, so you must be clear on what you can expect an agent to do legally. Some countries go to extremes in protecting their citizens from foreign companies.

Foreign distributors may sell on a commission basis or buy your goods directly. You and the distributor should work together to produce your marketing materials, because translating your packaging and promotional material into another language can be a problem.

Direct Exporting

With direct exporting, you do not use any intermediaries, as with indirect exporting. If you choose to use direct exporting as your method of selling your products in other lands, you have more control over the exporting process, greater potential profit, and direct contact with your customers. A point you must remember when considering any channel of distribution is that you can do away with the intermediary, but *someone* has to perform this function. If you choose not to use an intermediary for your exporting, then *you* have to perform those duties. You have to choose the target countries, arrange the most efficient channel of distribution, and market your product in the foreign country. Direct exporting is therefore riskier, more expensive, and more difficult than indirect exporting, but because you pay less in service fees or commissions, your potential profit could also be greater.

In direct exporting, one approach could be the use of sales representatives who sell your products and other (noncompeting) products on a commission basis. You may choose to use a distributor or to sell directly to the final consumer.

Selling your product in other countries may be a logical extension of your domestic business. Many business executives say that exporting is essentially no different from expanding into a new market in your own country. Of course, operating in other countries can create unique challenges, but first you have to go back to basics. You have to do your market research to determine who will buy your product and where they are. You have to determine your channels of distribution and your prices. Remembering these basics may take some of the intimidation out of "going international."

Bagels-To-Go—A *Long* Way

Many small business owners think their business is too small to export products. But Jerry Shapiro, president of Petrofsky's International, thinks that the success of small businesses trying to break into the trade game has more to do with courage than size.

Petrofsky's began as a family-owned neighborhood bakery in St. Louis that developed a way to quick-freeze uncooked bagel dough as a way to let bakers take weekends off. Next, they expanded by selling to supermarkets that would prepare and package the bagels as their store brand. Petrofsky's increasing success with this product led it to build a new factory with a production capacity of 1.5 million bagels per day. As a way to spread increased overhead over a larger market, Petrofsky's began to consider exporting.

In 1985, Shapiro attended a trade show in Japan, where he passed out 8,000 sample bagels. He also observed local customs and test-marketed his bagels to find out if any changes would be needed to sell the bagels in that country. (He found that softer and larger bagels sold best.) But when Petrofsky's made the decision to export, Japanese food inspectors refused to allow the bagel dough into the country because of the "active bacteria" in the dough. Of course that bacteria was yeast, which makes bread and bagels rise. To solve the entry problem, Shapiro joined forces with Itochu, a large Japanese trading company. Itochu used its local influence to get Petrofsky's product certified.

By 1993, Petrofsky's annual revenues were up to $12 million, with $1.5 million representing international sales. Not bad for a company that started as a neighborhood bakery! In 1994, the company opened its own retail bagel stores in Tokyo to complement its wholesale business.

Shapiro has learned that choosing the right partner is a critical decision when entering foreign markets. When he tried to expand into Europe, he says, he chose the wrong person—neither side trusted the other completely. After finally terminating that relationship, Petrofsky's found itself three years behind schedule for its European expansion.

Source: Adapted from Rob Norton, "Strategies for the New Export Boom," *Fortune,* 22 August 1994, 124–130.

Identifying Potential Export Markets

Successful marketing depends on your knowledge of the people and places with which you are dealing. In addition to marketing research you would conduct locally, marketing research in the international sector needs to include the following activities.

FIND COUNTRIES WITH ATTRACTIVE, PENETRABLE MARKETS. Sometimes the largest trading partners of the United States may not be the best countries for you or your products. For example, Harden Wiedemann of Assurance Medical, Inc., a provider of alcohol- and drug-testing services, was surfing around the Internet one day when he stumbled on information about growing alcohol-related problems in Argentina. A little more investigation revealed a sizable opportunity for his company.

Most small businesses begin their search for market information from U.S. government sources. The Department of Commerce's *National Trade Data Bank*

FIGURE 15.2
Top Ten Trade Partners of the United States

These ten countries represent 70 percent of U.S. imports and 66.35 percent of U.S. exports.

Source: www.census.gov/
foreign-trade/top/dst/2001

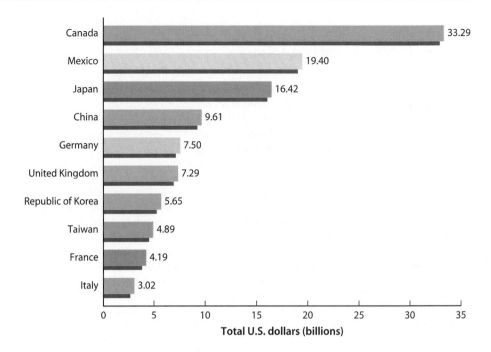

FIGURE 15.3
Canada at a Glance

For information about the United States' largest trading partner, go to country listing of *The CIA World Factbook* (www.cia.gov/cia/publications/factbook/index.html)

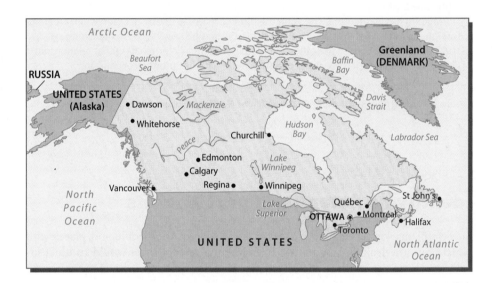

ECONOMY OVERVIEW

As an affluent, high-tech industrial society, Canada today closely resembles the United States in its market-oriented economic system, pattern of production, and high living standards. Since World War II, the impressive growth of the manufacturing, mining, and service sectors has transformed the nation from a largely rural economy into one primarily industrial and urban. Real rates of growth have averaged nearly 3.0 percent since 1993. Unemployment is falling, and government budget surpluses are being partially devoted to reducing the large public sector debt. The 1989 U.S.-Canada Free Trade Agreement (FTA) and the 1994 North American Free Trade Agreement (NAFTA), which included Mexico, have touched off a dramatic increase in trade and economic integration with the United States. With its great natural resources, skilled labor force, and modern capital plant, Canada enjoys solid economic prospects. Two shadows loom, the first being the continuing constitutional impasse between English- and French-speaking areas, which has been raising the possibility of a split in the federation. Another long-term concern is the flow south to the United States of professional persons lured by higher pay, lower taxes, and the immense high-tech infrastructure.

(NTDB) is a rich source of information. Available at federal libraries on CD-ROM, the NTDB contains more than 100,000 documents on export promotion and international economic information.[17] With the *Automated Trade Locator Assistance System (SBAtlas)*, the SBA provides current market information to small businesses on foreign markets where their products are being bought and sold, and on which countries comprise the largest markets. SBAtlas is available at your local SBA office.

Canada, Mexico, and Japan top the list of importers of products made in the United States (see Figure 15.2). More detailed information on foreign markets for small businesses is available through sources like the CIA World Factbook (see Figures 15.3, 15.4, and 15.5).

DEFINE EXPORT MARKETS THAT MATCH YOUR PRODUCT. After you have identified potential countries, you must find out if a need exists there that you can satisfy. You should ask yourself

- How does the quality of products in the foreign country compare with that of your products?

- Will your prices be competitive?

- Can you segment customers?

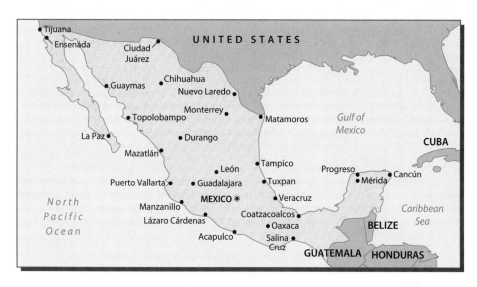

FIGURE 15.4

Mexico at a Glance

For information about the United States' second-largest trading partner, go to the country listing of *The CIA World Factbook* (www.cia.gov/ cia/publications/factbook/ index.html)

ECONOMY OVERVIEW

Mexico has a free-market economy with a mixture of modern and outmoded industry and agriculture, increasingly dominated by the private sector. The number of state-owned enterprises in Mexico has fallen from more than 1,000 in 1982 to fewer than 200 in 1999. The Zedillo administration privatized and expanded competition in seaports, railroads, telecommunications, electricity, natural gas distribution, and airports. A strong export sector helped to cushion the economy's decline in 1995 and led the recovery in 1996–1999. Private consumption became the leading driver of growth, accompanied by increased employment and higher wages. Mexico still needs to overcome many structural problems as it strives to modernize its economy and raise living standards. Income distribution is very unequal, with the top 20 percent of income earners accounting for 55 percent of income. Trade with the United States and Canada has nearly doubled since NAFTA was implemented in 1994. Mexico is pursuing additional trade agreements with most countries in Latin America and has signed a free trade deal with the EU to lesson its dependence on the United States. The government is pursuing conservative economic policies in 2000 to avoid another end-of-term economic crisis, but it still projects an economic growth rate of 4.5 percent because of the strong United States economy and high oil prices.

FIGURE 15.5

Japan at a Glance

For information about the United States' third-largest trading partner, go to the country listing of *The CIA World Factbook* (www.cia.gov/cia/publications/factbook/index.html)

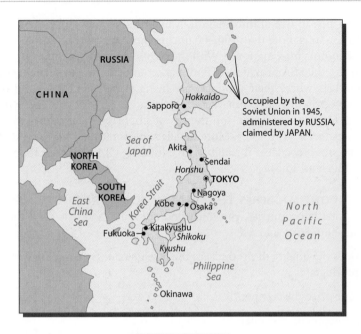

ECONOMY OVERVIEW

Government-industry cooperation, a strong work ethic, mastery of high technology, and a comparatively small defense allocation (1 percent of GDP) have helped Japan advance with extraordinary rapidity to the rank of second most technologically powerful economy in the world after the United States and third-largest economy in the world after the United States and China. One notable characteristic of the economy is the working together of manufacturers, suppliers, and distributors in closely knit groups called *keiretsu*. A second basic feature has been the guarantee of lifetime employment for a substantial portion of the urban labor force. Both features are now eroding. Industry, the most important sector of the economy, is heavily dependent on raw materials and fuels. The much smaller agricultural sector is highly subsidized and protected, with crop yields among the highest in the world. Usually self-sufficient in rice, Japan must import about 50 percent of its requirements of other grain and fodder crops. Japan maintains one of the world's largest fishing fleets and accounts for nearly 15 percent of the global catch. For three decades, overall real economic growth has been spectacular: a 10 percent average in the 1960s, a 5 percent average in the 1970s, and a 4 percent average in the 1980s. Growth slowed markedly in 1992–1995 largely because of the aftereffects of overinvestment during the late 1980s and contractionary domestic policies intended to wring speculative excesses from the stock and real estate markets. Growth picked up to 3.9 percent in 1996, largely a reflection of stimulative fiscal and monetary policies as well as low rates of inflation. But in 1997–1998, Japan experienced a wrenching recession, centered around financial difficulties in the banking system and real estate markets and exacerbated by rigidities in corporate structures and labor markets. In 1999, output started to stabilize as emergency government spending began to take hold and business confidence gradually improved. The crowding of habitable land area and the aging of the population are two major long-run problems. Robotics constitutes a key long-term economic strength, with Japan possessing 410,000 of the world's 720,000 "working robots."

■ Are there political risks in the country you are considering?

■ Will your products need any modifications?

■ Will tariffs or nontariff barriers (restrictions or quotas) prevent your entry into the market?

The Department of Commerce and the Small Business Administration produce various publications and reports to help provide this information. The Department of State gathers information on foreign markets through consulates and embassies. Foreign affiliates of the U.S. Chamber of Commerce, called American Chambers of Commerce (AmChams), also collect and disseminate information.

EXPORT PRODUCT CLASSIFICATION. To be able to gather data from government sources about markets for your product, you need to know their classification number or numbers. The U.S. government classifies products by a system called the Standard Industrial Classification (SIC). The Standard International Trade Classification (SITC) number assigned to your products will help you find data from international organizations. To export, all documentation will need to contain your product's Harmonized System (HS) classification number.

Importing ▰

When your small business is importing rather than exporting, the major focus of your activities shifts from supplying to sourcing. You need to identify markets making products for which you see a domestic demand.

Factors to consider when choosing a foreign supplier include its reliability in having products available for you, the consistency of product or service quality, and the delivery time needed to get products to you. A bank subsidiary office and the embassy of the supplier's home country are sources for this information.

As an importer, you must comply with the regulations and trade barriers of both the foreign country and the United States. You must make sure that your product can legally cross national borders. For example, cigars made in Cuba cannot be imported into the United States because of an embargo against that country. The United States also has import quotas that limit the amount of products like steel and beef that can be brought in. The intent of such quotas is to protect domestic industries and jobs, although their results are not completely positive. Debate over trade restrictions are a topic of political discussion and will be for years. You should try to stay as current as possible on trade and tariff regulations if you are involved in global trade.

Anthony Raissen knew from personal experience that he needed a product that could cleanse his breath, especially after eating the spicy foods that he loved. And it's a problem faced by many people. Yet he found that gum, mints, candies, and other breath aids didn't do the job. These products tended to mask the bad breath as opposed to eliminating it. During a trip to his native South Africa, Raissen was introduced to a group of chemists who had developed a formula of parsley seed oil and sunflower oil that worked like magic on the bad breath problem. Raissen bought the rights to the formula and returned to the United States to form BreathAsure, Inc., of Calabasas, California. Selling this product, Raissen's company has achieved annual sales revenues of nearly $18 million. In fact, responding to consumer demand, the company released Pure Breath, a version of the original BreathAsure product designed for dogs and cats—another obvious target market for this imported formula.[18]

▬ Financial Mechanisms for Going International

Once you decide to enter the international trade game, you face challenges such as how to finance your expansion, how to pay your debts and get paid, and where to find information and assistance.

International Finance

Selling overseas is only half the challenge; the other half is finding the money to fill the order.[19] Working capital may be needed for your new transaction level. Options for additional sources of capital include: conventional financing, venture capital from investor groups, and prepayment or down payment from overseas buyers. To start looking for export financing, contact the following.

THE EXPORT-IMPORT BANK (EXIMBANK). The Eximbank is an independent federal agency with a program that covers 100 percent of working capital for a commercial loan. It also offers export credit insurance to protect exporters, in case a foreign buyer defaults on payment. To get information on the Eximbank's programs, go to www.exim.gov

THE SMALL BUSINESS ADMINISTRATION. The SBA has several financial services for exporters, including an international trade loan program for short-term financing and the 7(a) business loan guarantee program for medium-term working capital and long-term fixed-asset financing. The SBA's free booklet on export finance is entitled *Bankable Deals*.

A problem for most small businesses is getting paid. Most small businesses do not have the financial resources to carry excessive accounts receivable, which can be amplified by selling in other countries. In the United States, the average number of days needed to collect accounts receivable is 42. That's quite a while for a small business to have money outstanding, but the international branch of the National Association of Credit Management says that there are countries that average much longer (see Table 15.1).[20]

Managing International Accounts

Your primary financial concern as a global operator should be to ensure that you get paid in full and on time. Keep in mind that your foreign buyers will be concerned about receiving products that meet their specifications on time. Thus terms of payment must be agreed upon in advance in a way that satisfies both parties.

The primary methods of paying for international transactions follow, ranked from most secure for the exporter to least secure:

PAYMENT IN ADVANCE. Requiring clients to pay in advance provides the least risk to you, but unless you have an extremely specialized product, the buyer can probably get a better deal from someone else. Still, it is reasonable to negotiate partial payment or progress payments.

TABLE 15.1 We'll Get Paid When?	Country	Average Days Outstanding
	Iran	310
	Syria	175
	Kenya	143
	Ethiopia	138
	Argentina	121
	Uruguay	120
	Tunisia	116
	Chile	109
	Ecuador	107
	Cameroon	106
	Morocco	105
	Algeria	103

Source: Jill Andresky Fraser, "How Bad Can Collections Get?" *Inc.,* March 1993, 94.

LETTER OF CREDIT. A letter of credit is an internationally recognized instrument issued by a bank on behalf of its client, the purchaser. It is a guarantee that the bank will pay the seller if the conditions specified are fulfilled.

DOCUMENTARY COLLECTION (DRAFTS). Drafts are documents that require the buyer to pay the seller the face amount either when the product arrives (called a "sight draft") or at a specified time in the future (called a "time draft"). Because title does not pass until the draft is paid, both parties are protected. Drafts involve a certain amount of risk but are cheaper for the purchaser than letters of credit.

CONSIGNMENT. Selling on consignment means that you advance your product to an intermediary who tries to sell it to the final user. If you sell on consignment, you don't get paid until the intermediary sells the product. Consignment is risky because there is no way of knowing when, if ever, the goods will be sold.

OPEN ACCOUNT. Although commonly used in selling products in the United States, delivering goods before payment is required is very risky for international sales. If the creditworthiness of the buyers or the political and economic stability of their country is questionable, you stand to lose your entire investment, possibly without recourse.[21]

Countertrade and Barter

A problem encountered in trading with many economically emerging countries (such as many Eastern European and former Soviet countries) is that their currency is virtually worthless outside their borders. A solution to this problem may be **countertrade.** Although countertrade takes several forms, it is basically substituting a product for money as part of the transaction. Although countertrade is not often a long-term solution, it may be a tool to make deals that could not be made otherwise.[22]

countertrade The completion of a business deal without the use of money as a means of exchange. Barter is a common form of countertrade.

The most common form of countertrade that small businesses can use is barter.[23] This type of trading has existed throughout history. In countertrade, some creativity may be needed to find a business that has complementary needs. Pepsico arranged creative trades within the former Soviet Union by trading soft drinks for vodka. The vodka was worth much more on the open market than the ruble and was much easier to sell. You may make deals just as creatively.

The key to making money in countertrade is to have somewhere to sell the goods you get in trade. Swapping your product for something you can't get rid of is no bargain.

Information Assistance

In addition to the information assistance cited throughout this chapter, help is available from your state export office (it may be listed under your state economic development office). The AT&T Export Hotline (800-872-9767) is a good "fax-back" service to provide demographics, industry reports that assess market conditions, competition, and the best sales opportunities for countries of your choice.[24]

reality check

Changes Here + There = International Opportunity

Small businesses often must react to volatile external changes—changes beyond their control that may threaten the way they have done business. Highly regulated businesses, like those producing medical supplies, have enjoyed relative stability and predictability for some time. But it is dangerous to think that a stable environment will stay the same forever.

Integrated Surgical Systems (ISS), Inc., manufactures the Robodoc surgical assistant system, a 3-D computer imaging and robotic arm which helps surgeons plan and perform total hip replacements. When ISS began producing medical devices in 1990, approval from the U.S. Food and Drug Administration (FDA) took two to four years. Although that may seem like a long time for a startup to wait to bring a product to market, ISS knew about it and planned for it. Because technologically innovative firms like ISS expect a high rate of return, investors are willing to underwrite them, anticipating certain delays. ISS planned to introduce products in the United States and then distribute them in Europe and the Far East.

Events over the next two years, however, dramatically altered ISS's plans. A new commissioner took over the FDA, and some well-publicized problems with medical devices (such as heart valves and breast implants) led to changes in the FDA's approval process. The approval process became much longer, and the environment was changing. ISS, which had initially planned on a three-year approval process, was now facing a best-case scenario of six years.

ISS's reaction? Radically reevaluate and change its rollout strategy for new products. ISS decided to introduce the new product in Europe first, then the Far East, and ultimately bring it to the United States. ISS became an international business much sooner than expected because other countries offered less stringent approval procedures. Today, this strategy is not uncommon for medical device firms.

ISS is another example of a small business that has successfully responded to an unexpectedly changing environment. Small businesses need to respond to market demands and conditions.

Online Global Power

Do you think of your business as a local, mom-and-pop operation? It may not be for long. No matter how small you are, once you create a web site, you may be attracting business from anywhere in the world.

Many small businesses create a web site by "concentrating on the English version first." This approach may be more expensive later, when you have to reengineer it for another language. Start by looking at major multilingual sites like Microsoft, MSNBC, ZDNET, and Symantec. See how they bring each language version into line with the base site. If you want to create a web site that uses multiple languages, you need to see www.glides.com, a company that translates languages on a web page from a single database.

Some other considerations:

- Keep the layout simple, and avoid cultural icons such as the American flag or the Russian hammer and sickle.

- Keep the page layouts and color choices similar throughout all the pages of your base site. This way you can use the base site as a template.

- Choose visual elements that can work across cultures.

- Do not lose sight of the purpose of your web site. You want to communicate the benefits of your products or services to the customer, with the purpose of stimulating a response—like a purchase.

Where can you go on the net for help going global?

- *U.S. Census Bureau (www.census.gov)*. Great site for international trade statistics, export classification assistance, and profiles of exporting companies.

- *U.S. Department of Commerce (www.doc.gov)*. One-stop shop for useful statistics on business, trade, and the world economic picture.

- *U.S. Small Business Administration (www.sba.gov)*. You've been sent here before, but this time you will find information on export assistance in the "Expanding" section.

- *Association for International Business (www.aib-world.org)*. Connect with other businesspeople around the world to exchange ideas and make new friends.

- *Export Hot Line (www.exporthotline.com)*. A leading destination for business executives dealing with cross-border trade. You will find everything from country and industry research to trade shows and shipping services.

- *Inside Ex (www.insidex.com)*. Claims to be the first site doing business abroad. You'll find tips of the trade, foreign exchange rates for 164 countries, and help in accessing target markets.

- *World Trade Zone (www.worldtradezone.com)*. This site is targeted toward small and medium-size businesses involved in international trade who wish to promote themselves inexpensively.

- *Tradenet's Export Advisor (link through sba.gov)*. Another one-stop shop for exporting. A joint venture with the SBA, Department of Commerce, and other agencies. Its credo is "no business is too small to go global."

Sources: Laurel Delaney, "A Crash Course in Doing Business Abroad," *Fortune Small Business,* April 2001, fsb.com; Kenneth Klee, "Going Global?" *Fortune Small Business,* March 2001, 98–103; and John Mulligan, "Prepare Your Site for Going Global," 20 June 2000, inc.com/articles

One of the best one-stop sources of addresses, telephone numbers, fax numbers, and office names for global assistance is a book copublished by the SBA and AT&T entitled *Breaking into the Trade Game: A Small Business Guide to Exporting*. This book also includes a step-by-step guide for developing your international business plan and is available online.

▬ The International Challenge

Success for many small businesses will depend increasingly on some degree of sales to markets in other countries. International business presents quite a few challenges, but then most entrepreneurs thrive on challenge. There are no hard-and-fast rules for going global, and space does not permit coverage of every situation you may face, but some issues you need to be aware of are cultural differences, global trading regions (especially NAFTA), WTO, and ISO 9000 quality certification.

Understanding Other Cultures

When marketing your product globally, you must think and act globally. This means that you need to be sensitive to cultural beliefs that vary from country to country. Every culture has different accepted norms and ways of doing business. Not understanding and not following these norms can lead to embarrassment for you at the least, to completely blowing your deal at the worst. In the United States,

Ted Goff Cartoons.

Goals for Globetrotters

manager's **notebook**

We continue to emphasize the importance of understanding other cultures before jumping into the global marketplace. If you want your small business to be successful in another country, you'd better do your homework first! There's a lot of available information about cultural aspects, but it's going to take effort on your part to locate and digest the information. Here are some hints:

Find Out All You Can About the Culture of the Country You're Looking At. The most important cultural factors you'll want to look at include language, religion, education, and social systems. Ask questions such as

- How do these factors differ from those in my home country?

- How does my business or product name translate into the language? (This could affect brand-name usage, advertising, and other promotions.)

- What are the recognized religious holidays and customs? (They could affect when, where, and how you conduct business.)

- What is the average educational level of your potential customers? (This could influence the type of employee training needed or packaging and advertising decisions.)

- What are the accepted and practiced social rituals, customs, and behaviors? (These could influence many different business decisions.)

And just where can you find this information? First of all, there are numerous books and other publications on cultural customs and the differences among countries. A trip to your local library can provide a wealth of sources. You could also contact international business professors or foreign language professors at a local college. These individuals are typically highly knowledgeable about cultural factors, or at the very least, they can point you toward other information. If you know someone who has traveled to or lived in the country you're investigating, most certainly talk to that person. Such firsthand knowledge is invaluable. Another source of information would be the U.S. Department of Commerce, which has a number of programs and services for companies interested in doing business in other countries.

Enroll in a Cross-Cultural Training Course. The first place to look for a cross-cultural training course would be at a local college or university. If there's no program of this type provided there, check with your local chamber of commerce or local Small Business Administration office. These local offices might offer a course or be able to steer you to one that's conveniently located. If these approaches yield nothing, you could always enroll in a training course offered by a professional training company. These professional courses are generally going to cost more than university or locally sponsored courses, but in return you'll be getting specific, intense training. Some selected courses and training companies include Global Interface Skills Training, offered by Moran, Stahl & Boyer International; Going Global, offered by ITAP International; and Global Perspectives, offered by Lawton International. For more information about professional global training programs, contact the American Society for Training and Development (703–683–8129).

Sources: Philip R. Cateora, *International Marketing*, 8th ed. (Homewood, IL: Irwin), 1993; Sylvia Odenwald, "A Guide for Global Training," *Training and Development*, July 1993, 22–31; and Mark Mendenhall, Betty Jane Punnett, and David Ricks, *Global Management* (Cambridge, Mass.: Blackwell), 1995.

This small U.S. company is finding a market for American-style beer by opening a brewery in Hong Kong.

for instance, a pat on the back says "attaboy," whereas in Japan it is a sign of disrespect. Nodding your head means "no" in Bulgaria, and shaking your head side to side means "yes," the opposite of American customs.[25]

Training the employees you send overseas can help them adjust to cultural differences so that they can perform their jobs better.[26] There are several types of programs available that provide cross-cultural training beyond training in foreign language. These global training programs generally involve six overlapping categories: cultural awareness, multicultural communication, country-specific training, executive development, language courses, and host-country work force training.[27]

Customs like gift giving are important to understand. Gifts from business partners are expected in some cultures, but they are considered offensive in others. Should you present the gift on the first meeting or afterward? in public or private? to whom? What kind of gift is appropriate? In Japan, gifts are exchanged to symbolize the depth and strength of a business relationship.[28] When dealing with a Japanese business, the first meeting is the appropriate time to exchange gifts; if you are presented with a gift, you are expected to respond with one in return. By contrast, gifts are rarely exchanged in Germany, Belgium, and the United Kingdom.

Exchanging business cards is no big deal, right? Wrong. Taking someone's card and immediately putting it in your pocket is considered very rude in Japan. You should carefully look at the card, observe the title and organization, acknowledge with a nod, and make a relevant comment or ask a question. Even presenting your business card has a proper protocol in Japan or South Korea. You should use both hands and present the card so the other person can read it. If English is not the primary language, you should print the native language on the reverse side.

Language is another obvious problem. You cannot depend on what you might think of as "easy" transitions. In England, what they call a "lorry," "petrol," and "biscuits" are what Americans call a truck, gasoline, and cookies. A rule of thumb in international business is to conduct business in the buyer's language.

You are not expected to speak another language like a local, but making an attempt to learn some of the language can be a sign of good faith. Most trade specialists recommend that you employ a professional translator for written communication and absolutely have one available when you travel for face-to-face meetings.[29]

Trade experts at Moran, Stahl & Boyer International, an international consulting firm, say that culture has two components: surface culture (fads, styles, food, and holidays) and deep culture (norms, attitudes, values, and beliefs). According to the tip-of-the-iceberg concept, only 10 to 15 percent of a region's culture is visible (see Figure 15.6).[30] This means you must look below the surface to identify forces that truly drive a culture.

You can see that the cultural aspects of international business are very complicated and confusing, but their importance cannot be overstated. Doing your homework can prevent serious mistakes.

Recognizing an increasing shift in attitudes—part of that "deep" culture—in favor of community planning and environmental protection was a key to the global success now enjoyed by Sheily Brady. As president of Brady and Associates, a small landscape architecture firm located in Berkeley, California, she fueled her company's push into the Asian market during travels to Vietnam and China. There she met with government officials regarding urban design and environmental planning services. Brady had recognized that these geographic regions had just finished a decade of unbridled and largely unrestricted economic and development growth. And she knew that public and governmental officials' opinions were changing toward the use of community planning to help manage growth. Brady was able to capitalize on her assessment of the cultural change and establish a solid foothold in this market.[31]

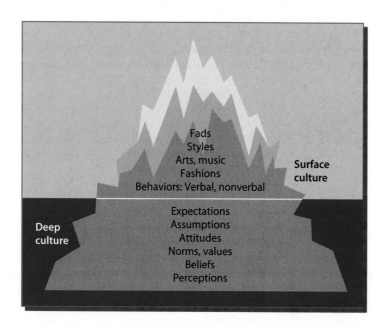

FIGURE 15.6

The Cultural Iceberg

Many important cultural factors are not easily seen.

Source: Kevin Walsh, "How to Negotiate European Style," *Journal of European Business,* July/August 1993, 45–47.

International Trading Regions

Since World War II, a major development in the world economy has been the creation of regional trade associations—the European Union, the Association of Southeast Asian Nations, and the alliance created by the North American Free Trade Agreement.

Since World War II, a major development in the world economy has been the creation of regional trade groupings. That trend has accelerated in recent years. A trade region is established through agreements to create economic and political ties among nations usually located within a close geographical area. These agreements reduce trade barriers among countries within the region and standardize barriers with countries outside the region. They also intend to increase competition within them, so that inefficient nationalized companies or monopolies lose their protective walls and are forced to come up to speed. Table 15.2 identifies major trading regions and the member countries.

What effect do world regions have on you and your small business? The passage of the North American Free Trade Agreement (NAFTA) was intended to open markets and to reduce barriers for you to send your products to Mexico and Canada. Regional agreements also change your strategy for dealing with businesses in those countries. For example, because the European Union (EU) has higher tariffs and barriers for products coming from countries outside the region than for products that come from within, it might make sense for you to establish operations in an EU country if you intend to do a lot of business there. Then you can sell in any of the 12 member nations under reduced barriers.

NAFTA. In 1993, Congress passed the North American Free Trade Agreement joining Canada, Mexico, and the United States in a free trade area. One of the primary goals of NAFTA is to ultimately eliminate tariffs and nontariff barriers between the United States, Canada, and Mexico on nearly all qualifying goods.[32]

A key word here is *qualifying*. Products will qualify for tariff elimination if they *originate,* as defined in Article 401 of NAFTA, in one of the three countries. For example, products that are made in Japan and are shipped through Mexico cannot enter the United States under preferential NAFTA duty rates. First, you need to determine if your products are originating goods. There are four primary ways for goods to qualify.

1. Goods wholly obtained or produced in a NAFTA country
2. Goods made up entirely of components and materials that qualify
3. Goods that are specifically cited in an article of the agreement (very few products are cited)
4. Goods that are covered under specific rules of origin for that product, as listed in NAFTA Annex 401. This is the most common way to qualify.[33]

TABLE 15.2 **Major Regional Trade Associations**	Association	Countries
	North American Free Trade Agreement (NAFTA)	Canada, Mexico, United States
	European Union (EU)	Belgium, Denmark, France, Germany, Greece, Ireland, Italy, Luxembourg, Netherlands, Portugal, Spain, United Kingdom
	MERCOSUR	Argentina, Brazil, Paraguay, Uruguay
	Andean Common Market (ANCOM)	Bolivia, Colombia, Ecuador, Peru, Venezuela
	Association of Southeast Asian Nations (ASEAN)	Brunei, Indonesia, Laos, Malaysia, Myanmar, Philippines, Singapore, Thailand, Vietnam

Your products need to be assigned a harmonized system (HS) number. The harmonized system classifies products so that their chapter, heading, and subheading numbers are identical for all three countries. For example,

Chapter 95	Toys, games, and sports requisites
Heading 95.04	Table or parlor games
Subheading 9504.20	Articles for billiards and accessories
Tariff item 9504.20.21	Billiard tables

Once you have determined the HS number for your products, you can find the specific NAFTA rule of origin that applies. Some specific rules of origin will call for additional requirements. Usually this is a test of the product's regional value content (RVC), which means that a certain percentage of the product's value has to originate in a NAFTA country. For example, if the rule specifies that a good must have at least 65 percent RVC, then you need to demonstrate that at least 65 percent of the good's value originated in either Canada, the United States, or Mexico.

If your products do qualify as originating goods, you need to complete a certificate of origin for each product. The importer of your products must have a valid certificate to claim preferential tariff treatment. The certificate of origin shows names and addresses of the importer and the exporter, a description of the goods, the HS number, the preference criteria (how it qualified), the producer, the net cost, and the country of origin.

Don't be intimidated by the documentation process required by NAFTA. Assistance at every step of the process is available. David Hirschmann, director of Latin American affairs for the U.S. Chamber of Commerce, says, "Small business should benefit the most, not just because tariffs will be lifted, but because there will be fair and reliable rules. Products won't be held up at the border for ten days because of costly, confusing regulations."[34]

For help in determining a product's HS number, exporters can call the Census Bureau Foreign Trade division (301-763-5210) or contact their Commerce Department district office. The Commerce Department's Industrial Trade Staff (202–482–5675) can determine the tariff rate and phase-out schedule for specific products. To understand NAFTA rules of origin and other important provisions, exporters should obtain a copy of the NAFTA agreement, available from the U.S. Government Printing Office (202-783-3238). U.S. Customs has set up a help desk for assistance on how NAFTA affects a wide variety of issues (202-927-0097). The Trade Information Center (TIC) is a convenient first stop for new exporters, offering information on the export process (800-USA-TRADE). Finally, companies new to exporting should buy a copy of *A Basic Guide to Exporting* from www.sba.gov[35]

WORLD TRADE ORGANIZATION (WTO). The first global tariff agreement began in 1947 with the General Agreement on Tariffs and Trade (GATT). The agreement, which originally included the United States and 22 other countries, has grown to include 134 member countries that represent over 90 percent of world trade. Since GATT's inception, it has gone through eight "rounds" of negotiations or meeting sites. The latest series of negotiations, called the Uruguay Round, lasted from 1986 until 1994. One of its provisions was to create a successor to GATT, called the World Trade Organization, created in 1995, which has broader authority over services and agricultural products.

"GATT created a safer, more stable environment in which to do business. Smaller companies without the resources to protect themselves in international markets will feel safer," says Mike Van Horn, president of Pacific Rim Consortium, a consulting firm that helps American businesses enter Asian-Pacific markets.[36] The WTO agenda focuses on nontariff barriers to trade.[37]

ISO 9000

Quality isn't a concern just among American managers who have adopted total quality management (TQM). It is also an international issue. The International Standards Organization (ISO), based in Europe, has established quality standards to show industrial customers that manufacturers' *methods* of product development and achieving quality standards are designed to ensure quality.[38] ISO has developed 13,000 international standards, with ISO 9000 standards relating to quality and ISO 14000 standards relating to environmental issues. The intent of ISO standards is to minimize the need for on-site visits by vendors to make sure their suppliers are producing quality products. In 2000, ISO developed and adopted new standards called ISO 9001:2000 which maintain a greater focus on customer satisfaction, user needs, and continuous improvement of quality management systems.[39]

The process of getting your business ISO certified is time consuming, complex, and expensive. The procedure works like this: After you document all the steps of your operations that ensure the quality of goods and services, an auditing firm visits your company to conduct a process audit and a financial audit to determine whether or not you pass. Two followup audits per year are required to maintain certification.

Why would a small business bother? Lori Sweningson, owner of Job Boss Software, is taking her company through the ISO certification process because she wants to sell software in Europe. To get certified, Sweningson has budgeted $30,000 to $50,000 for consultant and auditor fees.[40] The payoff is expected to be the marketing tool of being ISO certified. She believes that ISO certification will soon be the minimum requirement for many international sales.

Currently, large businesses and divisions of major corporations are the ones getting ISO certified, and small manufacturers are quickly following. Free information packets are available from the American Society of Quality Control (800-248-1946) or the American National Standards Institute (212-642-4900). Or, of course, go right to the source at www.iso.ch for a wealth of information on ISO standards, principles, and forms—even business plans for public review. We will revisit the topic of ISO 9000 in more depth in Chapter 18.

SUMMARY

The components of an international business plan.

In addition to your domestic business plan, you need to include how you intend to enter foreign markets, which markets are the best opportunity for your business, projected costs and revenues, any contacts you have in overseas partnerships or foreign investment, and any legal requirements or restrictions you must consider.

███ **The five ways for small businesses to conduct international trade.**

The five methods for small businesses to conduct international business are exporting, importing, licensing, joint ventures, and direct investment.

███ **The advantages and disadvantages of exporting for small businesses.**

The advantages of exporting are that it offers you a way to increase sales and profits, increase your market share, reduce your dependence on existing markets, increase your competitiveness in domestic markets, satisfy a demand for your products abroad, extend your product's life cycle, stabilize seasonal sales fluctuations, sell excess production capacity, and learn about foreign competition.

The disadvantages of exporting are the expense of changing your products and promotional material; the increased costs that cut into short-term profits; added administrative and travel costs; time needed to receive payment, which may be longer than for domestic accounts; the need for additional financing; and the increased paperwork involved.

Small business owners have two choices to approach exporting—indirect and direct. Indirect exporting involves the use of intermediaries such as agents and brokers, export management companies, export trade companies, piggyback exporting, and foreign-based distributors and agents. With direct exporting, the small business owner makes all contacts and handles the logistics and paperwork of exporting alone.

███ **Factors to consider when importing products and materials.**

The focus of a small business concentrating on importing changes to finding international sources of products to satisfy their domestic customers. The small business owner must consider the reliability of the foreign supplier, the consistency of the product quality, and the additional time that will be needed to ship products from another country.

███ **How small businesses can manage their finances in international trade.**

In managing your finances for international trade, you must plan how to raise additional funds and how to get paid. Funding can come from your current commercial bank, from the Eximbank, or with assistance from the SBA. Methods for payment include payment in advance, by letters of credit, by draft, on consignment, and by open account.

███ **The challenges of international small business activity.**

Some of the challenges you will face when going global include learning and adapting to cultural differences, dealing with provisions of trade regions and agreements like NAFTA and GATT, and ensuring the quality of your products to customers who are not familiar with you or your business, through international standards such as ISO 9000.

QUESTIONS FOR **REVIEW & DISCUSSION**

1. Discuss the difference between and the advantages and disadvantages of indirect and direct exporting.

2. What is the advantage of a strategic alliance over direct investment when entering a foreign market?

3. What information should a small business owner gather before deciding to export products?

4. Why is finding financial assistance for international expansion more difficult than for domestic?

5. Why would a small business choose to license its products in other countries?

6. Choose three foreign markets and find the customs and courtesies for greetings in those countries (possibly using the Internet as a source).

7. Imagine that you own a small manufacturing business. Identify the product that you produce and a foreign market that appears to be an opportunity. What country would pose a bigger risk?

8. Name a form of countertrade and when it would be appropriate to use.

9. Discuss the differences between and similarities of domestic- and foreign-based intermediaries.

10. What does the Eximbank do for potential exporters? for importers?

QUESTIONS FOR **CRITICAL THINKING**

1. Now that the Internet has opened international trade, especially for small businesses, what impact do you think it will have on trade standards for selling goods abroad? Do you expect an increase in nontariff barriers?

2. What countries are riskier markets for small businesses to enter? Why? Where would you find information regarding political stability, financial risks, and cultural differences?

Locate a small business in your area that conducts business in another country (you may be surprised to find who local global players are). Ask the owner what the greatest challenge has been in doing business across borders. Share your story with the class.

Experience this...

WHAT WOULD **YOU** DO?   No. 1

Roberto and Efrain Rodriguez have run a neon and electrical sign business in Miami since 1985. Recently, they've developed a lucrative sideline selling brightly colored neon lighting kits for cars and other vehicles. This sideline business—Motion Neon, Inc.—has reached sales levels of $2 million. However, with the passage of NAFTA, the two brothers see a lot of potential and want to expand their business into Mexico, where they think consumers will be attracted to the bright and colorful neon accessories. They've collected several pieces of information already. The main language spoken in the country is Spanish. The major religions are Protestant and Roman Catholic. Mexico's culture is characterized by a heavy dependence on family structures and community; high emphasis on titles, rank, and status; and strong emphasis on the acquisition of material goods. Economic and other trade information can be found in Figure 15.4. Oh, and one final thing, the value of the peso has been on a wild ride, reflecting the uncertainty of the country's economic stability.

QUESTIONS

1. Working in pairs, make a list of additional information that you think the Rodriguez brothers will need before expanding their business into Mexico and why you think they need this information. Also try to indicate where you think they could find this information.

2. Assume that the Rodriguez brothers have decided to expand into Mexico by licensing their product name and technology to a business based in Mexico City. They need to select that business—a critical decision. Using the cultural and economic information presented here, role-play an interview between the Rodriguezes and a potential licensee.

| WHAT WOULD **YOU** DO? | No. 2 |

Refer back to the chapter opener on Lonely Planet. You remember the story of the Wheelers' building the business of describing travel in many countries around the globe. In the process, they have created a web site (www.lonelyplanet.com) which offers an incredible wealth of information for entrepreneurs. Choose a country that you believe has potential to be a market for the small business you wish to own. Working in teams of two, use Lonely Planet online to become "experts" on this country. Use all their resources, like Worldguide, Theme Guides, The Thorn Tree, and The Scoop. Once you have gathered this valuable information on Iceland, Singapore, or anywhere in between, prepare a two-page executive summary on the opportunities you find for your chosen country, and present your findings to your class.

| CHAPTER CLOSING CASE | No. 15 |

International Windsurfing School S.N.C.

Situational Summary   "I like punctuality and I want people to receive good value for what they pay," said Benno Schmieder, "and that explains my success." It was the week before Christmas 1994 and Benno was enjoying his annual seven-month vacation. During past years, he had traveled across Asia and South America. This time he was in Cape Town, South Africa, and Benno was asked whether he would consider expanding his business internationally. If so, to ensure the continued success of his business, marketing communications would be a primary concern so potential customers in other markets could learn of his unique services.

Introduction   Benno Schmieder, a German national from Munich, did his military service during the early 1980s at a NATO base in Sardinia, Italy. There, he learned how to windsurf and took a liking to the sport. After completing his military duties, he decided to return to Italy and spend the summer of 1982 giving windsurfing lessons.

A problem arose, however, when Eppe Giua, the son of a wealthy Italian family, found Benno operating an unofficial school with no license to do so.

"I'll go to the police," said Signor Giua. "Or, if you want, you can pay me and use my license."

Benno had noticed that there was much more bureaucracy and corruption in Italy than in Germany. However, he understood that he lacked the connections to obtain a license on his own and therefore agreed to pay Signor Giua a percentage of the earnings of what he would call Benny's Windsurfing School.

Benno realized he could not make much money by owning only the four windsurf boats that he did. He convinced Signor Giua that the school needed more capital investment, and it was finally agreed to acquire another ten windsurf boats.

All went well for some time, with the school using Signor Giua's license, but two years later the windsurf boats were wearing out and needed to be replaced. However, Signor Giua refused to invest in more boats.

Frustrated, Benno approached Signor Giua with another offer. This time Benno would pay for the boats, but in return he wanted 75 percent of the school and its profits. Because the school had operated for nine years without any accounting or bookkeeping, no one knew the revenues or expenses of the enterprise. Therefore, Signor Giua demanded a flat rate for the summer for (unofficial) permission to use his license.

Up to 1990, operations went smoothly. In 1991, however, Italian port authorities sent officials to verify licenses. Unfortunately, Signor Giua had forgotten to apply for a renewal and, as a result, Benno's school was closed down for two weeks, causing annual income to fall by about 12 percent.

A Formal Business   Through the end of 1993, Benno was unofficially operating with Signor Giua's license. There were two problems, however. In order for the license to be valid, Signor Giua had to be on the beach, but, in reality, he came by only a couple of times during the year. And, although Benno had invested in the school, there was no written record of his participation. Seeking to protect himself, Benno proposed that they jointly incorporate International Windsurfing School S.N.C. of Eppe Giua with each shareholder holding 50 percent of the new company. It was agreed that this new corporate body would expand operations, and that Signor Guia would apply for a license to lease parasols and beach lounges. However, he missed a March 31, 1994, application deadline.

Benno would live all year from his summer income, but in 1994 his income dropped. He had to return to Germany for cancer surgery, which delayed his arrival in Italy, and because Signor Guia had missed the application deadline he did not have a license to rent parasols and beach lounges. He finally approached Signor Giua and demanded either that Signor Giua sell control of the enterprise to Benno or that Benno be allowed to dispose of his shares. Signor Giua agreed to sell his shares, giving Benno 99 percent control with a friend of Benno's obtaining a symbolic 1 percent. The official name of the school was changed to International Windsurfing School S.N.C. of Benno Schmieder.

Strategic Planning   Benno calculated an income of 600 DM (German deutsche marks, about $279 in United States currency) per day from renting his 15 boats (an average of two rentals per day at 20 DM), or 73,800 DM ($34,326) per season. Windsurfing lessons brought in an additional 30,000 DM ($13,953) each season.

Nevertheless, Benno found it a strain to stay on the beach from 8 A.M. to 8 P.M. for 123 days in a row (May 1 to September 30). The beach had neither toilets nor showers, and it had lost its appeal after several years. Security was another problem. Although he kept his equipment locked in a hangar, vandals ripped his sails one night and during another night the locks were forced open and equipment was stolen.

About this time, a windsurfing instructor from Peru arrived and Benno hired him to assist in windsurfing lessons. Since he lacked working papers, Benno paid him "off the books" on a commission basis.

Finding that the Peruvian's real passion was sailing, Benno proposed a joint venture: Each would pay half the cost of a new fleet of sailboats; the Peruvian would keep one-third of the profits and Benno, two-thirds. In addition, to provide protection for their investment, the Peruvian would sleep on the beach during the season; from October to April the boats would be placed in storage.

The Parasol Division   Benno's students included many Italian children, but very few adults. Over the years, Benno concluded that Italians were concerned with image, fearing embarrassment. They were more reluctant to be seen learning to surf or sail than were Germans of any age group. To reach this potential clientele he needed a different product. A few summers earlier, for example, Benno purchased some Swatch watches in Germany for 50 DM ($23) each and sold them in Italy for the equivalent of 200 DM ($93) each. This time to reach the elusive Italian adult market he considered renting out sunbeds and parasols. He could buy a set of two sunbeds with a parasol for 400 DM ($186) a set. Twenty sets would be affordable, and renting out each set for 30 DM ($14) per day could bring in an additional 4,200 DM ($1,953) weekly. He would need a license costing about 2,000 DM ($930) per season. Benno felt that his enterprise, now formally a legal corporate entity, was credible enough to obtain the license.

Advertising   Benno had never kept records, he did not remit V.A.T. (Italian sales tax), nor did he file income tax declarations. For this reason, he had sought a low profile and refrained from advertising. In 1995, Benno decided to keep proper books and to advertise.

This case study was researched and written by Leo Paul Dana, University of Canterbury, with the cooperation of Benno Schmieder, and was first used as an exercise for MBA students of the Graduate School of Management at the Academy of Economic Studies in Bucharest, Romania, during January 1995. It was also used as an oral examination at the Graduate School of Business in Nancy, France, during February 1995. Copyright © 1995 by Leo Paul Dana. Reprinted by permission of the author. All rights reserved. It is unlawful to reproduce any portion of this case without the written consent of the copyright holder. To read the entire case, visit the *Small Business Management: Entrepreneurship and Beyond* web site at http://business.college.hmco.com/students.

QUESTIONS

1. Using theories, concepts, and models from the course, explain to Benno *why* he should, and *how* he could expand beyond Italy.

2. Serve as a marketing communications consultant to Benno, creating a realistic advertising program consistent with a viable international marketing plan.

3. In reality, Benno decided *not* to internationalize. Justify his strategy and prepare a realistic advertising program consistent with Benno's decision.

16 Professional Small Business Management

After reading this chapter, you should be able to:

Describe the functions and activities of managing a small business.

Explain the stages of small business growth and their consequences for managing your business.

Discuss the significance of employee leadership and motivation to small business.

Compare the positive and negative aspects of total quality management (TQM) for small business.

Discuss the special management concerns of time and stress management.

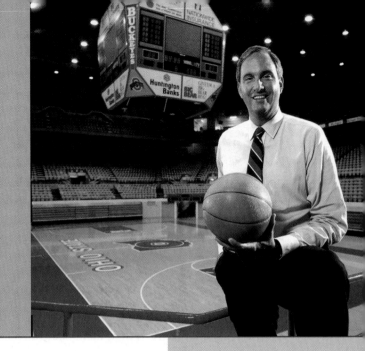

AS CEO OF VECTRA MARKETING Services, Craig Taylor is just as competitive as he was when he was captain of the Ohio State basketball team. He sees his employees as teammates and thinks of business as a game. When everyone is on the same team, information should be shared about *why* people have to perform on their jobs. Taylor is among the ranks of small business owners who are helping transform American management, focusing on teamwork rather than on individual effort.

Business can be seen as a game because *everyone* in a company, not just the key executives, has a stake in the business's succeeding, profiting, and growing. Everyone's livelihood is at risk if the company loses. This perspective is different from the traditional approach to management, which reacts to business problems like weak cash flow or low profit margins with memos, meetings, and orders. Instead, the game players set up a game with rules that everyone understands, offering some kind of payoff when the problem is solved and the game won.

At the end of 1992, Taylor gave his 54 employees two choices for the next year's bonus plan. They could take a 5 percent raise and be given the chance to share a $200,000 bonus pool if targets were met. Or they could forgo the raise and have a chance at a $400,000 pool. Bonuses in this latter case would be tied to hitting four targets: sales, operating expenses, inventory accuracy, and the current ratio. Employees voted 48 to 6 to go for the option with no guaranteed raise, bigger bonus pool, and nothing if the goals were not hit. At the end of the game, only goals for inventory accuracy and sales were hit, so employees shared only half of the bonus pool. Still, most did better than if they had gone for the raise. For 1994, targets were adjusted, and the game was started over. If employees won the game, bonuses could add 15 percent to 20 percent to their earnings.

If you are like Nancy Cohen of Published Image, a newsletter and publishing company, and don't care for the term *game,* fine—call it something else. What a game approach really is comes down to open book management. But Cohen's company still has teams and captains, coaches (not managers), and scoreboards (for teams to monitor progress). Since changing to this way of doing business (that is, teams with bonuses tied to sales and quality which allow players to win up to 40 percent over their base pay), Published Image's earnings are up 35 percent, and customer satisfaction is up 78 percent.

Open book management literally opens the books to show employees financial information, industry trends, quality reports, and customer service ratings. Proponents say that the practice enables companies to motivate employees and light a collective fire beneath tired workers. Some elements to make open book work include

- Provide access to critical business information
- Information provided must be timely
- Make sure people can interpret data
- Give everyone time to absorb the information
- Give everyone a stake in the outcome
- Give employees authority to act on the information
- Make sure that you (and the data) are believable

A game approach to managing a small business appears to change the company in two important ways. First, instead of different parts of the business being engaged in internal rivalry, everyone is on the same team—against the competition. Second, people not only help set their own goals, they can see how they are doing and what needs to be done to win.

Sources: John Case, "Games Companies Play," *Inc.,* October 1994, 46–56; Rick Maurer, "Open-Book Management," *Journal of Quality and Participation,* Spring 2001, 64; and C. J. Prince, "Does Open-Book Really Work?" *Chief Executive,* July/August 1999, 24.

▬ Managing Small Business

Businesses of every size must be managed or they will cease to exist. Although there are many similarities between managing a large business and managing a small one, significant differences also exist. Managing a small business is a complex job. You have to perform many activities well without the resources of your large competitors. The expectations of customers, associates, and employees are raising to the point where small businesses can rarely survive without understanding the tools and practices of professional management. In this chapter, we will investigate the processes of managing a growing business, of leading people, and of facing the concerns of a small business owner.

The Four Functions of Management

The functions of **management** are generally accepted to be *planning, organizing, leading,* and *controlling.* To some extent, these are the broad functions that a manager performs whether in charge of a large or a small operation, of a for-profit or a nonprofit organization, or of a retail, service, or manufacturing business. These four functions are *continuous* and *interrelated* (see Figure 16.1). Managers do each of them all the time. You don't have the luxury of getting out of bed in the morning and saying, "I think I am going to just organize today." Rather, you will have to do some planning, some organizing, a lot of leading, and some controlling every day.

These four functions are interrelated in that there is a progressive cycle to their achievement. Planning begins the process, as the manager determines what to do. Organizing involves assembling the resources (financial, human, and material) to accomplish the plan. Leading is the process of getting the most output possible from those resources. Controlling is comparing what was initially planned with what was actually accomplished. If a deviation exists between what was planned and what was done (which is almost always the case), a new plan is needed, and the cycle begins again.

management The process of planning, organizing, leading, and controlling resources in order to achieve the goals of an organization.

What Managers Do

Management is getting things done through people. When running a small business, you will have to spend a certain amount of time performing the actual duties and daily tasks of the business—probably more during the early stages in the life of the business and less later. You must decide where to strike a balance between doing and managing. This doesn't mean that managers don't "do" anything. It means that the time that you spend on the daily tasks like selling or writing new software or cleaning machinery is time when you are not managing. Those tasks have to be done, and the small business owner is usually the one who has to do them, but managing a business is more than a collection of tasks.

First-time managers and business owners often think of management as doing the job they have previously done, only with more power and control. Rather, to use

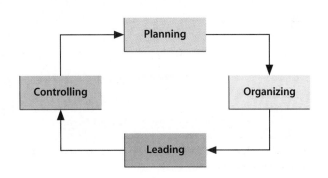

FIGURE 16.1

The Four Functions of Management

The functions of managing a business are continuous and interrelated.

the analogy of an orchestra, a novice business owner or manager must move from being a musician who concentrates on playing one instrument to being the conductor who brings the talents of all the musicians together and knows the capabilities of every instrument.[1]

Although the four functions are as generally true today as they were in 1916, when they were first articulated by Henri Fayol, there is more to describing what managers *do*. Henry Mintzberg has gone into considerable depth searching for descriptions of how managers spend their time.[2]

First, rather than being reflective, systematic planners, managers tend to work at an unrelenting pace on a wide variety of activities that are brief and have little continuity. The front-line managers in Mintzberg's study averaged 583 activities per eight-hour day—1 every 48 seconds. Half of CEOs' activities lasted less than nine minutes, and only 10 percent took longer than an hour.

Second, rather than managers' having no regular duties to perform, Mintzberg found that they spend a lot of time on regular duties, such as performing rituals and ceremonies, negotiating, and dealing with the external environment. Managers must receive visitors, take care of customers, and preside at holiday parties and other rituals and ceremonies that are part of their job, whether the business is large or small.

Third, even though management is often viewed as a technological science, information processing and decision making remain locked in the manager's brains. Managers are people who depend on judgment and intuition more than on technology. Computers are important for the business's specialized work, but managers still greatly depend on word-of-mouth information for almost all their decisions. A manager's job is complex, difficult, and as much an art as a science.

Portals like allbusiness.com can be a one-stop info shop for small business.

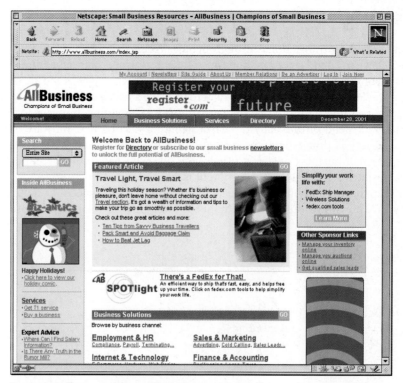

Screen shot of home page, from allbusiness.com. Reprinted by permission from Allbusiness. http://www.allbusiness.com

Any Portal in a Small Business Storm?

Where can a small business owner go on the Internet to get help? Is there anywhere an entrepreneur can gain insight into the daily nitty-gritty of running a business? A place to chat with others in difficult situations? Several small business portals have sprung up to go past advice and offer real online service. Portals are gateways to a wealth of resources. Portals are businesses in themselves and therefore have to make money to stay in existence. They do that in two ways: fulfilling business services (like processing payroll or hiring temps) and selling access to information.

Some big-time players are involved with small business portals. Citibank backs Bizzed.com, Microsoft is behind bCentral.com, General Electric is buying allbusiness.com As of this writing, the jury is still out on what works and what does not. Some are content heavy. Some have very little content and offer members-only discounts on goods and services. Some are broad based, some are niche oriented. One thing for sure is that small business owners want them. *Fortune Small Business* provides some analysis and advice. Allbusiness.com is FSB's top-rated portal. This site delves deeply into the minutiae of running a small business. You will find 350 ready-to-download forms. Partners offer services but few discounts.

- *Bizzed.com* Pass on this one. Few articles of any usable content. Services get one- or two-line descriptions that read more like advertising. No prices. Some product discounts.

- *Business Owner's Toolkit* Good portal for startups, not so much for existing businesses. Good information on marketing, taxes, incorporation, financing, employees—all the stuff you need for starting a business.

- *Workz.com* Good, comprehensive site for running an online business—from accepting credit cards to creating banner ads. More emphasis on content than services. You will find some free tools, for functions like checking your site for dead links, spelling errors (check their name), and browser incompatibilities.

- *Yahoo.com* Yahoo Small Business is not great by itself but is very good at steering you to top web resources.

- *ZdNet.com* Because this site is affiliated with *PC Magazine, PC Computing,* and other computer magazines, you can expect a lot of tech advice. Nothing on starting a business, but lots on leveraging technology for your business. Good e-commerce and web design.

Source: Alan Cohen, "The Virtual Business," *Fortune Small Business* (www.fsb.com/fortunesb/articles); and Alan Cohen, "Portal Players," *Fortune Small Business* (www.fsb.com/fortunesb/articles).

Mintzberg suggests several important skills a manager needs in order to plan, organize, lead, and control. A small business manager needs to

- Develop relationships with peers.

- Carry out negotiations.

- Motivate subordinates.

- Resolve conflicts.

- Establish information networks and then disseminate information.

- Make decisions in allocating resources under conditions of extreme uncertainty.

- Most important, a manager must be willing to learn continually on the job.[3]

As a manager, you must use your resources *efficiently* and *effectively*. The difference is more than an exercise in semantics. *Effectiveness* means achieving your stated goals. Having a helicopter fly you everywhere you go (across town to meetings, to the grocery store, to a ball game) is an effective way to travel. You get where you intend to go. But with the reality of limited resources, effectiveness alone is not enough.

Efficiency, by contrast, involves accomplishing goals and tasks while making the best use of the resources required. In running a small business, you have to get the job done, but you have to contain costs also. Wasting your limited resources—for instance, on helicopter rides—even though you achieve your goals will lead to bankruptcy just as fast as if you were not making sales. A small business manager must balance effectiveness and efficiency to be competitive.

Katherine Allen of Springfield, Missouri, runs a company that specializes in oil cleanup products and services. She estimates that half of her company's nearly $4 million in annual sales comes from exports to locations ranging from Singapore to São Paulo. Because her business is in a field traditionally dominated by men, she's had to expend significant time and energy building this global business. She says, however, that her company's success in global markets is due to her efforts to understand her markets and her customers. This type of knowledge is invaluable for any small business owner wanting to expand into global markets.[4]

Small Business Growth

Growth is a natural, and usually desirable, consequence of being in business. Growth of your business can be seen in several forms, but not necessarily all at once. You see it in revenues, total sales, number of customers, number of employees, products offered, and facilities needed. It is something to be expected and planned for as your business evolves, but it should not be an end in itself.

Growth brings change to what your business needs and does, but bigger is not necessarily better. A sunflower is not better than a violet.

As your business makes upward progress, you will experience "growing pains" like people do as they move through childhood, adolescence, and adulthood. Signals of growing pains can be jobs that are not delivered on time, costs that rise out of control, or feelings that chaos is reigning. Such signals can indicate that your business has grown to a point where your staff or operating structure can't match the rising demands. Breakdowns in customer service and product quality soon follow.[5] Managing growth is a difficult part of managing a small business because of the transitions needed as your business passes from one stage to another.

Your Growing Firm

When a business grows in size by increasing its number of employees and its volume of sales, the way it is managed must also change. As it evolves from a bare-bones startup to an expanded, mature firm, there are roughly four stages that it may

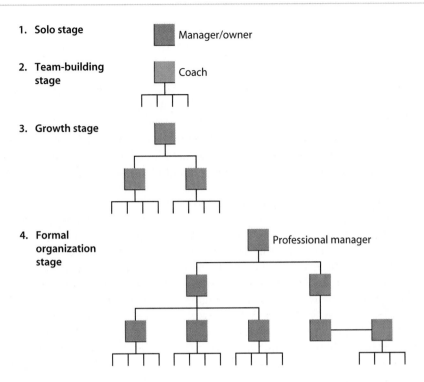

1. Solo stage — Manager/owner

2. Team-building stage — Coach

3. Growth stage

4. Formal organization stage — Professional manager

FIGURE 16.2

Stages of Business Growth

Businesses tend to evolve through four stages as they grow from single-person firms to full-fledged businesses.

pass through. Naturally, not all small businesses are the same size at startup, nor do they all seek to achieve the same level of growth in maturity. Yet these four stages provide a way to understand the changing needs of your business.

In the first, or solo, stage, the owner runs the business alone (see Figure 16.2). Although not every business begins as one individual running (and being) the entire business, it is not uncommon. In fact, technology is making the solo type of business much more common than ever (see Reality Check, "Flying Solo," in Chapter 1). Personal computers connected via modems and networks have allowed the creation of electronic cottage industries out of people's homes. So, although some people intentionally keep their businesses at the solo stage, it represents the first stage of growth.

A business enters the second stage of growth when other people are hired. Now the entrepreneur is no longer responsible just for his or her own efforts. Management begins because the entrepreneur must now get work done through other people rather than trying to accomplish everything that needs to be done alone.

When the business grows to the point where employees operate within several departments, the entrepreneur must either become a professional manager or hire managerial expertise. Stage 3 occurs when a level of supervision is added—hiring supervisors to lead departments or divisions. Care must be taken that these supervisors understand the culture of the business they are joining and will work toward building it. At this point, the entrepreneur is performing less of the daily production personally and may not be in direct contact with part of the company's efforts. The small business owner must turn loose more of the "doing" and assume more of the "managing." Turning loose in this way can be hard, but delegation of authority and responsibility is something an entrepreneur must do in order for the business to grow.

Carey Stacy began Dialogos International Corporation, a foreign language service company, as a solo business. The business prospered, and more teachers and staff were added, but Dialogos was typical of a business whose growth potential was stunted because it was dependent on one key individual—Stacy, the owner. Until Stacy was elected president of the National Association of Women Business Owners (NAWBO), she was a very hands-on owner. But because of the extensive travel she undertook for NAWBO, jobs were being lost waiting on Stacy's desk for her to return and make a decision. Stacy realized that she simply had to turn over the day-to-day decisions of Dialogos to employees. Although she didn't realize it at the time, she was creating a management system that functioned no matter who was staffing it—a key to growing a successful business. It turned out to be the best thing that could have happened to her and her business.

In the fourth, formal organization, stage, the business has grown to include multiple departments managed by numerous supervisors. As with the preceding stages, the owner is still the "head honcho" here, but now his or her responsibilities are more conceptual than technical in nature. In other words, rather than focusing on daily operations—making and selling the product or service—he or she will more exclusively focus on managing the bigger picture—through long-range planning and overseeing supervisors, for instance. The business now needs someone to establish policies, handbooks, job descriptions, training, and budgets, and the owner will now assume those executive duties. In this stage, the entrepreneur must either go through the difficult metamorphosis of becoming a professional manager, hire someone else to run the business and step out of the way, or sell the firm.

None of these four stages is inherently better or worse than any of the others. Competitive advantage can be drawn from the speed and adaptability of a solo business or from the muscle achieved from growing a larger organization. Problems also occur at every stage, but their magnitude is intensified when growth occurs too rapidly. Cash flow can turn negative, quality can suffer, and employees can lose sight of the vision of the business. Growth has to be managed, and it is not a heresy to try to limit the size of your business.[6]

Transition to Professional Management

The transition from entrepreneur to professional manager is difficult, because the skills or characteristics that were needed to establish and run the business in the startup phase are not the same skills needed to manage a larger business.[7] The transition from an entrepreneurial style of running a business to a managerial approach can be complicated by factors such as

- A highly centralized decision-making system in which few or none of the business decisions are made by employees.

- An overdependence on one or two key individuals, with little delegation.

- An entrepreneur's inadequate repertoire of managerial skills and training in all areas of the business.

- A paternalistic atmosphere within the company which leads to employees' reluctance to act without clearance from the entrepreneur.[8]

	Startup	Growth	TABLE 16.1
Obtain external financing	17%	1%	**What's Bugging You?**
Internal financial management	16%	22%	
Sales and marketing	38%	23%	
Product development	5%	2%	
Production and operations management	4%	8%	
General management	11%	14%	
Human resource management	5%	17%	
Economic environment	3%	2%	
Regulatory environment	1%	8%	

Source: David Terpstra and Philip Olson, "Entrepreneurial Startup and Growth: A Classification of Problems," *Entrepreneurship Theory & Practice*, Spring 1993, 5–20. Reprinted by permission of Entrepreneurship Theory & Practice.

In one study, 121 CEOs of Inc. 500 firms were asked about their most significant problem during their first year of operation and during a later period when their business grew rapidly (see Table 16.1).[9] Their responses provide practical insight into the differences in problems faced during those two periods of business development.

Note that problems associated with securing external financing and product development declined in the growth period. At the same time, problems related to internal financial management, sales and marketing, human resource management, and government regulations increased significantly.

A recent *Inc.* article identified attributes that distinguish professionally managed small businesses. To achieve professional standards you should

- *Be automated.* Computers can efficiently track items like inventory, expenses, and customers; use technology wisely.

- *Be competitive.* Being small no longer means you will have less competition— you have to produce quality.

- *Be resourceful.* There is no shortage of services available to tap for assistance and for tools you may lack.

- *Be planned.* Sophisticated marketing information like demographic mapping is no longer affordable by only the largest businesses.

- *Be experienced.* More "corporate refugees" are starting small businesses with incredible connections, talent, and management experience.

Small businesses can no longer operate unmolested in anonymity. Competition raises standards. As one small business owner put it, "Running a business is like playing a video game. You work and scramble to reach the next level only to find out that the game speeds up and everything gets even harder."

Balance: A Manager's Goal

One goal you will want to achieve as your business grows is to maintain a balance between retaining the innovation and flexibility of an entrepreneur and the admin-

Gotta Go Pro

Changes in almost every industry, from bookstores to funeral parlors, require running your business more professionally than has been possible for most "mom-and-pop" operations in the past.

In the spring of 1986, bookseller David Schwartz was preparing for a morning meeting with his banker, Bill Pattenson. He figured they would simply go over a few numbers—no big deal. Schwartz and his new partner, Avin Domnitz, knew that their business, Harry W. Schwartz Bookshops, was turning around. The year before, their six bookstores had lost $300,000, but currently they were close to breaking even. They had reduced their bank debt by over $100,000 and had missed no monthly payments. Unfortunately, Pattenson did not see the future for Harry W. Schwartz Bookshops to be anything rosy.

Pattenson recognized that the book industry was changing and growing, and that Schwartz was not keeping pace. Waldenbooks, B. Dalton, and Barnes & Noble had spread across the country, bringing sophisticated merchandising and computerized inventory and financial controls to an industry once dominated by small independent stores. Pattenson dissected the company's inventory turnover, salaries, expenses, and advertising. The banker leaned forward and asked the partners, "So when are you closing the company?" Hardly a simple review of numbers—rather, a wakeup call.

David Schwartz's father had started Harry W. Schwartz Bookshops in 1927. Although David grew up with the business and had been in charge since 1972, he didn't realize, until confronted by Pattenson, that he was "totally unlettered in the business part of my profession." Schwartz stated, "I knew how to buy books from the sales reps, and I knew how to sell them to people. And I knew nothing about the business in between."

If Schwartz and Domnitz did not become professional managers soon, they would be out of business. The partners took 10 percent pay cuts, required employees to pay for half of their health insurance costs, and required any purchases to be cleared through Domnitz, among other changes. In the transition to becoming professional managers, the partners realized they could no longer rely on intuition about ordering, hiring, and spending. They had to master the numbers of the business and "start doing structured, formal financial planning."

Before the meeting with Pattenson, for example, inventory turnover was below twice a year—well below industry standards. If Schwartz thought he would sell ten copies of a book, he would order ten copies and carry them until they finally sold. By ordering in smaller batches and tracking numbers with a computerized inventory system, inventory turnover rose to 2.8 in 1987, 3.2 in 1988, and 3.7 in 1989. Many other changes were made in the transition from a sleepy little father-and-son book business into a professionally run company. As Domnitz says, "We have to be the best retailers in the marketplace. We have to know our systems, our numbers, everything there is to know about this business. We have to bring people into our stores. We need this to be the most attractive, most well-stocked, best-serviced, most value-oriented, most selection-driven experience that anyone could possibly have."

Competition from larger players like Walmart, Home Depot, Waldenbooks, and Toys 'R' Us means that thousands of independent businesses, like Schwartz's, must come up to speed to survive.

Of course Amazon.com and BarnesandNoble.com change the book-selling landscape. While they account for about 2 percent of all books sold, they are increasing market share about fourfold per year. Online book sales topped $1 billion in 1999, but the number of books sold has not changed. Schwartz still has many changes ahead.

Sources: Tom Ehrenfeld, "The New and Improved American Small Business," *Inc.,* January 1995, 34–45; and Geeta Sharma-Jensen, "Online Sales Affecting Stores," *Milwaukee Journal Sentinel,* 13 May, 1999.

istrative skill of a manager. Stevenson and Gumpert illustrate these two opposing points of view as follows:

A manager with an *entrepreneurial focus* is one who would ask

- Where is the opportunity?
- How do I capitalize on it?
- What resources do I need?
- How do I gain control over them?
- What structure is best?

A manager with an *administrative focus* is one who would ask

- What sources do I control?
- What structure determines our organization's relationship to its market?
- How can I minimize the impact of others on my ability to perform?
- What opportunity is appropriate?[10]

Employee Theft: What's Walking Out the Back Door?

manager's notebook

Can you spot a thief in your business as easily as you can in the cartoons (you know, the guy with beady eyes, slick black hair, and droopy mustache)? Of course you can't. But employee theft accounts for greater financial losses than fire each year. And small businesses are especially susceptible because they have fewer defenses.

Fraud and other employee crime costs employers more than $400 million per year. Men commit three-fourths of the offenses, even though they are only 54 percent of employees. In 90 percent of the cases in which people steal from their company, the employer would probably have described the person as a trusted employee. So what is a small business owner to do?

- Get a good small business insurance policy covering outside theft, employee theft, and/or computer fraud.

- Screen out potential problem employees at the hiring stage by administering a standardized test that indicates level of integrity (available from career counseling centers).

- Create a culture of honesty with a written code of ethics and conduct. Instruct employees in how to spot problems and what to do about them (tell you). A culture of integrity is best created by your and other managers' demonstrating it.

- Minimize the amount of cash on hand, and put excess cash in a safe.

- Change the times and routes you take to the bank for making deposits.

- Never schedule an employee to work alone.

- Let everyone know that you look at every deposit and every check. Make sure that you get monthly bank statements delivered to your desk unopened.

- The most important point for small business: Divide up financial tasks. The person who keeps the books should not be the same person who keeps the money.

Sources: Pamela Rohland, "Caught in the Act," *Business Start-Ups,* June 2000, 86; Robert Gray, "Clamping Down on Worker Crime," *Nation's Business,* April 1997, 44–45; and Stephanie Gruner, "Are Your Employees Robbing You Blind?" *Inc.,* May 1998, 117.

■ Leadership in Action

Small businesses need managers who are also leaders, because building an organization requires every employee to contribute to productivity and efficiently use every resource. Owners of small businesses must be very visible leaders because they work closely with their people. Jim Schindler, CEO of ESKCO, Inc., says that leaders of small businesses are building a different foundation than their counterparts in large organizations. The small business owner's "character, his vision, what he brings to the equation has a lot more direct impact."[11]

Jim Kouzes, president of Tom Peters Group/Learning Systems, says that the foundation of small business leadership is credibility. He sums up his concept with one sentence: "If people don't believe in the messenger, they won't believe in the message."[12] How do you build credibility? Kouzes prescribes an acronym— DWWSWWD (Do What We Say We Will Do).

A lot of literature on management is devoted to an ongoing debate over management versus leadership. The debate began with a now-famous statement from Warren Bennis: "American businesses are overmanaged and underled."[13] Management has been depicted as unimaginative, problem solving, controlling, rigid, analytical, and orderly, whereas leadership is seen as visionary, passionate, creative, flexible, and charismatic.[14] Are these labels useful when running a business? Not really, for running a small business takes a combination of *both* qualities. Vision without analysis produces chaos, and structure without passion produces rigid complacency. **Leadership** is the inspirational part of the many things a manager must do through directing and influencing team members—along with an amount of planning, directing, and controlling.

leadership The process of directing and influencing the actions of members within a group.

Leadership Attributes

The magazine *Management Review* conducted a study to determine the attributes that business leaders need. Its findings included the following.

VISION. Having a mental picture of where the company is going will always be an important part of leadership. It also means describing that vision to others so that everyone is headed in the same direction. A person with a vision that can't be put into action is a dreamer, not a leader.

COMMUNICATION. Constant communication is needed for a leader not only to find out what is going on but also to let others know. The ability to clearly communicate ranks highly as one of the most important attributes a leader must possess.

INTEGRITY. Leaders must have inner strength and demonstrate honest behavior in all situations. People will not follow a leader who lacks integrity unless they are moved by fear. Leaders need a sense of dedication to doing what they know is right.

TRUST. The bond between leaders and followers must run in both directions. Leaders need to be able to trust their people, and at the same time they themselves must be trustworthy.

Six Styles of Entrepreneurial Management

There is more than one right way to run a new entrepreneurial business. Contrary to much management literature and many consultants, *any* of the many ways to run a business can work. The key is to recognize *your* style and match your strategy to your business goals.

To help business owners get a handle on the different management types, Merrill and Sedgwick identified six entrepreneurial styles. Three are individual oriented, and three are team oriented. Merrill and Sedgwick call the individual styles the Classic, the Coordinator, and the Craftsman. The team styles are called the Entrepreneur + Employee Team, the Small Partnership, and the Big-Team Venture.

Classic. Sue Scott of Primal Lite practices a Classic management style. Scott is involved in every aspect and every decision of the business. Many people are reluctant to admit they are Classics because of criticism for not delegating. Actually, this is a very legitimate way to run your business. Scott recognizes that the Classic style limits the size of her operation. The main problem with this style is not its lack of delegation, but when Classics delude themselves that they are using a team approach. Delegating is fine, not delegating is fine, but don't pretend to delegate, because no one will be happy.

Coordinator. As a Coordinator, you can build a good-sized business without a single employee—also called a *virtual corporation*. You can farm out everything from accounting, to sales, to manufacturing. Do what you enjoy or what you do well. Will Hills sees himself as a Coordinator of Craftsmen in his custom furniture business, Limitless Design. Hills realized that having employees meant overhead, whereas hiring contractors only when he had a job for them gave him larger capacity without full-time responsibility.

Craftsman. The Craftsman is the opposite of the Coordinator because he does everything himself. Stanley Herz runs his own executive search firm. Because his is such a personal service business, he feels that doing it all will keep him from having to compromise quality. There are many advantages to doing everything yourself—no payroll taxes, no unions, no workmen's compensation insurance, no hiring or firing. If you opt for a single-person business, you must first ask yourself how big you want the business to become. Because you will do it all, you may want to consider doing away with parts of the business that you dislike.

The Entrepreneur + Employee Team. This style gives the entrepreneur both control and the ability to grow. Authority can be delegated to key employees while final control is retained by the entrepreneur. Katharine Paine, CEO of Delahaye Group, is a self-proclaimed Classic entrepreneur who has empowered her people to create a consensus-driven team. In return, Paine has received more free time and higher profits.

Small Partnership. Entrepreneurs in Small Partnerships give up more control than those in other styles. When you start a business with two or three other equal owners, you have to share both tactical and strategic decisions with your partners. *Inside-outside partnerships* are a good way to split the turf. Inside partners are in charge of the inside tasks like operations and administration. The outside partners handle sales and marketing.

Big-Team Venture. Some business opportunities with rapid growth possibilities require substantial capital, resources, and a hot-shot team to take advantage, or the competition will take market share. Several owners are needed from the start, so setting up Big-Team Ventures is no time to scrimp. Terry Tognietti is part of the Big Team running Drypers (formerly number one on Inc. 500 list of fastest-growing U.S. companies). Five partners make up the executive team, each with complete responsibility for a business function. Tognietti says, "The critical challenge is to preserve individual accountability. All team members need to know exactly what they are expected to deliver. If you've got thin skin, you're going to have a tough time here. We think the critique makes each of us smarter and makes the company better."

Source: Excerpted from *The New Venture Handbook, 2/e.* Copyright © 1993 Ronald E. Merrill and Henry D. Sedgewick. Reprinted by permission of the publisher, AMACOM, a division of American Management Association International, New York, NY. All rights reserved. http://www.amanet.org.

Act Like the Boss

So you have your own business—now what? You may not get paid like a big-time CEO, but you need to act like one more than you realize. Thomas Bell, Jr., is CEO of Young and Rubicam Advertising, which conducted a research study of 2,600 stakeholders to create "the seven habits of highly regarded CEOs." Results included

- *Be believable.* People remember what you say, so you better tell the truth.

- *Have a vision.* The single strongest thing you can do is having a vision, then driving your organization toward it.

- *Lead a great senior team.* You need a strong core of top people around you for your business to survive after you have left it.

- *Understand global markets.* No matter what size your company may be, the world is still your market.

- *Embrace change.* As technology speeds the pace of change, you must be ready to adapt overnight.

- *Love your customers.* Survey says . . . number one answer. Putting the customer at the center of your bull's-eye is important for one reason—it works.

- *Communicate.* Let people involved with your business—customers, employees, and anyone else involved—know what you are doing and why.

Source: From "Discovering the Habits of Well-Regarded CEOs," by Michael Barrier. *Nation's Business*, March 1999, 15. Reprinted by permission of *Nation's Business.* Copyright 1999, U.S. Chamber of Commerce.

COMMITMENT.   Loyalty to one's company is more precarious in today's climate of economic uncertainty. With this being the case, leaders must be seen as even more caring. Passion for what is good for the business *and* for the workers can't be faked.

CREATIVE ABILITY.   Good leadership involves creating something that didn't exist before. A person must have a positive mindset to see creative opportunities and different ways to do things.

TOUGHNESS.   Often a manager is aware of the difficult choices or changes that must be made for the health of the business but is unable to make them. This indecisiveness is often perceived as lack of leadership. A leader needs a certain amount of toughness to make unpopular decisions or to stand against the majority. A successful leader can set high standards and not be willing to compromise them.

THE ABILITY TO TAKE ACTION.   Small business leaders must realize that, without action, all these attributes are merely academic rhetoric. These attributes need to be consistently practiced to be effective. Leadership is easy to talk about but a challenge to demonstrate.[15]

Negotiation

The art of negotiation is what you do in running your small business from the time the idea pops into your head until the day you harvest it. You may think you are raising money, hiring employees, shopping for computer systems, or signing contracts—but what you are actually doing is negotiating with others to get the job done.

Delegation

By delegating authority and responsibility, a manager gives employees the power to act and make decisions. **Delegation** allows the manager freedom from making every decision that has to be made, giving him time to concentrate on more important matters. Delegation also empowers employees, meaning that it increases employees' involvement in their work. By giving employees authority and responsibility, the manager is holding them more accountable for their own actions. Delegation allows managers to maximize the efforts and talents of everyone in the company.

Although delegation may be an important part of management, many small business owners are either unwilling or unable to do it for several reasons. For entrepreneurs who have started a business, giving up control is difficult. Owners often know the business more thoroughly than anyone else and feel as if they *have* to make all the decisions in order to protect the business. They may feel that subordinates are unwilling or unable to accept responsibility. In reality, this attitude may become a self-fulfilling prophecy. If employees' attempts to take responsibility or to show initiative are squelched too often, they will either stop trying or leave the business. Some small business owners simply misunderstand the meaning of management. These managers want to get the job done right by doing it themselves. That is a commendable attitude, but it can be counterproductive to being an effective manager—someone who needs to get things done through people.

Delegation is not the same as abdication. Nor is empowering people the same as instituting a pure democracy, where you simply count votes and the majority rules. In using delegation and empowerment, an effective leader is trying to encourage participation and take advantage of shared knowledge so that everyone can contribute. Consensus can't always be reached, so sometimes the leader has to make a decision and go with it.

When you assign tasks, make sure you clarify exactly what is expected, when the job should be done, the performance level expected, and how much discretion is allowed. Your employees need feedback control for their own sake and for yours. Controls help monitor employees' progress by letting them know how they are doing and preventing mistakes before they happen.

delegation Granting authority and responsibility for a specific task to another member of an organization; empowerment to accomplish a task effectively.

Motivating Employees

The word *motivation* comes from the Latin *movere,* which means "to move." For our purposes, **motivation** is the reason an individual takes an action in satisfying some need. It answers the question: Why do people behave the way they do? As a small business manager, you will be interested in how to motivate employees to perform.

MOTIVATION THEORIES. Some people say that one person cannot motivate another, that one can only create an environment for self-motivation. Still, many theories on motivation exist. Although a thorough examination of each of them is not appropriate for this text, you are encouraged to revisit any principles of management or organizational behavior text for more depth of coverage.

A small business owner can benefit from a knowledge of how to apply motivation theory. One of the best known is *Maslow's hierarchy of needs.* Psychologist Abraham Maslow stated that people have in common a set of universal needs occurring in order of importance. The lowest-level needs are *physiological* (food,

motivation The forces that act on or within a person that cause the person to behave in a specific manner.

Managing the Roller Coaster

Tomina Edmark started TopsyTail Company believing two things strongly: (1) Her hair-styling gadget would be a major success, and (2) her company would not turn into a big business of "suits" for her to manage. A one-time sales representative for IBM, Edmark had seen time and effort wasted on meetings, office politics, and trying to keep everyone happy. "In my own business," Edmark said, "I wanted to spend my time doing business rather than managing people."

Edmark has successfully met her own challenge. She has created an $80 million business and after three years has just hired her second employee. How can 3 people run the kind of volume which would normally require at least 50 full-time employees? By outsourcing. Edmark set up a network of 20 vendors who manufacture the products, sell them, distribute them, and service the accounts. She started with very little capital—the $25,000 severance pay she received from IBM—hardly enough to purchase the tooling and injection molding needed to make TopsyTails. Outsourcing has allowed her to be flexible and stay focused on the important parts of controlling her business.

Just because TopsyTail depends so heavily on outsourcing does not mean that it does not require management. Edmark retains control of the business by staying on top of new product development and marketing strategy. These two functions are the heart of a fast-growing company.

Although the company started with only one product, growth has been aided through new products. The My Pretty TopsyTail doll comes with a miniature version of the tool. Edmark has come up with another hair-styling gizmo: a line of hair jewelry and a book showing examples of hair styles that can be done using the TopsyTail.

A concern about outsourcing is that you will lose control of quality and delivery if you don't manufacture and distribute yourself. Edmark insists this is not the case, noting that if vendors do not perform to her satisfaction, they can be replaced. All contracts contain performance clauses that lay out minimum performance standards and time constraints. Everything was going well for TopsyTail, selling 3.5 million units at $12.95 a pop, until knock-off products started showing up in Walmart and K-Mart stores. These counterfeit products sold for $5 less than the original. Sales took a nosedive, and Edmark was devastated. She had spent four years getting a patent and had spent millions on promotion. Now large manufacturers were stealing her idea and coasting on her advertising.

Edmark was learning a distasteful truth about inventions—getting a patent is not enough. You have to be prepared to pay the legal bills to defend it. She discovered that unscrupulous companies exist to knock off products, assuming that they will never be sued because the entrepreneur responsible for the product can't afford excessive legal defense. If challenged, they usually settle out of court. If they can spend $150,000 in legal fees for a product that makes them millions with no development costs, they are way ahead.

Edmark did not roll over so easily. She brought suit against all five infringers and was willing to "fight to the death." She spent over $1 million in legal fees and lost an estimated $20 million in sales, but the emotional costs were higher. She got so caught up on the negative stuff that she even lost focus on her first love—inventing new products. After the lawsuits ended, she has purposely cultivated her reputation of being a hard hitter. She stated, "I wanted my competitors to think of me as this crazy woman so that they wouldn't mess with me!" Good defense.

Edmark is on the inventing track again and recently introduced the Halo, an ultralight, broad-brimmed woman's hat with interior foam that prevents "hat head." Bowrette is another device that uses scarves to create a wide variety of hair bows. She's back!

Sources: Sara Eckel, "Patent Perseverance," *Success,* February 1999, 32; Rusty Cawley, "Patent Protection," *Dallas Business Journal,* 12 June 1998, 1(3); Echo Montgomery Garrett, "Innovation + Outsourcing = Big Success," *Management Review* (September 1994): 17–20; and Julia King, "Farming out Everything but the IT," *Computerworld,* 23 March 1998, 41–44.

water, air, sleep, sex, and so on). *Safety and security* needs are the next level, followed by *social* needs, *esteem* needs, and the highest-level needs for *self-actualization.*

As a small business owner, you should understand that these needs do not occur in a rigid order. People will be at different levels of needs at different times—sometimes simultaneously—so a variety of ways to motivate their behavior is needed. The use of money to motivate is often misunderstood, especially in terms of Maslow's hierarchy. Money is generally seen as providing for basic physiological needs and not important to the higher-level needs. But money is actually a motivator because it buys the time and resources needed for self-actualization.

The biggest contribution of Maslow's theory to motivating employees is its recognition that people have needs that "pop up" and require attention until satisfied. If a lower-level need pops up for an employee, he or she will not be able to concentrate on a higher-level need until the lower-level need is fulfilled. For example, if an employee receives a phone call from a school nurse informing the employee that his second-grade child had an accident and broke her arm on the playground, a safety need has popped up. This employee will probably not be very productive on the job until he can be sure the situation is under control, either by going to the school in person or by making other arrangements. Any effort to interfere with his handling of this need will create frustration and antagonism, which will undermine your employee's motivation and damage his attitude toward work.[16]

Another important motivational theory is *Herzberg's motivation-hygiene theory.* This theory is important to the small business owner because it recognizes that factors producing job *satisfaction* are not the same as factors producing job *dissatisfaction.* Herzberg called things that cause people to feel good about their job *motivators* and things that cause people to feel bad about their job *hygiene factors.* By eliminating hygiene factors on the job (like unfair or inadequate company policies), you may create contentment among employees but not necessarily motivate them to excel (see Figure 16.3). For you to truly motivate your people, you need to create an opportunity for them to achieve.

Look at the factors listed in Figure 16.3 that cause satisfaction on the job: achievement, recognition, the work itself, and responsibility. These provide intrinsic rewards to people. The practical application of Herzberg's theory gives a small business manager some direction in keeping employees satisfied on the job. Satisfaction may not translate directly into motivation, but it is a significant component in keeping employees on the job.

MOTIVATION TECHNIQUES. A key to motivating the employees of your small business is to know what is important to them. For instance, if you provide a motivational reward that they do not want, it is a kind of inadvertent punishment. Say you promise a "sweet year-end bonus" for the top performer for the month of December. You will probably set up healthy competition that increases morale and achievement. But if your sweet bonus turns out to be a fruitcake—and your employees don't care for fruitcake—don't expect your next incentive to be motivational.

Bill Mork is the owner of Modern of Marshfield, a furniture maker located in Marshfield, Wisconsin. Mork followed the popular advice of using recognition instead of cash to reward participants in his new employee suggestion program. From the suggestions received, Mork and other managers picked a "colleague of the month," who was awarded with a special parking space and a big handshake in front of all the gathered employees.

FIGURE 16.3
Job Satisfiers and Dissatisfiers

The factors or experiences that cause people to feel satisfied with their jobs *(motivators)* are distinctly different from those that create job dissatisfaction *(hygiene factors)*. This chart records factors affecting job attitudes as reported in 12 investigations.

Source: Reprinted by permission of *Harvard Business Review.* From "One More Time: How Do You Motivate Employees?" by Frederick Herzberg, *Harvard Business Review,* September/October 1987, p. 112. Copyright 1987 by the Harvard Business School Publishing Corporation. All rights reserved.

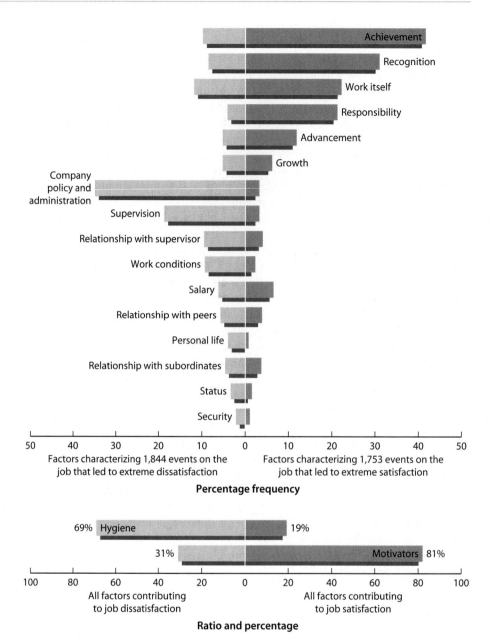

The number of suggestions that came in was underwhelming. One winner pleaded not to be chosen again, to avoid embarrassment and being called a "brown nose" by coworkers. As a result, Mork changed the whole program and added cash bonuses at each step. For any cost-saving suggestion made by an employee that was implemented by the company, the employee was given a bonus worth 10 percent of the estimated savings. An additional 10 percent of the savings was added to a fund to be split among all suggestion makers at the end of the year. Anyone who had contributed a suggestion was eligible for prize drawings, whether or not the suggestion was implemented. The "colleague of the month" is now chosen by previous winners rather than by managers.

Motivating More with Less

creating competitive advantage

Specialty coffee shops are typical of many small businesses—dependent on hourly employees for operation of the business and contact with customers. Think about what is expected of employees making $7 to $8 per hour. They are expected to spend eight hours a day providing quick, friendly, and superior service to every customer. They are expected to create perfect caffeine concoctions, wash dishes, wipe tables, and sweep floors. They are expected to be diligent, honest, and cut into their personal time (often with little or no notice) to cover a shift they were not scheduled for. The bottom line is that we expect our hourly employees to be as motivated about our businesses as we business owners are.

No surprise that a survey of 500 small and midsize business owners by Arthur Anderson's Enterprise Group showed that *retaining and motivating workers* is the biggest challenge. Over 48 percent of respondents placed this concern at the top of their problem list.

In response, many small business owners are creating "work/life" policies to sustain a competitive advantage in hiring employees. Work/life issues can include on-site child care, time-off policies, flextime, job share, and personal days. The problem is: How do you afford to offer such perks on limited revenues and razor-thin margins? The answer comes from the same source as many other solutions—creativity.

Tom Macon, owner of a chain of independent boutique coffeehouses in the metro Washington, D.C., area offers the following advice:

- *Give your staff a chance to believe.* Have staff meetings in which you share your plans and goals. Let employees provide help and ideas (then follow through). Let them suggest menu items (with the same constraints you operate under; they can pick only menu items that cost no more than 40 percent of the retail price). Participation in decision making leads to ownership of the process. As you know, ownership is a great motivator.

- *Get creative.* Recognize and reward employees' birthdays, pay something like $50 for recommending a new employee that you hire or free beverages and discounted food, for example. One year, Macon was short of cash for a decent Christmas bonus, but found an airline offering $59 round-trip tickets from Washington to Chicago. He loaded everyone up early one morning, flew to Chicago, rented cars, scored tickets to see Oprah (free), cruised Michigan Avenue, popped $20 a head for a nice lunch, kicked in another $20 for spending money, then headed back to D.C. This was quite an adventure for most of his young staff. About $100 created stories that lasted all year. Now it's a contest to see how far they can go for the least amount of money.

- *Tip jars.* When he started in the coffee business, Macon did not allow customers to spend more money than their bill on tips. Later, he softened his stance on letting customers show appreciation for quality service. A cup by the cash register at one of his establishments is labeled "Karma" rather than "Tips." Looks like Macon isn't the only creative one in the shop.

Source: Material adapted from "Motivating the Troops," by Tom Macon, from *Specialty Coffee Retailer,* March 1999, 10–11. Reprinted by permission of Adams Business Media.

Because the program was revised, Modern's sales have almost doubled. Each year Mork pays out $10,000 in rewards for the 1,200 suggestions submitted by 100 employees. Although this may sound like a lot of money, Mork estimates savings to be five times that amount. Employees have a very different attitude toward the program since bonus checks have been added.[17] This example provides evidence answering that long-asked management question: Does money motivate? Apparently, at a very visceral level, the answer is "yes."

MOTIVATION MYTHS. Although theories of motivation help managers to understand what drives employees, there are so many theories that confusion exists about what does and does not motivate people. Examples of misconceptions include

- *All employees need external motivation.* Some employees have such a strong internal drive that external techniques will not increase their motivation—but they still need your support, backing, and guidance.

- *Some employees don't need any motivation.* Motivation is the force that prompts every action—we all have to have motivation; it just comes from different sources.

- *Attempts to motivate always increase performance and productivity.* If our attempts to motivate involve incentives that employees do not desire, they can decrease performance. We can also increase happiness and morale without seeing an increase in productivity.

- *Money always motivates people.* Base salary is generally not a long-term motivator. A person who receives a raise may temporarily work harder but soon rationalize, "I'm *still* getting paid less than I'm worth" and return to his or her previous level of productivity.

- *Intrinsic rewards provide more motivation than money.* As seen in the Bill Mork example, money—as a one-time bonus—*does* motivate at a visceral level.

- *Fear is the best motivator.* Workers who are afraid of a boss will work hard in the boss's presence, but may not have the best interests of the business in mind. The best workers will also be looking for another job—so fear may drive out the very people the business needs the most.

- *Satisfied workers are always productive.* Happy people do not necessarily produce more. The goal of employee motivation is not to create a country club or amusement park atmosphere. The goal is to get everyone in the company to maximize his or her efforts in order to increase their contribution (and earnings).

- *This generation of workers is less motivated than the last.* Most generations think this of the following generation. While members of the so-called X generation have been mislabeled as "slackers," they have already produced notable entrepreneurs, including many who have been used as examples throughout this book.

Can You Motivate?

To determine how effective you are at motivating, ask yourself the following questions:

- Do you know what motivates each of the people who report to you?

- To what extent are they motivated by money?

- To what extent are they motivated by recognition?

- To what extent are they motivated by opportunity for growth?

- Have you done anything in the last week that was intended to motivate someone else?

- Have you done anything lately that would undermine an employee's motivation—such as embarrassing or criticizing an employee in front of others?

- Have you praised anyone today?

Total Quality Small Business Management

So much has been written over the past few years about quality and quality management that definitions have blurred and debate has increased over their meaning and worth. Total quality management (TQM) is a philosophy of management focusing on problem solving and control. It was *not* intended to be a panacea or a cure-all. TQM is based on the writings of W. Edwards Deming, who helped ingrain and teach the concept of quality to Japanese manufacturing managers after World War II. As outlined by Deming, the 14 points that serve as the foundation of TQM are

1. *Strive constantly for improvement.* The quality-centered business should aim to remain competitive, provide jobs, and stay in business—not just make money in the short run.
2. *Adopt the new philosophy.* Change comes from leadership. Western management must learn responsibility and not continue to tolerate inferior workmanship or service.
3. *Stop depending on mass inspection to ensure quality.* Quality products and services are built correctly from the beginning. Inspection tells you only what should be thrown out or reworked.
4. *Stop awarding business on the basis of price tag alone.* Rather than supporting inferior products by buying on price alone, minimize total cost by building long-term relationships of loyalty and trust with suppliers.
5. *Constantly improve the system of production and service.* Improvement does not start and stop. By always looking for ways to get better, you increase productivity and lower costs.
6. *Train everyone.* All workers need to learn how to do their job properly from the time they start.
7. *Institute leadership.* Leading is not just giving orders and applying punishment. Leading is helping, guiding, and teaching.
8. *Drive out fear.* People cannot perform at their best without feeling secure to ask questions or point out problems.
9. *Break down barriers between departments.* Different parts of the business should view competitors outside the business as the competition, not each other. All need to be part of the same team.
10. *Eliminate slogans, exhortations, and targets that demand zero defects.* These create adversarial relationships. Address quality and productivity problems by correcting the system rather than by badgering the work force.
11. *Eliminate numerical quotas.* Deming states that numerical programs like management by objectives (MBO) draw attention to numbers rather than quality.

12. *Remove barriers to pride in workmanship.* When employees (either salaried or hourly workers) feel that they are being judged or graded, they don't reach their potential.

13. *Start a vigorous program of education and self-improvement.* Continuous improvement must come from greater knowledge, so new methods of teamwork, processes, and techniques need to be taught.

14. *Put everyone to work on the transformation.* Transformation of a company to carry out the mission of quality takes every person in the organization. A few people, or even most of the people, can't do it—transformation is everyone's job.[18]

TQM is not just a set of tools and techniques that a business can pick up and use—it involves a change in the way of thinking about how the business is run. When so much attention is given to a topic, there is a danger of its becoming perceived as the latest management fad, buzzword, or quick cure for what ails American business. But if a small business owner has realistic expectations of what TQM is and what it can do, and if he or she is committed to involving every aspect of the business to produce a quality product or service, the philosophy can work. For TQM to have a positive impact, managers need to understand basic principles. They must

1. Strive to do work right the first time.
2. Be customer centered.
3. Know that continuous improvement is a way of life.
4. Build teamwork and empowerment.[19]

How can TQM programs and a company's quest for quality be criticized? Few would argue against quality, so the answer to that key question lies in making sure that the quality offered is the quality that customers want.[20] Of course, quality should be the focus of a business's operations, but programs can become so cumbersome that they replace the real reason a company is in business.[21]

Varian Associates, Inc., makes scientific equipment in California's Silicon Valley. From the beginning of the total quality movement in the mid-1980s, Varian was on the bandwagon. One thousand of its managers went through a four-day quality course, work teams were set up, and cycle times were discussed. They even had a mascot—Koala T, a manager dressed up in a koala bear suit who handed out quality homilies in the lunchroom. As a result, Varian's on-time delivery for the vacuum system department improved from 42 percent to 92 percent, and the service department for radiation equipment ranked first in the industry for speed of customer visits.

Varian appeared to be on top of the quality world, but not *everything* was improving. The people in the vacuum system department were so obsessed with meeting production schedules that they didn't return customers' phone calls. The service people in the radiation repair unit were working so quickly to meet their self-imposed targets that they would rush from one job to the next without ever talking to or explaining things to the customers. "Quality" was up, but everything else was down. Sales grew only 3 percent, and profits went from $39 million in 1989 to a $4.1 million loss in 1990.

A concerted push for quality can come from the best of intentions yet still be misguided. TQM programs can turn into expensive exercises that raise costs (therefore reducing profits) without creating anything of real benefit to the customer. Deming stated, "The trouble with Total Quality Management—failure of TQM, you call it—is that there is no such thing. It is a buzzword. I have never used the term, as it carries no meaning."[22]

Management guru Tom Peters cites three reasons for the failure of TQM. First, to be done right, quality must be a way of life, not a program. Second, the essence of offering quality is the belief in the abilities of your front-line employees—the people who meet your customers. Third, many quality programs are internally focused, not customer focused.[23]

Lifeline Systems, Inc., is a Massachusetts company that makes a home personal response system to summon emergency aid when the owner pushes a button. Quality is a serious issue for a product that *must* work every time. Lifeline overhauled operations to improve its quality, products, and systems. It realized improvements in productivity and waste reduction, but eventually sales dipped. John Gugliotta, vice president of operations, realized that continuous improvement in quality and productivity must be supported with increased sales.[24] The quality of Lifeline's process—it reduced wastefulness, for instance—was meaningless to customers and thus did not pay off in increased sales, profits, or market share. Quality in unneeded areas creates additional expense and wastes effort.[25] Because of the experience of companies like Lifeline, successful total quality management is evolving into *return on quality (ROQ),* which emphasizes that quality improvements must be ones that customers want and that will have a positive financial impact.

Special Management Concerns

Beyond the standard functions of management lie many other duties and responsibilities. Besides running your business, you also have personal, family, and social activities to tend to. You must be a good manager of time and be able to keep stress at acceptable levels.

Time Management

Management is the *effective* and *efficient* use of resources. What is a small business owner's most precious and most limited resource? Time. No one seems to have enough of it, yet everyone has the same amount—24 hours per day, 168 hours per week, 8,760 hours per year. You can't store it, rent it, hoard it, sell it, or buy any more of it. So you had better use it wisely.

Few of us use time as effectively or as efficiently as possible. The key to effective time management for a small business owner is investing time in what is important in life—including the business. This assumes that the small business owner knows what his or her priorities are—making time management a goal-oriented activity. To be an effective time manager, you must prioritize what needs to be accomplished in any given day. Indicators of possible time management problems are if you

- Are frequently late for or forget meetings and appointments.

- Are consistently behind in responsibilities.

- Don't have enough time for basics—eating, sleeping, family.

- Are constantly working and still miss deadlines.

- Are often fatigued, both mentally and physically.

> *You can't store, hoard, or buy time—so you had better use it wisely!*

"You've been working awfully hard lately.
If you need a little fresh air and sunshine,
you can go to www.fresh-air-and-sunshine.com"

© 1998 Randy Glasbergen www.glasbergen.com

How can you determine your effectiveness in using your time? A good starting point is to conduct a *time audit*. A time audit makes as much sense as conducting a financial audit, but few small business managers can account for their minutes as precisely as they can for their dollars. Why? They don't have time to conduct a time audit!

Begin your time audit by keeping a log to record your activities. Break days down into 15-minute intervals and keep track of what you do for about two weeks. When the log is complete, you can analyze how you have spent your time. Then you can prioritize activities according to their importance. Did you accomplish your most urgent needs? Which activities were a waste of time and could be eliminated? In the end, the time audit should help you set daily goals on a regular basis.

After you conduct your time audit, some additional tips are

■ *Make a to-do list.* Write down and rank by importance what you want to accomplish each day. The return you receive will be many times greater than the small amount of time you invest.

■ *Eliminate time wasters.* Combine similar tasks and eliminate unnecessary ones.

■ *Remember Parkinson's law.* "Work expands to fill the time available." If you schedule too much time to accomplish something, you'll probably set a pace to take that amount of time.

■ *Know when you are most productive.* We all have a daily cycle. Some of us are "morning people." Some are "night owls." Schedule your work so you handle your most demanding problems when you are at your best.

Stress Management

stress Emotional states that occur in response to demands, which may come from internal or external sources.

One of the most ambiguous words in the English language is **stress.** There are almost as many interpretations of the term as there are people who use it. Common usage leads us to think of stress as a negative thing, as if it were something to be avoided. The stress response is actually the unconscious preparation to fight or flee that a person experiences when faced with a demand. The negative side of stress, called **distress,** entails unfavorable psychological, physical, or behavioral consequences that may or may not result from stressful incidents.

For a situation to create distress for a person, two conditions are necessary: its outcome must be uncertain, and it must be a matter of importance to the person. Very few (if any) small businesses are "sure things" guaranteed to produce the outcome that the owner desires. Because small businesses are almost always the sole means of support for their owners, saying that they are important to the owners is not an understatement. Therefore, both conditions causing distress exist in running a small business.

Other sources of stress that small business owners encounter are role conflict, task overload, and role ambiguity. *Role conflict* exists when we are faced with a situation that presents divergent role expectations. For example, a two-day business trip to meet with a potential client could help you land a large new account and be very profitable for your business. But say the only days the trip can be made would make you miss your second grader's school play—creating role conflict for you. The desire to attend both the meeting and the play—to be both a focused entrepreneur and a loving parent—creates a stressful internal conflict.

Task overload is another common source of stress for a small business owner. More is expected of you than time permits—a common scenario in a small business. Unfinished work can be a sign of overload. In a business climate that calls for leaner organizations, work can pile up and more work taken on before existing jobs are finished. Unfinished work creates tension and uneasiness. If the pattern of taking on more and more continues, eventually an accumulation of unfinished work produces stress and decreases performance.

Role ambiguity occurs when you are not entirely sure what you should do in a situation. Owning a small business generally means that you don't have anyone to consult when problems arise and that you will have to make decisions on a wide variety of topics. Some people have higher tolerance or preference for ambiguity than others, but it is still stress producing.

Stress is cumulative—it builds up. Sales declining at the business, a key employee being unhappy, a child having discipline problems, and the transmission going out in the family car all combine to form a lot of stress. Individual stressors that could be handled by themselves may combine and become overwhelming.

Stress cannot, and should not, be eliminated from everyday life, but it must be managed. General recommendations for controlling your stress level include the following.

PREVENTIVE STRESS MANAGEMENT. Attempt to modify, reduce, or eliminate the source of distress. Any changes you can make in your schedule or role as business owner can help prevent distress from building to a dangerous level.

RELAXATION TECHNIQUES. A few minutes of concentrated relaxation will prevent a buildup of distress. Practice a five-step relaxation exercise. First, sit in a comfortable position in a quiet location. Loosen any tight clothing. Second, close your eyes and assume a passive, peaceful attitude. Third, relax your muscles as much as possible—beginning with your feet and continuing to your head—and keep them relaxed. Fourth, slowly breathe through your nose and develop a quiet rhythm of breathing. After each exhale, quietly say "one" to yourself. Fifth, continue relaxing muscles and concentrate on breathing for 10 to 20 minutes. Open your eyes occasionally to check the time. It will take practice for you to learn to ignore distracting thoughts during relaxation, but soon this exercise can help you reduce stress.[26]

distress The negative consequences and components of stress.

SOCIAL SUPPORT SYSTEMS. Working in an environment that provides social and emotional support can help us deal with distress. Relationships within the workplace, family, church, and clubs provide emotional backing, information, modeling, and feedback.

PHYSICAL EXERCISE. A person's physical condition affects his or her response in stressful situations. Aerobically fit people have more efficient cardiovascular systems and better nervous system interaction, which allows them to deal with and recover from stressful events more quickly.[27]

Stress can increase performance and quality of life if it is controlled. Many articles and books have been written on the subject of stress control, so comprehensive coverage is beyond the scope of this section.

SUMMARY

▬ The functions and activities of managing a small business.

Managers plan, organize, lead, and control. To accomplish these functions, they perform many activities, such as developing relationships, negotiating, motivating, resolving conflicts, establishing information networks, making decisions, and continually learning.

▬ The stages of growth and their consequences for your business.

In the earliest stage of many businesses, the entrepreneur acts alone. Many entrepreneurs even prefer to keep their businesses as one-person organizations. In the second growth stage, employees are added, so the entrepreneur often acts as a coach in getting work accomplished through other people. In stage 3, a new layer of supervision is added, so the entrepreneur does not directly control all the people or activities of the business. In the fourth, or formal organization, stage, the entrepreneur must transform himself or herself into a professional manager in order to run a complex business.

▬ The significance of employee leadership and motivation to small business.

Leadership means inspiring other people to accomplish what needs to be done. Leadership is part of a manager's job in providing the vision, passion, and creativity needed for the business to succeed.

Because management is getting things done through people, a small business manager must be able to motivate employees. The manager must therefore understand employees' behavior and what is important to them. Maslow's and Herzberg's theories provide small business managers with frameworks for understanding motivation.

▬ The positive and negative aspects of total quality management for small business.

A small business manager can use Deming's 14 points to focus on problem solving, control, and quality. If a small business manager adopts the way of thinking and running a business that is the heart of TQM, a constantly improving company can be operated. If TQM is approached as an internally focused program that raises costs without improving the quality of features that are important to customers, it may fail.

The special management concerns of time and stress management.

Besides running your business, you must be a good manager of time and be able to keep stress at acceptable levels.

QUESTIONS FOR REVIEW & DISCUSSION

1. Give examples of efficiency and effectiveness in managing your everyday life.

2. Discuss some of the skills or characteristics that are needed by a manager in the startup phase of a business that differ from those needed later to manage a larger, established firm.

3. Study the six styles in Manager's Notebook, "Six Styles of Entrepreneurial Management." Which one best describes you? Explain. Do you recognize a different style in managers you have worked for in the past?

4. What is motivation? Can managers really motivate employees?

5. How can TQM programs and a company's quest for quality be criticized? Elaborate on this question.

6. Are you a good manager of time in your personal life? How will this affect your ability to manage your time as a business owner?

7. Give examples of stress and distress.

8. How can the owner of a small business apply Maslow's hierarchy of needs to working with employees?

9. What are positive and negative aspects of delegation?

10. As a business owner, in which of the leadership attributes discussed in the text are you the weakest? How could you help yourself improve in this area? How could others help you? What is your strongest skill?

QUESTIONS FOR CRITICAL THINKING

1. As you read in the chapter opener, open book management can be a powerful motivational tool for a small business owner. Would you want to share all the financial information for your business with employees? Why? What are the possible negative implications?

2. Refer to Reality Check, "Gotta Go Pro." How would you have reacted if you were in David Schwartz's position when the banker asked, "So when are you closing the company?" How do you step back and evaluate a close situation from a different perspective?

Experience this . . .

Experience can be the best teacher—see what you can learn from others' experience. Contact five small business owners in your community for a one-question mini-interview. Ask them what they would do differently if they could build their business all over again. You—and they—may be surprised at the responses.

WHAT WOULD **YOU** DO?   No. 1

Chadwick's Manufacturing. It's a situation that no one ever likes to face, and a common one at large companies and small. Yet it seems to have a more profound impact on small businesses because of their size. The death of a popular and well-liked coworker can be devastating to workers' morale. At Chadwick's Manufacturing in Minot, North Dakota, employees were understandably upset over the unexpected death of the company's plant manager, who was well liked and respected by the 35 employees. In the month after his death, productivity was well below previous levels. As one employee was overheard saying, "It's hard for me to accept Roy's death. What's the use in working so hard when tomorrow I could be gone?" In such a situation, how can employees mourn the loss, and have their enthusiasm and motivation reignited?

Wizards of the Coast. Wizards' best-known product, Magic: The Gathering, is selling like hotcakes. Magic is a popular fantasy game designed for teens. Although the company keeps its financial figures a close secret, industry experts estimate that the company's sales totaled $50 million in its second year and probably doubled that in its third. With that type of incredible growth come management challenges. How can employee enthusiasm and motivation be maintained in the light of such growth rates?

QUESTIONS

1. Write a plan outlining how you would confront the employee motivation challenges presented in each of these situations. Focus on possible reactions of employees, alternative plans, and best- and worst-case scenarios.

2. Pretend you're the new plant manager hired to fill Roy's position at Chadwick's Manufacturing. Role-play your first meeting with all the plant employees. Then role-play a one-on-one meeting between yourself and one of the employees.

3. Pretend you're the supervisor of five software designers at Wizards of the Coast. Role-play a meeting between yourself and these designers over a loom-

ing deadline for a game update. Then pretend you're Peter Adkison, Wizards' founder and CEO. Role-play a motivational speech you're going to make at the company's annual employee retreat.

WHAT WOULD **YOU** DO?	No. 2

Ten years ago, Linda Turner was in an exercise class and saw a pregnant woman struggling through her routine. After class, Linda asked the woman if she knew of any products that would help her be more comfortable. Because none existed, she began developing a prototype of the Bellybra—a support device designed for women in their third trimester. The Bellybra has tank-top shoulder straps and fits snugly all the way down below the wearer's enlarged stomach area. Turner experimented with different fabrics, including white lace and CoolMax fabric that pulls heat away from the body.

The Bellybra prototypes tested well with consumers, but because Turner was a stay-at-home mom, she was not able to build a company at that time. She licensed the product to a company called Basic Comfort and became their first employee. As the success of the Bellybra increased, Turner eventually left on friendly terms to go out on her own. She sold 1,000 in her first year and 10,000 in her second. Some growth rate! She has now expanded her focus from obstetricians and gynecologists to her Internet site www.bellybra.com

QUESTIONS

1. Linda Turner will face different challenges as her company progresses through the four stages of growth described in this chapter. Describe how you believe her business would change in each of the four stages.

2. Business growth that occurs too quickly can present some significant problems and challenges compared with a business's growing at a slow, steady pace (of course, zero growth or decline makes for a whole new set of problems). Describe the challenges of hypergrowth that Turner could face and how she should respond as a small business owner.

CHAPTER CLOSING CASE	No. 16

Finding a Growth Plan for ERG

Four days after ERG International received the news that it had not won a key contract for a Department of Energy technical services hotline, company president Claude Robbins conducted a strategic planning meeting where he discussed plans for future growth and corporate reorganization.

Claude, 45, and his wife Sherrie, 45, founded Environmental Research Groups International, Inc., in 1980 as a two-person, summer-break operation. Claude was teaching at Florida A&M University and Sherrie was a chef at a Hilton hotel. That summer, they moved to Denver, where Claude had a job, and over the next few years he wrote two books that helped form the intellectual foundation for ERG's consulting services. In the meantime, Sherrie became an executive chef, managing kitchen staffs of more than 60 people.

In and Out of Partnership   In 1988 Claude and Sherrie quit their jobs to make ERG a full-time operation. Their first major client was Compaq Computer Corporation, and by early 1990, ERG had grown to 6 employees. That spring, ERG became involved with a venture capitalist who wanted to form a partnership to provide construction management services for the projects that ERG engineers designed. By mid-1990, ERG and the partnership venture employed a total of 34 people. However, managing two companies as one overwhelmed Claude and Sherrie, so ERG withdrew from the partnership at the end of that year.

The Compaq contract provided enough revenue to carry ERG through its early years. But when Compaq terminated the relationship in early 1991, ERG's business slowed to a virtual halt. By May, Claude and Sherrie had cut back to 3 employees—the office manager and two engineers. Letting people go was difficult. For several months, they clung to the belief that cutbacks would not be necessary because a number of major proposals were pending and new contracts might arrive any day.

In October 1991, a large utility in Utah awarded ERG a contract to provide technology transfer consultation and set up and maintain an information services bulletin board. By September 1992, ERG was back to 13 employees.

Keep the Corporate Structure Flat   ERG was divided into two areas: engineering and technical, which was Claude's domain; and administrative and management, which was Sherrie's. ERG's corporate structure was intentionally flat. Claude focused on marketing, project planning, raising and allocating capital, developing procedures manuals, and writing a business plan. Claude estimated that he spent 25 to 30 percent of his time soliciting and writing proposals, 20 to 25 percent composing operating procedure and policy manuals, and the rest managing the Utah project.

Sherrie spent most of her time managing the office and information systems, establishing accounting procedures, overseeing contracts and purchase orders, and managing personnel and benefits plans. She and Claude jointly conducted annual performance appraisals for all ERG employees.

Because ERG's "product line" consisted of technical reports and assistance unique to each client, it was essential that the staff work together to provide clients with accurate and timely reports. Everyone was responsible for typing his or her own reports; everyone had to submit final reports to at least one other person for editing. Everyone was expected to voice his or her opinion and to offer suggestions for improving the business. Training seminars were open to all. People dressed casually, and everyone shared in making coffee and cleaning up the kitchen area and conference room.

Let Employees Share in Management   Looking back on the partnership experience, Claude observed, "They were hung up on titles; they were hung up on power trips; they were hung up on dictating to people instead of building teams, building consensus so that you get things done."

In contrast, he and Sherrie wanted every ERG employee to feel and act like part of the decision-making process. "It's part of our planning to spread out management and let other people get into the decision-making process," he said. "We realize that if we want to make the company grow, we have to give up some of the authority in management of the company."

Effective information management was critical for keeping track of client records and sharing progress reports and technical information. New project teams had access to prior records so that they could maintain continuity for a particular client or project. ERG kept all project files electronically, and a spreadsheet showed who was working on which project.

Every employee carried a "Green Book" to track activities, document meetings and conversations with clients, and record ideas. As these books were filled, they became part of ERG's permanent records.

Looking Ahead   At the strategic planning meeting in September 1992, ERG's staff considered several ideas: create a board of directors, composed partly of influential industry insiders who were likely to be aware of pending projects; spread the marketing function by providing incentives to existing staff; and hire a marketing director to solicit new projects. With these changes, Claude and Sherrie believed ERG could achieve its growth goals.

Source: Adapted from Joan Winn, "ERG International, Inc.," University of Denver. From *Case Research Journal* 14(4), Fall 1994. Reprinted by permission of the author. To read the entire case, visit the *Small Business Management: Entrepreneurship and Beyond* web site at http://business.college.hmco.com/students.

QUESTIONS

1. How would you describe Sherrie's and Claude's management style?

2. What do Sherrie and Claude do to motivate ERG employees? Have they been effective?

3. What would ERG have to do to grow the company to the next level?

17 Human Resource Management

After reading this chapter, you should be able to:

- Discuss the importance of hiring the right employees.

- Define the job analysis process and the function of job descriptions and job specifications.

- Evaluate the advantages and disadvantages of six sources of employee recruitment.

- Describe the three steps of employee selection.

- Discuss the need for employee training and the seven methods of doing so.

- Explain the two components of a compensation plan and the variable elements of a benefits system.

- Profile an effective sequence for disciplining and terminating an employee.

NANCY RUDDY IS president of Cetra/Ruddy, a $2 million architectural and design firm in New York City with 20 employees. She had never heard of a professional employer organization (PEO) until she was urged to use one by her insurance broker. Outsourcing all the hassles of staying on top of employment laws, of shopping for and administering benefit plans, and of other HR functions was tempting, but Ruddy was skeptical. So, like any good entrepreneur, she spent six months of due diligence checking out PEOs.

Ruddy found that PEOs become co-employers with full legal responsibility for employees, including the final say in hiring, firing, and compensation. While the PEO handles benefits, 401(k) plans, and labor law compliance issues, the company is responsible for managing daily work assignments, on-site supervision, and ensuring production and service delivery.

The average PEO client employs fewer than 20 employees, and PEOs are most cost-effective for businesses with fewer than 100 employees. Above the 100-employee level, the cost advantage shifts to having a full-time HR staff. The PEO's fee is generally a percentage of the company's gross wages—typically $800 to $900 per employee per year.

Ruddy's first concern was insurance issues. She was reassured that her professional liability coverage would still stand with employees officially assigned to a PEO. Cetra/Ruddy's licenses to do design work in different states would also still be valid, even though the employees officially worked for the PEO. Her next questions related to legal issues. What would happen in the event of an employee lawsuit? Who would cover legal costs? Would the PEO be a codefendant?

Ruddy was finally convinced that using a PEO was the correct decision for her business and began the transition. Cetra/Ruddy is enjoying a 25 percent reduction in health insurance costs. Legal costs have plummeted also. Ruddy can now consult the PEO's staff lawyers (for employment law issues) rather than her own $300-per-hour legal team. And while costs went down, the overall benefits package increased. Employees now have access to a 401(k) that they did not before the switch.

Sources: Ilan Mochari, "Letting Go the Right Way," *Inc.,* December 1999, 151–152; Phaedra Brotherton and Gerda Gallop-Goodman, "HR Efficiency Without the Hassles," *Black Enterprise,* September 2000, 49; and "Buyer's Guide: HR Outsourcing" (www.buyerzone.com).

Hiring the Right Employees

Are human resource management (HRM) issues important to small businesses? Can small business owners afford the time and cost of developing formal recruitment, selection, training, and benefits programs? Perhaps the more appropriate question is: Can small business owners afford *not* to spend the time and money on such programs? In today's marketplace, some of the most valuable resources and competitive advantages a small business has are its employees.

According to a recent Roper Organization study, small business owners reported that their biggest problems were finding competent workers and motivating them to perform.[1] Part of the problem in finding employees is the cost involved. According to the Families and Work Institute, a nonprofit research group in New York, hiring and training costs to replace a nonmanagerial employee typically average 75 percent of a year's pay.[2] To make matters worse, 50 percent of all new hires last an average of only six months in their new positions.[3] As alarming as these figures are, they do not include other potential costs such as defending against charges of discrimination, the loss of customer satisfaction, low employee morale, and wrongful discharge suits. Once you find people to hire, you must find ways to retain and motivate your work force, which costs money. These costs may also be high as you increasingly implement various employee incentive and benefit plans.

All told, the costs and risks associated with human resource issues are too great for any company to ignore. Small business owners need to realize that their most valuable assets walk out the door at closing time.

The Job Analysis Process

job analysis The process of gathering all the information about a particular job, including a job description and a job specification.

The recruitment process involves attracting talented individuals to your company. To achieve this goal, you must be able to (1) define the positions to be filled and (2) state the qualifications needed to perform them successfully. This requires that you conduct a job analysis, prepare a job description, identify a list of job specifications, and identify alternative sources of employees.

The **job analysis** indicates what is done on the job, how it is done, who does it, and to what degree. It is the foundation on which all other human resource activities are based and, if necessary, defended in court. Although no single job analysis technique has been endorsed by the courts or the Equal Employment Opportunity Commission (EEOC), both entities urge, and in some cases require, that the information from a job analysis be used to ensure equal employment opportunity.

The first step in completing the job analysis is to gain the support and cooperation of employees, because they often know best what the job involves. The next step for you is to identify the jobs to be analyzed. Generally, the amount of time and money you have available, and the importance of the particular job to the company's overall success, will determine the order and the number of jobs you will analyze.

Step 3 involves identifying the job analysis technique or techniques you will use to obtain information about each job. Although numerous techniques exist, for reasons of cost, ease of use, and time savings, the most commonly used technique is the questionnaire. Job analysis questionnaires typically seek to identify the following: identification facts about the job, skill requirements, job responsibilities, effort demanded, and working conditions. Once you have analyzed your jobs, you are ready to prepare the job description and job specification.

Job Description

The purpose of the **job description** is to identify the duties, tasks, and responsibilities of the position. Although a standard format for the job description (increasingly being termed the *position description*) does not exist, it is generally agreed that one should include

- *A job identification section.* The job title, location or department within the company, and date of origin should be included in this introductory section. This section might also include the job code, salary range, pay classification, and analyst's name.

- *A job summary.* This summary should outline the jobholder's responsibilities, the scope of authority, and superiors to whom the jobholder is to report.

- *The essential duties to be performed by the jobholder.* Although this list may contain both essential and nonessential duties, the Americans with Disabilities Act requires that each be clearly identified, because employment decisions may be based only on the essential components of the job (see Chapter 10).

- *A list of tasks associated with each duty.* Task statements detail the logical steps or activities needed to complete the overall duties. These statements should focus on the outcomes or results rather than on the manner in which they are performed. For example, a loading-dock worker might "*move* 50-pound boxes from the unloading dock to the warehouse" rather than "*lift* and *carry* 50-pound boxes from the unloading dock to the warehouse."

- *Task statements.* Task statements help to identify the knowledge, skills, abilities, and educational levels needed to perform the job and help to establish performance standards for the position. In addition, these statements are valuable in complying with various federal and state employment provisions.

General working conditions, travel requirements, equipment and tools used, and other job-related data may also be included in the job description. To preserve your status as an at-will employer, which gives you the right to discharge an employee for any reason, you may also add a general duty clause, such as "and other duties as assigned," or write "representative tasks and duties" to indicate that your list is not comprehensive. Figure 17.1 shows an example of a typical job (position) description.

job description A written description of a nonmanagement position which covers the title, duties, and responsibilities involved for the job.

Job Title: Marketing Manager

Department: Marketing

Reports to: President

Status: Nonexempt

Summary: Plans, directs, and coordinates the marketing of the company's products and/or services by performing the following duties personally or through subordinate supervisors.

Essential Duties and Responsibilities: Include the following. Other duties may be assigned.

- Establish marketing goals to ensure market share and profitability.

- Develop and execute short- and long-range marketing plans.

- Research, analyze, and monitor internal and external factors in order to capitalize on market opportunities and ensure positive competitive position.

- Plan and oversee execution of advertising and promotion internally and through advertising agencies.

- Develop and monitor pricing strategies.

- Accountable for profit/loss ratio and market share in relation to preset standards.

- Establish controls and corrective actions needed to achieve marketing objectives within prescribed budget.

- Recommend changes of organization in marketing team as needed to respond to threats and opportunities.

- Conduct market research relative to target markets and product development.

- Prepare monthly marketing activity reports.

Supervisory Responsibilities: Manage three subordinate supervisors who supervise a total of five employees. Supervise two nonsupervisory employees. Carry out supervisory responsibilities in accordance with the company's policies and applicable laws. Responsibilities include interviewing, hiring, and training employees; planning, assigning, and directing work; appraising performance, rewarding, and disciplining employees; and addressing complaints and resolving problems.

Qualifications: The employee must be able to perform each essential duty satisfactorily. The requirements listed below are representative of the knowledge, skill and/or ability required. Reasonable accommodations may be made to enable individuals with disabilities to perform the essential functions.

- *Education and experience:* Master's degree or equivalent, or a minimum of four years' related experience and/or training, or combination of education and experience.

- *Language skills.* Ability to read, analyze, and interpret common technical and industry literature, financial statements, and legal documents. Ability to respond to common inquiries and complaints from customers, regulatory agencies, or members of the business community. Ability to present information to company or public groups.

- *Mathematical skills.* Ability to apply advanced mathematical concepts, such as exponents, logarithms, quadratic equations, and permutations. Ability to apply statistical operations, such as frequency distributions, determination of test reliability and validity, analysis of variance, correlation techniques, sampling theory, and factor analysis.

- *Reasoning ability.* Ability to define problems, collect data, establish facts, and draw valid conclusions using abstract and concrete variables.

- *Physical demands.* While performing the duties of this job, the employee is regularly required to sit and talk or listen. The employee is frequently required to use hands to finger, handle, or feel. The employee is occasionally required to stand, walk, and reach with hands and arms. Reasonable accommodations may be made to enable individuals with disabilities to perform the essential functions.

FIGURE 17.1

Sample Job Description

Source: Material adapted from "Sample Job Description: Marketing Manager," from www.jobdescription.com. Reprinted by permission of KnowledgePoint.

Job Specifications

A **job specification** indicates the skills, abilities, knowledge, and other personal requirements a worker needs to successfully perform the job. In writing the specification, take care to ensure that the stated requirements are truly necessary for successful performance of the job. For example, stating that a college degree is a requirement for a given job may be difficult, if not impossible, to prove if questioned by an Equal Employment Opportunity representative. For this reason, you may wish to add a qualifier, such as "or equivalent," and limit the specifications to those that are truly job related and necessary. Job specifications are often integrated into the job description, as shown in Figure 17.1.

job specification The identification of the knowledge, skills, abilities, and other characteristics an employee would need to perform the job.

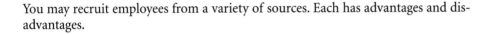

Employee Recruitment

You may recruit employees from a variety of sources. Each has advantages and disadvantages.

Small business owners must realize that the most valuable assets of a company are its employees.

Advertising for Employees

Help wanted ads placed in newspapers, trade publications, or storefronts generate a large number of responses, but generally the quality of applicants is not equal to that generated by other sources. Nevertheless, ads reach a wider, more diverse audience than other techniques, which may be needed to ensure equal opportunity representation or an adequate supply of employees with unique or specialized skills.

Employment Agencies

Located in all states and most large cities, government-funded employment agencies focus primarily on assisting blue- or pink-collar employees. On the positive side, they allow you to obtain screened applicants at no cost. On the negative side, the quality of applicants may not be equal to that generated by employee referrals. Private employment agencies can be useful in helping you find more skilled employees. Fees for professional and management jobs are usually paid by you, the employer.

Internet Job Sites

Monster.com charges $295 for a single posting for 60 days, yielding the most résumés and the largest pool of qualified candidates. HotJobs.com charges $195 for a single posting for 30 days. Headhunter.net charges $50 for an economy posting, $100 for a standard posting, and $150 for priority posting. JobsOnline.com postings are free and are good for 60 days. They are limited options, but you get what you pay for.[4]

Executive Recruiters (Headhunters)

These firms can be useful for small businesses looking for a key person or two rather than for the manual or lower-level positions that government agencies concentrate on. These firms search confidentially for people who are currently employed and not usually actively seeking another job. Their services can be expensive.

Employee Referrals

Because your employees know the skills and talents needed to work in your company, they can be a good source for finding people to fill slots. This inside-track approach to recruiting is not very costly and can generate qualified, highly motivated employees as long as your current employee morale is high and your work force is somewhat large and diversified. On the downside, an exclusive use of this source may perpetuate minority underrepresentation or create employee cliques. In cases in which the referral is not hired or does not work out, the referring employee may become resentful.

Relatives and Friends

The advantage of hiring relatives or friends is that you generally know beforehand of their abilities, expertise, and personalities. However, no approach is more laden with long-term repercussions. The effects of a poor decision may be felt long after the desk has been cleared and the nameplate changed. According to Peter Drucker,

- Family members working in the business must be at least as able and hard working as any nonrelated employee.

- Family-managed businesses, except perhaps for the very smallest ones, increasingly need to staff key positions with nonfamily professionals.

- No matter how many family members are in a company's management, no matter how effective they are, one top job must be filled by a nonrelative.

- Before the situation becomes acute, the issue of management succession should be entrusted to someone who is neither part of the family nor part of the business.[5]

Other Sources

Job fairs, trade association meetings, and specialized Internet sites run by professional organizations (accountants, environmental specialists, and so on) can be good sources of potential employees. Finally, don't forget the simple things like putting a help wanted sign in the window or a notice on the employee bulletin board.

Obviously, hiring employees in a foreign location presents special challenges. Unless you have a lot of firsthand knowledge about or experience in the country where you'll be hiring employees, you'd be wise to get assistance and advice from local experts. That's what Eli E. Hertz, founder of Hertz Computer Corporation in New York, did. In fact, when Hertz wanted to expand into Israel, he purchased a small distributor there to handle his computer equipment. Because of the nature of the business, potential employees would need technological as well as cultural understanding. Hertz felt that this was the best option for him in expanding into this market.[6]

Hiring decisions should not be made in haste, for several reasons. An incorrect decision can be costly to you and your business. Almost without exception, you are better off holding out for the *best* employee, rather than filling a position quickly. Some factors to keep in mind in order to hire the best include

- Keep your focus on hiring the best.

- Have a written job description.

- Use a written rating system so that you don't forget about attributes of early candidates.

- "Overqualified" is better than "underqualified."

- A person with a long history of self-employment will in all probability return to self-employment as soon as possible. Hire this person as a consultant if you need his or her skills.

- Test specific skills and industry knowledge. You want to observe the candidate performing the work to be done (as closely as it can be duplicated) during testing.

- Check the candidate's background and all references thoroughly.

- Keep a written record of all terms of employment.

Hiring Right

In a small business, the repercussions from hiring an incompatible employee can be devastating and demoralizing. Just ask Jody Wright, president of Motherwear, a $5 million-a-year catalogue company based in Northampton, Massachusetts. She faced that situation early in her company's history. The person she had hired had an impressive résumé, the job interview was a smashing success, and a job offer was made and accepted. However, it wasn't long before Wright discovered that the rest of the work team couldn't get along with the new employee. Since that disastrous hire, Wright has taken a new approach to bringing employees on board. She now allows her employees to interview and hire the individuals they'll be working with. In fact, more than 60 percent of Motherwear's 40-member staff have been hired that way. The disadvantage to this approach is that a consensus must be reached by the work team doing the hiring, and that can take up to two or three weeks. But, as Wright says, "Integrating the person into the job takes less time. Everybody has already bought in." But Wright doesn't use this open approach with every human resource decision. In fact, she still uses a mostly traditional process for promoting employees, in that the manager makes the yes-or-no promotion decision.

creating competitive advantage

Source: Adapted from "Employees Take Charge", by Donna Fedd, from *Inc.: The Magazine for Growing Companies,* October 1995. Copyright 1995 by Goldhirsh Group/Inc. Publishing. Reproduced with permission of Goldhirsh Group/Inc. Publishing in the format textbook via Copyright Clearance Center.

■ Selecting Employees

Once you have a pool of applicants from which to choose, you should match the applicants with the job requirements outlined in your job description and specifications. Three commonly used tools for selecting employees include the application form and résumé, the selection interview, and testing.

Application Forms and Résumés

Application forms and résumés contain essentially the same information. The difference between them is that applications are forms prepared by your company, and résumés are personal profiles prepared by candidates. Both contain the candidate's name, address, telephone number, education, work experience, and activities. The four purposes of the application form and the résumé are

1. To provide a record of the applicant's desire to obtain the position.
2. To provide a profile of the applicant to be used during the interview.
3. To provide a basic personnel record for the applicant who becomes an employee.
4. To serve as a means of measuring the effectiveness of the selection process.

The application form need not be complex or long to achieve these objectives. It must, however, ask enough of the right questions to enable you to differentiate applicants on the basis of their knowledge, skills, and ability to perform the job. In addition, the application form should provide the names of potential references and furnish the applicant's permission for you to contact him or her to discuss qualifications and prior job performance. Finally, it should include a notice that you are an at-will employer and may therefore discharge an employee for cause or no cause and that any misinformation provided on the application form is grounds for immediate dismissal.

A caveat on résumés: They are sometimes the best fiction written, so view them with some degree of skepticism. You want to believe what people tell you, but check out all the facts, and contact previous employers.

Time and money constraints will prevent you from interviewing every candidate. Applications and résumés give you a screening tool to decide whom to bring in for the next stage of the selection process—the interview.

Interviewing

Considered by many employers to be the most critical step in the selection process, the personal interview gives you a chance to learn more about the applicants; to resolve any conflicts or gaps in the information they provided; and to confirm or reject your initial impressions of them, drawn from the application or résumé. The interview also gives you a chance to explain the job and company to the applicant. Always remember that you are selling your company to the potential employee as well as determining his or her suitability to join your company. If the applicant is a good fit, you want him or her to join your firm. But even if you don't hire this applicant, the image you create may well lead to another suitable person through a word-of-mouth referral.

To conduct an effective interview, you should do the following:

BE PREPARED.   Start by thoroughly reviewing the job description and job specifications. You must know what your needs are before you can find a person to fulfill them. Next, review the candidate's application form. Look for strengths and weaknesses, areas of conflict, and questions left unanswered or vaguely worded.

SET THE STAGE FOR THE INTERVIEW.   Arrange to hold the interview at a time and location demonstrating its importance. The location should provide privacy and comfort, and present the right image of your company. It should allow you to talk without interruptions. Taking telephone calls, answering employee questions, or working on another task while conducting the interview does little to ease the fears of the applicant and simply does not facilitate good communication or a good image.

USE A STRUCTURED INTERVIEW FORMAT.   Develop a set of questions to ask each candidate, so that you can compare their responses. Your job description and specifications should be the source of the majority of your questions. Such a format will allow you to collect a great deal of information quickly, systematically cover all areas of concern, and more easily compare candidates on the basis of similar information.

USE A VARIETY OF QUESTIONING TECHNIQUES.   Although closed-ended questions are appropriate when looking for a commitment or for verifying information, they are very limiting. Consequently, you should use open-ended or probing questions that are related to the job. For example, rather than asking, "Do you like working with figures?" you may wish to probe with the question "What is it that you like about working with figures?" Open-ended, probing questions encourage the applicant to talk, providing you with a wealth of information and insight into the applicant's ability to communicate effectively.

NO MATTER THE TYPE OF QUESTION, IT MUST BE JOB RELATED.   The EEOC requires that all job interview questions be nondiscriminatory in nature. In other words, they must be devoid of reference to race, color, religion, sex, national origin, or disability, and they must be job related. You should be able to relate each interview question to one or more of the items in your job description or job specifications and to show how the information obtained from the questions will be used to differentiate candidates.

KEEP GOOD RECORDS, INCLUDING NOTES FROM THE INTERVIEW.   The EEOC construes any selection device as a test, and as is true of any test that results in underrepresentation of a protected group, the interview process must be validated. In the case of most small business owners, the problem is not one of questionable behavior or wrongdoing within this area, but one of inadequate documentation. (For a form that can help you document the interview, see Figure 17.2.) You must be able to show that your decision to hire or not to hire was based on a sound business reason or practice.

Please use this form to rate the applicant in each category listed. Study the job description and this form before interviewing and appraising the job applicant. First you are asked to weigh the value of each category to the job being applied for, then circle the applicant's ability rating in each category. Multiply the two scores to get the total for each category. Add the category totals to get the applicant's total score. Be sure to use the same value ratings for each applicant applying for the job.

VALUE FACTOR RATINGS

1 = No value to the job	**2** = Minimal value	**3** = Average value	**4** = Very important	**5** = Most important

APPLICANT'S ABILITY RATINGS

1 = Unsatisfactory	**2** = Barely satisfactory	**3** = Satisfactory	**4** = Above average	**5** = Outstanding

SKILLS AND KNOWLEDGE

The extent to which the applicant possesses the practical/technical knowledge required by the position. Makes effort to constantly improve.

Value factor	(Lowest)	1	2	3	4	5	(Highest)	Total	
Applicant's ability	(Lowest)	1	2	3	4	5	(Highest)	x Total	

CATEGORY TOTAL (Value x Ability)

RESPONSIBILITY

The extent to which the applicant has demonstrated integrity and responsibility in the workplace and community.

Value factor	(Lowest)	1	2	3	4	5	(Highest)	Total	
Applicant's ability	(Lowest)	1	2	3	4	5	(Highest)	x Total	

CATEGORY TOTAL (Value x Ability)

COMMUNICATION

The extent to which the applicant demonstrates oral or written communication skills. Ability to listen well and work as a team member. Pleasant personality.

Value factor	(Lowest)	1	2	3	4	5	(Highest)	Total	
Applicant's ability	(Lowest)	1	2	3	4	5	(Highest)	x Total	

CATEGORY TOTAL (Value x Ability)

INITIATIVE

The extent to which the applicant has the potential to work independently or with minimal supervision. Self-starter who seeks out opportunities.

Value factor	(Lowest)	1	2	3	4	5	(Highest)	Total	
Applicant's ability	(Lowest)	1	2	3	4	5	(Highest)	x Total	

CATEGORY TOTAL (Value x Ability)

FIGURE 17.2
Applicant Appraisal Form

Source: Material adapted from "Questions to Avoid During an Interview", by Donald A. Phin. From www.lawthatworks.com. Reprinted by permission of the author.

STABILITY

How stable is the applicant? (number of jobs in the past ten years, length of time at last jobs, emotional control)

Value factor	*(Lowest)*	1	2	3	4	5	*(Highest)*	Total	
Applicant's ability	*(Lowest)*	1	2	3	4	5	*(Highest)*	x Total	
								CATEGORY TOTAL (Value x Ability)	

MOTIVATION

How motivated is the applicant? Is he or she goal oriented? Will he or she work hard for our company?

Value factor	*(Lowest)*	1	2	3	4	5	*(Highest)*	Total	
Applicant's ability	*(Lowest)*	1	2	3	4	5	*(Highest)*	x Total	
								CATEGORY TOTAL (Value x Ability)	

FLEXIBILITY

Ability of the applicant to "roll with the punches," accept diverse assignments, and manage change.

Value factor	*(Lowest)*	1	2	3	4	5	*(Highest)*	Total	
Applicant's ability	*(Lowest)*	1	2	3	4	5	*(Highest)*	x Total	
								CATEGORY TOTAL (Value x Ability)	

CREATIVITY

How creative is the applicant? (problem solving, suggestions, innovation, etc.)

Value factor	*(Lowest)*	1	2	3	4	5	*(Highest)*	Total	
Applicant's ability	*(Lowest)*	1	2	3	4	5	*(Highest)*	x Total	
								CATEGORY TOTAL (Value x Ability)	
								TOTAL VALUE POTENTIAL (Sum of All Category Totals)	

Applicant's Name _____   Interview Date _____

Reviewer's Name _____   Date _____

Reviewer's
Comments: _____

_____

_____

Don't Even Ask!

EEOC and other government guidelines set parameters for what you can and can't ask in an interview. You are limited basically to information concerning how the person would handle the job and provide value to the company—no "small talk" for the sake of conversation. Unless clearly related to the job, avoid questions like

- "So, when did you graduate from high school?"
- "How many kids do you have?"
- "Where were you born?"
- "Do you own or rent your home?"
- "How long have you lived there?"
- "Have you ever been arrested?" (You *can* ask if the applicant has ever been convicted of a felony.)
- Questions regarding current or past assets, liabilities, credit rating, or bankruptcy.
- Questions regarding the applicant's state of health or medical conditions.
- "Have you ever filed a workmen's compensation claim?"
- "Can you leave a photo of yourself with us?"
- "Would any religious obligations prevent you from working any day of the week or holidays?"
- "Would your family object to your working at night?"
- "How do you people eat that kind of food? It gives me gas!"
- "You think you can keep up with these kids around here?"
- "Do you have any kind of disability that would require reasonable accommodation?"
- "How did you learn to speak that foreign language?"
- "Do you own a car?"
- "How did you lose that leg?"

Source: Material adapted from "Questions to Avoid During an Interview," by Donald A. Phin. From www.lawthatworks.com. Reprinted by permission of the author.

Testing

Employee testing has long been used by U.S. businesspeople to screen applicants. And, for the most part, prior to the 1971 Supreme Court *Griggs* v. *Duke Power Co.* decision, employers were fairly free to do as they pleased.[7] Today, however, employers must be able to prove that their tests and other selection criteria are valid predictors of job performance. This can be done, according to the Supreme Court and the Equal Opportunity Commission, through statistical or job-content analyses.

For small business owners, the process of statistically validating a test is generally far too time consuming and expensive. Therefore, short of eliminating all tests, two options remain: purchasing preprinted tests from commercial vendors who have conducted the necessary standardization studies to ensure test reliability (although ultimate liability still rests with the employer) or using content-based tests. Although it is not an absolute defense, you are more likely to be able to prove a test's validity if the test is a sample or measure of the actual work to be performed on the job. For example, if a clerk's job involves counting back change to customers, then asking an applicant to count back change as a test is probably content valid and its use is therefore permitted.

Regardless of the type of test used, in few cases should the results of a single test or indicator be used as the sole reason for hiring or not hiring an applicant. In addition, all test results should be kept strictly confidential and in a file other than the employee's personnel file. Commonly used tests include the following five options.

ACHIEVEMENT TESTS. Achievement tests are given to measure the specific skills a person has attained as a result of his or her experiences or education. These tests are easy and inexpensive to administer and score. Proving validity and job-relatedness, however, is another matter. Therefore, you should have a very compelling, business-related reason to justify their use during the selection process.

PERFORMANCE (ABILITY) TESTS. Performance tests are administered to assess the applicant's ability to perform the job. The tests provide direct, observable evidence of performance. They are also easily administered, relate directly to the job, and are relatively inexpensive to conduct. Validity is generally not an overriding issue with performance testing.

PHYSICAL EXAMINATIONS. Often considered the last step in the screening process, physical examinations are given to discover any physical or medical limitations that might prevent the applicant from performing the duties of the job.

"We do *so* hire people with disabilities!
Dan can't make a decision, Tina is a chronic whiner,
Jake is an obsessive-compulsive coffee drinker,
Katherine has no sense of humor...."

© 2000 Randy Glasbergen www.glassbergen.com

The Americans with Disabilities Act (ADA) states that physical examinations may be given only after a conditional offer of employment and only if they are administered to all applicants in the particular job category.[8] In addition, you may not disqualify individuals as a result of such examinations unless the findings show that the person would pose a "direct threat" to the health and safety of others.[9] All medical findings must be kept apart from general personnel files and be made available only to selected company personnel on a need-to-know basis.

DRUG TESTS. Organizations are increasingly using drug tests to screen applicants. According to a recent survey, 64 percent of reporting firms administered drug tests as part of their health and safety programs.[10] Although tests for illegal use of drugs are not considered tests under the ADA and are therefore not subject to its regulations, many state legislatures have imposed conditions under which drug tests may be administered, samples tested, and results used. Generally, to justify the cost and privacy concerns caused by these tests, you must be able to demonstrate a strong need for safety within your workplace or services.

HONESTY TESTS. The 1988 Employee Polygraph Protection Act essentially outlawed the use of voice stress analyzers and other devices in most business situations. As a result, employers have increasingly relied on paper-and-pencil honesty tests. However, to date, these tests are suspect in terms of their validity, and the courts have yet to rule decisively on their use. Several congressional committees are also looking into restricting or outlawing their use as a preemployment tool. Unless one has an overriding reason—for example, unless the employee will have ready access to merchandise or money—the use of an honesty test is not recommended without proper legal advice. Court rulings on honesty testing do vary from state to state.

Temporary Employees and Employee Leasing

Many small business owners are recognizing the benefits of hiring temporary employees. In the past, agencies such as Kelly Services and Manpower, Inc., were generally called upon only when someone in the company went on vacation or demand suddenly exceeded capacity. Although these are still the most popular reasons for using temporary services, other reasons include the need to fill new or highly specialized positions, to ensure a full work force during periods of labor shortages, and to take advantage of the growing pool of workers who like the flexibility and challenge of working for multiple employers. Today, temporary employees are being used by small and large businesses to perform tasks formerly done by permanent employees. According to the National Association of Temporary Services, 1.5 million people are working as temporary employees within the United States.[11]

The employment costs of temporary employees are often lower than those of permanent or full-time employees. The employment agency generally takes care of all federal and state reporting and record-keeping requirements, thus lowering the company's overhead costs. In addition, training and other costs, such as workmen's compensation, unemployment insurance, and fringe benefits, are paid by the agency, not by the company. Finally, once the job has been completed in the case of seasonal demands, temporary workers can be laid off quickly and with fewer concerns for wrongful discharge claims.

A relatively recent trend in human resource management involves leasing employees. In this arrangement, an employee leasing company becomes the legal employer, handling employee-related duties, including recruiting, hiring, payroll tax paperwork, and provision of benefits. The handling of benefit packages, especially health insurance, is usually what makes employee leasing attractive to small businesses.[12] Because employees with an employee leasing company are part of a larger group than they would be with a small business, they can get insurance coverage that is either unavailable or prohibitively expensive. Cost savings of benefits and other HRM functions may outweigh the leasing fee, making leasing employees cheaper for small firms than hiring employees.

But cost is seldom the only factor in such decisions. Many business owners are understandably reluctant to turn over responsibility of their most important assets—employees—to an outside company. Before leasing employees, check with your lawyer and accountant for legal and tax implications. Make sure the benefits provided by the leasing company are better than those you currently offer. Check the financial stability of the leasing company by finding out the years it has been in business, its capitalization, and its credit rating. If the leasing company goes out of business, you will face the problems of rehiring all your employees and finding a new insurance carrier. If the leasing company does not pay its insurance premiums on time, your leased workers could be left without insurance. Finally, the leasing company sets its own personnel policies, like performance appraisals and wage reviews—it does not administer yours. Make sure its policies are consistent with yours.[13]

Employee leasing may be a viable alternative for your small business if you can pick the right leasing company, but remember that you don't get anything for nothing. There are advantages and disadvantages. For assistance on choosing a leasing company, contact the National Staff Leasing Association, 1735 North Lynn Street, Suite 950, Arlington, VA 22209 (703-524-3636).

Placing and Training Employees

Every employee, no matter how experienced, will need to be introduced to the methods and procedures of the job and the rules of your company. This process of introduction is called **employee orientation.** Many organizations mistakenly leave orientation of new hires to coworkers on an informal, as-time-permits basis. Unfortunately, this casual approach often results in an incomplete orientation, and it cannot be formally documented in the event of a wrongful discharge claim. A formal orientation will, by contrast, ensure that the new hire is welcomed to the company in a positive, complete, and cost-effective manner.

employee orientation The process of helping new employees become familiar with an organization, their job, and the people they will work with.

The orientation should be comprehensive and spread over several days. The scope of topics should include both hard and soft issues. Hard issues, which are relatively easy to cover, include specifics such as how the job is to be performed, the company's policies and procedures, and a discussion of pay and fringe benefits. Soft issues might include the organization's interest in making a profit, producing a quality product, being socially responsible, and providing a safe, efficient, team-oriented work environment. These soft issues establish the tenor of the employment relationship and generally make the difference between an "acceptable" and a "good" employee. The sessions at which soft issues are discussed should be kept short, generally not exceeding two hours, and should be spread over several days if the employee is to truly learn and grow from the orientation experience.

FIGURE 17.3
Professional or Technical Employee Orientation Checklist

Source: Excerpted from *Effective Employee Orientation (A Worksmart Book)* by Linda A. Jerris, 43–44. Copyright © 1993 AMACOM. Reprinted by permission of the publisher, AMACOM, a division of American Management Association, New York, NY. All rights reserved. http://www.amanet.org.

- Provide employee with job description for position.
- Explain specific requirements and expected accomplishments.
- Provide overview of the organization and mission of the department, its relationship to other departments, and the employee's role as it relates to the goals of the department.
- Introduce employee to department staff.
- Provide tour of facility, and introduce employee to employees outside of the department.
- Review:
  - Working hours
  - Lunch period
  - Jury duty
  - Overtime
  - Probation period
  - Illnesses
  - Military obligation
  - Time and attendance reporting
  - Personal emergencies
  - Performance appraisals
- Review benefits:
  - Insurance (life, disability, medical, travel, accident, workers' compensation)
  - Tuition reimbursement
  - Holidays
  - Sick days
  - Vacation days
  - Career development
  - Employee assistance program
- Review paperwork for completeness:
  - Application
  - Signature on employment agreement
  - Personnel questionnaire
  - ID card
  - W-4 form
  - Sales forms
  - Insurance applications
- Provide employee with:
  - Employee handbook
  - "Where to Go" guide
  - Time card
  - Security procedures
  - Copy of newsletter
  - Organization chart
  - Building layout
  - History and product line
  - Telephone directory
  - Restaurant guide
- Make public announcement on bulletin board of new employee's name, position, and starting date.

An effective way to prioritize the order in which you present the orientation topics is to use a checklist (see Figure 17.3). When an employee reports to work for the first time, he or she has many needs, some of which are more immediately pressing than others. For example, the fear of not being at the right place at the right time or of saying the wrong thing to the wrong person generally far outweighs concerns over fringe benefits or the company's plan for future growth. Consequently, the order of the orientation presentation should be directed toward fulfilling the most pressing needs first. We can organize orientation by need level, following Maslow's hierarchy (see Chapter 16). According to Maslow, human needs fall into five categories: physiological, safety, social, esteem, and self-actualization.[14] These needs can generally be fulfilled through the following types of actions or discussions:

- *Physiological.* Draw a flow chart of the employee's typical day. Start by discussing the time when the employee should report to work, where to park his or her car or how to access public transportation, the location of his or her office, and so on. Your goal is to give the employee time to set up shop and become comfortable with new surroundings.

- *Safety.* Review the company's employee handbook, procedures manual, safety and health guidelines, and benefits package with the employee. Your goal is to give the employee a sense of security by letting him or her know the dos and don'ts of the organization and the safeguards available in the event of illness, disability, or discharge.

- *Social.* Introduce the employee to personnel outside his or her immediate work area; go over committee assignments; and inform her of special company events or days and other company traditions, norms, and standards. Your goal is to provide the employee with enough information so that he or she can interact comfortably with coworkers and others.

- *Esteem.* Review the company's employee performance appraisal and promotional processes, training programs and procedures, and any employee assistance programs. Your goal is to reassure the employee that his or her sense of self-worth and others' respect for him or her are supported by your company.

- *Self-actualization.* Discuss the company's past, present, and future plans, and the employee's participation in its evolution, along with opportunities for promotion and transfer within the company. Your goal is to instill within the employee the desire to achieve his or her fullest potential as both an individual and an employee.

It's particularly important for small businesses to employ individuals who are committed to providing outstanding customer service. This is particularly true for businesses in which employee turnover can be extremely high, as in food retailing. William Brodbeck, president and CEO of Brodbeck Enterprises of Platteville, Wisconsin, preaches the importance of employee training and orientation for reducing employee turnover and thus being able to keep service high. His company owns and operates eight supermarkets where a highly systematic training program is in effect for new hires. The company's basic training and orientation session is 6.5 hours long. Cashiers receive another 38.5 to 40 hours of training on top of that, deli employees get another 33 hours, and seafood workers get an additional 47.5 hours of training. Brodbeck feels strongly that his company's commitment to training and orientation makes a difference in the customer service his supermarkets provide.[15]

Employee Training and Development

An important means of motivating employees often overlooked by managers is **employee training** and **development.** Training involves increasing the employee's knowledge and skills to meet a specific job or company objectives. It is usually task and short-term oriented. Development, on the other hand, is more forward looking, providing the employee with the knowledge, skills, and abilities to accept a new and more challenging job assignment within the company.

A trained work force can give you a competitive advantage that, once gained, is not easily duplicated by competitors. That advantage can be maintained and enhanced through an ongoing training and development program. Training and development help to keep employees from becoming bored and unfulfilled, and increase retention of qualified personnel. Not only are turnover costs reduced but,

employee training A planned effort to teach employees more about their job in order to improve their performance and motivation.

employee development A planned effort to provide employees with the knowledge, skills, and abilities to accept new and more challenging job assignments within the company.

Training is critical to ensure that employees are happy and productive.

over a period of time, the overall level of employee morale is increased. Finally, training and development assure your firm a place in tomorrow's competitive environment. New employee skills and abilities will be required as the business expands into new product lines, acquires new technologies, and strives to maintain or reach a higher level of customer service.

According to the American Society for Training and Development, despite an annual investment of $210 billion in worker training, of which American companies contribute $30 billion, 50 million workers need additional training just to perform their present jobs.[16] Over 65 percent of all jobs require at least some special training and additional education beyond high school. Employee training will be not an option but a competitive necessity in the future.

Ways to Train

Depending on the objectives of your training program, there are several techniques available. Some of the more commonly used methods include on-the-job, lecture, conferences, programmed learning, role-playing, job rotation, and correspondence courses.

ON-THE-JOB (OJT). Everyone from mail clerks to company presidents experience OJT from the time they join a company. It is learning the job while you are doing it. OJT is effective, but try to ensure that it is not the *only* type of training you provide. The most familiar types of OJT are coaching and mentoring, in which a new employee works with an experienced employee or supervisor. This practice not only instructs new employees on how to operate equipment, but hopefully builds a bond between the employee, the mentor, and the business.

LECTURE. Lecturing involves one or more individuals' communicating instructions or ideas to others. The technique is often used because of its low cost, the speed with which information can be covered, and the large number of individuals that can be accommodated. Employee participation is limited, however, and no allowance is made for individual employee differences.

CONFERENCES. Also termed *group discussions,* this technique is similar to the lecture method, except that employees are actively involved in the learning. Although this technique produces more ideas than lecturing does, it also takes more time and limits the number of participants involved.

PROGRAMMED LEARNING. Programmed learning or instruction is achieved through a computer or printed text. The employee receives immediate feedback and learns at his or her own speed. This method is good for almost any type of training. However, outside materials must generally be purchased, and the learner must be self-directed and motivated for this technique to be effective.

Online Training

People you hire need to be trained. Training takes time. Small business owners do not have a lot of excess time. Solution? Online training. E-learning can fill multiple roles in a business's training and development plan. It can

- Provide access to broad learning opportunities for your employees.

- Provide comprehensive content coverage of a specific topic.

- Be closely aligned with your development plans or business objectives, or be a just-in-time, just-what's-needed learning resource for a global workplace.

- Be self-directed or self-paced.

Some selected service providers include the following:

Service Provider	Offerings	Course or Service Price
Brainbench Brainbench.com	Web-based skills testing and certification preparation	Online courses are $3 to $50 each; full-service account setup is $300
Click2learn.com	E-learning content for business, IT, and health and safety topics; strategic consulting, development systems integration, technical support, and placement services	Online courses range from $29.95 to $1,995
EMind.com	1,200-plus online courses for banking, securities, accounting, IT, and personal development	$25 to $395 per course
Hungry Minds University Hungrymindsuniversity.com	17,000-plus online courses ranging from how-tos to college courses	Prices vary

Sources: Donna Abernathy, "A Guide to Online Learning Service Providers," American Society of Training and Development (ASTD), (www.learningcircuits.org/oct2000/abernathy.html); and Nancy Bartlett and Brandon Hall, "Packaged E-learning: What You Are Buying," American Society of Training and Development (ASTD), (www.learningcircuits.org/oct2000/bartlett.html).

ROLE-PLAYING. In this method, employees take on new roles within the company, acting out the situation as realistically as possible. If videotaped, playing back the situation allows for employee feedback and group discussions. Some employees find the technique threatening, and not all business situations lend themselves to this type of training.

JOB ROTATION. Job rotation allows employees to move from one job to another within the company. In addition to providing employees with a variety of job skills and knowledge, the technique also provides management with trained replacements in the event that one employee becomes ill or leaves the company. However, the technique does not generally provide in-depth, specialized training.

CORRESPONDENCE COURSES. This technique is especially useful for updating current knowledge and acquiring new information. Generally sponsored by a professional association or university, the employee receives prepackaged study materials to complete at his or her own pace. In addition to providing individualized learning, the technique is applicable to a variety of business topics. The employee must be motivated to learn, and course costs may be high.

Compensating Employees

Wages and incentives—including health care and other benefits—are necessary to keep employees alive, healthy, and motivated.

Employees expect to be paid a fair and equitable wage. Determining what is fair and equitable is a challenging and ongoing task that involves primarily two components: wages and benefits.

Determining Wage Rates

Based on the Fair Labor Standards Act (FLSA) of 1938, employees are classified as either exempt or nonexempt. Exempt employees are not covered by the major provisions of the FLSA, which controls minimum wage, overtime pay, child labor laws, and equal-pay-for-equal-work regulations. Most exempt employees are paid on a straight salary basis. Nonexempt employees, however, must be paid a minimum wage set by Congress (or your state government, if higher). These payments may be in the form of hourly wages, salary, piecework rates, or commissions.

HOURLY WAGES. Most organizations pay their nonexempt employees an hourly wage (a set rate of pay for each hour worked).

ALL-SALARIED EMPLOYEES. Some organizations are moving to an all-salaried work force. These companies pay both exempt and nonexempt employees a salary (a fixed sum of money). Although still subject to FLSA provisions, this type of compensation plan removes the perceived inequity between the two "classes" of employees and fosters a greater esprit de corps.

PIECEWORK RATES. Unlike salaried or hourly wage rates, the piecework rate is a pay-for-performance plan. Under a piecework rate, the employer pays an employee a set amount for each unit he or she produces. Some employers pay, as an incentive, a "premium" for units produced above a predetermined level of production. For example, an employee might receive $2 per unit for the first 40 units produced and $2.25 for any units above 40. Other plans might pay a straight rate for all units—say, $2.15—once the standard output quota of 40 units has been surpassed.

COMMISSIONS. Commissions are another type of pay for performance. Some jobs, especially those in sales, are not easily measured in units produced. Under a straight commission plan, the employee's wages can be based solely on his or her sales volume. Because employees often cannot control all of the external variables that affect sales, employers are increasingly paying on a base-salary-plus-commission basis. Employees tend to favor this combination approach because they are provided with a degree of income security during slow sales periods.

Still other employers are allowing the employee to "draw" against future commissions. This means that the employee may draw an advance from the employer during a slow sales period and repay the advance (draw) out of commissions earned during the remainder of the pay period or, in some cases, future pay periods. Such draws are particularly effective if sales fluctuate from month to month or quarter to quarter.

Incentive Pay Programs

An incentive pay program is a reward system that ties performance to compensation. Two common types of incentive pay programs involve the awarding of bonuses and profit-sharing programs. **Bonuses** are generally awarded on a one-time basis to reward employees for their high performance. They may be given to either an individual employee or a group of employees. Bonuses are frequently awarded when an employee meets objectives set for attendance, production, cost savings, quality, or performance.

bonus A one-time reward provided to an employee for exceeding a performance standard.

To be an effective motivator, the bonus must be tied to a specific measure of performance. The reason for which the bonus is being awarded must be communicated to employees at the time they are informed that they will receive it. The bonus should be paid separately from the employee's regular paycheck to reinforce its specialness. In this way, the bonus is less likely to be viewed by employees as an extension of their regular salary and something to which they are automatically entitled.

Under most **profit-sharing plans,** employers make the same percentage of salary contributions to each worker's account on a semiannual or annual basis. The percentage of contributions varies according to the amount of profits earned, making the system highly flexible. Startup costs for a profit-sharing plan typically run about $2,000, with another $2,000 being incurred annually to administer the plan. Most employers believe these plans serve to motivate workers by giving them a sense of partnership with the employer. Profit-sharing plans are a mainstay of many small business owners' compensation plans. According to Mac McConnell, owner and president of Artful Framer Gallery, a $600,000 business with a staff of eight, "A company can never be too small to benefit from a well-designed profit-sharing plan."[17]

profit-sharing plan A plan in which employees receive additional compensation based on the profitability of the entire business.

Benefits

An employee **benefit** consists of any supplement to wages and salaries. Health and life insurance, paid vacation time, pension and education plans, and discounts on company products are examples. The cost of offering and administering benefits has

benefit Part of an employee's compensation in addition to wages and salaries.

increased greatly—from 25.5 percent of total payroll in 1961 to about 38 percent today. Often employees do not realize the market value and high cost of benefits.

According to a survey by the Employee Benefit Research Institute, Americans' satisfaction with their benefit packages is declining.[18] Less than 50 percent of survey respondents said that they were completely satisfied with their benefit package, down from a high of 70 percent satisfied in 1991. At the same time, the number of respondents satisfied with the level of benefits but wanting a different mix of benefits increased to 27 percent, up from 15 percent in 1991. Health care coverage, vacation or other time off, and life insurance were the three areas in which most respondents wanted to see changes made.

With this increasing discontent and call for a new mix of benefits, the challenge for small business owners is to provide a mix of benefits that is affordable for the employer and motivational for employees.

FLEXIBLE BENEFIT PACKAGES. Because all employees do not have the same needs, a flexible (cafeteria) benefit package allows each employee to select the benefits that best suit his or her financial and lifestyle needs. Employees generally favor such plans due to their flexibility and pretax benefits.

Increasingly, flexible benefit packages not only provide employees with a choice or menu of benefits from which to choose, they also include choices between taxable and nontaxable benefits. Under these latter, IRS-approved plans, employees are allowed to purchase benefits with pretax dollars. In this way, they can reduce their taxable income while at the same time increasing their benefit options.

The advantages of flexible plans are not realized without additional costs. As the number and mix of benefits increase, so do administrative costs associated with activities such as record keeping, communications with employees, and compliance with government regulations. A second, but no less important, concern is that employees may select the wrong mix or types of benefits. Often employees do not worry about their benefits until they are actually needed, generally in response to a major illness or accident. Yet the law does not allow benefit choices to be changed during the plan year, so employees often find that their benefit options do not match their immediate needs.

HEALTH INSURANCE. One of the most common and valued employee benefits is health insurance. According to Dallas Salisbury, president of the Employee Benefit Research Institute, "There's no question that workers value health insurance benefits above all others."[19] In response, employers are increasingly providing employee health care coverage, although many are also opting for a copayment plan of some type. Sixty-seven percent of all small private employers provide some form of medical care coverage.[20]

In order to hold down the growing costs of health insurance, many small business owners are joining cooperative health maintenance organizations (HMOs) or preferred provider organizations (PPOs). Under an HMO system, a firm signs a contract with an approved health maintenance organization that agrees to provide health and medical services to its employees. In return for the exclusive right to care for the firm's employees, the HMO offers its services at an adjusted rate. Unfortunately, employees often object to these plans because they are restricted to using the health care specialists employed or approved by the HMO. To overcome this objection, some companies are switching to preferred provider organizations (PPOs).

With a PPO, a firm or group of firms negotiates with doctors and hospitals to provide certain health care services for a favorable price. In turn, member firms then encourage their employees, through higher reimbursement payments, to use these "preferred" providers. Employees tend to favor PPOs because they have the opportunity and freedom to use the doctor of their choice.

PENSION PLANS. To assist employees in saving for their retirement needs, employers provide them with retirement plans. Pension plans present employees with an accumulated amount of money when they reach a set retirement age or when they are unable to continue working due to a disability. Five of the more common options are individual retirement accounts, simplified employee pension plans, salary-reduction simplified employee pension plans, 401(k) plans, and Keogh plans.

INDIVIDUAL RETIREMENT ACCOUNTS. Individual retirement accounts (IRAs) allow employees to make tax-exempt contributions of up to $2,000 per year into their own account. As of this writing, Congress is considering an increase to $5,000 per year. Although interest earned on IRAs remains tax deferrable, contributions are totally deductible from personal income taxes only if an individual earns less than $25,000 ($40,000 if married filing jointly) or if the individual is not covered by a company-sponsored pension plan. Eligible employees pay tax on the principal and accrued interest only when money is withdrawn. (There is a penalty for withdrawing funds before retirement.) As the name implies, IRAs are individual plans; contributions are at the discretion of the employee, not the employer. In addition to the obvious advantage of providing a retirement income, IRAs reduce eligible employees' current taxable income.

SIMPLIFIED EMPLOYEE PENSION PLANS. A simplified employee pension (SEP) plan is similar to an IRA but is available only to people who are self-employed or who work for small businesses that do not have a retirement plan. Those who are eligible may contribute up to 15 percent of their salary or $25,500 per year, whichever is less. There are few, if any, startup or administrative costs for the employer in establishing a SEP. In addition, there are no additional IRS reporting requirements for the employer, and he or she may change the percentage of salary contributions made from one year to the next. Employees are immediately vested (meaning that they are eligible to keep the employer's contribution without having to wait for a probationary period to end) and may withdraw funds from their account at any time (provided they are willing to pay income tax on the principal plus early withdrawal penalties if under age 59.5). In addition, any employee who has earned $396 or more in compensation, is 21 years of age, and has worked for the employer for at least three out of the last five years is covered. Thus most part-time workers are eligible for SEP plans.

401(K) PLANS. Named after Section 401(k) of the 1978 Revenue Act, 401(k) plans allow small businesses to establish payroll reduction plans that are more flexible and have greater tax advantages than an IRA. As was true of the foregoing plans, the amount deferred and any accumulated investment earnings are excluded from current income and are taxed only when distributed.

The contributory limits for 401(k) plans are the same as for SEP plans. Although not required to do so, many employers match employees' contributions on a percentage basis. The most common match is 50 cents for each dollar contributed by the employee, up to a cap of 5 percent or 6 percent of the employee's salary.[21] This 50 percent rate, according to a study by William Mercer, Inc., encourages almost as much employee participation as does a 100 percent match rate.[22] The funds are managed by a trustee overseeing the company's pension plans. In many cases, employees have the flexibility of selecting the investment vehicle for their investment or, in the case of mutual funds, of switching from one fund to another. Employers may establish vesting requirements. Loans as well as hardship withdrawals are available from the plan.

On the downside, 401(k) plans are expensive to develop and administer because they require IRS approval and must meet Labor Department pension guidelines. In response, some mutual fund companies are beginning to offer 401(k) packages that fulfill the basic needs of investment options, administration, communication to employees, and compliance with government requirements specifically to small business customers.[23]

KEOGH PLANS. A Keogh plan is a special type of retirement account for self-employed individuals and their employees. Currently, a self-employed person may contribute the smaller of $30,000 or 20 percent of self-employment income to a qualified money-purchase Keogh plan for himself or herself and the smaller of $30,000 or 25 percent of each employee's taxable compensation to an employee account. Contributions and accumulated investment earnings are tax exempt until the time of withdrawal.

Employers may, with IRS approval, establish various limitations and eligibility requirements for employee participation in these plans. However, once established, the employer is required to make yearly contributions at the stated contributory rate. As a qualified plan, Keogh plans require IRS approval, resulting in startup costs that range from $1,000 to $4,500 and administrative costs that may vary from $1,500 to $6,000 annually.

For a review of retirement plans, see Table 17.1.

CHILD CARE. As the number of dual-income families continues to increase and the concern over family values grows, more and more employees are looking to their employers for help. For example, a recent survey of employees showed that 68 percent of respondents said they would be willing to contribute to a benefit pro-

The Benefits of Education

It all started on a fishing trip for John Strazzanti, founder and president of Com-Corp Industries in Cleveland; his vice president of finance, David Wright; and Wright's son. Wright's son wanted to attend the University of Southern California, but the Wright family had saved little money. That's when Strazzanti came up with the idea of providing low-interest educational loans for his employees' dependents.

Strazzanti, upon learning that other employees in his auto parts manufacturing firm were experiencing similar concerns, called a companywide meeting to announce the loan program. Employees liked the program, but they wanted to limit Com-Corp's risk. At their suggestion, four safeguards were built into the system. First, employees were eligible only after three years of employment. Second, the company would never have more than $40,000 outstanding in loans. Third, dependents would repay the loan at 3 percent annual interest over ten years. Fourth, the company could take legal action if it got burned or, if legal action would cost too much, it could recover any losses from the company's profit-sharing fund.

The program cost virtually nothing to set up, and Com-Corp believes it helps account for its low 2.5 percent annual turnover rate. When Wright's son graduated from USC, he was the program's first beneficiary. His sister started college shortly afterward.

Source: Adapted from "Managing People", by Michael P. Cronin, from *Inc.: The Magazine for Growing Companies,* September 1993, 29. Copyright 1993 by Goldhirsh Group/Inc. Publishing. Reproduced with permission of Goldhirsh Group/Inc. Publishing in the format textbook via Copyright Clearance Center.

TABLE 17.1
Retirement Plan Preview

	Eligibility	Funding Responsibility	Annual Contributions per Participant	Vesting of Contributions	Administrative Responsibilities
SIMPLE IRA	Businesses with 100 or fewer employees who do not currently maintain any other retirement plan.	Funded by employee salary reduction contributions and employer contributions	Up to 100% of compensation, to a maximum of $6,500 (employer/employee combined up to $13,000)	Immediate	No employer tax filings
SEP-IRA	Any self-employed individual, business owner, or individual who earns any self-employed income	Employer contributions only	Up to 15% of compensation, to a maximum of $25,500	Immediate	Form 5498 and IRS testing
401(k)	Any type of public or private company; typically for companies with 25 or more employees	Primarily employee salary reduction contributions and optional employer contributions	Primarily employee design, could be up to 25 percent of compensation to a maximum of $10,500 (employer/employee combined up to 25% of compensation, to a maximum of $30,000)	Employee contribution vested immediately; different vesting schedules available for employer contributions	Form 5500 and special IRS testing to ensure plan does not discriminate in favor of highly compensated employees
KEOGH	Any self-employed individual, business owner, or individual who earns any self-employed income	Generally employer contributions only	Up to 25% of compensation, to a maximum of $35,000	May offer vesting schedules	Form 5500

Source: Material from Mie-Yan Lee, "May the Best Plan Win," *Entrepreneur Magazine,* April 2001, 86–87. Reprinted with permission from *Entrepreneur Magazine,* April 2001, www.entrepreneur.com.

gram that allowed them to set aside money before taxes to pay for health care or child care expenses.[24] Apparently employers are listening, as nearly eight out of ten major U.S. employers now offer some form of child care assistance.[25] This aid takes many forms, of which the most common types are flexible work schedules, flexible spending accounts that allow workers to set aside a portion of their pretax earnings to pay for child care costs, resource and referral services, and, to a much lesser extent, company-sponsored day care centers. Employers who offer child care assistance generally do so for one or more of the following reasons: to accommodate employee requests, thus increasing employee morale; to retain high-performing employees; to improve recruiting efforts; to reduce employee absenteeism and tardiness; and to increase employee productivity.

TABLE 17.2
Benefits Provided by Small Private Employers (percentages)[a]

Employee Benefit Program	All Employees	Professional, Technical, and Related Employees	Clerical and Sales	Blue-Collar and Service
Paid				
Holidays	80	86	91	71
Vacations	86	90	95	79
Personal leave	14	21	18	8
Funeral leave	51	60	60	42
Jury duty leave	59	74	68	47
Military leave	18	25	23	12
Sick leave	50	66	64	35
Family leave	2	3	3	1
Severance pay	15	23	19	9
Child care	2	4	2	>.5
Flexible workplace	1	4	1	>.5
Fitness center	4	6	5	3
Nonproduction bonuses	44	44	46	43
Educational assistance				
Job related	38	56	45	27
Non–job related	5	6	6	4
Section 125				
cafeteria benefits	23	31	29	16
Retirement				
All retirement[b]	46	56	53	37
Defined benefit				
pension	15	12	16	15
Defined contribution	38	51	46	28
Types of defined contribution plans				
Savings and thrift	23	32	29	16
Deferred profit sharing	12	13	17	9
Employee stock				
ownership	1	2	2	1
Money purchase				
pension	6	6	3	3

[a]These tabulations provide representative data for 32 million full-time employees in private nonagricultural establishments with fewer than 100 employees. The survey was composed primarily of small independent businesses, although about 25 percent of respondents were small establishments that were part of larger enterprises.
[b]Total participation is less than the sum of individual plan types because some employees participate in two or more types of plans.
Source: U.S. Department of Labor, Bureau of Labor Statistics, *Employee Benefits in Small Private Establishments, 1996* (www.bls.gov/special.requests) (Washington, D.C.: U.S. Government Printing Office, 2000).

MISCELLANEOUS BENEFITS. The number and variety of employee benefits are limited only by the generosity of the employer and his or her ability to pay. Benefits provided by firms with fewer than 100 workers represented 25.3 percent of total compensation, whereas those provided by firms with 500 or more workers amounted to 30.7 percent.[26] Table 17.2 summarizes the types of benefits provided by small private establishments.

When Problems Arise: Employee Discipline and Termination ▬

Although you can strive for harmony in the workplace, sometimes problems arise. When they do, you need policies laid out for discipline or dismissal of employees.

Disciplinary Measures

Discipline involves taking timely and appropriate actions to modify or correct the performance of an employee or group of employees. The purpose of discipline is to ensure that company rules and regulations are consistently followed for the well-being of both the company and its employees. A fair and just disciplinary procedure should be based on the four following tenets.

The first of these principles is a comprehensive set of rules and regulations. Expressed in the form of an **employee handbook** or policy manual, these rules and regulations should inform employees of their rights and responsibilities in the employment relationship. To be effective, the rules and regulations must be up to date, easily understood, and, most importantly, communicated to employees. An effective way to achieve this latter goal is to go over the employee handbook during employee orientation and have employees sign a statement acknowledging receipt of the document.

A well-designed **performance appraisal** system is the second essential component. Not only does a sound performance appraisal process document the need for possible discipline, but it also affords management the opportunity to address problem areas before they become disciplinary concerns. In addition, a well-defined performance appraisal process will help to fulfill the third tenet: a system of progressive penalties.

Increasingly, managers are moving away from the "hot-stove" principle of discipline, in which discipline is immediate and of consistent intensity, to the **progressive approach,** in which discipline is incremental and increasingly forceful. Under most progressive systems, managers first issue an oral (informal) reprimand, then a written warning (formal notice), followed by suspension, and finally discharge. Arbitrators and the courts generally favor progressive discipline over that of the hot-stove approach, except in cases of gross misconduct, such as theft or assault, when immediate discharge is warranted. We should note now that a record of any disciplinary action should be placed in the employee's file even if the reprimand is verbal. A written record is essential if termination occurs and to be sure that the discipline is in accordance with a union contract, if one exists. Write out what happened, what was said by both parties, and when it happened as soon as practical—memories fade.

The final component of an effective disciplinary program is an **appeal process.** The most common appeal process in nonunion companies is the open-door policy, a procedure whereby employees seek a review of the disciplinary decision at the next level of management. For such a process to be effective, it must involve a thorough and truly objective review of the facts of the case by an executive of higher rank than the supervisor who applied the discipline. Open-door policies are appropriate for companies with many employees and levels of management, but in the majority of small businesses, the only level of management is you—the owner. If an employee feels unjustly treated and is not satisfied with your decision, his or her only recourse is through the courts.

employee handbook Written rules and regulations informing employees of their rights and responsibilities in the employment relationship.

performance appraisal A process of evaluating an employee's job-related achievements.

progressive approach Discipline that is applied to employees in appropriately incremental and increasingly forceful measures.

appeal process A formal procedure allowing employees to seek review of disciplinary measure at a higher level of management.

manager's notebook

Employee Handbooks

How do you communicate your mission statement, your code of ethics, and your policies on topics such as discrimination and sexual harassment to your employees? Many small businesses are writing employee handbooks that explain company policies and help to orient employees while covering legal notification requirements to prevent lawsuits.

Wendy Rhodes, a partner with Hewitt Associates, a benefits and compensation consulting firm, suggests including the following sections in your employee handbook:

- *The disclaimer.* Every employee handbook should have a disclaimer (it's a good idea to include it at the beginning and the end) specifying that the handbook is not a contract of employment. Without such a notice, a fired employee might attempt to sue you for breach of contract. It's a good idea to have an attorney who practices labor law review your employee handbook to ensure you do not have any unintentional pitfalls.

- *Employment policies.* Describe work hours, regular and overtime pay, performance reviews, vacations and holidays, equal employment opportunities, and other items that affect employment.

- *Benefits.* Relate insurance plans, disability plans, workmen's compensation, retirement programs, and tuition reimbursement.

- *Employee conduct.* Explain your expectations on everything you classify as important, from personal hygiene to dress codes to employee development.

- *Glossary.* Every company has its own terms and jargon. Explain terminology important to your business. For example, Ashton Photo distinguishes between *late* ("not completed on time in a given department"), *delayed* ("production of a job has been suspended, awaiting information from the customer"), and *on hold* ("production of a job has been suspended for accounting reasons").

- *Organization chart.* Include charts and job descriptions to give employees a sense of their place in the organization and how all the parts of the business fit together.

In your employee handbook, don't try to spell out specifics on what people should do in every possible situation. You just want to communicate your broader principles of what the company believes in and how you expect people to perform.

You do not want to give the impression that providing an employee with a handbook guarantees lifetime employment, so lawyer Robert Nobile recommends including a disclaimer to the effect of "This handbook is not a contract, express or implied, guaranteeing employment for any specific duration. Although we hope that your employment relationship with us will be long term, either you or the company may terminate this relationship at any time, for any reason, with or without cause or notice."

Sources: Tom Ehrenfeld, "The (Handbook) Handbook," *Inc.,* November 1993, 57–64; and "Essentials of an Employee Handbook," How-To section (www.allbusiness.com).

Dismissing Employees

Because dismissing an employee is the most extreme step of discipline you can exercise, it must be taken with care. Your legitimate reasons for dismissing an employee may include unsatisfactory performance of the job or changing requirements of the job, which make the employee unqualified.

Productive Disciplinary Steps

- *Determine whether discipline is needed.* Is the problem an isolated incident or part of an ongoing pattern?

- *Have clear goals to discuss with the employee.* You should discuss the problem in specific terms. Indirect comments will not make your point clear. You must also state what you expect the employee to do. If the employee has no idea about your expectations after discussing a performance problem with you, the employee is likely to repeat past performance.

- *Talk about the problem in private.* Public reprimand is embarrassing for the employee and for everyone who witnesses it. If you chastise in public, you will lose trust and respect not only from that individual but also from those who observe the act.

- *Keep your cool.* A calm approach will keep a performance discussion more objective and prevent distraction by irrelevant problems.

- *Watch the timing of the meeting.* If the problem is not obvious and you schedule the meeting far in advance, the employee will spend time worrying about what is wrong. On the other hand, if the problem is obvious, the meeting should be scheduled to give the employee plenty of time to prepare.

- *Prepare opening remarks.* Performance meetings will be more effective if you are confident in your opening remarks. Think them out in advance and rehearse them.

- *Get to the point.* Beating around the bush with small talk does more to increase the employee's anxiety level than to reduce it.

- *Allow two-way communication.* Make sure the disciplinary meeting is a discussion, not a lecture. You can get to the heart of the problem only if the employee is allowed to speak. Your intent is to arrive at a solution to a problem, not to scold the employee.

- *Establish a followup plan.* You and your employee need to agree to a followup plan to establish a time frame within which the employee's performance is to improve.

- *End on a positive note.* Highlight the employee's positive points so that he or she will leave the meeting with a belief that you want him or her to succeed in the future.

Source: Material adapted from D. Day, "Training 101: Help for Discipline Dodgers," *Training and Development,* (May 1993), pp. 19–22. Reprinted by permission of American Society for Training and Development.

When it comes to discharging an employee, what you can and cannot do will be influenced to a large degree by two considerations. First, the decision to discharge an employee must be based on a job-related reason or reasons, not on the basis of race, color, religion, sex, age, national origin, or disability. Second, your ability to legally discharge an employee and the manner in which you may do so will be highly dependent on your at-will status. Over the past century, the prevailing law in the United States has been that, unless an employment contract is signed, either the employer or the employee can terminate the employment relationship at will. Under the **at-will doctrine,** an employer has great leeway in discharging an employee, in that he or she has the right to discharge the employee for a good reason, a bad reason, or no reason at all. Remember, though, that an employee cannot be fired for union-related activities, even if a union does not exist in the company.

at-will doctrine The legal restrictions on an employer's ability to discharge an employee without just cause.

Within the past decade, however, the courts and some state legislatures have imposed one or more of the following restrictions on at-will employers. Check the laws of your state to find which apply to your business.

IMPLIED CONTRACT. An employer may be restricted in discharging an employee if an implied contract exists as a result of written statements in the company's employment application, employment ads, employee handbook, or other company documents. Verbal statements by company representatives to employees may also erode an employer's at-will status, as may an employee's record of long-term employment with the firm.

GOOD FAITH AND FAIR DEALING. This exception holds that the employer must have acted fairly and in good faith in discharging the employee. For example, an employee may not be fired simply because he or she is about to become vested in the company's pension plan.

PUBLIC POLICY EXCEPTION. Under the public policy exception, employers may not discharge workers for exercising a statutory right, such as filing a workmen's compensation claim, or performing public service, such as serving on a jury. Nor may an employee be fired for refusing to break the law or engage in conduct that is against one's beliefs; for example, refusing to falsify an employer's records to cover up possible misconduct on the part of the company.

In the event that a terminated employee seeks legal redress by filing a lawsuit against you, whether or not you have acted in a manner consistent with the at-will principle will be decided by a judge. In all cases, you should be able to provide evidence of *just cause* for the dismissal. Just cause generally implies due process and reasonability on the part of the employer. You are likely to have just cause if you can

- Cite the specific work rule violation and show that the employee had prior knowledge of the rule and the consequences of violating it.

- Show that the work rule was necessary for the efficient and safe operation of the company and was therefore a business necessity.

- Prove that you conducted a thorough and objective investigation of the violation and, in the process, afforded the employee the opportunity to present his or her side of the story.

- Document that the employee was given the opportunity to improve or modify his or her performance (except in cases of gross misconduct or insubordination, when it is unnecessary).

- Show that there was sufficient evidence or proof of guilt to justify the actions taken.

- Show that you treated the employee in a manner consistent with past practices.

- Demonstrate that the disciplinary actions taken were fair and reasonable in view of the employee's work history.

- Document that the disciplinary action was reviewed by an independent party either within or outside the company prior to being implemented.

Firing an Employee

Despite the economic recovery, companies are continuing to use layoffs as a cost-cutting strategy. But even though firing employees is an all-too-common part of their duties, few managers handle the process well. That's because, whatever the facts of the dismissal, most managers feel bad about letting someone go. Ironically, expressing feelings of remorse can be cruel, because it gives the employee false hope. Instead, the best way to deal with the termination is to make it a quick, unambiguous act. Spell out exactly why you are letting the employee go, state clearly that the decision is final, and explain the details of the company's notice policy or severance. Then ask the employee to leave by the end of the week if possible (so that his or her presence won't demoralize the rest of the staff) and to sign a letter of acknowledgment, which will make it more difficult for him or her to reopen the discussion—or to sue. Above all, resist any attempts to turn the discussion into an argument.

Icebreaker. I'm sorry to have to give you some bad news: Your job here is being terminated. [*If for economic reasons:* I think you'll find the terms of the severance quite generous. I have also prepared a letter of reference, which I'll give you at the end of this meeting.]

Fired for Poor Performance. Please understand that this decision is final. You haven't made any real progress with the problems we discussed at your last two performance reviews. I'm sure you'll be able to put your skills to better use in a different position. If you'll sign this letter that says you understand our discussion, we can put this matter behind us.

Laid off for Economic Reasons. Unfortunately, this decision is final. Please understand that it's purely an economic move and no reflection on your performance. I'll be happy to make that clear to any new employers you interview with. If you'll just sign this letter outlining what I've just said, we can get this unhappy business over with.

Gets Angry. You've got some nerve getting rid of me this way. This company might not be in such a mess if it didn't treat its employees so shabbily.

Gets Defensive. You're singling me out. I've performed as well as anyone else—better, in fact, considering the new accounts I just landed.

Gets Personal. How could you do this to me? We're friends. You've come over to my house for dinner. Isn't there something you can do?

Absorb Anger. I'm sorry to hear that you feel that way. Everyone here, including me, wanted to see your position work out. Unfortunately, it hasn't. Why don't you take a few minutes to look over this letter and then sign it.

Deflect Defense. As I've said, this is purely an economic decision. You were simply the last one hired. **OR:** Your skill in lining up new clients doesn't make up for your consistent problems with our existing accounts.

Deflect Guilt. I feel bad about this, but it is strictly a business decision. My personal feelings don't count. As your friend, I'll do everything I can to help you land another job. For now, though, I need you to take a look at this letter and then sign it.

Demands More Severance. I'm not going to sign anything until we talk about this severance package. It isn't nearly enough, considering how long I've worked here.

Threatens Legal Action. I'm not going to sign anything until I speak to my lawyer. I think there are some issues that I need to get some legal advice on.

Asks for Another Chance. Isn't there something I can do to reverse this decision? I need this job. I promise my work will improve. Please give me another chance.

End Discussion. You're welcome to discuss the severance offer with someone higher up, although I have to warn you that they're the ones who set the terms. **OR:** Of course. You have every right to speak with your attorney first. I'll hold onto the check and the paperwork until I hear from you. **OR:** I'm terribly sorry, but the decision really is final. [*Stand up.*] Good luck in the future.

Source: Stephen M. Pollan and Mark Levine, "Firing an Employee," *Working Woman,* August 1994, 55. Reprinted by permission of Working Mother Media via Reprint Management Services.

SUMMARY

■■■■   **The importance of hiring the right employees.**

Some of the most valuable resources and competitive advantages a small business has are its employees. There are too many costs and risks involved not to pay attention to human resource issues.

■■■■   **The job analysis process and the function of job descriptions and job specifications.**

Job analysis is the process of determining the duties and skills required to do a job and the kind of person who should be hired to do it. A job description is part of the job analysis. It is a list of duties, responsibilities, and reporting relationships of a job. A job specification is another part of the job analysis. It identifies the education, skills, and personality that a person needs to have to be right for a job.

■■■■   **The advantages and disadvantages of six sources of employee recruitment.**

Help wanted advertising reaches numerous potential applicants, but many of them will not be right for the job you are trying to fill. Employment agencies screen applicants for you so that you do not have to deal with as many people. Those run by the government are usually appropriate only for positions requiring lower-level skills. Internet job sites offer limited resources, for a fee. Executive recruiters (headhunters) offer more expensive services but can help you find people with higher-level skills. Employee referrals are effective because your current employees know the skills and talents needed, but hiring in this manner can create cliques. It can also build resentment if the new hire does not work out. When hiring friends and relatives, you have the advantage of knowing their abilities and expertise, but personal relationships can be strained on the job.

■■■■   **The three steps of employee selection.**

When recruiting employees, you first need to generate a pool of applicants. In the selection process, you will try to narrow the applicant pool down to match the needs of your business with the skills of the person. Application forms and résumés, interviews, and testing are the three most common tools of selection.

■■■■   **The need for employee orientation and training and the seven methods of doing so.**

To become a better, more productive worker, every employee needs to have his or her knowledge and skills enhanced through orientation and training. On-the-job training, lectures, conferences, programmed learning, role-playing, job rotation, and correspondence courses are seven common techniques.

■■■■   **The two components of a compensation plan and the variable elements of a benefits system.**

Employees can be compensated for their efforts with hourly wages or salary, or on the basis of piecework or commission plans. Incentive pay programs are a way to motivate and reward employees above their base pay by paying bonuses or profit-sharing amounts. Common types of benefits, which are part of a compensation package, include flexible benefit plans, health insurance, pension plans, and child care accounts. The most common pension plans adopted by small businesses are individual retirement accounts (IRAs), simplified employee pension (SEP) plans, 401(k) plans, and Keogh plans.

■■■■ An effective sequence for disciplining and terminating an employee.

The progressive disciplinary system, favored by many managers today, begins with an oral reprimand, followed by a written warning, suspension without pay, and, finally, termination from the company.

QUESTIONS FOR **REVIEW & DISCUSSION**

1. What is the difference between a job analysis and a job description?

2. When would you, as a small business owner, prefer to receive a résumé rather than an application form?

3. How is the use of temporary employees different from employee leasing? What are the advantages and disadvantages of each?

4. What are the differences between hard and soft issues during a job orientation? Is one more important than the other?

5. List the advantages of a flexible benefit package to employees; to the employer.

6. Explain the four components of an effective disciplinary system.

7. Define "at-will" status.

8. Discuss three key pieces of legislation that are used to prevent job discrimination.

9. What factors influence the type and amount of employee benefits that a small business can offer?

10. Review the section on training new employees. Give examples of types of jobs that would best lend themselves to each training method.

QUESTIONS FOR **CRITICAL THINKING**

1. As a young entrepreneur, you may soon be in the position of hiring one or more of your college friends in your own business. What are the advantages of hiring your friends? What are the potential pitfalls?

2. Hiring an employee is a big step for a small business. How can you make a wise hiring decision if so many limitations are put on the interview questions you can legally ask?

Experience
this... Find a copy of a small business's employee handbook, either from your current job or from a local small business owner (it may be interesting just to find out how many don't even have one). Compare the sections with those listed in the Manager's Notebook in this chapter. Is everything that an employee would need to know included in this handbook? What is missing? Does everything included in this handbook appear to comply with employment law?

WHAT WOULD **YOU** DO?   No. 1

Magnet, Inc., is the world's leading manufacturer of refrigerator magnets in the specialty advertising products industry. You've no doubt seen examples of their products—in fact, you may even have a few stuck on your refrigerator. Bill Wood is the founder and chairman of the company. The company is growing rapidly, and Bill needs to hire a market research analyst to help him with marketing issues. Here's a copy of the job information that's been used in advertising the position.

Market Research Analyst. Individual with good market research and data analysis skills needed by fast-growing small company that specializes in making refrigerator magnets. College degree in market research desirable but will look at individuals without degree who have at least five years' experience in a market research position. Skills in computer data entry and data analysis an absolute requirement. Must be willing to locate to small town in east central Missouri. Salary is competitive and commensurate with education and experience.

The applicant pool has been narrowed down to the following three individuals. Information about the three applicants has been summarized from their job applications and résumés.

Flora Cheung. Flora is a recent graduate of a state university in California. Her undergraduate degree is in market research, and she participated in three market research projects for one of her professors while a student. Her grades are average (2.9 on a 4.0 scale), and she speaks French fluently.

Edward Fleck. Edward is a victim of corporate downsizing. He was employed for 22 years at Procter & Gamble, the last 7 years in the market research department. He doesn't have a college degree, but his reference recommendations seem to be good. He's been out of work now for 19 months and really wants to find a job.

Bill Hampton. Bill has been out of school now for five years. He graduated from Howard University in Washington, D.C., with an undergraduate degree in business administration. Since graduating, Bill has had four different jobs. His latest job was in sales, and he's tired of living out of a suitcase. He's proficient in computers.

QUESTIONS

1. Develop a job description and job specification for this market research analyst position.

2. Pair off in teams and discuss the three applicants. From the information provided, write down what you see as the pros and cons of each individual. Then develop questions that you would like to ask each individual during his or her interview.

| **WHAT WOULD YOU DO?** | **No. 2** |

Todd owns and manages a T-shirt shop in a small resort town. Todd has two full-time employees who have been with the business for at least three years. He also employs up to five part-time employees, depending on the tourist season. They help him keep the shop open from 10 A.M. to 9 P.M. seven days a week. Todd opens the shop every day but typically has his employees close. Whoever closes the store follows a checklist of closing procedures, including ringing out the cash register, filling out the bank deposit, and putting the daily receipts in the safe, with $300 in a separate cash bag for the next day's opening cash on hand. As with many businesses, the cash drawer is often off by a small amount, but usually it's within a couple of dollars. One day Todd opened the store and found that the cash drawer was short $35 for the previous day. Todd called a meeting that afternoon and told all seven employees that they would each have to chip in $5 to cover the shortage and that any time there was a shortage, they would have to split the reimbursement. Todd walked out of the room. The seven employees sat in disbelief.

QUESTIONS

1. Is Todd within his legal rights to take this action? If his actions are legal, what are some possible consequences?

2. How would you have handled the situation differently if you were Todd?

| **CHAPTER CLOSING CASE** | **No. 17** |

Playing a Great Game at Kacey Fine Furniture

With the downtown Denver neighborhood around the main Kacey Fine Furniture store dramatically changing, president Leslie Fishbein is bracing for the worst. "We are the front yard of the largest entertainment complex in a five-state area," she says. "Selling furniture is harder than it used to be, especially because downtown is no longer the furniture district that it used to be. When sales decline, employees become nonmotivated and are reluctant to initiate changes or take on new responsibilities."

Leslie's father founded Kacey in 1950, and she grew up in the business, starting to work full time there after college in 1974. Over the next decade, she and her husband, Sam, helped transform Kacey from a small family business into a four-store chain. By 1984 Leslie and Sam were running the business.

A Lack of Employee Initiative   During an economic downturn in the late 1980s, Kacey barely broke even, and employee morale was low. In 1990 Leslie and Sam sold their house and worked without a paycheck to avoid laying off any employees. Meanwhile, they found it increasingly difficult to get employees to take any initiative. They paid on a commission basis, which meant that employees were focused on making an immediate sale, with little thought for operational efficiencies, vendor relations, or the customer service that might bring repeat business.

"We were frustrated," says Leslie, "because I wanted people to take it upon themselves to handle problem situations and satisfy customers without coming to me or a manager for help all the time. I couldn't figure out why they weren't capable or comfortable making decisions. I was working 10- to 14-hour days and I didn't want to make all the decisions. I wanted people to have greater accountability and responsibility."

Establishing a New Corporate Culture   She found a way to encourage greater participation in a management seminar run by entrepreneur Jack Stack, the author of *The Great Game of Business* (Currency Books, 1992). The Great Game of Business is a companywide, open-book management system. Says Leslie, "It's become part of our corporate culture so that everyone shares the same mission and buys into the plan. We teach all of our employees cash flow analysis, income statements, balance sheets—based on their level of education or understanding. They are involved in decision making at all levels. We have a gain-sharing program based on what everybody achieves according to preset profit goals. We paid out over $700,000 in bonus checks in 1994. All employees received at least 11 percent in bonuses."

The Kacey income statement shows that, although sales rose every year from 1991 to 1995 (from $13.4 million to $27.6 million), net profit went from a loss of $18,946 in 1991 to a net pretax profit of $388,504 in 1993. After Kacey adopted the Great Game of Business, that figure leaped to $702,869 in 1994.

"When we started the Great Game of Business," says Leslie, "I was worried about certain parts of the company. I went to people in the warehouse and shop who are very important to the business and said to them, 'If you can understand arcane baseball statistics, you can understand business.' They looked at me wide-eyed because most people don't get any economics, any information about how a business runs, what impacts it, what expenditures are, how to balance it to make a profit or not."

Letting Employees Make the Decisions   Leslie and Sam tell employees, "This is the company you work in, this is what it does, this is how you impact everybody, this is what your decision will do. We're going to let you make that decision, and you'll have more information to make it." Leslie says that attitude changes everything. Sometimes an employee will come to her for advice "and I'll say, 'You can make as good a decision as I can. I've never done this before either.' Employees often know what they need to do better than I do."

Tom O'Donnell, Kacey operations manager, says the program shows employees how they can make a difference: "Last month we had a bad snow storm. Everyone was here at 6 A.M. We had no delays. No tow bills. Last Saturday we had seven trucks instead of six because one of our drivers volunteered for extra duty—and the chain set a record for a single day's deliveries."

As Great Game principles permeated Kacey, managers became coaches and trainers rather than schedulers and disciplinarians. Employees formed study groups to share information and ideas. The lines separating owners and managers from staff and customers became less distinct, as titles and job descriptions gave way to camaraderie and strategic planning. Cost-revenue projections and employee participation, not management preference, determined new programs. Employees at one store decided to change their hours to allow more evening shopping.

Leslie believes that education is key: "The more education my workforce has, and the more involved they are in understanding issues, the more responsible they will be."

Source: Adapted from "Kacey Fine Furniture: Human Resource Management in the Face of Change," by Joan Winn, from *Entrepreneurship Theory & Practice,* 05(2), Winter 2000. Reprinted by permission of the author. To read the entire case, visit the *Small Business Management: Entrepreneurship and Beyond* web site at http://business.college.hmco.com/students.

QUESTIONS

1. What is the biggest human resource challenge Kacey Fine Furniture faces?

2. Leslie states, "We want all employees to have greater accountability and responsibility." How can small business owners do that? Is it possible?

3. What has been the single strongest effect of implementing the Great Game of Business?

4. What would you recommend that Leslie do now?

18 Operations Management

After reading this chapter, you should be able to:

- Describe the elements of an operating system.

- Explain how manufacturers and service providers use operations management.

- Describe how to measure productivity.

- Recount the four methods of scheduling operations.

- Explain the role of quality in operations management.

- Identify the three ways to control operations.

KRISPY KREMES. Now, these are not your ordinary doughnuts. Although the mini-factory bakeries are now covering North America like a glaze, they started in North Carolina, and when people who grew up in the South talk about them, they get a far-off look in their eyes. Comfort food remembered from their childhood.

Krispy Kreme doughnuts have a glaze so delicate that it melts under your fingers. They are so airy that you can't lift one without denting it. You can't enter the store without smiling.

Krispy Kreme combines the science of operations management with the passion of art. Customers stand in line to watch the production process through multiple viewing windows. A parade of doughnuts floats through the fryer, flipping over automatically halfway through the cooking process. Once they are cooked, a conveyor whisks the doughnuts out of the hot shortening and into a waterfall of glaze.

Whether the doughnuts are kneaded, cooked, and filled in Toronto, Ontario, Las Vegas, Nevada, or New York City, every container of doughnut mix, icing, and filling comes by truck from the headquarters on Ivy Avenue in Winston-Salem, North Carolina. The fryers, conveyors, and proofing boxes are all made by hand in the company's equipment department. The Krispy Kreme goal comes down to one word—*consistency*—the hallmark of operations management. Customers want a doughnut purchased anywhere to taste exactly the same. They also want a doughnut purchased on July 13, 1937, to taste just like one purchased on July 13, 2002. That level of consistency is not as easy to achieve as you might think—it takes superb operations management.

Krispy Kreme is so obsessed with consistency that before a batch of wheat flour is allowed into the building, a core sample is taken to a second-floor lab to analyze moisture content, protein, and ash. If a 25-ton truckload of flour falls outside the parameters of set tolerance ranges, the whole delivery is rejected. And it happens a couple of times a month.

Consistency is not achieved via the lab alone. Adjacent to the lab is a baking lab where Ben Parker and Andrew Henry make doughnuts from every single 2,500-pound batch of mix that comes through each day. Batches that are rejected (which happens about once a month) become food for a lucky bunch of pigs. Patience is needed as much as diligence to achieve consistency. A warehouse the size of a Home Depot holds the mix to season for approximately one week.

Krispy Kreme stores average 4,000 square feet, with franchise fees ranging from $20,000 to $40,000 and 4.5 percent annual royalty. Krispy Kreme estimates that the investment for a new store, excluding land and pre-opening costs, is $550,000 for a building of approximately 4,000 square feet and $500,000 for equipment, furniture, and fixtures.

Mike Cecil, Krispy Kreme minister of culture (yes, his real job title), has some great stories of doughnut obsession. He tells of a guy traveling from Florida back out West with a car full of camera gear, equipment, and luggage. He also had a bunch of Krispy Kreme boxes. Someone broke into his car and stole all the doughnuts—but left all the expensive equipment. Three hundred and fifty cases of Krispy Kremes are loaded on a U.S. Army C–130 Hercules every Wednesday and flown to a NATO base in Keflavik, Iceland. They go into the commissary on Friday morning and are gone by noon. One last story. Whenever a fresh batch of doughnuts is done, a neon sign in the window lights up, proclaiming, "Hot Doughnuts Now." A woman driving by Krispy Kreme in Greensboro, North Carolina, when the light came on was in such a hurry that she turned too quickly and rolled her car. She wasn't hurt and still got her doughnuts—free of charge.

Some fun facts about Krispy Kremes:

- Vernon Rudolph sold the first one on July 13, 1937, from a rack in the back seat of his 1936 Pontiac.
- By February 2002, Krispy Kreme will have 214 stores in 32 states and Canada.
- In less than two minutes, enough doughnuts are made to stack as high as the Empire State Building.
- In one year, Krispy Kreme bakes enough doughnuts to circle the earth twice.

Sources: Charles Fishman, "The King of Kreme," *Fast Company,* October 1999, 262–278; Kevin Libin, "Holey War," *Canadian Business,* 21 August 2000, 34–41; Jacque White Kochak, "Another Go Around," *Restaurant Business,* 15 August 2000, 81–90; Scott McCormack "Sweet Success," *Forbes,* 7 September 1998, 90–91; Larah Lorge, "Kreme of the Crop," *Sales and Marketing Management,* March 1999, 18; and "Retail Entrepreneurs of the Year: Scott Livengood," *Chain Store Age,* December 2000, 84.

This chapter focuses on operations management (OM) and the processes associated with it. The function of operations management has evolved over the last few decades from a narrow view of production, inventory, and industrial management into a broader concept that includes services. The management of production and operations is critical to all small businesses; not just those involved in manufacturing. Every business performs an operations function—the processes and procedures of converting labor, materials, money, and other resources into finished products or services.

Elements of an Operating System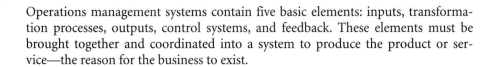

Operations management systems contain five basic elements: inputs, transformation processes, outputs, control systems, and feedback. These elements must be brought together and coordinated into a system to produce the product or service—the reason for the business to exist.

Inputs

The **inputs** in an operations management system include all physical and intangible resources that come into a business. Raw materials are needed as the things to be transformed. A company that makes in-line skates, for instance, must have polymers, plastics, and metal. Skills and knowledge of the people within the organization are other inputs. A management consulting firm, for example, needs people with special expertise. The in-line skate manufacturer needs trained workers to fabricate the product. Money, information, and energy are all needed in varying degrees. Inputs are important to the quality of the finished product of the business. Remember the computer cliché "Garbage in—garbage out." You can't produce high-quality outputs from inferior inputs.

inputs All the resources that go into a business.

Transformation Processes

Once we have identified the inputs of a business, we can look at the processes that are used to transform them into finished products. **Transformation processes** are the active practices—including concepts, procedures, and technologies—that are implemented to produce outputs. Dry cleaners, for instance, take soiled clothing (inputs) and use chemicals, equipment, and know-how to transform them into clean clothing (the outputs of the business).

transformation process What a business does to add value to inputs in converting them to outputs.

Outputs

Outputs, the result of the transformation processes, are what your business produces. Outputs can be tangible, like a CD, or intangible, like a doctor's diagnosis.

Since a business's social responsibility has become an even more serious matter, along with product liability lawsuits and other forms of litigation, we need to consider *all* the outputs a business produces—not just the beneficial or intended ones. When we look at the big picture of the transformation process, we see that employee accidents, consumer injuries, pollution, and waste are also outputs.

outputs The tangible or intangible products that a business produces.

Work Hard, Play Hard

At Alexander Doll Company in New York City, the Japanese principle of *kaizen*—or continuous improvement—is more than just child's play. As a manufacturer of collectible dolls, the company had gone into bankruptcy, and president Patricia Lewis was looking for a way to improve the firm's production efficiency and effectiveness. A consulting group, TBM Consulting Group, Inc., of Durham, North Carolina, felt that *kaizen* could turn the business around. TBM partners had studied Toyota's lean production system. Making dolls had to be simpler than Lexus LS400s, didn't it? Yes, but maybe not by much.

Alexander Doll Company had been around for over seventy-five years. It was founded in 1923 by "Madame" Beatrice Alexander, a daughter of Russian immigrants. The family lived over the father's New York City doll hospital. Each of the collectible dolls, which cost from $40 to $600, features a hand-painted face and elaborate costume. Sales began to falter in the mid-nineties. Enter TBM.

Implementing *kaizen* is a matter of evaluating the manufacturing system and involving employees in the search for greater efficiency and quality. At Alexander, operations were spread out over three floors, which wasted time and caused additional damage to the dolls. So TBM's first move was to set up a cross-functional team of ten Alexander employees charged with evaluating production line problems. The team observed 25 operations and measured each with a stopwatch. After this evaluation was complete, says William Schwartz, vice president of TBM and now a director at Alexander Dolls, "We physically moved the operation within the building and combined everything in one location on one floor. We started to flow the product so that each operation was carried out as each doll moved through the process."

As a result, the distance that each doll traveled from beginning to end of the process was reduced from 630 feet to 40 feet. The number of unfinished doll pieces shrank from 29,000 to 34, and the time required to complete a doll decreased from 90 *days* to 90 *minutes*. The square footage required for the production line went from 2,010 to 980. And productivity increased from 8 dolls per person per day to 25 dolls per person per day—a 212 percent improvement! Obviously, Alexander Doll Company wasn't just toying around with the Japanese principle of *kaizen*.

Sources: Alex Taylor, "It Worked for Toyota. Can it Work for Toys?" *Fortune,* 11 January 1999, 36; and Roberta Maynard, "A Company Is Turned Around Through Japanese Principles," *Nation's Business,* February 1996, 9.

Control Systems

control systems The means to monitor input, transformation, and output in order to identify problems.

Control systems provide the means to monitor and correct problems or deviations when they occur in the operating system. Controls are integrated into all three stages—input, transformation, and output (see Figure 18.1). An example of a control system would be the use of electronic monitors in a manufacturing process to tell a machine operator that the product is not being made within the allowed size tolerance. In service companies, employee behavior is part of the transformation process to be controlled. A bank manager, for instance, might hire people to pose as new bank customers and then report back to the manager on the quality of service they received from tellers or loan officers.

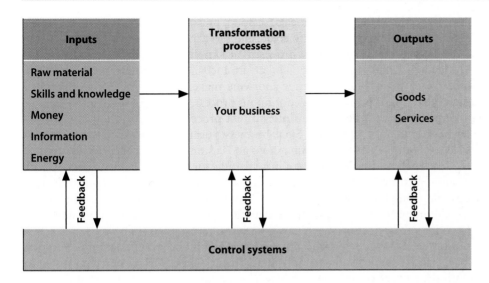

FIGURE 18.1
Control Systems

Every type of business takes inputs and transforms them into outputs.

Feedback

Feedback is the information that a manager receives in monitoring the operation system. It can be verbal, written, electronic, or observational. Feedback is the necessary communication that links a control system to the inputs, transformation, and outputs.

feedback Communication tools to connect control systems to the processes of a business.

Types of Operations Management ▬▬

Production broadly describes what businesses of all types do in creating goods and services. Computer hardware and software companies, health care providers, and farmers are all involved in production. Manufacturing is just one type of production, making goods as opposed to providing services or extracting natural resources. One of your highest priorities as a manager is to ensure that productivity remains high. **Productivity** is the measure of output per worker. It is important to measure productivity in order to control the amount of resources used to produce outputs.

productivity The measure of outputs according to the inputs needed to produce them; a way to determine the efficiency of a business.

Manufacturing Operations

Manufacturing businesses can be classified by the way they make goods and by the time used to create them. Goods and services can be made from analytic or synthetic systems, using either continuous or intermittent processes.

Analytic systems reduce inputs into component parts to extract products. Auto salvage businesses buy vehicles from insurance companies or individuals to dismantle them for parts or scrap iron to sell. **Synthetic systems,** by contrast, combine inputs to create a finished product or change it into a different product. Restaurants

analytic system Manufacturing system that reduces inputs into component parts to extract products.

synthetic system Manufacturing system that combines inputs to create a finished product or change it into a different product.

take vegetables, fruits, grains, meats, seafood, music, lighting, furniture, paintings, and a variety of human talents to create and serve meals.

continuous process A production process that operates for long periods of time without interruption.

Production by a **continuous process** is accomplished over long periods of time. Production of the same or very similar products goes on uninterrupted for days, months, or years. Microbreweries and wine makers are examples of small businesses that produce goods via a continuous process.

intermittent process A production process that operates in short cycles in order to change products.

Production runs that use an **intermittent process** involve short cycles and frequent stops to change products. Small businesses using intermittent processes are also called "job shops." Custom printing shops and custom jewelry makers are examples.

Can small businesses compete in a manufacturing sector long associated with gigantic factories? Yes, primarily because automation makes flexible production possible. Computers assist small manufacturers in determining raw material needs, scheduling production runs, and designing new products. Automation allows the retooling of production machines in seconds, rather than hours or days, so that shorter batches can be produced profitably. Machines can be programmed to perform many combinations of individual jobs and functions, rather than just one. With the help of computers, products and processes can be designed at the same time, rather than designing a product and then figuring out a way to make it.

Many small businesses are benefiting from the number of large businesses that are examining what they do best, determining that manufacturing is not exactly their strong suit, and farming out production to smaller specialty firms. For example, your new Dell computer did not come from a Dell computer factory—none exists. Dell concentrates on marketing, buying computer components from different companies, and assembling them in a warehouse.[1] This type of flexible contract production opens many opportunities for entrepreneurs

mass customization A production process that allows products to be produced specifically for individual customers.

Manufacturing is already evolving past flexible production, however, to **mass customization,** which means tailoring products to meet the needs of individual customers. An example of mass customization would see a customer in need of a new business suit stepping into a kiosklike device. An optical scanner would measure the customer's body. As soon as the choice of fabric and style are made, the order is beamed to the plant, where lasers cut the material and it is sewn together. The suit is ready and shipped directly to the customer in a matter of days.[2]

Operations Management for Service Businesses

Do both service providers and product manufacturers need and use operations management? Yes, they do. Both take inputs and produce outputs through some type of transformation process. However, operations processes differ from one product and service to another, and some overlap. Manufacturers often offer repair services. Restaurants offer food products as well as services.

Traditionally, all service businesses have been seen as intermittent process businesses, because standardization didn't seem possible for businesses like hair salons, accounting firms, and auto service centers. But, in an effort to increase productivity, some service businesses are adopting continuous processes. For example, Merry Maids house cleaners, Jiffy Lube auto service, Fantastic Sam's family hair-cutting salons, and even chains of dentists located in malls are all using manufacturing techniques of continuous production. A notable difference between service and manufacturing operations is the amount of customer contact involved. Many services, such as hair salons, require the customer to be present for the operation to be performed. Consider the examples of product and service operations systems in Table 18.1.

Inputs	Transformation	Outputs	Feedback	
Restaurant				**TABLE 18.1** **Product and Service Operations Systems**
Food	Cooking	Meals	Leftovers	
Hungry people	Serving	Satisfied people	Complaints	
Equipment				
Labor				
Factory				
Machinery	Welding	Finished products	Defects	
Skilled labor	Painting	Services	Returns	
Raw material	Forming	Waste products	Market share	
Engineering	Transporting		Complaints	
Management				
Buildings				

Small Business Robotics

Robots are making their way into small businesses to increase productivity and hold down costs. They were once considered a luxury that only large companies could afford. For example, Engineering Concepts Unlimited (ECU), of Fishers, Indiana, makes electronic boards and controllers, and sells about 5,000 units a year. The company uses robots to do the work of about ten people.

Adam Suchko, CEO of ECU, states that, "When we started building these, you put the parts in the holes, you put the boards in a rack, flipped them over, and soldered the connections. One every three or four seconds." Suchko bought the company's first robot for $350 at an auction in 1989. It took two months to rebuild the robot and get it into the production loop. Once the robot came online, production increased tenfold. Suchko's robot could solder connections at a rate of hundreds of connections *per second*.

ECU now has four robots, and the entire process can go for up to 50 hours at a time without people's intervening. Suchko programs the robots to perform as many tasks as possible. Then he and his three employees "do whatever's left," like reloading parts into the machines and making special adjustments.

Brannock Device Company of Syracuse, New York, is another ten-employee business that made the switch to robotics. Brannock produces cast aluminum foot measurement devices. It had long relied on outside vendors (who used manual methods) to sand and polish its products. If you have measured your foot in a retail shoe store, chances are you used a Brannock device to do it.

Vendors' prices continually increased, whereas quality ranged from fair to poor. Brannock never imagined that robots could be found in its price range but was pleasantly surprised to find it could not only afford robots, they were also simpler than expected to use.

Brannock went with a Fanuc Robotics material-handling robot and application-specific Handling Tool software. The six-axis robot picks up a part with a vacuum gripper and moves it into three different positions before placing the finished sanded piece on a tray. This sequence can be completed at the rate of 24 parts per hour with increased quality and productivity.

Sources: "Small Manufacturer Finds Savings with Robotics Sanding, Polishing," *Robotics World,* September/October 1999, 27–29; and John DeMott, "Look, World, No Hands!" *Nation's Business,* June 1994, 41–42.

■ What Is Productivity?

You read in Chapter 16 that, as a manager, you are involved in planning, organizing, leading, and controlling. But how do you tell if and when you are reaching the goals that you have set? You can measure and describe your success by your productivity or efficiency. Productivity, the measure of output per worker, can be described numerically as the ratio of inputs used to outputs produced, such as output per labor-hour. The higher the ratio, the more efficient your operating system. You should constantly look for ways to increase outputs while keeping inputs constant or to keep outputs constant while decreasing inputs.

Measurement of Productivity

Productivity can be measured for your entire business or for a specific portion of it. Because many inputs go into your business, the input you choose determines the specific measure of productivity. Total productivity can be determined by dividing total outputs by total inputs.

Total productivity = Outputs/Labor + Capital + Raw materials + All other inputs

If your software company sold $500,000 worth of software and used $100,000 in resources, your total productivity ratio would be 5. But you may not always want to consider all your inputs every time. For example, because materials may account for as much as 90 percent of operating costs in businesses that use little labor, materials productivity would be an important ratio for you to track.

Materials productivity = Outputs/Materials

If 4,000 pounds of sugar are used to produce 1,000 pounds of candy, the materials productivity is 1,000 divided by 4,000, or 0.25, which becomes a base figure for comparing increases or decreases in productivity. Stated simply, you can increase the productivity of your business by increasing outputs, decreasing inputs, or a combination of both. Most productivity improvements come from changing processes used by your business, from your employees' accomplishing more, or from technology that speeds production.

Productivity ratios can be used to measure the efficiency of a new process. Say that you run a furniture shop whose productivity ratio is

Output/Input = Number of tables/Hours = 100/100 = 1

You have invented a new process that will save 20 percent on your labor costs. Now you can still produce the same number of tables (100) yet take only 80 hours to produce them. Your new productivity ratio is

New productivity ratio = 100/80 = 1.25

Unfortunately, your new process ends up increasing defects in the tables. To correct these defects, you have to increase labor-hours to 120. Your productivity ratio is now

Corrected productivity ratio = 100/120 = 0.833

Your corrected productivity ratio shows that it is back to the drawing board for your new process.

Service Productivity

Productivity in the U.S. service sector has been flat over the last decade, with a growth rate averaging only 0.2 percent.[3] This statistic is even more significant when you remember that almost 80 percent of the U.S. work force is in the service sector.

Productivity in service-related businesses has not grown as rapidly as in manufacturing businesses because service businesses are more labor intensive. Factories can substitute machines for people and increase output. Can service businesses do the same?

Actually, to some degree they can. Rick Smolan, president of Wildfire Communications, has developed an electronic device that can totally automate your telephone communications. By blending computer, telephone, and voice-recognition technology, Wildfire receives and directs calls wherever you are, takes messages, and maintains your calendar and Rolodex—and does it all by responding to your voice. Smolan and others who are always on the phone but rarely in an office use Wildfire in place of a personal secretary. "Secretarial work is just not good use of a human being," according to Smolan.[4]

Besides technological innovation, another key to productivity in a service business is making sure your employees are comfortable. **Ergonomics** studies the fit between people and machines. "The human body is simply not designed to sit. Yet between 70 percent to 75 percent of today's work force is sitting and working on computers," says corporate ergonomist Rajendra Paul.[5] Lighting levels, furniture size and height, and the location of computers and telephones are important factors to consider in designing your work stations. With physical differences and varying employee needs, you may need to consider chairs with adjustable armrests and footrests, keyboards and mouse pads that adjust to the correct height and angle, and nonglare monitor screens.

ergonomics The study of the interaction between people and machinery.

> *Ergonomics is the key to worker productivity. Make sure that there is a healthy fit between people and equipment.*

Management style, too, is another key factor in improving the quality and quantity of service workers' output. At Mountain Shadows, Inc., in Escondido, California, owner H. Douglas Cook knew that keeping his employees' productivity high meant that he had to stay out of the way and let his employees do their jobs. And Cook has a special interest in Mountain Shadows, a residential facility for the developmentally disabled, because not only is he its owner, but his son Brian is a resident there. The facility's 105 residents range in age from 7 to 63, and almost all of them use wheelchairs. Mountain Shadows is, by necessity, a highly labor-intensive operation. Yet Cook doesn't interfere with the 170 employees. Instead he has introduced an open management style that recognizes the importance of the employees. By doing so, he has dramatically reduced employee turnover, which in turn has increased his workers' efficiency.[6]

What About Scheduling Operations? ▬

Scheduling is a basic operations management activity for both manufacturing and service businesses which involves the timing of production. The purpose of scheduling is to put your plans into motion by describing what each worker has to do.

Scheduling is necessary to maximize levels of efficiency and customer service. For example, if a beauty shop schedules one haircut every 30 minutes, although

"We were way ahead of schedule, so we revised the schedule.
Now we're way behind schedule because we lost too much
time revising the schedule. What we need is a schedule
to help us revise our schedules on schedule."

© 1998 Randy Glasbergen www.glasbergen.com

each could actually be done in 20 minutes with no decrease in quality, the operator could be working one-third more efficiently. Three haircuts could be produced per hour rather than two. But a shop that schedules too much work cannot complete jobs on time, resulting in poor customer service and probably losing future business from customers aggravated by having to wait for their appointments. If you can schedule the exact amount of work to meet your customer demand at a given time, you will optimize your resources.

Scheduling Methods

forward scheduling
Scheduling in which materials and resources are allocated for production when a job order comes in.

backward scheduling
Scheduling that involves arranging production activities around the due date for the product.

Most business operations use forward scheduling, backward scheduling, or a combination of the two methods. With **forward scheduling,** materials and resources are allocated for production when a job order comes in. Any type of custom production in which the product changes or in which demand is unknown in advance needs forward scheduling. **Backward scheduling** involves arranging production activities around the due date for the product. You take the date the finished product must be delivered, then schedule in reverse order all material procurement and work to be done.

Henry L. Gantt devised a simple bar graph for scheduling work in any kind of operation. Developed in 1913, it still bears his name: the Gantt chart. This chart can be used to track the progress of work as a product makes its way through various departments (see Figure 18.2). It allows you to see the time required for each step and the current status of a job.

Routing

routing Information showing the steps required to produce a product.

Scheduling involves routing, sequencing, and dispatching the product through successive stages of production. **Routing** shows the detailed breakdown of information

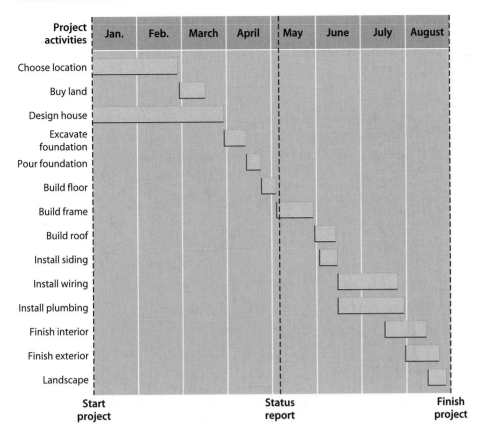

FIGURE 18.2

The Gantt Chart

Stages of work in building a house.

explaining how your product or service will be produced. Routing sheets are the paper copy, and routing files are the electronic versions of this information. Needed information could include tooling specifications and setups, number of workers or operators needed, the sequence in which steps are to be taken, and control tests to be performed.

Sequencing

Sequencing is the critical step of determining the order in which a job will go through your production system. Sequencing is most important when the job involves more than one department of your business, because a holdup in one department could cause idle time for another. Drafting a Gantt chart is a good way to track the flow of jobs between departments.

sequencing The order in which the steps need to occur to produce a product.

Dispatching

Dispatching is the act of releasing work to employees according to priorities you determined in planning the work sequence. Taxi companies often use *first-come, first-served* priority dispatching rules. A tailor may use an *earliest due date* rule, in which the order due first is dispatched first. A company that assumes that orders

dispatching Allocating resources and beginning the steps to produce a product.

How Good Is Good Enough?

If 99.9 percent accuracy were good enough,

- The Internal Revenue Service would lose 2 million documents per year.
- *Webster's Third International Dictionary of the English Language* would have 315 misspelled words.
- 12 newborn babies would go home with the wrong parents daily.
- 107 medical procedures would be performed incorrectly every day.
- 114,500 pairs of new shoes would be mismatched each year.
- 2,488,200 books would be printed each year with no words.
- Telephone companies would send 1,314 calls to the wrong number each minute.
- 5,517,200 cases of soft drinks would be made every year with no fizz.
- Two airplanes would crash at Chicago's O'Hare International Airport every day.
- 811,000 rolls of 35mm film would not take pictures each year.

that will take the longest will be the largest (and most profitable) will use a *longest processing time* priority dispatching rule. Companies that make significant profit from handling charges and that reduce costs by completing more orders will use a *shortest processing time* priority dispatching rule.

Quality-Centered Management

quality How well a good or service meets or exceeds customers' expectations, or the degree to which a product conforms to established tolerance standards.

defect rate The number of goods produced that are outside the company's boundaries of acceptable quality.

tolerance range The boundaries a manager sets in determining the acceptable quality of a product.

There is no quality more important to businesses today than just that—quality. Many U.S. businesses lost tremendous market share to foreign companies for one reason: They had not paid enough attention to quality. Now, few industries and businesses, large or small, can afford *not* to focus their attention on quality.

To manage a small business centered on quality, you must keep two things in mind about what the word **quality** means. First, from the customers' perspective, quality is how well your product or service satisfies their needs. Second, from your business's standpoint, quality means how closely your product conforms to the standards you have set.

Six Sigma in Small Business

A common way that companies measure the quality of a product is to keep close track of the **defect rate.** A defect rate is the number of goods produced that were out of the company's accepted **tolerance range**—the boundaries of acceptable

Six Sigma at Work

Many businesses have set a goal of six-sigma quality in production. Just what *does* this strange phrase *six sigma* refer to?

Six sigma has to do with the concept of near perfection in production and was initially introduced by the well-known quality expert Philip B. Crosby in his book *Quality Is Free* (1979). Motorola Corporation then popularized six sigma in the mid-1980s as a way to measure the probability that companies can produce any given unit of a product (or service) with only 3.4 defects per million units or operations. Motorola's goal was to manufacture defect-free products and to eliminate defects throughout its organizational processes. A six-sigma rating, therefore, signifies "best-in-class" status.

What are the components of a six-sigma quality program? Let's take a closer look at the basic components and the activities and tools needed to practice them.

Basic Components. The basic components of a six-sigma program include the actual improvement process and quality measurement. The actual improvement process involves the following steps:

1. Define products and services by describing the actual products or services that are provided to customers.

2. Identify customer requirements for products or services by stating them in measurable terms.

3. Compare products with requirements by identifying gaps between what the customer expects and what he or she is actually receiving.

4. Describe the process by providing explicit details.

5. Improve the process by simplification and mistake-proofing.

6. Measure quality and productivity by establishing baseline values and then tracking improvement.

Those quality measurements should include process mean and standard deviation, capability index, and defects per unit.

Quality Activities and Tools. The quality activities are ongoing management processes that businesses need to practice in a six-sigma program. These include participative management, short-cycle manufacturing, designing for manufacturing benchmarking, statistical process control, and supplier qualification. The improvement tools and analytical techniques include flow charts, Pareto charts, histograms, cause-and-effect diagrams, and experimental design.

The speed at which e-business is conducted fits like a glove with six-sigma principles, because these principles allow business to deliver just what customers need when they want it.

Small businesses that would like to achieve six-sigma status must work diligently to reduce and eliminate defects. The ultimate goals are improved manufacturing and increased customer satisfaction. It's not easy to achieve, but six sigma *can be* something more than just a strange phrase. It can provide a worthwhile target toward which to strive.

Sources: John Welch, "Timeless Principles," *Executive Excellence,* February 2001, 3–4; Fred R. McFadden, "Six-Sigma Quality Programs," *Quality Progress,* June 1993, 37–42; Gwen Fontenot, Ravi Behara, and Alicia Gresham, "Six Sigma in Customer Satisfaction," *Quality Progress,* December 1994, 73–76; and Jim Carbone and Thomas Pearson, "Measure for Six Sigma Success," *Quality Progress,* February 2001, 36–40.

TABLE 18.2	Sigma Level	Defects per Million
Sigma Levels and Defect Rates	3.0	66,810.0
	3.5	22,750.0
	4.0	6,750.0
	4.5	1,350.0
	5.0	233.0
	5.5	32.0
	6.0	3.4

quality. But how good is good enough? Is 99 out of 100 good enough? With a 1 percent defect rate, consider this: The U.S. Postal Service would lose over 18,000 pieces of mail per hour!

Perfection is not possible, but companies are striving for zero (or very near zero) defects. **Six sigma** is the term that has come to signify the quality movement, not just in manufacturing, but throughout entire organizations. In statistical terminology, *sigma* denotes the standard deviation of a set of data. It indicates how all data points in a distribution vary from the mean (average) value. Table 18.2 shows different sigma levels and their corresponding defects per million.[7]

With a normal distribution, 99.73 percent of all the data points fall within three standard deviations (three sigma) of the mean. Pretty good, but that is just for one stage of the production process. Products that have to go through hundreds or thousands of stages could still come out with defects.

If you choose six-sigma defects as your production goal, you will have 99.99966 percent of your products within your specification limits—only 3.4 defects per million! Even if your product has to go through 100 different stages, the defect rate will still be only 3,390 defects per million.

six sigma The tolerance range in which only 3.4 defects per million are allowed.

Six Sigma Online

www.6-sigma.com This site created by the Six Sigma Academy offers a good look within the academy and training provided. Start with a click on "What is Six Sigma?" A wealth of information on training and the six-sigma philosophy is provided. "News and Reviews" tells what companies have implemented the process and how it has impacted their operations.

www.iSixSigma.com This site will provide you with information on how to implement quality strategies into your business. Clicking on "Methodologies" will take you to a variety of papers with differing quality methodologies.

www.sixsigma.de Start with the site map link at the top of the page, where you will find an outline of site topics. It is easy to navigate from there. You may be interested in the detailed boundary conditions with graphics of six sigma.

www.thequalityportal.com Here you will find a wider range of quality-related items, but plenty of six sigma. Click on "Six Sigma" for a description, why it is important, when to use it, how to use it, and a definition of a black belt.

Source: "Online with Six Sigma," *Quality*, March 2001, 10–12.

The concept of six sigma is not limited to producing goods in your small business. You can also apply it to customer satisfaction in your service business. Consider a company with 1,000 customers and 10 employees (or stages) that can affect customer satisfaction. The difference between three sigma (499 dissatisfied) and four sigma (60 dissatisfied) is 439 dissatisfied customers. That represents 44 percent of your entire customer base![8]

Quality Circles

A popular technique for improving quality is the use of **quality circles** to involve everyone within the organization in decisions that affect the business. Small groups of employees meet regularly to discuss, analyze, and recommend solutions to problems in their area, after they receive training in problem solving, statistical techniques, and organizational behavior.

> **quality circles** The use of small groups of employees to analyze products and processes in order to improve quality.

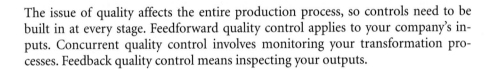

How Do You Control Operations?

The issue of quality affects the entire production process, so controls need to be built in at every stage. Feedforward quality control applies to your company's inputs. Concurrent quality control involves monitoring your transformation processes. Feedback quality control means inspecting your outputs.

Feedforward Quality Control

Control of quality begins by screening out inputs that are not good enough. **Feedforward quality control** depends strongly on the TQM principles that every employee is a quality inspector and is responsible for building better, long-term relationships with suppliers. When you have a long-term relationship with suppliers, they can help you achieve higher quality standards by continuously improving their products. Teamwork with your employees and cooperation with suppliers are keys to feedforward control.

> **feedforward quality control** Quality control applied to a company's inputs.

> *Small businesses must monitor their productivity closely to stay competitive, to remain profitable.*

Concurrent Quality Control

Concurrent quality control involves monitoring the quality of your work in progress. To facilitate this type of monitoring, many small businesses are realizing the value of the international quality standards known as **ISO 9000** (pronounced ICE-oh 9000). The purpose of the ISO 9000 standards is to document, implement, and demonstrate the quality assurance systems used by companies that supply goods and services internationally.[9]

ISO standards do not address the quality of your specific products. Rather, they are a way to show your customers (whether consumers or other businesses) how

> **concurrent quality control** Quality control applied to work in progress.
> **ISO 9000** The set of standards that certifies that a business is using processes and principles in order to ensure the production of quality products.

"We're Moving Where . . .?!"

For years, Loranger Manufacturing Corporation existed peacefully in Warren, Pennsylvania, making and supplying parts for major customers such as the Ford Motor Company. That changed in December 1991 when George P. Loranger, owner and CEO, decided to follow Ford and move to Szekesfehervar, Hungary. His decision to relocate the entire operation was a gutsy move for a small business, to say the least, and one that illustrates the pressure on small businesses to maintain long-term vendor and customer relationships and to operate internationally.

International expansion is difficult for the largest businesses and even harder for small businesses that usually have no experience or teams of lawyers and experts to blaze a trail. In retrospect, Loranger calls the move "one big roller coaster ride." Some of Loranger's hurdles included negotiating terms for leasing a building on a recently abandoned Soviet military base (complete with 2,000 sheep to trim the front lawn); dealing with rapidly rising inflation and Hungary's nonconvertible currency; unfamiliarity with the local language; and even the theft of underground telephone cables.

Why would Loranger make such a crazy move? The reason came down to his fear of losing Ford as one of the company's major customers. Ford rewarded such loyalty with a multiyear contract. The strategy is similar to a Japanese system called *keiretsu,* in which Japanese companies take suppliers with them when they expand into other countries. The intent of *keiretsu* is to reduce startup costs, keep the quality level of goods consistent, help transfer technology between the companies, and produce a product more in line with the needs of the host country.

Loranger got a call from Ford in late 1989 when Ford began talking of new operations in Spain and Portugal. He initially envisioned relaxing in his spare time on sunny beaches. But Ford's decision to locate the new plant in Hungary put him far from the nearest beach. Risks like moving entire businesses to other countries are extreme but may be part of "the way business is done" as large and small businesses begin forging long-term, mutually beneficial relationships.

By the year 2000, the former 650-acre military base is 75 percent developed by Loranger, has attracted more than $600 million in foreign investment with 27 companies, and has created 4,000 jobs. Loranger's 155,000-square-foot factory is doing well, employing 230 people. Assembly labor averages $3 to $5 per hour, but cheaper labor costs are offset by higher absentee rates—13.6 percent in Hungary versus. 4.2 percent in the United States.

Loranger is not finished with global expansion; in 2001, it opened an injection-molding plant in Guadeloupe, Mexico, to take advantage of a good work force and an attractive plastic processing market. Its experience in Eastern Europe made the transition to Mexico smoother.

Sources: Steve Toloken, "Loranger Factory Revitalizes Old Hungary City," *Plastics News,* 20 November 2000, 11; Dana Milbank, "It's Not Easy Being a Little Guy Overseas," *Wall Street Journal,* 15 September 1994, A11; and Rhoda Miel, "Loranger Opens Plant in Mexico," *Automotive News,* 26 March 2001, 26H.

you test your products, how your people are trained, how you keep records, and how you fix defects. ISO standards are more like generally accepted accounting principles (GAAP) than they are a spinoff of TQM.[10] Certification in the United States comes from the American National Standards Institute, 11 West 42nd Street, New York, New York 10035 (212-642-4900).

American Saw of East Longmeadow, Massachusetts, an 800-employee, family-owned business, was the first in its industry to receive ISO certification. Tim Berry,

Loranger Manufacturing took a big risk by relocating its operations to Hungary in order to build a long-term relationship with its major customer, Ford Motor Company. Fortunately, the gamble paid off.

quality control manager, believes that because the company took the steps necessary to become certified, its product defects have decreased, communication has improved, and workplace accidents have been reduced.[11] More important, meeting the standards will ease entry into foreign markets and cut costs. Unfortunately, the up-front costs of certification can be high for small businesses. American Saw laid out $60,000 for outside consultants and registrars.

Richard Thompson of Caterpillar states, "Today, having ISO 9000 is a competitive advantage. Tomorrow, it will be the ante to the global poker game."[12] Small businesses may find themselves between the proverbial rock and a hard place relating to certification and costs if the larger companies that buy their products require certification before they will purchase from the small business. Some suggestions for dealing with costs include

- *Negotiate consultation prices.* Different consultants and registrars charge different amounts. Consultation prices are on the way down, so shop around, but be sure the consultant you select is familiar with your particular industry.

- *Request customer subsidies.* If the company you are selling to is pushing its suppliers for certification, they may help you become certified. A primary customer of Griffith Rubber Mills of Portland, Oregon, paid the entire certification bill because it needed the technology.

- *Look for consultant alternatives.* A local college may be able to help set up an ISO networking group.

- *Consider your need for full certification.* You may be able to save money if it is more important to your suppliers for your business to meet ISO standards than to have full certification.[13]

Benchmarking Your Way to Competitive Advantage

In order to identify or measure a competitive advantage for your small business, you must have a comparison base. You have to compare your products, services, practices; almost anything related to your business that can be measured can be benchmarked. Benchmarking can be a powerful tool. Where can you find benchmark information? First of all, go to your local library reference section to find *Robert Morris Associates Industry Averages. RMA* is second to none for small business industry averages. Industry groups and trade associations often publish industry averages in journals, magazines, and newsletters. Check for your specific industry.

What you should compare is a different story. Benchmarking can be used to improve every facet of your business. Some examples include the following:

Defining the Consumer Need
- Market research
- Demographic considerations
- Competitor research
- Consumer satisfaction index
- Consumer trends
- Unique selling proposition

Design Process
- Materials needs
- Packaging needs
- Personnel requirements
- Competitor standards
- Sustainability issues
- Communication needs
- Design cycle time
- Future trends
- Cost considerations

Materials Purchase
- Vendor relations
- Quality of materials
- Delivery time
- Personnel needs
- Equipment needs
- Materials inventory management
- Storage needs
- Cost considerations
- Alternatives

Production Process
- Methodology
- Facility needs
- Equipment needs
- Personnel needs
- Assembly time
- Quality control
- Inspection
- Cost considerations
- Parts availability
- Returns and repairs

Packaging
- Consumer input
- Distributor input
- Materials needs
- Facility needs
- Equipment needs
- Personnel needs
- Labeling
- Instructions
- Quality control
- Inspection
- Cost considerations
- Returns and repairs

Inventory
- Routing needs
- Average time in inventory
- Just-in-time production
- Storage needs
- Inventory controls

Distribution and Delivery
- Distributor input
- Inventory control
- Methodology
- Personnel needs
- Quality control
- Inspection

- Facility needs
- Equipment needs
- Location of delivery
  - My place
  - Your place
  - Somebody else's place
- Cost considerations

Waste Management
- Recycling
- Low waste materials

Health and Safety
- Workmen's compensation and disability claims
- Equipment maintenance, repair, and replacement

Customer Service
- Goods and services availability
- Returns, repair, and replacement
- Feedback mechanisms (surveys, 800 numbers, etc.)

Marketing Issues
- Unique selling proposition
- Consumer education efforts
- Pricing considerations
- Advertising
- Direct mail
- Fax on demand
- Sales representatives
- Retail sales
- Telemarketing
- Catalogue sales
- Public relations
- Newsletters

Internal Communication Systems
- Use of computers
- Accounting systems
- Open book management
- Employee surveys
- Performance reviews
- Peer reviews

Personnel Issues
- Hiring
- Orientation
- Training
- Team building
- Performance review process

- Mechanisms for delivery
  - Direct presence
  - Mail/ship
  - Fax
  - E-mail
  - Software
  - Telephone
  - Truck/rail

- Cost considerations
- Alternative uses

- Wellness programs
- Ergonomics
- Absenteeism, lateness
- Health insurance claims

- Warranties and guarantees
- Cost considerations

- Joint venture and host possibilities
- Back-end sales
- 800 numbers
- Online marketing pagers
- Vendor and distributor assistance
- Cost considerations
- Alternatives
- Rebates, coupons, and other incentives

- Bulletin boards
- Newsletters
- Meetings
- Cost considerations
- E-mail
- Intranet

- Testing
- Outsourcing
- Retentions/turnover
- Terminations
- Rehiring

Sources: lian Mochari, "CEO Notebook—Significant Figures & Magic Numbers," *Inc.,* July 2000; and "Benchmarking Considerations" (www.inc.com/freetools), copyright 2001, www.lawthatworks.com

FIGURE 18.3
The Control Chart

Control charts are used to distinguish random from nonrandom variations in the production of goods.

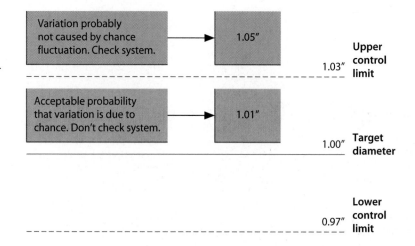

An important tool for monitoring the quality of a product while it is being produced is **statistical process control (SPC)**. SPC is the process of gathering, plotting, and analyzing data to isolate problems in a specified sample of products you make. Using statistical analysis, you can determine the probability of a deviation's being a simple, random, unimportant variation or a sign of a problem in your production process that must be corrected.

statistical process control (SPC) The use of statistical analysis to determine the probability of a variation in product being random or a problem.

For example, if you are producing titanium bars that need to be 1 inch in diameter, not every single bar will measure *exactly* 1 inch. You need to calculate the probabilities of various deviations' occurring by chance alone or because of some problem. If a sample bar measures 1.01 inches, you wouldn't be too concerned, because that amount of variation occurs by chance once in every 100 products (see Figure 18.3). But if a sample bar measures 1.05 inches, we know that the probability of that much variation's occurring by chance is only one in 10,000. What now? A problem needs correction in your production process, or more defective parts will be produced.

Feedback Quality Control

feedback quality control Inspecting and testing products after they are produced.

Inspecting and testing products after they are produced is called **feedback quality control.** Quality control inspectors may be used to check products. Rejected products will be either discarded, reworked, or recycled.

A problem with many types of product inspection is that the product can no longer be used. The product has to be cut up, taken apart, or disassembled to test and measure it. However, nondestructive testing of several metal and plastic parts is being perfected by using laser ultrasound and other electromagnetic and acoustic-based methods.[14]

SUMMARY

▬▬▬   **Elements of an operating system.**

In developing a system for producing your product or service, your business takes inputs such as raw materials, skills, money, information, and energy, and transforms them in some way to add value to product outputs. You need to receive feedback at every stage in order to control the process.

How manufacturers and service providers use operations management.

Operating systems used by manufacturers are either analytic (systems that take inputs and reduce them into component parts to produce outputs) or synthetic (systems that combine inputs in producing outputs). The processes that manufacturers use are either continuous or intermittent. A continuous process is one that produces the same good without interruption for a long period of time. An intermittent process is one that is stopped with some frequency to change the products being made. Service businesses also take inputs and produce outputs through some transformation process. Most have used intermittent processes, but some have adopted continuous processes in order to increase productivity.

How to measure productivity.

The ratio of inputs used to produce outputs is called "productivity." Productivity measures the efficiency of your entire business or any part of it. Productivity can be improved by changing processes used by your business, by getting your employees to accomplish more, or by using some type of technology that speeds production. To calculate productivity, simply divide outputs by inputs.

How to schedule operations.

Scheduling involves planning what work will need to be done and determining what resources you will need to produce your product or service. Forward scheduling is accomplished by having resources available and ready as customer orders come in. Backward scheduling is used when you plan a job around the date when the project must be done. Gantt charts are a useful backward-scheduling tool.

Building quality into operations.

A company's tolerance range denotes the boundaries of acceptable quality. The defect rate indicates the number of products made that fall outside the tolerance range. Six sigma establishes a tolerance range of only 3.4 defects per million products produced. Statistical process control (SPC) is a procedure used to determine the probability of a deviation's being a simple, random, unimportant variation or a sign of a problem in your production process that must be corrected.

How to control operations.

Controlling operations is how you measure what is being accomplished in your business. Feedforward quality control applies to your company's inputs. Concurrent quality control involves monitoring your transformation processes. Feedback quality control is inspecting your outputs.

QUESTIONS FOR **REVIEW & DISCUSSION**

1. Discuss the elements of an operations management system. What would happen if the control system were not included? the feedback?

2. What is the difference between flexible production and mass customization?

3. Define productivity.

4. How can ergonomics be tied to productivity? to motivation? to Maslow's hierarchy?

5. Explain the difference between forward and backward scheduling.

6. Define six sigma both technically and as used as a business standard.

7. What types of small business would benefit from having ISO 9000 certification?

8. Give examples of products that would be suited to each of the dispatching rules.

QUESTIONS FOR **CRITICAL THINKING**

1. This chapter concentrated on both productivity and quality. In running your small manufacturing business, can you increase both, or aren't they mutually exclusive?

2. The Reality Check "Small Business Robotics" is about small businesses' replacing manual labor with robots. When should management substitute capital for labor?

Experience this...

Some things are just better understood by seeing them, rather than reading about them or visiting them online. For this "Experience this," lobby your instructor for a class plant tour of a local manufacturing business. Write a two- to three-page paper describing its feedforward, concurrent, and feedback control systems.

WHAT WOULD **YOU** DO? | No. 1

Easy Living and the Salute to the Performing Arts. Every year, Savannah, Georgia, salutes organizations involved with the performing arts with a formal dinner and dance. The Savannah Symphony, Southern Regional Opera, Savannah Ballet, Community Theatre Association, and Savannah Visual Artists Alliance are among the organizations honored. Your party planning service, Easy Living, has been awarded a contract to plan this year's salute. You will be making all the arrangements for the food, drinks, entertainment, decorations, and advertising. In addition, you will have to coordinate the awards that are given to one person from each of the five community performing arts organizations. This year's salute is planned for April 28.

Super Sack Manufacturing Corporation. At Super Sack Manufacturing Corporation in Savoy, Texas, employees are elated to learn that they've received a huge order from a large, well-known animal feed producer. However, the order is for a product that they've never made before—a bag that has microscopic air holes so that air can circulate around the animal feed. The first order of 500,000 bags is due to the customer within three months, and the customer would like to approve the prototype before proceeding with actual production. Plant capacity is 25,000 bags per day.

QUESTIONS

1. Choose one of the businesses described and develop a Gantt chart timeline for it. Take into consideration the tasks that need to be done and the approximate amount of time that you think it will take to complete the task.

2. Divide into teams according to the business you've chosen. Compare your individual charts, and come to a consensus about the most reasonable time frame and sequence of activities.

WHAT WOULD YOU DO?   No. 2

Reread the chapter opener on Krispy Kreme. This vignette provides a lot of information about the company's products and processes. Find related articles about the company and visit its web site (www.krispykreme.com).

QUESTIONS

1. Using Figure 18.1 and Table 18.1 as models, describe Krispy Kreme's inputs, transformation process, outputs, feedback, and control systems.

2. How would you apply six-sigma principles to making doughnuts?

CHAPTER CLOSING CASE   No. 18

Building a Better Bicycle

John Sortino was disgusted that his $900 mountain bike needed brake and derailleur adjustments after he'd ridden it only twice. He was so dissatisfied that he founded the Chicago Bicycle Company to build a better bike.

Years earlier, John had founded the Vermont Teddy Bear Company and built it into the world's largest stuffed animal mail-order house. He took it public, retired from active management, and decided to use his equity, worth about $4 million, to fund the bicycle venture.

John wanted a high-end cruising bike with a comfortable seat, upright handlebars, fenders, and a hassle-free, internally geared hub. He envisioned a dependable bike that would be fun to ride and require minimal maintenance. "I studied the industry and was amazed that nobody made anything quite like that," says John. "I thought there would be a big market for people over 40 who don't like mountain bikes and can't find anything else."

Manufacturing in Chicago   He hired a technician to design his bike and recruited George Gregoire as chief operating officer. George had been chief financial officer of Cannondale Europe BV, a $40 million division of Cannondale Corporation, best known for its mountain bikes. And, although John lives in Burlington, Vermont (where the company's design center and marketing department remain), he leased manufacturing space in Chicago because it was once the bicycle-making capital of North America, "and we want to rebuild that industry."

John and George decided not to buy key components from Japanese giant Shimano, which dominates the market for derailleurs, crankshafts, and brake sets. "Not only must you pay Shimano cash up front," says George, "you have to order the parts 30 days before Shimano runs them. After 30 to 50 days in transit, the parts spend another month in your production system. You build the bikes and ship them to dealers, but most dealers can't afford to buy the inventory outright. The manufacturer ends up financing the receivables, often for four months or more."

As a result, 200 days might pass between the time the manufacturer pays for parts and the point at which it receives cash from sales. "When you have to make the bikes that far ahead," says George, "you can only guess which colors and style will be hot. By August, leftovers are deeply discounted because you're getting into your next season."

Selling Bicycles Directly to Consumers   John's strength is marketing. At Vermont Teddy Bear, he relied heavily on radio advertising and sold directly to customers who called a toll-free number. He plans to sell Chicago Bicycle products the same way. By building bikes to order and running the firm on a cash basis, John thinks he can be much more profitable than other bike marketers.

Direct manufacturing costs of Chicago Bicycle's first model averaged $432, versus an industry norm of about $300 for a comparable cruiser. Costs should drop as volume builds, but John plans to hold prices firm—$725 for a three-speed, up to $950 for a seven-speed bike. George argues that the high price won't deter the upscale consumers the company is targeting. High-end cruisers, he says, typically sell in the $800 to $900 range domestically and for $1,000 to $1,200 in Europe. He also believes that expensive mountain bikes have removed much of the price sensitivity from the bicycle market.

Bicycle dealers are not so sure. Andrew Kelly, general manager of Metro Bicycles, a seven-store New York City chain, says, "Almost every company out there is making similar bikes, from basic beach cruisers at $230 to models over $800. Obviously, some people will question spending almost $1,000 for a bike, so I think price will be an issue."

Establishing Relationships with Dealers   Most people will hear about Chicago Bicycle from a radio ad. Those who call the toll-free number will talk to a sales representative and receive a brochure and color chart. Customers can then order the bike directly from the factory. Those who want to see the bike first or who want to buy through a local dealer will be able to go to a bike shop in each of the advertising markets. Metro Bicycles, for example, is the New York dealer. "When a customer buys through us, we will special-order the bicycle," says Kelly, "and either assemble it here and deliver it or drop-ship it to their home."

Dealers get demo models only, so they don't have to carry inventory, saving on warehouse costs and floor space, and reducing the risk of unsold stock. For those savings, John expects dealers to settle for below-average margins of 20 percent instead of the usual 30 to 40 percent.

For prospects who ask how Chicago Bicycle, given the quality of the components, can retail a bike for less than $1,000, George offers three reasons: "We're not carrying finance costs like everyone else; we have much lower obsolescence losses; and dealer markups are lower. The customer makes out and we make out."

Source: Adapted from "A Bicycle Built for You", by Jay Finegan, from *Inc.: The Magazine for Growing Companies,* 80–89. Copyright ©1996 by Goldhirsh Group/Inc Pubg. Reproduced with permission of Goldhirsch Group/Inc Pubg in the format textbook via copyright Clearance Center.

QUESTIONS

1. What issues facing small business manufacturers does this case illustrate?

2. What are the two biggest problems Chicago Bicycle faces? How could they be solved?

3. John Sortino plans to concentrate on production of his bikes rather than distributing them through established dealers. Is this a mistake? Why or why not?

Complete Sample Business Plans

The following business plans are reprinted by permission. They were written by undergraduate business students at Mesa State College in Grand Junction, Colorado, as part of a class in small business management. These plans (one for a retail business, one for a service business) are about fictitious (at least for now) businesses and are included to serve as examples of structure, content, and format for your business plan.

Excalibur Traditional Men's Clothier Ltd. (Excalibur)

Executive Summary

*This is what quality is all about: the customer's perception of excellence.
And quality is our response to that perception.*
—Tom Peters

Excalibur Traditional Men's Clothier Ltd. (Excalibur) by and through its owners has created this comprehensive business plan in order to invite First of America Bancorp to assist Excalibur in raising the needed capital of $80,000 to begin the operations of a men's clothing store in Monroe, Michigan.

The Program

The development of Excalibur can be attributed to the two principal investors, B. Mark Springsteel and Karl E. Hall. A men's clothing store, yes, but that is where the similarity ends. By reintroducing an old concept— "customer service and satisfaction"— Excalibur intends to aggressively promote its *value-added* pricing policy to attract the professional businessman. It is the intention of Excalibur to assist the executive in image building through successful marketing of the proper apparel for his position in the company. Inasmuch as the only available service is off-the-rack-type purchasing, Excalibur intends to tailor-make to the needs of the customer. Excalibur will also provide the service of going to the office of the executive for proper measurements and selection of fabric, color, and styling, if need be. Excalibur is confident that the professional male is more than willing to pay for this type of value-added service. A survey of the Monroe area indicated there was no store that catered to the executive.

The principals of Excalibur are confident that there is a strong demand for this type of merchandise, which is not available in the Monroe area. Monroe is a bedroom community for both the Detroit Metro and Toledo areas; however, the principals discovered that executives preferred to shop in their home community as opposed to either metropolitan area, provided that the merchandise they sought was available to them.

The Plan

Financial projections for Excalibur indicate that an investment of approximately $80,000, in addition to the principals' investment of $100,000, is required for a startup cost in order to initiate operations. These funds will be committed to beginning inventory and store equipment and supplies, and will provide working capital for the first year of operations.

The Players

Excalibur has three distinct and complementary players. B. Mark Springsteel, president, brings to Excalibur his expertise in the area of finance and marketing, along with retail sales and management experience. Karl Hall, treasurer, with his varied background in accounting and finance, has the hands-on experience and know-how of the internal workings of a small business. Craig Hall, who will manage the store, in the past developed his own clientele base while employed with a men's retail store in the Monroe area. His ease with people and his ability to merchandise add to the diversity of this group.

The Game Summary

Collectively, the players have spent the past five months developing the concept and image of Excalibur. With confidence in their abilities, knowledge, and professionalism, the players anticipate a net profit in the first year of operations.

Table of Contents

Concept History and Background

Description of Product

The merchandise being offered by Excalibur Traditional Men's Clothier Ltd. will consist of men's professional wear: business suits of the finest quality along with dress slacks and sports jackets. In addition, Excalibur will offer accessories to complement the professional's image: dress shirts, ties, sweaters, vests, socks, belts, and undergarments. Seasonal wear, such as overcoats, gloves, and scarves, will also be available.

Idea History

The concept of Excalibur was first discussed in late 1993 by K. Evan Hall and his brother, Craig. However, the plan never proceeded beyond the preliminary discussions, and ultimately the idea never materialized. At the beginning of this year, K. Evan Hall approached Mark Springsteel with the business idea. Subsequent talks evolved into a decision to form the corporation.

Summary of Principals' Experience

K. Evan Hall completed his bachelor's degree in business administration with a finance major from Mesa State College, Grand Junction, Colorado. Mr. Hall's experience includes five years in retail sales, ten years in accounting, and seven years in personnel management.

B. Mark Springsteel also completed his bachelor's degree in business administration with a finance major from Mesa State College. Mr. Springsteel's experience includes six years in retail sales and three years in retail management. He also has broad experience in valuation of the stock of retail clothing companies.

Craig Hall is in the process of working toward a degree in business management. Hall's 19 years of retail sales experience will allow him to act in the capacity of sales manager for Excalibur. In addition, he has represented several retail stores, such as Neiman-Marcus, Bally, and Steve Petix, in the capacities of buyer, merchandiser, and advertising and sales manager.

Goals and Objectives

The main, long-term goal of Excalibur Traditional Men's Clothier Ltd. is to open a chain of men's clothing stores in the midwestern area of the United States. The initial capital requested will go toward the purchase of inventory, fixtures, and an initial place of business. After the first store is established in the Monroe County, Michigan, area, expansion into other areas of the Midwest will be implemented.

The final goal is to position Excalibur as the archetype of the finest in men's clothing retailers. This will be accomplished through sincere and unyielding service to our clientele and uncompromising dedication to selling quality products at prices that reflect the value-added features of our stores.

Management feels that the main target customer—namely, the professional male—is currently seeking such a store and has become frustrated with the lack of style and value currently available through retail outlets. This clientele will be willing to pay a premium for such value-added features as personalized attention, custom fitting, and "office-call" measurements (measurements done at the client's office or home).

The following one-year objectives have been determined by management:

1. Rent, remodel, and occupy the store in the Monroe, Michigan, area upon receiving debt financing.
2. Purchase fixtures and inventory.
3. Hire competent, professional sales staff.
4. Advertise innovatively and heavily toward our target market.
5. Establish immediate cash inflows sufficient to meet 18-month breakeven point.

Intermediate goals are to establish a strong base and system of operations at the Monroe, Michigan, location from which to launch other branches. This means establishing an early breakeven point and developing rapid profit growth at the Monroe, Michigan, store in order to support the expansions.

In addition, management has established the following five-year goals:

1. Average 20 percent annual growth rate as measured by revenues
2. Total sales over $5 million for the first five years combined
3. Net income before taxes expected to be $250,000 for that same period
4. The opening of a second Excalibur store

In order to establish our reputation as the finest in men's clothing, the following criteria for success will be kept in mind:

1. Focus on the value-added service features to our clientele and build within them an emotional attachment to Excalibur.
2. Incorporate a high-spirited, yet professional atmosphere among employees by respecting their skills and humanity, both monetarily and by treating them with autonomy.
3. Develop a culture and value system that pivots and grows from a passion for excellence in product and superiority in service.
4. Grow without becoming big. Be profitable without being greedy. Maintain sharp pencils and sharp minds without losing the gracefulness of flexibility.

Marketing Plan

Market Profile—Consumers and Demand

The typical customer for Excalibur products will be a professional male between the ages of 21 and 64 earning a median income of $37,500 annually. Management believes that any ancillary demand will be derived from this customer; therefore, any forecasted demand is inclusive of this group. In addition, the principal decision makers will be of this customer profile, and consequently any promotions will be directed toward this group. Within our customer group reside five subcategories segmented according to age. The following are descriptions of each subcategory:

Generation Xers

Age	21–24
Income	$20,000–$30,000
Family	Married, no children
Occupation	Salesman, intern, entrepreneur
Personality	Progressive, trendsetter
Percentage Demand	5 percent

In Betweens

Age	25–34
Income	$25,000–$35,000
Family	Married with young children
Occupation	Salesman, entrepreneur, middle manager
Personality	Risk sensitive, trend follower
Percentage Demand	15 percent

Young Baby Boomers

Age	35–44
Income	$30,000–$45,000
Family	Full nest or divorced single parent
Occupation	Manager, professional service provider (e.g., attorney)
Personality	Risk averse, conservative
Percentage Demand	25 percent

Older Baby Boomers

Age	45–54
Income	$40,000–$60,000
Family	Married or divorced with older children
Occupation	Manager, professional service provider
Personality	Risk averse, conservative
Percentage Demand	35 percent

The Old Guard

Age	55–64
Income	$50,000 and up
Family	Empty nest
Occupation	Senior manager, early retiree
Personality	Risk averse, conservative
Percentage Demand	20 percent

Management anticipates a strong demand for Excalibur products due to two important demographic features of the Detroit PMSA in which Excalibur is located. First, Monroe County itself has a relatively high median family income of $40,532, which management believes will help support demand for the premium-quality goods that Excalibur will market. Second, the city of Monroe is a bedroom community for both Detroit to the north and Toledo, Ohio, to the south. Management presupposes that much of the demand will come from the professionals who work in these cities but reside in Monroe. The following table shows the statistics and estimates used to calculate demand:

Monroe County statistics

Total population	135,962
Males per 100 females	97.2
Total males	66,077
Percentage within Excalibur's age range	56.40%
Males within Excalibur's age range	37,267

Age group	21–24	25–34	35–44	45–54	55–64	Totals
Percentage total males	5.30%	16.30%	15.50%	10.80%	8.50%	56.40%
Number of males	3,502	10,771	10,242	7,136	5,617	37,267
Estimated derived demand	8.00%	12.00%	15.00%	18.00%	12.00%	
Customer base by age group	280	1,292	1,536	1,285	674	5,067

As with the startup of any new business, the estimation of a product's demand is replete with assumptions; however, management believes this to be a conservative estimate of demand for Excalibur products. Additionally, the 5,067 customer base seems sufficient for revenue needs. This customer base is anticipated to stay fairly constant, due to a slow growth rate of approximately 1 percent per annum in Monroe County.

Market Profile—Competitors

The management of Excalibur used the following information to evaluate past and present competition:

		Reasons for Failure			
	Names	Competition	Poor Management	Under-capitalization	Lack of Knowledge
Top Hat					
Men's Wear	yes	no	yes	yes	yes
Uptown Clothing	yes	no	no	yes	no
J. C. Penney					
Southern					
Monroe City	yes	no	no	yes	yes
Creeks Brothers	no	no	no	yes	yes

Direct and Indirect Competition

	Price (H, M, L)	Location (B, W, S)	Facility (B, W, S)	Direct/ Indirect	Rank (1 = Most, 10 = Least)
T.J.'s Mens'					
Clothing	M	Same	Same	Direct	1
*Sears	L	Better	Better	Indirect	6
*J. C. Penney	L	Better	Better	Indirect	5
Sachs	H	Better	Better	Indirect	3
Macy's	H	Better	Better	Indirect	7
*Elder Berman	M-H	Better	Better	Indirect	2
*Hudson's	M-H	Better	Better	Indirect	4

*Indicates mall locations.

Four businesses offering approximately the same product as Excalibur are no longer in the competitive market. Three of the former competitors were located in or near downtown Monroe. Top Hat Men's Wear and Creeks Brothers were situated on the main street through downtown Monroe. Uptown Clothing was within walking distance of the downtown locale. Excalibur will be located in the same proximity as the former competitors.

Both Top Hat Men's Wear and Uptown Clothing were forced to close their doors because of poor management decisions. Both businesses attempted to leave their respective market niches and expand the existing product lines in order to compete with Sears and J. C. Penney. Sears and J. C. Penney both established new locations in a mall just north of the city of Monroe. Top Hat Men's Wear and Uptown Clothing were no longer able to meet the demands of their customers after adding to their product lines. Customers then sought other locations to fulfill their demands. Shopping in Toledo and the malls became the norm for local residents.

Both Top Hat and Uptown faced the same problems: outdated products, too large a product line to compete, and overpricing due to lack of business. Additionally, poor credit and accounts receivable management haunted both businesses.

Creeks Brothers Men's Wear recently closed its doors. The proprietor passed away, and the family lost interest in the retail business. Upon talking with the eldest son, he indicated a loss of market share because of outdated goods. Trying to deplete current inventory and reestablish an updated inventory was just not feasible at this time.

Creeks Brothers, Top Hat, and Uptown were all direct competitors. The only local indirect competitor to discontinue operations was J. C. Penney, located in southern Monroe County. This store was also in close proximity to downtown Monroe. J. C.

Penney continued to operate both stores because of the distance between locations. Although prices were about the same, the mall store continued to attract the business, and J. C. Penney finally made the decision to close the old store. Another factor prime to the decision was a fire that swept through half the shopping center where the old J. C. Penney was located.

The chart also shows how the management of Excalibur ranked both direct and indirect competition. Management believes that reestablishing a downtown Monroe location will produce enough business traffic to be successful. In the past, clothing stores in Monroe have all met with success. Keeping abreast of market demand, service, and quality goods has been the common denominator for these types of businesses.

New Business Strengths and Weaknesses

Strengths

1. Excalibur will supply the current demand for a quality product, which is nonexistent in Monroe County.
2. Commitment to professional personal service, along with custom fitting and quick turnaround tailoring for our customers.

Weaknesses

1. Excalibur will be selling at premium prices which will be recession sensitive. To combat this weakness, cash flows and retained earnings will be kept at higher levels than the industry average.
2. Reintroducing the concept of professional service and adding to it a premium price.

Excalibur will attack this problem head on by using aggressive ad campaigns and personal selling, and through the satisfied customers' word-of-mouth advertising.

Geographic Market

The geographic market for Excalibur will include a 20-mile radius from our location in downtown Monroe. Although this radius extends into other counties, we remain committed to establishing Monroe County as our geographic market, and any business that develops from outside Monroe County will be incidental and appreciated.

Although most of the competition, both direct and indirect, has mall locations and similar products, the management of Excalibur believes that the professional service and quality products offered will enable us to establish a customer base. Our intention is to draw the bedroom community workers away from the competition, both in Toledo and in the Detroit PSMA, back to Monroe to purchase their professional wear.

Pricing Policy

Excalibur will employ several pricing theories in the operation of its business.

1. The pricing strategy for our main product line, professional men's wear, will requisition a unique value-added price. The value-added price embodies personal service, custom tailoring, and delivery of a quality product.
2. The product lines of sports jackets and dress pants will entail a status quo pricing strategy, along with the value-added strategy for quality and service.

3. Accessories and complements to professional men's wear will be priced using a status quo pricing policy.

The value-added component of the pricing strategy for Excalibur will not remove us from the competitive market. On the contrary, we anticipate that the prestige pricing policy established at Excalibur will distinguish us from the rest of the competition. Most of the competition does not offer, on the same scale, the type of personal service or quality of merchandise of Excalibur. We firmly believe that our customer base is willing to purchase a quality product and professional service at a premium price.

Promotion

Excalibur's promotional strategy will focus on delivering a clear, concise message distinctly directed to the extent possible toward the previously described target customer. All advertising, personal selling, and merchandising will have a common core and fulcrum in the philosophy that, to sell quality, one must manifest quality in all that one does. The real-world application of this philosophy demands that all promotions communicate, both explicitly and implicitly, to the target market, our quality and value-added properties.

More specifically, Excalibur's advertising will focus on newspaper and radio. Management plans to utilize the daily newspapers, the *Toledo Blade* and the *Monroe Evening News,* along with the weekly *Frenchtown News.* Newspapers will be Excalibur's primary advertising medium, based on two assumptions. First, management concludes that the target customers are very apt to read the newspaper regularly. Second, because the demand for the products that Excalibur will market is based on visual appeal, newspaper advertising will have more impact due to its visual nature. For this reason, newspaper ads will be used somewhat uniformly and continuously throughout the year. A heavier emphasis will be placed on this type of advertising prior to and during high seasonally driven demand. During the seasonal demand times, radio advertising will be used to augment the base of newspaper advertising. The concentration of radio advertising will be on radio stations that appeal to the target markets. However, because radio audiences are segmented primarily by age, Excalibur will be able to target only a section of the whole target market with each advertisement. To use the medium of radio as a comprehensive demand inducer, a variety of radio stations will need to be employed. Primarily radio stations with an older listenership will be used, because the majority of the customer base is in an older category.

In addition to the above, Excalibur will sponsor an annual charitable fund raiser in the form of an auction of men dressed in suits from Excalibur. The bidders will bid for dates with these men, and the proceeds will benefit charities that the management of Excalibur deems appropriate at the time.

The service that Excalibur delivers with its personal selling will be the distinctive character of the business. The management wishes to position itself in the midst of consumers as the epitome of superior customer service. To do this, Excalibur will offer such services as "office-call" measuring, custom fitting, and quick-turnaround tailoring. Initial training and continual education of the sales staff will be of the utmost importance to support a high level of service. The management of Excalibur is committed to such training and education. These types of value-added services for our customers will initiate a word-of-mouth advertising campaign.

Legal Requirements

The law firm of Dewey, Cheatum, and Howe has been retained to serve as legal counsel for all of Excalibur's contracts, agreements, and other legal concerns. This law firm will also represent Excalibur in the event of a suit brought by or against Excalibur.

Contracts

The contracts that are relevant to the operation of Excalibur include a site lease agreement and licenses to sell certain products. The management expects to sign standard agreements with most suppliers with regard to shipping arrangements and agreements to sell. These will be reviewed and accepted on an individual basis. As of the writing of this plan, the signatures of both the president and the treasurer are required for a contract to be agreed to by Excalibur, but, as laid down in the bylaws, this requirement can be changed by vote of the shareholders.

Insurance

It is impossible to cover every risk contingency, but the management believes that ample insurance coverage is a necessity in today's litigious climate. Management also understands that the best way to deal with risk is to plan for it and work to reduce it. Under these considerations, Excalibur will carry a strong insurance package. Liability insurance will be carried to cover injuries to the person or property of customers. Workers' compensation will be carried in accordance to state statutes. In addition, key-employee insurance will be included to cover the contingency of the death or disability of key personnel. All employees with access to funds will be bonded.

Form of Ownership

The form of ownership that the management has elected to use is the subchapter S corporation form. There are numerous positive aspects to this form of ownership, including

- The fact that S corporations are taxed as partnerships.
- The limited liability faced by the shareholders.
- The transferability of ownership.
- The continuity of life of the corporation.
- The ability to increase equity capital by selling shares.

Each one of these advantages can be found in other forms of ownership, but the management feels that the mix of advantages found with this form are the best suited for this enterprise. A partnership would have left any general partners open to unlimited liability. The form of a C corporation would have entailed double taxation and reduced the ability of Excalibur to retain the earnings needed for growth. A limited-liability company would have been the next best option, but because its only advantage would be its ability to have unlimited shareholders and because we believe we will not need more than the 35 shareholders legally allowed to an S corporation, the limited-liability company seemed like an incorrect match for our purposes.

A copy of the articles of incorporation and the bylaws for Excalibur can be found on pages 618–620.

Financial Plan and Requirements

Initial Capitalization Plan

The startup costs required by Excalibur are outlined in the following pages. As indicated by the plan, the required financing to launch Excalibur into operation is $126,975. With capitalization from the principals of $50,000, along with the principals' loan to Excalibur for $50,000, the company requires additional financing in the amount of $80,000. We fully anticipate receiving the necessary funding from First of America Bancorp in Monroe, Michigan. The terms of the debt will be 1 percent over prime, or an 11 percent rate of interest on the principal. Required debt payments during our first year in operation will apply $12,700 to the principal balance and $8,172 to interest.

The principal players for Excalibur have agreed to accept responsibility for a portion of the required funding for startup costs. A schedule listing their respective liabilities for payment can be found in the Initial Capitalization Plan. The principals consider the "Total Other Costs" as sunk costs and accept the risk associated with these costs in the formation of a new business venture.

Projected Income

Forecasted net income for Excalibur's first year is expected to be $5,281. This takes into account the debt payment to First of America Bancorp. Other pertinent information regarding income and expense for 20— can be found in detail in the Forecasted Income Statement. The Projected Income Statement, Balance Sheets, and Statement of Cash Flows for Excalibur can be viewed in the following pages.

Pro Forma Statements

Excalibur Initial Capitalization Plan
Initial Capitalization

Inventory:

Suits	Sizes 36R to 48L	$ 58,000
Dress shirts	Sizes 14 to 18, Long & Short Slv	4,000
Ties	Assorted	3,600
Casual shirts	Sizes 14 to 18, Long and Short Slv	2,500
Dress slacks	Sizes 28 to 42, Assorted	5,000
Sport coats	Sizes 36R to 48L	7,000
Sweaters	Assorted Colors, Sm to XL	2,500
Overcoats	All Weather, Sizes 36R to 48L	7,500
Casual jackets	Assorted 36R to 48L	6,500
Belts	Assorted Sizes and Lengths	1,150
Socks	Assorted, Sizes 8 to 13	1,500
Undergarments:		
Briefs	Sizes 28 to 42	300
Boxers	Sizes 28 to 42	325
T-shirts	Sizes 28 to 42	300
Scarves	Assorted Colors and Lengths	900
Gloves	Assorted Sizes, Black and Brown	1,100
Miscellaneous	Tie-Tacks, Buttons, Cuff Links, etc.	1,200
Total Beginning Inventory		$103,375

Retail Store:

Equipment	(Desks, racks, file cabinets, mannequins, phone, shelves, etc.)	$ 20,000
Supplies	(Letterhead, envelopes, stamps, etc.)	3,600
Total Retail Store		$ 23,600

Other Costs:

Advertising, initial campaign	$ 4,500
Legal fees associated with license and registration	3,500
Heat, light, power, and telephone hookup, initial startup costs/deposits	2,000
Computer equipment deposit, secure equipment	1,000
Insurance deposit, fees associated with startup policy	300
Miscellaneous items (keys, alarm fees, safe setup)	450
Total Other Costs	$ 11,750
Total Initial Capitalization Costs	$138,725
Less Principals' Portion:	
K. Hall, 50% of 75% of Total Other Costs	(4,406)
B. Springsteel, 50% of 75% of Total Other Costs	(4,406)
C. Hall, 25% of Total Other Costs	(2,938)
Required Financing (Inventory $103,375; Retail Store $23,600)	$126,975

Excalibur
Forecasted Income Statement
20—

	Total	Jan	Feb	March	April	May	June	July	Aug	Sept	Oct	Nov	Dec
Sales	$810,000	$39,919	$32,756	$30,496	$35,107	$42,363	$52,894	$60,875	$76,707	$91,583	$102,141	$117,450	$127,709
COGS	283,500	13,972	11,465	10,674	12,287	14,827	18,513	21,306	26,847	32,054	35,749	41,108	44,698
Gross Margin	$526,500	$25,947	$21,291	$19,822	$22,820	$27,536	$34,381	$39,569	$49,860	$59,529	$66,392	$76,343	$83,011
Expenses													
Advertising:													
Mediums	$30,000	$2,500	$2,500	$2,500	$2,500	$2,500	$2,500	$2,500	$2,500	$2,500	$2,500	$2,500	$2,500
Postage	5,000	417	417	417	417	417	417	417	417	417	417	417	417
Depreciation	2,800	233	233	233	233	233	233	233	233	233	233	233	233
Wages:													
Employee	80,760	6,730	6,730	6,730	6,730	6,730	6,730	6,730	6,730	6,730	6,730	6,730	6,730
Commissions	20,250	998	819	762	878	1,059	1,322	1,522	1,918	2,290	2,554	2,936	3,193
Officers' Salary	100,000	8,333	8,333	8,333	8,333	8,333	8,333	8,333	8,333	8,333	8,333	8,333	8,333
Tailor Expense	81,000	3,992	3,276	3,050	3,511	4,236	5,289	6,088	7,671	9,158	10,214	11,745	12,771
Benefits	8,289	691	691	691	691	691	691	691	691	691	691	691	691
Payroll Taxes	30,152	2,409	2,382	2,374	2,391	2,418	2,458	2,488	2,547	2,603	2,643	2,700	2,738
Credit Card Expense	8,505	419	344	320	369	445	555	639	805	962	1,072	1,233	1,341
H, L, & P	11,800	983	983	983	983	983	983	983	983	983	983	983	983
Telephone	4,200	350	350	350	350	350	350	350	350	350	350	350	350
Store Supplies	3,200	1,500	155	155	155	155	155	155	155	155	155	155	155
Lease Expense, Computer	22,800	1,900	1,900	1,900	1,900	1,900	1,900	1,900	1,900	1,900	1,900	1,900	1,900
Repair/Maintenance	3,700	308	308	308	308	308	308	308	308	308	308	308	308
Miscellaneous Expense	4,300	1,500	255	255	255	255	255	255	255	255	255	255	255
Dues/Subscriptions	1,200	100	100	100	100	100	100	100	100	100	100	100	100
Travel/Entertainment	9,500	792	792	792	792	792	792	792	792	792	792	792	792
Donations	2,500	625	625	625	625								
Rent	22,592	2,884	1,792	1,792	1,792	1,792	1,792	1,792	1,792	1,792	1,792	1,792	1,792
Legal/Accounting	8,400	3,500	445	445	445	445	445	445	445	445	445	445	445
Insurance	3,500	292	292	292	292	292	292	292	292	292	292	292	292
State Sales Tax	48,600	2,395	1,965	1,830	2,106	2,542	3,174	3,653	4,602	5,495	6,128	7,047	7,663
Interest Expense	8,172	733	724	715	706	696	686	678	667	656	648	637	627
Total Expenses	$521,220	$43,959	$35,785	$35,951	$36,236	$37,672	$40,385	$41,342	$44,486	$48,064	$49,534	$52,574	$55,233
Net Income	$5,281	($18,012)	($14,494)	($16,129)	($13,416)	($10,136)	($6,004)	($1,773)	$5,374	$11,465	$16,857	$23,769	$27,778

Excalibur
Pro Forma Balance Sheet
January 31

Assets:
Cash	$ 52,325
Inventory	103,375
P, P, & E	20,000
Less: Depreciation	$ 0
Net P, P, & E	20,000
Prepaid Rent	4,300
Total Assets	$180,000

Liabilities:
Notes Payable:	
Shareholders	$ 50,000
Bank, Current Portion	12,700
A/P	32,213
LTD	67,300
Total Liabilities	$130,000
Owners' Equity	50,000
Total Liabilities and Owners' Equity	$180,000

Excalibur
Pro Forma Balance Sheet
December 31

Assets:
Cash	$ 47,335
Inventory	137,750
P, P, & E	20,000
Less: Depreciation	$ 2,800
Net P, P, & E	17,200
Prepaid Rent	2,508
Total Assets	$204,793

Liabilities:
Notes Payable:	
Shareholders	$ 50,000
Bank, Current Portion	14,170
LTD	53,129
Total Liabilities	$149,512
Owners' Equity	55,281
Total Liabilities and Owners' Equity	$204,793

Excalibur
Projected Income Statement
Year Ended 20—

Sales	$810,000
COGS	283,500
Gross Margin	$526,500
Expenses:	
Advertising	$ 35,000
Depreciation	2,800
Wages/Salaries	201,010
G, S, & A	194,645
Professional Fees	8,400
Rent	22,592
State Sales Tax	48,600
Net Income Before Interest	$ 13,453
Interest Expense	8,172
Net Income	$ 5,281

Excalibur
Statement of Cash Flows
Year Ended December 31, 20—

Cash flows from operating activities:			
Net Income, per Income Statement	$ 5,281		
Add:			
Depreciation	$ 2,800		
Increase Accounts Payable	32,213		
Decrease Prepaid Expenses	1,792	$36,805	$42,086
Less:			
Purchases	$ 103,375		
Increase in inventory	34,375	137,375	
Net cash flow from operating activities:	($ 95,289)		
Cash flows from financing activities:			
Cash received, Note Payable (Bank)	$ 80,000		
Cash received, Note Payable (Owners)	50,000	130,000	
Net cash from financing	$ 130,000		
Cash flows from investing activities:			
Less:			
Purchase P, P, & E	$ 20,000		
Payment of Note Payable,			
bank principal & interest	19,701	39,701	
Net cash flow from investing activities	($ 39,701)		
Increase/(Decrease) in cash flow	($ 4,990)		
Cash at beginning of the year	$ 52,325		
Cash at the end of the year	$ 47,335		

Organization, Management, and Staffing Plan

The Management and Organization

The management team of Excalibur represents an exciting mix of retail industry knowledge, business management skills, and experience in clothing sales. B. Mark Springsteel and Karl E. Hall will serve as president and treasurer, respectively, for Excalibur, and upon the inception of the corporation, both gentlemen will be the sole shareholders of the corporation. Craig Hall will serve as sales manager.

The résumés of all three gentlemen can be seen on the following pages, along with personal financial statements of the two equity shareholders.

Résumé
of
B. Mark Springsteel
Grand Junction, Colorado 81501

GOALS

My current goal is to become the co-owner and operator of a stable, growing men's clothier. I hope to see the company through the infancy and maturity stages, and then to divest myself of my share of the company, the proceeds of which I will use in other profitable ventures.

EDUCATION

I graduated from Mesa State College located in Grand Junction, Colorado, with a bachelor's degree in finance in 1990. My cumulative GPA was 3.96, and I received honors upon graduating.

WORK EXPERIENCE

Options Trader, Salomon Brothers Inc.   1993–1995

My main duty at Salomon Brothers was the trading of stock options on the Pacific Exchange. My main focus was stock options that derived their value from retail clothing stocks.

Stockbroker, Merrill Lynch & Co.   1991–1993

My duties at Merrill Lynch included the buying and selling of stock for over 40 accounts. I specialized in specialty retail clothing stocks, such as The Gap, and other broader retail stocks, such as Nordstrom.

Stockbroker Trainee, Merrill Lynch & Co.   1990–1991

During this time, I was trained specifically in the field of retail stocks for my subsequent duties as a stockbroker for Merrill Lynch.

Salesperson, Fridays Men's Clothing   1987–1990

This was a part-time position that I held during college. My responsibilities encompassed all duties in the retail sale of men's clothing, including measuring customers and selling, ordering, and stocking merchandise.

HONORS AND AWARDS

Rookie Broker of the Year, Merrill Lynch Co., 1991
Graduated Summa Cum Laude from Mesa State College
Who's Who Among Students in American Universities and Colleges, 1989
Third Place in Poetry, Mesa State College *The Literary Review,* 1989

Personal Financial Statements
of
B. Mark Springsteel

B. Mark Springsteel
Balance Sheet
April 30, 20—

Assets:			Liabilities:	
Current Assets:			Current Liabilities:	
Cash	$	756.00	Credit Card Debt	$ 532.00
Savings		2,193.00	Current Portion of	
Investments (value as of			Long-Term Debt	1,076.59
04/28/—):			Miscellaneous	
LSI Logic, 200 shares	$ 13,300.00		Short-Term Debt	152.36
Gap, Inc., 150 shares	4,781.25		Long-Term Liabilities:	
TeleEspana, 200 shares	5,493.75		Mortgage	58,263.54
Oppenheimer Fund,			Education Debt	7,638.00
GrowthA 500 shares	14,220.00			
Total Investments	$ 37,795.00			
Long-Term Assets:				
Condominium				
(appraised value)	$ 85,000.00			
Total Assets	$125,744.00		Total Liabilities	$67,662.49
Net Worth,				
B. Mark Springsteel	$ 58,081.51			
Total Liabilities and				
Net Worth	$125,744.00			

B. Mark Springsteel
Income Statement
Month Ended April 30, 20—

Monthly After-Tax Income	$3,256.25
Monthly Expenses:	
Mortgage	$ 820.27
Education Debt	256.32
Insurance	235.16
Automobile Lease	356.54
Telephone and Utilities	220.00
Food and Entertainment	321.54
Clothing	185.00
Miscellaneous Expenses	150.00
Total Monthly Expenses	$2,544.83
Monthly Net Income	$ 711.42

Résumé
of
Karl E. Hall
Parachute, Colorado 81635

GOALS

My current goal is to own a fine men's clothing store, catering to the executive. With my background and experience, I will provide the financial expertise to see the inauguration of the business and to guide the finances during its growth phase.

EDUCATION

I received my bachelor's degree in business administration from Mesa State College in Grand Junction, Colorado, and am in the process of working toward a master's of business administration. Other course work included financial planning seminars and banking seminars.

WORK EXPERIENCE

Financial Program Manager, U.S. Air Force   1992–1994

In this capacity, I developed and conducted comprehensive seminars on the effective uses of credit in today's society, and I wrote a financial guide for transitional and relocating military personnel based on the evaluation of personal finances, budgeting, and savings plans. In addition, I processed and disbursed funds for Air Force Aid Society (AFAS) loans to assist military personnel during emergencies and financial hardships.

Controller, Cutter Ceramics, Inc., MA   1990–1992

At this company, I was responsible for payroll, incoming and outgoing orders, and all financials. At this time I developed a spreadsheet program for tracking outstanding money orders, bank checks, and accounts payable checks.

Assistant to the Treasurer, Lexington Savings Bank, Lexington, MA   1989–1991

Among my duties were the completion of quarterly FDIC Call Reports, which included loan loss reserve calculation and the calculation of investment income for FNMA, FHLMC, Treasury bonds and notes, and other securities using computer software programs.

Customer Service Representative, Great Lakes Bancorp, Monroe, MI   1987–1988

In this capacity, I assisted new and existing customers in choosing financial products to meet their financial needs.

Military Experience   1982–1987

During my five years in the military, I received Air Force supervisory training as well as leadership training.

**Personal Financial Statements
of
Karl E. Hall**

**Karl E. Hall
Balance Sheet
April 30, 20—**

Assets:			Liabilities:	
Current Assets:			Current Liabilities:	
Cash	$ 1,050		Credit Card Debt	$ 1,076
Savings	13,596		Long-Term Liabilities:	
Investments:			Mortgages on Rentals	187,550
Current portion, LTD	$ 2,087		Education Debt	11,596
20th Ultra, 325 shares	3,54			
Berger 101 Fund, 475 shares	5,582			
Tenneco, Inc., 200 shares	9,224			
2 6-month CDs	2,096			
Total Investments	$ 20,448			
Long Term Assets:				
Real Estate Rental Property:				
Illinois				
(appraised value)	$136,850			
Michigan				
(appraised value)	104,900			
Total Assets	$276,844		Total Liabilities	$202,309
Net worth, K. E. Hall	$ 74,535			
Total Liabilities and				
Net Worth	$276,844			

**Karl E. Hall
Income Statement
For the Month Ended April 30, 20—**

Monthly After-Tax Income	$4,135
Monthly Expenses:	
Mortgage Payment	$1,958
Education Debt	325
Insurance	196
Auto Payment	225
Telephone and Utilities	215
Food and Entertainment	276
Clothing	100
Miscellaneous	75
Total Monthly Expenses	$3,370
Monthly Net Income	$ 765

Résumé
of
Craig R. Hall
Rochester Hills, Michigan 48309

GOALS

My current goal is to manage a men's retail outlet catering to the executive, in which I can best utilize my communication, organization, and merchandising skills. Future goals include assisting the executive in developing his image through the choice of proper apparel. I would also like to offer made-to-order clothing in situations in which it would not be necessary for the executive to leave his office to receive this service.

BUSINESS EXPERIENCE

Store Manager, Bally, Inc. 1994–Present

In this position I oversee all store operations, including staff management, inventory control, merchandising, promotional events, and daily business analysis.

Department Manager, Neiman-Marcus 1992–1994

Soon after I was hired, I became acting interim manager of men's clothing, during which time sales exceeded plan. I also initiated and implemented a program for special gift items and was responsible for contacting and arranging for personal appearances by designers. Within ten months after hire, I was promoted to manager of fashion accessories, a department grossing $1.2 million.

Duplication Specialist, Account Executive 1992

Chief duties here consisted of the management of major educational and municipal accounts.

Systems Specialist, Albin Business Copiers 1988–1991

During the time with Albin Business Copiers, I was Salesman of the Month five times.

ADDITIONAL EXPERIENCE

During the period 1982–1988, I was engaged in various retail and outside sales positions.

EDUCATION

I attended Monroe County Community College between 1980 and 1982, where I majored in marketing and management. In addition, I received training in Dallas with the Neiman-Marcus Sales Management Program as well as other intensive corporate programs which stressed sales and management techniques.

SUMMARY OF QUALIFICATIONS

Previous experience has proven my expertise in merchandising, buying, and display in a retail setting; success in managing and motivating sales associates through training, example, and leadership; strong organizational skills; the ability to compile and present reports concerning department status and fiscal goals; and excellent verbal and written communication skills.

Employee Requirements

Along with the above management, who will be active members of the sales team, two additional part-time employees will be required in order to serve the customer to the degree desired by management. The following chart is a tentative schedule which shows that at no time will there be fewer than three people on duty on any day. This is, of course, contingent on demand, and the principals have decided to err on the side of customer service and not on the side of cost cutting.

Tentative Weekly Schedule

	Monday	Tuesday	Wednesday	Thursday	Friday	Saturday	Sunday
President	O	O	O	O	O	O	X
Treasurer	O	O	O	O	O	O	X
Sales Manager	O	O	O	O	O	X	X
Salesperson 1	X	O	X	O	O	O	X
Salesperson 2	X	X	O	O	O	O	X

Note: O = on duty, X = off duty. Excalibur will be closed on Sunday.

The management believes that the human resource is the most valuable resource a business has. The people who work on the Excalibur team will be hired not simply on the merits of their experience and knowledge but also because of their potential to grow with the business.

The management of Excalibur has decided to outsource the tailoring services for a time, in order to see if demand for such services warrants hiring an in-house tailor. Again, the management will allow customer service to drive this decision.

Special Considerations

Facility Needs

The principals of Excalibur have signed an option to lease the facility located at 124 East Front Street, Monroe, Michigan. Due to the fact that this location was previously used as a retail clothing store, it will need very little reworking in order to fit Excalibur's needs. The location is 2,000 square feet, and the option states a lease price of $10.25 per square foot, the price of which includes building management fees.

Employee Training

Due to the high degree of customer service desired by the management, it is imperative that Excalibur have a highly trained staff. The goal is to ensure no less than 20 contact hours of training per employee per year. This training will focus on customer service, selling techniques, industry trends, teamwork, and management training. A battery of training sessions will be given to each new hire before any customer contact takes place. This training will include an introduction to the goals and direction of Excalibur and will attempt to instill an enthusiasm for the Excalibur team.

*Most people wish for riches, but few provide the definite plan and the burning desire
which pave the road to wealth.*
Napolean Hill

Articles of Incorporation
of
Excalibur Traditional Men's Clothier Ltd.

ARTICLE ONE
Name of Corporation

The name of the corporation is Excalibur Traditional Men's Clothier Ltd.

ARTICLE TWO
Period of Duration

The period of the duration of the corporation shall be perpetual.

ARTICLE THREE
Purposes and Powers

Purposes. The purpose for which the corporation is organized is the transaction of
all lawful business for which corporations may be incorporated pursuant to the Michigan Corporation Code.

Powers. The corporation shall have all of the rights, privileges, and powers now or
hereafter conferred upon corporations by the Michigan Corporation Code. The corporation shall have and may exercise all powers necessary or convenient to effect any of the
purposes for which the corporation has been organized.

ARTICLE FOUR
Capital Structure

Aggregate Shares, Classes, and Series. The aggregate number of shares that the
corporation shall have authority to issue is 1,000,000 shares of capital stock without par
value. The authorized shares are not to be divided into classes or series. There shall be
only one class of stock, which shall be common stock.

Consideration for Shares. Each share of stock, when issued, shall be fully paid and
nonassessable. The shares of the corporation may be issued for consideration as may be
fixed from time to time by the president and chief executive officer of the corporation.
Consideration may consist of money, property, services, or any consideration that the
president and chief executive officer of the corporation shall, in the absence of fraud or
bad faith, deem of appropriate value.

ARTICLE FIVE
Conditions to Commencement

The corporation will not commence business until it has received for the issuance
of its shares consideration of the value of $50,000.

ARTICLE SIX
Regulation of Internal Affairs

Bylaws. The initial bylaws shall be adopted by the shareholders. The power to alter,
amend, or repeal the bylaws or to adopt new bylaws shall be vested in the shareholders.
The bylaws may contain any provision for the regulation and management of the affairs
of the corporation not inconsistent with law or these articles of incorporation.

ARTICLE SEVEN
Initial Registered Office and Agent
The address of the corporation's registered office is 124 East Front Street, Monroe, Michigan, and the name of its agents at such address are Karl Evan Hall and Brian Mark Springsteel.

ARTICLE EIGHT
Cumulative Voting
Voting shall be done on a cumulative per-share basis. There will be no directors of the corporation, and the shareholders have sole power to repeal or amend the bylaws of the corporation.

ARTICLE NINE
Incorporators
The names and addresses of the incorporators are Karl Evan Hall, 1011 Main Street, Parachute, Colorado 81304, and Brian Mark Springsteel, 606 Chipeta Avenue, Grand Junction, Colorado 81501.

Incorporator Karl Evan Hall

Incorporator Brian Mark Springsteel

Sworn to on (date) by the above named incorporators.

Notary Public, Monroe County, Monroe, MI

Bylaws
of
Excalibur Traditional Men's Clothier Ltd.

ARTICLE ONE
Meetings of Shareholders

Annual Meetings. Meetings of the shareholders shall be held at the principal place of business of the corporation, located at 124 East Front Street, Monroe, Michigan, unless another place shall have been determined and notice has been given to all shareholders. Annual meetings shall be held on the twentieth day of the month of March, at 9:30 A.M., unless a holiday, and then on the next business day.

Special meetings. Special meetings may be called by any shareholder with a 10 percent or greater share of the total outstanding shares on 5 days' notice given personally or by telephone, telex, telegraph, or electronic mail, or on 14 days' notice by mail. Special meetings shall be pursuant on the aforementioned location and holiday requirements and restrictions.

Telephone or Video Meetings. The shareholders may participate in any meeting of the shareholders by means of conference telephone or similar communication equipment which enables all participants in the meeting to hear and speak to one another at the same time. Such participation shall constitute presence in person at the meeting.

ARTICLE TWO
Voting

Voting of Shares. Each outstanding share shall be entitled to one vote on each matter submitted to a meeting of shareholders.

Proxies. At the meeting of shareholders, a shareholder may vote in person or by proxy appointed in writing by the shareholder or by his duly authorized attorney-in-fact. Such writing must be shown at the meeting of the shareholders.

ARTICLE THREE
Informal Action by Shareholders

Any action required or permitted to be taken at a meeting of the shareholders may be taken without a meeting if consent in writing, setting forth the action to be taken, shall be signed by all of the shareholders entitled to vote with respect to the subject matter thereof.

ARTICLE FOUR
Officers

Number and Qualifications. The principal officers of the corporation shall be a president, a secretary, and a treasurer, each of whom shall be elected by the shareholders. Any two or more offices may be held by the same person, except the offices of president and secretary. The officers of the corporation shall be natural persons, 18 years of age or older.

Election and Term of Office. The principal officers shall be elected annually by vote of the shareholders at the annual meeting of the shareholders.

Removal of Officer. Any officer or agent may be removed by the shareholders whenever in their collective judgment the interests of the corporation shall be best served thereby. Such removal shall be without prejudice to the contract rights, if any, of the person so removed.

President. The president shall be the principal executive officer of the corporation and shall in general supervise and control all of the business and affairs of the corporation. The president shall, when present, preside at all the meetings of the shareholders. The president shall, at each annual meeting, present a report of the business of the corporation for the preceding fiscal year. The president may sign, with the secretary, certificates for shares of the corporation; any deeds, mortgages, bonds, contracts, or other instruments that the shareholders have authorized to be executed; and in general perform all duties incident to the office of president.

Secretary. The secretary shall (1) attend and keep the minutes of the proceedings of the shareholders; (2) see that notice of shareholder meetings is given; (3) be custodian of the corporate records and of the seal of the corporation, and see that the seal is affixed to any documents requiring the seal; (4) sign, with the president, certificates for shares of the corporation, or any deeds, mortgages, bonds, contracts, or other instruments that the shareholders have authorized to be executed; (5) keep a complete record of the shareholders on file and have general charge of the stockholder transfer books of the corporation; and (6) in general perform all duties incident to the office of secretary.

Treasurer. The treasurer shall (1) keep correct and complete books and records of account on file in the principal place of business of the corporation; (2) have custody of and be responsible for all funds and securities of the corporation; (3) receive monies due and payable to the corporation; (4) immediately deposit all corporate funds in a bank or other depository as may be designated by the shareholders; (5) disburse the funds of the corporation as may be ordered by the president or shareholders as a group; (6) render to the president and to the shareholders an account of all the transactions of the treasurer and the financial condition of the corporation; and (7) in general perform all duties incident to the office of treasurer.

Vice President. In the absence of the president or in the event of the president's death, inability, or refusal to act, the most senior vice president, but not if the vice president acts also as secretary, shall perform the duties of the president, and when so acting, shall have all the powers and be subject to all the restrictions of the office.

Salaries. The salaries of the officers shall be fixed from time to time by the shareholders, and no officer shall be prevented from receiving such salary by reason of the fact that he is also a shareholder of the corporation.

ARTICLE FIVE
Contracts, Loans, and Checks

Contracts. The shareholders may authorize any officer or officers, agent or agents, to enter into any contract or to execute and deliver any instrument in the name of and on behalf of the corporation, and such authority may be general or confined to specific instances or restricted as to time.

Loans. No loans shall be contracted on behalf of the corporation, and no evidence of indebtedness shall be issued in its name unless authorized by a voting of the shareholders. Such authority may be general or confined to specific instances.

Checks and Drafts. All checks, drafts, or other orders for the payment of money, notes, or other evidences of indebtedness issued in the name of the corporation shall be signed by both the president and the secretary of the corporation.

ARTICLE SIX
Certificates for Shares and Their Transfer

Certificates for Shares. Each purchaser of shares of the corporation shall be entitled to a certificate, signed by the president and secretary and sealed with the corporate seal or a facsimile thereof, certifying the number of shares owned in the corporation. Each certificate shall be consecutively numbered. The certificate representing shares shall state on the face that the corporation is organized under the laws of this state; the name of the person to whom issued; the number of shares; and a statement that the shares are without par value. Restrictions imposed on the transferability of the shares shall be noted conspicuously on the certificate.

Transfer of Shares. The name and address of the person to whom the shares represented thereby are issued, with the number of shares and date of issue, shall be entered on the stock transfer books of the corporation. All certificates surrendered to the corporation for transfer shall be canceled, and no new certificate shall be issued until the former certificate for a like number of shares shall have been surrendered and canceled. Transfer of the shares of the corporation shall be made only on the stock transfer books of the corporation by the holder of record thereof or by his or her legal representative, who shall furnish proper evidence of authority to transfer, or by an attorney thereunto authorized by power of attorney duly executed and filed with the secretary of the corporation, and on surrender for cancellation of the certificate for such shares. The person in whose name shares stand on the books of the corporation shall be deemed by the corporation to be the owner thereof for all purposes, except as otherwise authorized or provided in the bylaws.

ARTICLE SEVEN
Corporate Seal

The shareholders shall adopt a corporate seal. which shall be circular in form and shall have inscribed on the periphery the name of the corporation and the state of incorporation. In the center of the seal there shall be the word "Seal."

ARTICLE EIGHT
Miscellaneous

Fiscal Year. The fiscal year for the corporation shall run from March 1 to February 28, or 29 in the event of a leap year.

Shareholders' Inspection of Corporate Records. Any shareholder at any reasonable time may request to inspect and must be granted access within reasonable standards to the books, minutes, or other records of the corporation.

ARTICLE NINE
Amendments

The power to alter, amend, or repeal the bylaws or adopt new bylaws shall be vested in the shareholders. The bylaws may contain any provision for the regulation and management of the affairs of the corporation not inconsistent with law or the articles of incorporation.

BRONZE

Tanning Service & Salon

Business Plan

Business Plan Outline

Executive Summary

How many people do you know who enjoy having a suntan?

BRONZE Tanning Service & Salon is designed to target all of those people you know who love to worship the sun or just like to have a little color to their skin. *BRONZE* is an indoor tanning salon offering seven great tanning beds; a clean, friendly, warm environment; a masseuse; and a nail technician.

One of the major trends of the twentieth century is the importance of appearance. If you look good, you feel good. *BRONZE* immediately plays into this trend. People will do anything to enhance their appearance, and indoor tanning salons are a fairly inexpensive way of doing this.

Reprinted by permission of Lindy Casselman.

My main goals with this business are to maximize profits, satisfy my customers, and enjoy myself. It has always been a dream of mine to own my own business and be my own boss. *BRONZE* is the perfect way for all of these dreams to come true. I can enjoy myself and make a substantial living.

BRONZE will be located at 612 Main Street, in downtown Grand Junction, Colorado. This location offers great parking and accessibility, along with a very flexible floor plan. This property also has all of the electrical capabilities needed to open a tanning salon. With a few minor, inexpensive adjustments, this property will be quite suitable for the business I have planned. I enjoy the downtown area of Grand Junction and find it to be the perfect spot for a tanning salon.

Mesa County now supports three other similar tanning facilities. I plan to outprice these salons, while offering higher-quality equipment, additional salon services, and a superior atmosphere. The additional services I will provide consist of a subcontracted masseuse and a subcontracted nail technician. Both of these employees are somewhat on their own in terms of profit; however, they will rent space from me on a month-to-month basis. This is designed to give customers added enjoyment and convenience, while giving me an edge over my immediate competitors. Mesa County is growing at a fast pace and will be able to support another tanning salon.

Mesa County is my geographic market. My main target market consists of Caucasian females, ages 18 to 49. Through my research I have found that there are 27,912 people who fit this category in Mesa County. This makes my market penetration very easy. My goal is to get just 500 of these people to use my facilities twice a week for one year. This will allow me to reach and exceed my market penetration goal of 70 percent usage in the first year.

Grand Junction is a college town. Targeting college students along with high school students is also part of my business plan. I will offer special tanning package prices to these two groups of students. It is important to target these younger people. Word of mouth spreads very quickly among the school-age population, which can be a very beneficial and inexpensive source of advertising, crucial to a new business. My grand opening promotion consists of very inexpensive tanning services, designed to build a customer base as soon as possible.

I plan to break even financially with *BRONZE* after two years of operation. Utilizing 70 percent or more of my possible tanning hours is the key to paying my initial loan in full after two years of successful operation.

Tanning is an inexpensive service that is very appealing to a large majority of the population, especially in Mesa County. I am very excited about *BRONZE*. Many, many people enjoy being in the sun and having a bronze tan. With the right combination of marketing, management, and financial planning, *BRONZE* Tanning Service & Salon will be a success.

Business Description

Business Concept

People want to look great and feel great. Services that will help people acquire this feeling are a fine business choice.

I plan to open a tanning salon in the Grand Junction area. I will also offer a nail technician, a masseuse, a great atmosphere, and friendly service. Women as well as men take advantage of pampering. People will want to come in and enjoy this salon.

It is important for people to feel good about themselves and appreciate being who they are. Looking good is the first step in feeling better about yourself. Services such as tanning, manicure, and massage can help achieve the image people are looking for. I hope, by opening this business, to help people.

Business Name

The name of my business will be *BRONZE* Tanning Service & Salon. I will register this name through the Department of Revenue (see Appendix A). This name is available to use in the Grand Junction area.

Goals

BRONZE Tanning Service & Salon will be an escape from an ordinary job. Independence, profit, and enjoyment are my reasons for opening a business. I want the freedom to make my own decisions about business and life. Opening my own business is a huge commitment. With the right combination of attitude and business sense, *BRONZE* will be a huge success. I am willing to commit myself to this business and make things happen.

One of my goals is to break even in 24 months after opening *BRONZE*. My target breakeven date is January 1, 2004.

My main objective with *BRONZE* is to make a profit, while enjoying myself and my customers. I want to achieve customer satisfaction and gratification.

Industry Analysis

The indoor tanning industry is a large industry. The number of tanning salons nationally is outrageous. If there are 13 alone in Grand Junction, this means thousands, maybe even millions, of salons nationally. The average salon maintains a customer base of 2,053 patrons. As I said before, the trend nationally is that the better you look, the better you feel. Salons offering tanning and other services contribute to this trend.

In the Grand Junction area there are at least 13 indoor tanning facilities. Three of these facilities are tanning salons only. Ten of these facilities include hair, nail, fitness, massage, skin, chiropractic, spa, and even movie rental services. This is a large number of salons for a town this size. Therefore, the market is good in Grand Junction. The indoor tanning industry is growing on a local and national basis (see Appendix B).

Form of Ownership

BRONZE Tanning Service & Salon will be a sole proprietorship. I plan to open and run this business myself. Running my own business has always been a dream of mine. I see this as the perfect opportunity.

In order to run this business as a sole proprietorship, I have raised the necessary capital. I am liable for this business. I understand that being an entrepreneur is a risk.

I will also open a separate checking account for *BRONZE*. All business transactions will take place through this account.

Facility Requirements

In order to open *BRONZE* Tanning Service & Salon, I will need the following facilities:

- At least 2,000 square feet of space
- Electrical capabilities and installment
- Adequate parking

- Portable walls for separate rooms
- At least one bathroom facility

The location that I am aiming for is 612 Main Street in Grand Junction, Colorado. This space is currently for rent. It is a 3,000-square-foot unit, 25 feet across, containing one bathroom facility, with city parking directly across the street. Adequate electrical capability exists. Some minor wiring changes will have to take place. Portable walls may be installed and removed as I wish. I will also do some painting and redecorating. Other than these things, this facility is very adequate for this type of business. This facility will rent for $1,200 a month plus utilities.[1]

Sign

A sign will be necessary for the front of the building. I plan to order an Econo-Light sign for the storefront. This sign will be designed with as many colors as I wish. The sign will also be lit from behind. Econo-Light is a fairly new product which is inexpensive and long lasting. Many of the downtown businesses have gone to this type of sign for their storefronts. A sign like this runs anywhere from $800 to $1,000,[2] depending on the size of the sign.

Opening Date

BRONZE Tanning Service & Salon will open its doors on February 1, 2002. Opening on this day will allow us to work out any kinks in the system before the summer rush. The summer rush begins toward the end of February and the beginning of March. Customers will be preparing for the summer months. Proms for high school girls and spring break for college students are right around this time as well. This is the tanning industry's peak sales time. I want to make sure my doors are open and I am ready for business during this time.

Legal Requirements

There are several legal issues that I need to be aware of when opening my own business. Below is a checklist of things I need to do before opening my business:

- Register an employee tax identification number (see Appendix C).
- Register business through the Colorado Business Registration (see Appendix D).
- Contact OSHA.
- Find a licensed and certified masseuse and nail technician.
- Check into health codes and special permits.
- Inspect heating and electrical units in rental.
- Join the North American Alliance of Tanning Salon Owners.
- Update myself on new legislation in the indoor tanning industry.
- Have an accountant set up financial books, financial statements, and payroll.
- Have a lawyer look over or register me for lease agreement, retail sales tax, individual income tax, unemployment insurance, workers' compensation, property taxes, business insurance, and business liability.

---

[1]Quote from Grand Junction downtown property owner. Actual price of rental at 612 Main Street, Grand Junction.
[2]Quote from Angel Sign Company, Grand Junction.

Marketing Plan

Geographic Market

Mesa County, Colorado.

Customer Profile

My target market consists of Caucasian females, ages 18 to 49 (see Appendix B).

Potential Customers

The projected number of females, ages 18 to 49, in Mesa County is 28,540 (see Appendix E). In Mesa County, the Caucasian population makes up 97.8 percent of the total population (see Appendix F). Therefore, $28,540 \times .978 = 27,912.12$. My potential customer base is 27,912 Caucasian females.

Market Penetration

The projected market penetration number that I came up with reflects the possible number of tanning hours available at *BRONZE*. I will aim to use 70 percent of all possible tanning hours in the first year of operation.

My market penetration goal is 500 customers tanning twice a week for a year. This will give me 52,000 total tans in one year. This amount was calculated on the Market Penetration Worksheet (see Appendix G).

Competitive Analysis

Competition					
Establishment	**Quantity of Units**	**Types of Units**[a]	**Cleanliness**[b]	**Services Offered**[c]	**Overall Rating**[d]
Riviera Tanning	8	3 High 3 Medium 1 Standup	Satisfactory	Tanning only	8
Tan Perfection	7	4 High 3 Medium	Average	Tanning only	5
Tanfastic	6	6 Medium	Average	Tanning only	4
***BRONZE* Tanning Service & Salon**					
Establishment	**Quantity of Units**	**Types of Units**[a]	**Cleanliness**[b]	**Services Offered**[c]	**Overall Rating**[d]
BRONZE	7	3 High 3 Medium 1 Standup	Above satisfactory	Tanning, masseuse, nail technician	10

[a]There are many different types of units that are available to use in a tanning salon. They range from high-powered, hot beds to low-powered, cooler beds. Standup units are also available to maximize results.

[b]Cleanliness is very important to me as a consumer and as a business owner. Keeping a clean salon is one of my highest priorities. I graded each of my competitors by using above satisfactory, satisfactory, average, below average, and failing.

[c]My main competitors offer tanning services alone. I will offer a masseuse and nail technician as well.

[d]The final process in analyzing my competitors was to rank them on a scale from 1 to 10, with 10 being exceptional and 1 failing. The criteria consisted of overall service, technology, equipment, salon setup, results, convenience, decoration, and the desire I experienced to use their services again.

Pricing

Market penetration is my pricing strategy for the first month. Discounts will appeal to the customers, allowing us to show off the salon and establish a customer base.

I will offer a $5 discount on all tanning packages that I sell, along with a $1 discount on all individually purchased tans.

Grand Opening Promotion
(valid for February and March)

High-powered Unit	Packages
Individual tan $4	5 tans for $15
Medium-powered Unit	10 tans for $30
Individual tan $3	20 tans for $60
Standup Unit:	One-month unlimited tanning for $70
Individual tan $4	(all beds included in these prices)

I will use the market penetration pricing strategy for the first two months of business. March 1, 2002, I will begin using the status quo pricing approach, offering the same prices as my competition. I will incorporate some sporadic monthly specials or incentives into this pricing strategy.

Regular Prices

High-powered Unit	Packages
Individual tan $5	5 tans for $20
Medium-powered Unit	10 tans for $35
Individual tan $4	20 tans for $65
Standup Unit	One-month unlimited tanning for $75
Individual tan $5	(all beds included in these prices)

Promotion

The grand opening is a one-time event for a business. If done right, the grand opening can make or break your business. I will be opening on February 1, 2002. This is a prime time for people to start working on their summer tan. Included is a promotional flyer (see Appendix H). To promote my grand opening, I will do the following:

- Run a 1/4-page newspaper advertisement in the Grand Junction *Daily Sentinel* for one weekend prior to the grand opening (Friday, Saturday, and Sunday). This will cost $610.47 for Friday, $406.98 for Saturday, and $868.77 for Sunday ($610.47 + $406.98 + $868.77 = $1886.22).[3]
- Post grand opening promotion flyers throughout the Mesa State College campus. This will cost approximately $150.
- Submit a 1/16-page advertisement to the Quest Dex Phone Book yellow pages. This will cost $61 a month, or $732 a year.[4]

[3]Quote from the Grand Junction *Daily Sentinel,* display advertising office.
[4]Quote from Quest Dex Phone Book, yellow pages advertising.

Management Plan

Employees

Owner. As the owner of *BRONZE,* I am responsible for everything. It is my job to hire well-qualified and trusted employees. As owner, I have set aside duties for myself; they will be to

- Schedule and contact employees.
- Give proper job descriptions and schedules.
- Make sure facilities and equipment are running correctly.
- Make sure supplies are adequate.
- Clean and organize the store.
- Deal with promotions and advertising.
- Promote good customer service.
- Encourage employee morale.

Subcontracted Masseuse and Nail Technician. These two employees are on their own when it comes to profit. However, I still expect them to look after the store and encourage their customers to use the available tanning facilities.

Full-Time Employee. This employee will work 40 hours a week. He or she will do the following:

- Answer phones and make appointments.
- Solve problems among part-time and fill-in employees.
- Operate the computer unit.
- Reset tanning units.
- Clean tanning units when necessary.

Part-Time Employees. These employees will work approximately 20 hours a week. They will take over the full-time employee's job duties when the full-time employee is not working. They will be responsible for the following when they are working with the full-time employee:

- Sanitize units after they are used.
- Show new customers how to operate units.
- Show customers to tanning units.
- Assist full-time employee when needed.

Fill-in Employees. These employees will be utilized mainly in the busy season, from February through June. They will work approximately 10 hours a week and be used as a fill-in when another employee asks for time off from work. Their job duties are the same as those of the part-time employees.

Organization Chart

I will hire five employees and subcontract two employees at *BRONZE.* They include

- One masseuse.
- One nail technician.

- One full-time employee, working 40 hours per week.
- Two part-time employees, working 20 hours per week.
- Two fill-in employees, working 10 hours per week.

The chart below represents the chain of command I plan to use at *BRONZE.*

Employee Organization Chart

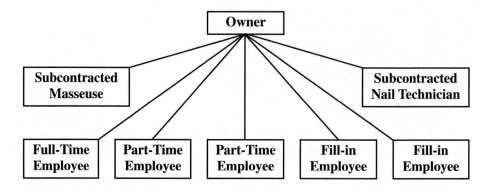

Résumé

I have included a current résumé, with three references, including one banking reference (see Appendix I).

Business Expertise

I have been a consumer in the indoor tanning industry since I turned 18 years old and it was legal for me to use tanning facilities without supervision. With the background of a consumer in this area of business, I feel I am very qualified and have the experience I need to make my own indoor tanning establishment profitable.

In the Grand Junction and Greeley, Colorado, areas, there are many successful indoor tanning facilities. I have made a point to use most of these salons. I have surveyed friends and relatives about their best tanning experiences. This research will allow me to establish a successful facility.

The indoor tanning industry allows people to feel good and look good. The demand for physical appearance in our society grows stronger every day. The tanning industry is a way of marketing to that growth.

Financial Plan

Initial Capitalization

Pro Forma Statement

Beginning Inventory:

Tanning Accelerator Lotions (various types and brands)	$ 1,000
Tanning Goggles (UV protection goggles in various colors)	200
Total Beginning Inventory	$ 1,200

Tanning Store:

Security Deposit (rental space, 1 month's rent)	$ 1,200
Sign (storefront sign)	900
Equipment (tanning beds, computer, desk, chairs, fans, massage table, manicure table, decor, portable walls)	63,750
Supplies (office supplies, towels, cleaning supplies, toiletries, UV stickers)	3,000
Tanning Bulbs (1st replacement tanning bulbs)	5,500
Total Tanning Store	$ 74,350

Other Costs:

Advertising (initial campaign)	$ 2,098
Accountant Fees (associated with payroll and books)	375
Legal Fees (associated with license and registration)	500
Heat, Light, Power, and Telephone Hookup (initial startup costs/deposits)	2,000
Insurance Deposit (fees associated with startup policy, general liability, and contents policy)	125
Misc. Items (keys, security locks, security lights)	500
Total Other Costs	$ 5,598
3 Months' Operating	$ 21,495
Total Initial Capitalization Costs	$102,643

Required Financing:

Total Inventory	$ 1,200
Tanning Store	74,350
Total Other Costs	5,598
Total 3 Months' Operating	21,495
Less: Principal's Portion (40% of Total Initial Capitalization)	(41,057)
Total Required Financing	$ 61,586

Term of Financing: 9% for 2 years

Total Financed	$ 62,000

Cash Flow Projection
12-Month Cash Flow Cycle – *BRONZE* Tanning Service & Salon

	Feb. 01 Estimate	Actual	Mar. 01 Estimate	Actual	April 01 Estimate	Actual	May 01 Estimate	Actual	June 01 Estimate	Actual	July 01 Estimate	Actual
Cash on Hand	$21,495		$29,584		$47,013		$56,086		$62,247		$66,179	
Cash Receipts												
Cash Sales[a]	$17,245		$26,826		$22,993		$15,329		$13,413		$15,329	
Product Sales[a]	108		168		144		96		84		96	
Subcontract Income[a]	600		600		600		600		600		600	
Total Cash Rec.	$17,953		$27,594		$23,737		$16,025		$14,097		$16,025	
Total Cash Avail.	$39,448		$57,178		$70,750		$72,111		$76,344		$82,204	
Cash Paid Out												
Wages[a]	2,736		2,736		2,736		2,736		2,736		2,736	
FICA	170		170		170		170		170		170	
Medicare	40		40		40		40		40		40	
Rent	1,200		1,200		1,200		1,200		1,200		1,200	
Utilities	500		500		500		500		500		500	
Advertising	61		61		61		61		61		61	
Bulb Maintenance	0		0		5,500		0		0		5,500	
Business Insurance	125		125		125		125		125		125	
Other Expenses	500		500		500		500		500		500	
Subtotal	$5,331		$5,332		$10,832		$5,332		$5,332		$10,832	
Loan Payment[b]	$2,832		$2,832		$2,832		$2,832		$2,832		$2,832	
Owner's Withdrawal	1,700		2,000		1,000		1,700		2,000		1,000	
Tot. Cash Pd. Out	$9,864		$10,164		$14,664		$9,864		$10,164		$14,664	
Cash Position	$29,584		$47,013		$56,086		$62,247		$66,179		$67,540	

[a]See Appendix K.
[b]See Appendix L.

	Aug. 01		Sept. 01		Oct. 01		Nov. 01		Dec. 01		Jan. 01		Total	
	Estimate	Actual	Estimate	Actual	Estimate	Actual	Estimate	Actual	Estimate	Actual	Estimate	Actual	Estimate	Actual
	$67,540		$71,772		$75,704		$75,136		$79,368		$83,300			
	$13,413		$13,413		$13,413		$13,413		$13,413		$13,413		$191,612	
	84		84		84		84		84		84		1,200	
	600		600		600		600		600		600		7,200	
	$14,097		$14,097		$14,097		$14,097		$14,097		$14,097		$200,012	
	$81,637		$85,869		$89,801		$89,233		$93,465		$97,397			
	2,736		2,736		2,736		2,736		2,736		2,736		32,832	
	170		170		170		170		170		170		2,040	
	40		40		40		40		40		40		480	
	1,200		1,200		1,200		1,200		1,200		1,200		14,400	
	500		500		500		500		500				5,500	
	61		61		61		61		61		61		732	
	0		0		5,500		0		0		5,500		22,000	
	125		125		125		125		125		125		1,500	
	500		500		500		500		500		500		6,000	
	$5,332		$5,332		$10,832		$5,332		$5,332		$10,332		$85,483	
	$2,832		$2,832		$2,832		$2,832		$2,832		$2,832		$33,989	
	1,700		2,000		1,000		1,700		2,000		1,000		18,800	
	$9,864		$10,164		$14,664		$9,864		$10,164		$14,164		$138,273	
	$71,772		$75,704		$75,136		$79,368		$83,300		$83,232			

Appendices

Appendix A

Trade Name Registration Form from the Colorado Department of Revenue

Appendix B

Growth trends reference, found online at http://www.sundash.com/sb05.htm

Appendix C

Application for Employee Identification Number Form SS–4

Appendix D

Colorado Business Registration Form CR–100

Appendix E

Mesa County census projection (2001) for females, ages 18 to 49, found online at http://www.dola.state.co.us/demog/widepro3.cfm

Appendix F

Mesa County census Caucasian population percentage, found online at http://quickfacts.census.gov/cgi-bin/county?cnty=08077

Appendix G

Market Penetration Worksheet

Market Penetration Worksheet

Business Hours

Monday–Friday 7:00 A.M. to 10:00 P.M. = 15 hours/day $\times$ 5 days/week = 75 hours
Saturday 9:00 A.M. to 8:00 P.M. = 11 hours/day
Sunday 10:00 A.M. to 6:00 P.M. = 8 hours/day

Operating Hours

Total operating hours/week = 75 + 11 + 8 = 94
Operate 360[5] days/year or approximately 52 weeks/year = 52 $\times$ 94 = 4,888 total tanning hours/year

---

[5]Salon operates 360 days a year. We close for Thanksgiving, Christmas Day, New Year's Day, Easter, and Labor Day.

Tanning Sessions

2 possible tanning sessions in each operating hour = 4,888 $\times$ 2 = 9,776 total tanning sessions/ year for one tanning unit
7 possible tanning units available = 9,776 $\times$ 7 = 68,432 tanning sessions available for *BRONZE* Tanning Service & Salon facilities

Market Penetration Number

BRONZE market penetration goal is to use 70 percent of these available tanning sessions = 68,432 $\times$ .70 = 47,902.4, or 47,903 tanning sessions to be used in order to operate *BRONZE*

Customer Market Penetration

Goal of 500 customers to tan twice a week for a year = 52 weeks/year $\times$ 2 times/week = 104 times/year
500 $\times$ 104 = 52,000 total tans/year, which exceeds my penetration goal of 47,903

Appendix H

Business Signage Sample

Appendix I

Current résumé with references

Appendix J

Initial Capitalization Worksheet

Initial Capitalization Worksheet

Equipment

Tanning beds
Solaris Plus 42 3F 3 beds $\times$ $8,099 = $24,297
Pro 28LE Series 3 beds $\times$ $3,699 = $11,097
Sun-Dome XL48 1 unit $\times$ $7,449 = $7,449
Total tanning bed cost = $42,843 + Installation fee + Taxes = **$45,000**
Computer
    Printer and software = **$2,000**
Computer desk = **$250**
Chairs = **$500**
Fans = **$400**
Massage table = **$1,000**
Manicure table = **$500**
Decor
    Pictures, posters, bathroom and tanning room decorations = **$5,000**
Portable walls
    Separate tanning beds, installation, and required parts and tools = **$9,100**

Supplies

Office supplies
    Letterhead, business cards, envelopes, stamps, pens, paper, etc. = **$2,000**
Towels = **$300**
Cleaning supplies
    For tanning beds and general cleaning = **$400**
Toiletries
    For customer use after tanning, lotion, deodorant, body spray = **$300**

Tanning Bulbs

Replacement bulbs (every two months)
    Case of 24 bulbs on average $500
    7 beds have 258 bulbs = 11 cases $\times$ $500 = **$5,500**

Associated Costs

Advertising
    Daily Sentinel advertisement = **$1,886.22**
    Promotional flyers = **$150**
    Yellow pages (monthly) = **$61**
Accountant fees
    5 hours $\times$ $100 = **$500**
Legal fees
    5 hours $\times$ $75 = **$375**
Insurance deposit
    No deposit required
    General liability $1,100 (annually) 1st month = **$92.00**
    Contents $400 (annually) 1st month = **$33.00**

Appendix K

Cash Flow Worksheet

Cash Flow Worksheet

Cash Sales

Market penetration = 47,903 tans/year
Multiplied by $4 average cost/tan = 47,903 $\times$ $4 = $191,612
Distributed over 12 months = February, 9%; March, 14%; April, 12%; May, 8%; June, 7%; July, 7%; August, 8%; September, 7%; October, 7%; November, 7%; December, 7%; January, 7%

Product Sales

Total inventory, tanning accelerator lotions = $1,000
Total inventory, tanning goggles = $200
Total inventory = $1,200, distributed over 12 months (using same distribution as tanning cash sales)

Subcontracted Income

Masseuse and nail technician ($300 each/month) = $300 $\times$ 2 = $600 $\times$ 12 months = $7,200

Wages

Full-time employee
    Salary = $15,000/year or $1,250/month
    FICA = $1,250 $\times$ 6.2% = $77.50/month
    Medicare = $1,250 $\times$ 1.45% = $18.13/month
2 part-time employees
    20 hours/week @ $6 hour = $12,480/year or $1,040 month
    FICA = $1,040 $\times$ 6.2% = $64.48/month
    Medicare = $1,040 $\times$ 1.45% = $15.08/month
2 fill-in employees
    10 hours/week @ $5.15/hour = $5,356/year or $446/month
    FICA = $446 $\times$ 6.2% = $27.65/month
    Medicare = $446 $\times$ 1.45% = $6.47/month

Appendix L

Amortization Table

Notes

Chapter 1

1. Small Business Administration, Office of Advocacy, "Facts About Small Business 1999," www.sba.gov/advo/stats
2. Ibid.
3. "Standard Industrial Classified Codes and Size Standards," *Federal Code of Regulations 13:121* (Washington, DC: U.S. Government Printing Office, 1995), 354–367.
4. *Standard & Poor's Register of Corporations, Directors and Executives*, vol. 1 (New York: McGraw-Hill, 1995), 161–173.
5. John A. Byrne, "How Entrepreneurs Are Reshaping the Economy and What Big Companies Can Learn," *Business Week, Enterprise Edition*, October 1993, 12–18.
6. Therese Eiben and Joyce Davis, "A New 500 for the New Economy," *Fortune*, 15 May 1995, 166.
7. Byrne, 14.
8. *Statistical Abstract of the United States* (Washington, DC: U.S. Government Printing Office, 1997), 560–561.
9. Ibid., p. 561.
10. "They Create Winners: The Boom in Entrepreneurial Education," *Success*, September 1994, 43.
11. Aida Alverez, symposia on "New Economic Perspectives on Job Growth," 8 June 1998, www.sba.gov
12. Small Business Administration, Office of Advocacy, "Facts About Small Business 1999."
13. *Competing in a Seller's Market: Is Corporate America Prepared? Workforce 2000* (Washington, DC: Towers Perrin, 1990).
14. "Workforce Diversity Stirs Little Concern," *Wall Street Journal*, 22 May 1992, B1.
15. Russell Mitchell and Michael O'Neal, "Managing by Values," *Business Week*, 1 August 1994, 46–52.
16. Faye Rice, "How to Make Diversity Pay," *Fortune*, 8 August 1994, 79–86.
17. Small Business Administration, Office of Advocacy, "Facts About Small Business 1999."
18. *Statistical Abstract of the United States*, 1997, 552.
19. Eiben and Davis, 170.
20. Myron Magnet, "The New Golden Rule of Business," *Fortune*, 21 February 1994, 60–63.
21. Tom Murphy, "Convenient Linking," *Ward's Auto World*, October 1997, 85.
22. Byrne, 12.
23. John Case, "The Wonderland Economy," *Inc. The State of Small Business*, 16 March 1995, 29.
24. Ibid.
25. Howard Gleckman, "Meet the Giant-Killers," *Business Week, Enterprise Edition*, October 1993, 68–73.
26. "Report Examines Small Business Innovative Activity," *The Small Business Advocate*, December 1993, 10.
27. George Gendron, Michael Hopkins, and David Birch, "Managing in the New Economy," *Inc.*, April 1990, 33–41.
28. "The Whiz Kids—Never Stop Learning," *Success*, September 1994, 38–42.
29. Michael Barbier, "Learning the Meaning of Measurement," *Nation's Business*, June 1994, 72–74.
30. David Greising, "Quality—How to Make It Pay," *Business Week*, 8 August 1994, 54–74.
31. Small Business Administration, Office of Advocacy, "Facts About Small Business 1999."
32. "Avoiding the Pitfalls," *Wall Street Journal Report on Small Business*, 22 May 1995, R1.
33. Case, 24.
34. James Aley, "Debunking the Failure Fallacy," *Fortune*, 6 September 1993, 21.
35. *1994 Information Please Almanac* (Boston: Houghton Mifflin, 1994), 839.
36. Small Business Administration, Office of Advocacy, "Facts About Small Business 1999."

Chapter 2

1. Robert Hisrich, "Entrepreneurship/Intrapreneurship," *American Psychologist*, February 1990, 209.
2. P. VanderWerf and C. Brush, "Toward Agreement on the Focus of Entrepreneurship Research: Progress Without Definition," *Proceedings of the National Academy of Management Conference*, Washington, DC, 1989.
3. Carol Moore, "Understanding Entrepreneurial Behavior: A Definition and Model," in *Academy of Management Best Paper Proceedings*, ed. J. A. Pearce II and R. B. Robinson, Jr., 46th Annual Meeting of the Academy of Management, Chicago, 1989, 66–70. See also William Bygrave, "The Entrepreneurial Paradigm (I): A Philosophical Look at Its Research Methodologies," *Entrepreneurship: Theory and Practice*, Fall 1989, 7–25, and William Bygrave and Charles Hofer, "Theorizing About Entrepreneurship," *Entrepreneurship: Theory and Practice*, Winter 1991, 13–22.
4. A. Shapiro and L. Sokol, "The Social Dimensions of Entrepreneurship," in *Encyclopedia of Entrepreneurship*, ed. J. A. Kent, D. L. Sexton, and K. H. Vesper (Englewood Cliffs, NJ: Prentice-Hall, 1992).
5. J. A. Schumpeter, *History of Economic Analysis* (New York: Oxford University Press, 1934).
6. William Gartner, "'Who Is an Entrepreneur?' Is the Wrong Question," *Entrepreneurship: Theory and Practice*, Summer 1989, 47. See also J. W. Carland, F. Hoy, W. R. Boulton, and J. A. C. Carland, "Differentiating Entrepreneurs from Small

Business Owners: A Conceptualization," *Academy of Management Review* 9, no.2 (1984): 354–359; and William Gartner, "What Are We Talking About When We Talk About Entrepreneurship?" *Journal of Business Venturing* 5 (1990): 15–28.

7. Steven Covey, *The Seven Habits of Highly Effective People* (New York: Simon & Schuster, 1989), 95.

8. Peter Drucker, *Innovation and Entrepreneurship: Practice and Principles* (New York: Harper & Row, 1985).

9. Christopher Caggiano and Susan Greco, "Boot Me Up," *Inc.*, November 1993, 44–45; "Start-ups From Scratch," *Inc.*, September 1994, 76–77. *Inc.* magazine publishes an annual issue on successful businesses that were start started with very little money.

10. Jon Goodman, "What Makes an Entrepreneur?" *Inc.*, October 1994, 29.

11. David C. McClelland, *The Achieving Society* (New York: Van Nostrand Reinhold, 1961). See also David C. McClelland, "Achievement Motivation Can Be Developed," *Harvard Business Review,* November/December 1965, 6ff., and David Miron and David McClelland, "The Impact of Achievement Motivation Training on Small Business," *California Management Review,* Summer 1979, 13–28.

12. Robert Brochhaus and Pamela S. Horwitz, "The Psychology of the Entrepreneur," in *The Art and Science of Entrepreneurship,* ed. Donald Sexton and Raymond W. Smilor (Cambridge, MA: Ballinger, 1986), 25–48.

13. Timothy S. Hatten, "Student Entrepreneurial Characteristics and Attitude Change Toward Entrepreneurship as Affected by Participation in an SBI Program," *Journal of Education for Business* (March/April 1995).

14. Michael O'Neal, "Just What Is an Entrepreneur?" *Business Week, Enterprise 1993,* 104–112.

15. *A Small Business Primer,* NFIB Foundation/ American Express Travel.

16. Jerome Katz, "The Institution and Infrastructure of Entrepreneurship," *Entrepreneurship: Theory and Practice,* Spring 1991, 85–102.

17. "They Create Winners," *Success,* September 1994, 43.

18. William Bygrave, *The Portable MBA in Entrepreneurship* (New York: Wiley, 1994), 2.

19. "Never Stop Learning," *Success,* September 1994, 41.

20. "Two Who Made Good," *Inc.,* June 1994, 40.

21. Geoffrey Brewer, "Siebel and Scopus: Will This Marriage Last?" *Sales and Marketing Management,* September 1998, 59.

22. Fred Steingold, *Legal Guide for Starting and Running a Small Business* (Berkeley, CA: Nolo Press, 1993), 1/9.

23. James Hopson and Patricia Hopson, "Helping Clients Choose the Legal Form for a Small Business," *The Practical Accountant,* October 1990, 67–84.

24. Steingold.

25. William Cohen, *The Entrepreneurship and Small Business Problem Solver,* 2nd ed. (New York: Wiley, 1990), 10.

26. William Copperthwaite, Jr., "Limited Liability Companies: The Choice of the Future," *Commercial Law Journal,* Summer 1998, 222–239.

27. James Hamill and Jennifer Olson, "Much Ado About 'Nothings,'" *Tax Advisor,* July 1999, 506–514.

Chapter 3

1. For a more complete discussion of corporate social responsibility, see Robert Kreitner, *Management,* 8th ed. (Boston, MA: Houghton Mifflin, 2001). See also Archer Carroll, "The Pyramid of Corporate Social Responsibility: Toward the Moral Management of Organizational Stakeholders," *Business Horizons,* July/August 1991, 39–48; and Richard Rodewald, "The Corporate Social Responsibility Debate: Unanswered Questions About the Consequences of Moral Reform," *American Business Law Journal,* Fall 1987, 443–466.

2. O. C. Ferrell and John Fraedrich, *Business Ethics: Ethical Decision Making and Cases,* 2nd ed. (Boston, MA: Houghton Mifflin, 1994), 67.

3. Milton Friedman and Rose Friedman, *Free to Choose* (New York: Harcourt Brace Jovanovich, 1980); and Milton Friedman, *Capitalism and Freedom* (Chicago: University of Chicago Press, 1963), 133.

4. Jack Gordon, "Rethinking Diversity," *Training,* January 1992, 23.

5. Anne Fisher, "Sexual Harassment: What to Do," *Fortune,* 23 August 1993, 84–88.

6. 29 CFR 1604.11 (a).

7. Gordon, 85.

8. Jan Bohren, "Six Myths of Sexual Harassment," *Management Review* (May 1993): 61–63.

9. T. Gordon Roddick letter, 22 September 1994.

10. Marjorie Kelly, "To Tell the Truth," *Business Ethics,* September/October 1994, 6–7; Jon Entine, "Shattered Image," *Business Ethics,* September/October 1994, 23–28; and Marjorie Kelly, publisher of *Business Ethics.* letter, Sept/Oct 1994.

11. Jeannine Reilly, "Charitable Works Sells at a Number of Firms," *Arizona Daily Star,* 11 September 2000, 16.

12. Quentin Hardy, "The Radical Philanthropist," *Forbes,* 1 May 2000, 114–121.

13. Anne Murphy, "The Seven (Almost) Deadly Sins of High-Minded Entrepreneurs," *Inc.,* July 1994, 47–51.

14. Ferrell and Fraedrich, 10.

15. George Manning and Kent Curtis, *Ethics at Work: Fire in a Dark World* (Cincinnati: South-Western Publishing, 1988), 74.

16. "Should You Put It in Writing?" *Nation's Business,* March 1998, 37.

17. Manning and Curtis, 77.

18. Scott Baca and Erin Nickerson, "Ethical Problems, Conflicts, and Beliefs of Small Business Professionals," *Journal of Business Ethics,* November 2000, 15–24.

19. Tom Peters, *Thriving on Chaos* (New York: Knopf, 1988).

20. Tom Ehrenfeld, "The (Handbook) Handbook," *Inc.,* November 1993, 58.

21. Robert Linnman and John Stanton, "Mining for Niches," *Business Horizons,* May/June 1992, 43–51.

22. Fran Tarkenton and Joseph Boyett, "Taking Care of Business," *Entrepreneur,* February 1990, 18–23.

23. Sheila Eby, "Pssssssst! (Do You Want to Know a Secret?)" *Inc. Magazine Guide to Small Business Success,* 1993.

24. M. A. Lyles, J. S. Baird, J. B. Orris, and D. E. Kuratko, "Formalized Planning in Small Business Increasing Strategic Choices," *Journal of Small Business Management* (April 1993): 38–50.

25. Kenneth Hatten and Mary Louise Hatten, *Strategic Management: Analysis and Action* (Englewood Cliffs, NJ: Prentice-Hall, 1987), 13.

26. Jill Andresky Fraser, "Plans to Grow By," *Inc.,* January 1990, 111–113.

27. Ferrell and Fraedrich, 114.

Chapter 4

1. George Gendron and Bo Burlingham, "Thriving on Order," *Inc.,* December 1989, 47–62.

2. Karl Albrecht, "The Power of Bifocal Vision," *Management Review,* April 1994, 42–46.

3. Bo Burlingham, "How to Succeed in Business in 4 Easy Steps," *Inc.,* July 1995, 30–45.

4. Roger Thompson, "Business Plans: Myth and Reality," *Nation's Business,* August 1988, 16–23.
5. Stanley Rich and David Gumpert, "How to Write a Winning Business Plan," *Harvard Business Review,* May/June 1985, 156–163.
6. "Did Somebody Say 'Small?'" *Fortune Special Issue,* Summer 1999, 142.
7. *Guidelines for Entrepreneurs,* pamphlet, Colorado Small Business Development Center.
8. Kayte Vanscoy, "Unconventional Wisdom," *Smart Business for the New Economy,* October 2000, 78–88.
9. J. Tol Broome, Jr., "How to Write a Business Plan," *Nation's Business,* February 1993, 29–30.
10. David H. Bangs, *Financial Troubleshooting: An Action Plan for Money Management in Small Business* (Dover, NH: Upstart Publishing Company, 1992), 46.
11. Ibid., 50.

Chapter 5

1. Thomas Dicke, *Franchising in America: The Development of a Business Method, 1840–1990* (Chapel Hill, NC: University of North Carolina Press, 1992), 13.
2. "The Wonder Years," *Entrepreneur,* January 1999, 180–184.
3. Robert Justis and Richard Judd, *Franchising* (Cincinnati: South-Western, 1989).
4. U.S. Department of Commerce, *Franchise Opportunity Handbook* (Washington, DC: U.S. Government Printing Office, 2000).
5. Joan Delaney, "10 Danger Signs to Look For When Buying a Franchise," *Black Enterprise,* September 1994, 118–222.
6. "Franchise Industry Resources," *Black Enterprise,* September 1994, 122.
7. Jenny McCune and Leslie Jay, "The Source," *Success,* October 1995, 43–48; and Phaedra Hise, "Click Here for Business Help," *Inc.,* November 1995, 101.
8. Heather Page, "No Substitute," *Entrepreneur,* January 1996, 192–194.
9. U.S. Department of Commerce.
10. Andrew Sherman, "Structuring the Financial Agreement," *The Franchising Handbook* ((New York: AMACOM American Management Association, 1993), 297.
11. Sherman, 300.
12. David Baucus, Melissa Baucus, and Sherrie Human, "Choosing a Franchise: How Base Fees and Royalties Relate to the Value of the Franchise," *Journal of Small Business Management*, April 1993, 91–104.
13. Andrew Sherman, "Hard Data on Franchisees," *Nation's Business,* February 1994, 54.
14. Kevin Butler, "Franchise Reform on Horizon?" *Investor's Business Daily,* 29 July 1999, A1.
15. Andrew Serwer, "Trouble in Franchise Nation," *Fortune,* 6 March 1995, 118
16. Jeffrey Tannenbaum, "U.S. Franchisors Expect NAFTA to Boost Mexican Business," *Wall Street Journal,* 17 November 1993, B2.
17. Meg Whittemore, "An International Touch in Expansion Plans," *Nation's Business,* January 1992, 62.
18. Alex Konigsberg, "Around the World with Franchise Legislation," *Franchising World,* May/June 1999, 18–27.

Chapter 6

1. William Cohen, *The Entrepreneur and Small Business Problem Solver,* 2nd ed. (New York: Wiley, 1990), 90–91.
2. Fleming Meeks and Nancy Rotenier, "Am I Going to Mind Sweeping the Floors?" *Forbes,* 8 November 1993, 142–148.

3. Gustav Berle, *SBA Hotline Answer Book* (New York: Wiley, 1992), 78–80. Also contact your local Service Corp of Retired Executives (SCORE) for a complete management consultants' checklist.
4. Joshua Hyatt, "Should You Start a Business?" *Inc.,* February 1992, 48–58.
5. *RMA Annual Statement Studies 1999* (Philadelphia: Robert Morris Associates, 1999).
6. Joseph Anthony, "Maybe You Should Buy a Business," *Kiplinger's Personal Finance Magazine,* May 1993, 83–87.
7. John Johansen, "How to Buy or Sell a Business," *Small Business Administration Management Aid,* no. 2.029 (Washington, DC: U.S. Small Business Administration, Office of Business Development).
8. Gary Schine, "How to Buy a Business Without Overpaying," *Home Office Computing,* August 1993, 26–27.
9. William Bygrave, *The Portable MBA in Entrepreneurship* (New York: Wiley, 1994), 63–66.
10. Wendy Handler, "Key Interpersonal Relationships of Next-Generation Family Members in Family Firms," *Journal of Small Business Management,* July 1991, 21.
11. John Ward and Craig Aronoff, "Two 'Laws' for Family Businesses," *Nation's Business,* February 1993, 52–53.
12. David Wold, ed., *Nxlevel Guide for Entrepreneurs,* 3rd ed. (Denver, CO: U.S. West Foundation, 2000), 108.
13. George Rimler, "How to Professionalize the Family Business," *Air Conditoning, Heating & Refrigeration News,* 19 June 2000, 28.
14. Wold.
15. Jeffrey Barsch, Joseph Gantisky, James Carson, and Benjamin Doochin, "Entry of the Next Generation: Strategic Challenges for Family Members in Family Firms," *Journal of Small Business Management,* April 1988, 49–56.
16. David Bork, "If Family Members Ask for a Job," *Nation's Business,* April 1992, 50–52.

Chapter 7

1. John Patrick, The Internet: More Than We Can Imagine," *Financial Executive,* May/June 1999, 14–18.
2. Amy Wilson Sheldon, "Strategy Rules," *Fast Company,* January 2001, 165–166.
3. Robert McGarvey, "Reality Check," *Entrepreneur's Start-ups,* September 2000, 53.
4. Carolyn Brackett, "Setting Up Shop in Cyberspace," www.inc.com articles.
5. Jan Gardner, "Web Site No-Nos," www.inc.com and *Inc. Technology,* 14 November 2000.
6. Melissa Campanelli, "At First Site," *Netpreneur,* special insert, *Entrepreneur's Start-ups,* June 2000, 12
7. Nichole L. Torres, "No Place Like Home," *Entrepreneur's Start-ups,* September 2000, 38.
8. David Bangs and Linda Pinson, *The Real World Entrepreneur Field Guide* (Chicago: Upstart Publishing, 1999), 474.
9. Nichole L. Torres, "No Place Like Home," *Entrepreneur's Start-ups,* September 2000, 38–45; Heather Lloyd-Martin, "Oh, Give Me a Home," *Entrepreneur's Start-ups,* October 2000, 42–45; and Pamela Rohland and Elaine W. Teague, "The Price Is Right," *Entrepreneur's Start-ups,* August 1999, 34–44.
10. "Work at Home in 1997," Bureau of Labor Statistics, www.bls.gov/newsrelease
11. "Data Mine," *Inc. 500,* 17 October 2000, 57–65.
12. Leslie Brokaw, "The Truth About Start-ups, *Inc.,* March 1993, 56–64.
13. Jeffry A. Timmons, Daniel Muzyka, Howard Stevenson, and William Bygrave, "Opportunity Recognition: The Core of

Entrepreneurship," in *Frontiers of Entrepreneurship Research, 1987* (Wellesley, MA: Babson College, 1987), 409.

14. Stephanie Mehta, "Small Talk," *Wall Street Journal Small Business Edition,* 22 May 1995, R16.

15. Diane Goldner, "Ahead of the Curve," *Wall Street Journal Small Business Edition,* 22 May 1995, R16.

16. David Kopcso, Robert Ronstady, and William Rybolt, "The Corridor Principle: Independent Entrepreneurs Versus Corporate Entrepreneurs," in *Frontiers of Entrepreneurship Research, 1987* (Wellesley, MA: Babson College, 1987), 259–271.

17. Karl Vesper, "When's the Big Idea?" in *Frontiers of Entrepreneurship Research, 1989* (Wellesley, MA: Babson College, 1989), 334–343.

18. Virginia Hutchins, "Artisians Honored for Idaho-made Products," *Twin Falls Times-News,* 27 June 1999.

19. Anne Murphy, "Where Great Business Ideas Come From," *Inc.,* September 1993, 59–60.

20. Phaedra Hise, "Where Great Business Ideas Come From," *Inc.,* September 1993, 59–60.

21. Neil A. Martin, "Invincible Spirit," *Success,* October 1994, 24.

22. Michael Treacy and Fred Wiesema, "How Market Leaders Keep Their Edge," *Fortune,* 6 February 1995, 88–98.

23. Lori Stones and Kelly Lynn, "Entrepreneurism + Customer Service = Success," *Management Review,* November 1993, 38–44.

Chapter 8

1. "Making Sense of Your Dollars," *Home Office Computing,* November 1993, 79–88.

2. For a concise source on reading financial statements, see Frank Evans, "A Roadmap to Your Financial Report," *Management Review,* October 1993, 39–47.

3. Kathryn Stewart, "On the Fast Track to Profits," *Management Accounting,* February 1995, 44–50.

4. For more depth on the use of numbers in running your business, see Tom Richman, "The Language of Business," *Inc.,* February 1990, 41–50.

5. Andrew Tanzer, "Your Passport, Please," *Forbes,* 6 November 1995, 252–253.

6. Jay Finegan, "Corporate Cost Cutters," *Inc.,* August 1995, 28.

7. Andrew J. Potts, "Cash Flow—The Oil That Keeps the Small and Family Business Organization Running Smoothly," *Journal of Small Business Strategy* 4, no. 2, Fall 1993, 63–71.

8. "Cash Flow: Who's in Charge," *Inc.,* November 1993, 140.

9. Leslie Manonson, "Cash Is King," *Management Review,* October 1990, 36–38.

10. "Cash Flow," *Inc.,* November 1993, 140.

11. Roberta Maynard, "Smart Ways to Manage Cash," *Nation's Business,* August 1992, 43–44.

12. For a more detailed treatment of inventory management, see Robert A. Mamis, "Money In, Money Out," *Inc.,* March 1993, 96–103.

13. Adapted from Maynard, 44.

Chapter 9

1. Dale D. Buss, "Growing More by Doing Less," *Nation's Business,* December 1995, 18–24.

2. For a more thorough explanation and example of the process of defining required assets, see Andy H. Bangs, Jr., *The Business Planning Guide,* 8th ed. (Chicago: Dearborn Publishing, 1998).

3. U.S. Small Business Administration, Office of Business Development, "The ABCs of Borrowing," Management Aids Number 1.001 (Washington, DC: U.S. Government Printing Office).

4. www.sba.gov/financing

5. Ibid.

6. Dun & Bradstreet, "Small Business Credit Survey," August 1994.

7. Joel Millman, "Imported Entrepreneurs," *Forbes,* 6 November 1995, 232–237.

8. G. Baty, *Entrepreneurship: Playing to Win,* (Reston, VA: Reston Publishing, 1990), 157–159.

9. Jeffry A. Timmons, *New Venture Creation,* 5th ed. (Homewood, IL: Irwin, 1999).

Chapter 10

1. William Dennis, *Small Business Primer,* National Federation of Independent Business (August 1993), 32–33.

2. 8 USC 1324 (a).

3. 8 USC 1324 (B) (g) (2) (B) (iv) (I)-(III).

4. Ibid., C4

5. Ibid., 19–20.

6. William Jackson, Geralyn McClure-Franklin, and Diana Hensley, "Sexual Harassment: No Immunity for Small Business," *Proceedings of 1995 Small Business Consulting Conference,* Nashville, TN, 161–165.

7. Jennifer Laabs, "HR Puts Its Questions on the Line: Sexual Harassment," *Personnel Journal,* February 1995, 36–45.

8. Jackson, McClure-Franklin, and Hensley, 164.

9. U.S. Department of Labor, Employment Standards Administration, Wage and Hour Division, *Compliance Guide to the Family and Medical Leave Act* (Washington, DC: U.S. Government Printing Office, 1993), 16.

10. Ibid.

11. 29 USC 651 (b).

12. Fred Steingold, *The Legal Guide for Starting and Running a Small Business* (Berkeley, CA: Nolo Press, 1992).

13. Alan Zeiger, "Bankruptcy Can Also Mean Smart Investment," *Management Review,* May 1992, 36–39.

14. Michael Blair, "Business's Plight, Lawyers' Delight," *New York Times,* 18 June 1995, F13.

15. "Constitution of the United States of America," Article I, Section 8, in Daniel J. Boorstin, *An American Primer* (Chicago: University of Chicago Press, 1966), 94.

16. David Pressman, *Patent It Yourself* (Berkeley, CA: Nolo Press, 1991).

17. Ibid., 6/41.

Chapter 11

1. Peter Drucker, *People and Performance: The Best of Peter Drucker on Management* (New York: Harper's College Press, 1977), 90.

2. Ibid., 91.

3. Tom Stein, "Scoring with Sportswear," *Success,* September 1995, 31.

4. Regis McKenna, *Relationship Marketing* (Reading, MA: Addison-Wesley, 1997).

5. Ibid.

6. Earl Naumann and Patrick Shannon, "What Is Customer-Driven Marketing?" *Business Horizons,* November/December 1992, 44–52.

7. David Cravens and Shannon Shipp, "Market-Driven Strategies for Competitive Advantage," *Business Horizons,* January/February 1991, 53–61.

8. Avraham Shama, "Marketing Strategies During Recession: A Comparison of Small and Large Firms," *Journal of Small Business Management*, July 1993, 62–72.

9. William Bygrave, *The Portable MBA in Entrepreneurship* (New York: Wiley, 1994), 85.

10. Pierre Loewe and Dominique Hanssens, "Taking the Mystery Out of Marketing," *Management Review*, August 1994, 32–34.

11. *The 1994 Information Please Almanac* (Boston: Houghton Mifflin, 1994), 748.

12. Anil Gupta, "Business-Unit Strategy: Managing the Single Business," in *The Portable MBA in Strategy*, ed. Liam Fahey and Robert Randall (New York: Wiley, 1994), 84–107.

13. Michael Porter, "Know Your Place," *Inc.*, September 1991, 90–95.

14. David Cravens and Shannon Shipp, "Market-driven Strategies for Competitive Advantage," *Business Horizons*, January/February 1991, 90–95.

15. Porter.

16. Robert Hartley, *Marketing Mistakes*, 5th ed. (New York: Wiley, 1992), v.

17. Leslie Cauley, "Perils of Progress," *Wall Street Journal Report— Technology*, 27 June 1994, R12.

18. Ibid.

19. Ibid.

20. Christopher Power, Kathleen Kerwin, Ronald Grover, Keith Alexander, and Robert Hof, "Flops," *Business Week*, 16 August 1993, 76–82.

21. John Czepiel, *Competitive Marketing Strategy* (Englewood Cliffs, NJ: Prentice-Hall, 1992), 41.

22. Michael Porter, *Competitive Advantage: Creating and Sustaining Superior Performance* (New York: Free Press, 1985).

23. Jenny McCune, "In the Shadow of Wal-Mart," *Management Review*, December 1994, 10–16.

24. Lee Iacocca, *Iacocca: An Autobiography* (New York: Bantam Books, 1984).

25. Oren Harari, "The Secret Competitive Advantage," *Management Review*, January 1994, 45–47.

26. Robert A. Mamis, "Second-Time Smart," *Inc. 500*, 17 October 1995, 47–50.

27. "New Marketing Research Definition Approved," *Marketing News*, 2 January 1987, 1.

28. J. Ford Laumer, Jr., James Harris, and Hugh Guffey, Jr., "Learning About Your Market," Management Aid No. 4.019, Small Business Administration Management Assistance Office.

29. Dina Bann, "Companies Use Shared Approach to Collect Low-Cost Marketing Data," *Denver Rocky Mountain News*, 21 February 1999, 46.

30. George Kress and John Snyder, *Forecasting and Market Analysis Techniques: A Practical Approach* (Westport, CT: Quorum Books, 1994), 29–54.

31. Vera Gibbons, "The Scoop on Info Brokers," *Inc.*, December 1992, 27.

32. Susan Greco, "Fact Finders for Hire," *Inc.*, December 1992, 27.

33. Fahri Karakaya, "Market Research: A Pocket Guide for Managers," *SAM Advanced Management Journal*, Summer 1991, 34–40.

34. "Do-It-Yourself Techniques to Solve Marketing Problems," *Profit-Building Strategies for Business Owners*, December 1992, 14–16.

35. Allan Magrath, *The 6 Imperatives of Marketing: Lessons from the World's Best Companies* (New York: AMACOM, 1992), 40–41.

36. Oren Harrari, "The Tarpit of Marketing Research," *Management Review*, March 1994, 42–44.

37. Ibid., 43.

38. Gary Hamel and C. K. Prahalad, "Seeing the Future First," *Fortune*, 5 September 1994, 70.

Chapter 12

1. Christopher Caggiano, "Fleet Delivery," *Inc.*, August 1995, 36.

2. Bos Isenhour and Kathryn Payne, "Getting Serious About Product Development," *Management Review*, April 1991, 19–22.

3. William Barbach, "Developments to Watch," *Business Week*, 28 June 1993, 85.

4. Roberta Maynard, "What's in a Name?" *Nation's Business*, September 1994, 54.

5. *Frozen Food Digest*, July 1997, 20.

6. Alexander Hiam and Charles Schewe, *The Portable MBA in Marketing* (New York: Wiley, 1992), 242.

7. Verona Beguin, ed., *Small Business Institute Student Consultant's Manual* (Washington, DC: Small Business Administration, 1992), Appendix F.

8. Donald W. Dobler, David N. Burt, and Lamar Lee, Jr., *Purchasing and Materials Management*, 5th ed. (New York: McGraw-Hill, 1990), 50–64; and Barry Render and Jay Heizer, *Principles of Operations Management* (Upper Saddle River, NJ: Prentice-Hall, 1995), 406–415.

9. Stephanie Gruner, "The Smart Vendor-Audit Checklist," *Inc.*, April 1995, 93–95.

10. Eliyhu Goldratt, "Late-Night Discussions," *Industry Week*, 5 August 1991, 28–29.

11. Leon Erlanger, "Small Office Software: The Essentials," *PC Magazine*, 13 June 1995, 120–121; Bronwyn Fryer, "How to Succeed with Software," *Working Woman*, November 1995, 55–60; Arden Hoffman, "Perfect Picks," *Working Woman*, November 1995, 63–68; and Dennis James, "Level the Field with the Accounting Equalizer," *Success*, January/February 1996, 58.

12. Otis Port, "A Cutting-Edge Strategy Called Sharing," *Business Week Special Report on Enterprise*, 20 November 1995, ENT4–ENT6.

13. Kathy Reilly, "EDI Requires Prudent Management," *Folio*, 1 August 1995, 45; Anne Knowles, "Electronic Commerce: Securing Transactions over the Net," *PC Week*, 30 October 1995, 102ff.; and Jenny C. McCune, "Stop, Thief!" *Success*, March 1996, 54.

14. Sang Lee and Marc Schniederjans, *Operations Management* (Boston: Houghton Mifflin, 1994), 256.

15. Michael Barier, "When 'Just in Time' Just Isn't Enough," *Nation's Business*, November 1992, 30–31.

16. Julie Candler, "Just-in-Time Deliveries," *Nation's Business*, April 1993, 64–65.

Chapter 13

1. John Case, "Where the Growth Is," *Inc.*, June 1991, 66.

2. "The Power of Buying Survey," *Sales and Marketing Management*, 30 August 1994, A6–A14.

3. James Aley, "Startup 'Hoods," *Fortune*, 18 October 1993, 24.

4. Richard Stern and Toddi Gutner, "A Helluva Place to Have a Business," *Forbes*, 21 December 1992, 114–136.

5. William Bennett, "A Great Place to Visit, But. . . ," *Fortune*, May 1993, 92–94.

6. CIA World Factbook, 2001 www.odcl.gov

7. Ellyn Spragins, "Working Far Afield," *Inc.*, July 1991, 79–80.

8. Gary Brockway and W. Blynn Mangold, "The Sales Conversion Index: A Method for Analyzing Small Business Market Opportunities," *Journal of Small Business Management*, April 1988, 38–48.

9. Michael Weiss, *The Clustering of America* (New York: Harper & Row, 1988).

10. Benjamin Weiner, "Sources of Information (and Misinformation)," *Management Review*, January 1992, 24–25.

11. Niklas von Dachne, "Ears to the Ground," *Success*, December 1995, 14.

12. Troy Segan, "Feathered Nests for Your Fledgling Business," *Business Week*, 19 February 1990, 24–25.

13. Bradford McKee, "Achieving Access for the Disabled," *Nation's Business*, June 1991, 31–34.

14. Jill Hecht Maxwell, "Home But Not Alone," *Inc.*, March 2001, www.inc.com/articles

15. Ripley Hotch, "All the Comforts of a Home Office," *Nation's Business*, July 1993, 26–28.

16. Robert Cunningham, "Ten Questions to Ask Before You Sign a Lease," *Inc. Guide to Small Business Success*, 1993 supplement issue.

Chapter 14

1. Edward Welles, "When Wal-Mart Comes to Town," *Inc.*, July 1993, 76–88.

2. Ibid., 79.

3. Gayle Sato Stodder, "Green Thumbs," *Entrepreneur*, November 1995, 100–105.

4. Paul Argenti, *The Portable MBA Desk Reference* (New York: Wiley, 1994), 313.

5. For a concise article on breakeven analysis, see Kevin Thompson, "Planning for Profit," *Black Enterprise*, April 1993, 93–98.

6. Michael Mondello, "Naming Your Price," *Inc.*, July 1992, 80–83.

7. Kelly Holland and Greg Burns, "Plastic Talks," *Business Week*, 14 February 1994, 105–107.

8. "Cardweb.com Predicts Holiday Credit Card Use Will Top $113 Billion," *Business Wire*, 21 November 2000.

9. Ibid., 107.

10. Timothy O'Brien, "Merchant's Ire Flares over Fees on Credit Cards," *Wall Street Journal*, 11 October 1993, B1.

11. Carolyn Brown, "How to Secure a Line of Credit," *Black Enterprise*, January 1994, 64–67.

12. Armin A. Brott, "How to Avoid Bear Traps," *Nation's Business*, September 1993, 49–50; and Paul J. Mignini, Jr., "The Globalization of Credit," *Business Credit*, April 1994, 3.

13. Jill Andresky Fraser, "Getting Paid," *Inc.*, June 1990, 58–69.

14. Jill Andresky Fraser, "The Outstanding Bill Collection System," *Inc.*, May 1993, 93–95.

15. Paul Hawkin, *Growing a Business* (New York: Simon & Schuster, 1987), 33.

16. Melanie Wells, "Making for Strange Bedfellows," *Advertising Age*, 29 March 1993, 30.

17. Minda Zetlin, "It's All the Same to Me," *Sales and Marketing Management*, February 1994, 71–75.

18. "The Cost of a Sales Call," *Inc.*, May 1991, 86.

19. Susan Greco, "The Art of Selling," *Inc.*, June 1995, 72–80.

20. Jane Applegate, "Building Your Business with PR," *Working Woman*, December 1993, 69.

21. Larry Light, "Promotion Has Bigger Role Than Ads, But 'Short-Term Bribes' Are Suicide," *Advertising Age*, 29 March 1993.

22. Rachel Miscall, "Pick a Card," *Denver Business Journal*, 23 October 1998).

Chapter 15

1. Johnathan Calof, "The Impact of Size on Internationalization," *Journal of Small Business Management*, October 1993, 60–69.

2. SBA News Release, "New Data Show Small Business Will Drive Exports in 21st Century," www.sba.gov/news; and Amy Barrett, "It's a Small (Business) World," *Business Week*, 17 April 1995, 96–101.

3. Michael Barrier, "A Global Reach for Small Firms," *Nation's Business*, April 1994, 66.

4. Ibid.

5. *Breaking into the Trade Game: A Small Business Guide to Exporting* (Washington, DC: U.S. Small Business Administration/AT&T Printing, 1993), 4–5.

6. Thomas Gaspar, "International Business Planning: A 'How-to' Workshop Sponsored by the New Jersey DEC," *Business America*, 28 June 1993, 16.

7. Anil K. Gupta and Vijay Govindarajan, "Managing Global Expansion: A Conceptual Framework," *Business Horizons*, March/April 2000, 45–54.

8. Ibid.

9. Ibid.

10. Ted Rakstis, "Going Global," *Kiwanis*, October 1991, 39–43.

11. Inga Baird, Marjorie Lyles, and J. B. Orris, "The Choice of International Strategies by Small Business," *Journal of Small Business Management*, January 1994, 48–59.

12. *Breaking into the Trade Game*, 3.

13. Ibid., 4.

14. Robert Mamis, "Not So Innocent Abroad," *Inc.*, September 1993, 110–111.

15. Clark Cassell, *The World Is Your Market: The Export Guide for Small Business* (Washington, DC: Braddock Communications, 1990), 20.

16. Ibid., 25.

17. Joseph Pattison, "Global Joint Ventures," *Overseas Business*, Winter 1990, 24–29.

18. Tom Stein, "The Sweet Smell of Success," *Success*, December 1995, 23.

19. Roberta Maynard, "A Good Time to Export," *Nation's Business*, May 1994, 24.

20. Jill Andresky Fraser, "How Bad Can Collections Get?" *Inc.*, March 1993, 94.

21. *Breaking into the Trade Game*, 86.

22. Margitta Wulker-Mirback, "New Trends in Countertrade," *OECD Observer*, April/May 1990, 63.

23. Matt Schaffer, "Countertrade as an Export Strategy," *Journal of Business Strategy*, May/June 1990.

24. Susan Greco, "Export Experts Close to Home," *Inc.*, July 1992, 117.

25. "Understand and Heed Cultural Differences," *Business America*, September 1992, 30–31.

26. Joann Lublin, "Companies Use Cross-Cultural Training to Help Their Employees Adjust Abroad," *Wall Street Journal*, 24 August 1992, B1, B9.

27. Sylvia Odenwald, "A Guide for Global Training," *Training and Development*, July 1993, 22–31.

28. Ibid.

29. Cassel, 90.

30. Kevin Walsh, "How to Negotiate European-Style," *Journal of European Business*, July/August 1993, 45–47.

31. Roberta Maynard, "Trade Tide Rises Across the Pacific," *Nation's Business*, November 1995, 52–56.

32. *Trilateral Customs Guide to NAFTA* (Ottawa, Ontario, Canada: Department of Customs, Excise, and Taxation, 1994), 1.

33. *NAFTA Rules of Origin* (Ottawa, Ontario, Canada: Department of Customs, Excise, and Taxation, 1994), 1.

34. Geoffrey Brewer, "New World Orders," *Sales and Marketing Management*, January 1994, 59–63.

35. Patricia Raiken, "Business Guide to Planning for the NAFTA," *Business America*, 18 October 1993, 33–35.
36. Kim Howard, "GATT Bridges the Gap," *Business Credit*, March 1994, 22.
37. Michael Albert, "A Q&A on the WTO, IMF, World Bank, and Activism," *Z Magazine*, January 2000, 24–29.
38. Leslie Brokaw, "ISO 9000: Making the Grade," *Inc.*, June 1993, 98–99.
39. "ISO 9000:2000 Quality Standards Approved," *Quality*, February 2001, 14–16.
40. Brokaw, p. 99.

Chapter 16

1. Linda Hill, "Hardest Lessons for First-Time Manager," *Working Woman*, February 1994, 18–21.
2. Henry Mintzberg, "The Manager's Job: Folklore and Fact," *Harvard Business Review*, March/April 1990, 163–176.
3. Ibid., 175.
4. Amy Barrett, "It's a Small (Business) World," *Business Week*, 17 April 1995, 96–101.
5. Jacquelyn Denalli, "Keeping Growth Under Control," *Nation's Business*, July 1993, 31–32.
6. John Case and Elizabeth Colin, "Second Thoughts on Growth," *Inc.*, March 1991, 46–57.
7. Donna Fenn, "When to Go Pro," *Inc. 500 1995*, 72.
8. Ibid., 4.
9. David Terpstra and Philip Olson, "Entrepreneurial Start-up and Growth: A Classification of Problems," *Entrepreneurship Theory and Practice*, Spring 1993, 5–20.
10. Howard Stevenson and David Gumpert, "The Heart of Entrepreneurship," *Harvard Business Review*, March/April 1985, 85.
11. Theodore Kinni, "Leadership Up Close," *Industry Week*, 20 June 1994, 21–25.
12. Theodore Kinni, "The Credible Leader," *Industry Week*, 20 June 1994, 25–26.
13. Warren Bennis, "Why Leaders Can't Lead," *Training and Development Journal*, April 1989, 35–39.
14. Genevieve Capowski, "Anatomy of a Leader: Where Are the Leaders of Tomorrow?" *Management Review*, March 1994, 10–17.
15. Ibid.
16. For examples of applying Maslow's hierarchy in small businesses, see Mark Hendrichs, "Motivating Force," *Entrepreneur*, December 1995, 68–72.
17. Michael Cronin, "Motivation the Old Fashioned Way," *Inc.*, November 1994, 134.
18. W. Edwards Deming, *Out of Crisis* (Cambridge, MA: MIT Press, 1986), 24.
19. David Bowen and Edward Lawler, "Total Quality-oriented Human Resource Management," *Organizational Dynamics*, Spring 1992, 29–41.
20. David Greising, "Quality: How to Make It Pay," *Business Week*, 8 August 1994, 54–59.
21. Oren Harari, "Ten Reasons Why TQM Doesn't Work," *Management Review*, January 1993, 33–37. See also related articles Selwyn Becker, "TQM Does Work: Ten Reasons Why Misguided Attempts Fail," *Management Review*, May 1993, 30–33; and Oren Harari, "The Eleventh Reason Why TQM Doesn't Work," *Management Review*, May 1993, 31–35.
22. Catherine Romano, "Report Card on TQM," *Management Review*, January 1994, 22.
23. Ibid., 23.

24. Howard Rothman, "Quality's Link to Productivity," *Nation's Business*, February 1994, 33–34.
25. Greising, 55.
26. Martha Davis, Matthew McKay, and Elizabeth Robbins Eshelman, *The Relaxation & Stress Reduction Workbook*, 2nd ed. (Oakland, CA: New Harbinger Publications, 1982).
27. Kenneth Hart, "Introducing Stress and Stress Management in Managers," *Journal of Managerial Psychology* 5, no.2, 1990, 9–16.

Chapter 17

1. *Wall Street Journal*, 20 March 1990, A1.
2. Asron Bernstein and Paul Magnusson, "How Much Good Will Training Do?" *Business Week*, 22 February 1993, 77.
3. Martin John Yate, *Hiring the Best: A Manager's Guide to Effective Interviewing* (Holbrook, MA: Bob Adams, 1998), 18
4. Jeffrey Seglin, "Rating Cyber Job Searches," *Fortune Small Business* (www.fsb.com), 1 May 2001.
5. Peter F. Drucker, "How to Save the Family Business," *Wall Street Journal*, 19 August 1994, A10.
6. Amy Barrett, "It's a Small (Business) World," *Business Week*, 17 April 1995, 96–101.
7. *Griggs* v. *Duke Power Company*, 401 U.S. 424 (1971).
8. John S. O'Connor and Carlene Warner, "How to Develop Physical Capacity Standards," *Personnel Journal New Product News Supplement*, May 1996, 8, 10.
9. Ibid.
10. "SHRM-BNA Survey No. 59: Human Resource Activities, Budgets, and Staffs: 1993–94," *HR Bulletin to Management*, 30 June 1994, 31.
11. Michael Barrier, "Now You Hire Them, Now You Don't," *Nation's Business*, January 1994, 31.
12. Marvin Selter, "On the Plus Side of Employee Leasing," *Personnel Journal*, April 1986, 87–91.
13. John Naisbitt, "Employee Leasing Takes Off," *Success*, April 1986, 12.
14. Abraham Maslow, *Motivation and Personality* (New York: Harper & Row, 1954).
15. Frank Hammel, "Tackling Turnover," *Supermarket Business*, October 1995, 103–108.
16. "Business Realities Clash with Training Needs and Turnover," *HR Focus*, January 1994, 1, 8.
17. Jill Andresky Fraser, "Financial Strategies," *Inc.*, November 1993, 137.
18. Stephen Huth, "The Perfect Storm?" *Employee Benefit Plan Review*, January 2001, 14–15; and www.ebri.org
19. *Public Attitudes on Flexible Benefits* (Washington, DC: Employee Benefit Research Institute, 1994), 10.
20. Lynn Miller, "Small Companies Pushed to Offer Health Benefits," *HR Magazine*, June 2001, 18.
21. Richard J. Henderson, *Compensation Management: Rewarding Performance* (Englewood Cliffs, NJ: Prentice Hall, 1994), 491.
22. "Employer Contributions Spur 401(k) Participation Modestly," *HR News*, April 1994, 13.
23. Mary Rowland, "Pension Options for Small Firms," *Nation's Business*, March 1994, 27.
24. *Public Attitudes on Flexible Benefits* (Washington, DC: Employee Benefit Research Institute, 1994), 20.
25. "Employees Pitch in for Working Parents," *Parents*, July 1994, 132.
26. Joseph S. Placentini and Jill D. Foley, *EBRI Databook on Employee Benefits*, 2nd ed. (Washington, DC: Employee Benefit Research Institute, 1992), 18.

Chapter 18

1. Shawn Tully, "You'll Never Guess Who Really Makes . . . ," *Fortune,* 3 October 1994, 124–128.
2. Otis Port, "Custom-made, Direct from the Planet," *Business Week, 21st-Century Capitalism Edition,* 18 November 1994, 158–159.
3. Ronald Henkoff, "Make Your Office More Productive," *Fortune,* 25 February 1991, 72–84.
4. Dan Gutman, "Always in Touch," *Success,* March 1995, 54.
5. "Office Ergonomics: Not the Same as in a Plant," *Industry Week,* 5 December 1994, 37.
6. Michael Barrier, "You Have a Purpose in Life," *Nation's Business,* September 1995, 13–14.
7. Gwen Fontenot, Alicia Gresham, and Ravi Behara, "Using Six Sigma to Measure and Improve Customer Service," *Proceedings of 1994 National Small Business Consulting Conference,* Small Business Institute Director's Association, San Antonio, 1994, 298–304.
8. Ibid., 303.
9. *Breaking into the Trade Game: A Small Business Guide to Exporting* (Washington, DC: U.S. Small Business Administration, 1994), 94.
10. Ronald Henkoff, "The Hot New Seal of Quality," *Fortune,* 28 June 1993, 116–117.
11. Michael Barrier and Amy Zuckerman, "Quality Standards the World Agrees On," *Nation's Business,* May 1994, 71–72.
12. Henkoff, "The Hot New Seal," 116.
13. Barrier and Zuckerman, 72.
14. Steven Ashley, "Nondestructive Evaluation with Laser Ultrasound," *Mechanical Engineering,* October 1994, 63–66.

Index

Assets (*continued*)
   tangible, 179–181, 184–185
   thinning, 187
   total asset turnover ratio, 248
Association for International Business, 485
Association of Independent Information
   Professionals (AIIP), 353
Assumptions, business plan evaluation of, 120
Assurance Medical, Inc., 477
AT&T, 486
Attard, Janet, 245
AT&T Export Hotline, 484
Attrition, 435
At-will doctrine, 300–301, 559–560
Audience for business plans, 109
Audits, 236
   before buyouts, 177
   independent, 177
   time, 522
   vendor, 374
Augmented product, 365
Auntie Anne's, 137–138
Auringer, Dave, 463
Austin, Nancy, 256
Authority, 36
Authorize.net, 206
Automated Trade Locator Assistance System (SBAtlas), 479
Automation, 507
Autonomy, 290
Average collection period, 247
Avocations, business ideas from, 214–215
Avrin, David, 457
Avrin Public Relations Group, 457

Backdoors, 85
Backward scheduling, 578
Baechler, Mary, 44
Baechler, Phil, 44
BAI International, 36
Balance sheet methods of valuation, 183
Balance sheets, 122–123, 237, 238, 241
Ballon, Marc, 463
Balloon notes, 280–281
Bankable Deals, 482
Bankruptcy, 310–312
   Chapter 7, 310–311
   Chapter 11, 311
   Chapter 13, 311–312
Banks
   cash flow management and, 261
   commercial, 280–282
   merchant, 206
   relationships with, 281
Banks, Kendall, 471
Bar codes, 381
Bardeen, Paul, 169–170
Bargaining power, 344
BarnesandNoble.com, 508
Barnett, Donald F., 9
Barot, Dilip, 286
Barrett, Amy, 334

Barrier, Michael, 98, 512
Barter, 483–484
Bartlett, Nancy, 549
Basic Guide to Exporting, A, 491
BassMasters, 471
Baty, G.B., 289–290
BCentral.com, 503
Behara, Ravi, 581
Beiler, Anne, 137–138
Bell, Thomas, Jr., 512
Bellenson, Joel Lloyd, 388
Bellybra, 527
Ben and Jerry's Ice Cream, 76, 451
Benchmarking, 93, 586–587
Benefits, 551–556. *See also* Compensation
   child care, 554–555
   flexible packages, 552
   401(k) plans, 553–554
   health insurance, 552–553
   IRAs, 553
   Keogh plans, 554
   pension plans, 553
   SEPs, 553
Bennett, Alvin, 443
Bennis, Warren, 510
Berkeley, Roger, 471
Berman, Lyle, 100–101
Berne Convention, 321–322
Berry, Jonathan, 338
Berry, Tim, 584–585
Better Business Bureau, 152, 172
Biddulph, Jennifer, 201
Big Business, 381
Big-team ventures, 511
Bill collection, 443–447
Billing software, 443
Birch, David, 25, 396
Bisharat, Jaleh, 434
Bizbuysell.com, 174
BizPlanit.com, 109
Bizzed.com, 503
Black box model, 339–342
Blackhurst, Chris, 410
Blair, Michael, 311
Blair Communications, 311
Blanchard, Pascal, 388–389
Block, Toddi Gutner, 17
Bloom, Paul, 368
Body Shop, The, 76
Boisset USA, 101
Bond, Sharon L., 272
Bonuses, 551
Book value, 184
Bootstrapping, 105, 287
Bork, David, 191
Boston Beer Company, 3–4, 7
Bowers, Brent, 272
Brady, Sheily, 489
Brainbench.com, 549
Brands, 228–229
   definition of, 321
   domain names and, 48
Brand Toolkit, 165–166
Brannock Device Company, 575

Brazilian American Wildlife Society (BAWLS), 64
Breach of contract, 314
Break-down methods, 335–336
Breakeven analysis, 125
   for pricing, 432–434
Breakeven point, 125, 432–434
Breaking into the Trade Game: A Small Business Guide to Exporting, 486
BreathAsure, Inc., 481
Breckenridge, Delo, 146
British Columbia Business Service Centre, 109
Brodbeck, William, 547
Brodbeck Enterprises, 547
Broderick, Larry, 217–218
Brodsky, Norm, 107–108
Brokaw, Leslie, 36, 43, 454
Brokers, 392
   export, 475
BRONZE Tanning Service & Salon, 621–635
Brook Furniture Rental, 454
Brooks, Mel, 51
Broome, J. Tol, Jr., 363
Brotherton, Phaedra, 532
Brown, Bruce, 404
B2BWine.com, 366
Buchalter, Gail, 36
Buchanan, Leigh, 31
Budgets, cash, 254–257
Building facilities, 419
Building services, 417–418
Build-up methods, 335–336
Bundling products, 438
Bunnell, Tom, 43
Buppert, Hoby, 64
Bureau of Labor Statistics, 11, 207
Burkwell Directory of Information Brokers, 353
Business Background Report, 442
Business brokers, 173
Business buyouts, 168–198
   advantages of, 170–171
   closing the deal in, 187
   disadvantages of, 171
   due diligence in, 172
   family businesses, 188–191
   finding businesses for, 172–174
   how much to pay in, 183–186
   intangible assets in, 181–182, 185–186
   personnel in, 182–183
   seller's plans and, 183
   tangible assets in, 179–181, 184–185
   terms of sale for, 187
   terms of sale in, 187
   what is bought in, 179–183
   what to look for in, 174–179
Business cards, 457, 488–489
Business Ethics, 76
Business failure, 21–26
Business-format franchises, 141
Business ideas, 209–212
   sources of, 212–216
Business Information Tracking System (BITS), 11